ANGLO-ASSAMESE RELATIONS

1771-1826

ANGLO-ASSAMESE RELATIONS, 1771-1826

A HISTORY OF THE RELATIONS OF ASSAM WITH THE EAST INDIA COMPANY FROM 1771 TO 1826, BASED ON ORIGINAL ENGLISH AND ASSAMESE SOURCES

S. K. BHUYAN

GYAN

Published by

GYAN

Gyan Publishing House
5, Ansari Road
Daryaganj, New Delhi-110002
Phone: 011-47034999, 9811692060
E-mail: books@gyanbooks.com

Distribution Network
gyanbooks.com
India, USA, Canada, UK, Australia

ISBN: 978-93-6920-431-1 (PB)

First Published, 1949

2nd Impression 2025

Printed at: Gyan Press, Delhi.

ANGLO-ASSAMESE RELATIONS, 1771-1826
Author: S. K. BHUYAN

ANGLO-ASSAMESE RELATIONS

BY THE SAME AUTHOR

ENGLISH

1. An Assamese Nur Jahan, Queen Phuleswari Devi, 1926.
2. Report and Conspectus of the Assam Research Society, 1927.
3. Early British Relations with Assam. 1928.
4. Preliminary Report on the Agency Records of the Assam Government, 1823-1874. Printed in Assam Secretariat File. 1930-31.
5. Bulletins of the Department of Historical and Antiquarian Studies in Assam, Nos. I, II and III. 1932-36.
6. Tungkhungia Buranji, with Glossary, Index, etc. 1933.
7. Assamese Literature: Ancient and Modern. Printed in Assam Secretariat File. 1936.
8. Dr. Francis Hamilton's Account of Assam. 1940.
9. Lachit Barphukan and His Times. 1947
10. Annals of the Delhi Badshahate. 1947.
11. Military System of the Assamese People. Prativa Devi Memorial Lectures, Fourth Series, 1941. *Ready for the press.*
12. Atan Buragohain and His Times, 1662-1681. *Ready for the press.*
13. Quintessence of Experience. *Ready for the press.*

ASSAMESE

1. Gopal Krishna Gokhale. 1916.
2. Nirmali, poems. 1918.
3. Ahomar Din. 1918.
4. Jaimati Upakhyan, poem. 1920.
5. Anundoram Borooah, Sanskritist. 1920 and 1924.
6. Rabindranath Tagore. 1920.
7. Barphukanar Git, old historical ballad. 1924.
8. Panchami, short stories. 1927.
9. Jonaki, lives of eminent men. 1928 and 1938.
10. Chaneki, lives of eminent women. 1928.
11. Assam Jiyari, Assamese women of history. 1935.
12. Kowanr Bidroh. 1948.
13. Buranjir Bani. *In the press.*
14. King Rajeswar Singha, 1751-1769. *Ready for the press.*

CHRONICLES, EDITED WITH INTRODUCTION IN ENGLISH.

1. Assam Buranji by Harakanta Barua. 1930.
2. Kamrupar Buranji. 1930.
3. Deodhai Asam Buranji. 1932.
4. Tungkhungia Buranji. 1932.
5. Asamar Padya-Buranji, with Synopsis in English. 1933.
6. Padshah-Buranji. 1935.
7. Kachari Buranji, with Synopsis in English. 1936.
8. Jayantia Buranji, with Synopsis in English. 1937.
9. Tripura Buranji. 1938.
10. Assam Buranji, S. M., with Analysis in English. 1945.

ANGLO-ASSAMESE RELATIONS

1771-1826

A history of the relations of Assam with the East India Company from 1771 to 1826, based on original English and Assamese sources.

S. K. BHUYAN,
M.A., B.L. (CAL.), PH.D. (LOND.)
Provincial Director of Historical and Antiquarian Studies in Assam; lately Director of Public Instruction, Assam.

Thesis approved for the Degree of Doctor of Philosophy in the University of London.

DEPARTMENT OF
HISTORICAL AND ANTIQUARIAN STUDIES IN ASSAM
GAUHATI
1949

TO

MY WIFE

SRIMATI LAKSHESWARI BHUYAN

PREFACE

The object of the present book is to describe the relations of Assam with the English East India Company from 1771 to 1826. It deals incidentally with Assam's contacts with Europeans in general prior to 1771 and during the period of survey. In Assam, as in other theatres of commercial adventure, the British had to compete with other European merchants. The trade was profitable, but not very flourishing, owing to the quarrels and disputes amongst the merchants, and to the civil strifes then raging in Assam. The British who had become masters of the neighbouring province of Bengal were ultimately compelled to interfere in the affairs of Assam in their own interest, and this led eventually to their occupation of the country. The different stages of the Company's Assam policy have been fully narrated, with details of the circumstances of disintegration, both external and internal, immediate and remote, which led to the decline and fall of the old Assamese kingdom. This book may therefore be regarded as a political history of Assam from the last quarter of the eighteenth century to the first quarter of the nineteenth, covering the reigns and times of the last five Ahom sovereigns,—Swargadeos Lakshmi Singha, Gaurinath Singha, Kamaleswar Singha, Chandrakanta Singha and Purandar Singha.

Glimpses into several phases of the past history of Assam can also be obtained in this book as the description of important events and developments is generally accompanied by retrospective surveys for the purpose of furnishing the necessary perspective so that it can be read with advantage by the uninitiated reader. The background is also set forth in the introductory chapter which deals with, among other matters, the ruling power in Assam, the Ahom system of administration, relations with neighbouring states and hill tribes, Assam's commercial and foreign policy, exports and imports, early European visitors to and writers on Assam. In the narratives, I have tried to throw as much light as possible on the details of the administrative machinery, economic resources, social conditions, religious developments, and the careers of the leading persons. My remote object has been to present an authentic and well-documented account of Assam which will enable future historians to make use of the extensive source-materials referred to in the footnotes, and thereby enlarge upon the topics I have but lightly handled. The analytical list of contents will convey an idea of the offshoots and ramifications of the major themes.

The materials used in the compilation of this book are principally the Consultations and Proceedings, and the miscellaneous records of the East India Company, deposited at the India Office Library, London, where, as the result of two years' exploration, 1936-1938, I came upon a large mass of correspondence relating to Assam. In 1930, I had visited the Imperial Record Department at Calcutta, and copies of important documents have been obtained from time to time. At the instance of the then Governor of Assam, the late Sir Laurie Hammond, I was appointed in 1930, to examine the old records at the Assam Secretariat, Shillong; and I submitted detailed proposals regarding the preservation and publication of those records, and the compilation of a catalogue, a hand-book and a press-list or calendar. I also pointed out the necessity of obtaining the originals or the copies of the Assam records deposited at the Bengal Record Room, the Imperial Record Department and the India Office Library.

My interest in the records of the East India Company first took an active form about the year 1926 after a perusal of the published records which had found their way into Assam. I had also an opportunity to examine the original India Office Library manuscripts of Dr. John Peter Wade's *Account of Assam* and *Geographical Sketch of Assam* which had been borrowed by the Government of Assam. A paper on Dr. Wade was read at the Twelfth Session of the Indian Historical Records Commission held at Gwalior in December 1929. I dealt with the whole subject of Assam records in a monograph entitled *Early British Relations with Assam*, which was published by the Government of Assam in 1928. I attempted in that book "to draw the attention of the public and of the authorities to the vast mine of historical information buried in the archives of the Bengal and the Imperial Record Rooms, the India Office Library, the British Museum and the District and Divisional offices of Assam." A comprehensive bibliography was appended to the book. It has been referred to in several compilations published meanwhile, including Prof. H. H. Dodwell's *Cambridge Shorter History of India*. I had also to deal with Assam's early relations with the British in the chapter entitled "British Occupation of Assam", in my book *Tungkhungia Buranji, or, A History of Assam,* 1671-1826 *A.D.*, published in 1933 by the Oxford University Press. A chapter on Assam's dealings with European merchants was compiled about that time and inserted in my *History of the Reign of Swargadeo Rajeswar Singha,* 1751-69, which is awaiting publication. A number of English documents and Assamese Buranjis or chronicles were borrowed from the India Office Library by the Department of Historical and Antiquarian Studies, Assam, since the year 1929, and some of them have been incorporated in that Department's publications.

Materials for this book have also been drawn from the indigenous Assamese Buranjis, written both in prose and verse. Several of them have been edited by me and published by the D.H.A.S., and many more are still unpublished, the manuscripts and transcripts being mainly deposited in the library of the above Department. It is interesting to note that Monsieur J. B. Chevalier, Hugh Baillie, George Lear, M. Laval, Daniel Raush, Captain Welsh and Lt. MacGregor occupy an important place in the contemporary Assamese narratives as in the records of the E.I.C. But the machinery of history-writing, like that of the other departments of the state, failed to function efficiently during the last half-a-century of Ahom rule owing to continued disturbances in the country. So the chronicles of this period are not so exhaustive and numerous as those of former times. The value of the narratives relating to Assam's contact with Europeans, in spite of their meagreness, is immense as they convey an impression of the other side of the picture and supplement the information available in the E.I.C. records.

Contemporary publications and secondary works have proved equally useful in the compilation of this book, and most of them were examined and could be examined only in the India Office Library as it contains the largest collection of books on the British period of Indian History. I have also drawn my materials from the books in the Library of the School of Oriental Studies, Royal Asiatic Society of Great Britain and Ireland, British Museum, and the London Institute of Historical Research. I traced the existence of valuable records about Assam at the Vatican Library in Rome, and the Bibliotheque Nationale in Paris, but they could hardly be consulted by me as my visits to both the libraries were brief. The published sources have been studied with thoroughness and care; but, though they have helped me in filling up unbridgeable gulfs, the comparative meagreness of the information obtained from them has led me to draw my data principally from the unpublished sources. The history of Assam of the period under review has thus been reconstructed by synthesising the information drawn from all possible sources, both indigenous and foreign.

The important sources of information have been enlisted in the Bibliography; and precise references to them have been cited in the footnotes. Now that the spade work of tracing and locating the sources has been accomplished to some extent, future scholars will be able to follow them up easily, and to prepare transcripts, and to edit and publish selections. I had a mind to publish at least one volume of such selections; and for this purpose, I had prepared in England typescripts of the entire correspondence of Captain Thomas Welsh, and of a number of other valuable documents including some letters of David Scott. But I have not been able to carry out my plan for want of time and of the requisite opportunities. I have however prepared a complete press-list of the documents examined by me during my two years' "digging" at the India Office Library, and of which I took full or partial copies.

It may be mentioned that this book represents the first attempt at a scientific handling of all available sources, Assamese and English, both published and unpublished. Most of the personalities and events have been subjected for the first time to a rigorous critical examination; and hence their evaluation may bear the traces of a pioneer attempt. In other places, historical landmarks have, through the attempts of succeeding writers, attained some degree of standardisation in value, which can be accepted or modified in the light of newly discovered data ; in Assam, these landmarks convey only a hazy impression of the actual realities, owing to the paucity of reliable details and the consequent absence of scientific discussions. I have in this book made a systematic attempt to throw as much light as possible on these dim pictures, in order that they may appear in their true colours. As I do not pretend to say the last word on any subject, I invite future labourers to fill up the landscape with more copious details. In the pages of this book they will at least have the skeleton and the dry-bones to work upon, together with an idea of the quarries wherefrom replenishing materials can be extracted.

Having worked for a considerable number of years in the field of historical research in Assam, I proceeded in 1936 on two years' Study Leave to England, in order to study the records and publications about Assam in a centralised institution like the India Office Library, and to fuse the results of this study in a constructive history. I joined the School of Oriental (also African at present) Studies in London where I worked for the Ph.D. degree of London University as an Internal Student, under the direction and supervision of the late Mr. H. H. Dodwell, M.A. (Oxon.), Professor of History and Culture of British Dominions in Asia with special reference to India. The compiler thus received the benefit of regular consultations with the learned editor of the fifth and sixth volumes of *The Cambridge History of India,* and at that time, the greatest living authority on the British period of Indian History. The book was approved in 1938 for the Ph.D. degree in History in the Faculty of Arts, the examiners being Professor Dodwell, Sir Edward Gait, and Professor P. W. Morrell of Birkbeck College and Reader in Imperial History in London University. The book has since been revised on the lines of the suggestions made by Sir Edward Gait and Professor Morrell. The sections dealing with the ruling power in Assam, its relations with the neighbouring states and hill tribes, have been newly added to the Introduction, as their knowledge is essential for properly understanding the trend of the historical narratives. The life-sketch of Dr. John Peter Wade, inserted as an appendix to Part II of Chapter VII, was compiled so recently as November 1948, with the help of the letters written to Francis Fowke, copies being obtained meanwhile through the courtesy of Dr. H. N. Randle, Librarian of the Commonwealth Relations Office, London. The thesis as submitted to London University in 1938 bore the title *East India Company's Relations with Assam* ; it has now been shortened into the present form *Anglo-Assamese Relations.*

The delay in the publication of the book is due to abnormal circumstances. Just when arrangements were in progress for printing it in 1941-42, with the help of a grant placed at the disposal of the D.H.A.S. by Shri Rohini Kumar Chaudhury, then Minister of Education, Assam, the proposal had to be abandoned owing to the strained financial position of

Assam mainly brought about by World War II. The scarcity of paper and the unusually heavy demands on printing presses rendered the publication of the book almost an impracticable proposition. The attempt was revived after the cessation of hostilities followed by the partial restoration of printing facilities. The Hon'ble Shri Gopinath Bardoloi, Premier and Education Minister of Assam, has been pleased to make a fresh grant for the publication of the book.

Assam and India have undergone momentous changes since the compilation of the book. First came the War during which Assam became a base for military operations against Japan. The world also witnessed the final Indian struggle for independence known generally as the "1942 Movement". On the 15th August 1947, India emerged into a sovereign republic from its position as a dependency of the British. The form and pattern of its future governance are being forged by its own constitution-makers. The different units of the Dominion of India have realised the benefits of merging into an undivided and cohesive whole; and Assam which in ages past had to fight its existence single-handed can now look upon the rest of India as an integral part of the same body-politic. Under the pressure of such changes it is but natural that our present-day way of thinking is sometimes different from that of ten or twelve years ago. It is believed that in spite of this change of outlook, the views and opinions expressed in this book will not lose their significance in the new set-up and in the ages to come.

On the other hand, the events have special meaning attached to them now that we are independent, when the responsibility of steering the ship of state rests entirely on our shoulders. The forceful logic of geography and economics being unrefutable, every event evokes in our mind fresh streams of thought when it is studied in the background of our present surroundings. The forces of disruption which brought the Assam kingdom to an end in 1822 will be once more released if the underlying circumstances are repeated and re-enacted ; and our present duty is therefore one of circumspection, and the inculcation of the habit of profiting by the blunders of our great-grandfathers of the late eighteenth and early nineteenth centuries. With the restoration of independence, the study of national history has become endowed not only with a higher academic value, but also with an intense practical utility, as every past event induces us to search for the lesson it has for the present. It is also indispensable for stimulating creative works of art and literature which are equally important in directing the energies of our people to the cultivation of those qualities which are necessary for retaining and utilising this hard-won independence.

In compiling this book I have attempted to transmit the spirit of the past by inserting in the narratives short extracts from contemporaneous documents, because a phrase or a sentence culled from the sayings or writings of a historical personage conveys the reflections of the age more pointedly than folios of reconstructed history. A few specimens are given below to enable the reader to have a foretaste of the realistic flavour latent in such utterances:

"The Dafala miscreants can be captured only if an elephant can enter into a rat-hole."—Premier Atan Buragohain, about 1672.

"Is it called trade if it be limited to the import of a few maunds of salt from Bengal, and the despatch of two or four boats from our place ?"—King Rudra Singha, about 1713.

"His Majesty should not listen to a man if he says that the Morans will retire to the woods after having once attained the position of Raja-Chakravarti."—Kirtichandra Barbarua, November 1769.

"The kingdom of Assam is totally and absolutely independent of any control from Bengal as the Empire of China is."—William Dow, Jugighopa, May 15, 1784.

" The civil dissensions still rage in Assam to the destruction and ruin of that once opulent kingdom."—Hugh Baillie, Goalpara, November 9, 1789.

" To-day we shall enter a kingdom [Assam] scarcely if ever trodden by Europeans before."—Dr. John Peter Wade, Goalpara, November 16, 1792.

" Three of us among the Maharaja's ministers, myself with the Barpatra Gohain and the Buragohain, are all engaged in the public service of the said Maharaja. If the Buragohain can be chief over Assam, then why not all the others of the Maharaja's ministers become chiefs also ?"—Malbhog Bargohain, Calcutta, January 29, 1820.

" The Burmese having obtained complete mastery of Assam, and a person of that nation having been appointed to the supreme authority, the country may now be considered as a Province of the Burman Empire."—David Scott, July 11, 1822.

" We are not led into your country by the thirst of conquest ; but are forced, in our defence, to deprive our enemy of the means of annoying us."—British Proclamation to the Assamese, March 1824.

" I wish you, gentlemen, to bear witness to Government, that I am no longer able to conduct the affairs of the country." —David Scott in his sick-bed, Cherapoonji, August 20, 1831.

I take this opportunity to acknowledge my indebtedness to those from whom I have received encouragement and help in various ways in the compilation and publication of this book : Sir Robert Reid, Governor of Assam, 1937-42 ; Sir Andrew Clow, Governor of Assam, 1942-47 ; Dr. H. N. Randle, Librarian, Commonwealth Relations Office, London, and the staff of the India Office Library of 1936-38 ; Sir Edward Gait, author of *A History of Assam* ; Dr. D. G. E. Hall, author of *Early English Intercourse with Burma, 1587-1743* ; Mr. G. W. Rossetti, Secretary, School of Oriental Studies, and the School and Library staff ; Dr. Lionel D. Barnett, O.M., formerly Keeper of Oriental Books and Manuscripts at the British Museum, London ; Dr. C. H. Philips, Dr. Purnendu Basu and Mr. Khurshid Muhammad Chistie, my colleagues in the Indian History class in the School of Oriental Studies, London; Dr. S. N. Sen, Director of the National Archives of India ; The Hon'ble Shri Gopinath Bardoloi, Premier and Education Minister of Assam ; Shri Rohini Kumar Chaudhury, formerly Education Minister of Assam ; Shri Mahendramohan Chaudhury, Parliamentary Secretary for Education, Assam ; Mr. S. K. Dutta, Honorary Deputy Director of Historical and Antiquarian Studies in Assam ; Srijut Debakanta Barua, B.A., LL.B.; Srijut Padmeswar Gogoi, M.A., Lecturer in Economics, Gauhati University ; Srijut Maheswar Neog, M.A., Lecturer in Assamese, Gauhati University ; Srijut Kamala Kanta Kakati, M.A., Historical Research Scholar, D.H.A.S., Assam ; Mr. Apurba Kumar Bardoloi ; Srijut Arun Chandra Bhuyan, M.A.; Srijut Jibeswar Barua, Principal, Assam Art School, Gauhati ; Srijut Sasadhar Rai Barua, student of Cotton College, Gauhati ; Srijut Dharmakanta Hazarika, student of the B.Com. Class, Gauhati University ; Srijut Keshab Chandra Das of the staff of the D.H.A.S. I am specially thankful to Srijut Madhab Chandra Baroowa of the D.H.A.S. staff for his enthusiastic help in the publication of this book ; and to Mr. G. Srinivasachari, B.A., Proprietor, G. S. Press, Madras, for his unfailing courtesy, and the promptness with which he has executed the work of printing.

I have now the sacred duty to gratefully record the names of those who are no longer in the land of the living, who gave me all possible encouragement in the study of old records, and specially in connection with the compilation and publication of this book : Sir Laurie Hammond, Governor of Assam, 1927-1932 ; Sir Michael Keane, Governor of Assam, 1932-1937 ; Sir Akbar Hydari, Governor of Assam, 1947-48 ; Prof. H. H. Dodwell, my tutor at the School of Oriental Studies, London ; Mr. C. E. A. W. Oldham, Honorary Secretary of the Royal Asiatic Society of Great Britain and Ireland; Lt.-Col. P. R. T. Gurdon; Nawabzada A. F. M. Abdul Ali, Secretary to the Indian Historical Records Commission; Professor Sir E. Denison Ross, Director of the School of Oriental Studies; Mr. W. Sutton Page, Reader in Bengali in London University; Mr. W. T. Ottewill, Superintendent of Records, India Office Library, London.

In conclusion, I would crave the indulgence of the reader for the irregularities which may be noticed here and there, as the book has been seen through the press at a time when for reasons of health I have been precluded from exerting myself to the extent required for bringing out a volume of this size in a perfectly flawless manner.

Gauhati, Assam, S. K. BHUYAN
July 11, 1949.

CONTENTS

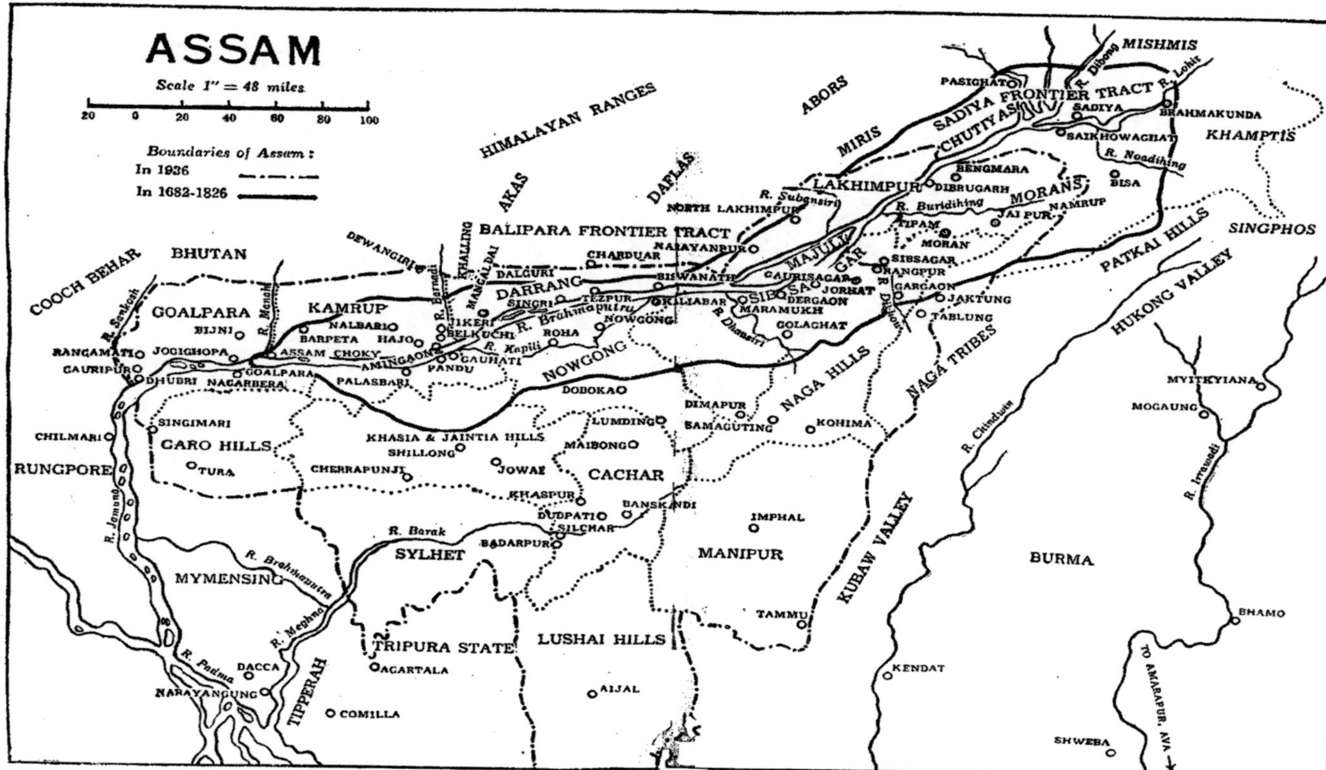

S. K. BHUYAN: *ANGLO-ASSAMESE RELATIONS*

ANGLO-ASSAMESE RELATIONS

1771 TO 1826

CHAPTER I

INTRODUCTION

Extent of Assam: The kingdom of Assam, as it was constituted during the last 140 years of Ahom rule, was bounded on the north by a range of mountains inhabited by the Bhutanese, Akas, Duflas and Abors; on the east, by another line of hills peopled by the Mishmis and Singphos; on the south, by the Garo, Khasi, Naga and Patkai hills; and on the west, by the Manas or Manaha river on the north bank, and the Habraghat Perganah on the south in the Bengal district of Rungpore. The kingdom where it was entered from Bengal commenced from the Assam Choky on the north bank of the Brahmaputra, opposite Goalpara; while on the south bank it commenced from the Nagarbera hill at a distance of 21 miles to the east of Goalpara. The kingdom was about 500 miles in length with an average breadth of 60 miles.[1] The above limits had remained stationary since 1682 when the Moguls were for the last time expelled from Lower Assam, and the old western boundary of the Manas river restored. The Ahom kingdom of Assam thus roughly corresponds to the five present districts of the Brahmaputra Valley Division,—Kamrup, Darrang, Nowgong, Sibsagar and Lakhimpur, and portions of the Sadiya Frontier Tract. The population of the kingdom before the commencement of the Moamaria revolt in 1769-1770 was estimated by Gunabhiram Barua to be about two million and a half.[2] There were about 80,000 *paiks* incorporated in the several official guilds or *khels*, both civil and military. As there were three sets of these *paiks*—*mul, dowal* and

1. William Robinson, *A Descriptive Account of Assam,* 1841, pp. 2-3; John M'Cosh, *Topography of Assam,* 1837, p. 1; Gunabhiram Barua, *Assam Buranji,* 1876, p. 1.

2. Gunabhiram Barua, *Assam Bandhu* journal, Calcutta, 1885, Vol. I, No. 1, p. 3. In 1826 the population was computed at about 8 or 9 lakhs, Adam White's *Memoir of the late David Scott,* 1832, p. 15. The Burmese are said to have diminished the population by half during the years 1817-1825, *Cambridge History of India,* Vol. V, p. 558. Similar reductions had occurred during the Moamaria disturbances.

tewal—we can compute the number of adult male effectives including the reserves to be 240,000. During the war with Ram Singha in 1669-1671, the infantry and cavalry under the command of the Ahoms were reported to have totalled about 100,000.[3]

The ruling power in Assam: During the period of our survey, namely, the end of the eighteenth century and the beginning of the nineteenth, Assam was ruled by the Ahoms. They had first conquered a portion of the eastern part of the kingdom in the beginning of the thirteenth century, and had gradually extended their dominions eastward and westward till they became the undisputed masters of the whole valley of the Brahmaputra.

The Ahoms are members of the Shan branch of the great Tai or Thai family of the human race. This Tai family extends from the Gulf of Siam northwards into Yunnan and thence westwards to Assam, and it comprises several divisions, namely, the Siamese, Laos, Shans, Tai-mow or Tai-khi (Chinese Shans), Khampti and Ahom. The prestige associated with the name *Tai* or *Thai*, literally, of celestial origin, is seen in the Ahoms still designating themselves by that name though most of them have been converted to Hinduism, and the recent attempt to rename the Siamese kingdom as *Thailand.*

The first Ahom conqueror of Assam was a prince named Sukapha who left his native Shan state of Maulung in Upper Burma about the year 1215 as a result of some quarrel with his kinsmen.[4] Having crossed the Patkai range which divides Assam from Upper Burma, Sukapha wandered for thirteen years about the hilly country of Patkai, after which he entered the eastern limit of the territory which came to be known as Assam. The date of Sukapha's conquest has been universally accepted to be 1228 A.D. In Assamese parlance the country and tribe of Sukapha's origin are both known as Nara.

In the dealings with the subdued tribes who had been in possession of the eastern part of the valley, Sukapha adopted a policy of appeasement and conciliation. He and his followers had left their womenfolk in their Shan homeland as being incapable of the

3. News-letter of the court of Emperor Aurangzeb, dated 10th December 1669, Akhbarat-i-darbar-i-Muala, Royal Asiatic Society Ms., 12-11, quoted in Sir Jadunath Sarkar's *Assam and the Ahoms in 1660*, J.B.O.R.S., 1915, p. 189-*n*.

4. Maulung was somewhere in the kingdom of Mungmau or Pong, the capital of which was Mogaung as called by the Burmese, and Munkong or Mongmarong or Moong-khoo-loung as called by the Shans. See Gait's *History of Assam*, p. 74; U. N. Gohain's *Assam under the Ahoms*, p. 1.

strenuous life of adventurers, and they were therefore compelled to marry from among the women of the conquered tribes, the Morans, the Barahis and the Chutias. Speaking of the relations of the Ahoms with these tribes, Atan Buragohain, prime minister of Assam from 1662 to 1679, said in one place,—"Sukapha had greater regard for the abilities and personal qualities of the Chutias, Barahis and Morans whom he met at different places, than towards his own followers. Since that time there was an admixture of blood, and children were of mixed origin as the Ahoms had not brought their wives when they first came from Nara, and as they accepted wives only when they came here."[5]

Another historian, Harakanta Barua, said in the same vein,—"King Sukapha managed to engage the Mataks [Morans] as fuel-suppliers and orchard-keepers, while the Barahis were employed as wood-cutters, valets, cooks, store-keepers, casket-bearers, physicians and poultry-keepers. These Barahis went on saying amongst the people,—"Though this prince [Sukapha] and his followers have made us so many servitors, yet we do not feel any resentment in our hearts; on the other hand, we long for serving and attending on them, and for meeting them as frequently as possible. They are therefore men of divine origin, and nobody is *sama* or equal to them, and they can be designated as *a-sama* or unparalleled."[6] It is believed by some that the word *Assam*, the name of the province, is derived from this circumstance, and that *Ahom* is a corruption of the word *A-sam*, as in the Assamese language the sibilant *S* in many cases becomes an aspirate *H*; others hold that Assam is so called because of the uneven character of the province composed as it is of hills and plains.

From the thirteenth to the fifteenth centuries the Ahoms were mainly busy in consolidating their power over the neighbouring tribes. Sections of the Nagas and the Kacharis were brought under Ahom domination, as well as some tribes of the Tai race who had settled in Assam long before Sukapha's invasion. But real expansion began from the sixteenth century when the Ahom king Suhungmung Dihingia Raja annexed the kingdom of the Chutias centering round their capital Sadiya. The same king drove the Kacharis from their stronghold at Dimapur. The Bhuyan chieftains who had been ruling in the north bank of the Brahmaputra were brought under Ahom control and made to settle in Bardowa in Nowgong,

5. S. K. Bhuyan, *Deodhai Asam Buranji*, which incorporates Atan Buragohain's chronicle, p. 91.

6. S. K. Bhuyan, *Assam Buranji* by Harakanta Barua, pp. 12-13.

though their complete subjugation was effected a hundred years later.

It was during the reign of Suhungmung that a new kingdom sprang up on the ruins of Kamata. Biswa Singha founded the ruling dynasty of Cooch Behar about the year 1515, and for nearly 150 years the relations between Cooch Behar and Assam reacted on each other's political life. In 1527 occurred the first Muslim invasion of Ahom Assam, but the name of the commander cannot be ascertained. It was followed in 1532 by the invasion of another Muslim commander named Turbak, who was killed in the expedition, and the Ahoms pursued the fugitives as far as the Karatoya river. Suhungmung's rule also witnessed the Vaisnava revival in Assam which had far-reaching effects on the social life of the people as well as on the continuance of Ahom domination.

The history of the Ahoms of the seventeenth century was mainly the history of the Assam-Mogul conflicts which arose out of the ambition of the Moguls to extend their territories further to the east, the intervention of the Ahoms in the affairs of the rival princes of Cooch Behar, and the violation by the Ahoms of the terms of the treaties entered by them with the Moguls. The main theatres of contest were Darrang and Kamrup; and Hazo, Pandu, Saraighat, Gauhati, Kajalimukh, Singri, Bharari, Simalugarh and Samdhara are as famous in the Persian versions of the conflicts as in the Assamese chronicles.

On the death of Biswa Singha about the year 1540 his son Naranarayan succeeded to the throne of Cooch Behar. Accompanied by his brother Chilarai as his commander-in-chief,[7] Naranarayan entered into a career of conquest as a result of which the Ahoms were compelled to acknowledge the suzerainty of Naranarayan, though no transfer of territories nor replacement of the authority of the Ahoms by that of Cooch Behar was involved in this submission. Chilarai died about the year 1578, and on his death the Cooch Behar kingdom was parcelled off into two portions, the western portion upto the river Sankosh being retained by Naranarayan for himself and his successors, and the eastern portion being made over to Chilarai's son Raghudeb. The western kingdom was thenceforth known as Cooch Behar, and the eastern part as Koch Hazo. In 1613, as a result of the quarrels between Lakshminarayan, son of Naranarayan, and Parikshit, son of Raghudeb, the Moguls obtained possession of Koch Hazo. Parikshit's brother

7. For further details about the Cooch Behar rulers, see "The Dynasty of Koch Rulers" and subsequent sections in Part III of Chapter VI, *post*.

Balinarayan sought the help of the Ahom king, which was accorded. This occasioned the invasion of the Ahom territories by the Moguls under Abu Bakar but the invading force was completely destroyed by the Ahoms. Balinarayan was installed by the Ahoms as tributary Raja of Darrang with the name Dharmanarayan. The Ahoms and the Moguls were engaged in continued hostilities for more than twenty years, 1617 to 1639, and the possession of Koch Hazo changed hands several times. It was during the early part of this period that an expert revenue officer of the Moguls undertook the fiscal organisation of Koch Hazo. The province, named *Koch Hazo Vilayat*, was divided into four Sarkars,—Kamrup, Dhekeri, Dakhinkul and Bangalbhum; and a Sarkar was divided into a number of perganahs. Traces of the Mogul system of revenue administration, known as the perganah system, can be seen in Kamrup even at the present time. In 1639 a treaty was concluded according to which Kamrup passed into the hands of the Moguls.[8]

In 1658, the Ahom king Jayadhwaj Singha took advantage of the commotions in Mogul India caused by the War of Succession. He recovered Koch Hazo and carried his inroads upto the neighbourhood of Dacca. The Moguls under Nawab Mir Jumla invaded Assam in 1662 and marched as far as its capital Gargaon. A treaty was enacted in January 1663 according to which Jayadhwaj Singha transferred Kamrup to the possession of the Moguls and promised to pay a heavy war-indemnity. Jayadhwaj Singha's successor Chakradhwaj Singha wrested back Kamrup from the Moguls in 1667, and the Ahoms, remained in undisturbed possession of their territories till 1679 when Laluk Barphukan the Ahom viceroy of Gauhati, entered into a collusion with Sultan Azamtara, the Subedar of Bengal, and made over Gauhati to the Sultan's deputy Nawab Mansur Khan. In July 1682 during the reign of King Gadadhar Singha, the Ahoms expelled Mansur Khan from Gauhati and re-established their possession over the territories extending up to the river Manas which remained the western limit till 1826.

King Gadadhar Singha, who had ascended the throne in July 1681, was virtually the first prince of the Tungkhungia dynasty. His son King Rudra Singha was a man of great ability and ambition. Having brought the neighbouring territories under his domination he turned his attention towards organising a confederacy of the Rajas of Hindusthan with a view to oust the Moguls from their sovereign power. Messengers were sent by Rudra Singha to several Rajas and Zemindars who sent him promises of support. An army of 400,000 was mobilised at Gauhati, and Rudra Singha

8. S. K. Bhuyan, *Kamrupar Buranji*, pp. 27, 51.

planned to march into Mogul territories in November 1714, but when preparations were on foot the king suddenly died at Gauhati in September 1714.

After King Rudra Singha's death his four sons sat on the Ahom throne one after the other,—Siva Singha, Pramatta Singha, Rajeswar Singha, and Lakshmi Singha. The last named monarch was succeeded by his son Gaurinath Singha and the latter by Kamaleswar Singha. During the reign of Siva Singha, Pramatta Singha and Rajeswar Singha, 1714 to 1769, there was peace and order in the land, and the monarchs found time to pay their attention to the patronage of literature and art; but from 1769 onwards the country was disrupted by civil dissensions, and the government had ultimately to seek foreign aid for the suppression of local disturbances.

Kamaleswar was succeeded in 1811 by his brother Chandrakanta Singha. Since 1783 the real authority of administration was wielded by the prime minister Purnananda Buragohain. The emergency measures which he employed for counteracting the grave situation of the country made him unpopular among the nobles, and several conspiracies were launched to murder Purnananda. The Burmese invaded the country in 1817 at the instance of Badanchandra Barphukan, the viceroy of Gauhati, but Purnananda died before the invaders entered the capital. Chandrakanta continued to rule till 1818 when he was replaced by Purandar Singha, a descendant of Rajeswar Singha. Chandrakanta regained his throne in 1821 through Burmese intervention, but being unable to tolerate the atrocities committed by the Burmese, he entered into hostilities with the invaders, and on his defeat in June 1822 he fled to Bengal, leaving the Burmese to the complete domination of Assam. But in 1824 the British entered Assam and expelled the Burmese from their commanding position up the river Brahmaputra. By the Treaty of Yandaboo enacted in February 1826, Assam passed into the hands of the East India Company. Purandar Singha was installed in 1833 as tributary ruler of Upper Assam, but as he failed to pay the stipulated tribute his country was resumed by the Company in 1838.

The Ahoms thus ruled in Assam for a little less than six hundred years. Lord William Bentinck, Governor-General of India from 1828 to 1832, referred to the long continuance of Ahom rule in Assam as "almost without example in history."[9] It should

9. W. H. Macnaughten, Secretary to Governor-General, to G. Swinton, July 18; and David Scott to Swinton, Aug. 4, Beng. Pol. Cons., Sept. 2, 1831, Nos. 2 and 3.

be pointed out that the Ahoms were one of the few races in India who could stem the tide of Mogul conquest. It was only for ten months during 1662-63 that Mir Jumla remained in possession of the Ahom capital; and Kamrup since its first annexation to the Ahom kingdom in 1615, was possessed by the Moguls for a total period of twenty-six years only, once from 1639 to 1658, and again from 1663 to 1667, and from 1679 to 1682.

The factor which enabled the Ahoms to consolidate their power in Assam and to maintain it for such a long period were mainly their militaristic cult, their highly developed political sense, and their religious toleration, detachment and neutrality. Political and military achievements were considered as the only path to fortune and to fame. The Ahoms were past masters in strategy and statecraft, and they were endowed with a keen sense of values in political matters. The first Ahom conqueror Sukapha was accompanied by a handful of followers, but he and his successors strengthened themselves by admitting into the Ahom fold members of the old martial races of Assam. Records were, however, maintained to show the distinction between the descendants of the original conquerors and of the newly affiliated Ahoms. For several centuries the Ahoms remained aloof from the Hindu influences of their surroundings. They followed their old rites and ceremonials, and maintained to some extent their intercourse with their original homeland in Upper Burma.

The political instincts of the Ahoms actuated them to record the chief events of the reigns of sovereigns in officially compiled chronicles or Buranjis. This system, which has conferred upon the Assamese the unique distinction of possessing historical masterpieces in prose, can be traced to Sukapha's command that "the Pandits should write down all particulars, whenever an incident takes place, when a person dies and when we acquire new followers."[10] The Buranjis served as a record of precedents, and also as an inducement to perform great deeds and desist from performing evil ones.

The Ahom system of administration: Lord William Bentinck inferred from the long domination of the Ahoms in Assam that there must have been something intrinsically good in the original constitution. The principle which governed the administrative system of the Ahoms was the right of joint conquest according to which the enjoyment of the soil was vested in the leader Sukapha and his commanders and camp-followers who had helped him to

10. S. K. Bhuyan, *Deodhai Asam Buranji*, p. 90.

establish Ahom domination in Assam. Sukapha's descendants enjoyed a hereditary title to the throne, and those of his companions to the principal offices of the state. Only the descendants of Sukaphas' Buragohain and Bargohain could be appointed to these respective posts ; and the Barbarua and the Barphukan must always be selected from among the members of the Lahan, Duara, Dihingia and Sandikoi families on the ground that their ancestors had been the compatriots of Sukapha in the conquest of Assam. Any appointment from outside these families was viewed with disfavour by the ancient aristocracy of the land as it meant a decided infringement of their vested interests. During Mir Jumla's invasion of Assam in 1662, the Ahom commanders in charge of the garrisons at Gauhati and Kamrup relaxed their resistance to the invaders as a protest against the appointment of a Kayastha—Manthir Bharali Barua of the Bezdoloi family—over their head as Sirdar of the army with the rank of Parvatia Phukan. In Lakshmi Singha's reign the Ahom nobles were seriously offended at the growing power of a non-Ahom—Kekeru Kalita Choladhara Phukan—though the monarch was personally in favour of allowing the Kalita to continue in power in view of the services he had rendered in the deliverance of the king from imprisonment at the hands of the Moran rebels. Captain Thomas Welsh who had stayed in Assam from 1792 to 1794 and had closely studied its affairs considered the confirment of the office of Barbarua on Rupchandra, on his son Kirtichandra and on the latter's grandson Jainath, as one of the sources of the prevailing discontent and disaffection, as Rupchandra did not belong to either of the families from which a Barbarua could be selected.[11]

The main trend of Ahom political ideology is embodied in the advice given to Khunlung and Khunlai at the time of their departure to rule over this earth,—"Just as a man loses his wife if he quarrels with his father-in-law and brothers-in-law, and just as a mother-bird guards her nestlings with her wings and protects them from rain and storm, and rears them up by feeding them herself, so you two brothers should protect your subjects and desist from quarrelling with your friends and supporters."[12] However engrossed they might be in the realities of political domination and government, the Ahoms cherished a noble conception of the ideal state or Utopia in which all men were happy and there was no distinction of brothers and strangers. The prime minister Atan

11. Capt. Welsh to Sir John Shore, Beng. Pol. Cons., Feb. 17, 1794, No. 20.
12. S. K. Bhuyan, *Deodhai Asam Buranji*, pp. 1-2.

Buragohain Rajmantri Dangaria said in one place about the *Satya-yuga* or the Golden Age,—"Love was the order of the time. Men used to take food in the same dish like sons of the same mother; and nobody entertained any jealousy or hatred towards any other person." The same Buragohain wrote about the reign of a descendant of Khunlung,—"During his rule the sufferings of the people came to an end, and they became happy as before. He governed his subjects as his own sons. There was no taxation in his time. He lived in the ways of righteousness according due punishment to every guilt, and rewards and honour to virtue and merit."[13]

The Ahom government was monarchical and aristocratical. The king, or Swargadeo or Swarga-Maharaja as he was called, was the supreme head of the state; and all honours, titles, offices, decisions and war measures emanated from him; but he had to act according to the advice of the three hereditary councillors of state, the Buragohain, the Bargohain and the Barpatra Gohain. The duty of selecting a king from among the qualified members of the existing princely families devolved upon these three nobles, and if united they could depose a monarch. A powerful sovereign could override the decisions of the three Gohains, and an astute Gohain could impose his will upon his colleagues, and upon the large body of Phukans and Baruas, and upon the king himself. The Barbarua was the head of the executive and the judiciary, but he could not act independently of the three Gohains; any matter placed before the monarch by the Barbarua would be considered in the presence of the Gohains, and if it was one of great moment the Phukans and Baruas would also be summoned to give their opinion.

The Barphukan lived at Gauhati as the king's deputy, and administered the territory from Kaliabar to the western frontier of Assam. He conducted the political relations with Bengal and Bhutan and the chieftains on the Assam passes. The Choladhara Phukan, or the master of the regalia, was in charge of foreign affairs, both political and commercial. The states of Jayantia, Cachar, Khyrim and Manipur were in friendly alliance with the Ahom government though some degree of subordination was accepted by the first two as a result of definite agreements. The province of Darrang enjoyed complete autonomy in its internal administration, as well as the other vassal states, Rani, Beltola, Luki, Barduar, Bholagaon, Mairapur, Pantan, Bangoon, Bagaduar,

13. S. K. Bhuyan, Atan Buragohain's Buranji, in *Deodhai Asam Buranji*, pp. 88-89.

Dimarua, Neli, Gobha, Sahari, Dandua, Barepujia, Topakuchia, Khaigharia, Panbari, Sora, Mayang, Dhing, Tetelia, Salmara, Garakhia, Baghargaon and Bhurbandha. Each state was ruled by a vassal chief who was bound to furnish a stipulated number of *paiks* to work on the king's account, or pay the commutation money if exemption from personal service was granted. In case of war the vassal Raja was expected to take the field at the head of his contingent of *paiks* by the side of his liegelord. The frontiers of the kingdom were protected from the inroads of the hill people by several wardens, the Sadiya-khowa Gohain, the Marangi-khowa Gohain, the Solal Gohain, the Jagialia Gohain and the Kajalimukhia Gohain, and they were always selected from the families of the three Gohains at the metropolis. The frontier tribesmen were allowed regular blackmail either in the shape of money or articles or servitors.

The adult population of Assam was divided into *khels* having to render specific service to the state, such as arrow-making, boat-building, boat-plying, house-building, provision-supplying, fighting, writing, revenue collecting, road-building, catching and training of elephants, superintendence of horses, training of hawks, and supervision of forests. Sometimes *khels* were composed on a territorial basis, e.g., the Dimaruguria *khel* consisted of the men of Dimaruguri. Each *khel* was like a guild to which lands were allotted for cultivation by the constituent members, free of rent in return for the service they rendered to the state. The strength of a *khel* varied from 3000 to 100. Each *khel* was placed in charge of a Phukan if it was an important one, and of a Rajkhowa or a Barua if it was of less importance. A Phukan commanded 6,000 men, and a Rajkhowa or Barua was in charge of two to three thousand men. A Barua was generally a departmental or administrative head or deputy; whereas a Rajkhowa was ordinarily a governor of a territory and head of the levies raised from his jurisdiction. Hence, in an expeditionary force there was a preponderance of Rajkhowas over Baruas, as the former, like feudal lords, joined the war with their respective contingents who had been in the habit of knowing him and receiving commands from him in the regular course of administration. The Rajkhowas also administered justice in their allotted districts. In the correspondence of the East India Company the head of a *khel* was sometimes designated as a *Kheldar*. He was assisted by a gradation of officers, Hazarikas or commanders of 1000, Saikias or commanders of 100, and Baras or commanders of 20 men. An adult male whose name was registered for state service was called a *paik*, and four *paiks* constituted a unit called a *got*. One man in a *got* had to serve the state for three months in a year at the end of which his place was taken by a second man from the same *got*, and so forth. The remaining three *paiks* looked after the cultivation and other domestic concerns of their absent comrade. In cases of emergency two men, and even three men, were recruited for state service from each *got*, or the *got* maximum was reduced from four to three *paiks*. The levy of one man from each got was called the *mul*, of two the *dowal*, and of three the *tewal*. The standing army at the capital was a very poor one; in 1809 it consisted of 300 up-country sepoys and 800 native troops. In case of war or other public occasions the officers in charge of the various *khels* mobilised their respective quotas of *paiks*. A *paik* could sometimes obtain exemption from personal service by payment of money, a privilege which was invariably enjoyed by all *chamuas* or the higher rank of subjects. On account of the marked similarity between the Ahom *khel* system and the Mogul *mansabdari* system, it is likely for the Ahoms to have obtained the cue from the Moguls whom they had known from their frequent political contacts. According to the *mansabdari* system, ranks were decided by the number of soldiers commanded by an officer, both infantry and cavalry; there were also *mansabs* below 1,000. There is some similarity also in the gradation of the insignias. The Ahom *khel* system was organised by Momai-tamuli Barbarua in 1609 under the direction of the reigning monarch Swargadeo Pratap Singha.[14]

The main sources of revenue were the commutation money realised from men who were exempted from personal service, rent paid by *paiks* when they cultivated lands in excess of those allotted to them free of charge, house-tax for houses and gardens, hearth-tax and hoe-tax, royalties on elephants and timbers, and rent paid by farmers of mines and frontier traders. The Muslim chronicler who accompanied Mir Jumla to Assam computed that if Assam were administered like the Mogul dominions it was very likely that forty or forty-five lakhs of rupees would be collected from the revenue paid by the ryots, and from the price of elephants caught in the jungles and other sources. He further calculated that the value of the gold washed from the sands of the Brahmaputra would come to rupees 80,000 to 108,000. The currency of Assam consisted of gold and silver coins and conch shells or *cowries*. Copper coins were not current in Assam.[15]

14. Ms. Assam Buranji, No. 8.
15. Sir Jadunath Sarkar, J.B.O.R.S., 1915, p. 187.

Succession to the throne was systematic in the beginning, being based on the law of primogeniture, with occasional deviations in favour of a brother or a nephew. Later on a powerful Gohain or a Barbarua could manoeuvre the support of his colleagues in placing on the throne any prince from the collateral branches. Normally, succession was determined during the life-time of a reigning sovereign and was announced immediately on his death. When succession was not previously fixed, the announcement of a monarch's death was postponed till a new king was selected. Succession to the throne was solemnised by the Gohains and the principal officers offering their prostration to the new sovereign; but the coronation, known as the *Singhari-ghar-utha* ceremony, which entailed elaborate and expensive arrangements, was performed a few months later. As any prince of blood royal could claim succession to the throne it was a custom to disqualify all possible rivals by mutilation. It was not unusual for a prince who had no deformity in his body to enlist the support of some minister and make a dash for the throne, or for a powerful potentate to harbour a prince and set him up as a claimant when opportunities offered themselves. There was thus in the country a vast body of ambitious princes who were secretly supported by powerful nobles and who thus provided ready-made materials for insurrection. On one occasion the princes were removed to segregation areas in the wilds of Namrup which being distant from the capital the sinister influence to which the princes were exposed could not be averted; they were then transferred to the vicinity of the capital which exposed them to the machinations of powerfully organised disloyal parties. In the absence of a proper solution of the problem of the princes the efficiency and internal harmony of the administration were imperilled to a very great extent.

The tenets of the Ahom faith, their correspondence to the faiths of the other Shan races, and the influences which had entered into the texture of those tenets have not yet been examined owing to the practically total absence of the necessary data. But from Pali chronicles corroborated by archaeological finds we learn that the Thais had come under Buddhist-Hindu influences, and the Ahoms as members of the Thai race had shared in that influence. Yunnan, the most powerful Thai principality, was called Nan-Chao by the Chinese, and Gandhara by the Indo-Chinese; its capital was known as Mithila, and a part of the kingdom as Videha-rajya. Yunnan adopted Buddhism through the preachings of an Indian saint named Avalokiteswara. In the ninth century A.D. it was visited by an Indian monk from Magadha named Chandragupta.

The Hinduised Thai kingdom of Gandhara or Yunnan flourished till 1253 when it was overrun and conquered by the great Mongol chief Kublai Khan. It is believed that the Thai states to the west and south of Yunnan, and to the east of the mountain ranges which border on Manipur and Assam had colonies of Hindus or had settlements of Hindus in large numbers. A writer has remarked "that the main spring of the civilisation of most of the Thai states lay in India and not in China."[16]

Definite traces of Buddhist-Hindu influence can be found in the Ahom scriptures, the most significant of which is *Phura-Tara-Alam,* known also as *Phura-Alang* and *Min-mang Phuralung,* which is held in high veneration by the priests even up to this day. The book expounds the virtue of non-violence in deed and thought, in the form of an exhortation given by the Almighty God Sikia to Lengdan and other deities to rule the earth according to the principle of *Ahimsa.* The discourse begins with the story of a disciple who participates in the flesh of a fowl during his short visit to his parental home, which involves a violation of his teacher's injunctions. This incident supplies an opportunity to the teacher to dilate on the virtue of *Ahimsa* of which non-slaughter and non-participation in animal flesh constitute the first step. According to the traditions of the Ahoms, *Min-mang Phuralung* which has been called the Bible of the Ahoms had been brought to Assam by the priests who accompanied the conqueror Sukapha. Another classic *Pung-Gao-Kham,* known ordinarily as the Ahom Ramayana, contains an account of Ramachandra, called by the Ahoms Chang-Gao-Kham.[17]

The wealth of old Ahom literature is unfortunately a sealed book to us owing to the great paucity of men who can read the manuscripts intelligently and translate them into tolerable English or Assamese. The Ahom priests called Deodhais, Mohans and Bailungs, conserved the original Ahom traditions, and conducted worship at the Ahom shrines according to their own sacerdotal code. The first Ahom king to accept Hinduism formally was Jayadhwaj Singha though Hindu tendencies had crept into the royal household since the days of Sudangpha Bamuni-kowanr. From 1648 to 1681 the newly Hinduised Ahom kings were all disciples of Vaisnava Gosains; and Sakta influence entered the

16. R. C. Majumdar, *Hindu Colonies in the Far East,* 1944, pp. 225-229.

17. S. K. Bhuyan, Bulletin I of the Department of Historical and Antiquarian Studies in Assam, 1932, pp. 20-21, 29. The *Phura-lung* Puthi was translated for the D.H.A.S. by the well-known Deodhai Pandit Srijut Nandanath Phukan.

Ahom court with the ascendency of the Tungkhungias. The Ahom princes and nobles patronised literature and art; and numerous Assamese classics, poems, dramas as well as treatises on useful subjects were written or compiled under the patronage of Ahom kings, queens and grandees.

Even after their acceptance of Hinduism the Ahoms did not completely give up their religion and their customs. On ascending the throne every king assumed two names, one in Assamese Hindu form and the other in Ahom, e.g., Jayadhwaj Singha, Rudra Singha, Gaurinath Singha and Chandrakanta were also given the Ahom names Sutamla, Sukhrangpha, Suhitpangpha and Sudingpha respectively. Coins continued to be struck in Ahom and Assamese scripts, and land-grants on copper-plates were inscribed in both the languages. Since the death of Rajeswar Singha the funeral ceremonies of the Ahom monarchs were performed in accordance with both the Brahmanical and Ahom codes.

The Muslims, and in fact all non-Ahoms, did not suffer any disability on account of their religious faiths. Upto the year 1772 the Gohains and the Phukans were all appointed from among the Ahoms; and the highest office to which a non-Ahom, whether he was a Hindu or a Muslim, could look forward to was a Baruaship. A large number of Muslims were appointed in several departments of the state, minting of coins, painting, carpentry, embroidery work, sword-making, gun-casting and the manufacture of gunpowder. Several learned Muslims generally known as *Parsi-parhias,* or Persian readers, were attached to the Ahom court, and their main occupation was deciphering and interpreting of Persian documents, drafting and supervision of the Persian correspondence of the government. Muslim religious leaders or *pirs* paid visits to Assam to minister to the spiritual needs of their co-religionists. The Ahom rulers encouraged these *pirs* to settle in Assam by the grant of revenue-free lands, known as *Pir-pal* lands. Some of them were known as Dewans and they exercised great influence upon the masses. Dr. J. P. Wade, who stayed in Assam from 1792 to 1794, has referred to a Muslim, "the gooroo-general of his persuasion in Assam from about the time of Roodur Singha. He had numerous attendants dressed in the high Mussleman dress. He resided at or near the capital and frequented the durbar; and the Swargadeos used to despatch him to pray at Hadjoo after the Mussleman fashion for their prosperity. He was usually succeeded by his nearest relations". The same writer found ten or twelve houses of instruction for Muslim children at Gauhati, and more than twenty at Rangpur, the capital of Assam. The Hindus and the Muslims lived in perfect amity and peace, and Shihabuddin Talish, who came to Assam with Nawab Mir Jumla, wrote,—"As for the Musalmans who had been taken prisoner in former times and had chosen to marry here, their descendants are exactly in the manner of the Assamese and have nothing of Islam except the name; their hearts are inclined far more towards mingling with the Assamese than towards association with Muslims."[18]

Ahom social outlook: The Ahoms were liberal in their social outlook, being dominated in their actions mainly by considerations of practical necessity and political expediency, unaccompanied by any desire to propagate their own view of life. The number of Ahoms who had come with the first conqueror Sukapha was very small, and those who came in later were restricted in number as Shans are reluctant to leave their homes where there is plenty of food and happiness in their own self-sufficient villages situated amidst pastoral surroundings. With such small numbers the Ahoms found it impossible to maintain their comparatively extensive dominions in Eastern India, peopled by heterogeneous races and tribes, with the powerful Muslim and Koch rulers on the west as a source of perpetual danger. The Ahoms were therefore compelled to increase their community by conferring upon the new entrants the status and privileges of the members of the ruling race. The records of these affiliations were very carefully maintained and they were checked in every reign, the most exhaustive scrutiny being carried out during the reign of Swargadeo Pratap Singha. From these records, some leading Ahom families appear to have been founded by patriarchs belonging to the following non-Ahom races, tribes and communities,—Barahi, Chutia, Garo, Koch, Kachari, Moran, Hindu Kalita, Hindu Dhoba, Miri, Mogul and Muslim.[19]

The non-Ahom families who were admitted to the Ahom fold owed their affiliation to some heroic and meritorious act done by the founders, or their particularly attractive manners and features, or indications of their potential capacity. These new families were thoroughly assimilated with the old Ahoms, and no disabilities were attached to their holding offices of rank, and their enjoyment of the other privileges to which the older Ahoms were entitled. The orthodox and the 'blue' section of the Ahoms were, however,

18. Sir Jadunath Sarkar, tr. of *Fathiyah-i-Ibriyah* in J.B.O.R.S., 1915, p. 193; S. K. Bhuyan, *Annals of the Delhi Badshahate*, Introduction, pp. 1-27, dealing with Assam's contact with the Muslim world.

19. H. C. Goswami, *Purani Asam Buranji*, pp. 24-25; S. K. Bhuyan, *Assam Buranji, S.M.*, unprinted portion; Ms. Assam Buranji, No. 14.

annoyed if too much prominence was given to the new entrants in the first stage of their affiliation; but their opposition became gradually relaxed as their new nationals proved their ability, earned some fame, and identified themselves with the ideals and aspirations, and successfully adopted the manners and customs of the members of the original stock.

The seven principal Ahom clans or *phoids* were distinguished under the name *Sat-gharia-Ahom*, literally, the Ahoms of the Seven Houses. The first three houses were the royal family, the Buragohain family, and the Bargohain family; and about the remaining four families there was always a difference of opinion. According to one section, these four *phoids* were the Deodhai, Mohan, Bailung and Siring families of priests and astrologers; while according to others, they were the secular families Lahan, Sandikoi, Dihingia and Duara. The Satgharia Ahom families, whatever their constitution might be, were exogamous groups each family being derived from one common ancestor. Each *phoid* was again divided into a number of sub-groups, generally named after the places where they settled after having branched off from their original families. There were seven sub-houses of the royal family; eight of the Buragohain family, sixteen of the Bargohain family; twelve of the Deodhai, seven of the Mohan and eight of the Bailung family.[20] The original Barpatra Gohain's family, known as Kenduguria Barpatra *phoid*, was absorbed in the family of the king, as its founder Kancheng was a prince of royal blood. The non-royal Barpatra Gohain families were Kalugayan or Gargayan Patar and Moran Patar.

In the beginning, the Ahom rulers married from the recognised Ahom families, including those of the new entrants. Towards the latter part of their reign they occasionally married from Hindu families as well. The lead, as far as we know, was taken by Sukhampha Khora Raja by marrying two Sonari Hindu girls who became great favourites of the monarch to the chagrin and resentment of their rivals, and the displeasure of the nobles. To humble the pride of his wives who boasted of a numerous family, the king conferred the status of a prince on a number of handsome youths, equipping them with gold-mounted muskets and declaring them as belonging to his own family. These 'princes' were given the title *Kowanr-Hiloidaris* or musketeer princes. Swargadeo Siva

20. Lt.-Col. P. R. T. Gurdon, *A Short Note on the Ahoms,* contributed to Hastings's *Encyclopaedia of Religion and Ethics;* Kasinath Tamuli-Phukan's *Assam Buranji Katha,* 1906, pp. 120-121.

Singha married an exceptionally beautiful and accomplished Nat girl, Phulmati; and after her death, her sister Damayanti. They were both elevated to sovereign ranks, when they assumed the names Pramatheswari Devi and Ambika Devi. They both became patronesses of art and literature. Their brother Harinath was made a Barpatra Gohain after being formally admitted to the Ahom fold. Their other relatives, including their mother Sita, were similarly honoured. Siva Singha's successor Pramatta Singha also took a number of Hindu girls to wife. About the year 1812, King Chandrakanta married Padmavati, the daughter of a devotee attached to Bengena-Ati Satra, in the teeth of opposition from the prime minister Purnananda Buragohain, which contributed to the growing estrangement between the king and the premier.[21]

Ahom religious policy: The same liberal and practical outlook also shaped the religious policy of the Ahom monarchs. In the beginning of their rule the Ahom priests known as Deodhais acted as political advisers, but they were gradually relegated to priestly functions and to the divining of events. The Deodhais and other Ahom priests were associated with all ceremonial occasions; and sacrifices in the orthodox Ahom fashion used to be performed even upto the end of their rule. These sacrifices were calculated to secure the welfare of the kings and the people, or were performed for bringing victory to Ahom arms, or to celebrate successes in war. The association of Ahom priests was indispensable in the coronation of a monarch whom they blessed uttering old-time verses in a musical tone reminding him of the primordial gods *Phura-tara* or creator, *Lengdan* or Indra, *Jasingpha* or the god of learning, *Phai* or god of fire, and *Kao-Kham* or god of water; and their own royal ancestors Khunlung and Khunlai, who were attributed a divine origin. The image of Chom-cheng which Sukapha had brought with him from his ancestral home was the tutelary deity of the Ahom rulers till the end of their rule, and there were regular provisions from the state for the maintenance of the worship of this image.[22] The Ahoms looked upon Charaideo, their first capital, as the most sacred place of their faith. It subsequently became

21. S. K. Bhuyan, *An Assamese Nur Jahan*, pp. 29-30; *Assam Buranji* by Harakanta Barua, p. 85; Ms. Assam Buranji, No. 14.

22. According to orthodox Ahom traditions *Chom* and *Cheng* were two images. The former was with Hkun-tai who founded a kingdom in Assam; and the latter was with the younger prince Hkun-lai who established a kingdom among the Nara tribes (Mung-Hkwan), Rev. W. W. Cochrane's "The Northern Shans" in *Shans at Home* by Mrs. Leslie Milne, London, 1910, p. 19.

their necropolis, and there were many shrines where Ahom worship was regularly maintained.

The Ahom kings were not bigoted adherents of their faith, and they did not force their religion on any one, and they warmly embraced all men into their social fold if such absorption was calculated to add to their political strength. They did not hesitate to punish the priests if their predictions were not properly fulfilled or if they produced untoward results. The rulers kept their eyes open to new influences, and yielded to them ungrudgingly if they were found to possess any practical value.

The Hinduisation of the Ahoms was partly the result of a number of accidental circumstances, and partly the outcome of a deliberate policy. Hindu influence first entered the Ahom court during the reign of King Sudangpha Bamuni-kowanr who had been brought up in a Brahman family. The influence was more marked in the reign of King Pratap Singha who was personally grateful to Brahman priests for ridding him of a "demon" which had possessed him during his princehood, and whose continuance was considered by that monarch to be distressful and undignified if he had to perform his royal duties with justice and equanimity. The first Ahom monarch to accept Hinduism formally was Jayadhwaj Singha who wanted to propitiate the gods by his devotion to religion and atone for his patricide. Jayadhwaj Singha and his successors upto Sulikpha Lora Raja took their initiation into Vaisnavism which was the predominant faith in Assam at that time.

But Gadadhar Singha who succeeded Lora Raja in 1681 had decided leanings towards Saktaism, as he considered Vaisnavism to be too passive and mild to be suitable for a ruling class who had to maintain their domination by the force of arms. He viewed with disfavour the wealth, grandeur and influence of the Vaisnava pontiffs whom he regarded as potential danger-spots capable of diverting the loyalty of the subjects to themselves and thereby reducing the monarchs to comparative nonentities. Gadadhar Singha therefore inaugurated a campaign of pillaging the Vaisnava monasteries and killing and expelling their heads. His son King Rudra Singha became towards the end of his rule an open supporter of the Sakta faith, and from his death onwards that faith became the creed of the Ahom sovereigns and of the principal nobles and officers.

The Ahom rulers, with probably a very few exceptions, showed at the same time due respect and courtesy to the Vaisnava monks, and made grants and endowments for the maintenance of the Vaisnava Satras or monasteries. They also patronised the

Ahom priests and allowed them to perform their rituals, and to participate in the royal ceremonies as prayer-men. By adopting the Sakta faith, by supporting the Vaisnava monks and Satras, and by maintaining the orthodox Ahom rituals and ceremonies the Ahom rulers encouraged a state or triarchy in religious matters, leading to a considerable amount of rivalry between the three groups. They also entertained Muslim priests to pray for their welfare at the principal Muslim shrine at Poa-Macca hill in Hazo.[23]

Many people hold the view that the adoption of Hinduism by the Ahoms was the result of a deliberate policy. They realised the dangers springing from their being in a hopeless minority in a kingdom where the majority were Hindus. They thought they would add to their strength if they became one with their subjects by embracing the latter's faith. The Ahoms did even give up their own language, and adopt Assamese, the language of the ruled. The history of the subsequent periods will demonstrate how far this adoption of the religion and language of the subjects was expedient and sound. It is at any rate unique in the history of the world. The Ahoms continued to extend their adherence to Hinduism and their patronage and support of its institutions even though they were not admitted by the older Hindus into their social fold, and to the unifying amenities of inter-marrying and inter-dining, a position which sometimes perplexed the Ahoms because they for themselves embraced their new entrants with open arms without attaching to them any social and political disability.

The Ahoms were catholic in their social and religious outlook, and extremely tolerant of the views of others. King Udayaditya Singha's infatuation of the up-country Sannyasi, Paramananda Bairagi, and the consequent pressure put by him upon the Assamese Vaisnava monks to become the Sannyasi's disciples, was an unusual deviation from the path of toleration; but it was the private action of the monarch, and it had not the sanction of the government. The Ahoms themselves opposed the growing influence of Paramananda, and in the revolution that followed the king lost his throne and his life. The Sannyasi was executed and his corpse exposed to public ridicule. Similarly Queen Pramatheswari's humiliation of some Vaisnava monks by compelling them to bow before the Durga image was an unpremeditated act of impulse. The queen's dislike of a particular order of Vaisnava

23. S. K. Bhuyan, "An Early Historian of the East India Company, Dr. J. P. Wade," in the Proceedings of the Twelfth Session of the Indian Historical Records Commission, held at Gwalior in December 1929.

monks, namely, the Mahantas of the Thakuria denomination, was however pronounced. Her attitude and actions can be explained as the zeal of a neophyte and the vagaries of a woman who was called upon to wield sovereign power for which she did not possess the requisite equipment, either of birth or of training.

The Ahom rulers considered themselves to be the guardians of the existing usages and customs, and they thought that this policy ensured peace and tranquillity in the kingdom; and that connivance of innovations of a drastic kind and the encouragement of heterodoxy in any form might lead to inter-communal discord and the growth of revolutionary propensities which might reappear some day in the political sphere as well. So they rigorously suppressed every disturbance of the social and religious order at the very moment its possibilities made their appearance.

During the invasion of Assam by the Koch general Chilarai, the Ahoms dressed up their soldiers in the guise of Brahmans, each wearing a sacred thread and seated on a cow, the killing of a Brahman or of a cow being tabu to a Hindu. Chilarai, out of respect for the Brahmans and dreading the obloquay of cow-slaughter, desisted from attacking the Ahom army. But the social consequences of this *ruse de guerre* resulted in serious confusion in society. Most of these 'war-Brahmans' refused to give up their sacred threads; they began to live the life of Brahmans to all intents and purposes, and claimed the privileges and respect due to that superior caste. King Pratap Singha appointed a commission with an Ahom officer named Lekai Chetia as its head, who went round the villages, scrutinised the claims, and separated the spurious Brahmans from the genuine ones. The doubtful claimants were given a special appellation to be used as a distinguishing mark.

The same monarch punished two hundred Brahmans by ordering their conversion to the Kaivarta caste, now designated as a Scheduled Caste under the Government of India Act of 1935. These Brahmans had accepted in their society a co-caste man and eaten with him though he had commerced with a Kaivarta woman. The offenders had of course subjected their gallant friend to a ceremony of purification, but it had not been regarded by the monarch to be capable of absolving the Brahman of his original guilt.[24]

A claim was made by five Sudra preachers that they could offer initiation to Brahmans. Protests were lodged with King Rudra Singha disputing this claim of the Sudra monks. In 1702, the

24. Ms. Assam Buranji, No. 8.

monarch summoned a convention of Pandits and Vaisnava abbots, where he asked the Sudra preachers concerned to produce texts from the scriptures or cite other sources to substantiate their claim. "The five priests", it is recorded in an old chronicle, "failed to refer to any *puthi* [manuscript, scripture], nor could they cite any authority. They also could not utter a single word. The Brahmans therefore became furious." The five preachers were severely punished by King Rudra Singha for having sponsord such a claim which appeared to him preposterous and heterodox, and he passed orders prohibiting Brahmans to stay in or visit Sudra monasteries. The head of the Mayamara Satra was subsequently punished for having allowed two Brahmans to live in his Satra.[25]

The contact of the Ahoms with different religious faiths reacted on their political concepts. In the beginning their political conduct was principally governed by the instructions which, according to the sacred books of the Ahoms, were given by Jasingpha, god of learning, to Khunlung and Khunlai on the eve of their departure to rule upon the earth as representatives of their grandfather Lengdan or Indra. During the later periods, the Ahoms were imparted systematic knowledge of Hindu political treatises,—Arthasastras and Dandanitis, through the learned Pandits attached to the royal court and to the families of the leading Ahom nobles. This can be illustrated by a few extracts:—

Jasingpha said,—"If there be a battle, inform me, and I shall send down eight lakhs of gods who will cut down all the enemies to pieces....I give you a sword; all the people of the country will pay you homage. You must always be alert in carrying out state affairs. At the end of a year, you must wash and sharpen the sword. I give you the rule of a wide country. You will never be overcome or defeated by others....I give you Somdeo [Chum-cheng]; you will never leave the idol.....You must be careful not to let the idol fall to the ground. You will then be endowed with long life. No king will disobey you." To this Lengdan added,—"There are innumerable number of people in the country. The country is full of Tais and slaves. They cannot distinguish right from wrong. They are in the habit of taking other's property and wives by force.....If a person commits a crime, do not kill him at once without fair trial.....There are people of various communities on the earth. It is very thickly populated. You must rule with a firm hand."[26]

25. S. K. Bhuyan, *Tungkhungia Buranji*, O.U.P., pp. 33-35.
26. Golapchandra Barua, *Ahom Buranji*, pp. 11-15.

To this may be compared the advice of Kirtichandra Barbarua given to the fugitive king Lakshmi Singha on November 24, 1769, suggesting that the monarch and his trusted followers should retire to Kaliabar with a view to collect an army to expel the Moran insurgents who had been successful in their operations against the royalist forces, and were at that time marching towards the capital Rangpur:—

"The duty of a Kshattriya", said Kirtichandra Barbarua, "is to fight as long as there is life in his body. If victorious he enjoys the powers and blessings of sovereignty; if dead he goes to heaven. If he desists from fighting he earns disgrace in the life hereafter, while in this world he has to lead a life of subservience to others. As he has perpetually to carry out the commands of others, he becomes subjected to fright, humiliation and pain. He has to live in eternal solicitation of death. This is certainly a dire distress. When a king becomes subjected to the monarch of another country, diplomatic measures should be adopted so that the conqueror may return to his own kingdom. On his retirement the subdued prince should remain in preparedness with his army; and when opportunities present themselves for action he should strike promptly and reinstate himself in his lost suzerain power.....The wicked have never consistently maintained their vows of friendship with the pious. The wicked have no forgiveness nor any piety: so none of the king's adherents will be spared by the rebels. If nothing untoward happens to His Majesty he will at least have some mental anxiety and displeasure; his nobles and followers also will share the same; it will then be impossible for the king to collect adherents like ourselves. A person acquires a petty job by parting with large sums of money and other articles; still he is reluctant to give it up. If any body asserts that the Moamarias will retire to the forest after attaining the position of a *Raja-chakravarti* Your Majesty should by no means believe in such words." [27]

External relations: The external relations of the Ahom government were concerned with the states and tribes contiguous to their immediate frontier, and occasionally with the territories situated at a distance from the Assam boundaries. These relations sprang from Assam's treatment of foreign demands for political and commercial concessions; or their mutual wishes to establish bonds of friendship and alliance, and to strengthen them if such

27. S. K. Bhuyan, *Political Wisdom of Kirtichandra Barbarua,* in Assam Sahitya-Sabha Patrika, Vol. II, Part 2, pp. 67-71. Ms. chronicle of King Lakshmi Singha's reign.

relations had existed before. Desire for friendship was inspired by an overt object, or dictated by the requirements of neighbourliness.

Relations with the Muslim powers in Bengal and with Cooch Behar were systematic and continuous, and more so after Cooch Behar came under the domination of the Moguls when they became neighbours to Assam; while relations with the hill tribes were casual and sporadic, as they had no territorial ambition, and their trading activities were conducted on a minor scale, though the commodities they brought into Assam were precious and unavailable in other parts of India. Besides, the hill tribes generally respected their agreements, while the established governments of the Moguls and the Koches flouted the agreements as expediency demanded, if they could support such transgression by the application of force. Contravention of treaty terms was not also an unusual feature of the strategy of the Ahoms. They held that a powerful enemy should be pacified and removed from the land by the acceptance of terms however humiliating they might be, and when opportunities permitted the treaty terms should be defied and hostilities resumed. The Ahoms followed the political adage that promises made under duress need not be fulfilled if such fulfilment puts the promiser-state in a serious disadvantage.

The states with which Assam had political relations were Mogul India including the Subah of Dacca and the Thana of Rangamati, Cooch Behar, Cachar, Jayantia, Dimarua, Khyrim, Bhutan, Manipur, Tripura, Nara and Munkang; and the principal hill tribes were the Duflas, Miris, Nagas, Khamptis, Singphos and Mishmis. The Ahom government's agents for conducting the negotiations were the disciplined, well-trained, erudite and astute body of envoys known as Katakis, who followed a highly developed technique laid down by their government, which left enough room for originality and inventiveness.

The basis of Assam's foreign relations was the remembrance of the limits of the ancient Hindu kingdom of Kamarupa, bounded on the west by the Karatoya river, including "roughly, the Brahmaputra Valley, Bhutan, Rangpur, and Behar".[28] The ultimate territorial ambition of the Ahoms was to restore the old limits up to the Karatoya river, and they succeeded at times to bring parts of the ancient territories under their domination or under their political influence.

28. Gait, *History of Assam*, 1906, p. 10,

The first move in this direction was taken by Suhungmung Dihingia Raja when his forces under Chankham Ghar-Sandikoi "washed their swords in the waters of the Karatoya river," by compelling the Padshah of Gaur to enter into a friendly alliance with the Ahom monarch. The phrase 'washing of swords' in the waters of a river in a foreign territory is an euphemistic equivalent for the extension of sovereignty to the limits of that river. Ghar-Sandikoi, as a symbol of his conquest, constructed a temple on the banks of the Karatoya and excavated a tank in its neighbourhood. But the Ahoms did not maintain a military garrison near the Karatoya. They retracted their limits further eastward and fixed their western boundary at the Manaha river, which remained as such till the occupation of Assam by the Burmese in 1822, and by the British in 1824. The selection of Manaha was dictated by reasons of strategy. There were hills in the neighbourhood on both banks of the Brahmaputra which were easy to fortify, and from which commanding position the Ahoms could, with convenience, oppose the progress of an invading army from Bengal. But when the Ahoms considered themselves powerful enough they aimed at restoring the old limits of the Karatoya. So the region between the Manaha and the Karatoya was like a buffer-state, governed by the Koches and sandwitched between Mogul India and Assam; and it thus enabled the Ahoms to divert the first brunt of a Mogul attack to Cooch Behar, during which they got sufficient time to perfect their preparations for resistance. The second rallying point of the Ahoms was Gauhati with hills on both banks of the river; and then Samdhara, with the same strategic advantage of hills in the neighbourhood. The Ahoms avoided contests on plains as they had a meagre cavalry, and level regions were not suitable for their guerilla tactics. The plains of the Karatoya-Manaha districts were therefore abandoned by the Ahoms in favour of the mountainous environs of Manaha.

The foundation and objective of Ahom foreign policy come out in an exhortation given by King Pratap Singha to his Katakis, and in a speech made by King Rudra Singha's prime minister when that monarch planned to invade Bengal with a view to restore the old limits of Assam. "During the reign of Dihingia Raja", said King Pratap Singha, "his army proceeded down the Brahmaputra in a fleet of seven *mar-naos* [mar-nao=several boats tied together], and Chankham Ghar-Sandikoi, son of Phrasengmung, marched along the banks. They washed their swords in the Karatoya river, and constructed a small temple, and excavated a tank on its bank as a mark of victory. They then established friendship with the Padshah of Gaur. They also established Biswa Singha in the government of Cooch Behar as a friend, and he paid his homage to Dihingia Raja with two pots of gold and silver. Our soldiers were rewarded with suitable presents, and Ghar-Sandikoi was given the title of Bar-Azam". It was on this occasion that the Padshah of Gaur presented to the Ahom king the princesses Khanbibi Harmati and Darmati with three *perganahs* as dowry.[29]

That the fixation of the western boundary at Manaha was a voluntary contraction on the part of Assam is illustrated in King Jayadhwaj Singha's overstepping the frontier in 1658 and carrying his victorious arms to the neighbourhood of Dacca.[30] The reprisal came in the shape of Mir Jumla's invasion of Assam in 1662-63. The attempt to restore the old limits of Assam was revived by King Rudra Singha, who launched elaborate preparations to invade Bengal. In the war council held in connection therewith, the Barpatra Gohain said,—"The territories bordering on the Karatiya are ours. The enemies have got possession of them only on account of our indifference and inaction. The duty of a king is to destroy the enemy, and to recover his lost possessions with a view to preserve the ancient boundaries of his kingdom." He was followed by the prime minister, Kuoigayan Buragohain, who said,—"The ancestors of our king had, by virtue of their prowess and courage, crossed the boundaries of Rangamati, and washed their swords in the Karatoya-Ganga. They found it inconvenient to fix the boundaries of Assam at the Karatoya, so they made the river Manaha the western limit of Assam, and established a garrison at Gauhati".[31] This sentiment found expression in the death-bed injunction of King Rudra Singha delivered to his five sons,—"Old and young, you shall all be kings successively. I have subdued the countries that surrounded my dominions; I proposed the reduction of the provinces contiguous to the Coroteea [Karatoya] river; but my design must perish with me; for who will be found capable to pursue my plans?"[32]

Dihingia Raja's expedition to Gaur took place during the days of the independent Afghan Sultans of Bengal, and the Moguls first established their supremacy over that province in 1576. Till about 1614 the Ahoms had no quarrel with the Moguls but hostilities

29. S. K. Bhuyan, *Assam Buranji*, S.M., pp. 23-29; Ms. Assam Buranji, No. 7.

30. Charles Stewart, *History of Bengal*, 1910, p. 317.

31. S. K. Bhuyan, *Tunghungia Buranji*, O.U.P., p. 38.

32. J. P. Wade, *An Account of Assam*, p. 136.

broke out in that year as a result of Mogul encroachments and raids, which Assam opposed. The war continued with varying fortunes till the year 1639 when a treaty was enacted according to which Lower Assam, from Gauhati to Manaha, passed into the hands of the Moguls. The Ahoms recovered this territory from the Moguls in 1658; ceded it again in 1663, and recovered it in 1667. The Ahom viceroy Laluk Barphukan, without any authority from his government, surrendered Lower Assam to the Moguls in 1679, and the Ahoms finally recovered it in 1682, and Manaha remained the western boundary of Assam till the termination of their rule.

The Ahom attitude towards the Moguls was one of watchful friendship in normal peace times, and armed preparedness to oppose the Moguls when it was necessary. Assam's hostilities with the Moguls were almost always successful, and the latter admitted the difficulties of a war against Assam in view of the natural disadvantages, combined with the organisation and intrepidity of the Assamese generals.[33] The Mogul attitude towards Assam was influenced partly by their general policy not to permit any independent state to exist in India, and partly by their desire to obtain an access to the forests of Assam which teemed with elephants, and wherein could be found *agar* wood and other precious articles. Assam's name for Mogul strategy was "*Mogulifandi*", which they tried to thoroughly master through Assamese messengers and agents despatched to Mogul India, both in an authorised and unauthorised capacity; and also through the numerous Mogul subjects who stayed on in Assam after the departure of the expeditions to which they had been attached.

Biswa Singha's submission to Dihingia Raja, just when he had founded the Cooch Behar kingdom on the ruins of Kamata, was regarded by the Ahoms as a great landmark, and as the basis of the Assam-Koch relations of the subsequent ages, according to which the Ahoms looked upon the Cooch Behar Raja as belonging to the category *thapita-sanchita,* a name applied to the rulers who were first settled by the Ahoms in the government of a particular state. This claim was repudiated by Biswa Singha's two sons, Naranarayan and Chilarai. They tried to bring under their sway practically all the states forming part of ancient Kamarupa, during the course of which they vanquished the Ahom king and compelled him to sue for peace. They also subjugated Cachar, Manipur,

33. S. K. Bhuyan, *Lachit Barphukan and His Times,* for a sustained treatment of the subject, pp. 152-158.

Jayantia, Tripura, Khyrim, Dimarua, and Sylhet, after which they marched towards Gaur where however they could not obtain any success. The rivalries between the sons of Naranarayan and Chilarai brought the Ahoms into the arena of Cooch Behar politics. The kingdom, as has been stated before, was split up into two portions; the western portion was known as Cooch Behar, and it continued to be governed by Naranarayan's descendants; and the eastern portion, known as Koch Hazo, fell to the lot of Raghudeb's sons and grandsons. The mastery of Koch Hazo changed hands between the Moguls and the Ahoms; but Koch princes ruled in Darrang and Beltola as vassal chiefs. The Rajas of Darrang however considered Kamrup or Lower Assam to be their natural heritage of which, they thought, they had been unjustly deprived by the Ahoms. This contention took the shape of a positive demand during the decadence of Ahom rule, specially under Krishnanarayan, a prince of Darrang; and the Ahom monarch Gaurinath Singha had to solicit the intervention of the East India Company for the suppression of that prince's open rebellion.

Cachar was another territory of the *thapita-sanchita* order, as after a brief interregnum, its ruler Nirbhayanarayan, had been placed on the throne by Dihingia Raja who also gave the Kachari Raja the paraphernalia of a ruler. Frictions between Cachar and Assam were of frequent occurrence, and at times the Cachar Raja assumed full independence and defied the authority of the Ahoms. King Rudra Singha re-subjugated Cachar, and its Raja was allowed a semi-independent status.[34]

Jayantia always proved to be recalcitrant, and it had to be frequently subdued. It raised its head whenever opportunities permitted till it was finally subjugated by King Rudra Singha. Jayantia's professions of friendship were not serious, though it declared times without number that "Jayantia and Gargaon are not separate and divisible". The refractoriness of Jayantia and the submissiveness of Cachar come out very well in a speech of King Pramatta Singha's prime minister in connection with that monarch's coronation ceremony held in 1745,—"The two principalities of Jayantia and Cachar have been recognised and protected by the Heavenly King since the days of his ancestors. The father [Rudra Singha] of Your Majesty, in order to punish their untoward attitude invaded their territories and brought down their chiefs together with their ministers and potentates. Cachar has abided

34. S. K. Bhuyan, *Kachari Buranji*, 1936, pp. 68-113.

by the terms settled with its ruler at that time, but Jayantia has failed to carry out the terms of the agreement. So its ruler has been imprisoned for fourteen years. Cachar should be invited to send its representative to witness the festivities of the coronation, but it is not proper that this privilege should be conferred upon Jayantia. If the consul for Jayantia be shown round the amusements now going on in full swing, then there was no necessity of imprisoning its ruler for fourteen years."[35]

The bone of contention between Assam and Jayantia was the intervening state of Dimarua which the latter claimed to be under its vassalage, though Assam repudiated this claim. About the year 1665, Jayantia promised to send a contingent to help Assam in its conflicts with the Moguls, but it suggested that the force must be taken to Assam by the route through Dimarua. The Ahoms however followed the route most suited to them. The Ahom claims on Dimarua were based on their occupation of that state after defeating the Moguls under Abu Bakar about the year 1615, and again by defeating Sayed Firoz Khan, Fauzadar of Gauhati, in 1667. The Ahom premier Atan Buragohain wrote to the Jayantia Raja in 1675, —"About your claim on Dimarua,—we have got possession of Darrang, Beltola and Dimarua, after having vanquished Sayed Babakar [Abu Bakar] and his twenty-two Omraos. Very recently we have obtained mastery over Dimarua after defeating Sayed Phiroz Nawab and other Omraos."[36]

The states bordering on Assam offered the stipulated aid to King Rudra Singha in his plan to invade Bengal. Jayantia, Cachar, Darrang, Naduar, Rani, Topakuchi, and Dimarua furnished in all forty thousand soldiers.[37]

The Ahom policy towards conquered territories and vassal states was the same as adopted by Hindu rulers in ancient times. The subdued princes were allowed to retain their autonomous powers in the administration of their respective dominions. They had to pay some tribute, in cash or in kind, or in both, and furnish allotted quotas of men and provisions when asked to do so by their paramount sovereign. They had besides to attend the ceremonial functions of their liegelords like coronations and victory celebrations. This custom can be illustrated by the message sent by King Rudra Singha to the Nawabs and princes of Bengal,—"We formerly possessed the provinces on this side of the Corotea [Kara-

35. S. K. Bhuyan, *Tungkhungia Buranji*, O.U.P., p. 47.
36. S. K. Bhuyan, *Jayantia Buranji*, p. 45.
37. J. P. Wade, *An Account of Assam*, p. 132.

toya] river, and we are now desirous to resume them. Do not prove inimical to us. If we remain friendly everything will succeed. Be yours the countries, the government and the Revenue; mine the name. Act in a manner to preserve peacé. Fear not our approach."[38]

The picturesque country of Manipur exercised a great fascination upon the Assamese mind on account of its antiquity, and specially for Babrubahan, the mythological founder of its ruling dynasty, who figures so prominently in the epic *Mahabharata,* and who is also the subject of a very popular Assamese drama performed almost in all parts of Assam in a spectacular form. But the Ahoms do not appear to have any diplomatic connection with Manipur till about the year 1765, when its ruler Jai Singha Karta-Maharaj visited the court of Swargadeo Rajeswar Singha soliciting the Ahom king's aid to expel the Burmese who had occupied Manipur. This request was supported by the offer of the Manipuri princess Kuranganayani to the Ahom monarch. A force was sent to Manipur under the command of Harnath Senapati Phukan, father of Badanchandra Barphukan, with specific orders to re-establish Jai Singha on his lost throne. But this Ahom force had to share the fate of the British contingent sent to Manipur in 1762 under Mr. Verelst. It could not make any headway in its march on account of the dense forests through which its route lay; it had therefore to return before reaching Manipur. Kuranganayani played a very gallant part in rescuing King Lakshmi Singha from his confinement at the hands of the Moran rebels, and in re-establishing him on the Ahom throne, usurped for a few months by the insurgent Moran leader Ramakanta. Some thirty years later Jai Singha came to Assam, on the invitation of King Gaurinath Singha, at the head of a small force, to assist in the suppression of the Moamaria disturbances. After this there is no trace of any diplomatic contact between Assam and Manipur. It came to limelight again during the invasion and occupation of Assam by the Burmese, owing to entanglements of the rival princes Marjit, Chaurjit, Govinda Chandra and Gambhir Singh in the affairs of Cachar, and their conflict with the nominees set up by the Burmese on the throne of that state.

As regards Tipperah, the Ahoms had no relations with this country till the year 1710, when King Rudra Singha sent an embassy to Raja Ratna Manikya soliciting his aid to a confederacy of the Rajas and Zemindars of Bengal which the king of Assam

38. J. P. Wade, *An Account of Assam,* p. 131.

was organising at that time to overthrow the Moguls from their power. The absence of any relations with Assam was pointed out by the Tipperah Raja when he received the Assamese deputation. Having heard of the position and power of the Ahom monarch from an intermediary named Anandiram Medhi, Ratna Manikya became anxious to establish friendly relations with Assam, but he said,—"Our men have never visited that country, and what will be the best method of sending my men now?" The last embassy left Assam in April 1714, but before the terms of friendship could be firmly and finally settled King Rudra Singha died at Gauhati, and Tripura itself suffered from serious palace intrigues and political convulsions.[39]

The relations with the Khasi state of Khyrim were mostly of a commercial nature, and they came to prominence in the reign of King Rudra Singha, when one Santosh Bangal of Pandua in Sylhet took shelter in Dimarua, the chief of which made him over to Kina Barua, a merchant of Khyrim. Santosh became rich and prosperous, and Kina Barua proposed to send him to Khyrim, obviously for the purpose of ousting the Pandua adventurer from the Assam trade in which he had become the Barua's rival. The other Khyrim merchants considered this incident to be an act of undue harassment and interference on the part of Kina Barua, and they attended the markets on the Assam frontier properly armed to oppose any eventual interference in their trading activities. The trade between Assam and Khyrim suffered considerably owing to this disquieting state of affairs. Negotiations for improving the situation commenced between Barmanik, Raja of Khyrim, and the Ahom government, and the first Khyrim embassy met the Barphukan at Gauhati in June 1704. This was followed by the deputation of an Assamese embassy to Khyrim two months later with assurances of Assam's friendly attitude towards the Khasi state. Another embassy from Khyrim came to Gauhati in 1786, and they were received with due honour and ceremony by the Barphukan under the orders of Swargadeo Gaurinath Singha. The Khasi embassy, led by Manurai and a Kharkowanr, represented the Khyrim Raja's solicitude for the protection of the Ahom government.[40]

The Katakis or ambassadors who represented the affairs of Assam in foreign courts were highly intelligent and educated persons, as upon their powers of advocacy and exposition depended the settlement of grave issues. The messages which they carried

39. S. K. Bhuyan, *Tripura Buranji*, D.H.A.S., 1938.
40. S. K. Bhuyan, *Jayantia Buranji*, pp. 140-152.

were embodied in written epistles, but they had always to elucidate and supplement the contents of the letters by *mukh-jevan* or oral explanations. According to the usages of diplomatic negotiations ambassadors are immune from the consequences of the messages they carry, but 'ill news infects the giver', and irritable monarchs or nobles sometimes mishandled the Katakis for carrying imperious or unpalatable tidings. The Katakis were expected to be strictly honest, and King Pratap Singha executed several of them for receiving gratification from Raja Dharmanarayan of Darrang, and from the Mogul commander Raja Satrajit. The Assamese general Lachit Barphukan punished some Katakis for accepting such tiny presents as wooden birds and for attempting to entice an Assamese astrologer to the Mogul camp. The diplomatic service of the Ahom government was placed on a proper footing by King Pratap Singha, who replaced Ahom Katakis by shrewd Brahmans the latter being gifted with nimble tongues and persuasive ways of speaking. He once explained to the Katakis the importance of their duties in the following words,—" I am highly pleased with the manner in which you have conducted yourselves and asserted your views in a foreign place [court of the Mogul commander Allah Yar Khan]. Katakis should be like shieldsmen. Your words alone constitute your rice and cloth; more specially the relations between ourselves and yourselves are like gold and borax ; the former is refined with the help of the latter. You have been able to vindicate your cause in a foreign Durbar, and thereby to protect the interests of your government, without paying any heed to your own personal safety. Therefore, O Bamuni-puteks [Katakis], have I got any one dearer to me than yourselves ? "[41]

Men versed in the affairs of Bengal, and possessing knowledge of Hindusthani were appointed for representing Assam in the courts of the officers of the East India Company, and the selection was extended to the members of the leading non-Brahman families. A knowledge of Persian was acquired by a large number of the Assamese gentry for cultural purposes, and also for ensuring high appointments under the government.

Relations with the hill tribes : The maintenance of peace and tranquillity in the country and its protection from foreign attacks constitute the common objective of every government. But the Ahom rulers of Assam were confronted with the additional responsibility of protecting the subjects from the inroads of the tribes

41. Ms. Assam Buranji, No. 7.

inhabiting the hills on the immediate borders, almost all of whom were of a most rapacious nature, and anxious for opportunities of plunder which might be offered by the slackness or imbecility of the government. Attempts were made to adjust the mutual relations, but their strict observance could not be usually enforced as the tribesmen lived in inaccessible hills and forests, and the conduct of an expedition against them was invariably a matter of extreme difficulty.

The tribesmen carried on their warfare with primitive weapons which were very effective in close-range fights, but could not be so very useful in engagements with the Ahom army who used matchlocks and guns; it was however in open contests that the success of these modern weapons could be assured, and such opportunities did rarely occur as the hillmen conducted their attacks from unsuspected woods and defiles, depending mainly upon such guerrilla and ambuscade methods. At the same time the invading Ahom force could hardly maintain an open line of communication, the paths, if there were any, being mainly tracks over precipices and slopes infested by the lurking hillmen in the neighbouring woods. The warning given by the very astute and farsighted prime minister Atan Buragohain in connection with the proposal to despatch an expedition against the Duflas sums up generally the policy of the Ahom government towards the hill tribes. King Udayaditya Singha proposed to send a force to punish the Duflas in the Subansiri area for having carried off a number of Assamese subjects including women and children. The premier said,—"The Dufla miscreants can be captured only if an elephant can enter into a rat-hole." His warning was ignored, and the expedition resulted in heavy losses of men and provisions. In the expedition to Manipur in 1765, to restore the throne to its lawful ruler Jai Singha Karta-Maharaj "two-thirds of the men and provisions were lost, only a third could come back." The explanation submitted by Harnath Senapati Phukan, the Ahom general, embodies the difficulties of progress in the mountainous regions of Assam. The Phukan submitted to the king,—"The Manipuri Raja promised to conduct us by showing the way, and so we undertook the march. On entering the forest we could not trace the way by any means. Besides, many of our soldiers died of blood dysentery, and our food-provisions also failed. There were no provision-suppliers, and the Nagas did not allow us passage; they used to roll down stones from hill-tops and kill our men by that method. We proceeded one month's journey by clearing the jungle, but could not find any clue whatsoever. So, I, His Majesty's slave, have been made liable to blame ".[42]

The whole brunt of tribal ferocity fell upon the inhabitants of the tracts lying between the foot of the hills and the extremities of the plains. This belt of land was very fertile, and produced abundance of rice, cotton and other staples valued by the neighbouring hillmen. It was intersected by a number of Duars or passes through which the hill people maintained their contact with the plains. The ownership of this belt was claimed by the Ahom government, but it could enforce its claim only when it was strong enough to expel the tribal intruders. But, when the government was weak the hillmen swept down the plains on marauding excursions, and carried off property and men from the Duars; and they did not even hesitate to claim ownership over this zone. Most of the tribesmen were deficit in labourers and certain necessaries of life; and the Duar people were forced into compulsory servitude in the hills, and their crops, cattle and other property were constantly at the mercy of the needy and rapacious hillmen. The Ahom government was compelled to be ever-vigilant, and its weakness was reflected in the increased transgressions of the stipulated limits.

The reforming zeal of the Vaisnava preachers extended only to the inhabitants of the Duars, and did not reach the hill tribes in the hinterland, with the result that the latter remained unhumanised, and consequently unamenable to rules of docile citizenship. The isolation of the hillmen from the formative influences of the religions of the plains accounts for the continuance of the border tribes in their own code of life brought to being by their environments and the influence of their primitive instincts. Whereas life in the plains is rapidly changing these hillmen are living as they used to do many thousand years ago. The existence of these tribes on the borders imparts a unique distinction to the province of Assam, in their representing different grades of civilisation, different origins, customs and languages, but they add considerably to the worries of the administrators. Only a strong government in the plains can keep these tribesmen within their proper bounds, by preventing their incursions undertaken partly to gratify their marauding propensities, and partly to acquire the goods which their hills do scarcely produce.

The policy of the Ahom rulers towards these tribes was one of conciliation, backed by the display of force when it could be

42. S. K. Bhuyan, *Tungkhungia Buranji*, O.U.P., pp. 59-60.

employed effectively. Complete subjugation of any of the tribes, and annexation of their territories to the Ahom kingdom was never envisaged by the rulers, for such attempts would make the tribes recede further and further into the backwoods, and the conquerors would find themselves masters of unpeopled hills and forests. The Ahom policy stated in plain words would come to something like this: "Conciliate these tribes by promising to furnish them their necessaries as far as possible. If they indulge in wanton pillages, pursue and capture the miscreants, but never overstep the limits." Violation of this policy by any frontier commander in an excess of enthusiasm was invariably followed by regrettable consequences. The policy of the Ahoms was essentially the same as the policy of their British successors, as embodied in the ever-reiterated command to frontier officers and commandants; "Conciliate these savages if you can. Be persistent in demanding surrender of murderers, but endeavour so to approach the tribes, that a basis may be opened for friendly intercourse in the future".[43]

Of the tribes on the Assam frontier the Bhutanese alone possessed a systematic government. Bhutan appeared at times to be subordinate to Tibet and indirectly to China through the pontifical hegemony of the Lamas. The Bhutanese kept up their intercourse with the plains through the usual Duars, of which there were eleven in Bengal and seven in Assam. There were two Duars in Darrang, —Buriguma and Killing; and five in Kamrup,—Gharkola, Baksa, Chapaguri, Chapakhamar and Bijni. These Duars were normally the property of the Assam government, but the Deva-Dharma Rajas of Bhutan took possession of them in the eighteenth century, and the feeble Ahom rulers of the time were hardly able to vindicate their claim. Complaints of oppressions and encroachments emanated from both governments, and when the British occupied Assam in 1826 they found the Bhutan Duars to comprise "the most fruitful elements of future discord".[44]

The government of the Ahoms had been compelled by circumstances to make over the Darrang and Kamrup Duars to Bhutan in consideration of an annual tribute, consisting of yak tails, ponies, musk, gold-dust, blankets and daggers, the total value of which was estimated at Rs. 4785-1. The tax-collectors of the two governments harassed the poor peasants of the intervening territory for the staples of Bhutan whose price was differently estimated to suit

43. Mackenzie, *North-East Frontier*, p. 369.
44. R. B. Pemberton, *Report on Bootan*, 1839, p. 52.

the extortionate agents. These oppressions led to endless disputes between the frontier officers of the two states.

East of Darrang there is another Duar, known as Kariapar Duar, which was independent of the Bhutanese government of Punakha. The Bhutias of Kariapar, known generally as Mombas, are governed by a council of chiefs designated as *Sat Rajas,* not always necessarily seven, who owed allegiance to Towang Raja, a tributary of Lhassa. All the Assam trade with Tibet passed through this Kariapar Duar at a place called Chouna, two months' journey from Lhassa; and in the first decade of the nineteenth century it amounted in value to about two lakhs of rupees per year. The Assam merchants used to be stationed with their commodities at Geegunsheer, distant four miles from Chouna. The articles offered for sale by the Lhassa merchants consisted of rock salt, woollens, gold dust, horses, chowries, Chinese silks etc. The Assam merchants carried the following goods,—rice, Tussa cloth or coarse silk woven by Assamese women; iron and lac; skins; buffalo horns; pearls and corals, etc. About the year 1820 the Lhassa merchants brought with them 70,000 rupees to buy Assam staples.[45]

To the east of Kariapar Duar there are two other Duars, known as Char Duar and Na Duar, which were protected from the independent tribes of Bhutias and Duflas by the grant of concessions in the shape of blackmail.

During the Moamaria and Burmese disturbances the Bhutanese carried off to their hills a large number of Assamese subjects for employment as slaves; and Captain R. B. Pemberton during his visit to Bhutan in 1838 received numerous applications from Assamese captives to effect their release and restoration to their own country.[46] During the period of anarchy and confusion many Assamese subjects had taken shelter in the Bhutan Duars. The Duars also offered an asylum to Assam princes and potentates who rebelled against the government or who wanted a safe retreat to mature their plans of revenge. Robbers and freebooters from Bengal also used the Duars as their rendezvous from where they could march to the Assamese villages on plundering excursions.

The first formal embassy from Assam was despatched to Bhutan by Pratapballabh Barphukan in 1802, to adjust the mutual relations which had become strained on account of the shelter given to some Assamese nobles and princes by the Raja of Bhutan. The deputation was composed of Pankaj Chaudhury, a Brahman

45. Mackenzie, *North-East Frontier,* p. 15.
46. Pemberton, *Report on Bootan,* p. 151.

of Pubpar Perganah; and Athir Bara and Kapchiga Lekharu, both of Kharangi. The Assamese envoys returned in the company of thirty-six Bhutanese, headed by two Jingkaps or messengers, Jiva and Dindu, who brought two epistles from the Deva-Dharma Rajas of Bhutan, one written in Persian and the other in Bengali. The presents included a silver box, a gilded saddle, two bales of blankets, two ponies, and four bullocks of Bhutanese breed. Similar presents were also brought by the Bhutanese chiefs, known as Jadungs, who accompanied the embassy. The Bhutanese envoys complained to the Ahom monarch of the oppression committed near the borders by the officers of Kamrup,—the Bujar-baruas, Barkaiths and Chaudhuris. They averred that the Bhutanese government had regularly delivered the stipulated articles, namely, musks, cow-tails, gold, ponies, blankets, and *chep-chongs* or daggers, at the passes fixed by the two states. The envoys also communicated the following message of the Deva-Dharma Rajas of Bhutan; "There had existed cordial and indissoluble friendship between the previous Swarga-Maharajas [of Assam] and the ancient Deva-Dharma Rajas [of Bhutan], on the strength of verbal messages and communications, though unlinked by any physical sight. There had however been no exchange of embassies and epistles. Now, as commanded by the Swarga-Maharaja, the Barphukan Barnabab of Barpani [Brahmaputra, *i.e.*, Lower Assam] had despatched envoys and letters making enquiries about our prosperity and welfare. From this, the Deva-Dharma Rajas have been convinced of the presence of inseparable ties of friendship [between the two kingdoms]. They have been exceedingly happy at the fulfilment of their heart's desire caused by the pleasure arising from personal sight. We Jingkaps have in consequence been sent by the Deva-Dharma Rajas to enquire about the peace and happiness of the Swargi-Maharaja. Our Rajas have also sent with us letters and presents".[47]

The task of protecting the Assam subjects from the inroads of the Bhutias devolved mainly upon the vassal Raja of Darrang. In 1805, the newly appointed Darrang Raja, Samudra Narayan, was instructed to "push back the Bhutias to their original limits", as reports had been received of "the Bhutias' occupation of some portion of His Majesty's dominions by transgressing the old boundaries".[48]

47. S. K. Bhuyan, *Jayantia Buranji*, p. 156; *Tungkhungia Buranji*, O.U.P., p. 154.

48. S. K. Bhuyan, *Tungkhungia Buranji*, O.U.P., p. 187.

The Akas, who call themselves Hrusso, live in the hills to the east of the Bharari river in Darrang District. They are divided into two clans,—the Hazari-khowas, or eaters of a thousand hearths, and Kapah-chors, or thieves who lurk amidst the cotton plants. The Akas, limited to only 260 families or so, are extremely fierce and primitive. To prevent their oppressions the Ahom government assigned to the Hazari-khowas a number of Assamese families from whom the hillmen could levy the stipulated quantity of articles as *posa*, consisting of a portion of female dress, one bundle of cotton thread, and one napkin from each such family. The assigned families were exempted by the Ahom government from the payment of taxes to the extent of the amount represented by the articles of *posa*. Members of these families, known as *bahatias*, had to serve as labourers under the Akas when they were required to do so. The *bahatias* were settled in the villages in the Aka Duars in order to restrict the annual visits of the hillmen to a fixed locality. The Kapah-chors were long a terror of Darrang, though they consisted of only eighty families. Their leader, known as Tangi or Taghi Raja, murdered the Assamese governor of Charduar, soon before the British occupation of Assam. He subsequently became the leader of both the clans and continued his depredations in Charduar for many years, till his surrender to the British in 1842.

The Duflas live in the hills situated between the Bharari river on the west and the upper courses of the Somdiri on the east. The intervening tracts in Darrang District leading to the habitats of the Duflas are known as Nao-duar; and those in Lakhimpur District as Chai-duar. The tribes near the Darrang Duars are known as Paschima Duflas; and those on the border of North Lakhimpur as Tangi Duflas.

The predatory habits of the Duflas made them very dangerous neighbours, and an expedition against them was always considered to be a hazardous enterprise. The Ahoms therefore attempted to conciliate them by assigning to them a number of *paiks* in the Duar areas. They were called *Dafala-bahatias*, or the serfs of the Duflas, and they formed an independent *khel*. They were generally culprits convicted of various offences, and the land occupied by them became gradually a penal colony peopled by convicts and their descendants. The Dafala-bahatias were originally Assamese by origin and custom, but they gradually adopted a Dufla way of living imbibing the rough manners of the hillmen. Every ten houses of Dafala-bahatias were to make over to the Duflas per year one double cloth, one single cloth, one napkin, one dao, ten heads of cattle, and four seers of salt. Each *got* of Dafalt-bahatia *paiks* paid to the Assam government only rupees three instead of the usual demand of rupees nine, the balance being remitted in consideration of the articles they delivered to the Duflas. The innovation of Dafala-bahatia assignment was first made by the Ahom monarch Gadadhar Singha, and it served the purpose of conciliating the rapacious Duflas by placing at their disposal a number of people upon whom they could concentrate their ferocity and greed; the system also acted as a deterrent to the commission of crimes the consequences of which would be forfeiture of lives to the mercy of the unrelenting hillmen.

During the weak rule of Gaurinath Singha and Kamaleswar Singha, the Dafala-bahatias in league with the Moamarias revolted in several places in the north bank, and once they proceeded as far as Duimunisila in Kaliabar. A tactful Assamese officer, the Baskatia Barbarua, managed to raise a contingent of Duflas, Dafala-bahatias and Miris, and placed it at the disposal of the premier Purnananda Buragohain to quell the Moamaria disturbances in the north bank.[49]

The Apatanangs or Ankas are a tribe with a comparatively high degree of organisation. They live in a well-cultivated plateau, ten miles by six miles, to the north of the Dufla hills. They are peaceful agriculturists, and their rice fields are highly cultivated and artificially irrigated terraces which are watered by the Kali river. The monotony of the plain is broken up by small hillocks and low pine-clad spurs. Primroses, violets and wild straw-berries are to be found in abundance in the woods and meadows. They have eight villages in the middle of rice fields in close proximity to one another. The Apatanangs number about 20,000 souls and can put into the field a body of fighting men at a short notice, to defend their villages against the attacks of an invading tribe. The people are governed by a council of elders. Their language differs considerably from Dufla and Miri. The Apatanangs disown any kinship with their neighbours, on the other hand, they claim to be one with the people of the plains.[50]

The Abors and the Miris represent the later and earlier migrations of the same tribe. The Abors as the last comers have retained their pristine ferocity, while the Miris have become docile and peaceful having lived long in the plains and the lower

49. S. K. Bhuyan, *Tungkhungia Buranji*, O.U.P., pp. 95, 98-99, 128-129, 142-143.

50. *Balipara Frontier Tract Gazetteer*, pp. 14-15; B. C. Allen's *Lakhimpur District Gazetteer*, pp. 74-75.

hills. The different branches of the Abor and the Miri tribes therefore represent different strata of civilisation. The Abors, commonly known as Padam Abors, occupy the hilly country between the Dihong and Dibong rivers, while their more intractable kinsmen the Bar Abors live in the interior lofty summits. The Ghasi Miris, also known as Parvatia Miris, are more turbulent than the Miris of the plains. The latter live in their own Arcadias, rearing mustard plants, plying their boats against the strong current of the Subansiri, weaving Miri-jims or blankets of cotton wool, and living a life of pastoral contentment in their riverain homesteads.

The Abors considered the Miris as their slaves and employed them as intermediaries in the Assam trade. The Ahom government accepted this claim, and relieved the Miris of all their taxes and obligations, so that they might be paid to their overlords the Abors. The latter also claimed a right to all the fish and gold found in the rivers flowing in their territories, and compelled the Bihia gold-washers, employed by the Ahom government, to deliver to them regular presents in the way of conciliatory offering. The Abors never allow any of their community to emigrate to Assam.

The Miris, ordinarily meek and submissive, proved at times to be fierce and aggressive. In the year 1683, the Sadiyal Miris set fire to the house of Kanu Gohain Rup Sandikai, the Ahom governor of Sadiya, and burnt the children and inmates to death. The Miris also killed 200 Assamese subjects and pillaged the neighbouring villages. Maupia Naobaicha Phukan, grandson of Baghchowa Neog Gohain, was despatched at the head of a strong force, and he succeeded in bringing the Miris to submission. The Phukan constructed ramparts terminating at the Brahmaputra and enclosing the villages inhabited by the Assamese, rearranged the allotment of *paiks*, and regulated the payment of taxes by the Miri subjects. It transpired afterwards that the Miris had been instigated to rebel by Bih Gohain who wanted to see the destruction of Kanu Gohain. Bih Gohain was executed, and Kanu Gohain dismissed from office.

The son of the Dihingia Phukan, a member of the Miri Sandikoi Bargohain family, was appointed governor of Sadiya, described in old chronicles as "Bargohain of Sadiya." The Naobaicha Phukan completed the regulation of Sadiya in 1687. A stone pillar found near Sadiya contains an inscription according to which Dihingia Bargohain fixed the habitation of the Mishmis to the hills near the Dibong river, *i.e.* in the neighbourhood of the present Nizamghat outpost.[51] The Dihingia Bargohain of the inscription was probably

51. *Sadiya Frontier Tract Gazetteer*, pp. 18-19; H. C. Goswami's *Purani Asam Buranji*, pp. 160-162.

the new governor of Sadiya appointed in 1687, and the restriction on the Mishmis was imposed by him for their complicity in the Miri insurrection of 1683.

The Mishmis occupy the hills to the east of the Abor country. They are divided into several clans, the most dangerous being the Chulikata and Mezho Mishmis. Their raids and incursions caused some annoyances to the governors of Sadiya. They have some interest in trade, and appreciate the opportunities offered by markets and fairs. They produce a kind of poisonous aconites called *Mishimi tita,* in return for which they obtain swords, woollen cloth and salt from the Tibetans. The fighting strength of the Mishmis was estimated in 1883 as 500 men; that of the Abors as 10,000; and of the Duflas and Miris as 3,000.[52]

The Khamptis belong to the same Shan stock as the Ahoms. They were originally inhabitants of the Bar-Khampti country, called Khampti-Long by the Burmese, the hilly region between the extremity of Assam and Irrawady valley. The Khamptis are Buddhists in faith and have their own literature. Their country abounds in pagodas, one of which is 95 feet in height and 125 feet in circumference.[53] They first came to Assam towards the end of the eighteenth century, and settled at Tengapani. But under the pressure of the Singphos they crossed the Brahmaputra, and about the year 1794 they expelled the Ahom governor of Sadiya. The Khampti chief assumed the title and authority of the Sadiya-khowa Gohain, and the weak government of Gaurinath Singha acquiesced in the usurpation. The British on their occupation of Assam in 1825 found the Sadiya tract entirely under Khampti control which was not interferred with by the new conquerors as the Khamptis agreed to maintain a force for the preservation of order. The old Khampti chief, Chou-salan Sadiya-khowa Gohain, respected the terms of the settlement with the British; but his son Chowrangfat Sadiya-khowa Gohain violated the terms and was deported in consequence in 1835, and a British officer assumed thenceforward the responsibility of administering the Sadiya country. Four years later the Khamptis numbering 500 led by their chiefs attacked the Sadiya post one night, murdered the sentries and Col. Adam White, the officer in command, and 80 other men. The suppression of the Khamptis was completed in 1843, when their chiefs were dispersed to different quarters, one being settled at Chunpura, another at Sai-

52. Capt. St. John F. Michell, *Report on the North-East Frontier of India,* 1883, p. 39.

53. W. W. Shakespear, *History of Upper Assam,* p. 130.

khowa, a third at Dhamaji, and the fourth at Bhadia in North Lakhimpur.[54]

Assam's most troublesome neighbours on the Sadiya frontier were however the Singphos, identical in race with the Kakus or Kakhyens of Burma. They are estimated to have a fighting strength of 10,000 men.[55] Their chief habitat was the great eastern branch of the Irrawady; but on the break-up of the northern Shan kingdom they spread themselves in the country lying between Upper Assam and Bhamo, and brought it under their virtual control. The Singphos belong to the Tesan clan of the Kakhyens. They first came to prominence during the weak rule of Gaurinath Singha. They drove the Khamptis from the Tengapani area, and settled in the Upper Buri-Dihing and in Namrup. The Moamarias found ready allies in the Singphos, and they together pillaged Assamese villages, sometimes with the aid of Burmese mercenaries. Purnananda Buragohain, the prime minister, in order to placate the Singpho leader Bichanong, presented to him an Ahom girl named Rangili, sister of Baram Duara Barua's father. Bichanong presented her in turn to the Burmese monarch Bodawpaya. The Singphos violated their pact with Purnananda Buragohain, and carried off a large number of Ahom subjects as captives, some 3,000 of whom were subsequently recovered by Captain Neufville, the first British Political Agent of Upper Assam. The Singpho chiefs who entered into an agreement with the British in May 1826 described themselves and their dependent Singphos as being formerly "subjects of the Assam State"; and they promised "not to side with the Burmese or any other king to commit any aggression whatever."[56]

The Nagas are one of the most numerous tribes inhabiting the borders of Assam. Their habitats extend along a large portion of the Brahmaputra valley, from the Kapili river on the west to the Buri-Dihing on the east. They thus occupy the whole hill country bordering upon the plains districts of Nowgong, Sibsagar and Lakhimpur. They are also to be found along the northern slopes of the Patkai mountain. The Nagas are divided into several tribes, each possessing distinct characteristics; and they have also entered into the composition of a few other tribes and races who are now known by altogether different names. All Nagas were originally head-hunters, and their women refused to respect men who had

54. Shakespear, *History of Upper Assam,* p. 148; Mackenzie, *North-East Frontier,* pp. 59-60.

55. Michell, *North-East Frontier of India,* 1883, p. 28.

56. Aitchison, Treaties, 1931, Vol. XII, p. 119.

not taken heads or demonstrated their valour by participating in raids.[57] This practice has however ceased in the areas comprised in and adjacent to the present districts. It is now to be found in the interior hills which are inaccessible for the purpose of exploration, or where planned settlement and administration are too hazardous and expensive.

The Naga tribes with whom the old government of Assam had to deal live mainly in the low hills south of the Sibsagar and Lakhimpur districts, from the Dikhow to the Buri-Dihing. These tribes were claimed as subjects of the Ahom government. They paid taxes of slaves, elephant teeth, spear shafts, cloths and cotton. Their chiefs were granted lands and retainers like the ordinary Assamese nobles. These states called Naga-khats were managed by Assamese agents known as Naga-katakis. The chiefs represented several sub-tribes, namely, Namchangias or Jaipurias, Bar-duarias, Banferas or Jabakas or Abhoypurias, Changnois, Tablungias, Mooloongs, Jaktungias and Paniduarias. There were several salt mines in this Naga area, and Raja Purandar Singha successfully asserted his claim to their produce.

Clashes with the Nagas were matters of common occurrence. About the year 1530, the Namchangia and Tablungia Nagas, living on the banks of the Dikhow river, defeated an Ahom force and captured several guns.[58] In 1692, the same Nagas killed 23 Assamese subjects. The severe measures of reprisal instituted by King Gadadhar Singha resulted in the submission of the Nagas. Their chief Latha Khunbao was executed; and the other leaders reaffirmed their allegiance to the Ahom sovereign by personally visiting the capital. It was followed by an insurrection of the Nagas living in the Dayang area. Tancheng Duara Phukan brought the rebels to submission, and the Nagas presented two of their princesses to King Gadadhar Singha. The explanation offered by the Nagas on this occasion reflects their sentiments of loyalty and devotion towards their Ahom liegelord and sovereign: "For ages past we have been eating the crumbs thrown off from the dishes of the Swargadeo. We have not committed this misdeed; the Abors have done it. But still as we have been defeated we shall offer to the Swargadeo two of our princesses with slaves and female attendants. The Phukan should intercede on our behalf at the feet of His Majesty and bring about our salvation." [59]

57. Shakespear, *History of Upper Assam*, pp. 198-199.
58. Shakespear, *History of Upper Assam*, p. 211.
59. S. K. Bhuyan, *Tungkhungia Buranji*, O.U.P., p. 27.

Sporadic clashes continued throughout the entire period of Ahom rule in Assam, up to the time of Purandar Singha, but they were mainly confined to the Nagas on the immediate frontier. The Ahoms constructed a Naga Ali or embankment to protect the country from the inroads of the hillmen.[60]

The Shan tribes of Upper Burma, specially the inhabitants of Nara or Mogaung, Maulung, Mantara and Munkong kingdoms, were more or less peaceful in their relations with the Ahoms. The Shan chieftains looked upon the Ahom kings as "Bhai-Rajas", or brother monarchs, as they were descended from the same Shan stock; and as Sukapha, the first Ahom conqueror, belonged to a ruling Shan dynasty of Upper Burma. The Shan chiefs, in their difficulties, appealed to the Ahom government for protection and help. The orthodox section of the Ahoms, specially the priestly clans, used to keep some sort of communion with their Shan homeland. Shan monks used to visit Assam on religious missions, and some of them established *Bapu-changs* or schools for teaching the Shan language and for imparting education in the tenets of the Shan faith. The Shan chiefs of Burma used to feel some degree of pride in the fact that one of their kinsmen was exercising sovereign power in a part of India. After the termination of Ahom rule in Assam, a Shan chief deputed agents to Assam to make enquiries about what had happened to their Bhai-Raja, namely the Ahom king, of whom the chief had not heard for a long time.

Sukapha, as a powerful conqueror and as a founder of a ruling dynasty in far-off India, was admitted into the Shan pantheon, and offered periodic worship in his original native city of Mogaung. His remains as well as those of his two brothers Chowpya-hoseng and Chow-sam-lung-hue were buried in a monastery at Mogaung. Their spiritual counterparts were brought out on all occasions of state ceremony and duly propitiated with offering. The Shan chieftains then took their oaths to keep the peace. The ceremony was concluded by the chiefs all sitting down together and eating out of the same dish. British officers who visited Mogaung in 1836 found the worship of Sukapha still prevalent at that place.[61] The messengers employed by the Ahoms in their intercourse with Munkong were known as Tsai-kaus, and they mostly lived at Namrup. The Ahom king Jayadhwaj Singha, having fled to Nam-

60. Shakespear, *Upper Assam*, p. 211; G. C. Barua, *Ahom Buranji*, pp. 386-7.

61. Hannay and Pemberton, quoted in U. N. Gohain's *Assam under the Ahoms*, 1942, pp. 2-6, 10-11.

rup when Mir Jumla occupied Gargaon in 1662-1663, threatened to go to Nara or Mogaung if his ministers failed to obtain the withdrawal of the Mogul invaders from Assam. It shows the king's belief that in the Shan homeland of his ancestors he would find a ready reception and opportunities for rehabilitation.

But, these sentiments of attachment towards their kinsmen in Nara did not relax the vigilance of the Ahoms, as Nara chiefs contemplated at times to extend their domination over the territories ruled by Sukapha's descendants in Assam. This need for vigilance is well brought out in a speech of Swargadeo Pratap Singha where he expounded his policy towards foreigners before his trusted emissaries the Katakis. The occasion was provided by one Bhelai's son having paid unauthorised visits to the camp of the Mogul commander Nawab Allah Yar Khan during which he promised to deliver to the Nawab elephants, communicated to him secret information about Assam, and brought two pearl-chains as presents to the Ahom Swargadeo.

"The Gargayan Raja, a predecessor of mine on this throne," said King Pratap Singha, "married the daughter of the Nara Raja by performing the Chaklang ceremony, and made her his chief queen. This happened after the defeat of the Nara Raja at the hands of the Mantara Raja. The Nara princess did not abandon her hostile attitude. While living at Gargaon she pretended to be ill, and attributed her ailment to her being possessed of the devil through the machinations of the Assamese people. She therefore threw many men into water, and killed others having first subjected them to severe tortures. About that time one Ratnakhari of Nara used to live at Gargaon; and there was no love lost between him and the Assamese astrologer or Ganak named Achit Doloi. The king conferred upon Ratnakhari the title of Sagarkhari, who received the honour by kneeling down before the Gargayan Raja. This roused the suspicion of my predecessor, and he said,—"This man professes to be a Ganak; but why did he kneel down before me? I am sure he is not a Ganak; he has come to our country with a definite ulterior motive." Still then, the Gargayan Raja did not take any step against Sagarkhari Ganak on account of his affection for the queen. The Ganak counted all the subjects of Namrup and communicated the information to the Nara Raja, on the strength of which the Raja invaded our territories. Chao-aikhek Bargohain proceeded to the Nara campaign riding on an elephant. When he approached the enemy's camp the Nara Raja accosted the elephant in the customary language, in response to which the animal lay itself flat on the ground, and the Nara soldiers cut the Gohain with scythes used for mowing grass. The elephant, afterwards, picked up the head and the body of the Gohain and brought them to our camp. We also suffered heavy losses of men. The Gargayan Raja then pursued the Naras and put them to the rout. So we cannot fathom the inner workings of the minds of foreigners. This slave [Bhelai's son] is as unreliable as the Paschima or western Dafalas. My brother-in-law [Momai-tamuli Barbarua] will please teach him a good lesson." Bhelai's son used to be given five blows on coming out and the same number on going inside.[62]

The Mikirs who call themselves Arlengs live mainly in the low forest-clad hills between the Kapili and Dhansiri rivers. They are thus to be found in the districts of Nowgong, Sibsagar and Kamrup, and at the base of the Jayantia and Cachar Hills, they being most numerous in the Nowgong district. Dabaka, one of the principal habitats of the Mikirs up to this day is believed to be a fragment of the Davaka kingdom forming part of the empire of the Imperial Guptas as we learn from the Allahabad Pillar Inscription of Samudragupta; and the remains of old buildings and sculptures in the adjoining areas point to the existence of a flourishing Hindu state during the time of Samudragupta and his successors. Docile and unwarlike as the Mikirs are they gave very little trouble to the Ahom rulers, and in fact a section voluntarily migrated to Ahom territories to escape from the operation of the matriarchal law of inheritance which prevailed in the Mikir hills.[63]

The Garos live mainly in the region west of the Khasi hills. The earliest communications of the East India Company were conducted entirely from the sides of Goalpara and Mymensing. The founders of the ruling family of Jayantia and some people of the Rani state in Kamrup are described in old Assamese chronicles as Garos. The old Assam government had practically nothing to do with the real Garos of the interior hills. The government's contacts were mainly with the Garos who lived in the vassal states on the extremities of Assam in the south bank of the Brahmaputra, whose chiefs have been described by Buchanan-Hamilton as being of Garo origin. "The art of war", Hamilton continues, "has hitherto made so little progress among the Assamese that they have not been able to strip these chiefs of their dominions. On the contrary, they have contented themselves with a moderate tribute,

62. Ms. Assam Buranji, No. 7.

63. S. K. Bhuyan, *Deodhai Assam Buranji*, pp. 209-214; E. Stack, *The Mikirs*, 1908, p. 5; L. A. Waddell, *The Tribes of the Brahmaputra Valley*, J.A.S.B., Part III, 1900, pp. 29-35.

and conciliated the friendship of the independent mountaineers by a free commercial intercourse." Though the Garos were an independent people the villages adjoining the Bengal districts were encroached on by the neighbouring Zemindars. They raised supplies of cotton from the Garos which they made over to the Mogul Fauzadar of Rangamati. Exorbitant exactions were made by the Zemindars of Karaibari, Kalumalupara and Mechpara, leading to frequent disputes with the Garo chiefs till ultimately the latter were "rendered not only tributary, but mere cyphers." The success of the Zemindars was believed to be due to their being considered as agents of the East India Company. Writing in 1807-14 Buchanan-Hamilton pointed out "the absolute necessity for treating with the Garos, at least with those of the mountains as with independent people".[64]

The old Assam government did hardly come in contact with the tribes now living in the Lushai Hills, though there is evidence to show that the Assamese did know the Kukis on their way to Tripura through the Cachar Hills. The two Assamese envoys deputed by King Rudra Singha to the Tripura court proceeded up the Barak river for four days and reached Lakhipur. "Having halted there for two days", wrote the two ambassadors, "we proceeded for five days and reached the mouth of the Rupini river which is the boundary between Cachar and Tripura. There is no human habitation in that place. There are hills on both sides. After three days we arrived at Rangrung within the jurisdiction of Tripura. The hills on both sides of the Barak river are inhabited by a tribe called the Kukis who are like the Dafalas and Nagas here. There will be about three hundred men at that place; their weapons are arrows, bows, shields and Naga spears. The Tripura Raja appoints a governor over this place, and he is called Halamcha, who is like the Naga Khunbaos in our country. He has under him one Galim, one Gabar, one Chapia and one Doloi. They eat and dress like the Nagas, but they do not eat beef".[65]

The relations with the tribes were conducted by duly appointed frontier wardens and governors. The Sadiya-khowa Gohain was in charge of conciliating the tribes of the Sadiya country; the Marangi-khowa Gohain and the Rahial Barua, of the Kacharis and Mikirs; the Jagiyalia Gohain and the Kajalimukhia Gohain, of

64. S. K. Bhuyan, *An Account of Assam* by Buchanan Hamilton, compiled in 1807-14, p. 86; Mackenzie, *North-Eastern Frontier*, pp. 245-249.

65. S. K. Bhuyan, *Tripura Buranji*, pp. 21-22, Lt.-Col. J. Shakespear, *The Lushei Kuki Clans*, 1912.

the Jayantias; and the Barphukan and the Darrang Raja, of the Bhutanese. They had in their respective establishments a number of men versed in the languages, customs and habits of the tribes. There were also tribal experts in the court of the king, and their services were utilised in connection with a peace mission or a military expedition. Whereas Brahman ambassadors were as a rule appointed in embassies to the states of Western India, they were replaced by these sturdy tribal experts in conducting negotiations with the bordering races; for in dealing with tribesmen there was greater need of a spirit of forbearance and understanding, of sincerity and straightforwardness than of subtle logic, sophistry and propaganda. The Ahom diplomatic families—Chiring, Chengeli, Naga, Bakatial, Ramu and Lailengia—were generally harnessed in missions to the tribal areas.

The general success of the Ahoms in their dealings with the hill tribes was admitted by the Mogul chronicler Shihabuddin Talish who accompanied Mir Jumla's expedition in 1662-63. He wrote,—"Although most of the inhabitants of the neighbouring hills pay no tax to the Rajah of Assam, yet they accept his sovereignty and obey some of his commands. The Dufla tribe alone does not place its feet in the skirt of obedience, but occasionally encroaches on his kingdom".[66]

That the Ahom policy towards the tribes proved highly successful can be inferred from their uninterrupted enjoyment of sovereignty in Assam for six hundred years. In a kingdom where ferocious hillmen are lurking in the border areas, occasional frontier troubles were unavoidable; but the Ahoms suppressed these troubles with tact and diplomacy and the application of force as circumstances demanded. They did not allow these troubles to become intensified to the extent of jeopardising Ahom domination. On the other hand, the Ahoms harnessed the valour and dash of the hillmen in martial enterprises against foreigners. A British officer wrote in 1883,—"The Assamese army appears at this time (1660) to have been largely recruited from Nagas and Miris, and it is evident that they were quite able to hold their own against the well-trained armies of Hindustan".[67] In his interview with the Mogul commander Raja Ram Singha, the Assamese ambassador Madhabcharan Kataki referred to the tribal legions of the Ahom army as follows,—"Numerous chieftains of the mountain-

66. *Fathiyah-i-Ibriyah*, tr. Sarkar, J.B.O.R.S., 1915, pp. 184-5.

67. Captain St. John F. Michell, *Report on the North-East Frontier*, 1883, p. 30.

ous regions have become our willing allies in the campaign. The consist of a total strength of three lakhs of soldiers. They are n amenable to any considerations of right and wrong. Their partic pation in this campaign has been directly sanctioned by H Majesty, and they rush furiously against the enemy without wai ing for the orders of the general. They are quick and sudden i their attacks, and their movements and actions cannot be pr saged."[68] The Ahoms admitted members of the tribes into the racial fold, and the new entrants enjoyed all the privileges ar prerogatives of the ruling class. One Banfera Naga's son becan Barphukan; and one Miri became Miri-Sandikai, and he and h descendants enjoyed the governorship of Sadiya.[69] One reason the Ahoms' success in their dealings with the tribes was the immunity from caste prejudices which is illustrated in the ca: of the Mikirs. During an expedition against this tribe the Aho: soldiers partook of the food and drink obtained by them in tl houses of the Mikirs. "These men," said the tribesmen, "eat tl things we eat; they are therefore men of our fraternity." Tl younger folk who had fled to the forests on the approach of tl Ahoms were recalled by their elders. The Mikirs also expresse their satisfaction at the system of inheritance prevalent in Aho: Assam. The result was the immediate migration of several famili of Mikirs and Lalungs to Ahom territories.[70]

The Ahoms regulated their tribal policy in a very realistic ar judicious manner. They were conciliatory no doubt; but the did not hesitate to employ coercive measures when necessary, le the offer of friendship and good-will was interpreted as a manife tation of weakness and imbecility. An officer or noble who coul bring a refractory tribe to submission by the minimum applicatic of force received very high credit at the Ahom court, and h example was ever afterwards cited as a precedent whenever tl government undertook an expedition into the hilly country.

Commercial policy of the Ahom rulers: The Ahoms wer promoters of trade just like other rulers, and their diplomat relations with the neighbouring states and tribes centered, in mar cases, round the object of introducing free commercial intercour: to the advantage of both the parties. The Ahom government aime at making their markets secure and free so that people of tl adjacent territories could frequent them with commodities ar

68. S. K. Bhuyan, *Lachit Barphukan and His Times*, 1947, p. 71.

thereby contribute to the maintenance of a steady income from market duties and customs revenue.

The old-time conception of a trader or *Bepari* is recorded in a conversation held about the year 1696 in the court of the Gauhati Barphukan. A Jayantia envoy compared a *Bepari* to a black-bee which settles wherever honey can be found. To this the Barphukan replied,—"What you have said is correct. The black-bee settles on a number of flowers with the object of sucking honey from them. Having extracted honey from these flowers it settles with the same object on a lotus. But suddenly the sun sets, the lotus folds up its petals, and the bee becomes shut up there. With the rise of the sun next morning the lotus unfolds itself again, and the bee sets itself on its wings."[71] This comment of the Barphukan points to the vicissitudes of profit and loss which a trader must be prepared to face in his commercial enterprises and stipulations which are made still more precarious by his subjection to political changes and unexpected slumps and depressions.

The Ahom government interested itself in the trade of the frontier tribes, though it was conducted on a small scale, as large-scale production was unknown to the frontier tribesmen. Protection was given to the traders by the frontier wardens known as Datiyalia Bisayas and Duarias. But when commercial states were concerned the Ahom government considered petty trading to be outside their scope and function. Free commercial intercourse with Bengal required governmental protection of the traders of both the countries, and the supervision and control of the frontier officers and collectors of duties. The Ahoms were unwilling to set up an elaborate machinery for the purpose of safeguarding small quantities of articles. This is borne out in the reply given by King Rudra Singha in June 1713 to a request made by the Mogul Fauzadar of Rangamati for establishing commercial relations with Assam in which a proposal was made for despatching only a few boat-loads of commodities. This idea was not viewed with favour by the Ahom monarch, and he said,—"Is it called trade if it be limited to the import of a few maunds of salt from Bengal, and the despatch of two or four boats from our place? If the Nawab is intent on the establishment of regular commercial intercourse with us he should send his merchants [Shah-Mahajans] to Jogighopa and Goalpara, and our leading traders [Bar-mudois] will proceed to Kandhar Choky with large quantities of valuable articles. If

71. S. K. Bhuyan, *Jayantia Buranji*, p. 62.

matters could be arranged on this line then only they can well deserve the status of *hat-bat* or trade."[72]

The Ahoms made a clear distinction between politics and trade, and they considered the former to be more important and serious than the latter. Some agents of the Rangamati Fauzadar were gently rebuked by the Gauhati Barphukan when they pressed for the discussion of some commercial matters in the full court. "It is an affair relating to trade," said the Barphukan, "and it is not a fit subject for being taken up in the Durbar. Still then, I must admit that our trading activities have become more vigorous than before. The agents have spoken about multiple trade, but we have appointed only one man for this purpose, namely, the Duaria." In doubtful matters the version of a Kataki was considered to be more reliable than that of a mere trader.

Merchants were prohibited from meddling in politics. Three Assamese traders had once assured the Dacca Nawab that they would establish friendly relations between the Nawab and the Ahom government. The traders brought with them to Assam a couple of diplomatic agents of the Nawab together with letters and presents meant for the Ahom monarch Pratap Singha. The king accused the leader of the merchants, saying,—"He is a merchant and he should have confined himself to trading activities. What business had he to bring envoys from Bengal?" The traders were executed along with forty oarsmen in their employ.[73]

The Ahoms were ever-vigilant of the merchants of foreign territories, and never allowed them to settle in Assam lest they, as secret agents of some designing state, created any disruption in the country. The foreign traders had to transact their business in all possible haste, and return to their own land after completing their commercial activities in Assam.

Trade centres: The agent of the Assam government, known as the Duaria Barua, resided at the Assam Choky situated at the mouth of the Manas river. He enjoyed the exclusive privilege of the trade with Bengal for which he paid to the Assam government an annual rent of 90,000 rupees. Occasionally the privilege was granted to two men at the same time. The administration of the district round the Assam Choky was entrusted to an officer called the Kandhar Barua.[74] The Duaria Barua or Baruas received the

72. Ms. Assam Buranji, No. 6.

73. S. K. Bhuyan, *Assam Buranji*, S.M., pp. lxxv, 67.

74. The Assam Choky was known amongst the Assamese as Kandhar Choky and Hadira Choky. The term 'Kandahar Choky' also occurs in the Company's records of the period.

goods of the Assam merchants and exchanged them for Bengal products. They realised the duties on all exports and imports. The rates equitably fixed by the government of Assam underwent fluctuations at the hands of different Duaria Baruas. They received advances from the Bengal merchants for the delivery of Assam goods, or accepted Bengal goods on credit. The high rates of duties demanded by the Duaria Baruas, the non-fulfilment of their contracts or their refusal to carry on trade with particular individuals led to constant frictions with the Bengal merchants.

Goalpara on the south bank, and Jugighopa and Rangamati or the north, were the three eastern outposts of Bengal from where its merchants conducted their trade with Assam. Goalpara and Jugighopa were populous towns and had streets of shops. There was a numerous Christian population at both the places consisting mainly of Topazes of a questionable character.[75]

Rangamati situated at a distance of two miles from the bank of the Brahmaputra was a Mogul outpost of considerable importance. It was the headquarter of a Fauzadar who administered the adjacent territory and conducted the relations with Assam on behalf of the Nawab of Bengal. The town was 5 miles in length and 2 miles in breadth, and about the year 1770 it contained nearly 1,500 houses several of which were inhabited by the Mogul chiefs and others by the Portuguese.[76] Frey Sicardo visiting Rangamati in 1606 found there two churches, one dedicated to Our Lady of the Rosary and the other to Our Lady of Guadelup.[77] Rangamati was visited in 1714 by Father Francisco Troyand Laynez an account of which was written by his companion Father Claudius Anthony Barbier. Yunnan in China was described by Barbier as lying at a distance of 15 days' journey from Rangamati. "The intervening country [Assam]," wrote Barbier, "is occupied by Princes who refuse to grant a way through to foreigners." Rangamati was notorious for its unhealthiness, and Barbier referred to the common Bengali saying "that of two persons who go to Rangamati there is always one to remain there."[78] One of the duties of the

75. Montgomery Martin, *Eastern India*, Vol. III, p. 477; W. K. Firminger, *Rungpore District Records*, Vol. III, No. 217. Topazes were dark-skinned or half-caste claimants of Portuguese descent.

76. Walter Hamilton, *East India Gazetteer*, 1828, Vol. III, p. 459.

77. *The Earliest Episcopal Visitation in Bengal*, in *Bengal: Past and Present*, Vol. VI, p. 221.

78. Father Barbier's letter of Jan. 15, 1723, *Bengal: Past and Present*, Vol. VI, p. 200; also *Lettres edifiantes et curieuses*, in 4 vols., Paris, 1838, Vol. II, p. 595; also the Lyon edition of 1819 in 14 vols., Tom XIII, p. 288.

Muhammadan military officers in charge of Rangamati and Goalpara was to encourage the growth of jungle and reeds as a protection against the inroads of the Assamese.[79] The territory of which Rangamati was the principal town was also known as Rangamati which name was applied to the first revenue district formed in 1781 and 1787 with Hugh Baillie as Collector.[80]

The Company's representative in the district of Rungpore, in which the three towns Goalpara, Jugighopa and Rangamati were then included, used to be the channel of correspondence between the governments of Bengal and Assam.[81] From 1770 to 1792 Rungpore was administered by a Collector. In 1793 the office of Judge and Magistrate was separated from that of the Collector, and Assam relations were conducted thenceforward by the new official.[82] The Commissioner of Cooch Behar, a tributary state on the north-east frontier of Rungpore, remained occasionally in charge of the Company's relations with Assam. The Ahom viceroy at Gauhati holding the title of Barphukan conducted the relations with Bengal on behalf of the Assam government. The Barphukans and Duaria Baruas were carefully selected as the maintenance of harmony and good-will between the two states depended in a great measure to their discretion and judgment. The Barphukans were always Ahoms, and as far as can be ascertained the Duaria Baruas of the period 1771 to 1826 were all Brahmans.

Exports and Imports of Assam: The exports from Assam to Bengal consisted chiefly of muga silk, stick lac, munjit or madder, elephants' tusks, cotton, pepper and mustard seed; while the principal imports were salt, copper, English woollens and spices. Muga cloth, usually called *muga-dhuti* and muga silk in the correspondence of the Company, was much in demand in Bengal on account of its durability and texture, and was a regular article of trade in the Coromandal and Malabar coasts. It was mentioned

79. Sir William Hunter, Imperial Gazetteer of India, 1885-7, Vol. V, p. 113.

80. In Rennell's map of Cooch Behar and Rungpore, Rangamati extends to both banks of the Brahmaputra.

81. To avoid confusion the Bengal district and headquarter have been spelt in this book as *Rungpore*, and the Ahom capital of Assam as *Rangpur*.

82. The names of the Collectors of Rungpore, 1770 to 1832, and of the Judges and Magistrates, 1793 to 1832, are given in E. G. Glazier's *Further Notes on Rungpore Records*, Vol. II, 1876, pp. 35-37.

by Purchas in his *Pilgrimage* first published in 1614.[83] Munjit or *majathi*, (*Rubia munjista*,) a creeper growing wild in the eastern hills of Assam, was employed in dyeing cotton fabrics into various shades of scarlet, coffee-brown or mauve. Another product of Assam was *Agar* or aloe wood, (*Aquilaria Agallocha.*) An oil known as *Agar-attar* is extracted from the resinous portion of the wood. Elephants' tusks and *Agar* wood were principal articles of export during the Mogul period. A noble of Cooch Behar had once said to a Mogul commander,—"If it is desired I can establish friendly relations between the Nawab and the Assam Raja and procure for him [Nawab] *Agar* wood and elephants' teeth."[84] There was very great demand for Bengal salt in Assam, and about 100,000 maunds used to be annually imported, though the quantity fell off considerably during the period of the disturbances. There were brine springs in Sadiya and Barhat in Assam, and the revenue derived from them by the government amounted to 40,000 rupees in 1809. The local salt was said to be purer but more expensive than that imported from Bengal. The Assamese could not work these mines efficiently with the result that salt was a scarcity, and this compelled the Assamese to depend for it on Bengal.[85] It is a custom in Assam to present salt to guests in Vaisnava gatherings. The prime cost of Bengal salt ranged from rupees 70 to 120 per 100 maunds about the year 1780, and 400 rupees for the same quantity twelve years later. In the first period the price at which Bengal salt was sold in Assam ranged from rupees 2 to 4 per maund; and in the second to rupees 5 to 10. It was the prospect of profit in salt which mainly attracted Bengal merchants to the Assam trade.[86]

A fair idea of the trade between Bengal and Assam can be formed from the following figures showing the exports of the two countries in the year 1808-1809:—

Exports from Bengal: Salt, 35,000 maunds, at 5½ rupees per maund,—192,500 rupees; ghee, 1000 maunds,—1,600 rupees; fine

83. *Purchas His Pilgrimage*, 4th ed., 1625, p. 1005, quoted in Yule's *Hobson-Jobson*, under *moonga*. For *muga* see Thomas Hugon, *Remarks on the Silk Worms and Silks of Assam*, *J.A.S.B.*, Jan. 1837, pp. 21-38; B. C. Allen, *Monograph on the Silk Cloths of Assam*, 1899, pp. 3-16; Martin, *Eastern India*, Vol. III, pp. 671, 679-80.

84. *Kamrupar Buranji*, ed. S. K. Bhuyan, 1930, p. 20.

85. R. B. Pemberton, *Report on the Eastern Frontier of British India*, 1835, p. 82; Martin, *Eastern India*, Vol. III, pp. 660-61.

86. For information on the trade and commerce of Assam see Report on the Administration of Assam for 1874-75 and 1875-76, Part II-A, Permanent Chapters, Chapter I, Sections 4-8, pp. 19; also the Adm. Report for 1882-83, Part II-B, Chapters IV and V, pp. 44-55.

pulse,—800 rupees; sugar,—1,000 rupees; stone beads,—2,000 rupees; coral,—1,000 rupees; jewels and pearls,—5,000 rupees; European cutlery and glass-ware,—500 rupees; spices,—1,000 rupees; paints,—500 rupees; copper,—4,800 rupees; red lead,—1,000 rupees; English woollens,—2,000 rupees; Tafetas,—2,000 rupees; Benares Khinkobs,—500 rupees; Satin,—1,000 rupees; gold and silver cloth,—1,000 rupees; shells,—100 rupees; and Muslin,—10,000 rupees; *Total*,—228,300 rupees.

Exports from Assam: Stick lac, 10,000 maunds,—35,000 rupees; muga silk, 65 maunds,—11,350; muga cloth, 75 maunds,—17,500 rupees; munjit,—500 rupees; black pepper, 50 maunds,—500 rupees; cotton with seeds, 7,000 maunds,—35,000 rupees; ivory,—6,000 rupees; bell-metal vessels,—1,500 rupees; mustard seed, 15,000 maunds,—20,000 rupees; iron hoes,—600 rupees; slaves, 100,—2,000 rupees; Thaikol fruit, 50 maunds,—150 rupees; *Total*,—130,900 rupees.

The balance of trade amounting to 97,400 rupees against Assam was paid in gold from the mines and in silver.[87]

Assam had a reputation for gold. It is believed that there is scarcely a river in Assam which does not contain more or less gold in its sands which is washed down from the auriferous rocks in the neighbouring hills. A special class of Assamese subjects called Sonowals were employed by the government in gold washing, and as much as 7,000 tolas used to be annually received.[88] The possibility of obtaining gold from Assam was an additional inducement to Bengal merchants to engage in the trade with that country. Dr. J. P. Wade wrote to his friend Francis Fowke,—"Assam is not a country for diamonds, but it is for gold dust. I think I shall do well in it.[89]

In addition to the Bengal trade the Assamese carried on a considerable commerce with the neighbouring hill tribes and with Tibet and China. The trade with Tibet amounted to 200,000 rupees a year. The exports from Assam were lac, muga silk, endi cloth and dry fish; and the imports from Bhutan consisted of woollen cloths, gold dust, rock salt, cow-tails, musk and Chinese silks. The

87. Martin, *Eastern India*, Vol. III, pp. 660-61; Pemberton, *Eastern Frontier*, pp. 80-81; M'Cosh, *Topography of Assam*, pp. 63-64.

88. Dewan, Maniram, *Native account of washing for gold in Assam*, and Capt. S. O. Hannay's *Further information on gold washings in Assam*, *J.A.S.B.*, July 1838, pp. 621-628.

89. Wade to Fowke, written from Goalpara, Nov. 16, 1792, Fowke Mss., India Office Records, Vol. 22, letter No. 95.

Assamese used to receive from Tibet smoking pipes of Chinese manufacture, woollens and rock salt. A caravan consisting of nearly 20 men used to meet the Assamese merchants at a place near Chouna, at a distance of two months' journey from Lhassa. The Assamese used to receive from the Lhassa merchants, or Khumpa Bhutias as they were called, silver in bullion to nearly a lakh of rupees, and gold to the value of upwards of 70,000 rupees. Assamese merchants also went to Yunnan in China by the line of trade through Sadiya, Bisa and across the Patkai range of mountains, and through the Hukong Valley to the town of Munkong from where they ascended by the Irrawady to a place called Catmow. The goods were disembarked at Catmow from where they were conveyed on mules over a range of mountainous country inhabited by Shans into the Chinese province of Yunnan. Assam having no silver mine depended for that metal on supply from China, Tibet and the Barkhampti country near the sources of the Irrawady. The Mishmis living in the hills to the north of Sadiya brought with them Lama swords and spears and the vegetable poison known as *Mishimi tita*, and these they exchanged for glass beads, cloths, salt and money. The Abors and Miris brought pepper, ginger, munjit and wax. The Singphos used to bring ivory in considerable quantities. The Nagas brought cotton, ginger, and a little salt produced in their own springs.[90] One of the objects aimed at by the Company in establishing commercial relations with Assam was to participate in the trade with the frontier tribes, and if possible with China.

Communications with Bengal: There were four routes from Bengal to Assam, one by water and three by land. The river route from Goalpara was down the Brahmaputra, and *via* the Jennai from Jamalpore, and then after some distance along the Pabna river, a navigable branch of the Ganges. After proceeding up the Pabna river for two or three days the boats came to the Ganges which they ascended for three or four days more till they came to the mouth of Matabanga or the Jellingi down either of which they proceeded to Calcutta. As these two rivers become almost dry during winter the boats follow the route through the Sunderbans. The boats took 25 to 35 days to complete the voyage from Goalpara to Calcutta, and from 33 to 43 days from Calcutta to Goalpara. The first overland route from Bengal to Assam lay through Murshidabad, Maldah, Dinajpore, Rungpore, Bagwa and Goalpara, and it

90. Pemberton, *Eastern Frontier*, pp. 78-83; M'Cosh, *Topography of Assam*, pp. 10-12, 66; Robinson, *A Descriptive Account of Assam*, pp. 242-44.

was the line of the Calcutta dak. The second route was *via* Dacca, Dumary, Pucuoloe, Jamalpore, Singimari and Goalpara. Both these routes were almost impassable during the rains. The third route passed through Sylhet, Cherra, Moplung, Nungklao, Ranigaon, Khanamukh and Gauhati. The most popular of these four routes were the one by the water and the first overland passage.[91]

Old Assamese attitude towards foreigners: It was a common remark of all European writers that the Assamese were averse to the admission of foreigners into their country. This aversion was principally due to two reasons. From the time of Muhammad bin Bakhtiyar Khilji's invasion in 1205 upto the final expulsion of the Moguls in 1682 Assam was subject to frequent attacks by the Muhammadans from Bengal; and consequently all men from Bengal and other parts of India were considered by the Assamese as a potential source of danger. No outsider was allowed to acquire a footing in Assam lest he should become too influential and disturb the loyalty of the subjects or bring in other complications. All people living in the countries to the west of Assam were labelled under one name—*Bangals,* a term applied even to Europeans.

The Ahom rulers had originally come from the Shan kingdom of Pong or Nara in Upper Burma, and they looked upon the inhabitants of Nara as their brothers and kinsmen with whom they maintained throughout regular social and political intercourse. Whereas the early Hindu rulers of Assam had regarded themselves as one with the princes and peoples of Hindusthan the Ahom conquerors materially reduced, if they did not totally destroy, Assam's communion with India. Nara priests frequented the Ahom court, and the monarchs married princesses of their parent kingdom. Ahom kings were for several centuries guided in their political actions by the advice of their orthodox priests who looked to their Nara compatriots for recognition and reinforcement. It was only after the Hinduisation of the Ahoms that they began to take some interest in the religion and culture of India. Ahom princes and nobles then began to depute Brahman priests to the shrines of India for making offerings on their behalf; they sent also commercial and political agents, mostly in disguise, to study foreign customs, manners and movements. But the old fear of an attack from the west continued, attended by the suspicion of all foreigners.

But there were exceptions to this rigid exclusion of strangers. The Ahom rulers encouraged men from India to come and settle

91. M'Cosh, *Topography of Assam*, pp. 8-9.

in Assam provided their introduction was of advantage to the country. Artisans, craftsmen, weavers, clerks, accountants, scholars and saints, both Hindu and Moslem, were freely admitted, and occasionally brought by special arrangement with the rulers of Hindusthan as there was an inadequacy of such men in Assam. But these licensed foreigners, after having come to Assam, had to cut off all connection with their mother country, and to become assimilated with the Assamese in language, manners and racial sympathy. They became subjects of the Assam government like the older inhabitants. The Assamese objected to the admission of foreigners who owed allegiance to other rulers and proposed to reside in Assam as a temporary measure. The Assamese made a sharp distinction between desirable foreigners who came to stay and become naturalised, and undesirable foreigners upon whom the Assam government could not exercise any degree of control. Europeans fell in the second category, and hence their entrance was almost always forbidden, and their movements closely watched even when they were permitted to enter the Assam territory.

King Rudra Singha, the most cosmopolitan of the Ahom monarchs, created two new orders, the Khaunds and the Bairagis, whose function was to visit important places of India and note beneficent foreign customs with a view to their introduction in Assam. He invited Bengali priests, scholars, musicians and merchants to his court and sent them back with presents so that his good name might be spread in their country which he was scheming to invade.[92] Even this monarch would not permit outsiders to quit Assam if he suspected that they had deliberately collected information which might one day be used to the prejudice of this country. An up-country architect named Ghansyam who had erected the masonry buildings at the new capital Rangpur was put to death by King Rudra Singha as papers containing a full account of Assam and its inhabitants were found in his possession.[93]

Early European visitors: Assam being thus a forbidden field for the exploration of Europeans the only opportunity for collecting direct information was during their visit to the country when parts of it were under Mogul occupation, or when they accompanied the Mogul expeditions as sailors, gunners or camp-followers.

92. *Tripura Buranji, ed.* S. K. Bhuyan, 1938, English Introduction, pp. *ix* to *xi*; text, pp. 1-2.

93. Sir Edward Gait, *A History of Assam*, 2nd ed., 1926, pp. 171-2.

There are reasons to suppose that the Venetian traveller Nicolo Conti who visited India in the first half of the fifteenth century had gone as far as Assam. From Cernove [Sonargram ?] Conti "sailed up the Ganges for the space of three months, leaving behind him four very famous cities, and landed at an extremely powerful city called Maarazia, where there is a great abundance of aloe wood, gold, silver, precious stones and pearls. From thence he took the route towards some mountains situated towards the east, for the purpose of procuring those precious stones called "carbuncles" [rubies] which are found there." Conti perhaps travelled up the river Brahmaputra, which he called the Ganges, and reached some town in Assam, because aloe wood was the special produce of Assam, and because his desire to obtain rubies indicates his having visited the north-eastern frontier adjoining Northern Burma which was the only area where rubies were known to be found.[94]

Leaving conjectures aside, the first Europeans on record to visit Assam were the two Jesuit missionaries Father Stephen Cacella and Father John Cabral. The two travellers set out from Dacca on September 5, 1626, with a view to go to Cathay or China. On September 26 they reached Hazo which was then the head-quarter of the Mogul Fauzadar of Kamrup. Hazo was an important town in those days. The travellers met Raja Satrajit at Pandu which was densely populated and was the scene of constant warfare between the Moguls and the Assamese. They abandoned the idea of going to China, and on October 6, 1626, they left Hazo for Cooch Behar where they arrived on October 21. Cooch Behar was a populous town containing many bazaars which were visited by merchants from Patna, Rajmahal and Gaur.[95]

Cacella and Cabral were not the first Europeans to enter Cooch Behar for it had been visited in 1536 by the London merchant Ralph Fitch belonging to the party of John Newbery who had been furnished with a letter of introduction to Emperor Akbar from Queen Elizabeth. Fitch saw in Cooch Behar a number of hospitals for sheep, goats, dogs, cats, birds and for other living creatures. Old and lame animals used to be looked after till their

94. R. H. Major, editor, *India in the Fifteenth Century, The Travels of Nicolo Conti*, published by Hakluyt Society, First series, No. 22, 1857, p. 10. The late Mr. C. E. A. W. Oldham, sometime editor of the *Indian Antiquary*, first drew my attention to this possibility during my stay in London in 1936-38.

95. Cacella to Father Albert Laertius at Cochin, October 4, 1627, in C. Wessels, *Early Jesuit Travellers in Central Asia*, pp. 123-124, and Appendix II, pp. 316-317.

death, and people received rewards for bringing animals to the hospitals.[96] Another European, Peter Heyleyn, wrote in the same vein about the care taken of animals by the people of Cooch Behar.[97]

The next European was a soldier serving in the Mogul army during its encampment at Hazo sometime in 1635. He was seen firing at a vulture at Sualkuchi near Hazo. The slaughter of vultures being tabu the European was seized by the Ahoms and sent up to the king.[98] Nothing is known of his subsequent fate.

Early European writers on Assam: Assam received wide publicity in Mogul India and among Europeans as a result of its invasion by Nawab Mir Jumla in 1662. European merchants in Bengal had been directly interested in the progress of the expedition led by the governor of Bengal as upon his support they mainly depended for their success in trade. Mir Jumla was accompanied by a number of Dutch, Portuguese and English sailors and gunners.[99] The general's physician in Assam was a Dutch surgeon named Gelmar Vorburg.

Glanius, a Dutch sailor of Mir Jumla, has left an account of his experiences in Assam; and as he was among the first batch of Europeans to proceed as far as the capital or its neighbourhood his account has a significance of its own. Aurangzeb's object in sending Mir Jumla to Assam has been stated to be an attempt to get rid of the great general, "the soldier's darling, the People's Favourite, a great Politician, a Wise and Valiant Captain, and the wealthiest in all the Empire." The Assamese worshipped cows and their temples were full of the images of cows. Glanius and his comrades pillaged and carried away a golden cow from a temple in the vicinity of the fleet. He refers to some Assamese, obviously the Vaisnavas, who would never eat anything endowed with life. "How great soever their hunger may be," observes Glanius, "they choose rather to dye [die] than to eat either Fish or Flesh."

96. J. H. Ryley, *Ralph Fitch, England's Pioneer to India and Burma*, 1899, pp. 111-12.

97. Peter Heyleyn, *India Intra Gangem and Extra Gangem, London*, 1652, extract in *Bengal: Past and Present*, Vol. II, p. 50.

98. *Deodhai Asam Buranji*, ed. S. K. Bhuyan, 1932, p. 71; Golapchandra Barua, *Ahom Buranji*, p. 118.

99. Sir Jadunath Sarkar, *History of Aurangzib*, Vol. III, 1916, p. 179.

Glanius mentions the products of Assam as pepper, aloe wood, sandalwood and medicinal herbs.[100]

Assam is also mentioned in the correspondence between the Dutch authorities of Hugli and Batavia and Mir Jumla, the latter being usually described as "Chanchannan Supphesalar", i.e., Khan-khanan Sipah-salar. In two letters to Matthew van den Brouke, Director of the Dutch Factories in Bengal, and received by him on December 18, 1662, Mir Jumla recounted his victory over the Assamese. Gelmar Vorburg writing from Assam on December 10, 1662, expressed his doubts if the Nawab would succeed in retaining his hold over Assam as he had lost two-thirds of his men and horses through want of provisions and the pestilential airs which there blow from the mountains. On the conclusion of the treaty Mir Jumla wrote to the Dutch Governor-General about his pursuit of the Assam Raja and his adherents to Namrup. The Raja was brought to such a pass, wrote Mir Jumla, that seeing no help but in the favour of the Emperor, he presented his own daughter and the daughter of the Tipam Raja to the Mogul harem, furnishing them with rich offerings of gold, silver and elephants from his own country and from the countries of the Rajas of Darrang, Dimarua and Beltola, and he agreed to the annual tribute imposed. Vorburg wrote again on February 10, 1663, about the terms of the treaty, and the delivery of the Raja's daughter and the daughters of his nobles, together with a portion of the indemnity consisting of 3,000 tolas of gold, 420 tolas of silver and 150 elephants.[101]

The Dutch Governor-General Joan Maetsuyker, unaware of Mir Jumla's death which had occurred in March 1663, addressed a letter to the general on August 29. Maetsuyker had learnt from Mir Jumla's letter that he had subjugated Cooch Behar and Assam and that the loss on the enemies' side amounted to 50,000 killed and wounded and 300,000 prisoners. The Governor-General congratulated Mir Jumla on his bringing such a large country as Assam under tribute to Aurangzeb. He expressed a desire to carry on business with Mir Jumla on the latter's return to Bengal and communicated the appointment of Rogier van Heyningen as

100. *A Relation of an Unfortunate Voyage to the Kingdom of Bengala, by Mr. Glanius, London*, 1682, pp. 158-177. The original in Dutch was pub. at Amsterdam in 1681. See also *Bengal: Past and Present*, Vol. XXIX, pp. 7-29, for Glanius's account of Mir Jumla's invasion of Assam, copiously annotated.

101. *Batavia Dagh-Register*, Anno 1663, compiled by J.A. van der Chijs, 1891, pp. 21, 107, 140, 168, 424; Niccolao Manucci, *Storia do Mogor*, tr. William Irvine, Vol. IV, p. 430. The abstract in English was checked by the late Mr. W. H. Moreland, author of *India from Akbar to Aurangzib*.

successor to Brouke. With the hope of establishing permanent friendship with Mir Jumla, Maetsuyker and his Council sent to him four of their best cannon.[102]

The three travellers Bernier, Tavernier and Manucci refer in detail to the Assam expedition of Mir Jumla and to the distress of the Mogul army in that country. "Under a less able commander," wrote Bernier, "the army could not have hoped to reach Bengal.[103] Tavernier points out that Assam was not properly known till its invasion by Mir Jumla. He attributes the invention of gun and gunpowder to Assam from where they possibly went to Pegu and China for which it was ascribed to the Chinese. Tavernier refers to the economic independence of the Assamese "who produce all that is necessary to the life of man without there being need to go for anything to the neighbouring states." He points out the superior quality of the Assam lac which was used for lacquering cabinets and was said to have been exported to China and Japan in large quantities.[104] Manucci mentions the products of Assam as pears, apples, peaches, cherries and grapes. Mir Jumla's subjugation of Assam has been stated to be a preliminary step to the invasion of China and Pegu, but he could not carry out this object as he had to retire from Assam in consequence of the sufferings of his army.[105]

An English sailor Thomas Bowrey (*circa* 1650-1713) describes Mir Jumla's death on his return from Assam as a great catastrophe to the people of Hindusthan and specially to the Moguls. "By his death," says Bowrey, "they lost the best of Nabob, the Kingdom of Acham, and by consequence many other privileges."[106]

The final contest between the Assamese and the Moguls took place at Gauhati in February 1682 which resulted in the defeat of the invaders with heavy losses. William Hedges, the first Agent and Governor of the English Factories in the Bay of Bengal, in

102. Francois Valentyn, *Oud en Nieuw Oost-Indien*, 5 vols., Amsterdam, 1726, Vol. V, *Keurlyke Beschryving van Choromandel, Pegu, Arrakan, Mocha etc.*, pp. 173-174, containing a map of Hindustan prepared by Matthew van den Brouke, showing 'Azo' and 'Chamdhara' in Assam. An abstract of Maetsuyker's letter was kindly prepared for me by Dr. Holden Furber, author of *Henry Dundas*.

103. Francois Bernier, *Travels in the Mogul Empire*, 1658 to 1668, tr. Archibald Constable, London, 1891, pp. 171-74.

104. Jean Baptiste Tavernier, *Travels in India*, tr. V. Ball, 2 Vols., London, 1889, Vol. I, p. 16, Vol. II, p. 277.

105. Manucci, *Storia do Mogor*, tr. Irvine, Vol. II, pp. 98-101.

106. Thomas Bowrey, *A Geographical Account of Countries round the Bay of Bengal*, 1669 to 1679, edited by Sir Richard Carnac Temple, Hakluyt Society's Publications, Series II, Vol. XII, 1905, pp. 143-144.

describing his interview with Nawab Shaista Khan at Dacca on October 29, 1682, refers to the preparations for a fresh war with Assam to recoup the losses suffered eight months before. Hedges found Shaista Khan "very busy in despatching and vesting divers principal officers sent with all possible diligence with recruits for their army lately overthrown in Asham and Silhet, two large plentiful countries, eight days journey from this city (Dacca)."[107]

Bartholomew Plaisted, a Surveyor in the Bengal establishment from 1745 till his death in 1767, was the first official of the Company to write about Assam. But his account has very little value as it is based on Tavernier, and repeats all the mistakes and misrepresentations of the earlier writer.[108]

The first official of the Company who surveyed the frontier of Assam and collected some information about that country was Major James Rennell, "the father of Indian geography." In 1765 he traced the course of the river Brahmaputra to about 400 miles above the conflux upto the point where the Bengal districts ended and those of Assam began. But he was not permitted by the Assamese to go up higher. The Assamese territory on the south bank of the Brahmaputra terminated at Nagarbera, 21 miles to the east of Goalpara, while on the north bank it stretched as far as the Assam Choky at the mouth of the Manas river, opposite Goalpara. From December 2 to 6, 1765, Rennell was engaged in tracing the Brahmaputra from Goalpara to Nagarbera, but he had to keep near the south bank of the river. He managed to proceed about ten miles beyond Nagarbera, and on the return journey coasted the Assam side on the north bank near enough to collect the information he wanted.[109] The results of his survey are embodied in his *Bengal Atlas, Memoir of a Map of Hindustan* and his *Journals,* 1764-1767. Rennell recognised the identity of the Brahmaputra with the Tsanpo river of Tibet. He referred to the visits paid to the Assam capital Rangpur by some European merchants engaged in the Goalpara trade. From the fact that the

107. *Diary of Sir William Hedges in Bengal,* 1681-88, edited by Col. H. Yule, 3 vols., Hakluyt Society Pub., 1877-89, Vol. I, p. 43.

108. Bartholomew Plaisted, *A Journal from Calcutta in Bengal by Sea to Busserah, etc., in the Year MDCCL.* 2nd edition, 1758, pp. 227-28; partly reproduced in *Bengal: Past and Present,* Vol. VI, p. 603.

109. Rennell, *Journals,* 1764-1767, edited by T. H. D. La Touche, Memoirs of the Asiatic Society of Bengal, 1910, Vol. III, No. 3, pp. 56-7. Rennell's *Bengal Atlas,* first pub. in 1779, was republished in 1914 by the Surveyor-General of India; the Assam frontier is shown in Plate 36, Cooch Behar and Rungpore.

French merchant Jean Baptiste Chevalier had gone on a very large embarkation to Rangpur, Rennell concluded that the Brahmaputra must be navigable for large boats up to the neighbourhood of that town.[110] Rennell's maps and account were for a long time the only source of information relative to the geography of Assam and the eastern frontier of Bengal though at present it is mainly historically that they are of value.

Early European merchants: The first European to trade with Assam was Colonel James Mill who had come to India as a subaltern in the service of the Ostend East India Company. This Company had been established in 1722 with a charter from the Holy Roman Emperor Charles VI. A factory was built at Bankibazar, near Barrackpore, and the trade went on prosperously for some time. But in 1727 the Emperor yielding to the representations of England, Holland and France, suspended the charter for seven years. In 1732 the Directors received a decree definitely abolishing the Ostend Company.[111] Having found that the Ostend Company was ruined Hill became a soldier of fortune and enlisted a small body of Europeans whom he trained to some guns. In 1742 the Mahrattas invaded Bengal to enforce their claim, sanctioned by the Emperor of Delhi, to the payment of *chouth*. Seeing that the whole country of Bengal had been thrown into confusion by the Mahrattas, Mill escorted a number of salt boats to Assam. He carried on business in salt with Assam for some years. A rebellion having broken out at the Ahom capital the king asked Mill for assistance. He marched with his soldiers and quelled the rebellion. The king always expressed a deep regard for him and gave him facilities for trade. But Mill was not permitted by the Ahom monarch to establish himself in Assam.[112] An Assamese chronicle refers to a visit paid by three Europeans to the court of King Siva Singha in 1739. Their names have been given as Gudimbill, Distirbill and Mistirbill.[113] One of them was perhaps Colonel

110. Rennell, *Memoir of a Map of Hindoostan,* 2nd ed., 1785, p. 95.

111. Grose, *Voyage to the East Indies,* 1772, Vol. I, Ch. VII, pp. 317-20; C. R. Wilson, *Old Fort William in Bengal,* Vol. I, pp. 178-79 *n*; *Cambridge History of India,* Vol. V, p. 115; Home Misc. Series, Vol. 74, No. 2.

112. W. S. Seton-Karr, *Selections from Calcutta Gazette,* 1864, Vol. I, pp. 153-54. In 1746 Col. Mill submitted a scheme to the Emperor of Austria for the conquest of Bengal from its rebel governor Ali Verdi Khan, who had in possession a treasure amounting to 30 millions sterling, and whose annual revenue amounted to two millions, Willam Bolts, *Considerations on Indian Affairs, Vol. III, Part II,* 1775, App. IV and V, pp. 15-19.

113. Golapchandra Barua, *Ahom Buranji,* p. 274. Gait mentions four names—Bill, Godwin, Lister, and Mill, *History of Assam,* 1st ed., p. 179.

James Mill paying a preliminary visit in connection with his salt business.

The next European merchant of note to engage in the Assam trade was Jean Baptiste Chevalier who afterwards became Governor of Chandernagore and Commander-in-Chief of the French Settlements in Bengal. In 1755 Chevalier was deputed from Chandernagore to carry on a trade with Assam for the French East India Company. He penetrated as far as Sylhet from where he proceeded to Goalpara. He established a trade and settled at the latter place. In 1757 he embarked a considerable property at Dacca on a fleet of boats and proceeded to the frontier of Assam. Having obtained the permission of the Assam government he advanced with his fleet to the capital Rangpur under an escort who deprived him of all intercourse with the inhabitants.[114] He made over his goods to the Assamese on credit to the amount of nearly a lakh of rupees.[115] Chandernagore fell into the hands of the English on March 23, 1757, and M. Courtin, Chief of the French Factory at Dacca, was "expecting every day to see M. Chevalier return from his journey to the king of Assam."[116] After the capture of Chandernagore the trade on the part of the French Company with Assam was discontinued; but Chevalier remained at Goalpara in the service of some English gentlemen as their agent for the salt trade with Assam. Chevalier left Goalpara in 1763 and the agency was delivered to John Robinson.[117]

The next European to establish a regular trade with Assam was Paul Richard Pearkes. In 1757 he had been appointed Chief of the English Factory at Patna from which office he was suspended in 1758 for unfaithful conduct. He was then appointed Accomptant at Calcutta. In September 1759 he went to Assam to collect some outstanding concerns and John Zephaniah Holwell was appointed Accomptant in his place.[118] Pearkes erected a factory at Jugighopa. He studied the products of the place which consisted of fir and other kinds of wood, particularly sassafras and "worm-

114. Rennell, *Memoir of a Map of Hindoostan*, 1785, p. 95; C. C. Roy, *Note on J. B. Chevalier and Col. Montigny* in *Bengal: Past and Present*, Vol. XVI, pp. 126-61; J. P. Wade, *Geographical Sketch of Assam*, printed in Martin, *Eastern India*, Vol. III, p. 626.

115. Ms. Assamese chronicle of the reign of Lakshmi Singha of Assam (1769-80) in possession of the American Baptist Mission, Gauhati.

116. M. Courtin at Calcapore to his wife Madame Direy in France, Ap. 20, 1758, S. C. Hill, *Three Frenchmen in Bengal*, p. 137.

117. E. E. Pote, Commercial Resident at Rungpore, to Hastings, Ap. 20, 1784, *Bengal: Past and Present*, Vol. III, p. 366.

118. Beng. Pub. Cons., Sept. 24, 1759, No. 131.

wood," and gold gathered from the sands of the Brahmaputra. "I am at present on my voyage to Assam," wrote Pearkes to a friend in England, "a country that only two Europeans have visited besides myself, and where a trade may, I am certain, be carried on greatly to the advantage of the Company and their servants, and doubt not I shall make it turn out to my present profit."[119] Nothing is known of Pearkes's success in the Assam trade.

Disputes with Mir Kasim, Nawab of Bengal: After Pearkes had established a factory at Jugighopa other European merchants appeared at Goalpara and Rangamati, the most prominent being John Robinson and Hugh Baillie. Robinson was the agent of Johnstone, Hay and William Bolts, and Baillie of Henry Vansittart, Governor of Fort William in Bengal. Soon there ensued a serious dispute with Mir Kasim, Nawab of Bengal, over the question of the inland trade. Mir Kasim who had been elevated to the Nawabship by the English in 1760 claimed that the Mogul Emperor Farrukhsiyar's *firman* of 1716 entitled the Company to exemption from the customary duties only with regard to their ship-merchandise, while the Company and its servants claimed the privilege also in respect of the articles of inland trade produced in and imported into Bengal and meant for consumption in the country, such as salt, betel and tobacco. The position of the English had been strengthened by the perwanas, issued by Mir Jafar during his first Nawabship of Bengal, 1757-1760, by which his officers were forbidden to levy duties from the Company and its servants on any kind of goods, whether shipping commodities or articles of inland trade.[120]

The trade of the districts bordering on Assam came to prominence in the disputes between Mir Kasim and the Company. In May 1762 the Nawab complained to Vansittart that his losses in the trade with Assam, Rangamati and Karaibari amounted to 40,000 rupees, and that the whole trade had been monopolised by the Company's people to the detriment of the inhabitants of those places. The Nawab referred particularly to the oppressive conduct of Chevalier in forcibly seizing the *talukdars* and *ryots* and making them draw timber for him.[121] Vansittart deputed one Gangaram

119. Pearkes at Jugighopa to Percival Bentley Reid, Dec. 4, 1759, sent per *Royal George*, Home Misc. Series, Vol. 92, No. 35, pp. 23-24. The two Europeans must be Col. Mill and J. B. Chevalier. By "wormwood" Pearkes perhaps meant the bitter plant of that name.

120. *Cambridge History of India*, Vol. V, pp. 170-173.

121. Mir Kasim to Vansittart, in Vansittart's *Narrative of the Transactions in Bengal*, pub. 1766, Vol. II, p. 166.

Metre to Rangamati and Goalpara to enquire into the alleged abuses and put a stop to them where possible.

In November 1762 a counter-complaint was made by Robinson alleging obstacles being thrown in way of his trade by the Nawab's Fauzadar at Rangamati and protesting against the authorisation of Gangaram to enquire into the proceedings of English merchants.[122] Another protest was made by John Cartier, Chief of the Council at Dacca, asserting that the Nawab or his Fauzadar at Rangamati "can have no more right to regulate the terms of our commerce with that country [Assam] than with those of China." He pointed out that no duties had ever yet been paid on lac and muga and other goods imported into Bengal from Assam.[123] He also opposed the idea of throwing the whole trade of Assam and Rangamati into the hands of one individual, the Fauzadar of Rangamati.[124]

Vansittart arranged with the Nawab that the English would pay duties on the articles of inland trade though at lower rates than other merchants The Goalpara traders were strictly charged to make their purchases and sales through the agents of the Nawab's government.[125] Vansittart specially enjoined Hugh Baillie, his agent at Rangamati, to take the *dustuk* of the country government and not to interfere in the Nawab's trade in cotton received from the mountaineers. Baillie's request for some sepoys to be employed in his business was refused by Vansittart.[126]

Vansittart's attempts to compromise with the Nawab were not supported by the Members of Council who had large stakes in the commerce of Bengal. The tension between Mir Kasim and the Company gradually increased and led to open hostilities between the two governments, followed by the restoration of Mir Jafar to the Nawabship of Bengal. The Court of Directors strongly disapproved of the proceedings in Bengal, and appointed Clive a second time as Governor of Fort William in Bengal where he arrived in May 1765. One of his earlier acts was to force the Company's servants to subscribe the covenants against the receipt of presents. They were also forbidden to engage in inland trade.

122. Johnstone and Hay to Calcutta Council, Jan. 24, 1763, in Vansittart's *Narrative*, II, p. 213; N. L. Hallward, *William Bolts*, pp. 10-14. Robinson's letter was dated Nov. 10, 1762.

123. Cartier to Calcutta Council, Jan. 10, 1763, in Vansittart's *Narrative*, III, p. 217.

124. Vansittart, *Narrative*, II, p. 244.

125. Vansittart, *Original Papers Relative to the Disturbances in Bengal*, Vol. I, p. 233.

126. Vansittart to Baillie, Jan. 10, 1763, Beng. Pub. Cons., Feb. 1, 1763; also Vansittart to Peter Moore, Dec. 12, 1762.

CHAPTER II

COMPANY'S TRADE WITH ASSAM, 1771-1779

Baillie, agent of the Society of Trade: The year 1771 witnessed the foundation of the East India Company's commercial relations with Assam, for in that year the possibilities of trade with that country were first recognised by the Court of Directors and measures were adopted to obtain preliminary information on the subject.

An earlier attempt to trade with Assam had been made under the auspices of the Society of Trade established by Lord Clive in 1765, during his second administration of Bengal, to compensate the chief officers for the loss sustained by them by strict observance of the covenants that prohibited acceptance of *nuzzeranas* or presents, and participation in inland trade consisting mainly of salt, betel-nut and tobacco. The Society was to deal only in these articles, and the profits were to be distributed, in allotted shares, to the Governor and Councillors and the senior civil and military servants.

The Committee of Trade which was responsible for carrying into execution the objects of the Society appointed European agents to transact its business in different parts of the country, and they were the only Europeans engaged in inland trade. The agents were required to abstain from any trade or commerce on their part either as agents or principals except for the benefit of the Society, and from any act in the way of oppressing or insulting the natives. In forwarding his plan of the Society of Trade for the confirmation of the Court of Directors, Clive suggested the expediency of withdrawing all the freemerchants from inland trade. As a measure of relief Clive recommended some of them, including Hugh Baillie and David Killican, for being appointed to the rank of Factors, to which they were, in his opinion, entitled by "their character, age, behaviour and experience."[1]

Of the eleven agents appointed on November 1, 1765, three were to reside in the district of Rungpore, Hugh Baillie at Goalpara, Tom Lewis at the town of Rungpore, and Hargreave at

1. Clive to Court of Directors, Feb. 1, 1766, Select Committee's Fourth Report, 1772-73, App. 3, p. 473.

Chilmari.[2] The selection of Baillie to the agency at Goalpara which was established to supply the articles of inland trade to Assam and other neighbouring countries was probably due to his previous experience of the trade with those areas in which he had been engaged as the agent of Henry Vansittart, Governor of Bengal, and other merchants, and which he had now to close under the orders of the Company. To this must be added the obligation felt by Clive to provide Baillie with a career as we learn from his recommendation to the Court of Directors. It is not at all known what success Baillie obtained in his exertions at Goalpara on behalf of the Society of Trade. There could not be any demand for Bengal betel-nut in Assam except in the few villages bordering on Rungpore, as the Bengal nuts were sold then, and even now, in a dried and hard condition, while the Assamese invariably use soft ones freshly plucked from trees or raised from pits where they are allowed to mature for months; and betel is grown in every Assamese family orchard. Tobacco is also a very common garden produce of the Assamese. The Society itself relinquished the trade in betel-nut and tobacco in August 1767, and confined itself to salt, the most important article of inland trade.[3]

The demand for Bengal salt in Assam was great and steady for the salt locally produced was not easily available and was therefore very expensive. The salt springs of Barhat and Sadiya in Assam could not be properly worked on account of the unsettled state of that part of the country. It was generally computed that the total quantity of Bengal salt yearly consumed in Assam amounted to 100,000 maunds.[4] The revenue from salt alone consisting of the duty of thirty-five per cent, payable to the Company which had now stepped into the position of the Dewan of Bengal, justified the establishment of the Society's agency at Goalpara.

The income from the Society's sales of the first year exceeded the expectation of the originators of the plan. As the whole scheme was based on a comparatively low rate of profit, the agency at Goalpara probably succeeded like the rest in contributing to the general prosperity of the Society. Clive had, however, come to realise the inconvenience of employing European agents in the trade and he dispensed with their agency altogether in the course

2. Committee of Trade to Clive, Nov. 1, 1765, Select Committee's Fourth Report, App. 41, p. 513.

3. House of Commons Reports, Vol. IV, App. 59, p. 526, cited in *Warren Hastings in Bengal* by Miss M. E. Monckton Jones, p. 59-*n*.

4. Capt. R. B. Pemberton, *Report on the Eastern Frontier of British India*, 1835, p. 82.

of the second year which commenced in September 1766.[5] He made arrangements for selling salt at Calcutta or at the place where it was manufactured to natives only who were allowed to convey it wherever they pleased.

The career of the Society was destined to be a shortlived one. In spite of Clive's persistent and vigorous defence of its objects as conferring upon the servants "gratitude for affluence in service and for an independence at the close thereof wherein will be found the strongest ties or motives to the faithful discharge of their duty,"[6] the Court declared the creation of any monopoly for the benefit of Europeans, whether private merchants or servants of the Company, as "an intrusion upon the natural right of the natives of the country who now more particularly claim our protection."[7] The Court accordingly forbade all servants of the Company as well as freemerchants to be concerned in the inland trade, and defined their chief province as the ancient limits of the export and import trade. The Society of Trade ceased to exist from August 1, 1768, and the inland trade was thrown open to all persons, Indians and Europeans.[8]

Baillie in England: After the withdrawal of Baillie from Goalpara and the abolition of the Society of Trade he sailed for England in the beginning of 1769, and remained there till 1773. Clive had already left Bengal in January 1767. The time formed a turning point in the affairs of the Company. The British people had heard of the rapid accumulation of territories by the Company, of the vast increase in their revenues, and had seen with their own eyes the immense fortunes taken home by the servants of the Company and private traders. Interest in the Company's affairs thus roused was stimulated by numerous pamphlets and books depicting different aspects of their administration mostly written by men who harboured some real or fancied grievances against the Company. The political influence wielded by India-returned merchants, *Nabobs* as they were called, had excited the jealousy of members of Parliament. Politicians began to ask

5. Sir John Malcolm, *Memoir of Lord Clive*, Vol. III, p. 104. The reasons for this inconvenience are not stated, though we believe the difficulty of preventing the agents in the districts from engaging in private trade might be one.

6. Secret Committee to Court of Directors, Jan. 24, 1767, Home Miscellaneous Series, Vol. 769, p. 30.

7. Court's Letter to Bengal, Nov. 20, 1767, Select Committee's Fourth Report, App. 61, p. 529.

8. Malcolm, *Clive*, III, p. 111; Home Misc. Series, Vol. 769, p. 530.

whether a private trading organisation like the East India Company should be allowed to continue political operations without interference from the British Crown. In the meantime the increased civil and military establishments in the three Presidencies of Bengal, Madras and Bombay had involved heavy expenditures which produced a fall of the Company's stock. The Directors were thus compelled to apply to the ministers for a loan which gave the latter their long-sought opportunity to examine the state of the Company's affairs in India. In 1772 two committees were appointed, the Select Committee and the Committee of Secrecy, "to enquire into the state, nature and condition of the Company and of British affairs in the East Indies." Clive himself had to answer a number of charges which were commonly attributed to Laurence Sulivan, Deputy Chairman of the Court, who bore Clive intense personal animosity. Clive eventually replied to these charges in a speech in the Parliament where he asserted that the Court of Directors and the General Court of Proprietors were themselves to blame for the evils complained of. In 1773 the two Committees brought out their reports mainly condemnatory in character, and the same year the Parliament passed two Acts: one empowered the ministers to lend £140,000 to the Company to discharge their obligations, and the other, commonly known as North's Regulating Act, gave the Company a new constitution "evolved on the basis of the eminent dominion of the Parliament over our every subject in every concern." The Act mentioned the names of the first Governor-General and the four Members of Council under the new constitution.[9]

It is not known if Baillie took any part in the disputes and enquiries of the period. At a time when almost all persons connected with India cast their weight on one side or the other, in support of their friends or condemnation of their enemies, in vindication of the acts of the Company or in denunciation thereof, it would be a matter of surprise if Baillie had remained a mute spectator of the contests. But in the reports of the two Parliamentary Committees his name does not appear among the witnesses summoned to give evidence. It is, however, known positively that his father Dr. Hugh Baillie "wrote a defence of his Lordship [Lord Clive] against calumnies thrown out against him in which, he believed, Mr. Sulivan had some concern." Dr. Baillie's petition claiming repayment of a sum of money deposited by his

9. Governor-General, Warren Hastings; Members,—Barwell, Francis, Monson and Clavering.

deceased son William Baillie in the Bengal Treasury in 1755 was withheld from submission to the Court so long as Sulivan was in power with the Company, and this postponement was advised by Clive "though his Lordship thought the petition to be just."[10]

Baillie's first memorial: Hugh Baillie, junior, in his turn, was not a man to left slip his opportunities. He intended to make use of his exclusive knowledge and experience of the Assam trade to advance his cause as well as that of the Company The inland trade had been laid open to all merchants, and a host of competitors had appeared in the trade with Assam. It was not difficult for Baillie to realise that without superior advantages over his rivals of dubious commercial integrity he would not meet with success. His first enterprise in that direction had been supported by the authority of Vansittart at once a private merchant and Governor of Bengal; while the second had been conducted under the orders of the Calcutta Council and the special backing of Lord Clive. Seeking to secure future profits by the continuation of such patronage he attempted to persuade the Directors that Assam and the countries adjacent to it offered a fair market for the sale of European commodities, and that the trade could be prosecuted with advantage to the Company provided a salaried agent was appointed to undertake it. No other man, he thought, had a better claim to such an appointment if the Court decided to create one. His recommendation by Lord Clive in 1766 for the Court's special favour, and the latter's influence which he expected would be exercised in his behalf, encouraged Baillie to cherish the highest hopes about his scheme.

With this object Baillie submitted a memorial to the Court on March 13, 1771, in which he recounted his acquaintance with the Bengal trade since 1749 and with that of Assam since 1762. He referred to the trade he had carried on from Goalpara first as an agent of Henry Vansittart and afterwards for the Society of Trade. "During the above time," he pointed out, "your memorialist embraced the opportunity of acquiring a knowledge of the Company's business at Rungpore, and also of the interior parts of Buttan and Assam, and countries adjacent to Gualparah, which had never been explored by any European before." From the experience gained by his long residence on the borders of these countries he hoped "that the Company's trade may be considerably extended in their exports from Europe, specially in

10. Dr. Baillie's petition to Court, Feb. 9, 1775, Miscellaneous Letters Received, Vol. 59, p. 181.

broadcloth, iron, copper, lead etc., provided a proper person is fixed upon for that purpose."

Baillie then asked the Court to consider whether from the nature of his opportunities he might not be deemed a proper person for that undertaking. Then came the last note evincing his personal interest in the proposal,—"If he is honoured with their approbation he humbly requests to be employed as their Resident at Gualparah (at which place there never had been a Company's servant) with what rank in the service may appear most agreeable to the Hon'ble Court." For information about his ability Baillie referred the Court "to Lord Clive or any gentlemen from Bengal for his character in every respect." [11]

It is not difficult to anticipate the action that the Court would take on Baillie's proposal. The Court had no information about Assam, Bhutan and the neighbouring territories, about their commercial requirements and resources, about the sale which could be expected for the Company's exports in those areas, and about the exchange and the existing facilities for transport. Baillie's memorial was vague as it did not give an estimate of the profit that would accrue to the Company after having defrayed the expenses of the Residentship proposed by him. At best Baillie's proposal was a commercial venture without any certainty of profit. The practical sagacity of the Court precluded their entrance into an uncertain career of commercial enterprise specially when their existing affairs were in a state of confusion.

On the 15th March the Court referred Baillie's memorial to the Committee of Correspondence.[12] The Committee discussed the proposal in their meeting held eleven days later where they arrived at the conclusion "that the memorialist's request cannot be complied with."[13] The Court at their meeting next day endorsed the opinion of the Committee.

The Court's refusal to appoint Baillie as Resident at Goalpara might be officially attributed to their lack of information about the Assam trade; but we may surmise that Baillie's reference to Clive probably damned his proposal in the eyes of the Directors. Though the Court rejected Baillie's petition for appointment as Resident they decided to take advantage of the information communicated by him about the possibility of opening trade with

11. Writers Petitions, 1775-79, Vol. 8, No. 26.
12. Court Book, Vol. 79, March 15, 1771.
13. Com. of Correspondence Report, Vol. 9, March 27, 1771.

Assam and Bhutan on which the Committee had, however, expressed no opinion.

The decision of the Court was embodied in paragraph 16 of their despatch of April 10, 1771. Without mentioning the source of their information or referring to Baillie's petition for appointment as a servant of the Company, the Court set forth his suggestions about the possibility of selling European commodities in Assam and Bhutan. They expressed their "earnest desire to extend the vend of the staples of this kingdom [Great Britain] to as great a degree as possible," and expressed their surprise that the Government of Bengal "have not already made an attempt to carry so desirable an object into execution." They concluded by asking the Bengal Government to procure the best accounts possible and give their opinion thereon.

Bengal Government's enquiries on Assam trade: The letter of the Court which conveyed a mild note of criticism spurred the Calcutta Council into action, and in December 1771 at a meeting presided over by John Cartier, Governor of Bengal, they decided to investigate the possibilities of establishing trade with Assam and Bhutan. The Board accordingly asked the Comptrolling Committee of Commerce to make particular enquiries into the subject.[14]

The efforts of the Committee of Commerce bore no ostensible result. Warren Hastings assumed charge of the Government of Bengal on April 9, 1772. The problems which confronted the new Governor, whether in foreign relations or internal reforms, left him very little time to renew investigation into the Assam and Bhutan trade. Besides, the invasion of Cooch Behar by the Bhutanese, which necessitated the mediation of the Company's arms, prevented peaceful enquiries into commercial matters; and Charles Purling, Collector of Cooch Behar, who with his colleague at Rungpore, constituted the only agents for such investigation, was absent from his headquarters with the expedition against the mountaineers. But it will be seen that the contest with the Bhutanese army ultimately placed in the hands of the Bengal Government a more substantial and accurate information on the commerce and resources of Bhutan and Assam than what could be collected through the customary official channels.

The enquiries about the trade of Assam and Bhutan set on foot by the Bengal Government at the instance of the Court of Directors were resumed after the return of Purling to his civil

14. Secretary Wm. Wynne to Committee of Commerce, Dec. 9, 1771, Bengal Public Consultations of same date, No. 1.

duties as Collector of Cooch Behar. In June 1773 the Board asked the Collectors of Cooch Behar and Rungpore to suggest measures by which the sale of British staples might be promoted in Bhutan, Assam and the adjoining countries.[15] Bhutan was included within the scope of the enquiries as the idea of sending a mission to that country occurred to the Governor only after the receipt of the Teshu Lama's friendly letter in March 1774. Charles Purling in his reply to Government expressed pessimism about the prospect of trade before concluding the treaty of peace with Bhutan. He further believed that as the Bhutias were accustomed to carry on trade mainly by way of barter it would not be advantageous to the Company to receive the articles of Bhutan in exchange of their own commodities.[16]

Herbert Harris, Collector of Rungpore, was better informed though he shared the pessimism of Purling. He began by saying that he had made enquiries into the subject from which he concluded that there was very little likelihood of establishing any mart worthy of consideration for the commodities of Europe. The Bhutias wove their own blankets and used no other kind of cloth; and they possessed a mixed kind of metal from which they made all their utensils. As regards the Assamese, Harris observed, that the quantity of cloth and metals taken by them was very inconsiderable, and that an exchange of muga-dhutis and stick lac for salt and a little cloth constituted the whole of their traffic. Harris affirmed that he had never seen European articles sent into Assam by the traders, who would have certainly done so if there had been any profit in that business.[17]

Baillie's second memorial: Before the report of the Bengal Government reached the authorities at Home. Hugh Baillie, who was still in England, submitted a second memorial to the Court on December 21, 1773, in which he set forth more forcibly his reasons for extending the Company's trade in Assam and Bhutan adding several fresh considerations not mentioned in his previous representation. The trade, Baillie observed, would particularly promote the sale of broadcloths and other European merchandise, which from the coldness of the climate in those countries were necessary to the Bhutias inhabiting the hills to the northward of Goalpara, as also to the natives of Assam who carried on a con-

15. Hastings to Purling and Harris, June 21, Beng. Pub. Cons., June 21, 1773, No. 10.

16. Purling to Hastings, July 6, Beng. Pub. Cons., July 19, 1773.

17. Harris to Hastings, Aug. 27, Beng. Pub. Cons., Sept. 13, 1773, No. 3,

siderable traffic with the countries situated to the northeast. Exclusive of the demand for woollen goods, there was a considerable trade in metals of all sorts. The memorialist pointed out that the Company's returns for this branch of trade would consist of lacs of all sorts, muga silk, black pepper and specie. In conclusion, he reaffirmed that the trade could be rendered highly beneficial to the Company provided a proper person was employed to set it on foot, and he was vested with authority from the Company to explore those countries which were at that time practically unknown. He then requested the Court "whether from the knowledge he has acquired of those countries he may not be deemed properly qualified to commence this undertaking, and to be received into the Hon'ble Company's service in any capacity the Hon'ble Court may be pleased to direct."[18] The prayer to be appointed a Resident which had been rejected by the Court in 1771 was eliminated from Baillie's second memorial though he repeated his request to be admitted into the Company's service.

Baillie appointed to Goalpara: The Court of Directors evinced greater interest this time in the possibility of extending their trade to Bhutan and Assam as well as in the personal well-being of Hugh Baillie. In their despatch to Bengal of January 7, 1774, they admitted Baillie to be the source of their information. They expressed their earnest desire to avail themselves of this valuable branch of trade, and accordingly directed the Bengal Government to make these matters the objects of immediate enquiry, and to report in what manner and to what extent the Company might be benefited by opening a trade to those countries. The authorities in Bengal were further asked that if they discovered good reasons to prosecute the trade with a prospect of success, Baillie should be employed in promoting the undertaking, provided he was found better qualified for it than any of their existing civil servants. The last clause was inserted as a matter of course to convey an impression of justice and fairness to the gentlemen already in the Company's employ, and it could not be meant to weaken the claims of Hugh Baillie as no other man could possibly be found who had shown greater interest in the Assam trade or possessed longer acquaintance with it. This softening of the tone of the Court of Directors may presumably be ascribed to the change in the personnel of the Company's Direc-

18. Misc. Letters Recd., Vol. 57, 1773.

torate, and the absence of Laurence Sulivan from it.[19] Baillie may have procured the special support of some of the Directors by convincing them of the advantage that would be derived by accepting his proposal. That Baillie was more earnest on this occasion is proved by the fact that he and his wife made themselves agreeable to Miss Frances Barwell, sister of Richard Barwell, the newly appointed Member of the Calcutta Council and induced her to request her brother in India to exert himself to promote the interest of Baillie. Another sister of Barwell, Mary Barwell, exercised some influence in official circles in London and was regarded by her brother as the guardian of his interests.[20] It can be fairly assumed that Baillie must have engaged Mary Barwell as well as her sister on his behalf in London.

In the meantime Barwell had written to his sister Frances promising to help Baillie on her account. "I am pleased to perceive by your letter," he wrote on August 19, 1773, "that you appear happy with Mr. and Mrs. Baillie's family. Their politeness and attention to you lay me under a great obligation to them, which on any occasion I shall be glad to show my sense of, and the opportunity Mr. Baillie has now given to me will, I hope, enable me in some small degree to convince them that I would willingly make them every consideration in my power for making your situation agreeable to you. You may be certain I will look into Mr. Baillie's affairs, and do him all the services you require. It is my duty, and it is the first request you ever made to me."[21]

Armed with the recommendation of the Court of Directors and the promise of assistance from Richard Barwell, Baillie returned to India in the summer of 1774. He applied to the Calcutta Council for permission to go to Goalpara and reside there with special licence. The Board at a meeting held on September 5, 1774, with Warren Hastings as President, concluded that no better method could be found for obtaining the information desired by the Court than to comply with Baillie's request, specially as he was recommended by the Directors. The Board accordingly permitted him to go to Goalpara, and assured him of suitable encouragement and reward if his discoveries tended in any shape

19. L. Sulivan was not a Director from Ap. 8, 1773 to Ap. 7, 1778, see Index to General Court Minutes : Elections of Directors, 1702-1846.

20. John Caillaud to Hastings, Nov. 20, 1775, B. M. Add. Ms. No. 29136, f. 345, cited in Dr. Sophia Weitzman's *Warren Hastings and Philip Francis*, p. 17-*n*, 121-*n*.

21. *Bengal : Past and Present*, Vol. XI, pp. 42-43.

to the advantage of the Company or to the trade of Bengal.[22] The Board's reply to the Court of Directors was framed in accordance with this resolution.[23]

Bogle's account of the Assam trade: The nomination of Baillie to Goalpara had been preceded by the despatch of George Bogle to Tibet entrusted with the collection of information about Assam as a subsidiary object of his mission.

The country of Cooch Behar which had become a dependency of the Company in 1765 was little noticed till the year 1772 when it was overrun and devastated by the Bhutanese under the leadership of their ambitious chief Deb Judhur. The ruler of Cooch Behar, Raja Dharendranarayan, applied to Warren Hastings for protection which was readily granted as it offered an opportunity of expelling the Bhutias from the outlying parts of Rungpore which had been exposed to their frequent incursions rendering the collection of revenue very precarious.[24] A detachment of four companies was despatched under Captain John Jones for the purpose of driving back the invaders to their mountain fastnesses. The operations took place in the cold season of 1772-73. Captain Jones soon repulsed the Bhutanese from Cooch Behar, and followed them into Bhutan where he captured several forts. The Company's force so pressed the Bhutanese that they were compelled to seek the aid of the Tibetan government at Lhassa. On the restoration of his territory the Raja of Cooch Behar agreed by the Treaty of April 15, 1774, to acknowledge subjection of the Company and pay a tribute. It is said that Deb Judhur attempted to form a confederacy against the English with the Rajas of Nepal, Sylhet and Assam, who promised to help him and would certainly have done so if he had not been defeated by the Company's force.[25]

The Doloi Lama, the pontifical ruler of Tibet, being a minor, the actual reins of government were wielded by the Teshu Lama who was the regent appointed by the Chinese court. By his integrity, intelligence and efficiency as an administrator, the Teshu Lama commanded great respect and authority at the court of the Chinese Emperor Kien-lung (1736-96) during whose reign the ascendancy of China over Tibet was completed. Being asked by the Bhutanese to intercede on their behalf, the Teshu Lama sent

22. Beng. Pub. Cons., Sept. 5, 1774.

23. Bengal Letter to Court, General Deptt., Oct. 17, 1774.

24. Bengal Secret Letter to Court, January 15, 1773.

25. C. R. Markham refers to this coalition in his introduction to the *Mission of George Bogle to Tibet*, p. lxvii, though he does not mention the source of his information.

a deputation to Warren Hastings under Puran Gir Gosain, a Sivaite Sannyasi. The Lama's letter requesting cessation of hostilities was received by the Governor on March 29, 1774.

"Having been informed," wrote the Lama, "by travellers from your country of your exalted fame and reputation, my heart, like the blossom of spring, abounds with gaiety, gladness and joy. Praise that the star of your fortune is in its accession." Of Deb Judhur, the Raja of Bhutan, the Lama said,—"I have been repeatedly informed that you have been engaged in hostilities against Deb Judhur, to which it is said, the Deb's own criminal conduct in committing ravages and other outrages on your frontiers has given rise. As he is of a rude and ignorant race—past times are not destitute of instances of the like misconduct which his own avarice tempted him to commit—it is not unlikely that he had now renewed those instances. .... I have reprimanded the Deb for his past conduct, and I have admonished him to desist from his evil practices in future, and to be subservient to you in all matters. .... As to my part, I am but a Fakir, and it is the custom of my sect, with the rosary in our hands, to pray for the welfare of mankind, and for the peace and happiness of the inhabitants of this country, and I now, with my head uncovered, entreat that you may cease all hostilities against the Deb in future."[26] The letter was accompanied by valuable presents which in themselves conveyed an idea of the commercial products of Tibet.

The desire for peace manifested by the paramount authority of Bhutan and the *de facto* ruler of Tibet, who was at the same time a great influence in the court of Peking, expressed in language of such dignity and humility, made a deep impression on the mind of Warren Hastings. Cessation of hostilities was advantageous from the Company's point of view, as the troops had suffered greatly in the pestilential mountain tracts. The object of the expedition was now attained: the Bhutanese had been defeated and reduced, Cooch Behar had been restored to its chief, and a treaty concluded with him placing the Company in a position of paramountcy. Under such circumstances, when peace was earnestly solicited, Warren Hastings accepted the proposal most readily. A treaty was concluded with Bhutan on April 25, 1774, which granted the Bhutias the privilege of trade in Company's territories free of duty, and permission to their caravan to go to Rungpore annually.[27]

26. *Bogle's Tibet*, edited by Markham, pp. 2-3.
27. Pemberton, *Report on Bootan*, 1839, Appendix, p. 100.

After having accomplished the immediate objects of the Bhutan expedition Warren Hastings resolved to use the opportunity of the Lama's professed friendship and good-will to reopen commercial and amicable intercourse between India, Tibet and Bhutan.[28] Friendship with Tibet carried with it the possibility of acquiring the good-will of the Chinese court where the Teshu Lama was held in great reverence, and of opening a way to China for English merchants through Bhutan and Tibet through the good offices of the Lama as an alternative of the sea-gate, the latter being regarded with suspicion by the Chinese.[29]

In May 1774 the Council resolved to send a deputation to the Teshu Lama under George Bogle of the Bengal Civil Service, with a view to negotiate for opening a mutual and equal communication of trade between the inhabitants of Tibet, Bhutan and Bengal. Bogle was instructed to take with him samples of such articles of commerce which could be introduced in that trade. He was asked to inform himself of the manufactures, productions and goods of the northern countries, specially such as were of great value and easy transportation, such as gold, silver, precious stones, musk, munjit, etc.

The tenth article in the private commissions entrusted to Bogle required him to ascertain the course and navigation of the Brahmaputra and the state of the countries through which it runs. This clause at once placed Assam within the scope of Bogle's enquiry, though from the accounts left by him it appears that he never visited Assam on such a mission.

Bogle left Bengal in May 1774, visited Tassisudon, the capital of the Deb Raja of Bhutan, and met the Teshu Lama at his capital Teshu Lumbo. The Lama showed great cordiality to Bogle, and expressed his readiness to establish an unrestricted commercial intercourse between his subjects and the inhabitants of the Company's territories, a project which was not heartily countenanced by the merchants of Lhassa who were always averse to the admission of foreigners into Tibet. The only way to remove the opposition of the Lhassa merchants was by appealing to the Chinese Emperor at Peking through the Teshu Lama.

Bogle returned to Bengal in June 1775, and submitted the account of his mission in several official reports, and in a well-

28. The trade, conducted through the Nepal passes had been almost destroyed by the persecution of the merchants by the exaction of enormous tolls and duties by the authorities of Nepal.

29. Capt. S. Turner, *Account of an Embassy to the Court of Tesho Lama in Tibet*, 1800, Introduction, pp. xii-xiii.

informed journal, which so pleased Hastings that he sent a copy to Dr. Samuel Johnson. But unfortunately the results of Bogle's mission were not known to the world for a hundred years, till 1876 when the *Narratives of the Mission of George Bogle to Tibet* collated from papers preserved by his family in Scotland, was first published under the editorship of Clements R. Markham.

Bogle prefaced his observations on Assam by referring to the narrow tract of fertile land at the foot of the Bhutan hills and sloping downwards to the plains, varying in breadth from ten to twenty miles, and extending over a distance of about 85 miles. A great part of this territory is covered with impenetrable jungles and dense forests of *sal* trees, and is intersected by a number of rivers all of which, except the Tista, fall into the Brahmaputra. The produce of this area consists of rice, mustard seeds, tobacco, some opium and 40,000 maunds of cotton annually; and on the borders of Assam it yields some black pepper and muga silk. The trade carried on with Bhutan is by way of barter. The region is unhealthy owing to the great moisture of the air, and the great and sudden changes of the weather causing intermittent fevers of the most obstinate kind. The English troops suffered a great deal in this quarter during their expedition against the Bhutanese. Bogle considered that war with Bhutan would always involve considerable difficulties, for though it could easily be conquered it could never easily be occupied. The same objection applied to Nepal and Lhassa for the difficulty of keeping a communication open.

Bogle then proceeded to point out the superior advantages of the Assam trade, as compared with that of Bhutan, Nepal and Lhassa. "An open and unrestricted trade with Assam, considered separately," said Bogle, "is an object of much greater consequence; but when it is known that it will include all the advantages attending the other, it must of course become a much more desirable object."

Bogle based his recommendation mainly on the accessibility to the country by land or by water. As the river Brahmaputra is navigable throughout the whole year it could be used either for purposes of war or for commerce. The communication could always be preserved in the case of Assam. Assam is an open country of great extent, well cultivated and inhabited, and it yields many valuable articles for exploration. Gold is a considerable article of inland trade; and Bhutan, Lhassa and Nepal supply the Assamese both gold and silver. The people of these countries and of many other countries lying north-west of the Brahmaputra carry on a constant trade to Assam. It was possible to sell European commodities and particularly broadcloths not only in Assam but in all the countries lying to the north-west of the Brahmaputra as well as to the eastward of that river by forming a settlement on its banks preferably near the capital. The boats required for carrying on trade with Assam could be built on the spot with the fine timber which covers the banks of the Brahmaputra. The Assam government had restricted the trade in such a manner that it was of little advantage to Bengal. The trade amounted, in Bogle's estimate, to nearly six or seven lakhs of rupees per year, mostly by way of barter; and in the event of a balance Bengal paid it in silver. The Assamese were permitted to trade in the territories of the Company; but Bogle regretted that the Assamese government did not concede the same privilege to the subjects of the Company.

As a preliminary to the establishment of a commercial intercourse with Assam he suggested that the government of Assam should be requested to grant liberty of trade in their country. Such a request would probably be refused, jealous as the Assamese were of all foreigners. But the demand of the Bengal Government could be enforced by sending an expedition to Assam; and in Bogle's opinion, it was bound to succeed as it would not have to encounter the difficulties that attended a similar enterprise against Bhutan, Nepal and Lhassa. The stores and provisions necessary for the expedition could be easily conveyed from Bengal by water; and once the troops had entered into Assam they would get ample supplies. Bogle further assured that "a few months after our entering Assam, the troops might be paid and provisioned without making any demands on the Company's treasury." After having gained a footing in Assam it would be possible for the Company to pursue enquiries into the trade of Assam and of the countries lying on its eastern confines. The scheme, Bogle observed, would open a trade and intercourse with countries unexplored by Europeans.

Bogle's account of the Assam trade and the facilities available for pursuing it conformed to the experience of those who followed it. But the proposal to launch a military expedition into Assam to enforce the Company's request to confer upon Bengal merchants the privilege of trading in that country certainly militated against Warren Hastings's foreign policy which, with regard to territories not owning any subservience to the Company, was highly pacific, though his official foes resolved not to admit that aspect of his statesmanship. This can be illustrated by the readiness with which he intervened when a Goalpara merchant, George Lear, entered into Assam with an armed force to recover some outstanding balance. "Should Mr. Lear," wrote Warren Hastings to the Collector of Rungpore, "be actually engaged in any measures the consequences of which may appear to you alarming, I recommend it to you to check them immediately."[30] The Assamese were shy of foreigners on account of the experiences they had in their long contest with the Moguls and posts were established on the frontier to check the free ingress of outsiders. Permission was always granted to desirable foreigners who wanted to come to Assam for purposes which were not prejudicial to the interest of the country; and Bogle himself referred to "people who had been permitted to trade to that country," and "reports of those who have visited that country." Bogle perhaps realised the unwarranted character of his proposal as we can infer from the conclusion of his observations,—"Probable conjecture has been found sufficient to stimulate enterprising spirits, and success has generally justified their undertakings of this kind when concluded with spirit, resolution, and prudence."

The success which had attended Bogle's mission to Bhutan and Tibet, mainly in the consolidation of the friendship with the Teshu Lama and the acquisition of a mass of information on the resources and manners of the people of those countries, encouraged Warren Hastings to maintain the intercourse by sending two missions in 1776 and 1777, both under Dr. Hamilton who had accompanied Bogle in 1774-5. A fair was established at Rungpore where the Bhutias could trade on conditions very advantageous to them. At the request of the Teshu Lama a plot of land was granted on the banks of the river Hugli, immediately opposite to Calcutta, where a Buddhist monastery was erected at the expense of the Lama which afterwards became a rendezvous and an inn for merchants and pilgrims from Bhutan and Tibet.[31]

Barwell's misgivings about Baillie's prospects: The commission given to Baillie to make enquiries into the trade of Assam and of the countries near Goalpara, with the possibility of the assumption of that trade by the Company, marks the first definite step taken by the Bengal Government in the matter of extending its commercial concerns in that quarter. Thus in 1774 two agencies were simultaneously at work entrusted with the object of collecting information about Assam trade, one under Bogle and the other

30. Hastings to Purling, Nov. 7, 1778, *Rungpore District Records,* edited by W. K. Firminger, Vol. I, p. 60.

31. An account of the monastery and of Puran Gir Gosain was given by Gaurdas Basak in *J.A.S.B.*, Vol. LIX, 1890, pp. 61-62.

under Baillie, with this distinction that while the former was a covenanted servant of the Company the latter was only an aspirant to such an appointment; while instructions to the former were elaborately drawn up, the latter was provided only with a general indication of the object of his mission. The difference in the treatment of the two agents showed a lack of enthusiasm in the Assam side of the investigation. There was no Teshu Lama in Assam to win the esteem of Warren Hastings by the manifestation of probity and good sense; no king of Assam could make his friendship a desirable object by the influence he was expected to exercise upon the Emperor of China. In fact the pacific letter of the Teshu Lama concealed an invitation to the Governor to send a deputy to strengthen the attachment which he had already cherished for the new dispensation in India, and Warren Hastings seized the opportunity as any other statesman would have done. Assam was still an unknown country: and the temper of its government and the manners of its people were still matters of conjecture. The best course was certainly to watch it from the borders and wait for an opportunity to establish an intimate contact.

As regards the personal benefit that Baillie would derive it was evident from the Board's resolution that his remuneration was only a prospective one dependent upon his own exertions in the trade and the proofs he could furnish that the trade would be profitable to the Company. There was nothing of great value in the licence given to him to reside at Goalpara; and in fact such were generally granted to all freemerchants who wanted to trade under the protection of the Company. What Baillie thought he gained was the right of trading under the supposed authority of the Company. In any case this slender safeguard would not protect him from competition with other merchants who had consolidated their position in the Assam trade during his absence in England.

A shrewd observer and businessman like Barwell, who had amassed a large fortune in India, could at once see that Baillie's scheme for making money out of the Assam trade, for himself or for the Company, was purely visionary. In his letter of November 30, 1774, addressed to his sister Mary Barwell in England, he said,—"Mr. Baillie is returned, and with him his very curious appointment. I conceive the whole to have sprung from his own bewildered imagination, and the idea of duping the publick. I told him very plainly that my wish to oblige him on account of my sister Fanny would induce to exert myself to obtain him a publick nomination to Gualparah, and in any other way to assist him his views there: but that I would, under no pretence, countenance any attempt he might make to possess himself of the Company's property to answer his own purpose. He is now nominated to Gualparah, and the prosecution of his trade left to his own discretion, with his own means, but I fear as the publick do not entrust their property to his management and engage not in his commerce of Gualparah, that Mr. Baillie will find himself extremely mistaken; and that Gualparah is not such a Peru as he wishes to make the Directors think that it might be made to the Company."[32]

Barwell's view of the Assam trade was nearer the truth than Baillie's exaggerated estimate of the same. The economic structure of Assamese society made the people more or less independent in all their necessaries of life, which were produced at home or purchased from neighbouring villages mostly by barter. The only article for which the Assamese were dependent on foreign supply was salt; and here too a merchant would have to compete with a number of rivals. To relieve the congestion of salt in the *golah* the merchant was compelled to sell it on credit or at reduced rates or in exchange of Assam products for which there was no immediate demand in Bengal. Once the Assamese debtor was securely sheltered in his wooded home in the midst of his brothers, relatives and co-villagers it was difficult for the Bengal creditor to trace him out. To cross the Assam frontier for the purpose of trade or for realisation of outstanding claims one had to apply for permission to the officers at the Assam Choky, and permission was generally withheld when apprehension of harassment of any Assam subject justified such a course. Any display of force was resented by the Choky officers, and the Ahom viceroy at Gauhati took immediate steps to check or retaliate upon high-handed acts of foreigners. The only recourse of Bengal merchants was the intervention of the Government at Calcutta, who sent letters requesting the king of Assam to settle the demands; but no potent instrument could be employed in these negotiations except the language of persuasion. The grievances of Bengal merchants became so acute at times that the enactment of a commercial treaty between the two states became a matter of constant solicitation on the part of the Company's Government.

Besides, from the year 1769 commenced those political convulsions in Assam which weakened the government and encour-

32. *Bengal: Past and Present*, Vol. XII, p. 73.

aged foreign freebooters to enter and devastate the country. In that year had died the good and conciliatory monarch Swargadeo Rajeswar Singha who was succeeded by his brother Swargadeo Lakshmi Singha. The new monarch who owed his elevation to the manoeuvres of the autocratic Barbarua Kirtichandra was not popular with a large section of his subjects. The Moamarias, the disciples of a Vaisnava Gosain whose influence and wealth had excited the jealousy of other religious heads as well as of numerous Ahom nobles and potentates, rose in open rebellion to avenge the insults inflicted upon their leaders by the haughty and imperious Barbarua. The king was imprisoned, and a Moamaria set up on the throne. The leading Ahom nobles and officials including Kirtichandra were executed, and Moamarias appointed in their place. With the help of his loyal adherents Lakshmi Singha succeeded in recovering his throne in April 1770. The revolt was suppressed for the time being, but it raised its head again whenever the recalcitrants, aided secretly by people who were royalists by profession, found an opportunity for assailing the established authority of the monarch. The Moamarias were scattered all over the country, and any body of mischief-mongers could set up an Ahom prince as a candidate for the throne and organise recruits to support his claims, promising that on the success of the plan the supporters would invariably be appointed to high offices in the new regime. From the restoration of Lakshmi Singha upto his death in 1780 we get numerous instances of princes yielding to the machinations of rebels, who in the event of failure in their major schemes established their authority, by threats and violence, over the interior districts in open defiance of the Ahom government. The rival princes were banished to pestilential regions and disqualified for the throne by the mutilation of their limbs, a measure which served to intensify their hostility to the throne converting them into so many centres of discontent and revolt. The task of quelling these disturbances engaged all the attention of the Ahom government and the demands of trade and commerce became matters of secondary importance. The spirit of disorder grew apace. Lakshmi Singha's son and successor Gaurinath Singha was expelled from the capital by the Moamaria insurgents, and he had to be re-established by a contingent of British sepoys deputed to Assam by the Bengal Government.

These political troubles, fostered by masked loyalty and remembrance of enormities committed on both sides, hindered the growth of commerce. The government in Assam, dependent as it was on the local levies for its military strength, could not at all times enforce obedience to its commands. The discharge of functions for which its officers enjoyed revenue-free lands and the services of retainers became a matter of choice as government was sure to be thwarted before its punishment reached the disobedient. The payment of dues to Bengal merchants and creditors, which had been formerly enforced by the Assam government, was now withheld as the authority of that government began to wane. This state of things was certainly not favourable to the growth of commerce, and Richard Barwell was correct in his judgment that Goalpara was not such a Peru as Baillie wanted the Court to believe. The verdict of Daniel Raush recorded fifteen years later confirmed Barwell's misgivings—"As I am perfectly well acquainted with the nature and situation of the Assam Trade, during my residence of above eighteen years at Gualparah, I most humbly beg leave to represent that the said trade—in whatever light Mr. Baillie may represent it—never will be of any advantage to the Hon'ble Company."[33]

Baillie's third memorial: It is not known what success Baillie had met in his trade with Assam. He paid occasional visits to that country, collected information about its trade and resources and tried his best to popularise British staples. He submitted reports to one Middles of the Council of Commerce but they were not attended to owing to the latter's continued indisposition.

On July 28, 1776, Baillie submitted from Goalpara a third memorial on the Assam trade. It was addressed to William Aldersey and other members of the Board of Trade. He repeated his conviction that the Assam trade if properly conducted would be a source of profit to the Company. He expected to sell for the Company in the first year, 100,000 maunds of salt, 400 pieces of broadcloth and 300 maunds of copper, and assured the Board of Trade that the sales would increase gradually, particularly in the two latter articles. The Assamese, observed Baillie, had to buy the cloth at a very high rate from a fourth hand which precluded their wearing it. He confidently hoped to clear for the Company an annual profit of 200,000 rupees. He also suggested that the accumulated quantities of salt lying in the Company's *golahs*, for which there was no market in Bengal, could be got rid of by disposing them in Assam. At the same time he pointed out that the limited business in salt had been destroyed by there being too many competitors in the Assam market. He therefore asked the

33. Raush to Board of Revenue, Sept. 1, Bengal Board of Revenue Proceedings, Sept. 25, 1789.

Government to give him the sole agency of the Company's sales in Assam, "the situation which the Directors positively assured me on my leaving England, I should have on my arrival in Bengal [in 1774]." Baillie's representation was discussed by the Board of Trade on August 12, and was sent up to the Court of Directors.[34]

The Directors in their despatch of April 16, 1777, admitted that in view of the large annual profit which, as Baillie had assured, was likely to accrue from the Assam trade it was "by no means an object undeserving of attention." They again asked the Bengal Government to take the matter into their serious consideration and determine on the expediency of adopting the whole or any part of Baillie's proposals, and pay him such attention as his merits might entitle him to, from his zeal on that occasion and from any future service which he might render to the Company. The Court further authorised the Bengal Government to carry out or enlarge the scheme, or adopt any other system of commerce that might promise advantage to the Company.

Though the Court of Directors had systematically referred to Baillie as "Resident at Assam,"[35] and he himself had described his nomination to Goalpara as an appointment "by the Hon'ble Court of Directors to be Resident for the Company in the Kingdom of Assam,"[36] he had not yet been admitted to any rank in the service of the Company. Being keen on entering into the position of a covenanted servant he applied to the Court of Directors on October 9, 1776, for appointment as Writer in the Bengal establishment. As Baillie was in India his memorial was signed on his behalf by his wife Mrs. Anna Baillie.[37] He embraced the opportunity of giving a short sketch of his services to the Company, first as a volunteer in the wars against Nawab Siraj-ud-Dowlah, and then in the repulsion of the Dutch. He referred to his deputation by Vansittart to Assam, a country at that time barely known to the English, to the good fortune he had to open a considerable traffic between that country and Bengal, and to the pains and expense he subsequently bestowed to acquaint himself with the commerce of not only Assam but of other countries beyond Assam which

34. Proceedings of the Board of Trade, August 12, 1776, copy obtained from the Keeper of the Records of the Government of Bengal.

35. *Court's Book*, Jan. 29, 1777; Court's General Letter to Bengal, April 16, 1777.

36. Writers Petitions, Vol. 8, No. 26.

37. In 1774, Baillie had returned to India alone, his letter to Court, No. 20, 1773; Writers Petitions, Vol. 8, No. 26.

traded with Bengal through it. He concluded his memorial by pointing out that the trade if assumed by the Company would bring in a clear annual profit of £25,000. On February 26, 1777, the Court appointed Baillie as Writer in the Bengal establishment, the usual securities being tendered by two London merchants, Aaron Franks and Moses Franks.[38]

Baillie remained for two years at Goalpara till his appointment in April 1779, on the recommendation of Warren Hastings, as Assistant to the Collector of Sarkar Saran in Bihar.[39] During his absence the Goalpara concerns were managed by his agent Kasinath Ghose.

The years 1771 to 1779 saw a decided advance in the way of establishing the Company's trade with Assam. As a result of Baillie's memorials of 1771, 1773 and 1776, the Court of Directors enjoined the Bengal Government to adopt measures for placing the trade on a proper footing. The enquiries of Baillie and Bogle and of the local officers supplied the Company with some information about the resources and trade of Assam. At the same time the withdrawal of restrictions on the inland trade following the abolition of the Society of Trade in 1768 brought to the field a large number of European merchants with whom a Company's agent was required to compete, and whose exclusion was therefore considered necessary to ensure success in any venture on the part of the Company. The limited nature of the trade and the imperfect knowledge of Assam created in certain quarters pessimism about the results that were likely to attend the Company's participation in the trade in spite of Baillie's assurance to the contrary. Unfortunately enough the year 1769, when European merchants first interested themselves seriously in the trade of Assam, saw the commencement of the internal troubles which greatly impeded the progress of that trade and ultimately brought ruin and desolation to that country.

38. Court Book, Vol. 85, Oct. 18, 1776; Nov. 13, 1776, and Feb. 26, 1777.

39. Beng. Rev. Cons., Ap. 13, 1779. Baillie's appointment was opposed by Philip Francis.

APPENDIX TO CHAPTER II

HUGH BAILLIE

Hugh Baillie, as the name indicates, came from a Scotch family. His father Dr. Hugh Baillie, Doctor of Laws, was for some time a Judge of the Vice-Admiralty Court in Ireland.[1] After his retirement in about 1772 Dr. Baillie settled in London as a lawyer paying occasional visits to his home in Scotland. His four sons William, Hugh, Lesly and Robert, had served in India, and 'with reputation' as their father asserted. Lesly died commander of the Company's fleet in the Persian Gulf in 1766 after having done his duty to the satisfaction of the Governors for twenty years.[2]

The three other brothers were present in Bengal during the conflicts with Nawab Siraj-ud-Dowlah in 1756-57. William Baillie was in 1756 a member of the Calcutta Council being eleventh in order of seniority, and also Military Store-keeper. Before this he had served as Chief of the Factory at Jugdea or Lakhipore, a town in Noakhali in Bengal. In 1754 during his residence at Jugdea he had received from the Indian *dalals* Rs. 32,000, calculated at 2½ per cent of the 15 per cent profit made by them on the Company's investment. This amount was supposed to be illegal and rendered William Baillie liable to dismissal from the Company's service. He defended his conduct by saying that the sum was accepted by him "on no other consideration but his taking the trouble to judge in the controversies between the brokers and the people of the country." This explanation was not supported by the *dalals*. In 1755, the Council at Calcutta, with Governor Roger Drake as President, directed Baillie to pay the amount to the Company's treasury in Bengal, and he accordingly paid Rs. 18,000 rather than quit the service.[3]

On June 13, 1756, Fort William was attacked by the Nawab's forces. Some of the women were sent on board and were embarked for Fulta. At 9 in the morning of the next day William Baillie, "who exerted himself on all occasions in a most disinterested and generous manner," undertook to see the women and

1. J. H. Grose, *Voyage to the East Indies*, 1772, Vol. II, p. 248.
2. Misc. Letters Recd., Vol. 59, 1775, p. 103-a.
3. Personal Records, Vol. 14, pp. 641-47.

effects sent away by boat. The Nawab's troops having pressed upon the Fort with great vigour the Armenians and Portuguese became mortally terrified to take part in the defence. It was only by the personal efforts of Drake, Holwell and Willian Baillie that even the Europeans could be persuaded to resume their arms. At about 10, Governor Drake, Commandant Minchin, and crowds of Company's officers, merchants and sea-captains, left the Fort and escaped on board the few ships which were still available at the river. The fugitives included Hugh Baillie.

William Baillie and the other two councillors Eyre and Holwell defended the Fort with the handful of men who now formed the remnant of the garrison. Baillie was wounded by a musket ball from the enemy on the side of his head, and was in that condition shut up in the Black Hole with 145 other Europeans. Holwell and Baillie were the first to enter the prison. Baillie himself suffering terribly from suffocation and thirst and the pain from his wound suggested one or two measures for the alleviation of the miseries of his fellow-prisoners. "Between 9 and near 11," wrote Holwell, "my friend Baillie, Messrs. Jenks, Revely, Law, Buchanan and Simson, and several others for whom I had a real esteem and affection, had for some time been dead at my feet, and were trampled upon by every corporal or common soldier." William Baillie's name appears in the list of the victims inscribed on the Holwell Monument at Calcutta.[4]

Hugh Baillie was appointed executor of his brother's estate.[5] A month before the siege of Fort William, William Baillie had written to his father that his property in Bengal was worth £14,000.[6] After the recovery of Fort William by Clive and Watson, Hugh Baillie submitted his deceased brother's accounts of cloth delivered for bandages, cartridges, etc., during the siege.[7] Mir Jafar the new Nawab of Bengal, according to his treaty with the Company, was to recoup the Company and individual Europeans for their losses. In September 1759 and February 1760 Hugh Baillie received on this account Rs. 6,892-2-0 and Rs. 4,965-12-0 respectively; part of these amounts was presumably received as compensation for the losses suffered by his deceased brother.[8] The

4. S. C. Hill, *Bengal in 1756-57*, Vol. III, pp. 136-140, Vol. I, pp. lxxix-lxxx.

5. Beng. Pub. Cons., May 30, 1757, No. 874.

6. Misc. Letters Recd., Vol. 59, 1775, p. 104.

7. Beng. Pub. Cons., May 30, 1757, No. 874.

8. Beng. Pub. Cons., Dec. 4, 1759 and March 3, 1760, cited in S. C. Hill's *List of Europeans in Bengal in 1756*.

father however admitted afterwards that he had received Rs. 28,000 as William Baillie's effects.[9]

The news of William Baillie's death and the circumstances attending it reached England in private letters. Dr. Hugh Baillie, indignant at the conduct of Roger Drake, submitted to the Court of Directors a vigorous indictment of the Governor's action. The charges laid were that Drake had given shelter and protection to a person who had incurred the displeasure of the Nawab, that he had not maintained the Fort at Calcutta in any position of defence, that he had deserted the garrison without taking with him the Company's books or effects, and that as a result of the Governor's delinquency valuable lives and property were lost. Then added Dr. Baillie,—"Amongst those who lost their lives miserably was my son. I hope the Hon'ble Court of Directors will not think I act an officious part in what I now say. I have done no more than my duty to my country, to the memory of my son and to my family obliged me to do."[10] Roger Drake answered to these charges in a letter addressed from Bath on December 11, 1759. As Dr. Baillie was not in a position to produce any positive evidence of the Governor's misconduct the Committee of Correspondence informed Drake "that they did not think fit to proceed further in the said matter." In fact Dr. Baillie's attempt to induce the Court to open an enquiry into Drake's behaviour constituted all that was done by the affected parties in the way of punishment for the loss of the finest settlement the Company possessed in India, and of so many lives and valuable properties.[11]

Dr. Baillie then set up his claim for the sum of Rs. 18,000 which his son William Baillie had deposited in the Bengal Treasury in 1755. This sum according to the rate of exchange at that time,—two shillings and three pence per rupee, would be equivalent to £2,025. The Court of Directors granted Dr. Baillie a gratuity of 500 guineas, and Sir George Colebroke, Chairman of the Court, told the petitioner that the Directors intended to give no more. On May 17, 1762, Dr. Baillie signed a deed of release affirming that he had no further claims upon the Company. After the return of Clive to England in 1767 Dr. Baillie wrote a fresh application claiming the balance of £2,025, but Lord Clive advised him not to submit it to the Court as Laurence Sulivan was then in power with the Company. It was feared that the claimant would not get

9. Misc. Letters Recd., Vol. 59, 1775, p. 103-a.

10. Dr. Hugh Baillie to Court, Oct. 1, 1759, Misc. Letters Recd., Vol. 41, 1758-59, pp. 216-23.

11. S. C. Hill, *Bengal in 1756-57*, Vol. I, page c.

justice in that quarter as he had written a defence of Lord Clive against calumnies thrown out against him in which Clive believed Sulivan had some part. In February 1775 Dr. Baillie submitted the petition to the Court of Directors along with the opinions of lawyers. On March 30, the petition was laid before the Committee of Correspondence and they confirmed the previous decision of the Court that no further sum could be paid to Dr. Baillie after he had signed the deed of discharge in 1762.[12]

Dr. Baillie who was then in the eighty-first year of his age died a few months later. In October 1776 his widow Frederica Charlotte Baillie, living in 35 Great Mary La Bone Street, London, submitted a petition to the Court renewing the request for relief, as she alleged "she was left in very narrow circumstances by Dr. Baillie whose income arose from the interest of money settled on his children." The Court rejected Mrs. Baillie's prayer.[13]

Robert Baillie, brother of William Baillie, was one of the sufferers during the siege of Calcutta, but it is not known what part he actually took in the defence or in the flight of the Europeans by boat to Fulta. One Baillie appears to have been captain of the ship *Wellcome*, and in the absence of the mention of Christian names in the documents concerned it is difficult to know whether it was Robert Baillie or his brother Hugh Baillie.[14] After the recovery of Calcutta, Robert Baillie applied to the Council to remit by bills on the Company a part of his deceased brother William Baillie's estate, which was refused possibly in view of High Baillie being already accepted as the executor.[15] In compensation for the losses suffered during the siege which were recouped by Nawab Mir Jafar, Robert Baillie obtained from the Bengal Council Rs. 27-0-0 and Rs. 303-7-0 respectively in October 1759 and February 1760.[16] In 1759 he was appointed Master of the Workhouse with an allowance of Rs. 20 per month. A jamadar and four peons were placed at his disposal as a guard on the House of Correction.[17] In 1773 he held the office of the Deputy Judge Advocate at Calcutta.[18]

12. Misc. Letters Recd., Vol. 59, 1775, p. 103; Personal Records, Vol. 14, pp. 641-47.

13. Misc. Letters Recd., Vol. 60, 1776, p. 145.

14. Hill, *List of Europeans in Bengal in 1756*, where both Hugh and Robert Baillie are described as Captain of *Wellcome*.

15. Beng. Pub. Cons., Nov. 14, 1757, No. 966.

16. Beng. Pub. Cons., Dec. 4, 1759 and March 3, 1760.

17. Beng. Pub. Cons., July 2, 1759, No. 1231.

18. Orme Mss., No. 167, W. Hosea, Chief of Hugli, to Robert Baillie, Nov. 26, 1773.

Hugh Baillie, the pioneer of the Company's commerce with Assam, came to India as the Captain of a vessel in 1749,[19] and resided in Bengal upto his final departure for England in 1792, paying only two visits to England in 1769 and 1784. He served as a volunteer in the defence of Fort William against Nawab Siraj-ud-Dowlah's forces. On the morning of June 19,1756, during the continuance of the siege he escaped with the Governor Roger Drake by boat to Fulta, where he shared the hardships of other European refugees.[20] He fought again in the retaking of the Fort by Clive in January 1757. On May 30, he was appointed Alderman in the Mayor's Court at Calcutta.[21] In 1758 his father applied to the Court of Directors for granting to his son some favourable opportunities either in the service or under the protection of the Company, in consideration of his patriotic conduct in the defence as well as in the recovery of Calcutta. The Court directed the Bengal Council to give Capt. Hugh Baillie, then in the sea-faring way, " option of residing in India under the protection of the Company by free-merchants' indentures or to be provided for in our service in the sea-faring way if you can find an employment for him in that manner." The Court further showed their eagerness to help Captain Baillie by recommending to the Bengal Government to fix him in such station as may render his services useful to the Company and at the same time be satisfactory to himself."[22] During the hostilities with the Dutch in Bengal who had brought a large body of troops from Batavia at the instance of Nawab Mir Jafar, Baillie served as a volunteer under Col. Francis Forde, and took part in the engagement at Bidara where on November 25, 1759, the enemy were completely defeated and repulsed.[23] On December 19, 1761, Hugh Baillie was appointed to the office of Mayor of Calcutta for the ensuing year.[24]

19. In the memorial submitted to the Court on March 13, 1771, Hugh Baillie stated his "having resided in Bengal 22 years." His residence in Bengal was again mentioned as having extended "for the space of 22 years" in his memorial of Dec. 21, 1773. Archdeacon Firminger stated that H. Baillie had come to India about 1756 as a sea-captain, vide *Rungpore District Records*, Vol. II, p. 49, and *Bengal: Past and Present*, Vol. V, p. 144.

20. S. C. Hill, *Bengal in 1756-57*, I, p. 41.

21. Beng. Pub. Cons., May 30, 1757, No. 844.

22. Court's Letter to Bengal, March 3, 1758, para 88.

23. Writers Petitions, Vol. 8, No. 26; Bidara was midway between Chandernagore and Chinsurah. S. C. Hill identified Bidara with Bhadreswar, *Catalogue of Orme Mss.*, p. 243.

24. Beng. Pub. Cons., Dec. 19, 1761, Nos. 1, 14, and 19.

In 1763 Baillie was at Rangamati near Goalpara carrying on trade on behalf of Henry Vansittart, Governor of Bengal, and other merchants. As a result of the disputes with Nawab Mir Kasim over the payment of duties on articles of inland trade by Europeans and the oppression of natives by the agents of European merchants, Hugh Baillie was instructed by his principal Henry Vansittart to obey the regulation newly introduced by which "the English were to pay the same duties as other merchants and take the Dustuck of the Country Government."[25] On the withdrawal of European merchants from the inland trade Baillie closed his concerns at Rangamati. In 1765 he was appointed agent of the Society of Trade at Goalpara.[26] During the second year of the Society's career Clive withdrew all European merchants from the several agencies.[27] The Society itself was abolished by the orders of the Court of Directors on August 1, 1768.[28] Clive left for England in January 1767, but a few months before his departure he had recommended Baillie and a few other merchants for appointment as Factors.[29]

On December 12, 1768, Baillie requested the Calcutta Council for orders to Captain George Stainforth, Commander of the vessel *The Queen,* to receive him and his family on board the ship for Europe.[30] On April 6, 1770, he applied to the Court of Directors for permission for his "black servant named Andrew to return to India on *The Duke of Portland,* the Company being at no charge thereby."[31] A year later, on April 3, 1771, his two daughters applied to the Court for the same permission.[32] While in England, Baillie submitted his first memorial to the Court of Directors on March 13, 1771, drawing their attention to the possibility of opening trade with Assam and Bhutan.[33] This was followed by another memorial, dated December 21, 1773, to the same intent and purpose.[34] He and his wife lived on intimate terms with Miss Frances Barwell and induced the latter to request her brother Richard

25. Beng. Pub. Cons., Feb. 1, 1763.
26. Select Committee's Fourth Report, 1772-73, App. 41, p. 513.
27. Malcolm, *Clive,* III, p. 104.
28. Malcolm, *Clive,* III, p. 111; Home Misc. Series, Vol. 769, p. 530.
29. Select Committee's Fourth Report, App. 3, p. 473.
30. Beng. Pub. Cons., Dec. 12, 1768.
31. Misc. Letters Recd., Vol. 53, 1770.
32. Misc. Letters Recd., Vol. 55, 1771.
33. Writers Petitions, Vol. 8, No. 26.
34. Misc. Letters Recd. Vol. 57, 1773.

Barwell to exert himself in Baillie's favour.[35] On November 20, 1773, he requested the Court for permission to return to India, because his presence was necessary in Bengal where he had a considerable part of his fortune.[36] He arrived in India in the summer of 1774, leaving Mrs. Baillie and the children in England.

Baillie had two children by his first wife Maria, Elizabeth baptised on October 2, 1762, and Hugh, baptised on April 27, 1765. On the death of Maria he married Miss Anna Pearce on January 30, 1766, by whom he had a daughter Ann, who was baptised on June 17, 1767. Ann was married to John Henry Davies on April 3, 1788, who succeeded Sir John Day as Advocate-General of Bengal.[37]

35. *Bengal : Past and Present*, Vol. XI, pp. 42-43 ; XII, p. 73.

36. Writers Petitions, Vol. 8, No. 26.

37. *Bengal : Past and Present*, Vol. IV, p. 492 ; V, pp. 328, 330 ; XXVIII, p. 203. The Appendix to Chapter II was read at the 24th Session of the Indian Historical Records Commission held at Jaipur in February 1948, the title of the paper being *The Baillie Brothers.*

Chapter III

FREEMERCHANTS AND ADVENTURERS, 1769-1779

Unauthorised adventurers at Goalpara: During the period when the Bengal Government was surveying the possibilities of the Assam trade and Baillie was residing at Goalpara with special licence from the Governor-General, a number of freemerchants and interlopers were engaged in commerce with the Assamese either on their own account or on behalf of their principals. The rivalries between these merchants, and the disputes with Assamese traders and officers, not infrequently accompanied by the exercise of force, produced conditions which were not favourable to the steady progress of commerce. Delay in payment of the claims of Bengal merchants, and the refusal of the Assamese to carry on trade with them led the aggrieved parties to take the law into their own hands, and enter the Assamese territories to enforce their demands. The disputes of the merchants of the two countries would have led to serious consequences had not they been averted by the forbearance and caution of the Assam king and the timely intervention of the Governor-General.

"The trade of Assam," observed the Supreme Board in 1780, "had long been subjected to a monopoly in the hands of a few unauthorised adventurers."[1] "This trade," wrote David Killican about the same time, "which was highly beneficial to Bengal is now in a great measure ruined by the mode in which it is conducted"[2] Hence Warren Hastings, in a letter to the Assam king written in June 1780, admitted the urgency of taking steps to remove "the various disputes amongst the Europeans who are settled at Gualparah,....and the more effectually to secure the peace of the country and the welfare of all parties,....and to protect the Assam traders from all freebooters and enemies whatsoever, that commerce may be carried on for the mutual advantage of both kingdoms."[3]

English merchants at Goalpara: Of the private merchants engaged in the Assam trade George Lear and Daniel Raush pos-

1. Beng. Rev. Cons., June 13, 1780, No. 411.
2. Killican to Hastings, June 9, Beng. Rev. Cons., June 13, 1780, No. 411.
3. Hastings to Assam Raja, June 14, 1780, *Calendar of Persian Correspondence*, Vol. V, No. 1911, copy obtained from the Imperial Record Department, Calcutta, in 1930.

sessed the most extensive concerns at Goalpara and its neighbourhood by virtue of which they exercised considerable influence in that locality thereby rendering their services indispensable to the Government of Bengal in times of emergency. Raush lived to play an important part in the political affairs of Assam by procuring aid from outside to suppress its internal disorders.

George Lear had arrived in India in 1755.[4] In 1763 he came to reside at Rungpore as the agent of Hugh Watts with the permission of the Government of Bengal.[5] In 1765 he was a freemerchant at Patna.[6] From 1765 to 1768 he served as Alderman of the Mayor's Court at Calcutta. On May 27, 1768, he served on the Grand Jury at a General Quarter-Session of Oyer and Terminer held under the presidency of Henry Verelst, Governor of Bengal.[7] In 1769 Lear came to Goalpara to carry on trade with the Assamese. He built a factory there at a cost of rupees 21,742. He had also warehouses and godowns at Dacca which was his headquarter.[8]

Daniel Raush has been variously described as a Dane, a German, a Hanovarian, and a Greek, and it is not known precisely to what nationality he originally belonged.[9] Before coming to India Raush had served as an officer under Frederick the Great of Prussia and had been wounded in the hand in the famous battle of Minden.[10]. He came to Bengal in 1766, and resided at Goalpara since 1769 without special licence from Government, and carried on trade at that place as the agent of David Killican, a Bengal Civil Servant and Calcutta merchant.[11] On July 19, 1782, Raush married Martha Mayo at Rungpore, the services being performed by Richard Goodlad, Collector of the district, owing to the absence of a person in holy orders. The tomb of Johan and Daniel, the twin children of the marriage, who died on June 24, 1783, within three hours of their birth, can still be seen at Goalpara.[12] Raush's elder daughter Charlotte Mary married Henry Droz, Chief of Cossimbazar Factory, and on his death in 1830 she married Colonel

4. Lear to Hastings, July 6, Beng. Rev. Cons., Sept. 5, 1780.

5. *Bengal: Past and Present,* Vol. IV, p. 629.

6. *Rungpore District Records,* Vol. II, p. 40-*n*.

7. Wm. Bolts, *Considerations on Indian Affairs,* Vol. III, pp. 485, 504-5.

8. Lear to Hastings, undated, Beng. Rev. Cons., Jan. 23, 1781.

9. E. C. Glazier, *Report on the District of Rungpore,* 1873, prefixed to *Rungpore District Records,* edited by W. K. Firminger, Vol. I, p. 47.

10. W. S. Seton-Karr, *Selections from Calcutta Gazette,* Vol. II, Feb. 4, 1796, p. 444.

11. Glazier's *Rungpore,* ed. Firminger, pp. 46-7.

12. *Bengal: Past and Present,* Vol. IV, p. 511.

Marmaduke Browne. The younger daughter Maria married one William Montgomery. Mrs. Raush died in 1830 having enjoyed an annuity of £100 from the Court of Directors since 1816.

Another merchant of note was William Dow who had come to India in 1773 with a relation Colonel Dow. He resided at Jugighopa with the permission of the Governor-General and carried on an extensive trade in cloth, and was also engaged in another trade known as the 'jars trade.'[13] In 1779 he entered into legal specific commercial engagements with the Assam agent for the year 1780, though the terms are not known. In addition to the Assam trade he established a factory at Kurigram in the district of Rungpore where he died in 1788.[14] William Dow is believed to be a brother of the orientalist Col. Alexander Dow.[15]

Robert Bigger and Bernard MacCullum were two other prominent merchants engaged in the Assam trade. Both resided at Jugighopa and had branches at Goalpara. The former acted as agent of a Bengali salt merchant named Ganganarayan Roy, and the latter of a Dacca merchant named Robert Hunter. Bigger died at Jugighopa in 1780.[16] MacCullum had no special permission to trade nor had his chief Hunter. MacCullum attained considerable notoriety by signing an address to the Court of Directors with five other merchants recommending the revival of the practice of purchasing the Bengal goods for the Company's investment through intermediate agents. Another signatory to this address was Hunter, MacCullum's chief. Richard Barwell, in a letter to Henry Savage, dated July 23, 1776, pointed out that such a proposal would operate to the prejudice of the Company's commercial interests. Of MacCullum he wrote,—"MacCullum is a person in the service of Mr. Hunter, not licensed by the Company. He was employed by him at Gualparah, and does not do any business that I know of independent of Mr. Hunter, so that in fact Mr. Hunter splits himself into Mr. MacCullum, and to swell the number of names to the address separates Mr. MacCullum from his own."[17]

Bernard MacCullum continued for many years in the Assam trade. In October 1784 he became one of the securities for the Hon'ble Robert Lindsay on his appointment as regular Collector

13. Probably the trade in earthen jars originally exported from Martaban, called 'Martaban jars', 'Pegu jars' or 'Martabans,' see *Hobson-Jobson*, under *Martaban*.

14. Glazier's *Rungpore*, ed. Firminger, pp. 46-47.

15. *Rungpore District Records*, Vol. II, p. 42-*n*.

16. Beng. Rev. Cons., Sept. 12, 1780.

17. Barwell's Letters, *Bengal: Past and Present*, Vol. XIV, p. 243.

of the Sylhet district upon the removal of the former Collector.[18] Upon the death of Raush in 1796 MacCullum was appointed by the executors of the estate as their agent. He was also permitted to reside at Goalpara for the purpose of trade as well as for the recovery of the balances and debts due to Raush's estate.[19] The Assamese merchants believed that MacCullum had been granted exclusive privilege of trade with their country. On the representation of Robert Brydie, a merchant of Jugighopa, the Governor-General Sir John Shore informed the Assam Raja that it was by no means the intention of the Bengal Government to grant to MacCullum any monopoly, "but merely to allow him to engage in commercial concerns upon the same footing as the late Mr. Raush, and in common with other merchants who have a similar licence to trade in your country."[20]

There were other English merchants engaged in the Assam trade, Williams, Wheatland, Cator and John Taylor. Cator was an agent of Lear and Taylor, and conducted Raush's affairs in Mogulhat on the road to Cooch Behar.[21] David Killican who obtained in 1780 the exclusive privilege of the Assam trade had also been engaged in the same for several years before that date acting through his agent Raush.[22] In addition to these merchants there was the Commercial Resident at Rungpore, Edward Ephraim Pote, who supervised the transactions concerning the Company's investment.[23]

French merchants: Besides the English merchants a number of Frenchmen resided at Goalpara carrying on trade with Assam, the most noted being Laval, Giblot and Campagnac. Laval had settled at Goalpara in 1767 as the agent of the English in partnership with Jean Baptiste Chevalier to carry on trade with Assam. The agency did not succeed and Laval's concern had to be closed. Laval became Chief of the French Factory at Dacca. The commanding position held by the English company led to the abandonment of that factory in 1774, and all Frenchmen were withdrawn

18. *Sylhet District Records,* Vol. I, No. 267, p. 199.

19. Shore to Assam Raja, Ap. 29, Beng. Pol. Cons., June 10, 1796, No. 43.

20. Shore to Assam Raja, June 16, Beng. Pol. Cons., June 26, 1797, No. 8.

21. Glazier's *Rungpore,* ed. Firminger, p. 47. There were two Cators, William and Joseph, both Bengal Civil Servants, appointed in 1771, and 1772 respectively. Joseph was a member of Barwell's household being his secretary and agent. William succeeded Haliburton in the office of Collector of Government Customs at Dacca, *Bengal: Past and Present,* Vol. VII, p. 164; *Personal Records,* Vol. 14, pp. 351, 472.

22. Beng. Rev. Cons., June 13, 1780.

23. Glazier's *Rungpore,* ed. Firminger, p. 46.

from Dacca. Laval came back to Goalpara to join the other French merchants and traded on his private account till 1778 when they were all recalled to Calcutta on the outbreak of war between England and France.[24] Giblot and Campagnac, the two other French merchants of Goalpara, were both arrested in 1778, and sent down to Dacca, and then to Chandernagore as prisoners. The orders for arresting the subjects of France had been communicated to the Collector of Rungpore on August 10, and the latter requested Lear to arrest Giblot and Campagnac at Goalpara. The two Frenchmen were then in Assam on a commercial visit. Lear deputed Raush to prevail on them to return to Goalpara, promising that they would not sustain any loss in their goods or effects, and that they would be given facilities to recover the balance due to them. The Frenchmen readily accepted the proposal as it came from "a person [Raush] whom they knew to be a man of probity," and they returned with him to Goalpara to Lear's house who renewed the offers previously made to them by Raush. They then set out to surrender themselves to the Chief of Dacca, John Shakespeare, where they wanted to remain for some time to collect "at least some wrecks of their fortune," and asked for permission for one of them to remove some goods which were detained in a warehouse at Goalpara.[25] The two were sent in 1781 as prisoners to Calcutta, along with Laval. The three names appear in the "list of Frenchmen to be confined in the upper apartments of the new building lately erected for a jail." Giblot and Campagnac were subsequently sent as "higher class" French prisoners to Europe.[26] It may be added that most of the acts of oppression, attributed to the European merchants, were believed to be the work of Frenchmen residing at or near Goalpara. These acts were committed with impunity as there was no officer stationed at Goalpara duly authorised to take cognizance of the conduct of the oppressors, "and whereby the whole trade had nearly been annihilated."[27]

24. *Bengal: Past and Present,* Vol. III, p. 366; XLII, p. 52. War was declared by Great Britain against France on March 18, 1778, and by France against England on the 30th of the same month,—*Sylhet District Records,* Vol. I, p. 33.

25. Beng. Pub. Cons., Jan. 7, 1779, No. 20, published in *Bengal: Past and Present,* Vol. III, p. 369.

26. Beng. Pub. Cons., Feb. 1, No. 4; March 13, Nos. 9-12; Ap. 14, No. 11; Ap. 27, 1781, No. 11, pub. in *Bengal: Past and Present,* Vol. VI, pp. 21-28.

27. Henry Lodge to Hastings, Nov. 15, 1784, Beng. Rev. Cons., Feb. 16, 1785.

Indian merchants: There were also a number of Indian merchants engaged in the Assam trade. Sooberam Palit and Gunny Sam Sarkar were granted *perwanas* for monopoly of trade in salt at Goalpara for three years by Muhammad Reza Khan, Naib Dewan of Bengal. This grant constituted the second of the five charges brought against Muhammad Reza Khan in his trial for mismanagement of the revenue affairs of Bengal, as the *perwanas* were alleged to have been given to Palit and Sarkar "of his [Muhammad Reza Khan's] own authority knowing the same to be contrary to the express orders of the Company and the regulations of the Select Committee." Reza Khan in his reply, dated May 26, 1772, denied having granted an exclusive three years' trade to merchants. He attempted to show that Palit and Sarkar had undertaken to pay the stipulated duties on account of the sale of salt at Goalpara, and hence, "Whatever they paid to the Royal cutchery exclusive of the regular duties, was an advantage and not a disadvantage to the Company."[28]

Ganganarayan Roy was a Bengali merchant who had purchased the salt of the 24-Perganahs for the years 1775-76 and 1776-77. He was granted general *rawannahs* which allowed him an unrestricted trade in salt throughout the provinces of Bengal, Bihar and Orissa, and particular *rawannahs* also for the Assam mart. His agent Robert Bigger erected a factory at Jugighopa with the special permission of the Governor-General. His trade extended to the Bijni state then in the Rungpore district.[29]

The firm of Jagat Seth, the famous bankers of Murshidabad had also trading concerns at Goalpara, Jugighopa and Gauhati, which continued upto 1815, and even later. The Marwari merchants in those places had also extensive commercial relations with Jagat Seth. The Assamese clients of Jagat Seth took advantage of the bankers' hospitality when they visited Murshidabad to bathe in the Ganges or for other purposes.[30]

Disputes and quarrels among Goalpara merchants: The records of the period refer constantly to the disputes and quarrels amongst the merchants trading at Goalpara and Jugighopa, and the warnings given to them in consequence by the officers of the Company's Government. The disputes arose mainly from commercial jealousy, and were occasionally attended by violence and aggression.

28. Sir George Forest, *Selections from State Papers*, 1772-85, Vol. I, p. 19.
29. G. Roy to Hastings, undated, Beng. Rev. Cons., Sept. 12, 1780.
30. *Life of Anandaram Dhekial Phukan*, in Assamese, by Gunabhiram Barua, 1880, p. 26.

In 1777 Lear seduced Ramram Datta and Baloram Ghose, the Banyan and Sarkar respectively of a servant of the Company named George Bright, who resided at Chittagong. Bright could not pay the sum of 77,810 rupees which he had owed to the Bengal Government as Baloram Ghose who had maintained the accounts and kept the key of the treasury had accepted service at Goalpara. The Supreme Board asked Lear to receive Baloram's answer to the charges and transmit them to the Government. Ramram Datta received an allowance of 200 rupees per month for transacting Lear's business at Goalpara.[31] In 1780 Lear's Sarkar transferred his services to David Killican and began to act in a manner prejudicial to the interests of his former master.[32].

In 1779 Lear, Dow and Raush were charged with the offence of preventing free access of merchants to the Assam Choky by placing men on the banks of the Brahmaputra. The Baruas or Assamese officers in charge of the Choky were thus kept practically under confinement. Charles Purling, Collector of Rungpore, acting on the representation of an English merchant named Williams warned Lear, Dow and Raush "how fatal the consequences of such conduct must prove to their own interest and even to their residence in those parts."[33]

In March 1780, the agents of Jagat Seth complained before George Bogle, Collector of Rungpore, that their boats had been stopped by Lear and Dow. The matter was investigated by the Nabob sent down to Jugighopa by the Collector for that purpose. Dow in his reply of March 17 attempted to show that the allegation arose from the apprehension that the Seth's boats might or would be stopped, and not that they had been actually stopped. He also showed that it was against his own interest to quarrel with the Seth's people because their trade at Jugighopa and his own business were intimately connected, and that "he was honoured with their friendly correspondence regularly." The Seths had commercial relations with the Assam Resident at Jugighopa, and Dow had entered into "legal specific commercial engagements" with him for the year 1780. Dow argued that even if he was prepared to fulfil his engagement the Assam Resident would not be able to fulfil his part of the contract if the Seths could not carry on business peacefully with him. The result, Dow asserted, would be to plunge him into serious loss.

31. G. Bright to Hastings, March 1, Beng. Rev. Cons., Ap. 7, 1777.

32. Lear to Hastings, undated, Beng. Rev. Cons., Jan. 23, 1781.

33. Purling to Lear, Dow and Raush, undated, *Rungpore District Records*, Vol. I, No. 131, p. 101.

Dow made several allegations of harassment against the Nabob.[34] The report that the Nabob had been authorised to enquire into the complaint of Jagat Seth's agents and to apprehend the two English merchants had hurt Dow's credit and his prestige which were greatly necessary for his success as a merchant there. The Nabob used to seize Dow's coolies and flog and imprison them on the slightest pretext, such as quarrelling with people like themselves. Dow alleged that it was "done ostentatiously to show his authority and to let all the poor people see that he can at his pleasure flog and imprison the servants of a European merchant with impunity." This harsh treatment by an outsider caused an insurrection in Dow's factory, and the coolies refused to work unless their employer secured them justice. It is with the utmost difficulty and persuasion that Dow could restrain his coolies for doing themselves justice after their own manner, and to prevail on them to return to their work.

In the aforesaid letter of Dow to George Bogle we get a glimpse of the activities of the factory of a merchant carrying on trade with Assam. There were 150 or 200 coolies engaged in Dow's business. Their work was to sort muga-dhutis and make them up into bales. Some were employed on black pepper and stick lac, and others as oarsmen. The coolies gradually formed themselves into a community and the insult inflicted on one of them was considered as a common injury.[35]

On June 6, 1780, Robert Bigger came with an armed force and possessed himself of some *golahs* and ground belonging to MacCullum at Jugighopa. Immediately after the incident MacCullum's assistant William O'Briyen, and his head Banyan Ramsundar Das reported the matter to the Collector of Rungpore and asked the latter to put a stop to Bigger's violent proceedings and order him to restore the *golahs* and ground of MacCullum.[36]

The quarrels among the merchants became so frequent that the Collector of Rungpore had to authorise Mir Afsud Ali, the Naib

34. Probably he was an official of the Nawab Nazim who had his court at Murshidabad. Nawab Mobaruttu-ud-Daula, son of Mir Jafar enjoyed that office since 1770 till his death in 1779 with Munny Begum as his guardian. In Aug. 1779 he laid charges against Robert Lindsay, Collector of Sylhet, for forcibly placing some Nizamut decoy elephants in the Company's *pilkhana*. *Sylhet District Records*, Vol. I, p. 71.

35. Dow to Bogle, March 17, 1780, *Rungpore District Records*, Vol. II, No. 57.

36. *Rungpore District Records*, Vol. II, No. 68.

of Rangamati, to seize and confine all men who committed violence on the person and property of other merchants.[37]

A common complaint of European merchants was the non-payment of dues by their Assamese debtors. The claims of Lear formed the subject of a letter from Warren Hastings to the king of Assam. The balance due to Chevalier was perhaps never paid at all. Giblot and Campagnac proceeded to Assam to recover their demands. Later on, the claims of Raush were renewed ever and anon even after the government of Assam had passed into British hands.

The attempt to recover the dues came to a head in 1777. The Bengal merchants pressed the Assam Barua to repay the balances, and on refusal they crossed the outposts and entered into the territory of Assam by force, and a party proceeded as far as Pandu, four miles west of the viceregal capital at Gauhati.

M. Laval's demands on Assam merchants : The first European to enter into Assam by force was the French merchant M. Laval. His first grievance was the refusal of the Duaria Barua, in charge of the Assam Choky, opposite Goalpara, to trade with him while the Barua carried on commercial transactions freely with other Europeans. As all goods imported into and exported from Assam had to pass through the hands of the Duaria Barua, who held the monopoly of the trade under the authority of the Assam government, his refusal implied the total ruin of Laval's concerns. It is not known why the Barua did not admit Laval to the privilege of trade with Assam. It might be due to some act of oppression and violence for which the French merchants of Goalpara were particularly notorious. Laval estimated his loss on this account at one lakh of rupees.

Laval's second grievance was the withdrawal of payment of the heavy outstanding balance due to Monsieur Jean Baptiste Chevalier who had visited Assam in 1755 and 1757, wherefrom he had to return abruptly as the government of that country had refused to permit him to carry on trade there. Chevalier had to dispose of his goods to Assam merchants mostly on credit, and there was a heavy outstanding still unpaid in 1777. Laval, as the agent of Chevalier, and as the leading French merchant engaged in the Assam trade, now renewed his claim for the payment of the dues.

Expecting to get no justice from the Duaria Barua, Laval proposed to go to Gauhati to set forth his grievances to the Barphukan or Ahom viceroy. In May 1777 Laval sailed along the south bank

37. *Rungpore District Records,* Vol. III, Nos. 59-60.

of the Brahmaputra with four boats. When questioned by the officers of the Assam Choky he said he was going to his *golah* at Kamarpota but came up to Nagarbera, the boundary between Assam and Bengal on the south bank. The Assamese officers posted at the various Chokies warned him of the consequences of further advance : but he disregarded their warnings and proceeded as far as Bhogpur about 15 miles from Gauhati. He acquainted the Assamese officers of his intention to sail up to Gauhati to lodge his complaint before the Barphukan.

The Barphukan easily realised that a clash with Laval was imminent. He adopted the necessary precautions and strongly guarded the garrisons on the river. Apprehending that forcible expulsion of the European merchant might lead to hostilities with the Company he referred the matter to King Lakshmi Singha asking for advice whether diplomacy or drastic action should be adopted to secure the return of Laval to the Bengal frontier. Haragovinda Kataki, coming in an express boat within four days from Gauhati, delivered the Barphukan's message to the king at Rangpur on June 11, 1777.

The king deliberated with the Barbarua and the three Gohains and despatched a reply by the same messenger Haragovinda. The viceroy was admonished for having permitted Laval to come up so far into Assam territory. "The Firingi [European]", observed the monarch, "should have been stopped from proceeding up before he had entered our waters. Now he must be pushed back by all means possible. If the Barphukan cannot keep the handful of Firingis at a safe distance how can he be expected to protect the kingdom ?"

The king commanded the Barphukan to send a man to Laval to persuade the latter to go back peacefully to the frontier. The messenger was to play the role of an independent adviser, and was not to convey the impression that he was an emissary of the viceroy. The king directed that the messenger should instruct and warn Laval in the following terms,—"As to the complaint regarding the refusal of the Duaria Barua to trade with you, you can obtain redress if you submit your grievance to the Choladhara Phukan, the minister in charge of commerce and foreign affairs. Instead of doing this, you have, against the usages of all friendly states, crossed the Chokies and entered into our territory. The Choladhara Phukan will be extremely indignant if he hears of these movements of yours. The king has posted an eminent officer at Gauhati, the Baranabab Barphukan, equipped with a regular army to convert enemies into friends. If he comes to know of your activities no one can say what the consequences will be. Moreover, if we report the matter to the Barasaheb of the Company [Governor-General] the result will certainly be unfavourable to you. About the balance alleged to be due to Monsieur Chevalier, it is now more than twenty years since that merchant came to our country. How can you demand payment after such a lapse of time? Anyway, your complaints will be properly investigated, and you may expect payment of your demand if you can produce the necessary proofs. We shall report these matters to the Choladhara Phukan, and his decision will be communicated to you in due course."[38] The Barphukan was further instructed to open negotiations with Laval by deputing some trusted agents if he had meanwhile arrived at Gauhati.

Before the orders of the king reached the Barphukan that officer had on his own initiative despatched an agent to Laval at Bhogpur. The agent drew the attention of the merchant to the discomfort he must have been experiencing at Bhogpur for want of food provisions. He was advised to go back to the Assam Choky with the two men sent by the Barphukan with instructions to enquire into the Duaria Barua's refusal to trade. On receiving this assurance Laval returned with the Barphukan's men to the Assam Choky. The viceroy sent another man to Hugh Baillie, described in the Assamese chronicle as "Beli Saheb who has been deputed as a Vakil by the Barasaheb and who says he has come to Assam for the purpose of trade." Baillie was then living at Goalpara. The Barphukan asked Baillie whether he would be able to prevent Laval from coming up again to Assam as the viceroy hoped to send the merchant back to Baillie's place this time by some means or other. "If he comes here", assured Baillie, "I will certainly restrain Laval from going to Assam again." The instructions despatched to the Barphukan by the king had therefore no occasion to be acted upon. The whole affair thus ended peacefully through the tactfulness of the Barphukan aided perhaps by the pacific intervention of Hugh Baillie. On July 2, 1777, the king received the news of Laval's departure from Bhogpur from the Barphukan's messenger Kemai Gajpuria Kataki. The monarch acting on the advice of the Barbarua, despatched strong injunctions to the Bar-

38. I have inserted this passage at length as it constitutes the only contemporary document to illustrate the diplomacy of the Assam government in its treatment of the affairs of European merchants.

phukan to adopt all possible means to prevent Laval or others from coming up again.[39]

Lear's armed entry into Assam: George Lear's attempts to recover the outstanding balance due from the Assamese merchant Sibram Sarma Bairagi assumed a graver aspect, but the consequences were averted by the mediation of Warren Hastings.[40]

So early as August 1773 Lear demanded payment of the sum that Sibram had owed to him for goods purchased to the value of one lakh of rupees. Lear asked the Assam Barua to pay the demand with interest within ten days, in default of which he sought permission to enter into Assam, search out the debtor and recover the balance. He further demanded the surrender of a Bengali merchant named Jagannath Sarkar who, he alleged, had taken shelter in Assam. Jagannath had also purchased from Lear goods to the value of one lakh of rupees.

Lear's request was communicated by the Barphukan to the king. It, however, transpired that the goods purchased from Lear by Sibram Bairagi were sold off to other people in Assam; and Rudram, son of Sibram, who had inherited his father's estate along with its obligations, found it difficult to recover the sums due to him from his Assamese customers. On September 10, 1773, the king in consultation with his ministers ordered that the sum claimed by Lear should be realised from the persons who had stepped into the possession of the houses, lands and retainers of Bhadrasen Barbarua after the latter's execution in July 1771 for high treason.[41] About Jagannath Sarkar the king observed that he had not gone to Assam. The monarch, however, promised to deliver Jagannath if ever he went to that country.

In September 1774 Lear renewed his demand for payment, and threatened Krishnaram Duaria Barua that he would be seized and punished if the payment was not made within a month, or if Rudram was not delivered within that period.

39. This episode relating to Laval's entry into Assam has been compiled solely from a manuscript Assamese chronicle of the reign of Lakshmi Singha (1769-1780), in possession of the American Baptist Mission at Gauhati, Assam.

40. This episode of Lear's demands and his forcible entry into Assam has also been compiled mainly from the Ms. Assamese chronicle of Lakshmi Singha. The facts are supported by Hastings's letter to the Assam king of April 22, 1777; to Charles Purling of Nov. 7, 1778; and Purling's letter to Dow, Lear and Raush, referred to in the text.

41. It is not known why the purchasers of Bhadrasen Barbarua's estate had to pay off Lear's demand. It is, however, recorded that Bhadrasen Barbarua had received a sum of 90,000 rupees for appointing Lahan Deka Phukan to the office of Barphukan of Gauhati. The latter might have paid the Barbarua in kind, *viz.*, the goods purchased by Sibram Bairagi from Lear.

In the meantime an imposter who described himself as a prince had been detained by Lear as a security for the debt. He was released from confinement through the intervention of Krishnaram who promised a ransom of 15,000 rupees. The so-called prince was sent up to the Assam capital Rangpur. In the enquiry that followed the prince was identified to be Phedela, son of a retainer of the Barpatra Gohain belonging to the guild of paddy-huskers. Phedela confessed his imposture and was executed.

In March 1775 Lear demanded payment of 70,000 rupees out of the total outstanding balance of one lakh. "If not," said Lear, "give us the country as far as Kaliabar; and if you do not agree to the cession of any territory we are prepared to fight." He seized two Bairagis or customs officials and kept them in confinement. But no substantial result was derived from these threats.

All measures for the recovery of the debt having thus failed Lear, who as a licensed freemerchant was entitled to the Company's protection, referred the matter to Warren Hastings. The Governor-General readily took up Lear's cause; and on April 22, 1777, he addressed a letter to the king of Assam requesting him to exercise his authority in securing payment of the debt.

It appears from Hastings's letter that in 1769 Lear had sold a parcel of goods to the amount of 57,000 rupees to Sibram Bairagi who engaged to make him returns in two or three months, but did not comply with his agreement, and instead sent his son with fair promises. Sibram died shortly after. According to the custom of the country his son Rudram as heir to his father became bound for the payment of Lear's demand. Rudram returned to Assam to collect the effects of his deceased father. At that time he was at the capital of Assam. He refused payment of the debt and set Lear at defiance. "As such conduct," concluded the Governor-General, "is not only contrary to every principle of Law and Justice, but moreover tends to the destruction of commerce which is of mutual benefit, I therefore request of you [Assam Raja] that out of regard to Justice and Friendship between us, you will enter heartily into this business, and oblige Ruborham [Rudram] to make satisfaction to the aforesaid gentleman [Lear] that he may sustain no loss, but receive the full sum with interest thereon from the time when the goods were delivered."[42]

42. Hastings to Assam Raja, Ap. 22, 1777, *Calendar of Persian Correspondence*, Vol. V, No. 518, full copy obtained from the Imperial Record Deptt., Calcutta, in 1930. *Sibram* and *Rudram* have been spelt in the copy as *Suborham* and *Ruborham*, obviously mis-transliterations in the Persian original.

Before the Governor-General received a reply to his letter, Lear advanced up the river with fifteen boats and one *jahaj* or ship, loaded with provisions and arms. He sailed up to Nagarbera and then to Bhogpur. The intention of Lear was easily surmised from his threats on previous occasions, and the Barphukan in order to gain time deputed some men to ask Lear to desist from coming up. But Lear was insistent, and expressed his willingness to wait at Bhogpur only for three days for receiving payment of the debt or the delivery of the debtor Rudram.

The Barphukan reported Lear's advance to the king who discussed the matter in a secret sitting of the ministers' council on July 2, 1777. It was resolved that Rudram should be delivered to Lear, and one Sindhu Ariadhara was appointed to execute the mission. To this Rudram protested saying,—"Why should I alone be made over to the Firingi [Lear]? The goods I purchased from him have been taken from me by many persons. If they do not pay up, do you think the Firingi will take my life? He will never kill me as I am a Brahman. The rest will see the consequences in time." Bailung Bargohain interceded on behalf of Rudram, and his son Krishnaram Choladhara Phukan stood surety for the debtor. Rudram was brought back and detained in custody.

In October 1777 Lear's party divided themselves into four sections; one halted at Hatbhaga, another at Rani, a third in Darrang and a fourth remained in front. On hearing of the advance of the party to the neighbourhood of Gauhati the king became concerned and entered into an investigation of the claims of Lear. It was found that his claims amounted to 62,000 rupees, of which 50,000 rupees constituted the principal sum. The king ordered the Barphukan to pay rupees ten thousand and send Lear back.

The negotiations with Lear continued for several months without any definite result. In February 1778, Lear sailed up and halted at Pandu wherefrom he demanded the delivery of Rudram and Jagannath Sarkar. "If not," said Lear, "we shall go in and search them out." Lear's men scattered themselves from Pandu to Rani. It was apprehended that they would attack Gauhati on Thursday, March 19, 1778. The Barphukan asked the king whether he should protract the negotiations or attack the fleet of Lear. The king ordered that Rudram should be made over to Lear; and accordingly sent him down under an escort of three men, Narayan, son of the Duaria Barua, Bhaluka Changmai and Gelai of Thenga.

In the meantime, Lear's men had erected their encampments at Sarai opposite Pandu, and had forcibly cut down bamboos from the estate of Abhaypuria Rajkhowa, a principal officer of the

Gauhati establishment. The Barphukan became highly exasperated at the aggressive conduct of Lear and his men. He wrote to the king,—"I have exhausted all my powers of persuasion, and I can no longer restrain the Firingi from acts of violence. I have everything ready. If Your Majesty permits I can fall upon the Firingi merchant in an instant. He has fifteen boats. They can be destroyed in no time and the wreckage made to float on the river."

The king realised that the Barphukan's proposal was far from being expedient. The Moamaria discontent had not been completely suppressed, and hostilities with European merchants could only end in disaster to the government. The king therefore proposed to send away Lear from Assam by pacific overtures. He sent Damodar Kataki to the Barphukan with a set of *chikan* or fine cloth for presentation to Lear in order to secure his peaceful return to Bengal.

Lear soon realised that in the face of Hastings's request to the Assam Raja for payment of his dues the continuance of violent measures against the Assamese would be indefensible. He therefore sailed down from Pandu after having locked up in a boat Krishnaram Duaria Barua, the debtor Rudram Bairagi, Narayan Kataki, and Bika Kakati of Panikauri family. Niramoy Tekela Bara and Gelai Duaria escaped by jumping from the boat into the river. This matter was reported to the king on April 23, 1778.[43]

The activities of Lear reached the ears of the Governor-General. The information might have been communicated by the Assamese monarch who had threatened Laval with such a course, or by Baillie who had gained the confidence of the Assamese and whose mediation had been solicited in restraining the French merchant Laval from re-entering Assam. Warren Hastings who systematically endeavoured to maintain friendly relations with the neighbouring states and thereby enhance the good name of the Company wrote on November 7, 1778, to Charles Purling, Collector of Rungpore, asking him to inform himself of every circumstance concerning the report that Lear, in order to receive some outstanding balance, had engaged in hostilities with the people of Assam and actually marched an armed force into their country. The Governor-General expressed his anxiety to know the truth of

43. Lear, perhaps, was the European from Bengal, who "advanced as far as Hatimoora with an intention to proceed to Gauhati. The Burro Fokun accompanied by the Prince of Darrangi repaired to the spot and the stranger immediately returned to Bengal," Dr. J. P. Wade, *Account of Assam*, ed. B. Sharma, p. 241.

the report so that he might either bring it before the Board or take such steps as might be proper. The Collector was ordered to check Lear immediately if he "was actually engaged in any measure the consequences of which appeared to be alarming."[44]

The action taken by Warren Hastings was evidently a belated one. Lear had left Pandu in April 1778. In August he was at Goalpara when he arrested the French merchants Giblot and Campagnac in pursuance of the Governor-General's orders.[45] It is not known whether any account of Lear's march into Assam was submitted by Purling as desired by Hastings. "No answer to this request for information," says Archdeacon Firminger, "can be found among the papers of the Home Department, but the letter [of Hastings] is valuable because it belongs to that horizon of statesmanship which lay beyond the ken of Hastings's official foes."[46]

Lear's forcible entrance into Assam from where he returned in April 1778 was not the last act of violence committed by him against the Assamese. As we have seen he along with Dow and Raush had to answer charges afterwards for preventing access to the Baruas of the Assam Choky. These high-handed actions served to intensify the mistrust of the Assamese towards Bengal merchants and made them readily believe any reports attributing hostile designs on the part of the Company.

Jayantia subdued by the British: The expedition against Jayantia under Captain Edward Elliker in 1774, resulting in the occupation of the Raja's capital by the Company's troops and his flight into the hills, had its repercussions in the politics of the neighbouring territories. The Assam government to which Jayantia was in a state of qualified vassalage regarded the successes of the Company's arms in that territory as a menace to the safety of its own kingdom. Exaggerated reports of the Company's intentions on Assam reached the Ahom court at Rangpur, and spies were sent to ascertain the true facts. An embassy was despatched to the Governor-General to strengthen the bonds of friendship between the two governments and thereby avert the impending conflict that was alleged to have been brewing on the Jayantia frontier. These precautions were supplemented by the

44. Hastings to Purling, Nov. 7, 1778, *Rungpore District, Records*, Vol. I, No. 61, p. 60.

45. Hastings to Purling, Aug. 10, 1778, requiring all subjects of France to be sent down to Chandernagore. *Rungpore District Records*, Vol. I, No. 55, p. 57.

46. *Bengal: Past and Present*, Vol. IV, p. 630.

preparation of an inventory of the men and war materials in the garrisons at Gauhati and the execution of repairs to face any eventual hostility with the Company's force. The fears of the Assam government were aggravated by the demands of the European merchants of Goalpara accompanied by threats to enter the country by force if the outstanding balances were not paid within a specified time.

The rulers of Jayantia were a constant source of trouble to the Assam government. Their frequent raids into the plains were checked by an officer specially appointed for the purpose known as Jagialia Gohain commanding a garrison on the frontier between Assam and Jayantia. In 1706 the Jayantia Raja Ram Singha imprisoned the messengers deputed to him by the Barphukan of Gauhati, and obstructed the Assamese merchants in carrying on their lawful trade with Jayantia and Sylhet. Ram Singha further exasperated the Assam government by imprisoning Tamradhwaj, Raja of Cachar, who also owed allegiance to the Ahom king. Rudra Singha, king of Assam, despatched an expedition against Jayantia under Surath Singha Barbarua. The Jayantias were defeated, and their chief Ram Singha and the heir-apparent, commonly known as Barkowanr, were taken as captives to Rangpur. Ram Singha died there of small-pox and Barkowanr was appointed by the Assam king to the musnad of Jayantiapur. The new Raja, who assumed the name of Jaynarain, promised to pay an annual tribute of six elephants to the Assam government, and received the insignia of his office with which he proceeded to his capital at Jayantiapur.[47] King Rudra Singha wrote in March 1708 to the Mogul Thanadar of Sylhet,—"Please see that there does not occur any misunderstanding between your government and mine. From now I am the lord of Cachar and Jayantia. I do not intend any further extension of my dominions and I wish you will remain within the limits of your ancient boundaries."[48]

Jaynarain who ruled from 1708 to 1728 respected the terms of his agreement with the Assam king. But his successor Chattra Sing withheld the payment of the stipulated tribute, and led occasional incursions into the Assam plains. During the coronation of King Pramatta Singha in 1745 the prime minister advised the monarch,—"Cachar has abided by the terms settled with its

47. *Kachari Buranji and Jayantia Buranji*, 1936, 1937, edited by S. K. Bhuyan, and published by the Govt. of Assam in the Department of Historical and Antiquarian Studies.

48. Collection of Assamese Historical Letters, Ms. in possession of the Department of Historical and Antiquarian Studies, Assam.

ruler [by King Rudra Singha], but Jayantia has failed to respect the terms of the agreement. Cachar should be invited to send its representative to witness the festivities of the coronation but it is not proper that the privilege should be conferred upon Jayantia."[49]

In 1768, the Jayantia Raja led an expedition against Cachar and occupied a number of villages by force. On receiving this news the Ahom king Rajeswar Singha deputed Kirtichandra Barbarua at the head of a numerous force. On the approach of the Ahom army the Jayantia Raja left Gobha where he had stationed his troops and returned to his capital without causing further depredations. In May 1769, Kirtichandra hurried back to Rangpur on receiving intelligence of the king's illness. The subjugation of the Jayantia Raja was thus left incomplete.

The depredations of the Jayantia Raja were not confined to the borders of the neighbouring native territories. Sylhet had come under the Company in 1765 with the grant of the Dewany. There was no representative of the Company in Sylhet though it was an important district specially on account of its *chunam* or lime which formed its staple product, more than one hundred thousand maunds being sent down annually. The district was managed from Dacca, and for its distance from the headquarters it was impossible to pay the necessary attention to secure its revenue or maintain its peace. Taking advantage of the slackness of the Company's administration in Sylhet the hillmen in the neighbourhood raided the fertile plains of the district at the foot of the hills with impunity. The most troublesome of the marauding chiefs was the Raja of Jayantia. His estates were situated on the bank of the river Surma a free passage through which was essential to the Company's trade. The boats carrying goods to and from Dacca were obstructed by the Raja who exacted tolls and looted their contents to the endless harassment and annoyance of the merchants.

In October 1772, William Makepeace Thackeray, the grand father of the novelist, was appointed Collector of Sylhet. He set his heart upon chastising the Jayantia Raja which he thought would serve as an example to the other turbulent chiefs. He submitted his views to the Calcutta Council, but questions of finance weighed heavily with the Board and they hesitated to sanction a military expedition against Jayantia. Thackeray, however, found

49. *Tungkhungia Buranji*, ed. S. K. Bhuyan, published by Oxford University Press, 1933, p. 47.

a sympathetic supporter in his immediate superior Richard Barwell, Chief of the Dacca Council. In February 1774 Barwell, without obtaining the sanction of the Board, deputed Ensign Leake with 50 men to put himself at the head of the troops stationed at Sylhet. The command of the Jayantia expedition was taken over by Thackeray's friend Captain Edward Elliker of the 7th Battalion of Sepoys, and Ensign Leake remained on duty at Sylhet.

On March 24, Captain Elliker took possession of Rajagunje, six miles from Jayantiapur. The Raja amused his enemies for some days with promises to come to terms, and threw up in the meantime an entrenchment extending for nearly half a mile and manned very closely by the hillmen. On the 29th March, the troops of the Company were fired at by the Jayantias, but the sepoys under Captain Elliker met the charge with great steadiness. The hillmen after having spent a few rounds were driven back. The Raja and his adherents fled into the hills and Captain Elliker took possession of the capital.

After deliberating for over two months as to the final disposition of the Jayantia territory the Calcutta Council decided to restore the Raja to his country on terms advantageous to the Company. He was to pay 15,000 rupees as compensation for the cost of the expedition, and to enter into an agreement to desist from offering any obstruction in the navigation of the Surma river. On June 12 Captain Elliker returned with his detachment to Sylhet.[50]

Assam's precautions against Company's attack: In the meantime reports of all descriptions had poured into the Assam court about the activities of the Company's troops in Jayantia and the neighbouring hills and they continued even after the withdrawal of Capt. Elliker's force from that territory. The Raja of Jayantia sent two deputations to Assam, one under Dhanrai Kataki and the other under Bathan Sirdar. Dhanrai related the discomfiture of his master at the hands of the Company's troops resulting in his utter destitution and poverty which compelled him "to eat his meal from only one bell-metal plate." Dhanrai also reported that the Raja was intending to come to Assam for shelter. Bathan Sirdar expatiated on the mutinous conduct of the Gobha Raja who had dealt a sword-cut on the neck of his liegelord the Jayantia Raja, pillaged a number of Jayantia villages wherefrom he had exacted a booty consisting of 3,000 rupees, 360 maunds of cotton,

50. F. B. Bradley-Birt, *'Sylhet' Thackeray*, 1911, pp. 154-172; *Sylhet District Records*, Vol. I, Nos. 11-25, pp. 10-20.

and 360 *daos* or short-swords. After having committed these atrocities the Gobha Raja had taken shelter in Assam, and the Jayantia Raja believed that the refractory chief had been secretly instigated by the Assamese. Bathan Sirdar now demanded on behalf of his master the extradition of the Gobha Rajá and the restoration of the plundered property. King Lakshmi Singha and his ministers resolved to send away the Gobha Raja from Assam as it was feared that "his retention would lead to complications with Jayantia."[51]

The Assam king sent several parties of spies to ascertain the true facts regarding the affairs of Jayantia. Mayaram Bairagi who had proceeded through Cachar was imprisoned by its ruler for not possessing the necessary credentials. The Kachari Raja, however, sent back a camp-follower of Mayaram to tell the Assam king that he would no longer be able to restrain the Raja of Manipur from carrying out his hostile designs against Assam. The messenger came and reported that a united force of Kacharis, Jayantias, Manipuris and Europeans, encamped at Demera, was contemplating to invade Assam. The king deputed Manmatha Tekela Bara and Bikina Kataki to the Kachari Raja to warn him of the consequences of disloyalty to the Ahom government. The Raja subsequently released Mayaram Bairagi who came and reported that Manipuri troops had been engaged in army manoeuvres in Cachar riding on ponies with sword and shield in their hands.

Another messenger conveyed the news that the Manipuris had strengthened their friendship with the Company by presenting a princess to one of the Europeans and by aiding the latter in subjugating the Jayantias.[52] The king despatched four swift couriers to investigate the situation on the Jayantia frontier and return within eight or ten days. They came back and confirmed the reports already received. The rumours alleging hostile intentions of the Company on Assam were evidently unfounded. The Company was not inclined to enter into hostilities with an independent kingdom like Assam which had offered no provocation of any sort whatsoever. The Jayantia expedition was mainly due to the initiative of Barwell and Thackeray. It is possible that the continued stay of Capt. Elliker's detachment in Jayantia from

51. This and the paragraphs following have been based on the Ms. Assamese chronicle of Lakshmi Singha's reign.

52. The Assamese chronicle says that this Manipuri princess was "the one who had been previously brought to Assam", referring possibly to Kuranganayani who had been presented by her father Raja Jai Singha to Rajeswar Singha, king of Assam, 1751-69.

March to June 1774, attended probably by the diversion of a small party to Cachar had originated vague rumours amongst the hillmen who were not aware of the policy nor of the actual state of affairs of the East India Company.

But the vigilant spirit of the Assam government, which had but recently emerged from the catastrophe of the Moamaria usurpation, would not permit it to remain inactive in the face of such wide-spread rumours, nor would it like to precipitate hostilities with the Company if such could be avoided by diplomatic negotiations. In September 1774, the Assam king deputed two envoys to Warren Hastings with friendly letters and presents consisting of two *barkapors* or double sheets, two elephant tusks, two ivory fans, one *satranj* and one box. The precise tenor of the Assam king's message to Warren Hastings and the results of the deputation are not known.

During the period from the commencement of the Jayantia expedition in March 1774 to the despatch of Warren Hastings's letter of April 22, 1777, requesting payment of Lear's dues, the Assam government followed the affairs of the Company with greater interest and concern. It is recorded that in 1775 a pair of ominous birds had perched on the palace at the ancient Assamese capital Gargaon and had screeched at night which was supposed to forebode disasters. After this it is chronicled that "the Barasaheb of the Firingis died as well as other eminent personages." The first event must have referred to the death of Lord Clive on November 22, 1774, which was heard in India during the course of 1775, as the term "Barasaheb of the Firingis" was uniformly applied by the Assamese to the head of the Company's administration in India.

An agent of the Governor-General had arrived at the Ahom court on March 31, 1777. On May 22, 1777, he was received by the Choladhara Phukan, the foreign minister. Some Kacharis used to live at the Assam capital forming part of the quota of retainers annually supplied by the Kachari Raja according to the terms of his engagement. The agent of the Governor-General confined them for not having paid courtesies to him. He said, "We have subjugated Jayantia and Cachar. These Kacharis do not come and meet me even when they know I am here! I shall see who can protect them." The Assam government remonstrated with the agent for his highhandedness, and the captives were set at liberty. The agent in a fit of resentment decided to leave the capital on June 1, 1777, and it was with great difficulty that he could be persuaded to remain.

On June 16, 1777, the Company's agent was received by the king at Rangnath temple in the vicinity of the palace at Rangpur. A large pavilion was erected for the occasion. At about two o'clock in the afternoon King Lakshmi Singha took his seat in the assembly attended by his ministers and nobles. The ceremony commenced with musical recital to the accompaniment of *pasouj* or long drums. The envoy had been waiting at the post near the Jaisagar tank, whereto he had been led from Mataimara and then through Namdang by boat. He was now taken to the presence of the king to whom he was introduced by the Choladhara Phukan. The Majumdar Barua, the king's private secretary, then put the usual question to the agent,—"Was the Barasaheb of the Calcutta Company in the enjoyment of good health at the time of your departure, offering protection to cows and Brahmans, virtuous and religious people ?" To this the agent replied,—"He was well at the time of our departure from Calcutta. We do not know what has happened meanwhile." The Governor-General's letter written in the Persian language was then read, after which flowers and sandal-paste were given to the agent. He was then permitted to leave the assembly.

The Jayantia rumours and the threats of the European merchants produced consternation in the Assam camp. It was a period of great anxiety for the Assam government. Sporadic revolts and conspiracies were the order of the day. Many of the princes allied themselves with the malcontents and attempted to subvert the authority of the Ahom monarch. The whole resources of the government were employed in stemming the growing disorders in the country.

The revolt of the Kalita Phukan added to the anxieties of the Assam government. He was originally a retainer of the Bargohain, but was raised to the office of Choladhara Phukan in recognition of his services in the extirpation of the Moamaria leaders which had led to the restoration of Lakshmi Singha to the Ahom throne. Kekeru Hazarika—for that was the name of the Kalita Phukan—was a Kalita, a caste Hindu ; and being practically the first Hindu to be appointed a Phukan was known as the Kalita Phukan.[53] He was a descendant of the Bhuyans, the

53. The earlier example was Manthir Bharali Barua of the Bezdoloi family, who was appointed Parvatia Phukan and despatched to Gauhati to oppose Mir Jumla's forces there in 1662. He is the famous "Bijdili Phukan" of the Persian chronicles dealing with Mir Jumla's invasion. The appointment was more or less an emergency measure.

pre-Ahom rulers of a part of Eastern Assam. During the period immediately following the restoration of Lakshmi Singha the Kalita Phukan became all-powerful in the state. He enjoyed the confidence of the monarch, lived in princely splendour and caused the dismissal and execution of Ahom officers for trifling offences. The Ahom nobles became jealous of the growing power of the Kalita Phukan and they feared that their Hindu colleague was secretly trying to revive the ascendancy of the Bhuyans in Assam. They poisoned the ears of the king against the Kalita Phukan and procured his dismissal from office and banishment to Tamulbari in the north-east confines of Assam. Secluded from official vigilance the Kalita Phukan collected a large number of followers, equipped them with arms, and was joined by the disaffected sons of Baruas and Phukans. He lived at Tamulbari defying the authority of the government, and it was believed his motive was to carve out an independent state for himself centering round the capital of Mriganka, an ancient king of Eastern Assam.

To add to these fears it was rumoured that a Padshahzada or Mogul prince, who had arrived at Dacca, was contemplating to march towards Assam at the head of a force consisting of 400 native sepoys and 200 European soldiers.

The Assam government took timely precautions to counteract any eventual hostility with the foreign powers. In May 1774 a capable officer named Lahan was appointed Barphukan to conduct the external relations of the government from his headquarters at Gauhati. This officer, before setting out for Gauhati, had asked the king to put him at the head of an expedition against the Kalita Phukan. The king refused the Barphukan's gallant request saying,—"I have appointed the Barphukan to Gauhati to meet any situation arising from our relations with the foreigners, and I cannot despatch him against the man called Kalita who is after all a person of no great consequence." The Barphukan was sent *posthaste* to join his new duties at Gauhati.

The office of the Duaria Barua who regulated the trade between Assam and Bengal was a very responsible one, as any indiscretion on his part, specially at that juncture, might lead to serious misunderstanding between the two governments. A very astute and capable man was appointed for that purpose in the person of Krishnaram of the Namlagowa family, and he was sent down to the Assam Choky with twelve Bairagis or customs officials.

As all conflicts with foreign invaders were decided mainly at Gauhati, the fortifications in that place were now repaired and the garrison strengthened. Two officers, Lahang Dolakasharia

Bara and Rangmal Barneog, were deputed from the capital to examine the military equipments at Gauhati and prepare an inventory of the forts and chokies there. Sometime later another batch of officers were despatched from the metropolis entrusted with the same mission.

During this period of anxiety the king instituted a rigorous watch in the capital. All the high officials including the Gohains, the Phukans and the Baruas were employed in guarding the palaces, fortifications and military stores of Rangpur. In addition to these precautions the Assam government deputed an ambassador, named Kalia Chaudhuri, to Bhutan with messages of friendship, avowedly in view of the menace from the western frontier.

Chapter IV

KILLICAN'S MONOPOLY OF THE ASSAM TRADE

David Killican, merchant and Bengal Civil Servant: In February 1777 Baillie was appointed Writer in the Bengal establishment. Two years later he left Goalpara to join his appointment as Assistant to the Collector of Sarkar Saran. His commercial concerns at Goalpara continued to be managed by his Bengali agent. Baillie did not, however, abandon his old idea of engaging the Company in the Assam trade to its benefit as well as to his own, for soon after we find him working out a plan through a merchant and Bengal Civil Servant who wielded considerable influence in the commercial and official circles in Calcutta.

Baillie's business colleague on this occasion was David Killican who figures prominently in the records of the administration of Lord Clive and of Warren Hastings. In 1766 Killican, along with Baillie, had been recommended to the Court of Directors for appointment as Factors as a compensation for their withdrawal from the inland trade in accordance with the orders of the Company.[1]

During the years 1765 to 1769 Killican served as Alderman of the Mayor's Court in Calcutta, and twice as Mayor.[2] The proceedings of the Court of this period have attained considerable publicity through the propaganda to discredit the Company's administration in Bengal carried on in India and in England by William Bolts, merchant and sometime Bengal Civil Servant. Killican, with other judges of the Mayor's court, had to share the attacks made by that unscrupulous Dutchman, the accuser of Governor Verelst and Raja Nobkissen. Bolts alleged that Killican was in the pay of the Raja and that his judgment in the trial of the Raja was vitiated by that circumstance.[3] On May 27, 1768, Killican served on the Grand Jury, with George Lear and Joseph Cator, in a General Quarter-Session of Oyer and Terminer with President Verelst and other members of the Council as justices.[4]

1. Clive to Court, Feb. 1, 1766, Select Committee's Fourth Report, App. 3, p. 473. Writers Petitions, 1770-74, Vol. 7, 1771, No. 2.
2. Committee of Secrecy Reports, 1772-73, App. 25 and App. 29.
3. Bolts, *Considerations on Indian Affairs*, Vol. III, App. F, pp. 504-5.
4. Bolts, *Considerations*, Vol. III, p. 485.

In February 1772 Killican's Gomostah Gunganaram Bose was accused of having seriously assaulted a molungi salt-maker for refusing to receive advances on account of Killican as he had received the same from another European salt merchant named Reed. Saun Bose, the Sikdar of the *perganah* where the dispute arose, was Killican's agent, and the business was carried on by his son Gunganaram Bose. As Saun Bose was vested with executive authority in the district his son practised acts of oppression with impunity. This dispute between Killican and Reed, and the oppression of the molungi salt-maker have been cited to prove the continuance of the evils which the Court of Directors had wanted to remove by throwing open the inland trade to natives only.[5]

In 1771 Killican applied to the Court of Directors, through his brother Samuel Blackwell, for appointment as Factor, on the strength of his experience of the trade in India, his services as Mayor in Calcutta, and Lord Clive's recommendation of 1766.[6] On April 7, 1773, Killican was appointed by the Court of Directors as Factor in the Bengal establishment.[7] In 1774 Killican succeeded Cotes as Sub-Export Warehouse Keeper under the Board of Trade.[8] The Court in their despatch of March 19, 1778, removed the bar to Killican's rising in Company's service in recognition of "the very satisfactory manner in which he had behaved himself." The Court directed the Bengal Government to appoint Killican to the rank of youngest Factor on the establishment, "and that he do rise to superior stations in the usual manner as vacancies shall happen in the service."[9]

Like other servants of the Company Killican was engaged in numerous trading concerns, but chiefly as a salt contractor. On March 16, 1776, Richard Barwell reported to one Lyde Browne about Killican's refusal to pay bills. Another report was transmitted to John Graham on March 24 about "Killican's strange unaccountable conduct" touching Graham's demand on Nobkissen, in spite of the fact that Barwell was himself one of the Attorneys of Graham. Killican, in partnership with another merchant named Burn, had taken a salt contract in the name of an Indian merchant

5. Miss M. E. Monckton Jones, *Warren Hastings in Bengal*, p. 228 ; Beng. Pub. Cons., Feb. 17, 1772, quoted by Miss Jones on pp. 246-7.

6. Writers Petitions, 1770-74, Vol. 7, 1771, No. 2.

7. Personal Records, Vol. 14, p. 475 ; Court's Letter to Bengal, April 7, 1773, para 17. Killican's arrival date has been mentioned as Oct. 18, 1773. Bengal Civilians, J-L, p. 1009.

8. Bengal Civilians, J-L, p. 1009.

9. Court's Letter to Bengal, March 19, 1778.

Ramtanu Dutt. Killican was also in charge of Thomas Rumbold's concerns in Bengal.[10]

In 1782 Killican was appointed Sub-Treasurer to the Board of Trade and Assistant to Export Warehouse.[11] In 1783 he was promoted to the rank of a Junior Merchant, holding the same offices.[12] The *Calcutta Gazette* of April 15, 1784, advertised for sale Killican's "large and beautiful garden on the road to Dumduma with 50 bighas of land."[13] In 1785 Killican was appointed member of the Police Commission and Head Assistant to Export Warehouse.[14] Killican died at Calcutta on October 25, 1785.[15]

Killican's proposal regarding Assam trade: In addition to his concerns in Bengal, Killican was engaged in the Assam trade for several years having conducted it mainly through his agent Daniel Raush. From the experience he had of that trade he thought it would be advantageous to the Company as well as to himself if he could conduct it as an exclusive privilege paying a fixed rent to Government. The eagerness with which merchants of all nationalities, French and Dutch included, had pursued the Assam trade showed that there were possibilities of profit in it. But the unscrupulous methods adopted by many merchants to oust their rivals from the field, leading to violence, with no courts in the neighbourhood to settle the disputes made the prospects of gain rather gloomy and uncertain. As the East India Company was primarily a trading corporation it was within its province to place the Assam trade under its direct control and authority.

On June 9, 1780, Killican submitted proposals to the Government of Bengal for the future regulation of the Assam trade.[16] He showed that the trade had formerly been beneficial to Bengal, and that its ruin was due to the want of any regulation in carrying it on. As the trade was in its nature limited, said Killican, it was properly an object for the Company either to engage in it directly themselves or farm the privilege to derive a revenue from it. He cited the example of the Assam government which farmed the privilege of Bengal trade to one single individual, the Duaria Barua.

10. Barwell's Letters, *Bengal: Past and Present,* Vol. XIII, p. 294; Vol. XIV, p. 224, p. 233.

11. Bengal Civilians, J-L, p. 1009.

12. *Ibid.*

13. Seton-Karr, *Selections from Calcutta Gazette,* Vol. I, p. 39.

14. *Rungpore Dist. Records,* Vol. II, p. 49-*n.*

15. Bengal Civilians, J-L, p. 1009.

16. Killican to Hastings, June 9, Beng. Rev. Cons., June 13, 1780.

Killican then set forth his proposal to pay to the Company 50,000 arcot rupees per year for the exclusive privilege of the trade to Assam for four years on condition that a Company's servant should be appointed to reside on the borders who would receive the revenue from the farmer, protect him in the exercise of his privilege, preserve peace and order in the locality, maintain a good understanding with the people of Assam, and conduct enquiries by which a door might be opened to extend the trade in the articles of the Company's exports from Europe. Killican pointed out in this connection that a proposal to increase the exportation of the Company's staple articles had been submitted to the Court of Directors some years ago by Hugh Baillie and that it was recommended by the Court to the Calcutta Council.

In the event of the acceptance of his proposal Killican asked the Government to prohibit salt or any other goods from being carried beyond Rangamati, and to give orders to the Company's servants to prevent any goods being carried clandestinely. About the persons who were then engaged in the Assam trade, Killican suggested that they should be allowed to settle their concerns by January 1781, and that after that period they should be recalled and not permitted to interfere in the Assam trade.

The object of his proposal, Killican stated, was to recover a ruined trade, to secure to the Company some revenue where it received none, to promote the sale of the productions of its own provinces, and to procure articles in return necessary for the foreign trade of Bengal which produced specie.

Killican granted exclusive privilege of the Assam trade: Killican's proposal was discussed by the Board in their meeting of June 13, 1780. They were of opinion that the trade of Assam which had for a long time been subject to a monopoly in the hands of a few unauthorised adventurers, could be conducted with advantage and credit to the Government and quiet to the neighbouring inhabitants by a regulation like the one proposed by Killican. The Board admitted that the proposal would place the Assam trade under the immediate control of the Bengal Government. An additional circumstance in favour of the proposal was the revenue to be derived from farming the exclusive privilege.

The Board therefore accepted the terms of the offer made by Killican. They appointed Hugh Baillie as Resident at Goalpara to regulate the trade and receive the revenue. The Resident's allowances were to be adjusted with the farmer.

On that very day the Board issued an advertisement announcing the grant of the exclusive privilege of trading to Assam to

Killican. As proposed by the farmer all persons engaged in the Assam trade were asked to close their concerns by January 1781. It was also notified that a Choky would be established at Rangamati to prevent the exportation of salt or any other goods to Assam except by the farmer. Orders were accordingly sent to George Bogle, Collector of Rungpore, to place a Choky at Rangamati and stop all boats not belonging to Killican. The Collector was also asked to assist the farmer with his influence and authority. The Board gave orders for the publication of the advertisement at Chilmari, Rungpore, Jugighopa, Goalpara and the Assam Choky. Information was also sent to the Chiefs of the Provincial Councils at Dacca, Chittagong and Murshidabad.

Hastings's letter to the Assam Raja: In order to obtain the co-operation of the Assam government in carrying out the object of the grant, Warren Hastings wrote a letter to Lakshmi Singha, king of Assam, referring briefly to the circumstances which led the Company to take the trade of Bengal and Assam into its hands, the chief reason assigned being the necessity to adopt some means to deal with the disputes amongst the Europeans settled at Goalpara. The appointment of Hugh Baillie as Public Resident at Goalpara was described as being calculated to effectually secure the peace of the country and the welfare of all parties. The Governor-General assured the king of Assam that Baillie had received particular instructions to protect the Assamese traders from all freebooters and enemies so that commerce might be carried on for the mutual advantage of both kingdoms. The Assam king was requested to inform his subjects trading with Bengal of the new arrangement, and to see that the Company's Resident might have no cause to complain of any obstructions from the officers of the Assam government. Copies of Hastings's letter to the king of Assam were also sent to the Assamese officers concerned, *viz.* the Barbarua or the chief executive officer, the Choladhara Phukan or the minister of commerce and foreign affairs, the Barphukan or the viceroy of Gauhati, and the Duaria Barua or the superintendent of the Assam Choky.[17]

Government control of the Assam trade established: The establishment of the Company's authority and control over the Assam trade was now an accomplished fact. The readiness with

17. Hastings to Assam Raja, June 14, 1780, *Calendar of Persian Correspondence*, Vol. V, No. 1911, copy obtained from the Imperial Record Department, Calcutta in 1930. King Lakshmi Singha died on Dec. 13, 1780, when he was succeeded by his son Gaurinath Singha.

which the Governor-General and Council accepted the terms of Killican's offer and adopted measures to give effect to the same shows that they had unofficially made up their minds to do so before they deliberated on the scheme at the Council table. Killican submitted his proposal on June 9, and the Council accepted it four days later. Killican and Baillie must have spent several months in maturing their plan, and enlisting support in its behalf. Killican had not directly asked for the appointment of Baillie to the Residentship at Goalpara, yet the Board appointed him to that position which implies that Baillie's consent had been previously obtained. It was possibly in anticipation of this appointment that Baillie resigned his duties as Assistant to the Collector of Sarkar Saran in March 1780.[18] The accepatnce of Killican's terms without any modification or alteration leads one to surmise that he presented them in a form to which the members of the Council and their departmental advisers had already expressed their consent. Killican's negotiations with George Lear to purchase the latter's concerns at Goalpara were initiated in December 1779, and from the transactions that followed, we can infer that the proposal to acquire Lear's property had in view the removal of influential merchants from the field whose protest might operate aganist the granting of a monopoly. The Board's indifference to the losses that a monopoly would inflict upon the private merchants at Goalpara betrays their willingness—or rather anxiety—to help Killican at any cost.

Apart from the addition of new revenues and the possibility of preventing the disagreements among Goalpara merchants which the new arrangement was intended to achieve, the Board's action may be justified by the repeated recommendation of the Court of Directors to place the Assam trade on a proper footing, specially those communicated in their despatch of April 16, 1777, authorising the Bengal Government to adopt "any new system of commerce with Assam that may promise advantage to the Company."

There was also the urgent necessity to station a Company's officer at Goalpara to prevent the disputes among the merchants which had at that time assumed a very violent shape. The Collector of Rungpore had to issue warnings to the merchants concerned that they would be arrested and confined by the Naib of Rangamati if they attempted to forcibly take possession of the property of other people. The court at Rungpore was too far removed from Goalpara, and the Naib of Rangamati was not

18. Beng. Rev. Cons., March 24, 1780.

sufficiently powerful to redress the grievances of European merchants.[19]

The trade in salt, which was the chief commodity on which Killican and other merchants based their calculations of profit in the Assam trade, was always held as a monopoly under the native regime in the hands of merchants upon whom the Nawab wanted to confer a favour, as Clive had pointed out in 1767 while justifying the establishment of the Society of Trade.[20] This monopoly was exercised by Nawab Shaista Khan, Governor of Bengal, as we learn from an old Assamese chronicle,—" Shaista Khan used to import by ship salt, betel-nut and other articles, and sold them in Bengal on profitable terms. He also sold salt and betel-nut to the merchants and traders in the city of Dacca. The latter were thus debarred from making purchases and sales on their own account. The merchants and traders complained to the Padshah at Delhi regarding Shaista Khan's acts of injustice..... [During the governorship of Sultan Azamtara] there were emporiums of salt worth 152,000 rupees at several places on the bank of the Bangsha river, which Shaista Khan could not transport."[21]

It is a known fact that Warren Hastings attempted to place the Company's revenue from salt on a stable basis. In October 1772 the Calcutta Council decided that no salt was to be made except for the Company. In 1775 Hastings was able to record that the Company's revenue from salt amounted to £120,000, four times as much as they had ever before received except in the time of the Society of Trade.[22] In 1780 a Comptroller of Salt was appointed with an agent in each district, and a total prohibition was once more laid on all imports of salt. In 1781 the profits rose to £321,912, against an average annual profit of about £80,000 during the three years 1770, 1771 and 1772. In 1782 and 1783 they amounted to £655,646 and £603,076 respectively.[23] Hastings spoke with feeling about the success of his measures in increasing the revenues of Bengal from the business in salt 'gained

19. Bogle to Lear, Dow, Williams, Raush, MacCullum, and other merchants of Rangamati, June 17, 1780, *Rungpore District Records*, Vol. IV, pp. 45-6.

20. Clive to Committee of Treasury and Correspondence, Aug. 28, 1767, Select Committee's Fourth Report, App. 59, p. 528.

21. S. K. Bhuyan, *Annals of the Delhi Badshahate*, pub. in *Islamic Culture*, Hyderabad, Deccan, April 1934.

22. Bengal Sec. Cons., Range A, 27, p. 1246, quoted in Jones, *Warren Hastings in Bengal*, pp. 229-30.

23. Home Misc. Series, Vol. 92, salt, p. 28, quoted in Jones, *Warren Hastings in Bengal*, pp. 230-31.

by the silent operation of official arrangement.' "The plan for the management of the salt," wrote Hastings in 1786, "was of my formation.....An uncertain collection has been gradually improved into a permanent and increasing revenue; and as long as Mr. Vansittart, or some other person of qualifications equal to his, shall preside over the office, and be allowed to conduct it according to the rules of its institution, I may venture to assure the Company of an annual revenue of fifty lacks of rupees from this department."[24]

The grant of the exclusive privilege to David Killican can thus be regarded as an offshoot of the Court's anxiety to regulate the Assam trade to the advantage of the Company, and Warren Hastings's scheme to stabilise the revenues of Bengal, and place the trade in salt on a proper footing.

As regards Baillie, he now achieved practically all the objects on which he had set his heart since 1771. The Company now assumed control and direction of the Assam trade. It would be possible now to promote the sale of British staples in Assam. Baillie became the Company's Resident and Killican's agent at Goalpara where he would have opportunities to make full enquiries into the Assam trade. But his present position was different from what he had prayed for in 1776, *viz.* "the Company's agency for their sales in Assam."[25] He had now two masters to serve, the Government of Bengal as his employers, and David Killican as his principal, whose interests though not antagonistic, would tend at times to clash. Anyway, Baillie was now on trial; and his success or failure would prove whether his original proposals were sound and wisely calculated or whether they had emanated from "his bewildered imagination."

According to the terms of the Board's resolution of June 13 Killican had to furnish securities for the performance of his engagements. On July 11, two Bengal merchants and servants of the Company, Herbert Harris and John Fergusson, were offered and accepted as securities.[26]

24. Warren Hastings, *Memoirs Relative to the State of India,* London, 1786, pp. 126-27.

25. Baillie to Board of Trade, July 28, 1776.

26. Beng. Rev. Cons., July 11, 1780. Herbert Harris was Collector of Rungpore in 1773, Sheriff of Calcutta in 1781, Mint Master in 1785, Salt Agent at Chittagong and Bullooah in 1794. He died at Calcutta on Jan. 22, 1810 after serving the Company for 45 years.—*Bengal: Past and Present,* Vol. XXVIII, p. 219. John Fergusson was a salt merchant supplying Ganjam salt—Beng. Rev. Cons., Jan. 22, 1781; described as a 'person of character' by Barwell in his letter to Savage, 23-7-1776, *B: P and P.,* Vol. XIV, p. 241.

Formal deed of Killican's grant: On July 25 the formal deed conferring the grant to Killican was executed by Warren Hastings and Edward Wheler.[27] The deed was worded in the customary legal language of indentures. The exact text of Killican's offer as it had been submitted by him on June 9, was incorporated in the deed. The reason for accepting the proposal was stated to be the necessity for reviving the Assam trade by placing it under proper regulations for the "interest of the Company as of general and public utility and benefit." In consideration of the payment of 50,000 rupees per year the Board granted, ordained and appointed "that from time to time and at all times hereafter during the said term of four years from the first day of January now next ensuing, the whole and sole trade, trafficking and merchandising to and from Assam shall be used, exercised and engaged, and shall be ruled, ordered and governed by the said David Killican, his executors, administrators and assigns, subject nevertheless to such reasonable and legal control and direction concerning the same as they the said United Company by themselves or their Council in Calcutta, or by or through the means of their Servant or Agent for the time being Resident at Gualparah aforesaid shall think it necessary or proper to exercise at any time during such term of years as aforesaid." The Board therefore agreed to appoint and keep a servant of the Company at Goalpara during the above term of four years to receive the revenue, to give due discharge for the same, as well as to protect the farmer in the Assam trade as far as the same can or may be lawfully had and done." The exgrantee David Killican was enjoined to "manage, transact, exercise and carry on the same trade in a fair and honest manner to the Natives of Assam and all others with whom he may have occasion to deal or trade, and shall not be guilty of any extortions or oppression towards the same Natives or any other person whatsoever in virtue of these presents or of the Grant hereby made or of anything herein contained." The deed further provided that in the event of any molestation or disturbance met by the farmer in carrying on his trade, which could be prevented by the Company, he would be entitled to withhold payment of the rent from the time of such interruption. It was also declared in the deed that David Killican had put his hand and seal in one part of the

27. The deed was executed in the meeting of the Council on July 25, 1780. Philip Francis was not present, and the Council ordered that the deed was to be presented to Francis for execution.—Beng. Rev. Cons., July 25, 1780. Barwell had left India in March 1780.

Present, and Warren Hastings, Governor-General, Philip Francis and Edward Wheler, Councillors of the Presidency of Fort William 'or the major part of them' had signed their names and put the common seal of the United Company to the other part.[28]

After having obtained the grant Killican applied for the posting of a company of sepoys to Goalpara to protect the Assam trade and to guard the Chokies and the factory, and undertook to bear the expenses. The Board ordered a company of sepoys from Dacca. On September 12 the Commander-in-Chief was requested to nominate an officer to the command of the company posted to Goalpara.[29]

Though the monopoly was to come into effect from January 1, 1781, Killican took steps to prevent the exportation of goods to Assam from after the date of the grant. The Collector of Government Customs at Calcutta, not having received official notice of the grant, had entertained applications made to him for *rawannahs* or permits to carry goods into Assam. Killican asked the Board to issue notices to the Collectors of Customs at Murshidabad, Dacca, Patna and Calcutta to stop the granting of *rawannahs* for Assam except to the farmer. In the meantime the Collector of Rungpore had established a Choky at Rangamati to prevent boats going into Assam.[30] The merchants engaged in the Assam trade were informed of the grant and asked to take due notice of the orders for closing their concerns.[31]

Lear's protest and Killican's reply: The consternation produced among the merchants of Goalpara and Jugighopa by the grant of the exclusive privilege of trade to Killican and the consequent orders for their withdrawal can be well imagined. Not knowing that the Assam trade would at any time be taken up by the Company they had deeply entered into it, built factories and *golahs*, contracted with the Assam merchants to sell Bengal goods and buy Assam products or had purchased them for disposal in future, had advanced goods and money and were expecting re-

28. It is not known whether Francis attached his signature to the deed afterwards. The proceedings contain at the end the signatures of Hastings and Wheler with a large blank space between the two, possibly left for the signature of Francis.

29. Beng. Rev. Cons., Aug. 4, and Sept. 12, 1780.

30. *Ibid.*, Sept. 12, 1780.

31. *Ibid.*, Sept. 15, 1780. The merchants to whom notice was served were Lear, Dow, Raush, Williams, Wheatland, MacCullum, Bigger, 'and other gentlemen merchants of Rangamati,'—Bogle to the above merchants, *Rungpore District Records*, Vol. IV, No. 61, p. 47.

turns and repayment. For them to retire from their respective stations with the goods undisposed of, balances unsettled and engagements unfulfilled, would certainly mean their utter ruination. The period of six months granted to them for winding up their concerns was obviously too short for such a purpose.

The man who was most adversely affected by the monopoly was George Lear. Engaged in the Assam trade since 1769 he had built *golahs* and warehouses etc. at Goalpara and Dacca to the amount of over 40,000 rupees. He had equitable outstanding claims upon the Assamese people coming upto 80,000 rupees. He had contracted with the Assamese to furnish them within 34 months with goods to the amount of three lakhs of rupees under stipulations and penalties for a breach of which they could sue him in the Supreme Court of Judicature. He had at the same time entered into a contract with several Bengal merchants to receive goods from them for being delivered to the Assamese and to supply them with imports from Assam. He had collected in his *golahs* Bengal goods to the value of 164,000 rupees, which he did not dare to deliver to the Assamese, for in view of the monopoly to be exercised by the farmer he could not entertain the least chance of recovering his demands. On the other hand, if he did not deliver Bengal goods to the Assamese he would make himself liable to penalties for a breach of contract.

On July 6, 1780, Lear submitted a memorial to the Board protesting against the grant. He described the losses and penalties he would be subjected to if he had to close his concerns at Goalpara after a period of six months. "Thus, Gentlemen," wrote Lear, "you see my ruin is complete, if I am compelled to put a stop to trade, and remove myself within the very short time allowed—I say very short time, because it is notorious to you and every man conversant in the trade of this place that returns are never made within the compass of 24 months, and that we risk our property upon the parole of the Assamese; and as we have no hold whatever upon them, should they once conceive our own rulers have withdrawn their protection from us, it cannot be expected they will ever perform their engagements. In short, Gentlemen, my distress is so complicated I can scarcely describe it; but my ruin will be certain and complete if the farm holds, or if a period of less than three years is allowed me to wind up my concerns."[32]

32. Lear to Hastings, July 6, Beng. Rev. Cons., Sept. 15, 1780,

Lear expected that when the Board were apprised of his hardships they would revoke the grant made to Killican. If again they adhered to their opinion that the trade should be pursued for the Company he asked the Board to provide some mode for the recovery of his fortune which was then chiefly in the hands of the Assamese, for reimbursing him for his factory and *golahs* and for his stock in hand, and also for guarding him against any legal consequences for a breach of contract on his part with the Assamese or the Bengal merchants. He concluded by saying that no less a period than three years would be necessary to enable him "to gather together some part of his scattered fortunes."

Lear's petition was forwarded to the Board by John Shakespeare, Chief of the Council at Dacca. Shakespeare recommended that some expedient might be found to grant the petitioner some relief in consideration of "his character, his exemplary good behaviour during a very long residence in the country, and his advanced time of life."[33]

Killican's reply to Lear's petition was submitted to the Board on September 29, 1780. Killican started by characterising Lear's statements as misrepresentations, and he prayed for time to lay before the Board 'a true and distinct account' of the manner in which the Assam trade had always been carried on. He, however, submitted some general observations to contradict the assertions of Lear. There could not be any balances in the Assam trade, stated Killican, as the Duaria Barua maintained a stock of Assam goods which he bartered for Bengal goods. If Lear had any balances, continued Killican, they were of many years standing of which he had no hope of repayment. Killican assumed that those balances had not arisen from Lear's intercourse with the Assamese who came to the Choky to receive Bengal goods, but from advances made to the hillmen for timbers.

Killican then proceeded to refute Lear's statement about contracts with the Assamese to furnish them with Bengal goods in 34 months. These contracts, alleged Killican, were always made with the Duaria Barua at the end of one year for the next. As a new Barua never respected the engagements entered into by his predecessor contracts had to be freshly made with the Barua when he came into office. Killican asserted that a new Barua had been recently sent to the Assam Choky by the Assam king so that Lear could not possibly make any engagement with him.

33. Shakespeare to Hastings, Aug. 15, Beng. Rev. Cons., Sept. 15, 1780.

About the goods lying in Lear's *golahs* said to value 164,000 rupees, Killican stated that from information supplied to him by Lear's Sarkar he had learnt that the goods consisted of 27,000 maunds of salt when the trade opened last year, and that the stock would be sold off by the end of December.

To Lear's statement, supported by Shakespeare, that his concerns could not be closed before three years Killican only replied that "it could not have a place in their letters had they really had any knowledge of the Assam trade." Killican then tried to show that Lear's engagements at Goalpara were far from being extensive. In December 1779 Killican had offered to purchase Lear's business. In his reply of January 19, 1780, Lear expressed his intention of returning to England and asked Killican to become the purchaser of his "small concerns." "I flatter myself," said Killican, "the Board will be sensible this requires no comment." About Lear's valuation of his house and buildings at 40,000 rupees Killican simply said that Baillie had assured him they might be worth ten or twelve thousand.

The whole tenor of Killican's first reply consisted of general contradictions based on information received from the persons interested in the promotion of his business at Goalpara—Lear's Sarkar who had proposed to accept or had already accepted service with Killican and Baillie who was Killican's agent and at the same time his official protector. Killican himself realised the insufficiency of his first rejoinder as he promised to give afterwards a fuller reply to Lear's letter. The Board agreed to wait for Killican's further remarks and proofs before any reply was transmitted to the Provincial Council at Dacca.[34]

Killican submitted to the Board his second and detailed reply on December 21, 1780, after an interval of about three months from the first.[35] The reply was based, as Killican himself avowed, on particulars supplied to him by Baillie about the state of Lear's concerns at Goalpara. He stated on Baillie's authority that Lear's factory was not worth more than one-third of the value specified by the owner. About the equitable outstanding claims to the amount of 80,000 which, as Lear had alleged, were due to him from Assamese merchants, Killican stated that the king of Assam had paid the debt between 60 to 70 thousand rupees to the European whom Lear had sent into that country to find out the debtor. The king of Assam, asserted Killican, then received from Lear an

34. Killican to Hastings, Sept. 29, Beng. Rev. Cons., Sept. 29, 1780, No. 698.
35. Killican to Hastings, Dec. 21, Beng. Rev. Cons., Dec. 29, 1780, No. 828.

acquittance in full of all demands which was in possession of the Barua at the Assam Choky.

Killican then pointed out that there was no reason why Lear should require three years to fulfil his contracts or he should complain of the time allowed to him, as the only contracts he had were with two merchants of Rungpore who had supplied him with Bengal goods which could be easily exchanged for Assam goods as they were always ready at the Choky. Killican then affirmed that he could add many other remarks but that he was unwilling to take up more of the Board's time. "I hope," said he, "from what I have already observed they [Board] are satisfied that Mr. Lear's representation is not well founded."

Killican concluded by informing the Board that he had made proposals to Lear to purchase his factory and the goods he might have remaining at Goalpara and to settle with him for the just balances or claims which he might have upon Assam. Killican's readiness to come to terms with Lear showed his moral conviction that the complainant's grievances were genuine, however vehemently the monopolist might characterise them as "unfounded" and as "misrepresentations."

The two replies of Killican, dated September 29 and December 21, were sent to Lear who had then been at Calcutta under the orders of the Board.

Lear's reply which was considered by the Board on January 23, 1781, was reasoned and forceful and full of sarcasms and invectives. The letter running to twenty folios is extremely valuable as a contemporary document illustrating some important phases of the Assam-Bengal trade relations of the last quarter of the eighteenth century.[36]

Lear justly indignant at Killican's representation of his statements as unfounded thought it incumbent upon him, "in vindication of his character," to authenticate every fact which had been called in question. The main issues raised in the controversy were;—balances incurred in the Assam trade, tenure of contracts with the Duaria Barua, unsold goods at Lear's *golah,* Killican's proposal to buy Lear's Goalpara concerns, value of Lear's houses and buildings, Lear's claims on the Assamese, Lear's contracts with Bengal merchants, sepoys stationed in Lear's ground, seduction of Lear's Sarkar and European agent, state of Lear's finances, and Lear's proposal for relief and accommodation.

36. Lear to Hastings, undated, Beng. Rev. Cons., Jan. 23, 1781.

To Killican's assertion that balances never arose in the Assam trade, Lear replied that they were always incurred in the same manner as in other places. The Duaria Barua received Bengal goods at the Choky for which he agreed to make returns at some future period. In November 1780 the balance of the Barua's account in Lear's favour was upwards of 10,000 rupees. Killican had himself admitted that Lear had sent a European to Assam to recover balances and find out the debtor, and that the Raja of Assam had paid the debt to the amount of 60 to 70 thousand rupees.

About the contracts made with the Assamese Lear reaffirmed that the period of such engagements or of the duration of the office of the Duaria Barua was not limited to one year, that he had a contract with the Barua for six annas or six-sixteenth of the whole trade for three years from the date of the agreement. Then said Lear,—"Hurrydeb with whom I contracted is now, was then and has been Buruah for more than two years."

Lear in his letter to the Board of July 6, 1780, had valued his goods remaining at the golah at 164,000 rupees. Killican in his reply of September 9, 1780, had estimated the value of Lear's stock at 108,000 rupees. Lear explained the difference as being due to the inclusion in his estimate of goods which he had ordered his Sarkar to purchase, and to the transfer by that Sarkar of a part of the newly purchased goods to some other account. In December 1780 Lear had 84,000 rupees in goods remaining unsold, though Killican had predicted that all the goods would be disposed of by that time.

About the proposal to buy the "small concerns" of Lear he admitted that in compliance with Killican's request he had balanced his books, and had sent in April 1780 the particulars through Cator. Baillie gave answer to Cator that Killican did not want to buy Lear's concerns. The purchase money that Lear had demanded for his concerns amounted to rupees 423,995 which Killican must have known at the time he addressed the Board. The term "small concerns", said Lear, was a relative one. "It is true", Lear pointed out, "that everything is large or small by comparison only; and though I might suppose that what appeared to me considerable might yet appear small to a gentleman of so much more extensive dealings than my own, and express myself accordingly; yet, to borrow Mr. Killican's words, I flatter myself the Hon'ble Board will be sensible this requires no comment."

The next remark of Lear related to Killican's undervaluation of his house and buildings, which were differently estimated on the authority of Baillie, first at ten or twelve thousand, and then at one-third of rupees 40,000. Lear's Dacca house had cost him rupees 25,558 and his Goalpara house and godowns 21,742. Lear added that the cost was out of the question, and that if he was permitted to enjoy undisturbed possession together with the privileges his "house alone at Goalpara, the place of all my [Lear's] commercial engagements is of much greater value to me [Lear] than 40,000."

To Killican's assertion that Lear had no outstanding claims upon the Assamese as the king of Assam had paid the debt between 60 and 70 thousand rupees to the European agent in 1778, and had received an acquittance in full of all demands, he pointed out that even if Killican's statement had been correct, the claims might arise from transactions between 1778 and July 1780. "Does he [Killican] suppose", asked Lear, "that I have had, no dealings in the intermediate time with the people of Assam?" Lear then explained how the claims mentioned as 80,000 in his letter of July 6 had arisen. The major part of the sum was not paid by the king of Assam, but advanced by Lear's own Gomostah to the Barua for that purpose on his promise that he would see the Gomostah reimbursed. The sum advanced by the Gomostah was included in the 80,000.

To Killican's statement that Lear's contracts were no more than a debt to two gentlemen at Rungpore who had furnished him with goods for Assam, he replied that he had received information from one of the contractors that by not complying with the conditions of his agreement he had incurred the penalty of 10,000 rupees.

Lear then adverted to the humiliation he had been subjected to by the posting of a Choky of sepoys in his own grounds at Panchratan under the orders of Baillie in addition to the one at Rangamati on the opposite side of the river. As a consequence Lear was greatly reduced in the estimation of the Assamese, and it operated to his disadvantage with his own people by lessening that confidence which they ought to place in him as their immediate master and protector.

Lear's discomfiture had not ceased there. His European agent and his Sarkar had both left his service. The European had been in his employ for ten years. The Sarkar whom Lear had appointed two years ago on the recommendation of Baillie had engaged himself in the service of Killican. "And from these," said Lear, "he [Killican] acquires—with what propriety I shall not enquire—that intelligence of all my concerns public and private."

About the sum which he required of Killican for making over his concerns in trade, outstanding balances and buildings, Lear said that the amount 423,995 rupees might look considerable, but the portion that would remain to his share after discharging his debts would be very small. Lear regretted that his enemies had spread a report that he was in easy circumstances with the object of withholding any relief from Government he would be entitled to.

Lastly, Lear requested the Board for permission to continue at Goalpara till he completed the remainder of his contracts, agreeing to pay any tax or duty that the Board might think proper to impose upon the Assam trade. He concluded his rejoinder by asking for the removal of the sepoys from his premises as his "credit and property much suffer while they are allowed to continue thereon."

From an examination of the issues involved in the replies and the counter-reply it appears that Lear's representation leaned more on the side of truth and justice than that of Killican. Balances did occur in the Assam trade as in similar concerns elsewhere. As we have seen Warren Hastings had to ask the Assam king in 1778 to exercise his influence in obtaining payment of the balances due to Lear for goods purchased in 1769. The Assam government had examined the papers and admitted the debt. It was also admitted by Killican in both his replies. In stipulating to purchase Lear's concerns he had promised to settle Lear's "just balances or claims upon Assam." After trading in Assam for two years under the terms of the exclusive privilege Killican discovered that his outstanding balances had amounted to a lakh of rupees. In the beginning of 1783 he had rupees 213,805 in goods remaining at the *golah*, consisting of rupees 184,000 in salt, and 29,804 in Assam products, while the balances due from the Assam Barua amounted to rupees 21,670, and from other merchants for Calcutta goods to rupees 74,681.[37]

About the duration of the period of contracts we have no independent evidence to go by except Lear's own statement that he had engaged with Harideb Duaria Barua for three years. But the difficulties of transport, the necessity of collecting the Assam products, *viz.* muga-dhutis, munjit and stick lac for which the Bengal goods were received as returns, rendered year-to-year trade a matter of considerable uncertainty, and merchants on both sides were naturally tempted to spread their engagements over a longer period. The incumbents who held the office of Duaria Barua enjoyed the same at the pleasure of the king. Krishnaram held that office from 1774 to 1778, and Harideb in 1779 and 1780; and

37. Killican to Hastings, March 20, Beng. Rev. Cons., April 8, 1783, No. 101.

subsequent Duaria Baruas continued in their office from ten to twelve years.

The stationing of troops in the ground of Lear at Panchratan which overawed his clients and his men was certainly an act of extreme highhandedness. It must be remembered that Baillie was not only the Company's Resident, but he was also Killican's agent; and occasions were bound to arise when the interests of his principal and consequently of himself would supersede his obligations as an official protector of merchants.

But it must be pointed out that Lear was not totally innocent as far as the employment of armed force was concerned. Three years before he had entered Assam by force, and Warren Hastings had to instruct the Collector of Rungpore to check his alarming activities. In 1779 Dow, Raush and Lear were charged with having prevented access to the Duaria Barua by posting men on the bank of the river Brahmaputra for which the Collector of Rungpore had to threaten them with the withdrawal of Company's protection in their Assam trade.

The Board's orders on Lear's representation were brief and non-committal. They agreed, "that the above letter do lie for consideration."

In fact the Board could not do anything in the way of relief to Lear at that stage. The deed had been executed and delivered to Killican, and the Court of Directors had been informed of the grant.[38] No modification of the terms could now be made without the consent of the grantee. It was upto the two parties concerned to come to an accommodation for which Killican had already expressed his willingness. There is evidence to prove that there was a compromise though the terms are not known. During the year 1781 Killican paid to Lear the sum of rupees 10,800 as gratuity. He had also purchased buildings at Goalpara and Jugighopa for rupees 54,451, possibly from Lear as a result of the negotiations carried on since the end of 1779.[39]

Ganganarayan Roy's protest: The case of Ganganarayan Roy, the Bengali salt merchant, was as hard as that of Lear. He had purchased the salt of the 24-Pergannahs for the Bengal years 1182 and 1183, A.D. 1775-77, and was granted general *rawannahs* allowing him an unrestricted trade in salt throughout the provinces of Bengal, Bihar and Orissa, and particular *rawannahs* for

38. Bengal Letter to Court, Revenue, November 25, 1780, paras 79-80.

39. "Account Current of Assam Trade from Jan. 1 to Dec. 31, 1781", Killican to Hastings, March 20, Beng. Rev. Cons., Ap. 8, 1783, No. 101.

the Assam market. He had given his bond for this salt to the Board of Trade, payable in nine months during which time he expected to dispose of it. After the above purchase was made, the Government introduced two measures which frustrated the expectations of Ganganarayan Roy and other merchants in similar circumstances. The Zemindars were allowed by Government a share of the salt trade in pursuance of Warren Hastings's policy "that the Zemindar or the land-farmer should also be the contractor [of salt] because he would be able to execute that business with greater advantage than another.[40] As the sole contractor of salt the Zemindar could always sell that article at a lower price than that at which the previous purchasers could. The result was that Ganganarayan Roy and other salt merchants were compelled to form new plans to sell the salt they could not dispose of at the new and reduced price.

Just when Ganganarayan Roy was carrying his plans into execution the exclusive privilege of trade with Assam was granted to Killican thereby closing all prospects of business to other merchants. Ganganarayan had established *golahs* at Jugighopa and other places at considerable expense. They now proved unprofitable as the salt could not be sold. Ganganarayan could not pay the Government the amount of the bond. The Board of Trade instituted rigorous proceedings against Ganganarayan to enforce payments, and he was threatened with imprisonment.

Ganganarayan submitted a petition to the Board of Trade setting forth his grievances. The acts of which he complained being acts of Government the Board of Trade expressed their inability to delay the proceedings without the orders of the Governor-General and Council. Ganganarayan then submitted a memorial to the Supreme Board asking for relief for the hardships brought upon him by the grant of the exclusive monopoly to Killican. "No deviation from existing commercial customs", said the petitioner, "or change in the regulations, shall take place without six months' previous notification of the same. Every man is then upon his guard, and no one will contract on terms that may be shortly destructive of his plan of profits."[41]

He then stated that he would not have engaged in the trade had he known the intention of Government to throw the salt trade into the hands of Zemindars almost immediately after a consider-

40. Minute by Hastings and Barwell, Ap. 22, 1775,—Jones, *Warren Hastings*, pp. 230, 284.

41. Ganganarayan to Hastings, undated, Beng. Rev. Cons., Sept. 12, 1780, pp. 485-98.

able purchase had been made by him of the Company's salt; and that he would not have sent up Robert Bigger, permitted by Government, at an immense expense to establish a factory for Assam and Bijni,[42] had he known of Government's intention to exclude every merchant but the present farmer Killican from the trade of those two countries. He alleged that the first act of Government, *viz.* the dispersion of the salt trade among Zemindars, had materially injured him and that injury should alone be considered as a sufficient reason for leniency in the matter of his debt to the Company. He held that the second act, viz. the farm of the Assam trade granted to Killican, evidently cancelled his engagements with the Company, "it being expressly contrary to the wording and intent of the *rawannahs* which gave him an unlimited trade throughout the Provinces and to Assam." He then claimed that the salt remaining unsold should be considered as henceforth lying at the risk and expense of the Company as he could not dispose of it for his exclusion from the trade of Assam to which the *rawannahs* had authorised him to trade. As a measure of relief he suggested that the Board should grant him a share of the farm of the Assam trade granted to Killican to buy the 40,000 maunds of salt which had lately arrived at Jugighopa. He was prepared to sell it at three rupees per maund of 93 sicca weight to the *seer*, which was two rupees less than Killican would sell it. In the event of the Board's refusal to accept the above proposal he prayed for extension of time beyond January 1781 to keep his agents in Assam to dispose of the remaining salt adding that orders should be issued to Baillie not to oppose the sale directly or indirectly.

Ganganarayan's petition was considered by the Governor-General and Council on September 12, 1780. They resolved not to allow him any right to leniency in the matter of paying the price of salt; and with regard to the prayer for the extension of time the Board considered that the period of six months allowed to him and to other merchants to settle their concerns in Assam was quite sufficient.

42. Ganganarayan repeatedly mentioned in his petition that Killican had been granted monopoly of trade in Assam and Bijni, which is obviously a mistake, as Bijni was outside the operation of the grant. Baillie aimed at establishing a monopoly in Bijni "to the utter ruin of numberless native merchants whose livelihood is derived from it"—Richard Goodlad, Collector of Rungpore, to Baillie, May 30, 1781, *Rungpore District Records*, Vol. IV, No. 105, p. 75.

Two months later he submitted another application stating "some additional reasons".[43] He pointed out that the *rawannahs* granted to him prohibited any Choky from demanding taxes or molesting his boats on their way to Assam; but that the advertisement issued by the Government in support of Killican's farm provided for the stopping of all boats attempting to pass Rangamati for Assam, except those belonging to Killican. He proposed to pay double the revenues to be paid by Killican for his farm and in proportion, in return for a share or any part of it, and furnish "unexceptionable security" for payment. He assured the Government that if he was allowed a share of the Assam trade he would be able to bring about an increase of revenue and security. As in the opinion of the Board the second petition did not contain any additional reason not covered in the first they resolved to adhere to their resolution of September 12, 1780.

The hardships of Lear and Ganganarayan Roy were shared in common by all the merchants of Goalpara and Jugighopa as the new monopoly upset all their arrangements in trade, and in some cases it involved violation of the terms conceded to them by the Company. Raush did not lodge any formal protest probably because he had been Killican's agent at Goalpara. The only way in which the Board rendered relief to the merchants was by extending the period upto nine months to enable them to dispose of the salt that remained unsold in their *golahs*.[44]

Baillie, Company's Resident at Goalpara: After the settlement of the preliminaries Baillie proceeded to Goalpara as Company's Resident and Killican's agent. On January 5, 1781, Killican applied to the Board for purchasing 100,000 maunds of salt of 82 sicca weights at Nullua and Gogodanga. He was ready to pay 100 sicca rupees for 100 maunds including the *rawannah* duties or to give security for the payment of the same within a year. He agreed to pay the duties when the salt was removed. He further engaged to take one lakh maunds annually. The Board "in consideration of the grant lately made to him, the advantages of which depend greatly upon the trade in this article," consented to allow him the quantity asked for on his paying the fixed price of 100 sicca rupees for 100 maunds with interest at the rate of 8 per cent from the date of delivery to the period or periods of payment and find-

43. Ganganarayan to Hastings, undated, Beng. Rev. Cons., Nov. 14, 1780, pp. 383-87.

44. Beng. Rev. Cons., April 8, 1783.

ing security for the same within the year.[45] Henry Vansittart, Comptroller of the Manufacture of Salt, wrote back that there was no salt remaining at Nullua and Gogodanga. In the meantime the price of salt had gone up to 110 rupees per 100 maunds. The Comptroller had even received offers for Nullua salt at the rate of 120 rupees per 100 maunds. Killican was asked to buy his salt from a salt merchant named Griffith.[46]

In the meantime Baillie had joined his appointment at Goalpara, from where he shifted his headquarters a few months later to Jugighopa to revert again to the original place.[47] On January 1, 1781, Baillie transmitted a Bill of Exchange on David Killican for arcot rupees 12,500 for the discharge of the first quarterly payment of the Company's revenue arising from the farm of the trade with Assam.[48]

Baillie's oppressive conduct: According to the terms of the farm granted to Killican his monopoly was confined to Assam. Bijni adjacent to the province of Kamrup in Assam, was outside the operation of the grant. The estate of Bijni lay on both banks of the river Brahmaputra, the northern portion being called Khuntaghat and the southern Habraghat. There was considerable trade carried on in Bijni with the Bhutanese and the Garos. Besides, Bijni forests teemed with elephants which used to be caught by farmers and sold in Bengal and other provinces of India. A part of Bijni was subordinate to the Bhutan government, and the British portion used to be administered by the Collector of Rungpore of which district it formed a part.[49]

It was convenient for the farmer of the Assam trade to have some degree of control over that of the contiguous territory of Bijni. From the beginning Baillie aimed at obtaining from the Bijni Raja or his officers the monopoly of the trade of that country, and he attempted to secure his object by the employment of the armed force at his disposal.

45. Killican to Hastings, Dec. 8, 1780, Beng. Rev. Cons., Jan. 5, 1781, pp. 388-89.

46. Vansittart to Hastings, Jan. 15, Beng. Rev. Cons., Jan. 23, 1781, pp. 401-404.

47. Baillie's letter to the Board, Jan. 1, 1781, was written from Goalpara,—Beng. Rev. Cons., Jan. 23, 1781. Richard Goodlad, Collector of Rungpore, in his letter of May 30, 1781, addressed Baillie as "Superintendent of the Trade at the Assam Choky, Jugighopa,"—*Rungpore District Records*, Vol. IV, No. 105, p. 75.

48. Beng. Rev. Cons., Jan. 23, 1781.

49. *An Account of the Burman Empire and the Kingdom of Assam*, Calcutta, 1839, p. 122.

In February 1781 the Collector of Rungpore received a complaint that Baillie had stationed a guard of sepoys at the house of the Bijni Raja. Baillie was asked to recall them and to apply in future either to the Fauzadar of Rangamati or the Collector of Rungpore to whom the Bijni Raja was immediately amenable.[50] Baillie did not reply to the charges till June of the same year.

In May 1781 a fresh complaint was lodged by the Bijni Raja accusing Baillie of violent conduct towards him and his officers. It was alleged that Baillie had demanded from the Raja's Dewan Lakshminarayan Chaudhuri the exclusive right to the trade of Khuntaghat and Habraghat, and on its refusal, he, under the pretence of a debt due from the Raja to one Gunderstrape, had confined the Dewan in the Company's guard till he had executed the deed. Richard Goodlad, Collector of Rungpore, in communicating the charges, pointed out to Baillie that his public instructions were widely different from what he had done, and that he was not possessed of the least authority either over the Raja or his officers. The Collector then added,—"I do declare to you that I am so convinced of the injustice and cruelty of the monopoly you are aiming at to the utter ruin of numberless native merchants whose livelihood is derived from it that [even if] the Rajah [had] given you his consent [I] would [not] have admitted of it taking place. Much less will I suffer it when you forcibly attempt to possess yourself of it." Baillie was warned that if he ever took on himself to confine the Bijni Raja or his officers, or employ the sepoys which Government allowed the farmer for the protection of his trade to any other use than what they were originally designed for, the Collector would immediately complain to the Governor-General and Council and issue orders to the Fauzadar "that would be exceedingly disagreeable."[51]

Baillie replied to the two charges on June 7, 1781. He accused the Collector for readily believing such an unwarranted story. "By all means, Mr. Goodlad," wrote Baillie, "do your duty. Honour and honesty demand it of you. But go no further than that line admits, which surely you have in this instance as well as exceeded the bounds of common justice in arraigning, judging and condemning a man of my character, permit me to say, Sir, a man of my character, without so much as paying me the compliment of asking if it was so or not." As regards the charges

50. Goodlad to Baillie, Feb. 24, 1781, *Rungpore District Records*, Vol. IV, No. 90, p. 63.

51. Goodlad to Baillie, May 30, 1781, *Rungpore District Records*, Vol. 4, No. 105, p. 75.

Baillie declared them to be utterly false. He admitted having asked the Dewan to mortgage Habraghat to some merchants for debts amounting to 40,000 rupees with the approval of Bogle, the former Collector of Rungpore, and the Bijni Raja. The allegation that he had extorted from the Dewan a deed conveying to him the monopoly of the Bijni trade was declared "to be a diabolical falsity of the first magnitude." The only transaction which could be regarded as a monopoly was the Dewan's agreement to mortgage five or six villages in return for some money which Baillie had been asked to lend the Raja. "As to the monopoly you have been told I was aiming at," wrote Baillie, "I abhor the idea as much as you do. The trade goes on as formerly. Every pykar carries on his own business, and I keep my golahs open to any fellow who may want even half a maund of salt." About the letter which Goodlad had written in February, Baillie stated upon his honour that he "neither ever saw or heard of it."[52]

Baillie appointed Collector of Rangamati: Baillie soon realised that unless he was vested with some degree of official influence he could not promote the interests of trade. There was a small *kutchery* at Jugighopa which managed the collections of the district of Rangamati amounting to 3,000 rupees per annum, and consisting of a small duty paid to the Choky at Jugighopa, together with a tribute from Bijni paid in elephants. The collection of the revenue was in charge of some merchant of Goalpara, and Baillie, Lear and Tomlin had at times made the above collection. In the absence of a regularly authorised Collector stationed at Jugighopa the peons and underlings of the *kutchery* at that place used to seize the Assam merchants and extort money from them by threatening to carry them to Rungpore unless they paid for their release. These practices discouraged the merchants and were detrimental to the trade. After the grant of the exclusive privilege to Killican a considerable volume of clandestine trade was carried on with Assam through Bijni with the connivance and even with the encouragement of the Revenue Collector of Rangamati. It was impossible for the Collector of Rungpore to prevent his underlings at Jugighopa from acting iniquitously.

In June 1781 Killican pointed out to the Board the advantage to his trade if Baillie was vested with magisterial power. He requested the Board to grant to Baillie the collections of Rangamati, and the small *kutchery* at Jugighopa "which will prevent

52. Baillie to Goodlad, June 7, 1781, *Rungpore District Records*, Vol. II, No. 156, p. 127.

the several inconveniences and oppressions now complained of."[53] The Board agreed to the proposal of Killican and asked the Collector of Rungpore to send a particular account of the collections concerned in order that they might be deducted from the Jumma of the land farmer."[54]

Richard Goodlad, Collector of Rungpore, foresaw the dangers that would result from placing magisterial powers or Fauzadari in the hands of traders. In 1780 he had been deputed by Bogle, Collector of Rungpore, to Jugighopa to see the manner in which the Assam trade was carried and he could therefore speak with precision on the subject. In 1775 Harewood, Collector of Rungpore, had made over the Fauzadari of Jugighopa to Baillie's Banyan Kasinath Ghose and it remained in his hands till 1779. Kasinath became notorious for his oppressions, and the Governor-General sent positive orders to Purling, Collector of Rungpore, for his removal. Since that time the Fauzadari had remained with people unconnected with trade, as the Assamese were subjected to endless harassments at the hands of merchants possessing Fauzadari powers. They were constantly threatened with vengeance from the Company to answer private ends. Bogle and Goodlad had rejected the repeated requests of Killican and Baillie to let them have the Fauzadari.

About Killican's allegations of the violent conduct of the peons and underlings of Jugighopa *kutchery*, Goodlad pointed out that no Assamese merchants had any occasion to go to Jugighopa. The trade of Assam, Goodlad alleged, was farmed by the Assam government to a Barua who came to the Assam Choky at particular seasons to dispose of his goods and receive his salt. His transactions at Jugighopa were conducted by two authorised Vakils. Goodlad stated with authority that "Mr. Bogle's people never sent a peon to the Choky, never touched a single Assam man," adding that had anything like that ever happened he should have heard of it from Baillie.

About Killican's assertion that the Fauzadar of Rangamati had encouraged clandestine trade with Assam through Bijni, Goodlad replied that all the avenues to Bijni were guarded by Baillie's Chokies, and that Baillie would have surely reported if the Company's Fauzadar had been accessory to the violation of the rights of Killican.

53. Killican to Hastings, June 25, Beng. Rev. Cons., July 5, 1781, and also in *Rungpore District Records*, Vol. II, No. 145, p. 189.

54. John Shore, member of the Committee of Revenue, to Goodlad, July 13, 1781, *Rungpore District Records*, Vol. II, No. 188, p. 144.

Goodlad concluded by saying that the allegations made by Killican against the Company's employees at Jugighopa and Rangamati implied either "connivance or want of care in him [Collector of Rungpore] which would be highly criminal," and that the Board's orders separating Rangamati from the Rungpore Collectorship left a censure against him on record which he did not deserve and that Killican's letter was "one continued error."[55]

The orders of the Government being positive the Collector of Rungpore had to take steps to give effect to them. He asked Raja Debi Sing, the farmer of the revenues of Dinajpore and Rungpore, to send the papers relating to the collections of Rangamati in order that the amount might be deducted from the Raja's *jumma.*[56] The Raja had entered into terms with the Committee of Revenue on a lease of ten years for collecting the revenues of Dinajpore and Rungpore, and the transfer of Rangamati collections to Baillie for no fault of the original farmer involved a breach of the terms of the lease. The Raja submitted his objections in a letter to the Collector of Rungpore. The collections of Rangamati, said the Raja, were very trifling; but he complained against the disgrace he suffered from the unwarranted transfer of a part of his farm. He feared that he might be similarly deprived of Dinajpore and Rungpore. For the collection of his revenues he counted upon the support of the Committee of Revenue; but the sudden alienation of Rangamati in favour of Baillie filled his mind with misgivings about the continuance of that support.[57]

The position taken up by Debi Sing was an unassailable one. After having granted the farm of Rangamati to him for ten years the Government could not transfer a part of it to a second farmer before the expiry of the lease. The matter could be settled only by a private accommodation between the parties concerned. Killican negotiated with the Raja and obtained from him the farm of the districts of Bijni and Bidyagong and of the Kheddamahal for the annual sum of rupees 6,000 with effect from the year 1781.[58]

55. Goodlad to Committee of Revenue, July 23, 1781, *Rungpore District Records*, Vol. IV, No. 130, pp. 87–8.

56. Raja Debi Sing was no other than the "Davy Sing" whose oppressions were eloquently described by Burke at the trial of Warren Hastings.

57. Debi Sing to Goodlad, undated, *Rungpore District Records*, Vol. II, No. 131, p. 89, enclosure to Goodlad's letter of July 23, 1781.

58. Goodlad to Baillie, June 7, 1783, *Rungpore District Records*, Vol. IV, No. 214, p. 158. The collections of Rangamati included the tribute of the two small states Bijni and Bidyagong which paid their revenue in elephants. The tribute was afterwards converted into a cash one,—Glazier's *Rungpore*, —p. 27.

Killican's success in the Assam trade: The success that attended Killican's commercial enterprise may be judged from his own statement submitted to the Board on March 20, 1783.[59] During the year 1781 he incurred, as he alleged, a loss of 43,541 rupees. He sold 82,870 maunds of salt mostly at 4 rupees per maund. The proceeds from the sale of salt came upto 329,152 rupees. His other source of income was the sale of copper and cloth which fetched him a profit of rupees 39,405. He had purchased 85,500 maunds of salt at Calcutta and Goalpara for rupees 265,192, of which 2,630 maunds remained unsold at the end of the year. His major expenditures came upto rupees 172,933 under the following different heads,—rupees 26,435 on factory charges, sepoys etc.; rupees 30,241 on interest; rupees 54,000 as Company's rent for the farm; rupees 10,800 as gratuity to Lear; rupees 54,450 on buildings purchased at Jugighopa and Goalpara. The gratuity paid to Lear was however not a just outgoing from the profit of the trade, and the amount spent on the purchase of buildings was not a decided loss. Killican did not also take into account the 2,630 maunds of salt remaining on hand which was worth about 10,000 rupees.

The figures for the year 1782 are not all available. He could sell only 40,000 maunds of salt representing less than half the quantity he had purchased for disposal during the year. At the end of the year he had goods to the value of 213,805 rupees remaining in the *golah,* consisting of 46,000 maunds of salt, 62 maunds of coarse muga, 97 maunds of pepper, 2,181 maunds of stick lac, 426 maunds of lump lac, 27 maunds of munjit, and 20 maunds of ivory. His outstanding balances due from several merchants for Calcutta goods amounted to rupees 96,350 as follows,—Mutichand, 9,244 rupees: Kamini Nandi, 13,853: Nandaram, 8,007: Daniel Raush, 16,110: Krishnanath Barua of the Assam Choky, 21,669: Hugh Baillie, 1,756: John Rodrigues, 1,705: Jar trade, 5,003: and cash 13,000.

The difficulties attending the Assam trade were pointed out by Killican in his letter to the Board dated March 20, 1783. He characterised this trade as being unlike all others, it being impossible to judge in what time any certain quantity could be sold at Goalpara owing to the frequent disturbances in Assam which always put a stop to the trade till they were all settled. Another cause which affected the trade was "the strange capriciousness of the people of Assam" who for many months did not carry on

59. Killican to Hastings, March 20, Beng. Rev. Cons., April 8, 1783.

any commerce while at other times they crowded down with their goods.[60]

Annulment of Killican's exclusive privilege: Killican could have perhaps made profits in the Assam trade if he had been allowed to exercise the exclusive privilege granted to him for the originally stipulated period of four years. But the Court of Directors held a different view from the Governor-General and Council. "Grants of this nature," wrote the Directors in their despatch of July 12, 1782, "are so repugnant to every principle of commerce, so detrimental to the revenue, and so prejudicial to the interest of the natives and others who ought to be allowed a free and uncontrolled trade over India on paying the customary duties to Government that we cannot hesitate a moment in declaring our condemnation of them."[61] This sentiment struck the Court more forcibly because Killican's farm was to be supported by a military force stationed under the Company's Resident who was at the same time the farmer's agent.[62] The Court accordingly directed that the agreement with Killican was to be forthwith annulled. They prohibited the grant of monopolies in future and declared that the Governor-General would be held responsible for the consequences of any breach of their positive orders in that respect.[63] In March 1783 the orders of the Court annulling the grant were communicated by the Supreme Board to Killican; and the powers granted to his agent Baillie were consequently withdrawn.[64] Baillie, who had been appointed to Goalpara principally on Killican's account was immediately recalled, and John Atchinson was sent by Killican to that place to serve as his new agent.[65]

Killican at once submitted a representation to the Board setting forth his losses in the Assam trade during the years 1781 and 1782, and praying for an extension of time till December 1783 to enable him to settle his concerns and to dispose of the quantity of salt he had on hand at Goalpara and for which he had paid rent to the Company. The Board accordingly granted the extension of time till the end of 1783 and advised the Collector of Rungpore to give public notice of this fact in his district and to

60. Beng. Rev. Cons., Ap. 8, 1783.
61. Court's Letter to Bengal, July 12, 1782.
62. Court's Letter to Bengal, March 14, 1786.
63. Court's Letter to Bengal, July 12, 1782.
64. Beng. Rev. Cons., April 8, 1783.
65. Killican to Hastings, Ap. 18, Beng. Rev. Cons., April 25, 1783, No. 153.

continue to assist Killican with his influence and authority during the above period.[66]

Though orders recalling Baillie from Goalpara were issued in April 1783 he continued in that place till the end of July promising to return after delivering over charge to Atchinson.[67]

On February 20, 1783, the Committee of Revenue had, in anticipation of the discontinuance of Killican's monopoly, ordered the restoration of Bijni and Bidyagong to the Collectorship of Rungpore. Killican was still then in enjoyment of his exclusive privilege of trade to Assam; and on the assumption that he would be in uninterrupted enjoyment of the same till the end of 1783, Baillie raised a protest against the reamalgamation of the aforesaid districts with Rungpore. He held that the proposed arrangement would greatly and materially injure the farmer's interests, not so much from the loss of profit but from the consequence that attended his official position as a collector of revenue vested with Fauzadari power. A Fauzadar of Goalpara or Jugighopa unconnected with the farmer might render things extremely inconvenient in the prosecution of the trade. He might seize the people in the farmer's employ for frivolous and trifling causes. Baillie affirmed that he had experienced such vexations before. He requested that the orders should be suspended. The Committee however did not think it necessary to alter their previous orders on the subject.[68] On June 9, 1783 Richard Goodlad, Collector of Rungpore, wrote to Baillie requesting the latter to deliver the charge of the districts of Bijni and Bidyagong etc. to William Kennell Amherst deputed to Jugighopa for that purpose.[69] Killican's factory at Goalpara with all its appendage was purchased by Daniel Raush.[70]

Oppression of Assamese merchants revived: The withdrawal of Baillie, the Company's Resident at Goalpara, was followed by the revival of the oppressive conduct of the Company's underlings towards the merchants of Assam. On May 15, 1784, Birnarayan Roy, the Naib of Rangamati who had his *kutchery* at Jugighopa, sent some sepoys and peons to the Assam Choky with

66. Beng. Rev. Cons., April 8, 1783, and Bengal Letter to Court, October 25, 1783.

67. Beng. Rev. Cons., July 25, 1783.

68. Baillie to Committee of Revenue, March 8, Beng. Rev. Cons., April 25, 1783.

69. *Rungpore District Records*, Vol. IV, No. 216, p. 159.

70. Raush to Cornwallis, Sept. 1, Beng. Rev. Cons., Sept. 25, 1789, and *Rungpore District Records*, Vol. V, No. 128, p. 77.

orders to seize the Assam Baruas till they paid a certain sum of money.[71] The presence of the force vested with such orders created great uproar and confusion in the Assam Choky and put a stop to all business. Dow had sent 300 maunds of salt to the Assam Choky which could not be delivered. His gomostah had gone to the Choky to buy goods to the amount of three to four thousand rupees. 'He could not receive a *chatak* of goods' and the boats had to return empty. The desertion of the Choky was prevented by Dow's assurances to the Baruas that such acts of violence were committed without the least shadow of authority, and that Birnarayan would be properly punished by the Government. Dow reported the incident to Peter Moore, Collector of Rungpore, and transmitted the original *dustaks* given by the Naib to his sepoys and peons, together with the letter of complaint that the Baruas had written to Dow, as well as their reply to Dow's assurances.[72]

Dow's letter to Peter Moore contains a clear indication of the prevalent attitude towards the people and government of Assam, specially of the disastrous effects to trade produced by the violence repeatedly committed upon the peaceful Assamese traders. Dow assumed that it was unnecessary for him to acquaint the Collector, "who is so well informed in the history and geography of every part of India, its connections and dependencies, that the Kingdom of Assam is totally and absolutely independent of any control from Bengal as much as the Empire of China is." "The report of such violence," continued Dow, "will go into Assam; and the *moodies* [Assam merchants] will be intimidated and will not bring their goods to the Choky (—Give me leave just to observe here that the people of Assam are perhaps, the most timid and pusillanimous races of people in the face of the earth—) for seeing such violence acted with impunity. They know not from what authority it proceeds, and conclude that possibly the step next will be to take their goods from them by force without any exchange." Dow believed that if the Assam trade were conducted with mutual confidence a large quantity of salt—the staple article of Bengal—might be annually taken off by the Assamese. In the total absence of confidence on the part of the Assamese the trade

71. Birnarayan was subsequently dismissed from the Naibship for arrears of revenue. He was ordered into confinement until the balance would be paid. Report of D. H. MacDowell, Collector of Rungpore, June 11, 1786, *Rungpore District Records*, Vol. VI, p. 72.

72. Dow to Peter Moore, Jugighopa, May 15, 1784,—*Rungpore District Records*, Vol. III, No. 257, pp. 157-9.

had dwindled to the supplying of their mere necessities. "This recent act of violence," Dow pointed out, "at a time when prudence and policy dictated and directed the most lenient and candid measures to endeavour to gain their confidence, has greatly increased that jealousy and mistrust." Dow requested the Collector to issue positive orders to every European merchant residing at Goalpara or Jugighopa, himself not excepted, that on no account or pretence whatever they should use any force or violence, or anything that has the appearance of force or violence, over the merchants of Assam or at the same Choky, but to conduct their business in peace, quietitude and mutual confidence as merchants should do, and if they had any unsettled claims or demand upon, or from Assam, to represent them to the authorities at Rungpore who would judge of their propriety and justness and give directions accordingly. Dow was of opinion that it was not necessary to deal on credit with the Assamese, as they generally gave their goods in advance. Balances arose only when a Bengal merchant forced the Assamese to accept larger quantities of goods for which they could not deliver ready returns in the shape of Assam products. Dow believed that in such cases the creditor merchant had nothing to depend upon but the good faith of the Assamese. "He has not power of himself to ensure payment," said Dow, "and Government cannot be expected to embroil itself with an independent kingdom to recover the pecuniary demands of a private individual."

The annulment of Killican's monopoly and the withdrawal of Baillie from Goalpara marked the termination of the second stage of the Company's relations. They were of a purely commercial character though political disturbances in Assam greatly hindered the trade which was the avowed intention of the Company to promote. In the first stage Baillie introduced the Company to the advantages of opening a commercial intercourse with Assam. He was permitted to reside at Goalpara and encouraged to explore the possibilities of vending the Company's staples in Assam. But his prospects were destroyed by the rivalry of the freemerchants and interlopers who quarrelled amongst themselves, and entertained no scruple in using violence against the peaceful merchants of the independent state of Assam. In 1776 Baillie applied for the sole agency for the sale of Company's goods in Assam which, he assured, would fetch a profit of rupees 200,000. Soon after, he persuaded an influential merchant to obtain the exclusive privilege of trade to Assam with himself as the active worker of the scheme. The Company was now assured of a definite revenue from the Assam trade amounting to 50,000 rupees per annum.

Though the farmer's loss at the end of the first year was shown to be 43,541 rupees there were the buildings in his possession to the value of rupees 54,450. The first year's business thus ended in a decided gain. The trade of the second year was equally profitable when we take into account the unsold goods and the outstanding balances due from sundry merchants. On the whole the Assam trade was not an utterly unprofitable venture and no one realised it better than the merchants who were engaged in that business. The Court of Directors who took a detached view of the situation also admitted that "both the British and native merchants as well as French and Dutch have at all times pursued, even with a degree of eagerness, the traffic of the country of Assam." [73] One of the reasons for which the benefit of the trade could not be fully reaped by the Bengal merchants was the mistrust caused in the minds of the Assamese by the violent conduct of the former as well as of the Company's underlings. The presence of a Company's officer at the frontier relieved the Assamese of the oppressions but they were revived as soon as he was withdrawn from that locality.

73. Court's Letter to Bengal, March 14, 1786.

CHAPTER V

COMPANY'S MONOPOLY OF THE ASSAM SALT TRADE

Lodge's proposal regarding Assam trade: After his recall from Goalpara, Baillie sailed for England determined this time to carry into execution his original idea of establishing a market for the Company's staples in Assam with himself as its director and superintendent. The Assam trade, with an assured sale of 100,000 maunds of salt per year, in addition to that of other articles, had attracted merchants of all description from Bengal. The only impediment in the way was the mistrust of the Assamese mainly brought about by the untoward treatment they used to receive at the hands of private merchants and the servants of the Company. It was generally believed that if the trade could be conducted peacefully and the confidence of the Assamese regained, it would lead to mutual and lasting benefit to the people of both Bengal and Assam. To achieve this object it was necessary that a properly authorised servant of the Company should reside on the Assam frontier to give protection to the traders and remove the suspicions and fears that might exist among the Assamese. A treaty with the Assam government to ensure beneficial commercial intercourse between the two states was regarded as a desirable object by the authorities of the Company.

Baillie's plans were anticipated by Henry Lodge, who had held important positions in the Bengal establishment as a member of the Dacca Council and as a Resident at Belluah.[1] On November 15, 1784, he submitted a proposal to the Board urging the propriety of the Assam trade being taken into the hands of the Government under the management of a Resident at Goalpara who should also be entrusted with the collections and Adawlat of Rangamati, Karaibari, Sherpur and Susang.[2] The objects which he hoped

1. Lodge became Collector of Rajshahi in 1785, Judge of the Dewany Adawlat in May 1793, and Collector of Sylhet in Dec. 1793 from where he was recalled for his oppressive conduct towards the Raja of Cachar. He continued in India till 1799. There is a complete sketch of Lodge's official career in Vol. 9 of the Personal Records in the India Office over the signature of Thomas Fisher, Searcher of the Records, Aug. 15, 1826.

2. Lodge to Hastings, Nov. 15, 1794, Beng. Rev. Cons., Feb. 16, 1785, pp. 248-54.

to achieve by his proposal were, to place the administration of justice in a remote country like Goalpara and its environs on a proper footing, yet without subjecting Government to any expense, thereby removing the disadvantages experienced by the inhabitants from the distance of any court where they could prefer their complaints; to secure the revenues without the necessity of deputing sepoys to quell the disturbances that so frequently happened among the Zemindars who were notorious in those parts for refractory conduct; and to effect a permanent advantage annually of four lakhs of rupees to the Company.

The amount which Lodge estimated as the probable annual profit to the Company was calculated on the assumption that the Assam market would absorb 250,000 maunds of salt every year, of which 6,250 maunds must be deducted for wastage in the transportation, and 41,927 maunds for the difference in the Company's measure of 82 sicca weight and the Assamese measure of 96 sicca weight. The salt would be sold at 4 rupees per maund; and 201,823 maunds would fetch a gross annual income of 807,292 rupees.

The expenses, according to Lodge, would come upto 407,292 rupees as follows:—175,000 rupees, the prime cost to Government for 250,000 maunds of salt of the Belluah manufacture at 70 rupees per 100 maunds; 87,500 rupees, the cost of transporting salt from Belluah to Goalpara at the rate of 35 rupees per 100 maunds; 18,000 rupees, Resident's salary at the rate of 1,500 per month; 3,600 rupees, Resident's house rent; 12,000 rupees, charges for collections, Adawlat, establishment for servants; 7,500 rupees, for 100 militia raised and paid by the Resident; 80,729 rupees, commission to the Resident, of 10 per cent, the customary allowance of merchants to their agents, in lieu of all factory charges, *golahs*, etc., buildings, gomastahs, weighmen, boat hire, etc.; 20,000 rupees, indemnity for risk in the transportation of salt; 2,963 rupees, Hoondwan to shroffs in exchange for bills on Calcutta, etc., in remittance.

There was annually a surplus quantity of salt of the Belluah manufacture which Government had no immediate means of selling, and according to Lodge Assam would furnish a ready market for what otherwise would continue deposited in *golahs*. Lodge alleged that the small profits which individuals had made in the Assam salt trade were not equivalent to the risk they ran in carrying it on, a military force being necessary to secure their property. He further believed that a duly authorized servant of the Company stationed at Goalpara would be able to prevent acts of oppression by foreigners, specially French, should they ever again return to that place. The French, previous to the war in 1778, had committed acts of violence with impunity as there was no officer at Goalpara to take cognizance of their conduct. It was also hoped that through the influence of the proposed Collector the inhabitants of the Garo mountains would be made amenable to administrative control and induced to cultivate the waste lands of Rangamati and the adjoining places which would lead to increase of Government revenues.

Lodge concluded his representation by a request that in the event of his proposal meeting the concurrence of the Government, he should be entrusted with the charge of the Residentship for five years from January 1785. He assured the Board that by his integrity, assiduity, attention, and rectitude of conduct in every department of his station he would be able to obtain the confidence of the Assamese and promote the welfare, happiness and prosperity of the inhabitants, and procure a further profit to Government.

In view of the orders of the Court of Directors issued at the time of abolishing Killican's monopoly the Calcutta Council felt restrained from taking action on Lodge's proposal. It was transmitted to the Court with the Governor-General's despatch of February 22, 1785. The Calcutta Council presided over by the interim Governor-General Sir John Macpherson, refrained from giving any opinion upon the subject except that the proposal appeared to be favourable to them at first sight.[3]

Court's views and orders on Assam trade: Soon after Lodge's proposal had reached the Court the lattter wrote to the Bengal Council on September 21, 1785, expressing their wish to open a trade in salt within the kingdom of Assam for which returns might be made in gold dusts and other articles.[4] As proposals of this nature had been made at different times by Baillie and Killican, and lastly by Lodge, it is not known precisely from which particular quarter the Court derived their desire this time to prosecute 'a beneficial trade' in salt with Assam. Baillie was then in England, and it is possible that the Court's present recommendation to the Bengal Government emanated from some representation on his part.

Six months later the Court issued orders to the Bengal Government to open the trade with Assam to all merchants reserving the traffic in salt to the Company, to appoint Baillie as the Company's Resident at Goalpara to conduct the salt trade on behalf

3. Bengal Letter to Court, Feb. 22, 1785. Warren Hastings attended the Council meeting for the last time on Feb. 1, 1785.

4. Court's Letter to Bengal, Sept. 21, 1785.

of the Government and to give protection to merchants. The Bengal Government was also authorised to form a new Collectorship with districts near Goalpara and with Baillie as the incumbent.

The Court's despatch of March 14, 1786, conveying the above orders is a document of great importance as it contains a minute examination of the whole problem of the Assam trade, based on the representations of Baillie, Killican and Lodge, and the protests of Lear and Ganganarayan Roy, and the orders and resolutions of the Bengal Council made at different times since 1773.[5] The Court admitted that the advantages which might result from a trade to the country of Assam had been first suggested to them by Baillie in 1773. They expected that broadcloth and other European commodities might be disposed of to the people of Assam who would make returns in muga silk, black pepper and specie. Notwithstanding these advantages they learned from Killican's representation of 1780 that the commerce which had formerly been extremely beneficial to Bengal was then in a great measure ruined by the mode in which it was conducted and for want of due regulations in carrying it on. Killican's proposal of an exclusive privilege which aimed at providing the needed control over the Assam trade had been accepted by the Bengal Council; but the Court abolished it as all monopolies appeared to them "repugnant to the general principles of commerce." The losses reported to have been sustained by Killican during the first two years of his monopoly appeared after a careful scrutiny of the details to be only nominal.

Lodge's proposal was considered by the Court as unacceptable in view of the heavy expenses which the Government establishment would involve, specially because there was no guarantee that 250,000 maunds of salt could be disposed of annually at the Goalpara market. Killican had sold only 85,000 maunds during 1781, and Lodge did not assign any reason to show the probability of an increase.

Lodge's proposal to assume into the Company's hands the exclusive privilege of trade to Assam was regarded by the Court as contrary to the general principles of commerce as they had affirmed while abolishing the monopoly of Killican. The Court, however, held that such a principle might admit of exceptions under the circumstances of particular cases; but the Directors were not satisfied that such circumstances existed in the present case. The argument contained in the Board's resolution of June 13, 1780, which assigned as a reason for complying with Killican's request that the

5. Court's Letter to Bengal, March 14, 1786.

trade had been for many years in the hands of a few unauthorised adventurers, appeared to the Court as a contradiction in terms. Neither Killican nor Lodge had assigned any reason why the trade might not be carried with advantage by individuals except the smallness of the profit and the necessity of a military force to secure their property. The first has been contradicted by the memorials of Baillie, Lear and Ganganarayan Roy, and the second would have been obviated if the protection of the Government was given to those who engaged in the Assam trade.

The Court affirmed their conviction that salt was unquestionably an important object for Bengal, more specially because salt was then in the hands of Government and had become a great source of revenue. But it was also equally important that measures should be adopted to promote amongst the people of Assam a demand for the other products of Bengal, or of the woollens and other manufactures of Great Britain, which in the year 1773 Baillie had represented to be very considerable.

Baillie appointed Superintendent of the Assam trade: The Court then set forth their decision to nominate one of their covenanted servants to Assam. They considered Baillie to be the fittest person to serve as Resident on the part of the Company at Goalpara as he was the author of the original proposals for opening a trade with the Assamese, as he had the experience of eighteen years' residence in that country, and as he was supposed to have suffered great losses by being recalled from Goalpara in consequence of the annulment of Killican's grant. The Court directed the Bengal Government to appoint Baillie accordingly.

The Court asked the Board to instruct Baillie to investigate the causes which had stood in the way of a beneficial commerce with Assam, to obtain a general knowledge of the extent, government and products of Assam and its probable communication with China, and to form a commercial treaty with the king of Assam "upon mercantile principles without any appearance of power or assumption of superiority that might give offence or alarm the Assamese." Baillie was to be entrusted with a Collectorship to be formed with the perganahs of Rangamati, Bijni, Bahirbund, Karaibari and Bhitarbund or any other districts, to give efficiency to his service and to put him in a situation to conciliate the inhabitants of the mountainous countries. The Court were not sure whether much benefit would arise from establishing an Adawlat at Goalpara as the inhabitants were not used to the regularity of judicial processes. The Court laid down that the other objects of the Resident's duties should be to give protection to merchants of every description, to cultivate an intercourse with the Assamese "upon principles of good faith and honour worthy of the British character."

The Court, however, proposed to retain the trade in salt in the hands of their Resident at Goalpara. They feared that though British subjects were restrained by law from trading in salt there would not be wanting persons to transport that article to the Goalpara market which, as a result of competition would lead to a fall in the established selling price of that article at that place. The Court's decision was based on the additional ground that salt was at all times a monopoly of the Government and there was a similar practice in Assam. The Court declared the trade in all other articles to be completely free and open, and threatened the Resident with punishment if he attempted to monopolise it for himself.

About muga-dhutis which formed a principal part of the returns from Assam and which were usually sent to the Coromandal and Malabar coasts by private merchants, the Court instructed the Bengal Government to consign to Madras or Bombay such quantities of muga-dhutis as could be disposed of in the two latter places. This measure was expected to prevent the sending of specie from Bengal and the drawing of bills on the same.

The Calcutta Council could not give immediate effect to the orders of the Court as Baillie had not returned to India. It was in the spring of 1787 that Baillie left England by the *Rodney* and arrived in Calcutta in the beginning of July 1787. The Court had written another letter on March 27 asking the Governor-General to grant to Baillie reasonable commission or percentage on the exports and imports as a means of "quickening his diligence and increasing his attention to the important object committed to his charge."[6]

The Court's despatch of March 27, 1787, contains a clear indication of their increasing interest in the resources of Assam. The list of investments sent to the Calcutta Board on April 11, 1785, had included the following products of Assam and the neighbouring countries:

> 20 double corge of Sylhet muga-dhutis packed in two bales, one bale containing 10 double corge of natural colour, and the second bale containing 5 double corge dyed of a dark blue colour and 5 of red colour; the above muga-dhutis were intended for an experiment for the African markets, and the

6. Court's Letter to Bengal, March 27, 1787.

Governor-General was asked to specify the charges for dyeing;

20 double corge of Goalpara muga-dhutis packed and dyed in the same manner as the Sylhet muga-dhutis, but marked "G.M. Dhutis" to distinguish them from the others;

20 seers of the muga silk that came from Assam; and a small quantity of munjit or madder, an article used in dyeing.

The Court expressed their regret that their requisition had not been complied with though they know full well that the articles were procurable at all times and available even in Calcutta. The Directors now declared,—"We shall consider our new Board as remiss in their duty if the same are not complied with." They desired that on the return of Baillie to Assam he should be called upon to furnish the above articles, and also to send to the Court specimens of any other growth, produce and manufacture of Assam likely to be introduced with advantage in England.

Soon after Baillie's arrival in Calcutta the Governor-General asked the Board of Revenue to report how many and which of the districts mentioned by the Directors might be made into a Collectorship for Baillie.[7] On July 9, 1787, the Bengal Government published a notification announcing Baillie's appointment at Goalpara and prohibiting the trade or vend of salt into Assam by any individual from March 1, 1788.[8] On July 12, 1787, Baillie recommended to the Government that the Company should not only interdict private merchants from selling salt in Assam but that they should not carry it higher than Rangamati. "Otherwise," he added, "it will be impossible for me, even with the utmost vigilance to prevent their smuggling that article into Assam." He also desired that every description of merchants should be excluded from trading in Assam except the Company. If not, he believed, broadcloths and other articles of Europe would be brought from the French and the Dutch and sent into Assam to the utter destruction of the Company's hopes. He advocated the limiting of the trade to Assam to one person. "So sensible," he said in this connection, "the Government of Assam is of this, it is conducted solely by one person [Duaria Barua] on their side, which has given them vast advantages over a number of competitors."[9]

7. Beng. Rev. Cons., July 4, 1787, pp. 13-14.

8. Seton-Karr, *Selections from Calcutta Gazette*, Vol. I, p. 191, July 19, 1787; and *Rungpore District Records*, Vol. V, No. 320, p. 202.

9. Baillie to Cornwallis, July 12, Beng. Rev. Cons., July 13, 1787, pp. 1093-95.

Government's instructions to Baillie: On July 18, 1787, the Governor-General in Council issued formal orders appointing Baillie as Superintendent on the part of the Company at Goalpara.[10] He was authorised to proceed to Gauhati or any other part of Assam for which he must obtain the previous sanction of the king of that country. Baillie was asked to try to form a treaty with the Raja or any agreement with the merchants of Assam of a purely commercial nature. The instructions issued to Baillie by the Government of Bengal amplified the general intentions of the Court of Directors. The Board asked Baillie to communicate to them information on the following points:

(1) The manner in which the trade is carried on between the subjects of Assam and those of Bengal.

(2) The qualities and quantities of the goods, the produce of Bengal or of Europe which may be wanted annually for the Assam market.

(3) The periods at which it will be necessary to despatch these goods.

(4) The manner in which Baillie proposed they should be despatched to him.

(5) An estimate of the expense attending the despatch of these articles.

(6) An estimate of the amount of the produce of their sales in Assam formed upon an average of Baillie's own experience.

(7) Whether the markets of the Assam trade are in general variable, and the cause of that variation if it subsisted.

(8) Whether Baillie deemed it more for the advantage of the Company to receive their returns for the commodities disposed of on their account in Assam in goods or in specie, and whether such an option was in his power.

(9) If the returns are made in the commodities of Assam, in what manner and at what places could they be disposed of most to the advantage of the Company.

(10) If any and what force would be required for the Resident's protection and that of the trade entrusted to him.

The above information was required to enable the Board to report to the Court of Directors on the probable extent to which the trade in general with Assam might be carried on, as well as in the particular article of salt.

10. Cornwallis to Baillie, July 18, Beng. Rev. Cons., July 18, 1787, pp. 1108-1112.

The Board informed Baillie that by his present appointment he became a Factor for the trade of the Company, and as such he was forbidden to conduct any private trade directly in his own account, or indirectly on the part of any other person. His personal allowance was fixed at 1,000 rupees per month. The amount of the commission on the trade entrusted to his management, as well as the names of the districts to be put under his jurisdiction, were to be communicated to him later.

Cornwallis's letter to Assam Raja: Lord Cornwallis, Governor-General of India, addressed a letter to the king of Assam notifying the appointment of Baillie and requesting the Raja's co-operation in fulfilling the objects of the appointment. The Governor-General referred to the state of harmony and good neighbourhood which had so long subsisted between the countries of Assam and Bengal. Baillie's appointment was described as being made for the regulation and protection of the trade, for cultivating and establishing on a firm basis that friendship "which the English have ever been and will continue solicitous to maintain in terms of perfect equality and justice as becomes the governments of states so closely connected by local situation." Baillie was to address himself more minutely to the king of Assam on his arrival at Goalpara, and had instructions to proceed to Gauhati or the Assam capital to concert measures which would secure to the subjects of both states the greatest commercial advantages. The letter ended with a request to the Assam king to recognise Baillie as the representative of the British Government. The letter was to be accompanied by some suitable presents for the Assam king and his principal nobles.[11]

The other details in connection with Baillie's powers and emoluments were fixed in the meantime in consultation with the Board of Revenue and the Board of Trade. In addition to his allowance of 1,000 rupees per month Baillie was to receive a commission of 7 per cent on the sale of goods effected by him. He was also granted a monthly allowance of 200 rupees for maintaining a *kutchery*[12] with the regular establishment of clerks and revenue officials. A small collectorship with the districts of Karaibari, Bijni and Rangamati including the Tope-Khana mahals of the latter was newly formed and transferred from the jurisdiction of the Collectors of Rungpore and Mymensing and placed under the management of Baillie. The whole collection barely exceeded the annual

11. Cornwallis to Assam Raja, July 18, Beng. Rev. Cons., July 18, 1787, pp. 1112-1115.

12. Beng. Letter to Court, July 31, 1787.

sum of 20,000 rupees.[13] The Board of Revenue were asked to prevent any loss of revenue accruing from the transfer of the management. The Collector of Rungpore was directed to deliver over the above districts to Baillie when the latter would declare himself as ready to take charge.[14] Baillie was asked to attend on one of the Judges of the Supreme Court of Judicature, previous to his departure for Goalpara, for the purpose of taking the oath prescribed for Revenue Collectors. On July 31, 1787, the Governor-General communicated to the Court of Directors the actions that were taken with regard to the establishment of a Residency at Goalpara.[15]

Baillie's recommendations regarding Assam trade: On the establishment of the Residency at Goalpara Baillie witnessed the fulfilment of the objects on which he had laboured since 1771. He was now the Company's official representative on the frontier of Assam with full power to adopt measures for the promotion of commercial intercourse between the two countries. He also became a Collector of Revenue which would give him a considerable degree of importance in the eyes of the people with whom he had to deal.

Baillie entered into his work with enthusiasm. On July 24, 1787, he addressed a letter to Lord Cornwallis promising to strictly obey the commands of the Government and indicating briefly the nature of the Assam trade.[16] He admitted the inadvisability of going into Assam without previously having obtained "the free and absolute consent and concurrence of that Government." With regard to his dealings with the Assamese he promised to be conciliatory in spirit. He informed the Governor-General that the trade of Assam was carried on partly by barter and partly for the specie of that kingdom, gold and silver. The Assam government entrusted the trade to one man called the Barua. The goods received in return for salt were black pepper, muga-dhutis, muga silk, stick and lump lac and munjit, the quantity of the different articles varying according to the year's produce in the country. The Assam market took off about 100,000 maunds of salt in a year. There was also a sale in the Assam Choky for some broadcloth, copper, etc. Baillie recommended that the salt to be sent to Assam should be of the best sort from Khulna or Dacca. He would want 50,000 maunds of salt in the month of November, 25,000 maunds in

13. Wm. Cowper, Bd. of Rev., to Cornwallis, July 17, Beng. Rev. Cons., July 23, 1787.

14. Cornwallis to Cowper, July 23, Beng. Rev. Cons., July 23, 1787.

15. Bengal Letter to Court, July 31, 1787.

16. Baillie to Cornwallis, July 24, Beng. Rev. Cons., July 27, 1787, pp. 5-11.

the latter end of December, and another 25,000 maunds about the latter end of July. He estimated the expense of transporting salt to Goalpara from Dacca to be about 25 rupees per 100 maunds. According to his calculation the amount of sales in Assam for the first year after the commencement of the trade would not be above 350,000 rupees. He asserted that the markets of Assam were always in his time rather steady particularly in respect of salt. A part of the Assam goods received in lieu of salt used to be disposed of by Baillie to the merchants of Chilmari and Murshidabad, etc., and the rest were sent to Calcutta where they always sold for a profit. As regards the force, Baillie believed that 100 sepoys or invalids commanded either by an officer and a sergeant, or possibly by a sergeant and a corporal, would be sufficient to protect the warehouses, boats, and the trade in general, and also to form the different necessary Chokies. Baillie was of opinion that the districts to be put under his administration, though small in respect of revenue, were of consequence to the Commercial Resident as they "give him an appearance in the eyes of the Assamese and offered him frequent opportunities of obliging them by preventing the borderers from insulting them and plundering their boats." He did not see the necessity of a Court of Adawlat as the Common Court of Kutchery would answer every necessary purpose. Baillie concluded his letter by pointing out the absolute necessity of preventing every description of merchants from carrying salt higher than the borders of Rangamati, otherwise, he thought, the object of his appointment would be subverted as it would be impossible for him to prevent the smuggling of that article into Assam.

Protests by Dow and Raush : It should be pointed out that the exercise of the monopoly in salt by the Company and the opening of the trade in other articles to individuals were a contradiction in terms. Baillie himself admitted that the Assamese generally offered the produce of their country in exchange for salt. As private merchants were not authorised to trade in that article they would not obviously get any Assam goods except what would remain with the Assamese after they had purchased their salt. Though Baillie was strictly forbidden to trade in other articles except salt he would have to find means for disposing of Assam goods that he would receive in exchange for that article. A clash with the private merchants of the place would therefore be unavoidable.

On receiving information from the Collector of Rungpore respecting Baillie's appointment William Dow at once lodged a formal protest against the virtual monopoly of the Assam trade which the

Company now proposed to exercise.[17] He believed that the privilege of trading in all articles except salt which the Government had granted to all other merchants was more specious than real. He foresaw the ruin that would come upon himself and many other industrious individuals now concerned in the Assam trade. He predicted that the new arrangement would not bring any sort of advantage to the Company, and he was confident that "of this the Honourable Board will be fully convinced in a very short time."

Daniel Raush who had renewed his trading activities at Goalpara after the abolition of Killican's monopoly was also adversely affected by the appointment of Baillie. He submitted a representation to the Collector of Rungpore pointing out that the exclusive sale of salt to Assam merchants comprehended the whole trade with that country, for every article of commerce was bartered for salt and nothing was sold for ready money.[18] "Therefore", said Raush, "Mr. Baillie's appointment must of course be the ruin of many individuals as well as of myself without the least advantage to the Company, which they will experience in one year's time." The Supreme Board did not take any action on the two protests.

On August 16, Baillie requested the Bengal Government that salt of the first quality available at Khulna should be sent for sale at Goalpara. It would, he expected, impress the Assam government of the Company's justice and of the advantage they would derive from trading with the Company instead of private individuals, who used to mix the salt, a practice which ultimately led to the ruin of the trade. He requested the despatch of 50,000 maunds of Khulna salt by October 15, 1787, 25,000 maunds in July, and a further quantity of 25,000 maunds by the middle of August 1788.[19]

Governor-General's presents to Assam Raja: The preliminaries which Baillie had to settle before leaving for Goalpara included the purchase and provision of the presents for the king of Assam and his principal nobles, and the arrangements about the transportation of salt to Goalpara.

On September 27, 1787, Baillie submitted a list of articles to the Board which he regarded as suitable for presents to the Assam court.[20] They were selected to convey a fair idea of the products

17. Dow to Day Hart MacDowall, Collector of Rungpore, Aug. 10. 1787, *Rungpore District Records*, Vol. V, No. 336, p. 215.

18. Raush to MacDowall, Aug. 12, 1787, *Rungpore District Records*, Vol. V, No. 337, p. 215.

19. Baillie to Cornwallis, Aug. 16, Beng. Rev. Cons., Aug. 17, 1787, pp. 609-11.

20. Baillie to Cornwallis, Sept. 27, Beng. Rev. Cons., Sept. 28, 1787.

of Europe and the East forming the principal commodities of the Company's import and export trade. They consisted of:—2 pairs of looking glasses, 2 cubits long and proportionately broad; 6 pairs of looking glasses about a cubit in length and breadth in proportion; 3 pairs of pictures of Europe in handsome frames; 1 pair of handsome silver-mounted pistols; 2 pairs of plain pistols in brass or iron-mounted; 2 handsome fowling pieces; 2 handsome small swords; 4 plain small swords; 1 piece of crimson-flowered velvet; 1 piece of broadcloth, one side scarlet and the other green; 2 pieces of superfine scarlet cloth; 2 pieces of common red cloth; 2 pieces of China flowered silk; 10 pieces of Zumdaum Dacca cloth; 10 pieces of middling mullmulls; 6 dressing boxes with razors; 4 Tweezera cases; 2 dozen of razors; 2 dozen of scissors; 2 dozen of penknives; 2 dozen of water-chauk; 1 box of China toys; 4 seers of cardamoms, mace, cloves, cinnamon, and nutmeg; 1 maund of sandal wood; and 1 maund of red wood.

The greater portion of the articles was purchased from the Calcutta bazaar at a cost of rupees 1,000.[21] The Export Warehouse furnished 10 pieces of *chameanahs*, 10 pieces of muslin and 1 maund of red wood, while the Import Warehouse provided 2 pieces of superfine scarlet cloth and 2 pieces of common red cloth. Baillie was directed to forward Lord Cornwallis's letter together with the presents to the king of Assam with a request from himself for permission to go into that country.[22]

Transportation of salt to Goalpara: On August 31, 1787, the Government had published an advertisement inviting tenders for transporting 50,000 maunds of salt from Narayangunge to Goalpara. The first and the only proposal came from a Greek merchant named Constantine Theodosius. He offered as his securities Arratoon Petruse, son of late Petruse, Mavrody Kyreakous, the head merchant of the Greeks in Bengal, G. Hamilton and Aberding, inhabitants of Calcutta.[23] The Greek merchants had been employed in the navigation of the river Brahmaputra between Narayangunge and Goalpara, and therefore the applicant claimed that his experience would enable him "to promise the business being done with due expedition and security equal if not superior to what can be

21. The purchase was made by Baillie's Attorney George Robinson through his Sarkar. Some slight alteration can be noticed between the list submitted by Ballie and the list of final purchase.

22. Baillie to Cornwallis, Sept. 27, and Cornwallis to Stuart, Sept. 28, Beng. Rev. Cons., Sept. 28, 1787, pp. 400-403.

23. Theodosius to Shore, Beng. Rev. Cons., October 2, 1787, pp. 451-54.

expected from other persons whatsoever." He offered to transport the salt at the rate of 70 sicca rupees per 100 maunds taking the risk of the safe delivery upon himself; and at the rate of 45 rupees for the same quantity if the Company took the risk upon themselves. He undertook to deliver the salt within the space of 80 days from the day of contract. The Board forwarded the proposal to Baillie and asked him to supply information regarding the expenses of transportation.

The estimate quoted by Baillie was much lower than the rates at which the Greek merchant was prepared to undertake the contract. According to Baillie the cost of transportation per 100 maunds of salt would come upto rupees 26 only, *viz.*, for boats 20 rupees, wastage and damage 3 rupees, and Heyals and Burdars 3 rupees.[24]

Constantine Theodosius submitted another representation to the Board agreeing to take off 10 rupees per 100 maunds from his former proposals from "an ardent desire to promote the interest of the Honourable Company as much as lay in his power." He explained the difficulties of transport caused by the high price of boats at Narayangunge. He would have to provide two empty boats to each fleet of 10,000 maunds with a European conductor for the purpose of protection directing the navigation independent of peons and lascars. The risk of the river from its rapidity was also very considerable, and boats were frequently lost to guard against which additional expenses in cordage and other equipment would be necessary. Robert Lindsay, Resident at Sylhet, used to pay rupees 35 per 100 maunds in sending his *chunam*, and another merchant named Robinson used to pay the same amount in transporting salt from Soolaliver to Rajmungal. The contractor further proposed to accept 50 rupees per 100 maunds as charges for transport if the value of the salt were reduced to 200 rupees per 100 maunds. The Board referred the proposals of the Greek merchant to Baillie with directions to transport the salt on the cheapest terms for the Company consistent with its safety; and for that purpose he was authorised to do it either at the Company's expense immediately or by contract.[25]

On October 18, 1787, Baillie who was still then at the Presidency submitted final proposals for the transportation of salt. He admitted the risks attending salt fleets, which, he believed, were

24. Baillie to Thomas Short, Asst. Rev. Secy., Oct. 5, Beng. Rev. Cons., October 16, 1787, pp. 582-3.

25. Theodosius to Bd. of Rev., undated, Beng. Rev. Cons., October 16, 1787, pp. 583-6.

no means so great as set forth by the Greek merchant. Baillie proposed to engage with two men who had been accustomed to that business for the transportation of 50,000 maunds immediately from Narayangunge to Goalpara at the rate of 26 rupees per 100 maunds. Baillie requested the Board to ask the Collector of Dacca to furnish the contractors with money for the above purpose, and to examine the boats before the loading of the salt to see that they were in proper condition to retain the quantity, and after the loading to see that the boats were not too deep. The Board authorised Baillie to adopt the measures proposed, and issued the necessary orders to the Collector of Dacca.[26]

Baillie's boat disaster: Towards the end of October 1787 Baillie left Calcutta by boat to join his new duties at Goalpara. On the 2nd November there took place a cyclone on the river Padma and affected the districts round the river. At about 4 o'clock in the morning the wind began to blow from the north-east with great violence attended by a heavy fall of rain, which continued to increase until about 3 o'clock in the afternoon, when changing suddenly to the east there came a most furious hurricane that lasted with different degrees of violence for ten hours. At Rungpore, the headquarters of the district, trees were torn up by the roots, the Resident's bungalows were almost all unroofed and there was scarcely a thatched house left standing in the place.[27] Baillie lost in that storm all his boats and with difficulty escaped with his life. His total loss which included the presents for the Assam king as well as his own personal effects amounted to 10,000 rupees.[28] Baillie went back to Calcutta, and on November 6, 1787, he made his application to the Board for a second provision of the presents. He proposed this time to despatch the presents by water under the charge of his Banyan, and to prosecute his own journey by land. The Supreme Board directed the Board of Trade to furnish Baillie with presents "in like quality and similar quantity." The purchases were made by Baillie's attorney, George Robinson, and Baillie left for Goalpara in December 1787.[29]

26. Baillie to Thomas Short, Asst. Rev. Secy., Oct. 18, Beng. Rev. Cons., October 19, 1787, pp. 963-5.

27. Glazier's *Rungpore*, ed. Firminger, p. 23.

28. Seton-Karr, *Selections from Calcutta Gazette*, Vol. I, p. 214; Baillie to Cornwallis, Nov. 6, Beng. Rev. Cons., No. 8, 1787, pp. 216-18; Bengal Letter to Court, Dec. 15, 1787.

29. Robinson to Ed. Hay, Rev. Secy., undated, Beng. Rev. Cons., Dec. 7, 1787.

Baillie as Collector of Rangamati: On December 23, 1787, Baillie was at Chilmari where he received charge of the district of Karaibari. He arrived at Goalpara in the first week of January 1788 and received charge of Rangamati and Bijni from Day Hart MacDowall, Collector of Rungpore. The three districts which constituted Baillie's Collectorship were Rangamati, Bijni and Karaibari, and included the Tope-Khana Mahals of those places. The district newly formed was called Rangamati, and Baillie was addressed at different times by the Board of Revenue as Collector of Rangamati or as Superintendent in the Collections of Rangamati. The total jumma for the district amounted in the Bengali year 1195, 1788-89 A.D., to rupees 14,469, and in the ensuing year 1196 to rupees 13,922-10-4. Karaibari was separated from Mymensing, and Rangamati and Bijni from Rungpore.[30]

The principal Zemindar of Rangamati was the Kanungo Bulchand Barua, who at the time of Baillie's arrival at Goalpara, was a prisoner at Rungpore for complicity in the revolutions at Cooch Behar.[31] A Sezawal had to be appointed to receive the revenue on behalf of the Government in the absence of Bulchand Barua. The total jumma for this district was rupees 3,674-10-4 in the Bengali year 1196. Rangamati, in respect of its revenue, was on the same footing with the other territorial possessions of the East India Company. Baillie affirmed that the revenue was assessed agreeably to the abilities of the very poor inhabitants.[32]

Karaibari was a tributary mahal and paid annually 8,200 rupees in five different *kists* or instalments. The Zemindar was one Mahendranarayan Chaudhuri and his family had been in possession of the Zemindari from time immemorial. Baillie found the country in very great distraction in consequence of the disputes between Zemindars and farmers. A Sezawal was appointed to supervise the collections on behalf of the Company.[33]

Bijni was like Karaibari a tributary mahal. The Zemindar was one Mukundanarayan, a descendant of Raja Parikshit, the

30. Statement signed by A. Caldecolt, Acct. Bd. Rev., Jan. 21, Bd. Rev. Proceedings, Jan. 25, 1790.

31. The present Raja of Gauripur is in direct line of succession to Bulchand. In 1905 the Gauripur estate consisted of the perganahs of Ghurla, Jamira, Aurangabad, Makrampur, Gola Alamgang, Kalumalupara, Noabad Faturi and Dhubri. The first five perganahs were acquired by Bulchand, to which his grandson Dhirchandra added the last three. Dhirchandra's son was Pratapchandra, whose widow adopted the Raja Prabhatchandra Barua. *Goalpara Gazetteer* by B. C. Allen, 1905, p. 117.

32. Baillie to Shore, Sept. 25, Bd. Rev. Proceedings, Oct. 29, 1788.

33. *Ibid.*, Mackenzie's *North-Eastern Frontier of Bengal*, p. 246.

grandson of the famous Koch general Chilarai. Bijni used to pay to the Company an annual tribute of about 40 elephants. As the elephants delivered were not always of the desirable kind, most of them having usually died before they reached Rungpore, the Government asked the Collector in July 1787 to settle the tribute in money.[34] A part of Bijni in the Eastern Duars was subordinate to Bhutan, the government of which claimed a tribute from Bijni which consisted of an exchange of the productions of the two countries, the advantage being considerably in favour of the Bhutanese.[35]

The estate of Bidyagong immediately adjacent to Bijni was constantly subject to the intrusions of the Bhutanese. It was obliged to deliver 40 elephants to the British Government, but it was found impossible to enter into any terms with the Zemindar the estate having gone entirely into the hands of the Bhutanese.[36]

Mechpara, or Mahespara or Mespara as it was sometimes called, was at that time a petty Zemindari included in the jumma of Karaibari.[37] It was of considerable importance as the town of Goalpara lay in it.

In addition to the ordinary land revenues or tribute of Rangamati, Bijni and Karaibari, Baillie was entrusted with the management of the Tope-Khana mahals. These mahals were a relic of the old Mogul administration during which an assignation for the payment of the artillery parks at Dacca had been granted on Karaibari, Mechpara, and on a part of Burripore and Sherpore. These districts were known as Tope-Khana mahals. It is not known what amount was paid to the Company by Karaibari and Mechpara as Tope-Khana contribution. The estate of Burripore in Ghoraghat Zemindari in Mymensing paid rupees 398-2-9, and Sherpore in Rungpore paid rupees 529-5-5. The Tope-Khana collections were under the management of a Sezawal. It was anomalous that the ordinary land revenues were paid by Burripore and Sherpore to the Collectors of Mymensing and Rungpore

34. *Rungpore District Records,* Vol. V, No. 306, p. 191. During the years 1776-87 only 90 elephants were received by the Company out of 816 which ought to have been supplied, Gait's *Koch Kings of Kamarupa, J.A.S.B.*, 1893, p. 307.

35. *An Account of the Burman Empire and the Kingdom of Assam,* 1839, p. 126.

36. Baillie to Shore, Jan. 31, Bd. Rv. Proceedings, Ap. 18, 1788.

37. Baillie to Shore, Oct. 23, Bd. Rv. Proceedings, Nov. 14, 1788.

respectively while their Tope-Khana contributions were to be paid to the Collector of Rangamati.[38]

Baillie was also in charge of the Abwab Fauzdari collections of Rangamati. Under the Moguls, the Thana of Rangamati being a frontier station, was a place of great consequence, and the Fauzadar in charge of it was always a person of high rank. He exercised a civil and criminal jurisdiction in the districts comprised in the Thana, and the Tope-Khanas, and deputed his agents to the mofussil who imposed fines on persons committing petty offences. The Zemindars finding that this was attended with bad consequences agreed to pay a sum of money annually in lieu thereof under the denomination of Abwab Fauzdari which became an article of the jumma. The Zemindar of Sherpore paid on this account rupees 698-5-6 to the Collector of Rangamati, and of Baritala rupees 601 though the two estates formed part of the districts Mymensing and Rajshahi respectively.[39]

On his arrival at Goalpara Baillie found the districts under his administration in the grip of a terrible famine. The year 1194 B.S., A.D. 1787-88, was a disastrous year for Rungpore of which Rangamati was a part. In July 1787 the rivers had overflowed their banks three times and inundated the whole country. Multitudes of men, women and children perished in the fields. The calamities culminated in a famine, and numbers of people who had escaped the floods died of starvation. Rice which used to be sold at 3 or 4 maunds per rupee was now sold at 12 seers per rupee, and even that was not to be had. Then there came the great cyclone of November 1787. It was estimated that during the year 1787-88 Rungpore had lost one-eighth of its inhabitants.[40] On June 13, 1788, Baillie asked the Government to grant rupees 600 or 1,000 for the relief of the distressed people, and the Board eventually granted rupees 1,000 for that purpose.[41] In spite of the floods and famine Baillie was prompt and regular in realising his revenue, and he received repeated letters of approbation from the Board of Revenue for his punctuality in realising the *kists*.

The conduct of the Zemindars was of considerable anxiety to Baillie. Mahendranarayan Chaudhuri, the Zemindar of Karaibari, was engaged in constant hostilities with the Garos. He compelled

38. H. Douglas, Com. of Coch Behar, to Bd. Rev., Aug. 30, Proceedings, Sept. 22 and Oct. 29, 1790.

39. Bd. Rev. Proceedings, Oct. 29, 1788; June 18 and 25, 1789; and Oct. 29, 1790.

40. Glazier's *Rungpore*, ed. Firminger, pp. 21-23.

41. Baillie to Shore, June 13, Bd. Rev. Proceedings, June 27, July 11, 1788.

the Garo chief Rengta to bring all the cotton produced in his hills to market in Karaibari and to deliver a certain proportion of it at a fixed rate to the Zemindar who on his failure always took recourse to oppressive measures. The Karaibari Zemindar had no just right to compel the Garos to trade with him, but his conduct had received the sanction of custom which had existed for upwards of forty years. The Garos opposed the imposition and raided villages in Karaibari. Mahendranarayan allied himself with Ranaram, Zemindar of Mechpara, invaded the Garo hills and entered on a career of conquest. They remained in the hills for two or three years, and brought large sections of the tribe under their control. Rengta opposed the aggressors with vigour, but he was captured by Mahendranarayan and kept in confinement till 1790. On his release Rengta offered to become a Zemindar under the Company. This proposal was accepted by the Company. But the negotiations fell through as Mahendranarayan arrested the messengers sent to conclude the arrangements.[42]

The Zemindar of Karaibari was involved in several boundary disputes with his neighbours causing riots and loss of life. It was difficult on the part of the Collectors to settle these disputes as the Ameens sent forth from each authority to enquire into the cases "gave always dismetrically opposite reports," and Baillie expressed his opinion in very forceful language,—"I am convinced that it [Karaibari dispute] can never be settled by black ameens; they are far too venal to settle the right of controverted property."[43]

The Zemindar of Mechpara, Ranaram Chaudhuri, was equally unruly and turbulent. In 1776-77 he had conquered several Garo villages compelling their chiefs to deliver cotton on terms favourable to himself. His revenue was included in the jumma of Karaibari. As the Mechpara Zemindar always evaded paying his share to the Karaibari Zemindar the latter had to pay the Mechpara revenue to the Company from his own funds. The Karaibari Zemindar submitted several petitions to Baillie for ejecting the Mechpara Zemindar and putting his perganah entirely under Karaibari. The Government did not pay serious considerations to Baillie's recommendations on the Karaibari Zemindar's request. Considering it unbecoming to press the Government further Baillie kept the Karaibari Zemindar in good humour by kind words and promises. There were other charges laid at the door of

42. Mackenzie's *North-East Frontier of Bengal*, pp. 244-5.
43. Glazier's *Rungpore*, ed. Firminger, p. 39.

Ranaram Chaudhury. "He is a villain," wrote Baillie to the Board of Revenue on October 23, 1788, "who commits depredations and robberies both in the river and his neighbourhood, and contumaciously refuses to come in though I have sent repeated perwanahs to that purpose."[44]

Baillie's relations with the Raja of Bijni were more cordial this time than in his previous incumbency seven or eight years before. Bhutanese incursions into Bijni were matters of frequent occurrence. The mountaineers swept down the plains of Bijni and carried off men and cattle. Baillie issued warnings to the Bhutanese, and he regretted that he could not do much with his force of 39 invalids. "Twenty of these," he wrote on July 19, 1788, "were ill with jungle fever."[45] The old Raja of Bijni Mukundanarayan died in August 1788. He was succeeded by Haridebnarayan whom Mukundanarayan had nominated as his successor.[46]

The task of inducing the Bijni Raja to agree to pay on annual tribute in money instead of elephants fell unon Baillie. After an "infinite deal of trouble for any sort of settlement for ready money," Baillie was able to write to the Board of Revenue on January 31, 1788, that the Zemindar of Bijni had agreed to pay rupees 2,000 for 1787-88, instead of the elephant tribute. He affirmed that the measures adopted by him were conciliatory in character which alone enabled him to bring about that desired change.[47] Baillie could not however obtain similar terms for Bidyagong which was completely under the domination of the Bhutanese government. The Governor-General declined pressing any settlement with the Zemindar of Bidyagong as the amount involved was trivial and might lead to disputes with the Bhutan people.

The years 1787 to 1790, from the appointment of Baillie as Collector of Rangamati to the abolition of that office, saw momentous changes in the revenue administration of Bengal. Previously to this the Committee of Revenue at Calcutta concluded settlement of the different districts by deputing special officers. The Collectors were mere figure-heads. The Zemindars paid their revenues directly to the Khalsa or exchequer at Calcutta. The reforms of

44. Baillie to Shore, Oct. 23, Bd. Rev. Proceedings, Nov. 14, 1788.

45. Baillie to Shore, July 19, Bd. Rev. Proceedings, Aug. 1, 1788.

46. Sept. 19 and Dec. 4, 1788. Haridebnarayan's father Hemnarayan and Mukundanarayan's father Bijoynarayan were both brothers, being sons of Raja Sibnarayan who was the grandson of Vijitanarayan, the founder of the Bijni ruling dynasty,—*Goalpara Gazetteer* by B. C. Allen, p. 113.

47. Baillie to Shore, Jan. 17, Bd. Rev. Proceedings, Feb. 5, 1788.

1786 made the Collectors completely responsible for the revenues of their respective districts. They made the settlements and collected all the revenues. The Board of Revenue which was created after the abolition of the Committee of Revenue exercised a general control over the work of the Collectors. They sanctioned the settlements made by the Collectors.[48]

The regulations for the Decennial Settlement were introduced in 1791, and Baillie had to follow the interim revenue regulations of 1786. In making the settlement for 1195 B.S., 1788-89 A.D., Baillie realised the difficulty of granting regular *pattahs* to the ryots. They were mainly of the nature of squatters and migrated freely from one place to another as in the opinion of Baillie there were "upwards of hundred times more land than is cultivated or used in any way." The ryots settled in some place promising to pay to the Zemindar something which they could avoid as "it was easy for them to move themselves and families in a night into the districts of other Zemindars where they are made welcome." He proposed to issue a proclamation commanding all Zemindars in settling with the ryots to give them a Kabuliyat signifying that they would require no more from them than the sum agreed for, and when any part was paid for the ryots to get a receipt for the same.[49]

As officer in charge of the Company's treasury at Goalpara the Collector was required to keep a sufficiency in hand to make advances to the Commercial Agent. On January 8, 1788, he was asked to advance money as follows: rupees 30,375 in February for raw silk, rupees 200 in March for muga-dhutis, rupees 15,187-8 in April for raw silk, and rupees 200 in May for muga-dhutis.[50]

On March 27, 1789, the Government of Bengal asked all the Collectors to submit reports on the thread, cotton and tobacco produced in their respective districts. Baillie in his report to the Board of Revenue, dated May 22, stated that Rangamati did not furnish any cotton, that the tributary districts of Bijni and Karaibari produced annually 20,000 maunds which were purchased by paikars in exchange for rice, dried fish and other things. The price of cotton varied from rupees 4½ to 5 per maund. The cotton was cultivated, as Baillie said, "by a wild savage race of mortals called Rabbahs who are the only people who inhabit the mountains." He informed the Government that no cotton thread was

48. F. D. Ascoli, *Early Revenue History of Bengal*, Chapters III and IV.
49. Baillie to Shore, June 13, Bd. Rev. Proceedings, June 27, 1738.
50. Shore to Baillie, Jan. 8, Bd. Rev. Proceedings, Jan. 8, 1788.

spun in the districts under his charge. Tobacco was not grown there in any quantity, that article being imported there from the districts of Bahirbund and Bhitarbund in Rungpore. He did not hear of any munjit or madder being found in any of the districts. D. H. MacDowall, Collector of Rungpore, stated in his report that Rungpore imported nearly 10,000 maunds of cotton from Bijni and Bidyagong, and that considerable quantities of the same article were brought from Sonapur and Sadiya in Assam to the Assam Choky from where they were retailed to the Bengal districts.[51]

Baillie's career as Collector of Rangamati was not marked by any singular achievement, except the settlement made with the Bijni Raja for payment of the tribute in money instead of elephants. His Collectorship was designed to give efficiency to his duties as the Company's Resident at Goalpara charged with the task of establishing a beneficial commercial intercourse between Bengal and Assam. But it must be admitted that the Collectorship brought the north-east frontier of Rungpore within one district organisation making the work of subsequent administrators easy. In 1822 Rangamati, corresponding roughly to the limits of Baillie's jurisdiction, was formed into a separate district under the designation of North-East Parts of Rungpore. In 1826, the same district, then called Goalpara, became provisionally a part of the Assam Valley Division. In 1867 it was placed under the Commissioner of Cooch Behar, and in 1874 it was finally incorporated in Assam. It now forms one of the six districts of the Assam Valley Division. The grouping of the Rangamati territories into a separate district was primarily due to the repeated representations of Baillie made since the year 1771.

Baillie's success in the Assam trade: What Baillie achieved as the promoter of the Company's trade in Assam can be judged from his own reports submitted to Government from time to time. The expectations which he had made could not be realised owing to the ravages of a civil war and a dreadful famine in Assam. The Moamaria rebels renewed their hostilities with greater violence. They were however suppressed. The king of Assam, Gaurinath Singha, promulgated orders to massacre the Moamarias whenever and wherever they could be found. They rose again in open arms and succeeded in capturing the capital Rangpur in Upper Assam. Gaurinath Singha fled to Gauhati in January 1788 with most of his officers leaving the management of affairs in Upper Assam to

51. Baillie to Shore, May 22, and MacDowall to Shore, June 1, Bd. Rev. Proceedings, June 15, 1789.

the prime minister Purnananda Buragohain. Assam was reduced to such serious distraction that a large part of the inhabitants fled from the country and took shelter in the neighbouring territories Cachar, Jayantia and the Bengal district of Rungpore. The Moamarias, soon after the occupation of the capital Rangpur, placed Bharath Singha, a relation of their spiritual leader, on the throne.[52]

The flight of Gaurinath Singha to Gauhati was regarded by Baillie as his abdication which precluded the idea of despatching the letter of Lord Cornwallis addressed to that monarch. The usurpation of the Moamarias was restricted to the territory immediately surrounding the capital Rangpur, and to Bengmara, their stronghold east of the Dihing river. Gaurinath Singha was still the king of the country. Lower Assam with its headquarters at Gauhati and a large part of Upper Assam where the premier Purnananda Buragohain still wielded the reins of government and organised operations against the insurgents were still in possession of the Ahom sovereign.

Baillie did not understand the real character of the situation in Assam. He considered the Moamaria usurper at Rangpur to be the successor of the 'deposed' Gaurinath Singha. Baillie proposed to send back Lord Cornwallis's letter to Calcutta as soon as he would be able to transmit the name and title "of the present man," so that another letter might be written. For transmitting the name and title of "the present Rajah" Baillie intended to wait until the new money was struck and "not before he was universally acknowledged." It is not known when Baillie sent the Governor-General's letter and the presents to Assam. Bharath Singha, the usurpur at Rangpur was not certainly "universally recognised". The real monarch Gaurinath Singha could not, nor did the distracted condition of the country permit him to give effect to the sentiments expressed in the letter of Lord Cornwallis.[53]

The signal failure of Baillie's expectations was seen in the astounding discrepancy between the quantity of salt he had hoped to dispose of annually and that which he actually sold to the Assamese. During the year 1788 Baillie sold only 9493 maunds of salt at Goalpara, whereas he had expected to sell 100,000 maunds.

52. The circumstances of the Moamaria rebellion leading to Gaurinath Singha's flight to Gauhati will be described more fully in a subsequent chapter. Coins struck by Bharath Singha, bearing the dates 1791, 1792, 1793, 1795 and 1797 are still extant.—Gait, *History of Assam*, p. 200.

53. Baillie to Cornwallis, May 17, Beng. Rev. Cons., July 21, 1788, pp. 994-6.

The first consignment of salt consisting of 50,000 maunds arrived at Goalpara in March 1788, of which Baillie received only 46,873 maunds, the deficit being due to wastage and loss in transit. He sold 6,266 maunds of salt to the Assam Barua and 3,227 maunds to sundry paikars at the rate of 6 rupees per maund. The sale proceeds amounted to rupees 56,957. The balance remaining undisposed of at the *golah* at Goalpara on the 31st December amounted to 37,380 maunds. He also sold Assam goods to the value of rupees 24,664 to a merchant named Dayalchand Misra at prime cost realising for the Company a profit of 7 per cent which amounted to rupees 1726. The Assam goods to the value of rupees 15,142 sold to sundry paikars at different percentages brought in a profit of rupees 165. The Company's total earnings during the year 1788 came upto rupees 58,849.

Of this amount the sum of rupees 33,459 was sent in two bills drawn on Baillie's attorney George A. Robinson in favour of the Governor-General in Council. Of the balance the sum of rupees 920 was spent in purchasing sundry Assam goods and despatching them to the Presidency under instructions of the Board of Trade. Baillie had made advances to merchants as follows: rupees 2,896 to the Assam Baruas; rupees 5,777 to sundry paikars; and rupees 501 to Dayalchand Misra. These advances were considered by Baillie as 'good outstanding debts'. The prime cost of the Assam goods that remained at the *golah* at Goalpara at the end of the year amounted to rupees 1,233. He had also a cash balance of rupees 7,133. The expenses included rupees 2,942 as factory charges consisting of servants' wages, repairs of *golahs,* boats, etc. Baillie's own commission amounted to rupees 3,987 calculated at the rate of 7 per cent on the sale proceeds of salt.

Baillie's transactions in Assam goods during the first year of his Residentship amounted to rupees 41,959. Part of it he sold at Goalpara, and part he despatched to Calcutta for disposal by the Board of Trade. Some portion of the Assam goods was possibly received by him from the Baruas and other purchasers of salt. He procured for the Company a profit of about 7 per cent on the Assam goods disposed of by him. The orders of the Government forbidding him to trade in any other Bengal articles except salt were strictly obeyed by Baillie.

In February 1789, Baillie went to Calcutta after settling the accounts of his business for the year 1788. On February 23 while at Calcutta he submitted his report to the Government on the trade of the previous year.[54] He attributed his failure to the ravages of a civil war and a dreadful famine in Assam—"calamities which could neither be foreseen nor prevented." Previous to his departure for Calcutta he had learnt that the evils in Assam had in a great measure subsided from which he expected that the trade for the current year 1789 would be worthy of the attention of the Company. He hoped that the Government would concur with his opinion that the trade had not had a fair trial during the preceding year owing to "the unsettled and disturbed state of Assam." He urged the Government to continue the trade for another year at the end of which he would report whether that business could be made an object deserving of the future consideration of the Company. He pointed out in this connection that the expense to Government in keeping up the establishment at Goalpara was trifling, that as his emoluments arose from a commission on the sales the Company could not lose, and that he alone would suffer by a second failure. The Governor-General in Council in the meeting of the Board held on March 18, 1789, resolved to comply with Baillie's proposal for conducting the trade for the year 1789. The Board communicated their decision to the Court of Directors in their despatch of August 10, 1789. The Directors approved of the Board's decision, and at the same time expressed their regret that interruption should have been occasioned in the experiment which they had launched with the intention of giving a fair trial to Baillie's proposition for establishing a commercial intercourse with Assam.[55]

Raush's views on Assam trade: A fair criticism of Baillie's commercial enterprise is available in the letter addressed by the merchant Daniel Raush to the Government on September 1, 1789.[56] Though there was a tinge of self-interest in Raush's representation as it was accompanied by the request to lay open the Assam trade in salt, his note embodied the results of his long experience in Goalpara—facts which Baillie could not discover or which he had concealed from the Government.

After the abolition of Killican's monopoly Raush had attempted to rehabilitate his Goalpara concerns. He had purchased Killican's factory with all its appendage. He had also erected an indigo manufacture near Goalpara. After Raush had invested a con-

54. Baillie to Cornwallis, Feb. 23, Beng. Rev. Cons., March 18, 1789, pp. 306-11.

55. Bengal Letter to Court, Aug. 10, 1789; Court's Letter to Bengal, May 19, 1790.

56. Raush to John Shore, Sept. 1, Beng. Rev. Cons., Sept. 25, 1789.

siderable sum of money in these ventures hoping to recoup his lost fortune Baillie reappeared at Goalpara with the monopoly of salt which amounted to an exclusive privilege of trade to Assam as he alleged that "nothing can be done here without salt." Raush had to abandon his concerns at Goalpara leaving his factory and all the property in and about that place to the mercy of Baillie trusting in the latter's professions of friendship in which, he alleged, he was greatly disappointed.[57] Raush then pointed out "that the said trade—in whatever light Baillie may represent it—never will be of any advantage to the Hon'ble Company, for the Assamese will never submit to be forced into trade, but they will have a free and open intercourse with every individual of Bengal, and this, Sir, [John Shore, President of the Board of Revenue], will be obvious to you by Mr. Baillie's having done no material business for the Hon'ble Company within these two years, and I presume to say, that he never will if he is continued at Gualparah."

Raush then referred to the loss suffered by the Company by having such a large quantity of salt as 30,000 maunds lying useless at Goalpara, and the further loss of 150,000 maunds which the Assamese would have taken from other individuals during the time Baillie had been at Goalpara. Raush alleged that by appointing Baillie to Goalpara the Company had caused "the loss of the whole Assam trade to Bengal in general which is about five and a half lakh of rupees per annum, and lastly the ruin of many individuals for the sake of a single individual."

Raush asked the Government to lay the trade of Assam open again, and he agreed to buy the 30,000 maunds of salt remaining in the Company's *golah* at Goalpara, at any price the Board would think proper. He then reaffirmed that his proposal, if accepted, would save needless expenses to the Company and prevent the ruin of himself and many others. The Governor-General in Council did not pass any opinion on Raush's representation; he ordered it to lie for consideration.

Though Raush solemnly declared his representation to be the real truth, yet it must be admitted that the failure of Baillie cannot be wholly attributed to the Company's exercise of the monopoly in salt, or to lack of enterprise, or inefficiency on Baillie's part. During 1788 Baillie had sold nearly 10,000 maunds of salt; Raush alleged that the Assamese would have taken 100,000 maunds if

57. Raush does not mention what these 'professions' were. They were, perhaps, promises to buy his concerns, or to afford him concessions as a salt paikar.

salt was sold by individuals. The difference, *viz.* 90,000 maunds, is too large a quantity to be ascribed to the mere accident of the Company's monopoly. If the Assamese wanted to buy or had the capacity of buying more salt they would have certainly done it from individual merchants or from the Company. The purchase would have been certainly restricted if the Assamese merchants did not enjoy the free choice of merchants to whom they could sell their own produce and buy salt in return, but never to the extent of 90,000 maunds. Baillie dealt justly with the Assamese and there was no complaint of any harassment or coercion during his Residentship. The real truth is that on account of the disorder and confusion in Assam, the depredations of freebooters from Bengal, and the ravages of a famine, the purchasing power of the Assamese became greatly reduced.[58] The men could not leave their homes for purposes of trade on account of insecurity of life and property in the country. Those who desisted from playing the role of active political partisans watched the results of the conflicts that were going on in the country. In fact the economic life of the people became completely upset owing to the tension that was in full swing. The Bengal salt was a useful article in the dietary of the Assamese, but it was not indispensable. The Assamese had their own local salt. Those who could not get it used the ordinary substitute for salt consisting of a decoction prepared chiefly by distilling the ashes of burnt roots of plantain trees. The Bengal salt was comparatively dear for the purse of the Assamese, and many went and still go without it taking recourse to their own local produce. It will be seen that a few years later Raush himself obtained the monopoly of the Assam trade from the Baruas, but he could not fare much better than Baillie. The growing disorders in Assam impeded the progress of trade. Raush had to enter Assam with an armed force to recover his dues in which unwise adventure he was eventually murdered.

Baillie recommends abolition of Goalpara Residentship : Baillie himself realised the grave character of the situation in Assam unattended by any prospect of the country being restored to tranquillity and order. The king being a fugitive at Gauhati hemmed in by foes from all quarters, Baillie could not enter into any negotia-

58. This is how the famine of 1789 is described in an old Assamese chronicle,—"The price of rice went upto one rupee per lime-pot. One mango cost one rupee. A bundle of arum used to be sold for one rupee or one rupee and eight annas. The sufferings of the people thus knew no bounds, and a large number of men died on that account."—*Tungkhungia Buranji*, O.U.P., page 116.

tions with the Assam government for placing its trade with Bengal on a proper footing which was one of the primary objects of his appointment.

To add to his disappointment the climate of Goalpara seriously affected his health. On July 9, 1788, he reported to Government on the "excessively unhealthy" climate of Goalpara and the indifferent state of his own health. He requested the Board's permission to go to Dacca for medical assistance. A year later he again fell ill, and was confined for sometime by a severe fever which left him in a very weak and helpless state. He proceeded to Dacca for treatment and change of air, stayed there for two months returning to Goalpara on November 7, 1789.

On November 8, Baillie received a letter from the Barphukan or viceroy of Gauhati, in the name of the king of Assam, asking for assistance to quell the disturbances in that country. Baillie was now confirmed in his opinion that as long as the troubles continued his appointment at Goalpara could not be of any utility or advantage to the Company. On the very next day he wrote a letter to Lord Cornwallis recommending the abolition of the Goalpara Residentship. "The civil dissensions," said Baillie, "still rage in Assam to the destruction and ruin of that once opulent kingdom." He did not see any possibility of the speedy conclusion of the disorders. He believed that even when the troubles were over "little can be expected for sometime after from a country destroyed by the calamities attending an implacable civil war." He then declared his opinion that under those circumstances his appointment at Goalpara had become unnecessary.

He recommended that in the event of the Government abolishing his appointment the districts of Rangamati and Bijni should be placed under the Commissioner of Cooch Behar, they being more contiguous to Cooch Behar than any other Collectorship, and that Karaibari should be put under Mymensing as formerly. As to the salt on hand he proposed to dispose of it to the best advantage "without any further dependence on Assam." The balances were now realised and he had about a lakh of rupees in silver which he intended to take down with him to Calcutta or send under the conduct of a proper guard. He concluded his letter by observing that the failure of his enterprise was due to "extraordinary casualties" and not to any fault on his part.[59]

Mechpara Zemindar's attack on Goalpara factory: The events at Goalpara moved rapidly towards a critical termination. A few

59. Baillie to Cornwallis, Nov. 9, Beng. Rev. Cons., Dec. 9, 1789.

days after Baillie had despatched his letter proposing the abolition of his Residentship there occurred an incident which proved that the spirit of disloyalty and rebellion was abroad, and that it was not safe for a Company's servant to reside in an out-of-the-way place like Goalpara without sufficient protection. Ranaram Chaudhuri, the refractory Zemindar of Mechpara, against whose conduct Baillie had reported several times to the Government, attacked the Company's *golahs* at Goalpara before daylight in the morning of November 22. He was accompanied by a force of 500 Burkendazes led by one Raghunath Sing, late a Havildar in the Company's service. Ranaram's intention was to cut off Baillie and his men, and Baillie did not receive any notice of his design until midnight. Before advancing upon Baillie in the factory Ranaram's people delayed for sometime in plundering and destroying the Dewan's house and the salt *golahs* so that daylight soon appeared. Baillie with his 29 men, rank and file—invalids with several unable to carry their arms—offered a vigorous resistance to Ranaram's force and succeeded in repulsing them from the neighbourhood of the factory. Ranaram lost 50 men most of whom had served in the Company's army. Raghunath was wounded with a ball through his thigh, but he managed to escape. Baillie imprisoned four men of Ranaram who were all ex-servants of the Company. The loss on Baillie's side was one European killed with several natives and some wounded. At 9 o'clock Ranaram went off with his force to about a *coss* from Goalpara into a jungle. Baillie apprehended a second and a more vigorous attack during the course of the night on the 22nd or in the morning of the 23rd. The inhabitants of Goalpara seized all the boats and fled with them on the first alarm.

Baillie took all possible precautions to oppose Ranaram's renewed attack. He crossed over to Jugighopa on the opposite bank of the river Brahmaputra to enquire about men and ammunition, and came back within two hours with some of both. He had one lakh of rupees in the treasury to guard which he proposed to post all the sepoys at his disposal. He wrote at once to MacDowall, Collector of Rungpore, to despatch 30 or 40 sepoys with a sufficient quantity of ammunition "to repel the infamous villain who has long been accustomed to such atrocious conduct." He requested MacDowall to write to Raush or whoever might be at Kurigram to forward the men and ammunition overland to Batamari and from thence by boats to Goalpara.[60]

60. Baillie to Cornwallis, Nov. 22, Beng. Rev. Cons., Dec. 9, 1789.

On the very day of occurrence Baillie wrote a letter to Lord Cornwallis describing Ranaram's attack on Goalpara. "My Lord," Baillie added, "he [Ranaram] is a villain of the greatest magnitude, and has long carried on the business of a principal dacoit both by land and water," He informed the Governor-General that any reinforcement from Rungpore would be of no effect if the second attack took place that night. He concluded by saying, "If I am spared I will take the most early opportunity to inform your Lordship of the result."

Baillie's reinforcement from Jugighopa and the loss sustained by Ranaram during the engagement in the morning of the 22nd prevented the latter from repeating his attack. He lurked for some days in the jungles in the vicinity of Goalpara, and on the 26th Baillie was definitely informed that Ranaram had left the place and retired to his hills. Baillie communicated the news in a subsequent letter to Lord Cornwallis.[61]

On receipt of Baillie's letter MacDowall immediately despatched a Havildar, a Naik, 15 sepoys, 1 Jemadar and 30 Burkendazes. He also requested H. Douglas, Commissioner of Cooch Behar, to despatch some sepoys to Baillie's assistance. The Commissioner immediately sent to Goalpara 20 sepoys under a Havildar. This diversion of forces outside their allotted jurisdictions was subsequently condoned by the Government; and the Commissioner of Cooch Behar and the Collector of Rungpore were both empowered to do so in future when such emergency would arise.

On hearing of Ranaram's attack on Goalpara the Supreme Board ordered that the lands of that Zemindar should be attached and confiscated and put up to public sale. They instructed the Collector of Rangamati to declare a reward of 500 rupees to be offered to any person who would apprehend and deliver Ranaram to him, or to the Collector of Rungpore and Mymensing or to the Commissioner of Cooch Behar. They also asked the Commander-in-Chief to detach a force sufficient to enable Baillie to apprehend Ranaram and restore the peace of the districts under his charge. The four persons whom Baillie had imprisoned were to be delivered over to the Fauzdari Court for trial.[62]

As Baillie needed a force immediately to quell the disturbances in Mechpara he engaged a great number of Burkendazes who had however to be disbanded on the arrival of the detach-

61. Baillie to Cornwallis, Nov. 26, Beng. Rev. Cons., Dec. 9, 1789.
62. Beng. Rev. Cons., Dec. 9, 1789; Bd. Rev. Proceedings, Dec. 24, 1789.

ment of sepoys sent up by the Commander-in-Chief. Baillie permitted the Burkendazes to proceed to Assam for the assistance of the Raja, "when," as Raush pointed out two years later, "it happened unfortunately for the Rajah of Assam as well as for his country and the trade that most part of the Bengal Burkendazes had engaged themselves by Kistenarain, the pretended Rajah of Dring [Darrang] in Assam, in order to possess himself by force of arms of all the Pergunnahs of Camrup and Dring."[63]

It is not known if Ranaram delivered himself up, or if he was arrested and imprisoned. His property was immediately confiscated. But before the investigations were completed Ranaram Chaudhuri died sometime in February 1790. His family at the time of his death consisted of his mother Sobun Chaudhurani, two wives, his son Mahiram aged 9, another son Gumburam aged 4, a third son aged 1½, an illegitimate son aged 12. After Ranaram's death his mother wrote to Baillie imploring the mercy of Government for herself and her grandson; and Baillie recommended them to the compassion of the Governor-General in Council as the best means of settling and establishing peace and quiet in these districts.[64]

Government abolishes Goalpara Residentship: In the meantime Baillie's proposition regarding the abolition of the Residentship at Goalpara had been considered by the Governmment. On December 9, 1789, the same day when the subject of Ranaram's attack first came up before the Board, they expressed their concurrence with the view of Baillie and abolished the appointment from the expiration of the Bengali year 1196.[65] Baillie was directed to deliver over the charge of the districts under his superintendence to such person on the Board of Revenue might think proper to order. He was asked to proceed to Calcutta and to take with him the invalid sepoys stationed with him in order that they might go from thence to join their corps at Munghyr. The Commander-in-Chief was requested to order the European sergeant upon duty at Goalpara to proceed to Sylhet after Baillie's departure, and to obey such orders as he might receive from the Collector of that district. Baillie was further directed to dispose of the unsold salt as well as he could and to send the proceeds together with the balances of each in his hands to Calcutta under a proper guard. An advertisement notifying the withdrawal of the restrictions

63. Raush to Cornwallis, Sept. 17, Beng. Pol. Cons., Oct. 3, 1792.
64. Baillie to Bd. Rev., Feb. 14, Bd. Rev. Proceedings, March 1, 1790.
65. This year ended on April 13, 1790 A.D.

imposed on salt and throwing open the Assam trade to all persons was published in the Gazette.[66]

The decision of the Government of Bengal was communicated to the Court of Directors in their despatch of February 13, 1790. The removal of the restrictions was described "to be the most likely measure for establishing a flourishing commerce advantageous to both countries." The Court concurred in the propriety of the Board's resolution of December 9, 1789, abolishing the Residentship at Goalpara. The Directors expressed their wish to be accurately informed of the state of the Assam trade after the withdrawal of the restrictions imposed upon salt since Baillie's appointment.[67]

On January 25, 1790, Baillie was directed to deliver charge of the several mahals under him to Henry Douglas, Commissioner of Cooch Behar, taking special care that no anticipation be made of the ensuing year's revenue by the existing renters. Baillie was asked, as usual, to furnish Douglas with all accounts and records in his possession relative to the districts in question.

Baillie's health had been completely undermined by his long residence on the Assam frontier. He fell ill again towards the end of 1789. On December 21, he proceeded to Calcutta for medical help before receiving the permission of the Government, his bad health obliging him to quit Goalpara immediately.[68].

Baillie returned to Goalpara for the last time in the first week of February. He busied himself in realising the arrears of revenue and getting things ready for delivering over the districts to the Commissioner of Cooch Behar.

Baillie's last significent act at Goalpara was his recommendation to Government that Mahiram, the eldest legitimate son of Ranaram Chaudhuri, should succeed to his father's Zemindari. "As the boy is quite guiltless," wrote Baillie in his letter of April 5, 1790, "I hope you will extend your compassion to him, and as it will be very agreeable to the inhabitants, his being put in possession restoring the Zemindary to him will be the means of insuring permanent peace and quiet, as also the recovery of the losses sustained by the Hon'ble Company by fire and pillage in November last." Baillie had been waiting for orders regarding the settlement of the Mechpara state as to whether it should be restored to the son of the deceased Ranaram or otherwise. He had com-

66. Sir Wm. Hunter, *Bengal Ms. Records,* Vol. I, Nos. 1153-54.
67. Court's Letter to Bengal, Dec. 15, 1790.
68. Baillie to Shore, Dec. 21, 1789, Bd. Rev. Proceedings, Jan. 4, 1790.

pleted all the arrangements for that purpose and would have been glad to have put the finishing hand to that business and delivered over the districts to his successor in a perfect settled state. Mahiram and other members of the family of Ranaram and also the prisoners were with Baillie. As his time had nearly expired he hoped the Commissioner of Cooch Behar must execute Government's final orders regarding Mechpara.

Baillie then concluded his letter which marked the termination of his labours at Goalpara,—"There remains now nothing further for me to do, but to deliver over the districts to Mr. Douglas, which shall be done at the end of the Bengal year [April 13, 1790] and I proceed to Calcutta according to your instructions."[69]

As directed by Government Henry Douglas, Commissioner of Cooch Behar, received charge of the Rangamati Collectorship from Baillie in the second week of April 1790. Two months later he submitted to the Board a list of the family of Ranaram Chaudhuri, the deceased Zemindar of Mechpara.[70] On July 21 the Supreme Board directed the Board of Revenue that Mahiram, the eldest legitimate son of the late Ranaram, be allowed to succeed his father in the Zemindari of Mechpara after the usual publication was made in the district and at the Khalsa.

The rules for the Decennial Settlement were issued by the Bengal Government on February 10, 1790.[71] The Commissioner of Cooch Behar asked the Government to be informed whether or not it was intended that the districts of Karaibari and Bijni which paid a fixed tribute should be included in the ten years' settlement. As regards Rangamati the Commissioner appointed a Sezawal named Birnarayan for making the collections and managing the *sayer* or transit duties at an expense of rupees 122 per month which was to be borne by the Zemindars. This step was taken in view of the difficulty of collecting the revenues of the place which was so very remote. The appointment of the Sezawal was approved by the Board of Revenue in their meeting of July 9, 1790. In respect of Karaibari and Bijni the Board directed that engagements for two years should be taken from the Zemindars if there was the custom of their executing annual engagements for the amount of their yearly tribute, in absence of which no decennial engagement was thought to be necessary.[72]

69. Baillie to C. Stuart, Ap. 5, Bd. Rev. Proceedings, Ap. 22, 1790.
70. H. Douglas to Bd. Rev., June 17, Bd. Rev. Proceedings, July 7, 1790.
71. F. D. Ascoli, *Early Revenue History of Bengal*, p. 70.
72. Douglas to Bd. Rev., June 14, Bd. Rev. Proceedings, July 9, 1790.

In October 1790 the Bijni Raja expressed his desire to pay his annual tribute in elephants as before as he was unable to pay rupees 2,000. The Commissioner of Cooch Behar proceeded to Goalpara and induced the Raja to agree to pay an annual tribute of rupees 3,000 in money in spite of the Board's definite prohibition to obtain an increase on rupees 2,000. When the increase was reported by the Commissioner the Board at once ordered the relinquishment of the increase of 1,000 rupees on the Bijni Raja's tribute.[73]

Henry Douglas, Commissioner of Cooch Behar, recommended the removal of the anomaly in the payment of the Tope-Khana mahals. He explained their origin and nature and asked the Government to sanction their transference to the Collectors to whom the land revenue was paid. In October 1790 the Board of Revenue recommended to the Governor-General in Council that the revenue of Burripore and Sherpore, then included in the Tope-Khana mahals of Rangamati, be added to the land revenue paid by the Zemindars of Ghoraghat and Sherpore to the Collectors of Rungpore and Mymensing and that the distinction of Tope-Khana be discontinued.[74]

In the meantime the specimens of Assam muga silk despatched to the Court in compliance with their requisition of April 11, 1785 and March 27, 1787, had arrived in England by the vessel *William Pitt*. The silk was examined by the buyers, who approved it in quality, though they objected to its having been packed in the *bird's-nest* manner, as they could not examine the inside which when opened was found to be of an inferior quality. The Court asked the Calcutta Board to send 10 bales by way of further trial to be made up in skeins similar to the other silk.[75]

Baillie's return to England: On his return to Calcutta after delivering over his charge to the Commissioner of Cooch Behar, Baillie was appointed Garrison Store Keeper at Fort William.[76] He also served as a Director of the Bank of Bengal.[77] Baillie stayed in Bengal till the spring of 1792 when he resigned his service and proceeded to Europe in the Company's ship *Lord Camden*. He entertained some desire to come back to Bengal where he had

73. Douglas to Bd. Rev., Oct. 20 and Nov. 15, Bd. Rev. Proceedings, Nov. 19 and 24, 1790.

74. Douglas to Bd. Rev., Oct. 7, Bd. Rev. Proceedings, Oct. 29, 1790.

75. Court's Letter to Bengal, May 19, 1790.

76. Bengal Public Consultations, June 4, 1790,

77. India Register, 1792, p. 62.

spent forty-three years, 1749 to 1792. The Bengal Government recommended that if he wished to do so the Court should permit him to return to India without prejudice to his rank and on his making application for it.[78] After this we do not hear of Hugh Baillie any more.

The return of Hugh Baillie to England marks the termination of a long and useful career devoted entirely to the service of the Company and English commerce in Bengal. As a young man he fought against the forces of Nawab Siraj-ud-dowlah and of the Dutch. He selected Goalpara to be the scene of his life's labours in spite of its inclement climate and all the dangers of a distant and unprotected station. From his experience of the place he realised the possibilities of a commercial intercourse with Assam, and he repeatedly urged the Company to take up that trade in all seriousness. He returned to England and used his influence in convincing the Court of the beneficial results of his scheme. He lived at Goalpara as a private merchant but could not achieve much success owing to the rapacious conduct of other traders. He then collaborated with an influential merchant and covenanted servant in the prosecution of the Assam trade but he was withdrawn before he could attain any degree of success. He went again to England to persuade the Directors to appoint a regularly authorised officer of the Company on the Assam frontier. He now obtained what he had been asking for so long, but before the experiment could be given a fair trial circumstances so developed in Assam that he himself had to recommend the abolition of his appointment.

One positive result of Baillie's long residence on the borders of Assam, whether as a private merchant or as an authorised agent of the Company, was the interest that he roused in that kingdom, on the part of the Government in Bengal and the Company's authorities in England, by his several proposals, reports, correspondence and personnal representations. Assam occupies not a very inconspicuous place in the records of the period, 1763 to 1790, which mark the two limits of Baillie's residence at Goalpara. Successive heads of the Bengal administration—Henry Vansittart, Lord Clive, Warren Hastings and Lord Cornwallis, as well as the Directors in London, had taken an interest in the affairs of Assam; and so when subsequently, matters of vital political significance came before them for decision they could marshall the necessary equipment and knowledge to view those questions in their proper

78. Bengal Letter to Court, April 27, 1792.

perspective. In fact it was Baillie who first revealed Assam to the East India Company. A dogged perseverance which is so characteristic of Scotchmen enabled Baillie to adhere to the one object of his life which entitles him to the credit of being the pioneer of English commerce in Assam.

Whatever might have been his material gain from his long residence at Goalpara Baillie enjoyed throughout the trust and confidence of the Assamese. "Beli Saheb"—the name by which he was known to the Assamese—was regarded by them as the authorised agent of the Company, and his mediation was invariably solicited whenever they wanted to be relieved of the oppressions and harassments of Bengal merchants. In 1777 the Barphukan applied to Baillie to stop the French merchant Laval from again entering Assam. In 1789 the same officer, in the name of the Assam Raja, asked Baillie for a contingent of sepoys to suppress the rebels. In 1791, after Baillie had left Goalpara, Assamese officers wrote to him to exercise his influence at Calcutta in bringing Raush and the Darrang prince Krishnanarayan to punishment for having invaded Assam with a force of Bengal Burkendazes. Whereas almost all other Bengal merchants were accused of violence towards the Assamese no such complaint was ever made in respect of Baillie. The confidence of the Assamese in the moderation, justice and helpfulness of the Company's Government was in a great measure created and fostered by the good treatment which they uniformly received at the hands of Baillie, and to his respect for Assam—"that once opulent kingdom."

Chapter VI

PART I

DISTURBANCES IN ASSAM

King Lakshmi Singha's Expulsion and Restoration

Character of the disturbances: The disturbances which had been responsible for the abolition of Baillie's appointment in Goalpara continued for more than three decades, and changed the whole character of the relations between the East India Company and Assam. Hitherto, the Company was solicitous of the friendship and co-operation of the Assam government for the purpose of promoting commercial intercourse between the subjects of Bengal and of Assam. Representatives of the Company resided at Goalpara to regulate the trade and maintain order and peace among the merchants of both countries. Now, when the troubles in Assam became acute its king and officers made repeated applications to the Company for assistance to quell the disturbances. The first petition to this effect was received by Baillie at Goalpara on November 8, 1789. Assamese rulers and nobles looked upon the Company as the only asylum for help for relieving them of their internal and external enemies or their personal foes. The relations which had hitherto been purely commercial now assumed a political shape, and thirty-five years after Baillie's departure from Goalpara, Assam became incorporated within the territories of the East India Company.

The disturbances in Assam were threefold in character,—the insurrection of the Moamarias, the rebellion of the Darrang prince Krishnanarayan, and the depredations of the Burkendazes. Taking advantage of the commotions in the land the local chieftains raised their heads and assumed virtual independence; and frontier tribes carried on plundering inroads into the outlying Assamese villages. The central government being weak owing to the inadequacy of the standing army, could not effectively enforce its orders, nor bring to punishment the refractory elements, nor protect the inhabitants from the oppressions of tyrants, freebooters and marauders. Life and property became insecure, trade and commerce came practically to a standstill, and a large section of the people deserted their homes, and those who remained were compelled to play the role of opportunists. The restoration of peace and order became the sole concern of the monarch or of a handful of patriotic nobles.

Genesis of the Moamaria revolt: The first to inflict a death-blow upon the solidarity and invulnerability of the Ahom government were the Moamarias, who were disciples of the Mayamara Satra, founded about the year 1601 by Aniruddhadeva at the instance of Gopaldeva. The Mayamara Satra was one of the twelve Satras under the episcopal hegemony of Gopaldeva; six of them were presided over by Brahman and the other six by Sudra Mahantas or pontiffs. The first six were Ahatguri founded by Sriram Ata, Kathpar by Purushottam, Khaura-mochar by Ramchandra, Ikarajan by Ram Sarma Sannyasi, Habung by Paramananda, and Charaibahi by Murari; the Sudra Satras were Bahbari or Dihing founded by Bar-Jadumani Ata, Haladhi-ati by Narayan, Gajala by Saru-Jadumani, Mayamara by Aniruddhadeva, Nagaria by Sanatan, and Doloi-po by another Sanatan. These twelve Satras and their branches and offshoots came to be known as Kala-Samhati Satras, a name applied to them after Gopaldeva's own monastery Kaljar Satra where he died in 1611.[1]

About the same time twelve Satras were established under the orders of Sankardeva's grandson Purushottam Thakur, and another twelve by Chaturbhuj Thakur, also a grandson of Sankardeva. The first twelve were known as Bar-Barejania Satras and the other twelve as Saru-Barejania Satras. These twenty-four Satras belonged to an order called Purusha-Samhati, as they were founded by preachers belonging to Sankardeva's line or Purusha.[2]

The Kala-Samhati Satras claimed some degree of superiority over the Purusha-Samhati Satras, inasmuch as the former were associated with Gopaldeva who had become the head of the Vaisnava church in Assam after the demise of Madhabdeva, the successor appointed by Sankardeva. This apostolic continuity claimed by the Kala-Samhati Satras was however not accepted by the other Satras, specially by those of the Purusha-Samhati order. Besides, the Kala-Samhati Satras, though they adhered firmly to the teachings of Sankardeva and Madhabdeva, developed separatist tendencies as far as practices were concerned, owing to the impressive

1. A deeper meaning is attached by some to this name. Gopaldeva was believed to have extracted religious truths from the bosom of *Kala* or eternity, which he revealed to mankind with his faith in the godship of Srikrishna.—Preface to *Gopaldeva Charit*, compiled by Jogeswar Mahanta, p. 12.

2. Srikrishna the Great Being or *Purusha*, in an earlier birth during the Padma-kalpa age, revealed the character of the true faith to his devotees. Sankardeva as the incarnation of Srikrishna repeated the message to the world. Madhabdeva further propagated the message with his faith in Srikrishna. This interpretation is given in the Preface to *Gopaldeva Charit*, compiled by Jogeswar Mahanta.

personality of Gopaldeva and the surroundings in which they had to flourish. These tendencies were manifested in the more democratic principles on which the Satras were run, the more intimate social contact between the Gurus and their disciples, and the inordinate reverence shown to the Gurus who were considered as higher than temporal overlords. The Kala-Samhati Satras adopted the hymns composed by Sankardeva and Madhabdeva, but supplemented them by those written by their own Gurus. The anxiety to acquire greater individual distinction and influence was inspired by the opposition of the Purusha-Samhati and the common rivalry with the Satras of the Brahmanical order. The differences became more noticeable in the case of the Mayamara Satra which had acquired great power and wealth, and had thereby caused the jealousy of the other monasteries and the misgivings of the government. The Mayamara Mahanta had thus to thrive in an atmosphere of hostility and suspicion; and after centuries of suffering its disciples, the Moamarias, first raised the standard of revolt against the Ahom government to avenge the insults which they and their Gurus had received at the hands of their countrymen and their rulers.

To understand fully the story of the Moamaria uprising one has to go to the very foundation of the Vaisnava movement in Assam.

Tantricism in Assam: It is generally believed that Kamarupa or Assam was at one time the home of Tantricism.[3] The Kamakhya temple at Gauhati, the Kechaikhati temple at Sadiya, the Mahadeva temple at Dergaon, and the net-work of Sakta temples in North Lakhimpur area bear proofs of the extent of Tantric influence in Kamarupa. It is but natural that Hindu or Buddhist preachers would tolerate and sanction the rites of the aboriginal tribes, read an esoteric meaning into them, and absorb them into their respective cults. It is not definitely known whether Hinduism or Buddhism first imparted to the rites of the primitive people the status of a regular religious faith. It is held that Mahayana Buddhism, propounded by Nagarjuna in the first century A.D., assumed a new character on the recrudescence of Brahmanism during the early Gupta period, and gradually developed into Tantricism from the eighth century during the rule of the Pala kings of Magadha

3. H. H. Wilson in the Preface to his translation of *Vishnu-Purana* says,—"It is a singular, and yet uninvestigated circumstance that Assam, or at least the north-east of Bengal, seems to have been in a great degree the source from which the Tantrika and Sakta corruptions of the religion of the Vedas and Puranas proceeded." Page *cvii*, London, 1840.

and Gauda. Images of Buddhas and Bodhisatwas with their female energies were worshipped; and other Buddhist gods gradually came in which developed into mysticism and sorcery. The magic rites began to be tolerated by the teachers of spells called Mantracharyyas. Hinduism, ever anxious to imbibe the spirit of the time, absorbed the Buddhist Tantric rites into its system.[4]

Tantric rituals in their debased forms were practised in Assam in the centuries preceding the Vaisnava revival. They included the sacrifices of ducks, pigeons, goats, buffaloes, and even men, to Sakti or Durga. Magic rites, wine drinking and divination by ripping open the entrails of a pregnant woman were the striking features of Tantric worship in Assam.[5] These rites gained popularity in Assam by the preachings of peripatetic Buddhist monks. Two such preachers were found roaming about in Eastern Assam; and Sankardeva is said to have vanquished them in arguments which made them flee the country.[6] The whole body of Tantric rituals was known in Assam by the name *Bauddhachara* or the usages of Buddhists. Whether the name was applied to the Tantric rituals for their accepted Buddhist origin, or whether orthodox Hindus refused to recognise them as a part of their cult and ascribed them to their rivals the Buddhists, is a point which yet remains unsettled.[7]

Sankardeva's crusade against Tantricism: It is against this *Bauddhachara* that Sankardeva [1449-1568], the great Vaisnava reformer of Assam, waged a life-long crusade.[8] He dispensed with the worship of all other gods except Vishnu in his several manifestations, and as such his creed was one of qualified monism as propounded by Ramanuja. He did away with the worship of images, the elaborate rituals and sacrifices and the esoteric rites practised

4. J. A. S. B., vol. x, 1914, p. 346.

5. L. N. Bezbarua, *Lives of Sankardeva and Madhabdeva*, in Assamese, p. 30.

6. Gunabhiram Barua, Assam Buranji, 1876, pp. 38 and 269.

7. Whether Buddhism was ever a popular religion in Assam is still a subject of controversy. But Buddhist and Hindu tendencies got so inseparably mixed up in some of the social and semi-religious customs that it is difficult to ascertain whether they emanated from direct Buddhist influence or filtered through ever-compromising Hinduism.

8. "In Bengal, Tirhut, Orissa and Assam the Vaishnavism preached by Chaitanya and Sankardeva (an Assamese saint unconnected with Chaitanya) conquered the majority of the Hindu population. The new creed introduced an unwonted gentleness and fervour, and tamed the rude manly savagery of Tantric worship and animism that used to prevail in many of these places before."—Sir Jadunath Sarkar's *Chaitanya's Life and Teachings*, 1932, p. 12.

by Saktas.[9] He enjoined simple ceremonials consisting of *Nama* or recitation of hymns and prayers, and *Bhakti* or incessant devotion based on implicit faith which, combined with two other elements, *Guru* or teacher, and *Hari* or Vishnu, constituted the fourfold path of salvation. He based his teachings principally on the *Bhagavata-purana* which deals with the life and teachings of Srikrishna, and hence his creed is known as *Bhagavati Dharma.* He translated several cantos of the *Bhagavata,* wrote numerous metrical episodes, dramas and hymns to popularise his creed. He established *Satras* or monasteries, and thereby perpetuated the prosecution of his faith. The negative aspects of his creed were summarised in the following passages,—"There is one God and one devotion, and there is no other but that One", and "Do not worship other gods, do not go to their temples, and do not take the offerings made to them. If this injunction is violated your devotions will be of no avail."[10] Of the four kinds of passions or forms of attachment Sankardeva selected *Dasya,* or servitude, as the guiding principle of devotion, discarding the other three as inappropriate, viz., *Sakhya,* or personal regard or friendship for the deity; *Batsalya,* or tender affection for the divinity of the same nature as parental love; and *Madhuryya,* or passionate attachment of the milk-maids towards their beloved Srikrishna.[11] The form of attachment, *Dasya,* emphasised by Sankardeva, governed the relations between the Vaisnava Gurus and their disciples. Sankardeva admitted a Muslim and several hillmen into the circle of his intimate followers.

The Vaisnava reformation in India, which had its counterpart in the teachings of Sankardeva, was a protest against the monopoly of the Brahman caste and against the exclusive spirit of the caste domination. The Vaisnava reformers in Assam and other parts of India asserted the dignity of the human soul quite independently of the accident of a man's birth and social rank. It raised the Sudra classes to a position of spiritual power and social importance almost equal to that of the Brahmans. A parallel is always drawn between the history of the Reformation Movement in Western Europe and the contemporaneous Vaisnava revival in India. In

9. In Assamese Vaisnava traditions it is held that on Sankardeva's birth the gods in heaven began to tremble at their approaching deprivation of sacrificial offerings.

10. K. L. Barua's *Mahapurushia Dharma-mat,* published in *Banhi* and inserted in L. N. Bezbarua's *Sankardeva* and *Madhabdeva,* p. 407.

11. H. H. Wilson, *Religious Sects of the Hindus,* 1846, p. 102.

Europe men ceased to believe that a priest was necessary to establish communion between God and man for purposes of salvation; and in India the belief that the Brahmans were entitled to the service and worship of other castes, was shattered to a considerable extent, and men and women, high and low, came to feel that they could attain salvation by faith and love in whatever position in society they might have been born.[12]

Sankardeva's democratic teachings were vehemently opposed by the Brahmans, first, because he dispensed with the rites and ceremonies including the worship of images, which constituted the principal occupation of the priests; and secondly, because he translated the scriptures into the vernacular and thus rendered them comprehensible to all people whereas the privilege of reading and interpreting them had hitherto been the virtual monopoly of Brahmans.[13] The Brahmans were destined to lose their importance if success attended the preachings of Sankardeva. They lodged complaints before the Ahom monarch Suhungmung Dihingia Raja alleging that Sankardeva was bringing disaster to the country by the prohibition of the time-honoured Vedic rituals. Sankardeva defeated the Brahmans in arguments, and the Ahom king appreciating the forceful logic of his doctrines dismissed him from the court with presents.[14]

But the hostility of the Brahmans increased day by day, and they took every opportunity to insult Sankardeva's followers. Sometime afterwards Sankardeva incurred the displeasure of the Ahom king for alleged neglect in keeping watch over the royal elephants entrusted to his care. He fled from his village before the arrival of the royal messengers despatched for his arrest. They arrested Sankardeva's apostle Madhabdeva and his son-in-law Haricharan. The latter was executed, but Madhabdeva was released as he was a bachelor, and there would be no one to weep for him if he were killed. Sankardeva left Assam and retired to Cooch Behar where he continued to live under the patronage of its enlightened ruler Maharaja Naranarayan (1540-1584). He established his reputation there as a saint and a scholar, and vanquished the Brahmans in arguments on several occasions. He refused to give initiation to the king on the ground that as a monarch he could

12. M. G. Ranade, *Rise of the Maratha Power*, 1900, pp. 149-172.

13. In asking Sankardeva and other scholars to translate the Sanskrit classics and scriptures into Assamese, King Naranarayan said,—"These translations will be presently read with eagerness by women and Sudras, and after some time by Brahmans as well."—*Darrang-raj-Vamsavali*, p. 117.

14. L. N. Bezbarua, *Sankardeva and Madhabdeva*, p. 83.

not do away with the worship of gods and goddesses.[15] When Naranarayan pressed further Sankardeva declared that personally he had resolved not to become the Guru of a monarch, of a woman, and of a Brahman of the sacerdotal order.

Democracy in Kala-Samhati Satras: On the death of Sankardeva in 1568 the leadership of the Vaisnava church in Assam devolved upon his chief apostle Madhabdeva (1489-1596). Hitherto, Vaisnava preachings had been mainly confined to Western or Lower Assam owing to the encouragement which they received from Naranarayan, the king of that territory. Madhabdeva deputed several of his followers to Eastern or Upper Assam which was governed by the Ahoms. Gopaldeva of Bhabanipur (1541-1611) spread the message of the *Bhagavata* among the Ahoms, Morans, Kacharis and Chutiyas, in addition to Brahmans, Kayasthas and Kalitas. Twelve Satras, as we have said before, were established under the auspices of Gopaldeva; six of them were presided over by Sudra Mahantas, and six by Brahman Mahantas. On Madhabdeva's death there were differences of opinion between his followers of the Brahmanical and of the Sudra orders. Bangsi-gopaldeva, a leading Brahman Vaisnava preacher, founded two Satras in Upper Assam, named Garamur and Kuruabahi which, together with Auniati and Dakhinpat, were hereafter known as "Bamunia Satras," as opposed to the twelve Satras established under the authority of Gopaldeva, and the twenty-four Satras founded by Sankardeva's two grandsons.

The Dihing Satra and the Mayamara Satra were the most prominent of the six Sudra monasteries of Upper Assam, associated with Gopaldeva.[16] As they admitted converts from the non-Aryan tribes and placed the disciples on an elevated footing, these two Satras became extremely popular. Though they had caste Hindus in their fold, such as Brahmans, Kayasthas and Kalitas,

15. That political exigency would not permit a monarch to tie himself to any creed was illustrated in King Naranarayan's own time. Before starting on his expedition to conquer Assam he performed many Hindu sacrifices calculated to bring him victory. But the Kacharis or Meches demanded that due honour should be shown to their tribal gods as well. The king performed their rites where the Meches were treated to feasts with wine, pork and fowls, and other articles of food prohibited to Hindus.—*Darrang-raj Vamsavali*, p. 64.

16. In reference to the Satra or the Gurus the word *Mayamara* has been used, for that is the name by which the Mahantas want their Satra to be called. The term *Moamaria* is universally applied to the disciples. The Dihing Satra was first known as Bahbari Satra, and then as Silikhatal Satra, after their successive headquarters.

their disciples consisted also of Kacharis, Ahoms; Kaivartas and Brittials; and in the case of the Mayamara Satra, Chutiyas and Morans as well. The democratic basis on which the Satras were run drew new converts to their fold from the influence of the caste-ridden Satras, specially of the Brahmanical order. In course of time the Dihing and the Mayamara Satras grew to be strongholds of Sudra Vaisnavism in Upper Assam as opposed to the Brahmanical monasteries. On account of the characteristic physical vigour of the large majority of disciples of the two Satras they were likely to make a more enterprising band of soldiers than the comparatively ease-loving and refined followers of the other Gosains.[17]

The Dihing and the Mayamara Satras shared the distinctive features of the other Satras of the Kala-Samhati order.[18] Their procedure of initiation, the relationship between the disciples and their Gurus, and between co-disciples, differed to some extent from that followed in other monasteries. The hymns used in Kala-Samhati Satras varied from one Satra to another; the original ones were composed by Sankardeva, Madhabdeva and Gopaldeva, but there were always a number of additional hymns composed by the pontiffs themselves. The Mahantas were regarded as supermen and they appropriated all the honours due to human beings. The expressions used in reference to the Mahantas were highly euphemistic in tone. When the Mahanta was ill or had an attack of smallpox the disciples usually referred to that circumstance in such phrases,—"Illness or smallpox has paid its homage to His Holiness." The Mahanta never "died"; he simply "closed the drama of his life."[19]

The autonomy enjoyed by every Kala-Samhati Satra made each of them grow on distinct lines conforming as far as possible to the general tenets of the Samhati. Nowhere was this dissidence of dissent better manifested than in the growth of the Mayamara Satra. The Morans, whose affinities with the Bodo tribe have been well established on linguistic grounds, are supposed by some to be

17. The author of *Fathiyah-i-Ibriyah*, the chronicle of Mir Jumla's invasion of Assam, 1662-63, drew a contrast between "the hardy, meat-eating, beer-drinking, fighting tribesmen, Hinduised or primitive, and the effeminate subjected Hindus."—J. A. S. B., 1872, p. 82.

18. The other Vasnava orders were *Brahma-Samhati*, *Purusha-Samhati* and *Nishtha* or *Nika-Samhati*.

19. For similar "tabu language," see R. O. Winstedt's *Shaman, Saiva and Sufi*, p. 49.

the autochthons of Assam.[20] They lived in the Bengmara territory in Eastern Assam lying between the Brahmaputra and the Buri-Dihing. They had accepted the domination of the Ahoms without much opposition, and they used to supply necessaries to the royal household and the public stores. The Morans were the earliest disciples of the Mayamara Satra as Aniruddhadeva first preached amongst them from his monastery at Tengapani in the heart of the Matak country.[21] Living in this compact and homogeneous territory comprising about 1,800 square miles, the Morans found it easier to organise a mass movement than was possible for the scattered disciples of any other Gosain. The Mayamara Mahanta ministering in a territory like this peopled by his own disciples found himself in the position of a temporal lord which he had to retain by being more democratic in his dealings with them. The Morans rewarded the liberal views of the Mahanta by placing implicit faith in him and considering him as the only object of veneration. They refused to bow their heads before any other object, not even before their king.[22] The entrances to their houses were cut in the gable-ends, and not in the transepts, because in the latter case they would have to lower their heads at the doors which would mean prostration. The Mahanta's disciples grew in number, and were found outside the Matak country, and the Guru became prosperous and wealthy. The inventory of the Mahanta's property in the reign of Rajeswar Singha has been given as follows: several wickerbarrels loaded with gold and silver, ten to twelve thousand *bhakats* or monks, eight to ten thousand attendants and maids, ten to twelve *khats* or estates, and four to five thousand buffaloes.[23]

The message of the Kala-Samhati Satras reached the very masses of the Assamese nation. Those castes which are now denominated as "depressed" were freely admitted into the fold of

20. Lt.-Col. P. R. T. Gurdon, Notes on the Morans, J. A. S. B., 1904, Part I, No. I; and Rev. S. Endle's *Kacharis*, p. 87.

21. The Matak country, the habitat of the Morans, lay between the Brahmaputra on the west and north, and Buri-Dihing on the south.—Pemberton, *Report on the Eastern Frontier of India*, 1835, p. 68. Capt. S. O. Hannay wrote in 1838, that the Morans occupied the same section of the country as they did in former days, J. A. S. B., 1838, p. 675. *Matak* is the name given to the Morans by the Khamptis.

22. "The Moamarias belong to that category of men who regard the words and actions of their Gurus as those of the great God."—Gunabhiram Barua, *Assam Buranji*, p. 147.

23. Maniram Dewan's manuscript *Assam Buranji*.

these Satras, and they gradually imbibed refined and enlightened ways of living.[24] In other parts of India, the humiliation to which these unfortunates were subjected, drove them to the bosom of other religions; in Assam, the liberal policy of the Kala-Samhati Satras endowed them with a sense of self-respect and individual value. These Satras made a great appeal to the unsophisticated Assamese people and thus they commanded unprecedented popularity.

But the history of Assamese Vaisnavism, like that of every other religious development, is a long chapter of strifes and conflicts. Sometimes this warfare overstepped the limits of abstract argumentation and polemics, and assumed the shape of mutual vilification and recrimination. The Kala-Samhati Satras, on account of their great popularity, became the special target of attack; and of them the Mayamara Satra and its several branches excited the envy of the other Vaisnava Satras and also of the Satras of the Kala-Samhati order. Certain heterodox practices observed by isolated groups of disciples, in their individual or collective capacity, were attributed to the entire body of disciples, and in the hostile propaganda carried on against him the Mayamara Mahanta was depicted as the promoter of unholy rites and ceremonies.

The myths and stories invented to bring the Kala-Samhati Satras into ridicule were freely circulated in the country, and were readily believed by the uncritical masses; and the loud protestations of the Kala-Samhati Mahantas could but make a dim impression upon the poisoned minds of the credulous people. Some of these stories were embodied in a book named *Adi-charit,* supposed to have been written by Madhabdeva, the successor of Sankardeva. But the transcendal personality of Madhabdeva, and the empyrean height in which his metaphysical intellect always soared, make it impossible to believe that he could dip his pen in scrolling such vilification and abuse against pontiffs of his own following. Besides the stories can hardly stand the scrutiny of chronology and geography.

The first story describes Aniruddhadeva as the audacious pilferer of a Tantric book, named *Kalpataru Sastra,* from the possession of Sankardeva. According to the second story, Sankardeva passed orders of ostracism against Aniruddhadeva as he had betrayed Sakta leanings, though he was a youth of fifteen when the

24. The adherents of the Moamaria sect "were mainly persons of low social rank, such as Doms, Morans, Kacharis, Haris and Chutiyas".—Gait, *History of Assam,* 2nd ed., p. 59.

great reformer died. The third story describes Aniruddha's ostracism for having treated Gopaldeva and Bar-Jadumani Ata with forbidden food during their stay in his house. The fourth story depicts Gopaldeva as the unholy claimant of the full knowledge of Vaisnava religion against the partial perfection of Sankardeva and Madhabdeva. The fifth story attributes Gopaldeva's ostracism by Madhabdeva.

The sixth story makes Gopaldeva the patron-saint of the Rati-khowa Sampradaya, or the fraternity of night-worshippers, the members of which form a sort of freemasonry, and rigidly exclude outsiders from participating in their rites which are always held at night in strict secrecy.[25] In the chronicles of the Ahom court there are many references to the Rati-khowa rites of the Moamarias. They are said to have been usually performed at the commencement of a campaign to ensure success in arms. We often come across passages like this,—" The Moamarias initiated hostilities after they had met in diabolical conferences and performed unapproved rites."[26] The Moran leader Nahar Khora Saikia received a copperplate containing magical incantations from a scavenger's daughter named Ramali. His two wives Bhatuki and Bhabuli, both of the fisherman's caste, were consecrated as Radha and Rukmini—the mistress and consort of Srikrishna—and led into the battle as twin war-goddesses. Another Moamaria leader named Tati dismayed the royalists by his magical feats which he had practised with the help of prayers engraved on copper. The deification of mortal women and the seeking of perfection in magic had usually to be preceded by " diabolical conferences " and " unapproved rites." Another name usually applied by the royalists to the Moamarias was *Aritiya,* which literally means, a practiser of unholy rites.[27] These stories of the observance of *Aritiya* practices

25. For an account of the Ratikhowa Sampradaya, see S. C. Goswami's *Night-worshippers* in the *Work of the Kamarupa Anusandhan Samiti,* 1920, pp. 36-47. The sect may be compared to the Vamacharis, and their rites to the ritual *Purnabhisheka or Full Initiation*, see H. H. Wilson's *Religious Sects of the Hindus,* pp. 164-166.

26. Tungkhungia Buranji, O.U.P., pp. 61, 99, 115.

27. So late as the year 1931, the head of the principal Mayamara Satra has disavowed all connection with *Aritiya* rites. He said,—" I swear by the name of God that such a practice as unholy night-worship (Aritiya Ratisewa) is not in vogue amongst us.....People say whatever they like out of malice and spite against our Satra. Not to speak of *Aritiya* practices, even wine-drinking is severely punished....Partaking of chicken and pork is out of the question,"—Postscript dated 8-10-1931 to *Mayamara Satrcr Vamsavali,* p. 75.

by the Moamarias are to be taken with a great deal of caution as they had emanated from the hostile camp.

Anyway, the religious acrimonies and bitternesses led to tragic consequences in the political field, and an attempt is made in the following pages to describe these consequences tracing them from the first Mayamaria Guru Aniruddhadeva.

Aniruddhadeva, the first Mayamara Mahanta: Aniruddhadeva (1553-1624) was the son of a Bhuyan named Gondagiri and his wife Ajali Devi, the daughter of Sankardeva's paternal uncle. He translated the fourth and fifth cantos of the *Bhagavata* and composed a large number of hymns in Assamese which bear testimony to his religious fervour and scholastic attainments.

Aniruddha is said to have been in possession of a Tantric book named *Kalpataru Sastra,* or the tree of desire, also known as *Dhatu-tamrakshari* as it was engraved on copper. It was supposed to contain incantations and prayers by reciting which the devotee could bring down the sacrificial fire and obtain the conferment of any gift he might ask for. The manuscript was an heirloom in the family of Sankardeva whose ancestors were worshippers of Sakti. According to *Adi-charit,* which contains an account of the Bhuyans, the manuscript was stolen by Aniruddhadeva from the possession of Sankardeva.[28] This is denied by Aniruddha's successors who say that the manuscript passed from Sankardeva to Madhabdeva, and from the latter to Gopaldeva.[29] Aniruddhadeva received it from his Guru Gopaldeva at the time of his ordination in 1601 as the head of the Mayamara Satra. No body knows what the actual contents of the book were, but the Mahantas of the Mayamara Satra claim that the success of Aniruddha in rapidly converting the Morans and others to his discipleship was the possession of this *Kalpataru Sastra,* with which he is said to have performed miracles.[30]

The Ahom king Sukhampha Khora Raja invited Aniruddha to his court and asked him to show some magical feats for which he had gained reputation in the country. The king put some articles in a pitcher, and having covered its mouth with a cloth asked Aniruddha what it contained. He replied that it contained a cobra.

28. *Adi-charitra,* analysis in Gait's *Progress of Historical Research in Assam,* pp. 20-21.

29. *Mayamara Satrar Vamsavali,* or chronicle of the Mayamara Satra, in Assamese, 1933, p. 19.

30. It is regarded by some as being the well-known treatise on archery and warcraft commonly known as *Dhanurveda Tantra.*

On the removal of the cloth a cobra actually came out from inside the vessel. At the instance of the king Aniruddha hushed the serpent to death by merely touching the sides of the vessel. Aniruddha is said to have performed this miracle with the help of some verses of the *Kalpataru Sastra.* The monarch being satisfied permitted his subjects to follow the teachings of Aniruddha.[31] Aniruddha's monastery came to be known from that day as *Mayamara* Satra, as he *killed* the serpent brought to being by his *maya* or magic. The name became afterwards corrupted into *Moamara* or *Moamaria,* from that of a lake in Majuli which abounded in a description of a small fish called *Moa* and where the second headquarters of the Satra were erected.[32]

Moamarias refuse to salute the king: The first clash between the Mayamara Mahanta and the Ahom government occurred in the reign of Pratap Singha, who ordered a prominent disciple of the Mahanta to be executed for having said of the king's great hall that it would make a commodious place for religious recital and prayer. Four disciples of the Mahanta refused to bow their heads before the king including the Barpatra Gohain, one of the three cabinet ministers, and Neog-Phukan or the commander-in-chief. The king in order to test the sincerity of the devotion of the officers to their Mahanta asked them to gallop their horses under a sword fixed horizontally between two posts at the height of a mounted man's neck. The Neog-Phukan was the first to try the ordeal. He galloped his horse towards the sword which severed his head from his body. The king then ordered the other three officers to desist from the experiment. The king sent his messengers to the Moamaria villages to investigate if all the disciples held their Guru as the only person before whom they should lower their head. The messengers discovered that the Moamarias not only regarded their Guru as superior to their king, but refrained from lowering their head before any other earthly object. The doors of their houses were cut at either of the gable-ends, as doors at the eaves or transepts would be low, and thus necessitate the lowering of their heads at the time of entering the houses. The king thus realised that all

31. This story is repeated in *Adi-charit* and in *Mayamara Satrar Vamsavali.*

32. *A Short Account of the Moamorah Sect,* J. A. S. B., 1838, p. 671. The present Mayamara Satras are Dinjay, Madarkhat, Puranipam and Garpara. A large number of Morans are adherents of the Tiphuk Satra founded by the Mayamara Mahanta Astabhujdeva (1748-1770). There are Moran disciples also in the other Satras.

the Moamarias were of one mind in respect of their refusal to prostrate before any one else but their Guru.

The power and influence of the Mayamara Gosain grew apace. He had a vast following in the country including practically the entire body of the Morans. Myths were invented to show that complete separation from Aniruddhadeva had been enjoined by Sankardeva. The Moamarias themselves admitted that such a separation had indeed taken place between Sankardeva and Gopaldeva, and that the latter alone had formulated the creed which was followed by the Moamarias. The myths were gradually enlarged and they gained further popularity from a book named *Adi-charit* supposed to have been written by Sankardeva's successor Madhabdeva. The result of all these myths, exaggerations, suspicions and allegations was the complete ostracism of the Mayamara Mahanta and his disciples by the vast body of Vaisnavas in Assam.

Mayamara Mahanta killed by the Ahoms: During the reign of Surampha Jayaditya Bhaga Raja, the Mayamara Mahanta Nityananda was invited to the capital as well as other religious heads on the occasion of the annual Sraddha ceremony of the late sovereign. Nityananda's retinue was larger than that of any other Gosain. The Mahanta, elated at the sight of his superior following, remarked,—"The other Mahantas cannot stand comparison with me in point of influence and power. My only equal is the Ahom sovereign descended from the great god Indra. The monarch should adhere to his kingly duties and a Mahanta to his spiritual ministrations. All the Mahantas cast an envious look on us, and if we do the same there will be trouble in the country." This remark was repeated to the king by the Bezdoloi Bhandari Barua. At the end of the ceremony at night the Mahantas retired to their respective camps accompanied by torch-bearers. Some of them had 10 or 12 torches, but the Mayamara Mahanta had 120 torches, thus exceeding the customary number accompanying the king. The king had remembered the remark, which combined with his present exasperation, incensed him furiously. An executioner was despatched to kill the Gosain. The Gosain was cut with a sword and his body was thrown into the Dikhou river. An old woman rescued the dead body and made it over to the disciples for the funeral rites. The Moamaria disciples, indignant at the ruthless slaughter of their spiritual leader, took a vow to avenge their Guru's murder. They desisted from taking any active step for rebellion for the absence of a leader, as for four years Nityananda's brother Jairamdeva lived in exile out of fear for the king. He was appointed to the Mahantaship in 1654 through the intercession of the mother of King Jayadhwaj Singha.

Saktism in the Ahom court: The Ahom king Gadadhar Singha during whose reign the Mogul wars with Assam came to an end, held the view that Vaisnavism was an effeminate creed, and that it was bound to bring about the speedy downfall of his kingdom. The great power which the Mahantas exercised over their disciples was regarded as a menace to the authority of the Ahom sovereign. Gadadhar Singha confiscated the Mahantas' property, drove them from their Satras, killed some and mutilated others. Baikunthanathdeva, the Mahanta of the Mayamara Satra, was killed in 1691. The Mayamara Satra like many others remained without a head for five years, till 1696 when Gadadhar Singha's successor Rudra Singha restored the monasteries to the survivors or their heirs. Baikunthanath's brother Chaturbhuj became the Mahanta of Mayamara Satra.

The Brahmans questioned the authority of the Sudra Mahantas to initiate Brahmans. They submitted a petition to Rudra Singha to decide the point. The king accordingly summoned the Sudra Mahantas to a synod to show from what scriptures they derived their authority to initiate Brahmans. Chaturbhuj Mahanta of Mayamara Satra and four other Sudra Mahantas accepted the challenge and promised to point out the authority. But they failed to do so in the royal presence. They were expelled from the court with earthen pitchers painted with lime hung from their necks.

King Rudra Singha evinced Sakta tendencies towards the end of his reign. He sent agents to Bengal to find out a good Sakta teacher. The selection fell upon Krishnaram Bhattacharya Nyayavagis of Nadia. The humble bearing of the Bengali priest did not inspire the king with reverence. He sent Krishnaram back to Bengal. The subsequent illness of the king and the occurrence of a series of earthquakes were interpreted by the king's Sakta advisers as the result of the insult shown to the Brahman of Bengal. Krishnaram was recalled, but Rudra Singha died at Gauhati before the Pandit's arrival. The monarch on his death-bed is said to have instructed his son and successor Siva Singha to take initiation from Krishnaram Pandit.

The adoption of Sakta Hinduism by the Ahom monarch followed by the conversion to that faith of his principal nobles introduced a new factor in the social and political life of the people tending towards the acceleration of that decline which had already commenced. State obligations began to play a secondary part. The king and his nobles cherished the ambition of becoming devout

Sakta worshippers, spent more time in religious observances, patronised Brahmans, made endowments, erected temples, and became direct and indirect propagandists of Saktism to increase their fold. The over-zealous Saktism of the Ahoms brought an estrangement not only with the Vaisnavas but also with the orthodox Ahom priests, Deodhais and Bailungs, who as custodians of the ancient traditions of the Ahoms or Tais, had kept the rulers in their martial ardour and outlook. The effects of this innovation were soon felt.

The astrologers and priests found out from the scriptures that Siva Singha's stars were on the wane, and that he would soon be dethroned. The only remedy suggested was the propitiation of the gods and the monarch's retirement from active participation in state affairs. His consort Phuleswari Kuanri was vested with *de facto* sovereign powers during the period of her husband's astrological disability; and coins were struck under the joint names of the royal couple.

Insults to Mayamara Mahanta : Phuleswari Kuanri, now known as Pramatheswari Devi, was a staunch devotee of Saktaism. She invited the Vaisnava Mahantas to attend the celebrations connected with the worship of Durga. They were asked to bow before the image of the goddess, which they obviously could not do by the articles of their faith. The queen indignant at the disobedience of the Mahantas, who were after all her subjects, is said to have ordered their foreheads to be besmeared with the blood of the sacrificial goats and buffaloes; and they were also forced to eat the offerings made to Durga. The other Mahantas being of a meek disposition could not do anything to avenge this grave insult and desecration. But the powerful Mayamara Mahanta summoned his disciples and planned schemes of vengeance. In 1731, the Mayamara Mahanta further exasperated the queen by prophesying that she would soon be the mother of a monstrous child contrary to the flattering prediction of her Sakta preceptor regarding her future offspring. The queen attributed the Mayamara Mahanta's evil forebodings to his ingrained ill-feeling and disloyalty. She handed over the Mahanta to the executioners; but he was rescued from his fate by the intercession of Krishnaram Nyayavagis and the king.

Siva Singha was succeeded by his brother Pramatta Singha. The most powerful official at that time was Kirtichandra Barbarua who was a disciple of Kaivalyanandanadeva Mahanta of Dihing Satra which was almost as influential as the Mayamara Satra. Chaturbhujdeva, Adhikar of the latter Satra, died in 1748 and was succeeded by his son Astabhujdeva.

Pramatta Singha was succeeded on the throne by his brother Rajeswar Singha, the fourth son of Rudra Singha. The succession ought to have passed to Mohanmala Gahaindeo, the third son of King Rudra Singha. Mohanmala, commonly known as Barjana Gohain, was a very popular prince to whom the nobles and officials were deeply attached. Kritichandra Barbarua contrived to set aside Mohanmala's claims on the flimsy pretext of his face being pock-marked. The Barbarua obviously foresaw the loss of his autocratic powers if Mohanmala with his influence on the nobles was allowed to sit on the throne. Mohanmala and his family were banished to the wilds of Namrup. The prince could never forgive Kirtichandra for the deprivation of his lawful claims to the Ahom throne.

Kirtichandra, though highly efficient, was very unpopular with the Ahom nobles, as he did not belong to the leading Ahom families. The story of his origin, and his father's servitude in the house of a Muhammadan were narrated in a chronicle compiled by Numali Bargohain. The episode was also incorporated in other contemporary accounts. Kirtichandra ordered a vigorous search to be made of all the chronicles, and destroyed all those which were found to have any reference to his plebeian origin. This added to the already prevailing unpopularity of Kirtichandra. Some of the nobles, with the active support of the king's sons and the connivance of the monarch, plotted to murder Kirtichandra. The conspirators attacked him one evening and wounded him in the neck, but Kirtichandra recovered through the treatment of a clever physician.

Kirtichandra raised his own Guru, the Mahanta of Dihing Satra, to eminent position at the royal court. The Mahanta of Dihing was as powerful as that of Mayamara, and his friendship was regarded as an effective measure to counteract the growing influence of the Mayamara Mahanta. The Mahanta was appointed a royal page—a legal fiction to authorise the Mahanta to enter the king's council chamber. Kirtichandra used to inflict deliberate humiliation on the Mayamara Mahanta by publicly acclaiming the superiority of the musicians of Dihing Satra and depreciating those of Mayamara Satra in performances held before the king and court. The greatest insult inflicted by Kirtichandra on the Mayamara Mahanta was on the occasion of the king's journey from Dergaon to Rangpur. The king was followed at some distance by Kirtichandra. As the king reached the gate of the Mayamara monastery the Mahanta's eldest son Gagini Deka-Mahanta, *alias* Saptabhuj, greeted the monarch with 200 trays of presents. The usual procedure required the previous sanction of the Barbarua on every occasion when one proposed to offer presents to the monarch; but it could not be followed as the king would pass the Mahanta's gate if one had to wait for the arrival of the Barbarua. The Deka-Mahanta obtained the permission of the Baruas and Phukans who formed the personal guard of the king. The Barbarua on reaching the monastery gate was greeted with 80 trays of presents. The Barbarua became highly incensed when he heard that the king had been approached without his permission and caused four blows to be inflicted on Gagini Deka-Mahanta.

Having received this insult the Deka-Mahanta summoned the Gaonburhas, or the headmen or Sirdars of the Moamarias, and explained to them his plans of revenge, which aimed at extermination of Kirtichandra Barbarua and the occupation of the Ahom throne. To measure the numerical strength of the Moamarias the Deka-Mahanta employed the disciples in erecting a prayer-hall and residence for the monks at the swamps known as Maloupathar. Each man was asked to throw a clod of earth on the site. After working for five days they raised the high plinths necessary for the foundation of the buildings. The sight of such a multitude of disciples, able-bodied and ardently devoted to their Guru, inflamed the Deka-Mahanta's passion for immediate action.[33] Astabhuj Mayamaria Mahanta dissuaded his son and the Gaonburhas from involving themselves in such a dangerous affray. "Why do you seek for political power?"—said the Mahanta, "I am the owner of unlimited property. A single individual like Kirtichandra Barbarua can do us but little harm. A hill stream does frequently leave its channel; but the ocean remains confined within its limits, but when it once transcends its shores countries become devastated. King Rajeswar Singha is like my father. If you launch any warfare the king will have anxiety and suspense. Wait for sometime. Better opportunities are bound to come sooner or later."

King Rajeswar Singha died in 1769 having left three sons Charusingha Majugohain, Ratneswar Sarugohain, Patkowanr, and a brother named Kalsilia Gohain. There was besides Mohanmala Gohaindeo, an exile in Namrup, waiting for an opportunity to assert his claims to the Ahom throne. Of these princes Charusingha had been nominated as the successor and installed as Juvaraj during the lifetime of his father. Kalsilia Gohain, the youngest son of King Rudra Singha, was dark in complexion and did not possess the presence and dignity of a sovereign, for which the Parvatia Gosain had refused to accept him for initiation into the Sakta fold. The stigma of illegitimacy was also fastened on to the Kalisilia

33. Maniram Dewan's Ms. *Assam Buranji*.

Gohain. Kirtichandra, by diplomatic machinations, set aside the claims of Charusingha and installed Kalisilia Gohain on the throne when he assumed the name Lakshmi Singha.

The accession of Lakshmi Singha attended by the ascendency of Kirtichandra Barua was viewed with grave forebodings of disaster by the Mayamara Mahanta. Two events now occurred in quick succession which exceeded the limits of the forbearance of the Mayamara Mahanta and of his disciples. In both cases the provocation was given by Kirtichandra Barbarua.

After the demise of Rajeswar Singha, Kirtichandra mutilated his sons and procured their banishment to the wilds of Namrup, for alleged complicity in the attempt to murder the Barbarua during the reign of their father. The wives of Rajeswar Singha, numbering 24 in all, were exiled to Barkola, another penal colony. They were all placed in a boat, with only two maids to attend on them, and a few utensils. Their ornaments were all taken away under the orders of the Barbarua. In their journey the boat, which was piloted by a disciple of the Mayamara Gosain, was stopped near the monastery. The Mayamara Mahanta seeing the plight of the widowed queens foresaw his own impending destruction at the hands of the autocratic Barbarua. He supplied to the ex-queens sufficient quantities of food, clothes and utensils, and treated them with the utmost civility and respect during the two days when the boat had stopped at the Mayamara Satra. The Mahanta supplied his own escort to reach the ladies at Barkola. On receiving this news Kirtichandra became highly infuriated. He gave out a report that the hospitality accorded to the widows by the Mahanta and his son had been actuated by ulterior objects to which the ladies had been compelled to yield though still in their period of mourning. The usual monthly *Nirmali* or presents of flowers sent by the Mayamara Mahanta to the king were returned, and the messenger taken to task for having brought such tokens from the unholy Mahanta. This was too much for the Mahanta to bear. He permitted the Deka-Mahanta to summon his disciples, but instructed him to concentrate on the destruction of the Barbarua and to avoid precipitating a crisis. This happened in July 1769.

The preparations for an open rebellion continued during the months of August and September. In October the Mayamara Mahanta received fresh insults from the Barbarua. King Lakshmi Singha and Kirtichandra in the course of a journey by boat halted for a few minutes at the landing *ghat* of the Mayamara Satra. The Mahanta saluted and blessed the king, but he ignored the presence of the Barbarua altogether, who thereupon reprimanded the

Mahanta severely in the presence of his disciples and the king's attendants.

The immediate provocation for the revolt was the punishment which Kirtichandra inflicted on Ragha Neog, a leading Moran and a prominent disciple of the Mayamara Mahanta. According to custom the Morans paid no revenue in lieu of which they were called upon to supply the king's household with different articles. The Morans were divided into several units or *khels* according to the nature of the supplies they had to furnish. The *Hati-chungis* supplied the king with elephants, the *Rangjoganiyas* with the colouring vegetable matter known in Assam as *Rang*, the *Dhari-bowas* with mats, and the *Mau-joganiyas* with honey, and so forth. On September 15, 1769, Ragha Neog and Nahar Khora Saikia delivered to the Barbarua the usual supply of elephants. They knew the haughty and irritable character of the Barbarua; and for his pacification they brought this time the best elephants. The Barbarua was not a man to be easily satisfied. He found the elephants defective, and ordered Ragha Neog to be flogged. He was pressed to the ground with bamboos and given 20 lashes. Ragha fell prostrate with pain. He shouted out,—"This land is infested with devils. The sun, the moon, the air and the clouds are standing spectators of this injustice and cruelty. Retribution is writ large on the forehead of the wrong-doer." Ragha under heavy bandage was taken to the presence of the Mahanta and his son. The Deka-Mahanta sent orders to the Gaonburhas to come with the disciples properly armed for a fight.

The Mayamara Mahanta, after a great deal of hesitation, is said to have accorded a qualified sanction for the revolt. His instructions on this occasion bear evidence of his statesmenlike forethought and sence of realities. "The Ahom rulers," said the Mahanta to his son, "conquered this country after undergoing great hardships and difficulties. They deserve our gratitude for having converted this forest-clad wilderness into a settled habitation. They have besides supported us in our spiritual leadership. A prince of the Tungkhungia royal family should therefore be placed on the throne, and you should never aim at capturing suzerain power for yourselves. The families of the Ahoms of the Seven Houses should be preserved, and the Gohainships should be conferred on the members of the respective families who are adherents of our Satra. You can hold offices as Phukans, Baruas, and Saikias. The Khels should not be dislocated. You should live in peace and concord with the disciples of the other Satras, and show due reverence to the saints and preachers. As you are not aware of the art of administration you should take the counsel of the Katakis and the Kakatis, and reward them handsomely. Man-slaughter should be confined to soldiers actually engaged in hostilities. If you violate these instructions you are sure to cause the destruction of all of us including our hallowed Satra.[34]

First Moamaria insurrection, 1769-70: In November 1769 the Morans raised the standard of revolt after having collected an army of 7,000 including 3,000 effectives. The nocturnal rites were performed to ensure the success of the enterprise. Bhatuki and Bhabuli, the two wives of Nahar Khora Saikia, were renamed Radha and Rukmini, and made to undergo the ceremonies investing them with supernatural powers. The Moran army pitched their camp at Secha and remained prepared for action under the command of Ragha. The Morans induced the three exiled princes Mohanmala, Churusingha and Ratneswar, to join their camps on the promise that one of them would be placed on the throne. This make-believe silenced to a great extent the opposition of the loyal subjects of the Ahom king as the princes were extremely popular and their banishment was regarded as an act of injustice and high-handedness on the part of Kirtichandra Barbarua.

A force of 2,000 was despatched against the Morans under the command of a Tekela Bara named Bez. The royalists were put to flight with heavy casualties and the loss of a vast quantity of provisions.

A fresh army of 8,000 strong was despatched under the command of Harnath Senapati Phukan, father of Badanchandra Barphukan. The Morans dashed towards the Phukan's fort placing Mohanmala, Charusingha and Ratneswar on elephants' back in the vanguard of their army. Mohanmala attempted to convince the Phukan that as a member of the ancient Duara family he should not obstruct the prince's elevation to the throne which was the primary object of the Moran enterprise. Mohanmala further pointed out that his revenge would be directed against the Barbarua, and that the other officials and nobles would be permitted to remain in their customary dignity and position. The Morans then attacked the fort of Harnath Phukan and seized his person and kept him under watch at a distance from their own camp.

Elated with this success the Morans formed a government of their own. Ramakanta, son of Nahar Khora, was declared as Raja,

34. Maniram Dewan's manuscript *Assam Buranji*. The late Adhikar of Mayamara Dinjay Satra, Hridayananda Goswami, said in the Preface to *Mayamara Satrar Vamsavali*,—"Astabhujdeva Mahanta never permitted anybody to revolt; on the other hand, he prohibited such a course. But it is regrettable that the others did not listen to his prohibition.

and Ragha as Barbarua. Charusingha and Ratneswar were poisoned. The subjects of the Ahom king were, however, informed that Mohanmala's son had become king. This not only swelled the number of Moamaria adherents, but also increased the discomfiture of the royalist forces in the matter of provisions and supplies.

Then there ensued engagements with the Morans at several places in all of which the Ahom detachments met reverses. In many cases the royalist forces walked over to the side of the rebels, or deserted their camps out of fear. Some disciples of the Mayamara Mahanta served as attendants on the Barbarua. They communicated to the Mahanta all the war-plans of the king and the Barbarua. The king then ordered the Barphukan at Gauhati to send up some detachments composed of men from the three vassal states Rani, Luki and Topakuchi, as they were not supposed to be tainted with sympathy for the rebels. Ragha encountered the forces sent by the Barphukan at the Dhai-ali, and completely routed them inflicting very severe losses. The rebels then made preparations for attacking the capital Rangpur.

King Lakshmi Singha's expulsion: On November 21, 1769, King Lakshmi Singha left Rangpur with the object of proceeding to Gauhati. He was accompanied by Kirtichandra Barbarua, Bhagi Buragohain, the Duara Barphukan, and a number of leading nobles. The fugitives were compelled to halt for the night at Chintamani-garh on the bank of the river Sonai as no boats could be obtained to take them down; and as the boatmen were all disciples of the Mayamara Mahanta they would not agree to ply the vessels for the benefit of the Ahom king and his followers. The Barbarua proposed flight to Kaliabar where it would be possible to collect an army with the help of the local officers. "To be dominated by others," said the Barbarua, "is the worst suffering on earth. When a king becomes subjected to the monarch of another country, diplomatic measures should be adopted so that the conqueror may return to his own kingdom. On his retirement the subdued prince should remain in his preparedness with his army; and when opportunities present themselves for action he should act promptly and reinstate himself in his lost suzerain power. The Morans are wicked people and many other wicked people have joined the ranks of the rebels. Their promises will have no value and they will never refrain from committing atrocities. If they once taste the prestige of sovereign authority they will never stoop to play the role of subjects. The report that their resentment is solely directed against me should never be believed. They will extend their cruelty to all alike. Many loyal subjects have joined the Morans on the assumption that Mohanmala's son has become king. They are all guilty of treason having joined the rebels whatever their reasons may be."

The Barphukan opposed the Barbarua's proposal by pointing out its futility as no boats were available to take the king and his party to Kaliabar. "Even if they procured a few boats," said the Barphukan, "the Moamaria fishermen are over ready to seize on enemy vessels. It will be impossible for the king to sail down unnoticed. The fishermen as well as their religious head have no sense of right or wrong. They are sure to attack the royal boats, plunder the goods and assault the occupants." The Barphukan proposed that negotiations should be opened with the Moamarias in order to gain time.

Just when Lakshmi Singha and his nobles were discussing the rival proposals the Morans led by Ragha occupied the capital Rangpur at midnight. A detachment of 400 Morans besieged the king and the nobles in their shelter at daybreak and made them all prisoners. The king was confined at Jaysagar temple. The Barbarua and his sons were chained with iron fetters.

A Moamaria placed on the throne: The Morans now became masters of Rangpur. The actual administration of affairs was conducted by Ragha Barbarua. Mohanmala Gohain was killed by the Morans for alleged sympathy with his brother Lakshmi Singha. Ramakanta, son of Nahar Khora Moran, was set up on the throne. On the advice of Madan Kakati Chaliha, Raja Ramakanta struck novagonal coins in imitation of the octagonal ones of the Ahoms.[35] Ragha occupied the house of Kirtichandra Barbarua, and his seraglio consisted of a hundred ladies who were the daughters of Ahom Baruas and Phukans. He took to his harem Kuranganayani, the Manipuri princess who was the widow of Rajeswar Singha. Lakshmi Singha and Kirtichandra Barbarua were presented one day before Mayamara Mahanta who showed the prisoners some commisseration. Ragha became indignant at the mild disposition of the Mahanta. He further exasperated the Mahanta by laying his hand on the person of Lakshmi Singha. The Mahanta uttered the following imprecation,—"Well, Ragha, this power has made you mad. Like a comet you will cause the destruction of all of us. Know for certain that your days are numbered. The coming *Bihu* [new year's day, Baisakh 1, 1692 *saka*, April 12, 1770] will see the end of your mortal existence."

Ragha appointed new officers, almost all selected from the Morans. The Barphukan of Gauhati and the principal officers of

35. The Moran rupee, struck on February 11, 1770, weighed 1½ *tolas*, Ms. chronicle of Lakshmi Singha.

his establishment were also Morans. The Vaisnava preachers were summoned to the presence of the Mayamara Mahanta and made to pay donations. Ragha proposed that all Vaisnavas should accept the Mayamara Mahanta as their Guru. But the Mahanta restricted his initiation to those who had not been formally admitted as disciples of other Gosains.

In the meantime division had taken place in the Moamaria camp. Ragha claimed the insignias of royalty as he thought the success of the Morans was due to his initiative and enterprise. Similar claims were made by Gagini Deka-Mahanta. Ramakanta refused to hand over the honours conferred on him. The partisans of Ragha concentrated themselves at a place named Sagunmuri under the leadership of one Govinda Gaonburha. The Morans had meanwhile put to death Kirtichandra Barbarua, Bhagi Buragohain, Madurial Bargohain and the other principal officers of the old regime.[36]

Restoration of Lakshmi Singha: Towards the end of March 1770 the surviving Ahom nobles and the deposed officers met together to deliberate on the situation of the country which they summarised as follows:—"The Morans had declared formerly that the son of Mohanmala Gohain would be the Raja, but now we see that a Moran has assumed sovereign power. The Swargadeo has also been removed from the throne: the Mahantas also have been made to pay money under compulsion; the Dangarias, the Baruas and the Phukans have been murdered, deposed or expelled. The Morans have set up an independent sway. Since Sukapha's advent to this country till now only the members of the royal family have become kings, and not others of inferior blood. Besides, the Baruas, the Phukans and the Rajkhowas were appointed from among Ahoms. The king as an act of favour occasionally raised others [or non-Ahoms] to power, yet they could not be independent."[37]

After a few days of deliberation the Ahom nobles decided upon a course of action for the extirpation of the Moran usurpers. According to the custom of Assam bands of men go about from house to house on the last day of the year and the weeks following, singing *Huchari* or folksongs appropriate to the occasion. The householder kneels before the singers by placing a tray of betel-nut and leaf and receives their blessings. As previously arranged the royalists, dressed like *Huchari* singers, each concealing a sword

36. Kirtichandra Barbarua was executed on January 22, 1770, by being pressed between unpolished wooden cylinders. His son Magha Singha was also executed on the same day.

37. *Tungkhungia Buranji*, O.U.P. p. 72.

in his clothes, appeared in front of Ragha's house on the night of April 11, 1770. Kuranganayani, who had been already tutored to do the needful, induced Ragha to come out and kneel before the singers, by representing that the revellers were no other than his own supporters, viz., the followers of Govinda Gaonburha. Ragha had a sword in his hand which Kurunganayani transferred to her own hand alleging that bowing with a sword would mean disrespect to the congregation. Ragha who was unacquainted with the civilities of the Ahom court thanked Kuranganayani for instructing him the proper line of conduct on such occasions. As Ragha knelt to offer his respect Kurunganayani dealt him a severe blow on the calf. He fell with his face flat on the ground. The *Huchari* singers who were waiting for their turn came up and finished the work which the valiant Manipuri princess had begun. The hundred virgins who composed Ragha's seraglio came up sword in hand and joined in the massacre of Ragha's companions. Nahar Khora was wounded at Rangnath temple, but he fled and concealed himself in an arum bush where he was subsequently discovered and killed. Radha, wife of Nahar Khora, who had assumed the role of the Goddess of War was pierced to death.

The royalists after having taken possession of the palace brought the king from his confinement at Jaysagar temple. The king then issued an order that the Morans should be killed whereever and by whomsoever they were found or brought as captives. This order was proclaimed from all the roads throughout the country by men on horseback, in pursunce of which the Morans were captured and put to death. Many were tied in pairs and made over to the state gaoler. The Barphukan and other Moran officials of Gauhati were also captured by a stratagem and killed. The Mayamaṛa Mahanta Astabhujdeva and his son Gagini Deka-Mahanta were killed, and the Satra remained without a head for fourteen years, 1770-1784. Soon after his restoration King Lakshmi Singh rewarded his supporters by appointing them to high offices. Ghanasyam, son of Bhagi who had been murdered by the Morans, was made Buragohain; Bailung was appointed Bargohain; Bhadrasen became Barbaṛua, Kasi was made Barphukan, and Kekeru Kalita Hazarika became Kath Bhandari Barua. The services of the Manipuri princess Kuranganayani were publicly acknowledged by the king in her presence at a sitting of the full court. She was restored to the estates and the privileges which she had been enjoying before as the queen-consort of Rajeswara Singha, accompanied by the grant of additional rank and honour.

Results of the first Moamaria revolt: Thus ended the first phase of the Moamaria hostilities. The Morans had remained in possession of the capital for about five months, November 21, 1769, to April 11, 1770. Being unacquainted with ordinary principles of administration they could not make their regime stable and acceptable. The dismissal and execution of the older officials and the latter's replacement by new ones who did not know the rudiments of administration constituted a blunder of the highest magnitude. The coercive measures adopted against the spiritual heads who commanded the reverence of the vast majority of the Assamese Hindus rendered the new order extremely odious and unpopular. The forcible introduction of a hundred maidens into Ragha's seraglio at once demonstrated that the Moran leader was out for enjoyment and not for the foundation of a steady, orderly and disciplined government. The Mayamara Mahanta and his son, who had been experienced in the organisation and administration of religious estates, and more accustomed to command and exact obedience, would have certainly proved more capable of the task than Ragha Barbarua and his confederacy of elephant-catchers.

The rebellion was on this occasion confined to the Moran country lying between the Buri-Dihing and the Brahmaputra. It gained strength from the fact that the Moran country contained settlements of princes who had been maimed and thereby rendered disqualified for the throne. Namrup and its neighbourhood had become a hotbed of disaffection, and all revolutionary activities were hatched in that quarter.

The weakness of the Ahom government was seen in the absence of discipline among its officers and soldiers who could not distinguish between the authority of the standing government which they served and the would-be power in the country, *viz.* Mohanmala Gohain or his sons and nephews or the Moran leaders. The Morans declared that their vengeance was directed only against Kirtichandra Barbarua, and as a large section of the ancient nobiliary of the land were interested in his downfall they connived at the conspiracy of the rebels while it was in its inception. "Let the bamboo tops be submerged under water," said the rivals and foes of Kirtichandra, "and we shall watch the scare of the panic-stricken and shelterless crows."[38]

The success of the Morans, short-lived though it was, greatly affected the sanctity of the Ahom throne. Never before in the history of the Ahoms in Assam had a plebeian sat on the throne. The people now realised that the Ahom monarchy was not invio-

38. Maniram Dewan's Ms. *Assam Buranji*. "He [Kirtichandra Barbarua] expressed his conviction that all the Nobles had conspired to accomplish his destruction."—J. P. Wade's *Account of Assam*, ed. B. Sharma, p. 172.

lable, and that any one who had a determined and organised force at his disposal could place himself on the throne and reward his supporters by the grant of rank and position. The many princes who had been living in exile now looked for opportunities similar to those which had fallen to the lot of Mohanmala Gohain which, however he could not manipulate to his own advantage.

The general massacre of the Morans which was instituted after the restoration of Lakshmi Singha was a suicidal policy as they formed the best recruits for the Ahom army. Rancour and embitterment which would have died away in course of time were now perpetuated. Moran survivors considered it to be a sacred duty to avenge the death of their brothers who had perished by the sword of the Ahoms. Moran family life and village life became shattered, and the stakes which had tied them to civil life were now removed. They in their desperation sought vengeance, till a kind of blood-feud was installed between the Morans and the loyalists. "To this indiscriminate massacre," wrote Capt. Hannay in 1838, "may be attributed the subsequent civil wars of Assam, which in the end have brought it to its present degenerate and comparatively impoverished state."[39]

The most unrelenting advocate of repressive policy in respect of the Moamarias was Lakshmi Singha's premier Ghanasyam Buragohain. In a speech before the king and the council he stated his opinion as follows,—"The men who commit treason against the king thereby perpetrate a crime against their countrymen. The rigorous measures adopted against such men in previous reigns are on record. Every man's person is sacred, and it cannot be surrendered even to God Vishnu if He asks for it. Even if one's spiritual head tries to hurt your body a Kshatriya is justified in raising his sword against him. Enemies should be killed and destroyed. Such a policy alone will remove disturbances from the land, by creating fears in the hearts of all potential miscreants, and by dissuading loyal citizens from sympathising or collaborating with rebels. We have killed the Moamaria Guru and a large number of his adherents. I have killed many Moamarias with my own hand. The survivors can never entertain friendly feelings towards us. The king should execute those whose loyalty is questionable; and no one should be spared. His Majesty should not listen to the counsel of his pacific and time-serving ministers. The king's predecessors had established peace and quiet in the country by executions and massacres. We should also institute enquiries into the movements

39. Capt. S. O. Hannay, *A Short Account of the Moamorah Sect*, J.A.S.B., August 1838.

of the Moamarias who have taken shelter in the neighbouring territories."[40]

Revolts and conspiracies marked the remaining years of Lakshmi Singha's reign. But the officers of his government were capable of grappling with them from their experience of the ordeals of the late revolution brought about mainly by the indifference and inaction of their fathers and uncles. The king himself was watchful; and he knew when to give way to his ministers and when to make them yield to his wishes. He governed with a strong hand and every element of disorder and potential defection was crushed in time.

In 1773, Bhudhar Singha, son of Charusingha Juvaraj, conspired to seize the throne, with the help of Bhadrasen Barbarua. But it was detected by Kekeru Kalita Phukan; and both Bhudhar and Bhadrasen were executed. A similar attempt was made by Malou Tipamia Gohain, son of Pramatta Singha, which was also detected by the same Kalita Phukan, and Malou was banished to Namrup. A number of Muhammadans under the leadership of one Hazari Dewan, tried to organise a conspiracy to set up a son of Mohanmala on the throne. The conspirators were let off with light punishments. In 1775 several exiled princes of Namrup, including Bijoy Barmura Gohain, son of Ratneswar, took up the cause of their fellow-sufferer Malou Tipamnia Gohain, but the attempt was frustrated by the death of that prince. Several Satras harboured princes to set them up as claimants to the throne when any opportunity occurred. Vigorous searches were made of such Mahantas, and specially of the relations of the Mayamara Mahanta. Namrup being a hotbed of disaffection the princes were transferred to Tokolai, near the present town of Jorhat, for more effective surveillance.

The orthodox Ahom priests and the Vaisnava Mahantas were averse to the conversion of the king and his nobles to Saktism. Siva Singha, Pramatta Singha, and Rajeswar Singha had accepted initiation from Krishnaram Nyayavagis or his descendants, and many nobles had followed suit to be able to associate with the monarch in religious observances. Lakshmi Singha took initiation from an Assamese Gosain, named Ramananda. On Ramananda's death his sons Gangaballabh, Gangadhar and Gangasekhar, became known as Na-Gosains. The change led to the formation of a schism in the Sakta camp between the followers of the Parvatia Gosain and the Na-Gosains. The Parvatia Gosain being thus slighted by

40. Ms. chronicle of Lakshmi Singha's reign.

the king had supported the conspiracy of Bhudhar Singha and Malou Tipamia Gohain. The king expelled the Parvatia Gosain from the land and promulgated an order that acceptance of *mantras* from the Parvatia Gosain would amount to treason, and that the transgressor would be duly punished. The order of expulsion was subsequently withdrawn.

Barpatra Gohain's warning: The redeeming feature in that age of political and religious acrimony was the solitary voice of the Barpatra Gohain, one of the three principal counsellors. The Gohain foresaw that preoccupation with religious observances would divert men's minds from their duties to the state. The Kalita Phukan had once sent a messenger to the Barpatra Gohain to persuade the latter to accept initiation into Saktism as had been done by the other Gohains and principal nobles. The Barpatra Gohain who was a Vaisnava, following the teachings of the *Bhagavata,* regarded Saktism as an encumbrance to officials who had always to remain ready for state duties. He rebuked the Kalita Phukan for taking part in religious propaganda at a time when the affairs of the country demanded his undivided attention. This is what the Barpatra Gohain told the Brahman messenger of the Kalita Phukan,—"I am the son of an Ahom. What *mantras* [Sakta incantations] have we got? We are all bewildered by the bait of worldliness. If we accept *mantras,* and sit down for a moment to utter them, the children will cry, the womenfolk of the house will break the silence of the atmosphere by their gossip and shout, our retainers and tenants will give out a vociferous howl, and commands will come from the king to proceed to his presence at once. So, how will one bring his *mantras* to perfection? So we, the sons of the Ahoms, have all agreed to cherish the religion as propounded in the *Bhagavata.* Hence, we should not be offered the *mantras.* Please tell the Phukan that the disturbances at Gauhati, Sadiya and other places have not been completely suppressed, and we have received reports regarding treasonable activities on the part of the prince Tipamia Gohain. Why should not the Phukan direct his attention to these matters? If he subordinates state duties to religious enthusiasm it is better for us to retire from office and sit quiet at home. Know it to be my express order that the Kalita Phukan should not interest himself any more in Sakta propaganda. If he does he will be awarded condign punishment."[41]

41. Ms. chronicle of Lakshmi Singha's reign; S. K. Bhuyan, *Assamese Historical Literature,* in *Indian Historical Quarterly,* September 1929.

PART II

King Gaurinath Singha's Flight to Gauhati

Coronation of Gaurinath Singha : Swargadeo Lakshmi Singha died on December 13, 1780, leaving a son named Lokenath Gohain and two daughters. To ensure the succession of his son, King Lakshmi Singha, with the concurrence of the nobles, had appointed Lokenath Gohain as Juvaraj or heir-apparent in 1777. There had been several conspiracies during the life-time of Lakshmi Singha to kill him and his son. They lived and moved very cautiously, and the conspirators once regretted that all their designs had been frustrated as the royal pair refrained from taking any medicine.[1]

On ascending the throne Lokenath Gohain assumed the name Gaurinath Singha. He was then a youth of fifteen, and no special provision having been made for properly educating him to shoulder the responsibilities of government at such an immature age, Gaurinath soon evinced those propensities which ultimately brought ruin to the kingdom and earned for him the notoriety of being "the most incompetent, blood-thirsty, disreputable and cowardly of all the Ahom kings",[2] 'a cruel tyrant', and head of 'the most corrupt, cruel and despotic government of which history could not afford a better example'.[3]

The usual diversions of the young monarch consisted of presenting 1,000 rupees to a man who could eat a vulture, 500 rupees to the eater of a crow, and 400 rupees to one who could eat 10 pounds of rice at one sitting. He used to be absent from the palace at unseasonable hours, and was on several occasions refused admittance by palace guards who could not recognise the monarch in the darkness of the night. When going out he sometimes left his retinue and made for houses where royal presence was the least expected.[4]

As regards the affairs of the administration Gaurinath became a puppet in the hands of Sibram Barbarua of the Adabaria Sandikoi

1. Ms. chronicle of Lakshmi Singha's reign.
2. Sir Edward Gait, *History of Assam*, 2nd edition, p. 215.
3. Welsh to Cornwallis, Feb. 4, Beng. Pol. Cons., Feb. 15, 1793, No. 15.
4. Maniram Dewan's Ms. *Assam Buranji*. The amours of Gaurinath Singha and Taravati, daughter of Sondhar, a scavenger by caste, form the subject of a popular Assamese ballad.

family, commonly known as Hekera Barbarua. There was a long-standing enmity between Sibram Barbarua and Bailung Bargohain. The Barbarua contrived to place an incriminatory letter in the house of the Bargohain to show that the latter was secretly plotting to place a rival prince on the throne. The king, acting on a report received from the Barbarua, deputed emissaries to search the house of Bailung Bargohain. The letter in question was discovered, and the king at once ordered the execution of the Bargohain who had taken a leading part in the restoration of Lakshmi Singha. The Bargohain was executed along with his sons, one of whom was Krishnaram Choladhara Phukan, who had married an elder sister of the king.[5] The Barbarua's son was appointed Choladhara Phukan. The vast property of Bailung and Krishnaram for which they had been specially noted was confiscated to the state.

But a monarch like Gaurinath Singha could not long brook the usurpation of his powers by a minister. He represented to some of his older officers about the annoyance and mortification to which he was subjected by the officiousness and arrogance of the Barbarua and they promised him their support. The Barbarua's sons were accused of entering the king's apartments with swords, of seducing the king's slave girls, and of riding on horses within the palace walls.[6] In March 1782 the king dismissed the Barbarua and his sons from their respective offices and expelled them to their ancestral home at Adabari. One Bhagati of the Namtial Sandikoi family, who had married the king's second sister, was appointed Barbarua.

In the same month the king accepted Sakta initiation from Gangadhar Na-Gosain, the second son of Ramananda Acharya, the preceptor of Lakshmi Singha, and became from that moment a staunch and lavish patron of Brahmans and Brahmanical rites. The unusually heavy expenses incurred by the king in the daily and periodical Sakta sacrifices, specially in the donations made to his Guru, began to tell heavily upon the royal exchequer. At the same time the growing affluence and power of the Na-Gosain were viewed with jealousy by the Bengali Parvatia Gosain who had a large following in the country and who had been the royal pre-

5. Krishnaram's love for his wife was a proverbial one. On her death he offered to be burnt on her funeral pyre from which he was dissuaded with great difficulty. He spent 300,000 rupees on her *Sraddha*.—Maniram Dewan's Ms. *Assam Buranji*.

6. David Scott's Historical Notes, Beng. Sec. and Pol. Cons., July 14, 1826, No. 2.

ceptor during the reigns of Siva Singha, Pramatta Singha and Rajeswar Singha, 1714-1769.[7]

In April 1782 the coronation of King Gaurinath Singha took place at the ancient capital Gargaon. The house where the ceremony of enthronement took place was known as *Singarighar* as the major portion of the wood employed in the building was of the Singari or *Castanea* tree. The hall was a spacious one measuring 210 feet in length. Images of the king, and of his nobles and officials, were carved on the pillars and beams and on every visible piece of timber. The ceiling was draped with velvet and *satin*. The house on this occasion had been constructed by Sibram Barbarua, but the organisation of the ceremony fell upon his successor Bhagati Barbarua. It was the usual practice for the king to live in the precincts of the *Singarighar* for one year after the coronation ceremony. The coronation hall was kept intact for four years though the costly trappings and decorations used to be removed after the king had left the place. The initial rites of the coronation were performed in two smaller houses *Patghar* and *Holong-ghar*. The entire body of functions was called *Singarighar-utha* ceremony or the ceremony of ascending the *Singarighar*. A monarch who had not been admitted to this ceremony was called a Sulung Raja, and he was not entitled to the privileges of a fullfledged sovereign. The ceremony cost four lakhs of rupees.[8]

Coronation building burnt by Moamarias: In the meantime the Moamarias had been planning to kill the king and seize the throne, actuated by the fact that he was young and without a powerful relative to protect him. The Moamarias had discovered the mistake of sparing the life of Lakshmi Singha. On April 21, 1783, the king had gone out to spend the day in amusements in the neighbourhood of Gargaon. As he was returning at night a number of Moamarias mixed with the king's torch-bearers and attendants and entered the royal camp. They set fire to the houses occupied by the guards, and attacked the royal sedan which was empty as the king had deftly made his escape in the meantime on an elephant and taken shelter in the underground compartments of the brick-built palace at Gargaon. The Moamarias struck several

7. Maniram Dewan's Ms. *Assam Buranji.*

8. Padmeswar Singh Naobaicha Phukan's Ms. *Assam Buranji.* For an account of the Ahom coronation ceremony see William Robinson's *Descriptive Account of Assam*, pp. 194-96; *Tungkhungia Buranji*, pp. 45-48; Martin's *Eastern India*, Vol. III, pp. 611-12, and Golapchandra Barua's *Ahom Buranji*, pp. 336-37.

blows on the pillow in the empty sedan, and cut off its bearers and a few other attentdants. The rebels then set fire to the coronation buildings and the residences of the Bargohain and the Barpatra Gohain as well as the king's audience hall. In the confusion that followed combined with the darkness of the night the rebels thought the king had been slain as well. Gargaon being open on all sides and thus exposed to attack from all quarters the Moamarias left for the new capital Rangpur where they met a stubborn resistance from the guards of the city. In the meantime Ghanasyam Buragohain and Harnath Senapati Phukan had traced out the king in his retreat, left him at the palace with a few guards, and dashed towards Rangpur. The Moamarias were defeated and repulsed with heavy slaughter. On the next day the king returned to Rangpur. It transpired that this attack on Gargaon had been incited by the sons of the deposed Sibram Barbarua, who had accompanied the rebels and taken an active part in the attack during the night. Having received conclusive proofs regarding their complicity the king punished the four sons of Sibram by having their eyes extracted.

Massacre of the Moamarias: On April 23, the king deliberated with his ministers as to the best means of putting an end to the revolt. Ghanasyam Buragohain who had played an important part in the restoration of Lakshmi Singha and in the late expulsion of the rebels from Rangpur two days ago, pleaded with vehemence that nothing but a policy of rigorous repression accompanied by a general massacre of the Moamarias would prevent them from contemplating rebellion in future. The other counsellors did not whole-heartedly support this proposal; but they had ultimately to give way before the eloquence of the Buragohain.[9] On that very day the king promulgated an order "that the Moamarias should be killed with their sons and friends by whomever and at whatever place they were met." This order was proclaimed throughout the country by messengers of the king. "Having heard this dire command of His Majesty", writes a contemporary historian, "our men captured and killed the Moamarias in all the villages with their sons and wives. Some of them fled into the territories of the Dafalas, the Bhots, the Kacharis and the Jayantas and thus saved

9. "The opinion of an eloquent man frequently influences the decrees of the Gohaigns. Eloquence is, therefore, in high estimation at court and leads to fame and honours even under a Government, not in any degree democratic." —J. P. Wade, *Account of Assam*, p. xiv.

their lives".[10] Many Moamarias of their own accord surrendered to the royalists and begged for an opportunity to share the fates of their murdered relatives and comrades. Prestige and rank used to be decided by the number of Moamaria heads a royalist could take. The massacre continued for one month and a half. A recent head of the Mayamara Satra had calculated that 700,000 Moamarias had perished by the sword of the royalists during those six weeks of terror.[11] Maniram Dewan, writing in 1838, thus describes the ravages of this massacre,—"The waters of the rivers could not be drunk and people could not walk along the roads. Even the water and fish of the Brahmaputra became tainted with the stinking smell of corpses. Half the country was depopulated. Thus was vengeance wreaked upon the Moamarias for burning the Singarighar and attempting to kill the king. From that period the kingdom became thinned and light. The *paiks* or servitors attached to different *khels* or units became reduced. If a Matak [Moamaria] was captured he would shout to his friends—'Oh, my comrades, I have been arrested'. Having heard this his friends would come forward and offer themselves to be apprehended and killed."[12]

Seeing the plight of the country the Bargohain, the Barbarua and other principal officers advised the king to suspend the massacre. They pointed out that the kingdom was going to be destroyed altogether and that innocent people had been ruthlessly killed along with the guilty. Ghanasyam Buragohain gave as his opinion, —"I intended to exterminate the poisonous nest of the Moamarias. My colleagues now desire the suspension of the slaughter after half the enemy have been destroyed. I predict that the Mataks will rise again and again and devastate the country. My colleagues will then remember me and realise the wisdom of my present action."[13] The Buragohain very reluctantly acquieseed in the proposal of the ministers and nobles to suspend the massacre, and the king issued the necessary orders.

Purnananda appointed prime minister: Towards the end of June 1783 Ghanasyam Buragohain fell ill. Seeing the approaching

10. *Tungkhungia Buranji*, p. 95.

11. Hridayananda Goswami, head of the Mayamara Denjay Satra, 1890-1934, in the Assamese magazine *Banhi*, Vol. XIX.

12. Maniram Dewan's Ms. *Assam Buranji*.

13. Maniram Dewan's Ms. *Assam Buranji*; *Matak* is the name given to the Morans by the Khamptis. It was loosely applied to all Moamarias, whether Morans and non-Morans. It is now used in reference to a man with a robust and vigorous physique combined with a strain of roughness and brutality.

end he obtained the king's orders for the appointment of his eldest son Purnananda as his successor in the office of Buragohain and prime minister. Ghanasyam summoned Purnananda to his death-bed and instructed him as follows: "Greater distinction is in store for you than what fell to my lot. Think not evil of the king. The Mataks are the source of all troubles. Seize those who, in your opinion, will rise to leadership and create mischief in the country. This course alone will enable you to carry on the work of administration smoothly. Do not accept any consideration from parties to a suit except the customary offer of betel-nut and leaf; then only your decisions and orders will have the validity of an inscription on a stone tablet. The people regard all judgments as vitiated if they receive reports of the corruption of a single judge. Finally, do not move from your country even if it be deserted by the king, and perish in the bosom of your own motherland."[14] The events of the subsequent decades will show that Purnananda Buragohain acted up to the wishes and instructions of his illustrious father. After the suspension of the massacre comparative peace prevailed in the kingdom for two years. Harnath Senapati Phukan, during his viceroyalty at Gauhati, offered 100,000 sacrifices, consisting of buffaloes, goats, ducks, pigeons, sugarcanes, pumpkins etc., to the temple of Kamakhya for propitiating the gods through whose wrath confusion and disorder were supposed to have occurred in the country. On Harnath's death in 1784, one Gogoi of the Sandikoi family was appointed Barphukan at Gauhati, and the king's maternal uncle Bhadari was appointed to the office of Choladhara Phukan. The king passed his days in amusement, visiting the principal monasteries, participating in hunting excursions and witnessing dramatic performances. In 1785 he married the daughter of one Kalia Deka of the Dihingia family.

In February 1785 the king passed a few weeks in his camp at Garamur on the north bank of the Brahmaputra and near the Luhit or Sabansiri river. The king's principal occupation during his holiday at Garamur was hunting of elephants, buffaloes, tigers and deer. The Mahanta of Narwa Satra who came to greet the king accompanied by the usual retinue of musicians was severely reprimanded for having harboured a prince in his monastery.

Fresh Moamaria revolt under Tati: In the meantime the Moamarias and Dafala-Bahatias living at Japaribhita at the foot of the Dafala hills had combined under the leadership of a Matak

14. Maniram Dewan's Ms. *Assam Buranji.*

named Tati.[15] An inscribed copper-plate had been found by a fisherman among the ruins of Arimatta's capital while being washed away by the Brahmaputra.[16] Tati got possession of the copper-plate ; it contained magical incantations the utterance of which was calculated to produce terror and bewilderment in the hearts of one's enemies. Tati got the *mantras* by heart, practised them day and night, and collected a large number of adherents, and imprinted on their foreheads a mark which was supposed to protect them from bullets and spear-thrusts. He then began to harass the people in the neighbouring villages, who now came in a body to complain before the king in his camp at Garamur. Bhagati Barbarua, the minister in attendance on the monarch, advised him not to pay any attention to the complaint as raids were a matter of common occurrence in that part of the country. The villagers were accordingly dismissed from the royal presence and no measures were adopted to enquire into the truth of their complaint. Tati's followers began to swell in number and their depredations continued unabated. The Moamarias who had left their villages during the massacre now returned and rallied round the banner of Tati.

The king then made preparations for leaving Garamur. At the moment of departure he was suddenly seized with the Nerovian impulse of seeing houses on fire. He gave orders for setting fire to the houses in his camp. The sight of house-burning is supposed to be very ominous, and the people predicted that disasters were awaiting the king and the kingdom.[17]

The king returned to Rangpur in April 1786. Reports about Tati's ravages poured upon the court almost daily. The rebels had destroyed four villages and killed a large number of people. The king took Bhagati Barbarua to task for taking no cognizance of the revolt in its early stage when it could have been suppressed without much difficulty.

A force was immediately despatched to Japaribhita under the command of the Marangi-khowa Gohain, the Dihingia Phukan of

15. Dafala-Bahatias were the Assamese subjects inhabiting the villages on the outskirts of the Dafala hills, whose services were made over to the Dafalas as blackmail.

16. Arimatta was an ancient king of Kamarupa, who figures very prominently in the traditions of the Assamese, though his identity, date and jurisdiction have not been ascertained with any degree of accuracy.—Gait, *History of Assam*, pp. 18-19.

17. Maniram Dewan's Ms. *Assam Buranji*.

the Rangpur establishment and Helimeli Solal Gohain. The Moamarias lured the royalists to encamp in the vicinity of a lake called Solmari Bil. Helimeli Solal Gohain left his command on the pretext of illness. In the engagement that followed Tati appeared in the field wearing a charmed cloth which he flung towards the royal force who, seized with fright, became completely incapable of wielding the weapons in their hands. The Marangi-khowa Gohain and the Dihingia Phukan were both killed in the resistance which they had offered with their handful of unswerving soldiers. Tati won the day after having caused severe casualties among the royalists. The survivors in their flight got themselves bogged in morasses. The victors obtained in this campaign a very large quantity of provisions and ammunition, and it was believed that these newly acquired supplies enabled the rebels to continue the struggle for such a length of time.

The Dihingia Phukan of the Gauhati establishment and the Naobaicha Phukan were then despatched against the insurgents. They were subsequently joined by forces under the Barpatra Gohain who was also appointed commander of the entire army. This supersession was resented by the Phukans who had already been in command. There were sporadic engagements at several places between Garamur and Japaribhita without any decisive result. The Moamarias then crossed the Subansiri river and pitched their camp at Garamur.

To strengthen their cause the Moamarias persuaded their spiritual leader Pitambar Mahanta to join them. Pitambar, after having performed the *Brahmaghna* or Brahman-slaying sacrifice, joined the side of his disciples. The insurgents then attacked the monastery of Garamur which was presided over, as at present, by a Brahman. The resistance offered by the monks and their head was of no avail. The contingent of soldiers recruited from Rani, Luki and Topakuchi in Kamrup were defeated by the Moamarias at Pahumara.

Rangpur attacked by the rebels: The rebels then crossed the Brahmaputra and spread themselves in the territory round the capital of Rangpur. The force commanded by the prime minister in person was defeated at Sagunmuri. He retreated to Gaurisagar. The Moamarias pursued him to that place and burnt a number of villages. The principal commanders including Purnananda Buragohain then retired to the fortifications of Rangpur. The rebels now advanced to Bhatiapar, three miles to the west of the capital, where they were attacked by the royalist commander Aka Bailung, who succeeded in arresting the progress of the enemy. The rebels were compelled to halt at Bhatiapar for three days before deciding on their next move.

Purnananda Buragohain posted garrisons at the different entrances to the capital. The Buragohain along with the other two cabinet ministers, the Bargohain and the Barpatra Gohain, guarded the three principal gates of the city. The Mahanta of Dihing leading a contingent composed of his disciples and monks attacked the rebels when they were engaged in burning the neighbouring villages. The Mahanta fought very bravely, but his soldiers who were not accustomed to the discipline of the battlefield, deserted their leader and fled in different directions. Another contingent composed of the Ahom priests, Deodhais and Bailungs, was defeated by the rebels with very heavy casualties. Aka Bailung was slain in an engagement at Jengerai. Then there followed several skirmishes in the neighbourhood of Bhatiapur. The Moamarias began to realise that an attack on the capital at that time would spell disaster to them.

Then there ensued the popular Assamese festival known as the *Maghar Bihu* which is held in the middle of January at the conjunction of the two Hindu months Poush and Magh. The *Maghar Bihu* marks the end of the harvesting season, and is next in importance to the *Bahag Bihu* which takes place at the beginning of the Hindu new year. The festivities commence with the burning of small lightly-thatched huts, temporarily erected for the occasion on banks of rivers and lakes. Friends are entertained with refreshments and juniors pay their respects to their seniors. It is a season of universal rejoicing, and men who have to live away from their homes come back to spend a week or two of amusement and feasting with their relatives and friends.

The Moamarias retreated from Bhatiapar on the pretext of going back to their respective villages for the *Maghar Bihu*. They were joined by fresh reinforcements. The Buragohain and the other royalist commanders now moved towards Gaurisagar some four miles west of Bhatiapar. The *Maghar Bihu* came to an end and the rebels advanced by the road along the Janji river.

The rebels then proceeded by the Maskhowa-garh towards the capital. The opposition offered by the royalists at different stages of their advance was easily repulsed. The Moamarias then arranged an attack on the capital from the east, and encamped at Meteka and Jaysagar in the immediate vicinity of Rangpur. They met only with a feeble resistance at the gates of the capital; and it is recorded that a more vigorous encounter was rendered impossible by a hail-storm which raged furiously at night.

Gaurinath's flight to Gauhati : When the rebels were knocking at the gates of the capital King Gaurinath Singha was conferring with his ministers regarding the course to be adopted. "The hearts of the people are not well disposed", said the nobles, "and so we think going down to Gauhati is the most reasonable thing to do." So at midnight, January 19, 1788, the king left the palace by a secret passage and embarked at Amgurighat in boats belonging to the Choladhara Phukan. The king was accompanied by the Na-Gosain, Bhadari Choladhara Phukan, the Dhekial Phukan, the Bhitarual Phukan, Bhimbal Siring Phukan, the Tipamia Rajkhowa, the Bailung Dulia Barua, and a few attendants. During the course of the same night the queens with their maids proceeded to the east, and so did the Buragohain and the Barbarua. The Barpatra Gohain sailed down to Gauhati. The other Phukans and Baruas deserted the capital and went to different directions. Thus within the course of a few hours Rangpur which had a population of 10,000 souls, became a deserted city. The treasures in the capital were plundered by the slaves and servitors of the king and of his nobles during the remaining hours of the night. They carried as much as they could and buried the rest for removal in future. The Moamarias enterd the evacuated city next morning, January 20. The rebels remained without action for seven days. In the meantime they sent for Pitambar Mahajan, but he left Rangpur as a result of a quarrel with a section of the Moamarias. Their affairs were now managed by the leaders Tati, Howha and Prasad. Tati and Howha soon retired to their own localities in the north bank where they assumed independance. Pitambar was recalled, and Bharath Singha, a relative of the Moamaria Gosain in the male line, was placed on the throne at Rangpur, and Pitambar continued to live at the capital.[18]

On the king's arrival at Gauhati the viceroy of that place, Gogoi Barphukan, received him with the pomp and honour due to a sovereign. Gaurinath despatched Kaliman Rajkhowa and Anandiram Kataki to bring down the queens from their retreat at Lechang. He then deliberated with the Gauhati officers and sent

18. Capt. S. O. Hannay mentions three Rajas as predecessors of Bharath Singha at Rangpur,—Dafala-Bahatia, Bura Phukan and Agni Kowar.—*J.A.S.B.*, August 1838, p. 672. The chronicle of the Mayamara Satra says that Howha Tati ruled at Rangpur for three years with the title Jogendra. Maniram Dewan says that immediately after the occupation of Rangpur the affairs of the victors were conducted by the two leaders Howha and Prasad who soon afterwards sent for Pitambar Mahajan.

up the Paniphukan and the Dhekial Phukan at the head of a large army to the assistance of Purnananda.

Purnananda opposes Moamaria advance: After the desertion of the capital Rangpur by the king and his officers the task of opposing the rebels was taken up by individual leaders and officers. The chief queen, known as Dihingia Barkuanri, during her stay at Lechang, appointed one Manjay of the Bakatial family as Barbarua, and despatched him at the head of 4,000 soldiers mainly recruited from the villages. Another leader Bhogai joined Manjoy's army, which was further reinforced by 2,000 *kowanrs* or 'princes.'[19] The united force under the command of Manjoy hurried towards the older capital Gargaon, and encamped at the Panichoky gate in its immediate vicinity. Another leader named Merkai Senapati advanced against Rangpur at the head of 2,000 soldiers; but he was confronted by the Moamarias at Jaysagar. A large number of the royalists were massacred and Merkai's soldiers dispersed to different directions. The Dihingia Barbarua attacked the rebels with an army of 20,000 soldiers at Darika. In the engagement that ensued the Moamarias were defeated and driven off to Rangpur. There was a further encounter near Sibsagar where the Dihingia Barbarua's men were attacked from the rear. The rebels inflicted heavy casualties on the royalists. There ensued a hand-to-hand fight where the Dihingias were completely routed and their Barbarua slain.

Manjoy Barbarua halted at Gargaon for eight days being joined meanwhile by Purnananda Buragohain and other royalist leaders including his brother, and the two Brahman officials the Tamuli Phukan and the Jalbhari Phukan. Bhogai's detachment was attacked by the rebels at Alikekuri. His men offered a stubborn resistance. Bhogai died fighting in the battle, on which the soldiers became disheartened and deserted the field. The Moamarias then set fire to the villages and encircled Manjoy Barbarua's forces as if by a ring of fire. Manjoy fled from Gargaon to Bakata. The Moamarias then entered Gargaon and burnt all the houses within the walls of the city. They then advanced to Charaideo which was the principal place of Ahom worship and destroyed the temples

19. There were two regiments of Kowanrs or 'princes,' known as *Kowanr-Hiloidaris*, which were first created by Khora Raja (1552-1603). "The king selected the handsome youths of the land, gave them a feast and affiliated them to his own family. These newly made princes were provided with gold-mounted guns and formed into distinct regiments employed mainly in the protection of the Raja's palace and enclosures, the capital and its environs."—*Tungkhungia Buranji*, Glossary, p. 241.

there. At the sight of these ravages the villagers were seized with fright and they came to the Moamarias and offered their submission. The Buragohain sailed down to join the king at Gauhati.

At Kajiranga the Buragohain met the Paniphukan who had been sent up to his assistance. The Paniphukan's army was now divided into three sections: the Bacha and Opar-Dayangia regiments were placed under the Dhekial Phukan, the Majiu-Dayangias under the Paniphukan, and the Nam-Dayangias under the Buragohain. In the meantime one Min Senapati collected a number of recruits and attacked the rebels at several places. This leader was now invited to join the Buragohain's division. The combined army of the Buragohin, the Dhekial Phukan and Min Senapati halted at the three stockades near a stream called Mitangjan. The Paniphukan proceeding along the Bar Ali raised a stockade at Kupoukhat on the other side of the Chintamani rampart. The Moamarias stormed the Paniphukan's camp and killed a large number of his soldiers. The Phukan then retired to a camp in the neighbourhood wherefrom he sent a message to the Buragohain to come to his rescue or take him to Mitangjan. The Buragohain sent for the Paniphukan who encamped in the vicinity of the premier's stockade. The Buragohain then despatched messengers in search of the soldiers who had deserted their camps and taken shelter in the neighbouring villages. On the return of these fugitives the soldiers in the camp of the Buragohain, the Dhekial Phukan and Min Senapati, deserted their garrisons and fled in all directions under the impression that the people who were approaching their camps were no other than Moamarias.

In March 1788 the Buragohain left Mitangjan and retired to Namdang five miles to the west of Rangpur. He erected five stockades within gun-shot distance from each other, and himself remained in charge of the fort on the bank of the Namdang river. The rebels failed in their efforts to dislodge the Buragohain from Namdang. In the meantime fresh reinforcements arrived from Gauhati under the Barpatra Gohain and the Bargohain.

Prince Patkowar's temporary successes: Then there appeared several royalist leaders who organised vigorous measures to counteract the influence of the rebels and oust them from their position at Rangpur. The first was Patkowar, the fourth and the only surviving son of King Rajeswar Singha. The prince had been living as an exile in Namrup since the death of his father in 1769. He now obtained the support of several Ahom princes including Dighala Gohain and Barmura Gohain, and a numerous body of Ahom nobles and ex-officers, and managed within a short time to recruit a large army from Tipam and Abhaypur. He erected twenty stockades at Panichoky in the vicinity of Gargaon, where he halted for some time, while his lieutenant Prince Japara Gohain encamped at Deobil near Athkhel and Hudupara. Purnananda Buragohain remained ready for action at Namdang with his commanders, the Paniphukan, the Dhekial Phukan and the Neog-Phukan.

Sporadic engagements with the rebels commenced from the latter half of April 1788 with no decisive result in the beginning. The rebels attacked the army of Japara Gohain, but were soon repulsed and compelled to fall back upon Rangpur. Japara then advanced towards Kharikatia Ali.

Patkowar's engagements with the rebels resulted on the whole in his favour. He now proceeded towards Rangpur and encamped at Sibsagar, at a distance of two miles east of the capital. In the meantime the Nara Raja had despatched to the aid of Patkowar 8,000 soldiers with the object of expelling the usurpers and restoring the Ahom monarch with whom the Nara Raja claimed common descent.[20] The Moamarias being hemmed in from all sides suffered from scarcity of provisions, and it was believed that if Patkowar had pressed upon them from Sibsagar the rebels could have been driven from Rangpur or compelled to surrender. Dissensions however broke out in Patkowar's camp rendering concerted action impossible. In the month of August the Moamarias stormed the fort of Patkowar who fled to Lechang where he was ambushed by the rebels and killed. The Patkowar's eldest son was then set up as Raja, but it was at best a nominal distinction. It is said that elated with his initial success, Patkowar had styled himself as *Swargadeo* and that he had once addressed a letter to Gaurinath Singha with the superscription "From the reigning monarch Patkowar to the fugitive prince Gaurinath Singha." Gaurinath communicated this fact to Purnananda Buragohain who, it is said, secretly contrived the undoing of Patkowar.[21]

Purnananda Buragohain at Jorhat: One Pahar Senapati placed himself at the head of the Gharphalias, and encamped at

20. The Ahoms looked upon the Nara country or Mogaung beyond the Patkai as their parent kingdom, as the first batch of victors under Sukapha came from there. The Nara Raja, as well as other Shan chiefs were addressed as *Bhai-Rajas* as brother-kings. After the occupation of Assam by the British the Nara Raja sent emissaries to enquire what had happened to their *Bhai-Raja*.

21. Maniram Dewan's Ms. *Assam Buranji.*

Samaguri where he was attacked by the rebels.[22] The insurgents were repulsed with heavy casualties and compelled to retreat to Rangpur. Pahar Senapati with his Gharphalias then joined the army of the Barpatra Gohain. The Moamarias beseiged the royalists in their stockade on the bank of the Namti river. Japara Gohain then appeared on the scene and fell upon the Moamarias who were made to retire with heavy losses.

Then two leaders of Lakhimpur organised a force of rebels and enlisted recruits after having performed the usual rites. They encountered the army of the Barpatra Gohain on the bank of the Janji river; but both sides retreated without any serious contest. Having received report of the rising of the Lakhimpurias the Buragohain despatched men from his fort at Namdang, who succeeded in capturing the rebels by a strategem. The two leaders managed to escape. Their followers were put to death after being subjected to various forms of torture. This happened towards the end of March 1789.

In April the rebels besieged the Ahom fort at Gaurisagar for two months, keeping their passage open to Rangpur. The beleagured garrison of the royalists underwent extreme privations for want of food supplies. Many died of starvation, and several prominent nobles including the Bargohain, the Paniphukan and Naobaicha Phukan perished in action. The Buragohain then retreated to Taratali, and then to Dichoi in the vicinity of the present town of Jorhat. He erected a stockade at Dichoi which he placed under the command of Japara Gohain and the Brahman Parvatia Barua. The Buragohain then retired to Kacharihat where he collected the Dayangias and placed them in a fort at that place. He then proceeded to Bacha where he summoned the 3,000 men who by law were obliged to render service to the government. The Bachas replied that they could not leave their wives and children, nor could they take up arms against the Moamarias. They directed the prime minister to leave the place in the same manner as he had come. The Buragohain then proposed to attack the Bachas. The latter placed themselves under a leader named Jabar Saikia and attempted to seize the Buragohain. There ensued a division in the Bacha camp; half the men veered round the Buragohain, and the other

22. The Gharphalias were an Ahom clan created by Rudra Singha (1696-1714) by selecting the stout and strong men of each family and separating them from their original families. *Ghar*, house or family, *phalia*, separated.—Golapchandra Barua, *Ahom-Assamese-English Dictionary* under *Phu-pha-ren*, the Ahom name of the Gharphalias.

half led by Jabar Saikia and a new leader named Tiktiki Neog proceeded to Gajpur and waited there for action. Japara Gohain who had been so long a royalist now changed his mind; he won over the recalcitrant Bachas to his side, augmented his followers, and began to behave like an independent chief. The Buragohain, however, was more than a match for this imposter. He pretended friendship with Japara Gohain, had him arrested and extracted his second eye, the first one having been already removed. Jabar Saikia and Tiktiki Neog were executed with their sons. The Buragohain then retired to Chungighat and from there to Charaibahi. Early in April 1790 the Buragohain encamped at Dichoi.

The Buragohain's encampment at Dichoi became the nucleus of the town of Jorhat which continued to be the capital of the Ahoms till the end of their rule. There were two *hats* or markets on the two banks of the river Dichoi. The eastern *hat* was under the Parvatia Phukan and the western one under the Raidangia Phukan; and hence the place came to be known as *Jor-hat* or couple-market.

Meanwhile the Buragohain sent Bajia Kataki with his despatches to the monarch at Gauhati and represented through him that there were many seditious persons in the kingdom who were ill-affected to the government but cloaked their deeds under the garb of patriotism, that if the king would delegate to him authority for the purpose he would bring such to condign punishment and establish the means of subduing the Moamarias. The king was not disposed to place such implicit confidence in the Gohain and arranged to bring a Burkendaz force from Bengal for service under the Buragohain.[23]

Gaurinath procures troops from Bengal: King Gaurinath Singha remained at Gauhati for six years from February 1788 to January 1794. Kaliman who had been sent to escort the queens from Upper Assam was confronted by the Moamarias at Suffry. Patkowar's son who had been elevated to Rajaship was killed in the engagement as well as a large number of Kaliman's followers. Kaliman, however, managed to escape with the ladies of the king's harem. The Buragohain supplied the necessary provisions and sent them down to the company of the king at Gauhati. Many Baruas and Phukans accompanied the ladies to Gauhati.

The king had despatched messengers to the Rajas of Jayantia, Cachar and Manipur asking for aid to suppress the disturbances.

23. David Scott's Historical Notes, Beng. Sec. and Pol. Cons., July 14, 1826, No. 2.

The first two Rajas gave evasive replies, and pleaded inability to send soldiers alleging that the strength at their disposal was necessary for the protection of their own territories.[24] The Raja of Manipur, Jai Singha Karta-Maharaj, who had been helped by King Rajeswar Singha in 1765, sent his Dharmadhi or high-priest at the head of some soldiers; but on their arrival in Assam the Manipuri force, instead of proceeding to the Buragohain's camp as directed by Gaurinath Singha, returned suddenly to their own country after having plundered the Assamese villages on the Assam-Cachar frontier.

In October 1789 the king asked Gogoi Barphukan and Bhagati Barbarua to arrange a force of Bengal Burkendazes so that he might be escorted by them to the Buragohain's camp at Jorhat. The two officers were lukewarm in their support of the king's proposal. The Barphukan pretended illness, and the Barbarua summarily refused to execute the king's wishes saying,—"I, your servant, can neither arrange for soldiers from Bengal, nor can I conduct Your Majesty to Upper Assam as long as the Moamarias are alive. The person who will undertake to escort the king should be appointed Barbarua." The king dismissed both the officers: one Medhi of the Dihingia family was appointed Barphukan, while the office of Barbarua was conferred on Jainath of the Bakatial family. Gogoi, the dismissed Barphukan, left Gauhati, with a large quantity of goods and treasures, but he was killed at Dopgar in Sibsagar by the Chutia-Kanris who wanted to seize his property. Medhi Barphukan wrote a letter, in the name of the king, to Hugh Baillie, the Company's Resident at Goalpara, asking for military assistance.[25]

Baillie could not send any assistance to Assam as he was soon confronted with troubles in his own factory at Goalpara which was attacked on November 22, 1789, by Ranaram Chaudhuri, Zemindar of Mechpara. Baillie engaged a number of Burkendazes to quell the disturbances in Mechpara, but he had to disband them owing to the arrival of a detachment of sepoys under the orders of the Commander-in-Chief. Baillie permitted the Burkendazes formerly in his employ to proceed to Assam for King Gaurinath Singha's assistance.[26]

24. Gunabhiram Barua, *Assam Buranji*, pp. 151-2.

25. Baillie to Cornwallis, Nov. 9, 1789, where he said,—"I yesterday received a letter from the Burah Fogun in the name of the Raja requesting assistance."—Beng. Rev. Cons., Dec. 9, 1789.

26. Raush to Cornwallis, Sept. 17, Beng. Pol. Cons., Oct. 3, 1792, No. 18.

In the meantime troubles had begun in Kamrup and Darrang. A conspiracy was set on foot by Haradatta Bajarbarua, a Chaudhuri of Kamrup, and Hangsnarayan, the Deka-Raja of Darrang. Gaurinath executed Hangsanarayan in January 1790, but his son Krishnanarayan at the instigation of the fugitive Haradatta and a Darrang noble named Phatik Hazarika, devised measures to avenge the death of Hangsanarayan and to recover possession of Darrang and Kamrup by force of arms. Most of the Burkendazes sent to Assam by Baillie were intercepted by Krishnanarayan and engaged in his service. Gaurinath then wrote to Raush for Burkendaz troops, and the latter was able to despatch 700 men from Dacca under one Chait Sing Subedar. Raush even advanced the pay and the supplies to the troops destined for Assam, and assured Gaurinath that if the force proved inadequate he would write to Calcutta for more.[27]

Gaurinath Singha thought it unsafe to continue longer at Gauhati. He proceeded to Nowgong under the escort of the troops sent by Raush. On reaching Dimou in Nowgong Gaurinath asked Medhi Barphukan to send the Burkendazes to the Buragohain's camp at Dichoi leaving a small guard of 40 men for his protection. The king then moved to Hahchora near Samaguri, and then to Khutarmur. While at the latter place he despatched in July 1790 a fresh deputation to the Manipuri Raja Jai Singha with a request for military aid. Jai Singha came personally at the head of 800 effectives and several thousands of irregulars, and met Gaurinath at Khutarmur in December 1790. Jai Singha was sent with his army to the Buragohain's camp.

Gaurinath's expulsion from Nowgong: The people of Nowgong felt themselves harassed by the king's long residence in their midst. They had to supply food grains and other articles to the king and his numerous camp-followers.[28] The officers used to forcibly bring down betel-nuts and leaves from the trees in the orchards of the villages. They also carried away virgins from their parents' protection. Many of the officers acquired *khats* or estates and engaged the surrounding inhabitants in compulsory labour. The people of

27. David Scott's Historical Notes, Beng. Sec. and Pol. Cons., July 14, 1826, No. 2; Wellesley to Assam Raja, No. 20, 1802, Barlow to same, Oct. 2, 1806, Beng. Pol. Cons., May 2, 1805, No. 97, and Oct. 2, 1806, No. 18 respectively.

28. Bakhar Bara, a local official of considerable eminence, was killed by the Nowgong rabble for alleged extortions in raising supplies for Gaurinath Singha. The ballad describing the circumstances of his death is still sung by villagers in Nowgong.

Nowgong were ultimately roused to action. They placed themselves under the leadership of Sindhura Hazarika, and proceeded to the royal camp armed with spears and swords. They destroyed the bridge on the river Rupahi, and surrounded the king's quarter one day in February 1791 soon after his return from Leterimukh where he had gone to bathe in the Brahmaputra. The Nagayans demanded that the king should depart from that place or appoint a new Barphukan and a new Barbarua, adding that they had been compelled to take that extreme measure on account of their continued oppression. The king promised to dismiss Medhi Barphukan and Jainath Barbarua and to appoint new officers in their place. After nine days the Nagayans submitted a counter-petition to retain the older officers which was accordingly done. The people of Nowgong received from that time the appellation of "Raja-kheda", or king-expelling, Nagayans.

A few months later there was a second attack on the royal camp at Khutarmur. One Bairagi organised a large force at Panisangal, near Biswanath, on the north bank of the Brahmaputra, and confronted the Moamarias at several places. Having attained some success the Bairagi declared himself as Raja and appointed a member of the Lahan family as his Barbarua. The Barbarua secured the sympathy of the local Ahom governor Helimeli Solal Gohain who permitted the Nagayans and Kharangis serving under him to join the rebels. The Barbarua then crossed the Brahmaputra at Kaliabar, won over the soldiers despatched against him, and beseiged the royal camp one midnight. The king escaped through a secret passage, but he was confronted again by the Lahan Barbarua. The king ordered a Burkendaz named Nathu Singh Jamadar to open fire upon the rebels on which they proceeded to the royal camp and plundered it. The king finally left Nowgong on June 11, 1792, and returned to Gauhati where more serious complications were waiting for him.

Purnananda's patriotic exertions: Purnananda Buragohain continued to direct operations against the Moamarias from his camp at Jorhat. He had erected an outpost at Meleng which was destroyed by the rebels in April 1790. The commanders Bacha Rajkhowa and Majiu-Dayangia Rajkhowa were killed in action, and the survivors retreated to Jorhat.

On receiving this news the king, as we have seen, sent up from Dimou the Burkendaz sepoys. The Buragohain erected a stockade at Teok and halted there with the Burkendazes in June; but on the advent of the rains he returned to Jorhat. In September the rebels attacked the Ahom fort near the river Kakila. The Burkendazes despatched by the Buragohain to the rescue of the garrison were defeated in an action on a field near Jorhat and were cut up to a man.[29] The royalists under the command of Kadam Dighala Charing Raja were attacked by the Moamarias at his fort at Bar Ali. The insurgents were put to flight and they returned to Rangpur.

In this way the Moamarias committed ravages in the country. Pillage and rapine constituted their normal occupation. Sometimes they entered the villages by the rivers Kakadanga and Dhansiri and returned with boat-loads of plunder. To counteract their designs the Buragohain organised bands of local volunteers in the respective villages who opposed the rebels in their plundering raids and outrages. But these defensive rural militias, or *Gayali-muths* as they were called, could not achieve permanent success for lack of co-ordination with neighbouring bodies.

The people had lost their heart since the flight of King Gaurinath from Rangpur. They would have readily accepted the domination of the Moamarias but for the ceaseless exertions of the prime minister Purnananda Buragohain who now became the *de facto* ruler of that portion of Upper Assam which had not yet been conquered by the rebels. He collected men from different parts of the country, equipped them with weapons brought from Kaliabar and Gauhati, and despatched them to fight against the Moamarias who could not advance further from Rangpur on account of the net-work of forts erected by the Buragohain at different places. The people of Majuli, Abhaypur and Rangpur, including the heads of the monasteries, deserted their homes and took refuge in the neighbouring territories. The Buragohain deputed agents to persuade the fugitives to return to their villages. The price of foodstuffs went up high, and rice used to be sold at the rate of five seers for a *tola* of gold. Men perished by hundreds for want of food. Wives and children were deserted by their husbands and fathers and left to die of starvation.[30] The Buragohain's camp at Jorhat became an asylum for refugees. He gave them food and raiment, and enlisted the able-bodied ones as soldiers, some of whom were retained in his army and the rest sent down to Gauhati to the assistance of the king. Presents were given to soldiers to induce them to proceed to action, or punishment in case they refused to take up arms . "During that period of affliction and misery," says a contemporary historian, "the Mahamantri Bura-

29. William Robinson, *Descriptive Account of Assam*, p. 170.
30. Golapchandra Barua, *Ahom Buranji*, p. 349.

gohain Dangaria [Purnananda] protected the people like a mother-bird guarding her nestlings under her wings."[31]

In the meantime the Manipur Raja Jai Singha accompanied by his son Madhuchandra Juvaraj arrived with his force at Jorhat. The Buragohain conducted the Raja to Teok from where he was despatched to attack the Moamarias at Rangpur. The Manipuri force halted at Gaurisagar. Madhuchandra went in advance with his detachment towards the capital. The Moamarias had concealed their batteries in the lofty grass and impenetrable reeds that covered both sides of the road. The prince avoided the route, effected a *detour,* and proceeded unmolested. He succeeded in forcing his way into the Rangpur fortress where he massacred the Moamarias of every age and sex. But his triumph was short-lived as he received the news that the rebels had opened their guns upon his father's army slaughtering a great number of Manipuris. The prince returned and experienced a similar fate. The old Raja Jai Singha personally conducted the attack riding on his horse Hayraj, but was compelled to retire before the well-directed fire of the Moamaria cannon. The Raja returned to his country leaving 1,000 men for service under the Buragohain.[32] Before reaching Manipur Jai Singha received the intelligence that the king of Burma had taken possession of his country and his capital.

About this time Purnananda constructed an earthen rampart enclosing the Dichoi forts and extending from the Kaliani Hill to the foot of the Naga Hills. The rampart was strongly barricaded with wooden posts. The Buragohain conducted the war-operations against the Moamarias from his shelter within this rampart which was called *Bibudhi-garh,* literally, the perplexing rampart.

The Moamarias continued their ravages in full vigour. The Baskatia Barbarua collected a force of Miris and Dafalas and offered to attack the Moamarias provided the Buragohain placed them under a good commander. The Buragohain despatched Kadam Dighala Gohain Charing Raja to the north bank at the head of the Baskatia Barbarua's force; but the soldiers defied the authority of the Charing Raja who consequently returned to Jorhat. The Moamarias attcked Dergaon and killed several Ahom officials. They could not, however, penetrate into the district within the

31. *Tungkhungia Buranji,* O.U.P., p. 120.

32. Dr. J. P. Wade, *Memoir of Gowrinath Sing,* a few fragmentary leaves found at the end of his *Geographical Sketch of Assam,* India Office European Mss. Srinath does not admit that Madhuchandra entered the fort of Rangpur. He advanced as far as Ouguri Choky, an outpost of the capital, *Tungkhungia Buranji,* p. 128.

fortification of Dichoi, and the Buragohain managed to keep the territory upto Ladoigarh immune from Moamaria depredations.

Self-styled Rajas: As an offshoot of the general anarchy and confusion there appeared a number of petty rulers in different parts of the country. Bharath Singha ruled at Rangpur with Sukura as his Barbarua and Pitambar Mahajan as his chief adviser. At Bengmara or the Matak country the Morans had set up one Sarbananda as their ruler and Godha as their Barbarua. At Japaribhita, in the districts from the foot of the Dafala Hills to the Luhit river, Tati continued to exercise an independent sway, while Howha ruled over Majuli as far as the Brahmaputra. The district of Sadiya was ruled by two Khampti chiefs with the titles Burha Raja and Deka Raja. They had ousted the Ahom governor Sadiya-khowa Gohain and assumed his name, dignity and jurisdiction, and reduced his subjects to dependence or slavery. In the district of Nowgong Sindhura Hazarika had succeeded in instigating the people to defy the authority of the Ahom government. Besides the above there cropped up a number of mushroom Rajas with or without any territory. "In this state of anarchy and confusion," said Gaurinath Singha to Capt. Welsh, "any man who can pick up a hundred desperate fellows sets himself up for a Raja."[33] The only places which had for a long time remained immune from Moamaria uprisings were Darrang and Kamrup; but as we shall see the commotions which soon disturbed the peace of those provinces were far-reaching in consequences, specially with regard to the relations of the Assam government with the East India Company.

General survey of the Moamaria disturbances: Before proceeding to the next stage of the disturbances I must give a brief résumé of the circumstances which originated the Moamaria revolt and maintained it with such tenacity and vigour. The first Mahanta of the Mayamara Satra preached his gospel among the Morans who lived in a territory subsequently known as the Matak country. They were a rude Kachari tribe and were not easily amenable to the discipline of Vaisnavism or of any other humanising process. The Mahanta had therefore to shape his articles of faith to suit the temperament of his new disciples. To remove the prospect of their deviation from his influence and to make them submit to his teachings with unflinching obedience he taught them to regard him as superior even to the greatest gods, to say nothing

33. Welsh to Cornwallis, Nov. 27, Beng. Uol. Cons., Dec. 17, 1792, No. 47.

of any mortal king. He overpowered them by his alleged powers of magic which at once raised him in the estimation and reverence of his followers. He was in possession of a book with the help of which he was supposed to be capable of fulfilling any desire. The Mayamara Mahanta became in course of time more than an agent ministering only to the spiritual needs of his disciples: he became the virtual sovereign of the Morans, and as he had a numerous following in other parts of Assam he could command great resources. This pre-eminence of the Mahanta was not disturbed even after he had shifted his hearquarters from the heart of the Moran territory. His disciples were mostly newly Hinduised converts capable of enduring great physical exertions, and thus they represented the warlike elements in the Assamese population.[34] Equipped with such a devoted and sturdy band of adherents the Mayamara Mahanta's transition from prelatical to temporal leadership was tempting and easy.

The numerical superiority of the Mahanta's following excited the jealousy of the other Gosains. He was despised for his offering initiation to unrefined tribesmen, and for his intimate communion with his disciples, which, his rivals believed, must have coarsened his manners, affected the purity of his Vaisnava faith and contaminated his spirit. The prevalence of degraded Tantric rituals among some of his followers, though in a suppressed form, and confined to isolated groups and individuals, was attributed to the Mahanta's connivance and even to his active support. These rites had been pursued by the tribesmen in Assam and elsewhere for ages past; the humanising influence of both Hinduism and Buddhism having failed to eradicate them, they had been absorbed into the systems of the two religions under a dignified nomenclature. The Mayamara Mahanta as a true Vaisnava discountenanced such practices. But in the eyes of his rivals the Mahanta was a suspect, a promoter of heterodoxy, a separatist, and a dissenter from the original cult of the great Vaisnava leader Sankardeva and from all pure forms of Hinduism. Attempts were made to show that dissociation with the Mahanta had been commanded by Sankardeva and his great apostle Madhabdeva in consequence of the clash between the monism and *Bhaktism* of the two Vaisnava reformers and the alleged heterodoxy of the Mayamara Mahanta. To this must be

34. "The Morans are by no means that degenerate and weakly race that the Assamese in general are. They are rude and rough in their manners, robust in their person, and hitherto not addicted to opium."—Wm. Robinson, *Descriptive Account of Assam*, 1841, p. 331.

added the spirit of rivalry which was generally seen between the Brahman Gosains and the Sudra Mahantas including the Mayamara prelate. This spirit was more pronounced against the Satras of the *Kala-Samhati* order whose creed was more democratic, less caste-ridden and avowedly more opposed to orthodoxy.

The Mayamara Mahanta's rise to prosperity and influence roused the misgivings of the Ahom government. The Mahanta gave indications of his political intent by comparing his eminence to that of the Ahom sovereigns. His disciples would not bow their heads to the Ahom king, a circumstance which could not be reconciled to their position as a subject people. The Bhuyans, of whom the Mayamara Mahantas were descendants, had ruled in a portion of eastern Assam before the advent of the Ahoms. The movements of the Bhuyans were therefore closely watched by the conquerors. After their subjugation, Suhungmung Dihingia Raja settled most of them at Bardowa in Nowgong in the hope that they would repel the incursions of the Kacharis. He hoped further that the spirited and enlightened Bhuyans, when exposed to the ravages of the marauding Kacharis, would not find time to organise any opposition towards the Ahom government.[35] The Bhuyans rebelled from time to time till they were finally crushed by King Pratap Singha. Their leader Uday was executed, and his principal adherents transferred to the south bank of the Brahmaputra. The Bhuyans were forbidden to cross to the north bank on penalty of death.[36] This suspicion, which continued ever afterwards, found expression in the case of a Bhuyan official, the famous Kalita Phukan, who wielded great political power in the reign of Lakshmi Singha and who contrived the execution of several Ahom princes and nobles for alleged complicity in seditious crimes. The Ahom nobles in a body expatiated before the monarch on the Phukan's suspected designs to revive the authority of the Bhuyans, and demanded on that ground his dismissal from office.[37] This fear obviously governed the policy of the Ahom rulers towards their predecessors, the Bhuyans, and was at the root of the execution of the Mayamara Mahanta Nityanandadeva during the reign of Surampha Jayaditya Bhaga Raja. To ensure effective surveillance and control the Bhuyans were divided into *khels* and placed directly under the three great ministers, the Buragohain, the

35. M. N. Ghose, *Religious Beliefs of the Assamese People*, pp. 15-17.
36. Gait, *History of Assam*, 2nd ed., p. 119.
37. Ms. chronicle of Lakshmi Singha.

Bargohain and the Barpatra Gohain. The attitude of the Ahom government towards the Mayamara Mahanta was therefore, one of suspicion and fear; and hence the reduction of his power was a matter of common political expediency.

The execution of Nityanandadeva marked the commencement of the atrocities committed against the Mayamara Mahanta and his disciples. King Gadadhar Singha dissolved the Vaisnava monasteries as they had been developing into small but powerful bodies likely to cause trouble and embarrassment to the government. The Mayamara Mahanta suffered martyrdom as did several other Vaisnava preachers; many were either banished or suffered mutilation. Though his successor King Rudra Singha withdrew the order of banishment and reinstituted the monasteries, the Brahmans still questioned the authority of the Sudra Mahantas to give initiation to twice-born men. The Mayamara Mahanta took up the challenge; but having failed to produce any scriptural text in support of the practice, was expelled from the king's presence with humiliation and disgrace. During the reign of Siva Singha his Sakta consort Phuleswari Devi, who was also the queen regnant, insutled the Mayamara Mahanta and other Vaisnava leaders by ordering their foreheads to be smeared with the blood of sacrificial victims. The Mayamara Mahanta further incurred the queen's wrath by making uncomplimentary predictions about the child in her womb. She ordered his execution which was, however, stayed through the intercession of her Sakta Guru.

During the reign of Rajeswar Singha his minister Kirtichandra Barbarua so insulted the Mayamara Mahanta and his son that they summoned their disciples and deliberated plans of revenge. The king diplomatically allayed the vindictiveness of the Mahanta; and further strengthened himself by conferring political favours upon the Mayamara Mahanta's rival the Mahanta of Dihing Satra and associating the latter in plans to counteract the Moamaria designs. During the reign of Kirtichandra's nominee Lakshmi Singha the Barbarua heaped further insults upon the Mayamara Mahanta and accused him of moral turpitude. The culminating stage was reached when Kirtichandra flogged the influential Moran leader Ragha Neog on the pretext of supplying defective elephants to the Ahom court. The Mahanta's son whose schemes of retaliation had hitherto been held in check by the forbearance and counsel of his aged father now obtained the long-solicited permission, though reluctantly given, to launch war against the Ahom government with the co-operation of Ragha and other Moran leaders. The revolt was primarily directed towards the destruction of Kirtichandra, but it soon exceeded its bounds, and produced a complete though temporary collapse of the old Ahom regime. Lakshmi Singha regained his throne, but his expulsion and the usurpation of the Morans showed the vulnerability of Ahom authority.

The insurrection of the Moamarias was nurtured on the disaffection of several sections of the Assamese people which made concerted royalist action a matter of comparative difficulty. There were numerous exiled princes, the sons, nephews and grandsons of reigning sovereigns, living in the pestilential wilds of Namrup. Most of them had suffered mutilation for no offence but for the reason that they were prospective claimants to the throne. The Ahom court had adopted the rule that no man, however nearly related to a late monarch, could ascend the throne if he had upon his person any blemish or scar, no matter whether caused by a wound received in play or military action, or by smallpox.[38] Wrongful advantage was taken of this rule when an heir-presumptive or a near relation of the last sovereign was reduced to the position of an impotent rival by having his eyes put out, or his nose or ears slit, or a finger, a hand or a foot cut off. Such mutilated princes were often banished to Namrup so that they might enjoy no opportunity of influencing the affairs of the capital. But these cruel precautions often failed in their object, and worked in a manner prejudicial to the interests of the government. Namrup was an unfrequented and isolated tract, not very far from the Moran country; and people who were ill-disposed towards the reigning monarch or his officials made of the princes convenient cat's-paws in maturing their disloyal designs. They exploited the affection which the Assamese entertained towards the near relations of the reigning sovereigns, and the sympathy caused by the sufferings of the princes, and in many cases, by the violation of their just claims to the throne of their fathers. The appearance of an exiled prince at the head of a rebel force paralysed the hands of the royalist soldiers who thought that the prince was only asserting his just rights and that he might one day sit on the throne. Those whose loyalty to the government was a matter of convenience deserted the field, or went over to the side of the prince, and became his supporters, and thus swelled the rank of the Moamarias.

During the first stage of the rebellion the Morans had declared the handsome and popular prince Mohanmala Gohain, the third son of King Rudra Singha, as Raja. This prince had been deprived

38. Dr. John M'Cosh, *Topography of Assam*, p. 17.

of his lawful succession to the throne through the machinations of Kirtichandra Barbarua. By this means the rebels avoided popular opposition. Many of the royalist soldiers left the field, and the villagers offered submission to the champions of Mohanmala's cause. After occupying the capital the Morans, however, conferred the Rajaship and other important offices on their own men. Mohanmala was poisoned as well as several other princes who had joined the rebels in hopes of preferment.

After Lakshmi Singha's restoration in April 1770 it became a common practice to set up a prince as a claimant to the throne, recruit followers in his name, and launch preparations to seize the king and his nobles in imitation of the Morans. If no genuine prince was available it was easy to fake one, provided the preparations were made in a place where the imposter's identity could not be detected. The organisers hoped, if success attended their enterprise, to enjoy the loaves and fishes of state, or at least some political consequence by having a nomineee on the throne. Several Mahantas, besides the head of the Mayamara Satra, harboured princes in their monasteries with the same object. A number of Muhmmadans plotted to place a son of Mohanmala on the throne. "How do you make your livelihood ?", said an enthusiast to a prospective recruit. "I sell betel leaves", was the reply. "How long can you live by selling betel leaves ?", said the first, "come and join us. We are setting up Mohanmala's son as Raja. The sons of many nobles have assembled for this purpose at Meteka. An office will be given to you, and your privations will come to an end."[39]

But Lakshmi Singha was an astute monarch, and his nobles, chastened by their late experiences, had learnt to act with promptness and vigour. All disloyal manouvres were instantly detected and condign punishments inflicted on the rebels. The princes were dispersed from Namrup and settled at Tokolai, nearer the capital, to permit the exercise of more effective surveillance over their movements. But during the reign of Lakshmi Singha's week-kneed successor Gaurinath Singha the princes revived their seditious practices and intensified the commotions in the land. The absence of a proper solution of the princes' problem greatly affected the stability of the Ahom throne.

The initiation of the Ahom rulers and nobles into the Sakta faith attended by their enthusiastic patronage of Sakta priests and

39. Ms. chronicle of Lakshmi Singha. Meteka is a village in the immediate vicinity of the capital Rangpur.

their ceremonials irritated the non-Sakta section of the community. The faith of the Vaisnava Gosains and disciples had evolved out of the peculiar requirements of the Assamese temperament and society, and had become a part and parcel of their life through the medium of the extensive mass of Vaisnava literature and song. The Vaisnavas felt aggrieved at the recrudescence of the old Sakta cult under the patronage and support of the kings and nobles. The Vaisnava Gosains lived in a sort of detachment from the court, always shrinking from causing embarrassments to the rulers by influencing their political conduct. The Sakta priests lived close to their royal converts and established an intimate contact with them through the numerous Sakta sacrifices, and did not hesitate to interfere in affairs of political consequence. The insult given to the Vaisnava Gosains by Gadadhar Singha caused misgivings with regard to their ultimate fate under full-fledged Sakta influence.[40] The humiliation suffered by them at the hands of the Sakta sovereign Phuleswari Devi confirmed them in their belief that religious neutrality which had been the characteristic of the Shan rulers of Assam was now a thing of the past.

Among the disaffected Vaisnavas none were so aggrieved as the Ahom priests, who had maintained the language and traditions of the great Tai race, and had thus helped to keep together the ragged fabric of Ahom racial solidarity. The spread of Sakta influence and the preference given to the advice and counsel of the Sakta priests chagrined the hearts of their Ahom rivals, who looked upon the Ahom government as their own handiwork brought to being and to power by their spiritual ministrations. Their resentment was full when in violation of Ahom customs King Rajeswar Singha's corpse was cremated. The subsequent disorders were attributed to this departure from the Ahom custom of burial. The disaffection of the Ahom priests found expression in the following imprecation which they uttered when they saw the king, descended, according to their traditions, from the great god Lengdan or Indra, bow his head before the Sakta priests of Bengal,—"The raven has plucked out the two eyes of Garuda; his wings have dropped off into the

40. Gadadhar Singha had evinced Sakta proclivities, but he was not formally initiated into the Sakta fath. His son Rudra Singha ended by showing some predilection for Saktaism. Rudra Singha's son Siva Singha was the first Ahom monarch to accept the Sakta faith. Siva Singha and his four successors, Pramatta Singha, Rajeswar Singha, Lakshmi Singha and Gaurinath Singha, were the only Sakta Ahom kings.

sea. What can he do now with the mutilated remnant of his body ?"[41]

There ensued a schism even in the Sakta camp. The Bengali priest, known as Parvatia Gasain, was the Guru of three successive sovereigns Siva Singha, Pramatta Singha and Rajeswar Singha. Many of the nobles had deserted the Assamese Vaisnava Mahantas and accepted initiation from the Parvatia Gosain and thus enjoyed the honour of being *Satirthas* or co-disciples of the monarchs. The Gosain, however, had refused to give initiation to prince Kalsilia Gohain by reason of his dark complexion and alleged illegitimacy. The prince was initiated into Saktism by his tutor, an Assamese Brahman named Ramananda Acharyya. On ascending the throne the prince, now known as Swargadeo Lakshmi, Singha, heaped honours and wealth upon his *Guru,* erected a costly establishment for him, and the *Guru* was thenceforward known as Pahumaria Gosain or Na-Gosain. The nobles followed suit and swelled the ranks of the Na-Gosain's disciples. The followers of the Parvatia Gosain looked upon the Na-Gosain as a usurper of the honour which had so long been the exclusive possession of their spiritual leader. The Parvatia Gosain supported several conspiracies to kill Lakshmi Singha, the patron of the Na-Gosain. They were however detected and suppressed; the Bengali Gosain was expelled from the kingdom; and the king issued an order that none of his subjects should have any dealing with that Gosain.[42] The Na-Gosain's prestige and wealth greatly increased during the reign of Gaurinath Singha. The rivalry between the two Sakta Gosains had led to considerable acrimony between their followers. It was held by the disciples of the Parvatia Gosain that the confusion and anarchy in the country were due to his removal from the Guruship of the king.

Of the attitude of the general masses towards the Ahom government it is not easy to form any definite idea. The average Assamese subject looked upon the Ahom connection as a dispensation of fate to which he tamely submitted according to the traditions of the land. As the Ahoms did not upest the old social structure, nor introduce any drastic reform, and adjusted their government to the

41. The original passage in the Ahom language was given to me some years ago by an old Ahom Deodhai priest Srijut Nandanath Phukan. Garuda, conveyance of Vishnu, is a fabulous bird frequently mentioned in Hindu mythology.

42. The order of expulsion was subsequently rescinded, and the descendants of the Parvatia Gosain still possess large estates in Assam.

customs and usages of the people, and themselves became completely assimilated in language, manners and religion, their rule was regarded as tolerable. Besides, the people observed the complacent doctrine,—"Whoever might be the Raja, we are his subjects." As to their positive sympathies the people certainly entertained affection for the Ahom king and his person, and had extreme veneration for his lawful authority, but not for the system of government of which he was the head. They tolerated that government as long as it gave them peace and protection to pursue their normal avocations. But when it failed to carry out these primary obligations its iniquitous measures naturally involved it in popular hatred. For example, the Ahom penal law was extremely severe. Heavy punishments were inflicted for comparatively trivial offences. The penalty of death was meted out to the whole family of a rebel. The forms of execution were inhuman and cruel. "Offenders were put to death in various manners, by cutting their throats, by impaling them, by grinding them between two wooden cylinders, by sawing them asunder between two planks, by beating them with hammers, and by applying burning hoes to different parts."[43] A person who incurred the particular displeasure of the king might be made to eat his son's flesh. Extraction of knee-pans and eyes and slicing off of noses and ears were common practices. Though most of these punishments were in vogue in other parts of India,[44] in Assam they produced the inevitable impression that the government of the Ahoms was inhuman and cruel, and this impression exists even amongst the present-day Assamese. The common people hold that the downfall of the Ahoms was due to their cruel treatment of offenders with whom innocent people were sometimes yoked. The masses had no positive political opinion; and what little they had was marked by lack of fervency for the Ahom connection—a condition very favourable to the interposition of the authority of any powerful schemer.

As regards the thinking class, the nobles and the officials, who constituted the steel-frame of the administration, their political sympathies were mainly governed by personal considerations. Loyalty to the state as an abstract entity was unkonwn. There were isolated instances of Ahom nobles fighting to the last to justify the trust imposed upon them by the reigning monarch; but their

43. Buchanan-Hamilton, *Account of Assam,* written in 1808-09, M. Martin *Eastern India,* Vol. III, p. 672.

44. Rev. J. Long, *Selections from Government Records,* Vol. I, Introduction, p. 51.

bravery did not produce the desired effect upon the rest who had relations among the families of the princes or among the Moamarias. The nobles were more interested in seeing the ruin of their rivals if that could be brought about by the sword of the Moamarias. Where it could not be thus effected they sought independent means to cause their rivals' destruction. To insert a couple of treasonable letters in the house of an enemy, and get them discovered by the king's emissaries sent to the spot at the instance of the accuser, was a very popular method of incrimination. Unless a king was strong in his judgment and determination he could always be induced to act according to the wishes of an intriguing minister.

The rivalry of the nobles blinded them of their duties to the state. The Moran revolt could have been nipped in the bud if the ministers had wanted to do so; they remained inactive though they had full cognizance of the secret preparations of the enemy. Their primary desire was to witness the destruction of Kirtichandra Barbarua through the agency of the rebels as they had repeatedly failed in their own attempts in that direction. During the confinement of Lakshmi Singha by the Morans the Ahom nobles did not exert themselves so earnestly for the expulsion of the usurpers. The extirpation of the Moran leaders followed by the restoration of Lakshmi Singha to the throne was principally due to the ingenuity of a non-Ahom official, subsequently known in history as the Kalita Phukan. This was admitted by the king in his reply to the demand made afterwards by the Ahom nobles for the Phukan's dismissal,—"I still recollect with horror the atrocities committed by the Moran rebels after their occupation of the country. There were my Ahom nobles living in comfort and luxury and enjoying the titles and honours conferred on them by us. But none of them came forward to rescue me and my throne from the hands of the Morans. It was through the ingenuity of a solitary Hindu lad that my life was saved. The nobles have continued to enjoy their old privileges, holding offices as Bargohain and Buragohain. Why should not they tolerate the favour I have conferred on a Hindu in recognition of his destruction of the Morans? Should they speak like that in my presence? Who can protect them if I do something to them?"[45]

The extreme callousness with which the Ahom nobles viewed the disturbances was due to the fact that they found in those commotions opportunities for satisfying their ambitions and their

45. Ms. chronicle of Lakshmi Singha.

animosities. Subordination of individual passions to the exigency of the state became a thing of the past. It became increasingly difficult for the nobles to put their heads together, devise a common policy and act up to it. The religious schisms helped to maintain this disintegration. When the troubles became intolerable the nobles, instead of deliberating measures to counteract them, begged exterior powers to come to their rescue, or deserted their homes and sought refuge in neighbouring territories.

There was a time when the Ahoms could conceive great political ideas and face national emergencies with firmness and determination. They rose to the height of their efficiency during the golden age of their administration, the period of the Muhammadan wars in the seventeenth century. During Mir Jumla's invasion of Assam, 1662-63, many Assamese subjects had gone over to the side of the Moguls. On the retirement of Mir Jumla from Assam the Ahom king proposed to punish all the traitors. "I shall not allow the king to do this", said the king's father-in-law, "if a few hairs of the head are gray it is soothing to pluck them, but when the whole head is gray who ever thinks of undergoing that painful operation?" The king stayed his orders for general prosecution and devised other methods of restoring stability to the government.

According to the terms of the treaty enacted with Mir Jumla the Ahoms had to pay a heavy indemnity and tribute, and to cede the whole of lower Assam to the Moguls extending from Gauhati to the Manas river. The fulfillment of the treaty fell upon Chakradhwaj Singha. "It is better for me to die," said Chakradhwaj, "than to continue as tributary to the Moguls." Proposing to expel the Moguls from Lower Assam he issued commands for immediate resumption of hostilities. The prime minister Atan Buragohain supported the king's patriotic proposal, but he uttered a note of warning,—"His Majesty has only voiced the sentiments of his ministers when he declares that we should fall upon the Moguls this very moment. But we must provide the army with sufficient quantities of food provisions and war materials, and must hold in stock a sufficient reserve to enable us to replenish the stores of the expeditionary force. We shall have to take the necessary steps now and provide for all future contingencies. When the three batches of oarsmen, posted at the middle and the two extremities of His Majesty's barge strike their oars simultaneously, the sight becomes pleasant to look at, the rowers feel inspirited, the boat glides on swiftly, and the helmsman wields the steering with convenience and ease. But if on the other hand, there is no harmony and synchronism in the strokes of the three batches of rowers, the helmsman is inconvenienced in steering his shaft, the boat does not make any headway, and the spectators are far from being delighted. If the king directs his measures on the lines indicated above he will be able to vanguish his enemies and extend his territories to the old limits." All departments of the government acted in perfect co-ordination; and Atan Buragohain and Lachit Barphukan succeeded in expelling the Moguls from Gauhati and recovering possession of Lower Assam in 1667.

A year later, Ram Singha, son of Mirza Raja Jai Singha of Amber, was deputed by Emperor Aurangzeb to oust the Ahoms from Gauhati. The Ahoms held tenaciously to their position and frustrated the diplomatic manouvres as well as the armed designs of the Rajput general. King Chakradhwaj Singha accused the Gauhati commanders for protracting the conflict, and issued positive orders to attack the Mogul army encamped near Alaboi Hill, some fourteen miles to the north-west of Gauhati. The king's mandate was obeyed though the commanders were doubtful of success in such an encounter. The Rajput cavalry rushed towards the Assamese foot soldiers and massacred ten thousand of their stalwarts within the course of one single day. The Barphukan sat depressed in his camp lamenting for the loss of so many soldiers each of whom was to him "a pillar of strength." The Buragohain gave him counsel saying,—"Well, general, such a reverse should never shake your confidence in our ultimate victory. Eventualities of this character are normal in a protracted warfare. When you agitate the waters of a pond for catching large fishes, the fish-catchers will be pricked by the thorny scales of the smaller fries. You should judge your success by the number of large catches." The Ahoms succeeded soon after in inflicting a crushing defeat upon the Moguls in the naval battle of Saraighat, and Ram Singha returned crest-fallen to the Mogul territories muttering praises of the valour and versatility of the Assamese.

The conduct of the Ahoms during the Moamaria revolt was an ignoble sequel to their great achievements of the seventeenth century.[46] A reverse in the battlefield now completely unnerved them; and instead of grappling with realities and devising means

46. The Assamese were one of the few races in India who successfully resisted the imperialism of the Moguls. *Cf.* "The Assamese were to the Moslems what the Numidians and Mauritanians were to the old Romans—*genus insuperbile bello.*"—*Calcutta Review*, 1867, Vol. XLVI, p. 78. See S. K. Bhuyan's *Lachit Barphukan and His Times*, 1947.

of rehabilitation they completely surrendered themselves to the hands of fate which they had been taught to do by their customary advisers. Soon after King Gaurinath Singha's flight to Gauhati, Bhagati Barbarua said to Purnananda Buragohain,—"Fighting with these archers and shieldsmen our sovereigns had vanquished the Moguls on numerous occasions, but the very same soldiers become terrified and demoralised at the sight of the Moamarias and take to their heels. All this has taken place because the gods have so ordained it. The Wheel of Time being so powerful nothing can be presaged."[47] Such a defeatist sentiment would not have been countenanced in the camp of Atan Buragohain and Lachit Barphukan.

We may investigate the causes which brought about the demoralisation of the soldiers as complained of by Bhagati Barbarua. The Ahom soldiers recruited, as a rule, from peasants and cultivators, derived their inspiration from the example of the commanders. The demoralisation of the latter infected the rabble. This aspect of things had been realised by the Phukan Buragohain who said in a war-council of King Rudra Singha,—"Arms and ammunitions, materials and supplies are torpid and impotent: the followers and subordinates of the king are symbols of life and animation: they alone can infuse into the immobile war-provisions a dynamic force."[48]

Since the death of Rudra Singha in 1714 the Assamese had not known any real war. The nobles, being accustomed to ease and comfort during this long-continued peace, became reluctant to undergo the arduous exertions of military operations. Their bread was secure as long as their fields were cultivated by their bondsmen and dependants. The office which they held was an ornamentation to give them power and prestige. In the preceding centuries a man's excellence was judged by his service to the state: in the eighteenth it was usually estimated on the basis of the patronage he offered to the Brahmans and the number of sacrifices he performed. This new attitude of life completely altered his springs of action, and debarred him from realising hard facts and finding out their solutions.

Sukapha, a Shan prince, had conquered Assam with only 1,000 followers. The circumstances of conquest and rank, with the pride and power of place had made the Ahoms consider them-

47. *Tungkhungia Buranji*, pp. 110-11.
48. *Tungkhungia Buranji*, pp. 38-39.

selves as a superior people to the other inhabitants of Assam. This habit of thinking had in a great measure preserved their superiority by giving them manliness, independence and intelligence.[49] But by intimate intercourse with the members of the subject races, and adopting their language and their manners, and ultimately their religion, the Ahoms lost their imperiousness and other distinctive traits, and became one with the governed imbibing the latter's defects. The highest offices continued in the hands of the Ahoms; but the officers were influenced by their Aryan subordinates and advisers who by their subtle methods found it easy to ingratiate themselves into their masters' favour. The views of the conquered races were transmitted to the conquerors through political contacts and social intercourse. The Ahoms who, in the words of the *Aalamgirnamah*, had never "bowed the head of submission and obedience to the most powerful monarch [the Great Mogul], who have curbed the ambition and checked the conquests of the most victorious princes of Hindustan",[50] became in course of time a Babel of discord, ease-loving, cowardly, priest-ridden, selfish and intriguing. Buchanan-Hamilton wrote in 1809,—"Hitherto the Assamese had been a warlike and enterprising race, while their princes had preserved vigor that in the east is not commonly retained for so many generations; but their subjection to the Brahmans, which was followed by that of most of the nation, soon produced the usual imbecility, and the nation had sunk into abject pusillanimity towards strangers and into internal confusion and turbulence."[51] The Assamese historian Gunabhiram Barua said to the same intent,—"In course of time the Ahoms gave up the manly and arm-strong character of the Kshatriyas, and imbibed the lip-strong traits of the Brahmans."[52]

The decline of the Ahoms was accelerated by some fundamental defects in their administrative system. Since their conquest of Assam in the beginning of the thirteenth century they had held to the bulk of the people the same relation as the Normans did for

49. Francis Jenkins, Governor-General's Agent, North-East Frontier, to the Secretary to the General Committee of Public Education, Sept. 30, 1838, Assam Secretariat Records.

50. Henry Vansittart, *A Description of Assam from the Alamgir-Namah, Asiatick Researches*, Vol. 2, 1807, pp. 179-180.

51. Martin, *Eastern India*, Vol. III, p. 604.

52. Gunabhiram Barua, *Assam Buranji*, 1876, p. 138.

generations in England.[53] They were the feudatory lords in the country, and all appointments, as far as practicable, were retained amongst them, the higher situations being hereditary in the descendants of those chiefs who were leaders in the invasion and conquest of Assam.

A feudal lord together with the men of the villages under him constituted a division called *khel,* the strength of which ordinarily ranged from three to six thousand. The *khels* were organised on an occupational and territorial basis, and consisted of men of all denominations and castes. Hence it was possible for a section of any particular *khel* to transmit its political sympathies and antipathies to the other members of that *khel.* For considerations of neighbourliness there prevailed a sort of comradery among the members of a *khel.* Thus Moamarias found it easy to tamper with the loyalty of the non-Moamaria section of a *khel.* When conflicts arose the non-Moamarias felt compunction in striking against their whilom comrades. At the same time the attachment of the subjects to their immediate overlords, *viz.*, the *Kheldars*, to whom they were tied by hereditary obligations, was greater than to their distant government at the capital. The *Kheldars* could therefore divert the loyalty of their men to their own advantage if they so wished. The opportunities of the semi-independent *Kheldars* to defy the authority of the government were possessed equally by provincial governors, frontier wardens and tributary princes.

Most of the *khels* were reduced in number during the period of unrest due to death of their members in the ravages, wars, and massacres, transfer of the Moamarias' allegiance from the Ahom government to their own leaders, migration of non-Moamarias to the side of the Moamarias and flight of people from their villages to neighbouring territories. The *khels* had specific functions to discharge. Some were employed in the army, others were employed as labourers in the construction of royal camps, public buildings, tanks and roads, while a large majority had to supply necessaries to the royal household and the public stores. These supplies con-

53. "The Buragohain, the Bargohain and the ministers, and the seven noble houses of the tribe of Ahom (from which tribe the Rajahs had the high dignitaries are elected) possess as well hereditary right in the soil, and are supported equally therefrom. The Rajah possesses an interest of two shares; the ministers one; and the rest of the nobility one. Ever since the reign of Rajah Sukapha [first Ahom conqueror] until that of Chandrakanta [last Ahom king] this quadruple division of interest in the soil has prevailed and obtained."—Application of Trilochan Deka Phukan, son of Purnananda Buragohain, to Government of Assam, Oct. 21, 1834, Assam Secretariat Records.

sisted among others of gold, food provisions, saltpetre, bows and arrows, boats, and elephants. The reduction of the *khels* led to decrease of the supplies both in men and provisions which greatly affected the proper functioning of the government. The Sonowal or gold-washers' *khel* of Upper Assam had to furnish six to seven thousand *tolas* of gold annually to the government; but during the reign of Gaurinath Singha the quantity was reduced to four thousand *tolas*.[54] The normal strength of that *khel* was 1,829 men, the number now came down to 738. The absconders had fled to the Matak country, and were obviously Morans or newly initiated Moamarias.[55] It was estimated that out of 80,000 *paiks* usually under the charge of the Buragohain there remained only 43,000 after the Manipur expedition in the reign of Rajeswar Singha and the civil wars of the Moamarias.[56]

In addition to the dangers arising from the semi-independent state of the Ahom feudal lords who regarded their possessions as matters of right rather than of favour, there was the drawback arising from the numerical inferiority of the standing army at the beck and call of the government. It was employed in guarding the government buildings and the city outposts under the command of the Bhitarual Phukan. It was quite sufficient for normal times, as in the event of an emergency any of the feudal commanders might be asked to come forward with his militia or *khel;* and if necessary there would be demand made upon his reserves. This system had the advantage of obviating the feeding and housing of large numbers in peace times, and it caused the least disturbance to the pursuits of the villagers. But when a feudal baron or his regiment proved refractory the standing army was not sufficient to reduce them to obedience. A fellow baron despatched against them would possibly enter into a collusion with them in view of past or potential obligations. When troubles broke out simultaneously in several parts of the country, as during the insurrection of the Moamarias, the government was in a worse predicament. The 'mighty army' at the disposal of Purnananda Buragohain in 1793-94 has been described by an eye-witness as a "miserable band of cowardly and undisciplined peasants amounting perhaps to six or seven hundred men, armed with awkward weapons which they dare not and cannot use, the small body of

54. *Tola* is an Indian weight for gold and solver equal to 180 grains troy.

55. Maniram Dewan's *Account of Washing for gold in Assam, J.A.S.B* July 1838, pp. 821-22.

56. A. J. Mills, *Report on Assam,* 1854, Appendix K-B, p. lxxviii.

unwilling and unpaid Burkendazes not exceeding the number of sixty or seventy Bengal subjects."[57]

The standing army acting in conjunction with the local levies did fairly well when they had to fight against a common enemy like the Moguls, the Kacharis or the Jayantias; but there was generally treachery and collusion when they were despatched against their own countrymen. Hence during the last few decades of Ahom rule the government had to seek the assistance of sepoys from Bengal. But no body of foreign mercenaries could bring success to the Ahom arms as long as the commanders were corrupt and pusillanimous. Capt. Welsh found at Gauhati a magazine containing enough to arm 20,000 men, and also 3 European and 110 country guns of different calibres, but they were lying useless as no man was found to organise and equip an army.[58] The supreme need of Assam at that time was of selfless and patriotic commanders, a fact which was pointed out to an Assamese noble by the victorious Burmese general Kiamingi,—"You have stalwart fighters in your land; but we have been able to vanquish you because you have no commander worthy of the name to lead them."[59] So every petition for military assistance made by the Ahom government to the Governor-General was accompanied by a request to send an English officer.

The Moamarias on the other hand acted like one man from beginning to end. They met with occasional reverses in the battle-field, followed by massacres which included unarmed men; but not a single act of treachery, wilful desertion or flagrant cowardice can be laid at their door. Those who escaped the sword of the royalists voluntarily offered to be despatched off like their comrades who had perished in the cause of their Gurus. Women took up the gauntlet and challenged the royalists and kept them at bay. It was this cohesion, unity and determination which enabled the Moamaries to maintain the struggle in their favour, expel Lakshmi Singha and his successor Gaurinath Singha from the capital and the latter from his refuge in the viceregal headquarters at Gauhati, carve out four idependent states, one at Rangpur, another at

57. Fragmentary pages of the lost manuscript of *Memoir of the Reign of Gowrinath Sing* by J. P. Wade, found at the end of the India Office Ms. of his *Geographical Sketch of Assam.*

58. Welsh to Conwallis, Nov. 27 and Dec. 4, Beng. Pol. Cons., Dec. 17, 1792, Nos. 47 and 50.

59. S. K. Bhuyan, *Asamar Padya-Buranji,* or a metrical chronicle of Assam, pp. 281 and 305.

Japaribhita, a third at Majuli, and a fourth at Bengmara. The last retained its independence for about 40 years having exacted recognition from the Ahoms; and it maintained its position when the rest of Assam fell into the hands of the Burmese, protected it against the incursions of the Singphos, and on the arrival of the British in Assam in 1825, the Barsenapati, as the ruler of the Matak country or Bengmara was called, "was found with all the semblance of an indepndent province and the head of a country with upwards of 50,000 inhabitants."[60] His alliance was eagerly sought and utilised by the first British conquerors in subjugating the predatory Singphos.[61]

The transformation of the Moamarias from a religious sect into a fighting and ruling body was not the outcome of accident or the successful enterprise of any individual adventurer. It was the culmination of an urge coming spontaneously from the hearts of the whole population bound together by common sufferings at the hands of the enemy. There was never a tribe called the Moamarias, but their unification for the purpose of resistance to the Ahom government was so complete that they appeared to have possessed all the characteristics of a regular tribal organisation.[62] The Moamarias were all disciples of one Satra or its few branches; but they belonged to separate tribes and communities, Morans, Chutiyas, Kacharis, Bihias, Ahoms, Kaivartas and Brittials; and many caste Hindus, Brahmans, Kayasthas and Kalitas were found among the Moamarias. The disciples were confined to no particular territory, but were scattered over the whole country as far as Goalpara.

Except a small section of the old Hindus all the Moamarias had a pronounced Mongoloid or non-Aryan strain in their blood, and that accounts for their general robustness and power of physical endurance. In their mental habits the Moamarias were marked by roticence, craftiness, subdued resentment, and doggedness, which were the characteristics of the ethnic group to which they belonged. The word *Matak* by which the Morans, and loosely the Moamarias,

60. *J.A.S.B.*, August 1838, p. 674.

61. Col. L. W. Shakespeare, *History of Upper Assam*, p. 153; Sir Alexander Mackenzie, *Relations with the Hill Tribes of the North-East Frontier of Bengal*, pp. 74-5; and William Robinson, *Descriptive Account of Assam*, pp. 326-32.

62. A writer in the Government Gazette for June 1835 designated the Moamaries as a tribe to which Capt. Hannay replied,—"The Moa Murreahs are not a distinct tribe, but a religious sect of the Assamese population, composed of individuals from most of the known tribes of Assam."—*J.A.S.B.*, August 1838, p. 676.

are known, is also applied to a robust and sturdy man lacking in refinement and not easily amenable to reason. The Moamarias derive the term *Matak* from two words, *Mat*, opinion, will or creed, and *Ek*, one ; and they believe the epithet is justly applied to them as they pride themselves in being of one persuasion, will and mind.

The Moamarias all knew Assamese. The Morans and Chutiyas spoke their tribal dialect which belonged to the Bodo group. But being bilingual they spoke Assamese with as much ease as their mother-tongues. Their hymns and prayers and religious books were all written in Assamese mostly by their own Gurus. The singing of those hymns was a part of their daily life, and the books were read out to them by their learned men according to the custom in Vaisnava congregational worship in Assam. Common religious practices and social usages further strengthened their bonds of union which prepared the ground for joint political action at a later stage of their history.

The refusal of the Moamarias to prostrate before any other man except their Guru combined with the superior reverence in which he was held led them to cast their lot on his side in the conflict that occurred between him and the government. In fact, in the early stage of their history the Moamarias, as subjects of the Ahoms, had not received any particular provocation from the government. Nityananda Mahanta who was their first Guru to be executed was regarded by the disciples as a martyr, and the cause of the Mayamara Mahanta became from that time the cause of the Moamarias. They took a vow to shed the last drop of their blood in avenging his death, and it was embodied in their war-cry "I shall kill or I shall be killed, and thereby I shall discharge my obligation to my Guru." This common purpose now set before the Moamarias gave the necessary stimulus in making their unification complete and in endowing them with the attributes of a military race. They were now divided into groups each under a Gaonburha who was like a local Sirdar. He acted as the representative of the Guru, collected his tithes and communicated his wishes to the disciples. Many Ahom nobles accepted the office of Gaonburha under the Mayamara Mahanta.[63]

Fifty years after the execution of Nityananda another Mahanta, Baikunthanathdeva, was put to death by the Ahom king Gadadhar Singha. The Moamarias could not dare to strike at the authority

63. The Mahanta recommended a member of the Ahom Duara family, who was his Gaonburha to the office of Barbarua when it would fall vacant by the death of Kirtichandra.—Maniram Dewan's Ms. *Assam Buranji*.

of the Ahoms who had just emerged victorious from their war against the Moguls. But when that power was on its wane owing to the imbecility of its rulers and the jealousy of the nobles the Moamarias found their opportunity for revenge. The intervening period was spent in marshalling their resources, and in spreading the ideas of self-respect and self-possession which lie at the root of all political upheavals.

The solidarity of the Moamarias was kept up by their common desire to avenge the insults heaped on their Gurus by Ahom sovereigns and nobles to which several new fctors were afterwards added. Having once succeeded in ousting the Ahom king from the throne and in enjoying the prestige and pride of domination for a brief interval in 1769-70 it became the principal motive factor in their subsequent hostilities. Kirtichandra Barbarua had predicted the introduction of this new phase in Moamaria politics in his advice to King Lakshmi Singha and his nobles before their capture by the rebels,—"His Majesty should not listen to a man if he says that the Morans will retire to the woods after having once attained the position of a *Raja-Chakravarti* or supreme ruler."[64] The ruthless massacre of the Moamarias by Lakshmi Singha in 1770 and by his son Gaurinath Singha in 1783 kept alive their passion for retribution.

There is evidence to show that the Moamaria discontent was promoted not only by oral propaganda but also by a literature which was revolutionary in tone. The hymns of the Mayamara prelates, like those of Shivaji's Guru Ramdas, were characterised by a political and martial odour. Some glimpse of this literary propaganda was obtained in the proceedings against conspirators during the reign of Lakshmi Singha. One Bhogananda arranged to sing a song just when his companions would approach the royal premises in order to seize the king and the Barbarua,—"The camp is well-barricaded, and the guardsmen are formidable. Renounce your love for your body, otherwise you will be caught in the meshes of your Ego. Your conduct is to be regulated in recollection of your Guru's injunctions." Another conspirator named Baga Deka was reported to have possessed a manuscript with the help of which all could be subdued, including kings and nobles.[65]

The transformation of the Moamarias into a military body has its parallel, though in a much larger scale, in that of the Sikhs

64. Ms. chronicle of Lakshmi Singha.

65. Ms. chronicle of Lakshmi Singha: also S. K. Bhuyan's Introduction to H. C. Goswami's *Descriptive Catalogue of Assamese Mss.*, p. xix.

who contributed to the subversion of Mogul authority in India. In both cases the fighting element in their sectarial organisations was introduced as a result of the clash of the Gurus with the government of the land. The Sikhs abandoned all things for the sake of their Guru: to him were to be surrendered body, mind and worldly wealth.[66] The Moamarias were taught to regard their Gurus as equal to Brahma, Vishnu and Maheswara. Aniruddha the first Mayamara Mahanta gave his disciples a distinct existence by organising his Satra on a more democratic and popular basis. Nityananda and Baikunthanath suffered martyrdom in upholding their creed which animated their disciples with a common mission; Chaturbhuj and Astabhuj added the use of arms and a military system. The organisation proved its mettle when it was pitted against the Ahom rulers in 1769, and it continued to work on the momentum it had acquired from its past triumph.

66. J. D. Cunningham, *History of the Sikhs*, 1903, p. 35.

PART III

KRISHNANARAYAN AND THE BENGAL BURKENDAZES

Foreign elements in Assam troubles: The rebellion of Krishnanarayan, prince of Darrang, introduced a new element in the disturbances in Assam. The Moamaria revolt was confined to the subjects of the Ahom government; the rebels fought with whatever resources they could command within the kingdom; and for many years they did not bring in any force from outside the country to supplement their own organisation. But Krishnanarayan asserted his claims with the help of soldiers recruited in Bengal from a class of professional marauders whose ravages had caused grave unrest in the territories of the Company, and whose suppression had engaged the serious attention of its administrators. The Burkendazes and Sannyasis who constituted the army of Krishnanarayan committed the most barbarous atrocities upon the people of Assam, and its government with its dilapidated resources found it difficult to suppress Krishnanarayan and expel his followers. It had, therefore, to apply to the Government of Bengal who thought it to be their duty to stop the depredations committed by their own subjects in a neighbouring friendly state. When peaceful methods failed the Government of Bengal had to despatch an armed force to Assam to effect the expulsion of the Burkendazes.

Affairs in Assam had become so distracted that the expulsion of the banditti provided only a partial relief. The British Government, prompted by considerations of humanity, as well as by a desire to see the revival of trade between Bengal and Assam, attempted to remove the root causes of the disturbances and restore the kingdom to stability and order. The expedition, the primary object of which was to expel the Burkendazes from Assam, succeeded in suppressing the Moamaria rebels, and in restoring the Ahom king to his ancestral throne at Rangpur. But before permanent measures could be adopted for preventing the recurrence of the disturbances from which the country had been rescued the detachment was withdrawn from Assam. The disorders which had called forth the intervention of the Company then reappeared reducing the country once more to the verge of destruction.

The rebellion of Krishnanarayan was symptomatic of the spirit of discontent that had prevailed in various parts of the country and among various sections of the people as a result of the rapacity of the rulers and the oppressions of their nobles. The revolt was launched not merely to gratify the ambition of a single adventurer; it was provoked by years of misrule, and fomented by leaders who had received injury and insult from successive representatives of the Ahom government. "The inhuman proceedings", declared Captain Welsh in his manifesto to the people of Assam, "that occasioned the rapid decline of Surgy Deo's authority to the Eastward, had produced a total extinction of his power in this quarter [Western Assam] at the period [November 1792] of my entering Assam."[1]

The province of Darrang: The Ahom province of Darrang as it was constituted in the eighteenth century, was bounded on the north by the high causeway at the foot of the Bhutan Hills known as the Gohain Kamala Ali, on the west by the river Barnadi, on the south by the Brahmaputra and on the east by the district of Chariduar. The principality of Darrang formed a square of about thirty miles in length and breadth,[2] and was more or less conterminous with the Mangaldoi sub-division of the present day.[3] The jurisdiction of the ruler of Darrang remained continually shifting in the seventeenth century. Sometimes it included the whole of Kamrup on both banks of the Brahmaputra, and sometimes a part; and again it extended on the east as far as the river Dikrai and included the district of Chariduar, and a portion of Naduar which lay between the rivers Bharali on the west and Dikrai on the east. The general tendency of the Ahom overlords was to curtail the powers and privileges of the Darrang Rajas as well as to reduce the dimensions of their territory.

The dynasty of Koch rulers: The dynasty of the Darrang rulers, of which Krishnanarayan was a member, was a branch of the famous Narayan family of Cooch Behar founded in the beginning of the sixteenth century by Biswa Singha. Nilambar, the last of the Khen rulers of Kamata, was overthrown in 1498 by Hussain Shah, the Nawab of Gauda,[4] who after that triumph styled himself "Sultan conqueror of Kamata and Kamarupa".[5]

1. Welsh to Cornwallis, Feb. 4, Beng. Pol. Cons., Feb. 15, 1793, No. 17.
2. J. P. Wade, *Geographical Sketch of Assam*, India Office Ms., partly produced in Martin, *Eastern India*, Vol. III, p. 637.
3. Gait, *A History of Assam*, 2nd ed., p. 69.
4. Gait, *Koch Kings of Kamarupa*, *J.A.S.B.*, 1893, p. 279; Buchanan-Hamilton's sketch of the history of Kamarupa, India Office Ms., inserted in S. K. Bhuyan's *Kamrupar Buranji*, pp. 138-42.
5. C. J. Brown, *Coins of India*, p. 80.

Hussain Shah left his son Daniel to complete the conquest. During an expedition to Assam Daniel with his entire force was killed by the Assamese.[6] Kamata, which extended from the Karatoya to the Barnadi, was now divided into small principalities ruled by a number of chieftains known as Saru-Bhuyans. Biswa Singha, a Koch leader, subjugated the Saru-Bhuyans and made himself master of the Kamata kingdom.

Biswa Singha died about the year 1540, and was succeeded by his son Naranarayan (1540-84). He appointed his brother Sukladhwaj as commander-in-chief. The two brothers proceeded on a career of conquest and compelled the rulers of Manipur, Jayantia, Tipperah, Sylhet, Khyrim, Dimarua and the Ahom king of Assam to accept the Koch suzerainty. These triumphs were mainly due to the skill and enterprise of Sukladhwaj, known also as Chilarai.[7]

Chilarai died about the year 1577 leaving a son named Raghudeb. Naranarayan married late in life. Raghudeb who had been regarded as the heir to Naranarayan lost hope of succession on the birth of a son to his uncle Naranarayan. He left Cooch Behar with his family and adherents and settled at Barnagar on the Manas river where he built a fort at an auspicious site which was thenceforth known as Ghila-Bijaypur. Raghudeb began to behave like an independent prince, and Naranarayan, unwilling to wage war with his nephew, divided his kingdom into two parts, keeping the portion west of the Sankosh river to himself and his successors, and giving the territory to the east of that river upto the Barnadi to Raghudeb, who undertook to pay a tribute to his uncle and acknowledge him as his overlord. This happened in 1581. The western portion of the kingdom retained by Naranarayan was known as Cooch Behar, and the eastern portion made over to Raghudeb as Koch Hajo from the name of an important town where the latter built the Manikut temple in 1583.

Naranarayan died about the year 1584, and was succeeded by his son Lakshminarayan. Raghudeb now assumed independence, stopped payment of tribute to Lakshminarayan and struck coins in his name. The king of Cooch Behar was not powerful enough

6. Translation of *Fathiyah-i-Ibriyah* in Blochmann. *Koch Bihar, Koch Hajo and Asam, J.A.S.B.*, 1872, p. 79.

7. The wars of Naranarayan are fully described in Gait's *History of Assam*, pp. 51-55 and *Koch Kings of Kamarupa, J.A.S.B.*, 1893, pp. 287-91, and also in *Darang-raj Vamsavali*, ed. by H. C. Goswami, pp. 62-113. Gait's account was based on *Darang-raj Vamsavali.*

to reduce Raghudeb to submission. Raghudeb died in 1603 leaving four sons, Parikshitnarayan, Balinarayan, Indranarayan and Mansingha. After his succession Parikshit removed his capital to North Gauhati on the eastern extremity of his dominions where he built his palace near the Aswakranta Hill.[8]

The struggle for independence was continued by Parikshit involving him in incessant hostilities with Lakshminarayan. They both approached the Ahom king for mediation, but the latter was too busy with the Kachari wars to pay any attention to the feuds of the Koch princes. In 1608 Parikshit gave his daughter Mangaldoi to the Ahom king Pratap Singha.[9]

Lakshminarayan had in the meantime solicited the assistance of the Moguls in subduing the refractory Parikshit. In 1596 he made his submission to the Mogul Emperor Akbar and in the next year he gave his daughter to Raja Man Singha, governor of Bengal.[10] But these solicitations did not bear any fruit, and Parikshit continued his depredations in Cooch Behar.

In 1602 Lakshminarayan went in person to Dacca and complained of Parikshit's conduct to the Nawab Alauddin Fathpuri Islam Khan. Raghunath Rai, Zemindar of Susang, whose family Parikshit had imprisoned, lodged similar complaints of Parikshit's highhandedness.[11] Mukarram Khan was despatched at the head of a large army to invade Koch Hajo. Parikshit being defeated at Dhubri sued for peace. Nawab Islam Khan demanded his submission in person as well as the secession of Koch Hajo to the Moguls.

Parikshit now turned to the Ahom king Pratap Singha for assistance to which the latter agreed on condition that the Koch prince would undertake to rule on the north bank allowing the Ahoms to rule on the south. Parikshit did not agree to the proposal and continued his hostilities singlehanded. In 1614 he was once more attacked by the Moguls. He was chased up to Pandu near Gauhati; and being hardpressed by both the Moguls and

8. A visitor to North Gauhati can still see the ruins of Parikshit's ramparts and palace enclosures.

9. Gait, *History of Assam*, p. 64. Gunabhiram Barua says that Parikshit's brother Balinarayan gave Mangaldoi to the Ahom king and that she was a relation of the Koch prince, *Assam Buranji*, p. 69. According to a Ms. *Assam Buranji* Mangaldoi was the daughter of Raghudeb. Balinarayan's daughter is mentioned in one place as Mukur.

10. *Akbarnamah*, Lucknow edition, III, p. 762, quoted in Blochmann's *Koch Bihar and Assam*, *J.A.S.B.*, 1872, pp. 52-3.

11. *Padishahnamah*, quoted in *J.A.S.B.*, 1872, p. 53.

Lakshminarayan he surrendered himself and all his possessions.[12] Parikshit was taken to Dacca from where he was sent to Delhi. Emperor Jahangir promised to restore him to his kingdom on payment of a sum of four lakhs of rupees. But Parikshit died on his way home at Allahabad. Koch Hajo, the kingdom of Parikshit, was then annexed to the Mogul Empire. One of Parikshit's nobles named Kabisekhar, son of Kabindra Patra, was appointed by the Emperor kanungo or registrar of Koch Hajo, and was granted large estates. Soon after, Sheikh Ibrahim Karori was deputed from Delhi to carry out the settlement of Koch Hajo on the lines of the existing system in Bengal. It was divided into four sarkars, *Uttarkol* or *Dhekeri* north of the Brahmaputra, *Dakhinkol* south of that river, *Kamarupa* containing Gauhati and Hajo, and *Bangalbhum* west of the Brahmaputra containing Bahirbund and Bhitarbund.[13] A gradation of officers, such as Chaudhuris, Patwaris and Thakurias were appointed, to conduct the revenue administration. The entire territory of Koch Hajo was called by the Assamese *Dhekeri Rajya ;* and the term *Dhekeri* was applied to its people as well as to the inhabitants of Darrang. Parikshit's son Chandranarayan, *alias* Bijitnarayan, was confirmed by the Moguls as Zemindar of the territory between the Sankosh and the Manas. He lived at Bijni and was the founder of the ruling family of Bijni.

Balinarayan now sought for assistance to recover possession of his brother Parikshit's kingdom. He had been living for a year in the house of a Bara-Bhuyan in the village Maniari in Darrang. In March 1615, Balinarayan visited the Ahom court and applied for help in order to expel the Moguls.[14] The Ahom king Pratap Singha promised to give the aid solicited, and provided him with estates, wives, servants, ornaments and provisions befitting a prince of Dharmanarayan's lineage.[15]

In the meantime hostilities had commenced between the Ahoms and the Moguls. A number of Mogul subjects led by a merchant named Ratancha had been purchasing *Agar* wood at Singari for the Mogul Emperor. Their boats were plundered by the Assamese

12. *Kamrupar Buranji*, edited by S. K. Bhuyan, pp. 13-14.

13. *Kamrupar Buranji*, pp. 27-29, 145; and Martin, *Eastern India*, Vol. III, pp. 416-17.

14. This date is given in *Kamrupar Buranji*, p. 14.

15. Buchanan-Hamilton says that after Parikshit's death his brother "was confirmed in the government of Darang," *Eastern India*, III, p. 417. According to *Padishahnamah*, Balinarayan fled to his friend the Assam king after Parikshit had surrendered himself to Mukarram Khan, *J.A.S.B.*, 1872, p. 54, and also 1893, p. 298.

and two of the men cut off. On receiving the report Shaikh Qasim, governor of Bengal, deputed Sayid Hakim and Sayid Abu Bakar with 10 to 12 thousand horse and foot and 400 large ships to Hajo and ordered them to invade Assam. They waited in Hajo till the end of the rains, after which they marched three or four stages into Assam.[16] The Moguls pitched their camp on the bank of the river Bharali and the Ahoms halted at Samdhara. Sporadic engagements continued for one month in December and January 1616. The Ahom king Pratap Singha conducted the war in person from his camp at Agiabandha, and urged his captains to storm the Mogul garrisons on the Bharali. The Ahoms constructed bridges across the river and suddenly fell upon the Mogul army before day-break on January 27, 1616.[17] The Moguls were not prepared

for this sudden attack, and the feeble resistance which they offered was easily repulsed. The prisoners were kept in an enclosure of reed grass, and were cut off on the following day. Several commanders including Abu Bakar were executed. Ten Hindu Rajas including Jagadeb, son of Raja Todarmal, offered their submission to the Ahoms. The king had expressed a desire to see the "Omraos who had ventured to fight with him", and hastened from his camp to the place of engagement. But the king being disappointed, as the Mogul commanders had been beheaded before his arrival, executed Chaolai Kowanr, his own uncle, for having ordered the massacre.[18] A Muhammadan historian has described the engagement as follows:—"The enemy fell upon the army of Islam from all sides in different groups and batches and made the brave warriors drink the wine of martyrdom. The market of the angel of death became very brisk and it became a veritable Day of Resurrection....About seventeen hundred men were killed consisting of the martyrs as well as those who sank in the lane of nonentity through cowardice. The group of men who escaped from the field of battle with two or three wounds and died in the adjoining fields will be double of this number, and nine thousand men were taken as captives. About three thousand men came out half-dead and kept themselves concealed in the jungles and deserts and

16. *Padishahnamah,* translated by Blochmann, *J.A.S.B.*, 1872, p. 55.

17. The Hindu date is Magh 15, 1637 *saka*, Saturday.

18. *Kamrupar Buranji,* pp. 17-18. The *Padishahnamah* attributes this disaster to the shortsightedness of Quasim Khan for which he was deposed from his office of governor of Bengal.

tried to escape."[19] The small remnant of the Mogul army retraced their steps to Hajo.

Dharmanarayan appointed Raja of Darrang: The province of Darrang from the Barnadi to the Dikrai was now cleared of the Moguls. The Ahom king appointed Balinarayan as tributary Raja of Darrang. His brothers also took shelter with the Ahoms who gave them estates for their maintenance; of them Gajnarayan was set up as a tributary chief of the Ahoms at Beltola.[20] The chief of Dimarua on the Jayantia border made submission to the Ahom king. This took place during the months of September and October 1616. The Ahom king gave a new name to Balinarayan, *viz.* Dharmanarayan, in appreciation of his pious disposition. The inhabitants of Koch Hajo, living in Uttarkol and Dakhinkol, offered their assistance to King Pratap Singha in order that the Moguls might be expelled from their headquarters at Hajo.[21]

In November 1617 Pratap Singha, accompanied by Dharmanarayan, advanced with an army against the Moguls. The Ahoms captured some Mogul forts in Kamrup, but they were soon defeated in their attack on Hajo. Soon after the Ahoms led by the Barphukan and Dharmanarayan defeated the Moguls at Hajo and captured their garrisons in Kamrup. Their commander Abdussalam was taken to the Ahom capital Gargaon. In a great part of Goalpara also the Mogul rule was thrown off. Many of the chiefs on the north bank acknowledged the supremacy of the Ahoms.[22] A chronicle mentions that Abdussalam was escorted to Gargaon by Raja Dharmanarayan, and that the Ahom king gave to that Raja the government of Dhekeri Rajya or Koch Hajo.[23] The conferment of Koch Hajo on Dharmanarayan on this occasion became afterwards the basis of the Darrang Rajas' claims to Kamrup.

In the wars that followed Dharmanarayan fought on the side of the Ahoms with zeal and vigour. In 1637 the Ahoms were defeated in several engagements in the vicinity of Gauhati. Dharmanarayan fled to Darrang, but being pursued by the Moguls he

19. Mirza Nathan, *Baharistan-i-Ghaybi*, translated by Dr. M. Islam Borah, and published by Department of Historical and Antiquarian Studies, Assam, Vol. I, pp. 396-99.

20. In the genealogical table prefixed to H. C. Goswami's *Darang-raj Vamsavali* Gajnarayan has been shown as the great-grandson of Parikshit. Gait in his *Koch Kings of Kamarupa* describes him as brother of Balinarayan which is more likely to be the fact, *J.A.S.B.*, 1893, p. 29.

21. *Kamrupar Buranji*, p. 19.

22. Gait, *History of Assam*, pp. 114-5.

23. *Kamrupar Buranji*, p. 27.

retreated to Singari where he was killed along with his two sons. The Moguls then consolidated their rule in Kamrup. A treaty was enacted in 1639 between the Mogul commander Allah Yar Khan and the Ahom general Momai-tamuli Barbarua under which the Barnadi on the north bank and Asurar Ali on the south near Gauhati were fixed as the boundary between the Ahom and Mogul territories.

Dharmanarayan's successors in Darrang: Darrang thus continued to remain in the hands of the Ahoms, being governed at that time by its tributary ruler Mahendranarayan,[24] son of Dharmanarayan. His jurisdiction extended also to a portion of Kamrup consisting of the narrow strip of land between Asurar Ali and Kajalimukh on the south bank. It could not have extended to the whole of Kamrup which was then in the hands of the Moguls. Mahendranarayan died in 1643 and was succeeded by his son Chandranarayan. He fixed his residence at Mangaldoi. Chandranarayan opposed the inroads of the Bhutias with the help of the Ahom army. The Bhutias were subdued and were made to pay an annual tribute to the Ahoms and confine themselves to the Gohain Kamala Ali road. Chandranarayan died in 1660 and was succeeded by his son Suryyanarayan.

In the meantime the Ahom king Jayadhwaj Singha taking advantage of the War of Succession among the sons of Emperor Shah Jahan had recovered possession of Kamrup. In 1662 the Mogul general Mir Jumla marched against Assam, and reached Gauhati in the beginning of February. "At this time Makardhaj, Rajah of Durang, who is subject to the Rajah of Assam, came and paid his respects to the Nawab, and presented an elephant, received a *khelat*, was promised protection and was ordered to travel with the army."[25] Under the terms of the treaty concluded next year the Ahom king agreed to cede to the Moguls, "Sirkar Durang,

24. Sundarnarayan is mentioned as Dharmanarayan's successor in Gait's *History*, p. 69, Wade's *Account*, p. 224; Robinson in his *Descriptive Account*, p. 156, mentions Dharmanarayan's successor as Mahendra which is supported by the genealogical tree prefixed to H. C. Goswami's *Darrang-raj Vamsavali*. Gait in his paper *Koch Kings of Kamrup*, *J.A.S.B.*, 1893, p. 307, supported Robinson on the basis of the information obtained in Prasiddhanarayan's *Vamsavali*. Wade put the reign of Mahendra and Chandra together under one name 'Sundar Narain' which was probobly the English form of Chandranarayan. It may be Mahendranarayan had an alternative name Sundarnarayan.

25. *Fathiyah-i-Ibriyah*, tr. by Blochmann, *J.A.S.B.*, 1872. Makardhaj might have been an alternative name of the Darang Raja Suryyanarayan. The contemporary Rani Raja was also named Makardhaj, Gait, *History of Assam*, p. 131-*n*.

bounded by Gawhatti on one side and by the Ali Burari [Bharali river near Tezpur] which passes Fort Chandhurah on the other side."[26] Darrang has been described by the chronicler of Mir Jumla's expedition as abounding in wild elephants and *Khedas* or enclosures for catching them. After the expulsion of the Moguls from Kamrup in 1667 Darrang passed again into the hands of the Ahoms. In March 1679 Laluk-sola Barphukan, the Ahom viceroy, in collusion with Sultan Azamtara, Governor of Bengal, made over Gauhati to the prince's deputy Nawab Mansur Khan, who was appointed Fauzdar of the newly acquired territory of Kamrup. Darrang remained with the Ahoms as before. Mansur Khan made repeated applications to the Ahom king for permission to catch elephants in Bargaon, Balipara and Singari in Darrang. The Ahom government refused to give the permission saying that the three places were covered with reed jungles where elephants did not live, but that they were to be found in the Dafala hills, where operations to catch them could not be conducted on account of the ferocious hillmen who would not spare any stranger.[27] In 1682 Mansur Khan invaded Darrang, captured the Raja Suryyanarayan and conveyed him to Delhi. His brother Indranarayan, who was then only five years old, was placed on the masnad of Darrang. Towards the end of 1682 Mansur Khan was expelled from Gauhati, and the Ahoms recovered possession of Kamrup. During the minority of Indranarayan Darrang was distracted with internal dissensions of which advantage was taken by the Ahoms to strengthen their hold on the country. The six thousand *mul* levies of Darrang, commanded by six Hajarikas or chiliarchs were transferred to the establishment of Gauhati and placed at the disposal of the Barphukan. The inhabitants who were exempted from personal service had to pay taxes in gold, cowtails and blankets of Bhutan. The subjects of Darrang were placed under the Barbarua. The Raja was deprived of all territories which formed part of Kamrup. Darrang alone remained to him for which he had to pay an annual tribute. The country was surveyed and a register formed to ascertain the number of paiks fit for manual service under the government as soldiers and labourers, as well as of non-paiks or *Chamuas* who obtained exemption from such service by paying taxes. Raja Indranarayan accompanied the Barbarua to fetch the daughter of the Jayantia Raja for the Ahom king. In

26. *Ibid., J.A.S.B.*, 1872, p. 94.

27. Ms. *Assam Buranji*, in possession of the Dept. of Historical and Antiquarian Studies, Gauhati,

1713 during Rudra Singha's stay at Gauhati on the eve of his proposed expedition to invade Bengal Raja Indranarayan joined the army with his quota of soldiers, which, with the levies from Jayantia, Cachar, Beltola, Rani and other tributary princes amounted to forty thousand.[28] Suryyanarayan had in the meantime escaped from captivity, and on his return to Darrang he expressed his surprise at the reduction of the Darrang Raja's powers during his absence. He recalled the *mul from* Gauhati; but Raja Indranarayan and the Barphukan reported the matter to the Ahom king who despatched his admiral with a number of gunboats to destroy Suryyanarayan. The prince was taken to the Ahom court where he complained " that Swargadeo formerly deprived him of Camroop and had now rendered the prince of Darrang still less independent by transferring the *mool* of that province to the department of the Burro Fokun." He desired his brother Indranarayan to retain possession of Darrang only on condition that the grievances were redressed. As Indranarayan did not insist on his rights Suryyanarayan came back to Mangaldoi with the 80 men granted to him by the Ahom king, and established his residence on the eastern side of the town. His father's personal property was divided between the two brothers in equal portions.[29]

Indranarayan died in 1725 and was succeeded by his son Adityanarayan. His territories now dwindled down to that portion of the present Mangaldoi sub-division which lies to the south of the Gohain Kamala Ali. In 1728 his younger brother Modnarayan seized upon two-thirds of the little kingdom and proclaimed himself *Burha* or senior Raja relegating Adityanarayan to the position of the *Deka* or junior Raja. From this time onwards Darrang was governed by a couple of rulers, one called the Burha Raja and the other the Deka Raja, on the lines of the dual monarchy prevalent in the contiguous territory of Bhutan.[30] From the time of Adityanarayan and Modnarayan the ruling family of Darrang, "sank into comparative insignificance. They were now mere subordinates of the Ahoms, and exercised no powers except such as were conferred on them by the Ahom prince."[31]

28. J. P. Wade, *Account of Assam*, pp. 130-32, 233-36.

29. J. P. Wade, *Account of Assam*, pp. 236-7. It is also said that Suryyanarayan refused to resume the reigns of government "from a sense of shame," Robinson, *Descriptive Account of Assam*, p. 156.

30. The dual rulers of Darrang are clearly indicated in the genealogical table prefixed to the H. C. Goswami's *Darrang-raj Vamsavali*. Two rulers of Bhutan were known as the Deva Raja and the Dharma Raja.

31. Gait, *Koch Kings of Kamarupa*, *J.A.S.B.*, 1893, p. 308.

Adityanarayan died in 1732 and was succeeded in the Deka-Rajaship by his brother Dhwajnarayan. In 1744 Modnarayan's place was usurped by Dhirnarayan, son of Suryyanarayan, but in 1747 he was compelled to give up his possession. Dhwajnarayan gave offence to the Barphukan by claiming the same pillar in the Hall of State as that officer. He was banished into Bhutan with his son Hemnarayan. The latter married a Bhutanese lady through whom he became father of a prince named Bhotar Kowanr. Dhirnarayan taking advantage of the Moamaria disturbances committed depredations in Darrang. On Modnarayan's death in 1778 the Rajaship of Darrang was held conjointly by his two sons Mahatnarayan and Durlabhnarayan, the former as Burha Raja and the latter as Deka Raja. Upon the death of Durlabhnarayan in 1783 his son Hangsanarayan was appointed Deka Raja. Mahatnarayan died in 1787 and was succeeded by Kirtinarayan, son of Dhirnarayan. Kirtinarayan died in the same year and was succeeded in the Burha-Rajaship by his brother Hangsanarayan, son of Bhirnarayan.[32]

So in the year 1787 Darrang was ruled conjointly by two Rajas both named Hangsanarayan. The Burha Raja Hangsanarayan, whom we shall call Hangsanarayan I, was the son of Dhirnarayan and brother of Kirtinarayan; and Hangsanarayan II, the Deka Raja, was the son of Durlabhnarayan, and the father of Krishnanarayan who rebelled against the Ahom government with the aid of Burkendazes recruited in Company's territories. There were three other prominent princes living at that time, Bishnunarayan and Amritnarayan, sons of Kirtinarayan, and Samudranarayan, son of Mahatnarayan.

Discontent in Darrang: The discontent in Darrang arose out of several causes. The Rajas chafed under the gradual reduction of their territories, including Kamrup. The transfer of 6,000 paiks to the Gauhati establishment for employment under the Barphukan reduced the Darrang Raja's man-power. Besides, the Raja had to supply to the Ahom arsenal at Gauhati a large quantity of saltpetre. He had to attend the Barphukan and the Ahom king in person when called upon to do so. The Raja's humiliation became more poignant when he remembered that his ancestors Raghudeb and Parikshit held absolute possession of Koch Hajo, which included Kamrup and Darrang, besides Goalpara and some more territories stretching southwards from the Goalpara boundary. Dharmanarayan, the founder of the dynasty, was a trusted and faithful ally

32. Capt. Welsh to Cornwallis, May 28, Beng. Pol. Cons., June 14, 1793, No. 11, Robinson, *Descriptive Account of Assam*, pp. 156-7; Gait, *Koch Kings of Kamarupa, J.A.S.B.*, 1893, pp. 307-8.

of the Ahoms for whom he fought against the Moguls for more than 20 years. The Ahoms asserted in 1669 that they had obtained possession of Kamrup from the Koches or members of the Narayan family.[33] It was not taken from Raghudeb or Parikshit, for upon the latter's death Kamrup passed into the hands of the Moguls. It was wrested gradually from Dharmanarayan and his successors whose demand for restoration was of no avail as it could not be backed by military power. Krishnanarayan was insistent in declaring that "there never was a distinction between the Rajaship of Kamrup and Darrang, both were held by one person, until the Assam Raja, possessing superior power, separated them and appropriated Kamrup to himself."[34] The Darrang Raja's grievances came to the forefront during the troublous times of the Ahom government; and men were not wanting in the Darrang court to set forth or magnify the iniquities of the Ahoms and to point out that the opportunity to strike had arrived.

To the disaffection of the Darrang Raja was added the discontent of his subjects. Darrang was surveyed once in 1707 by an Ahom officer named Dhaniram.[35] A new rent-roll of the revenues of Darrang was drawn up again during the reign of Rudra Singha's successor Siva Singha (1714-44).[36] The higher rates of assessment which these successive surveys and settlement operations introduced told very heavily upon the taxpaying power of the poor subjects of Darrang. They dared not raise any protest during the reigns of Pramatta Singha (1744-51) and Rajeswar Singha (1751-69) when the Ahom government was sufficiently strong to suppress any opposition to its decrees. But after Lakshmi Singha's restoration to the throne, when sedition became the order of the day, 4,000 subjects of Darrang marched in a body to the Ahom capital Rangpur to set forth their grievances before the Barbarua. They crossed the Chokies at different places by mere force of number, and appeared in front of the palace gate in violation of the orders which banned the entrances of Darrang and Kamrup subjects into the Ahom capital. There was a skirmish between the Darrang subjects and the king's constables who had been despatched to disperse the intruders. The men of Darrang expressed their determination to

33. S. K. Bhuyan, *Assamese Historical Literature*, *Indian Historical Quarterly* for Sept. 1929.

34. Krishnanarayan to Welsh, Ap. 16, Beng. Pol. Cons., May 1, 1793, No. 17.

35. Gait, *Koch Kings of Kamarupa*, *J.A.S.B.*, 1893, p. 303, n.

36. Robinson, *Descriptive Account*, p. 168, and Col. Jenkins's Report on Lakheraj Tenures, in Mills's *Report*.

die on the spot if their grievances were not listened to and redressed. Two days later the Barbarua, the Bargohain and the Majindar Barua deputed the Na-Gosain to explain the situation to the king who suspended the settlement of Darrang.[37]

The Darrang subjects were pacified for the time being, but soon they had fresh causes of discontent. During the troubles in the reign of Gaurinath Singha many inhabitants of Upper Assam had left their homes and taken shelter in Darrang. The fugitives lived by plundering the fertile province of Darrang of grain, betel-nut and other articles of daily use as others had done in Nowgong. The people of Darrang soon felt the scarcity of foodstuffs, and their village headmen assembled to consult on measures for counteracting the oppressions of the Upper Assam refugees.

In the meantime King Gaurinath Singha staying in his camp at Gauhati had ordered the two Rajas of Darrang, Hangsanarayan I and Hangsanarayan II, to march with their forces against the Moamarias. The Rajas halted at a place called Ghiladhari, at a distance of about ten miles to the west of Biswanath, from where they sent a detachment to the northward against the rebels. The Moamarias sent a letter to the Rajas saying that they were unwilling to fight against the two princes who were descendants of the illustrious Narayan family and against whom they had no cause of enmity. The rebels added that they would gladly agree to a partition of Assam, keeping the eastern provinces to themselves, and making over the countries west of Kaliabar to the Darrang Rajas. The two princes now began to waver between their allegiance to the Ahom king and the temptation of sovereignty over Kamrup. They would have accepted the offer of the Moamarias if they had not received at this juncture fresh orders from Gaurinath Singha to proceed with the duties entrusted to them.

The heads of Darrang villages, as a protest against the oppressions of the refugees from Upper Assam, determined to recall their 6,000 mul from Gauhati. The latter obeyed the summons of their countrymen. The Darrangis now took an oath that no assistance should be given to the Ahom king, and that anybody who supported the Ahom government in any shape would be excommunicated, expelled from the province and killed if he tried to re-enter it by force. The leaders of the Darrangis were Swarup, Mainapowa, Kalia, Phatik Hajarika, and Bhotar Kowanr, son of Hemnarayan. A message was sent to the Burha Raja and Deka Raja to return

37. Ms. chronicle of Lakshmi Singha.

to Darrang and assist their countrymen in opposing the tyranny of the people of Upper Assam. The princes proposed to abandon the field. The Solal Gohain, the Ahom governor of Darrang; asked them to stay. But they refused on which the Gohain imprisoned some followers of the two Rajas who likewise treated some of the Gohain's men. The Gohain was compelled to release his prisoners. The princes then returned with their men to Darrang.

An agent was sent by Gaurinath Singha to investigate the situation in Darrang and to demand the return of the 6,000 paiks as well as the presence of the two Rajas at Gauhati. The agent came back and informed the king that the Darrangis had taken advantage of the weakness of the government, and that the Rajas were not well disposed towards him as could be known from their refusal to repair to Gauhati. Hangsanarayan Burha Raja sent his nephew Bishnunarayan, and the Deka Raja's son Krishnanarayan, aged fifteen, to the Ahom king at Gauhati to explain that the return of the Darrang detachment had been necessitated by the shortage of food supplies.[38]

Discontent in Kamrup: In the meantime signs of disaffection became visible in Kamrup which had till now remained the main stronghold of the Ahom government. The people of Kamrup living for a long time under the domination of the Khen and Koch rulers looked upon the members of the Narayan family as their natural overlords. They considered the Ahoms as outsiders, and the Ahoms generally regarded them with suspicion and distrust. The feelings were severely strained during the reign of the later Swargadeos who could not check the oppressions of the local officers, nor suppress the troubles at their outset.[39] The Kamrupis and the Darrangis were not ordinarily allowed to enter the Ahom capital. In Gauhati, the viceregal headquarters, this restriction was rigidly enforced. No Kamrupi was allowed to spend the night at Gauhati. The gates used to be closed at dusk by which time all Kamrupis were required to evacuate the place and halt somewhere outside the enclosures if they wanted to come to the town next day. This restriction caused great inconvenience and humiliation to the Kamrupis whose business required constant presence at Gauhati. The social relations between the people of Kamrup and Darrang and those of Eastern Assam were also not of an intimate order, as one aspect of it was pointed out by Capt. Welsh on information received

38. J. P. Wade, *Account of Assam*, pp. 242-45.
39. Gunabhiram Barua, *Assam Buranji*, 1876, pp. 167-8.

from Bulchand Barua, a descendant of Parikshit's kanungo Kavindra Patra,—"The distinction between the natives of Kamroop and Deringh remains to this day in so much that the Brahmin to the eastward of Kollabar (properly denominated Assam) will not be suffered by him of Kamroop and Deringh (which have never been considered as part of Assam) to join in his social or religious ceremonies."[40] The differences between the people of Eastern Assam and Kamrup are also seen to some extent in the dialectal variations of their respective speeches.

Kamrup, which was contiguous to the territories of the Moguls and later to those of the East India Company, was regarded by the Ahoms as more or less a buffer-state. This sentiment found expression in 1675 when the Ahom officials of the Gauhati establishment left Kamrup and proceeded to Upper Assam to counteract the designs of the autocratic Debera Barbarua, who had raised an army of foreigners consisting of the remnants of the different Mogul expeditions. The Gauhati officials were taken to task for deserting their posts thereby exposing Kamrup to the attacks of the Moguls to which Atan Buragohain, the leader of the Gauhati party, replied,—"The foreigners have entered into the casket of gold; what is the harm if we expose outer Assam to their invasions.[41]

The administration of Kamrup after its occupation by the Moguls on the death of Parikshit was organised on the lines of the Bengal Sarkars. The same system was adopted by the Ahoms when Kamrup subsequently passed into their hands. There were 26 perganahs each under the charge of a Chaudhuri who wielded great influence in his locality, and at times eclipsed the paramount power of the Ahoms.

Rebellion of Hangsanarayan Deka-Raja: Such a Chaudhuri was Haradatta Bujarbarua of Jikeri. The exploits of the two brothers Haradatta and Biradatta, and the rivalry for the hand of the former's daughter Padma Kumari are sung in the form of a ballad in the villages of Kamrup even up to this day. Haradatta taking advantage of the weakness of the Ahom government and the dormant disaffection of the Kamrupis organised secret manoeuvres to expel the Ahoms from Gauhati who had now entrenched themselves more firmly at that place round the person of the king Gaurinath Singha. Not finding any opportunity in Kamrup he crossed over to Darrang and instigated the two Rajas, Hangsanarayan I and II, to commence hostilities promising to put

40. Welsh to Cornwallis, July 20, Beng. Pol. Cons., Aug. 12, 1793, No. 8.
41. Ms. Assam Buranji recovered from the family of Sukumar Mahanta.

them soon in possession of Kamrup of which they believed to have been unjustly deprived by the Ahoms.

The Deka Raja, Hangsanarayan II, agreed to Haradatta's proposal, while the Burha Raja opposed it, but the latter was persuaded at last to remain friendly with the Deka Raja. The two princes proceeded to a place called Sundarikola Khetra, accompanied by their army which was commanded by one Nurhama. The commander advanced to the pass of Hindughopa, some eight miles west of Mangaldoi. In the conflict that ensued the Darrang forces were defeated, and abandoned the field. Hangsanarayan fled to Kaliapani at the foot of the Bhutan hills.

Bolai Barbara, a trusted official of the Ahom government, was then despatched into Darrang at the head of a considerable force.[42] The Barbara seized Hangsanarayan Deka Raja in his retreat in Bhutan, and came back to Gauhati loaded with the plunder of Darrang. King Gaurinath Singha ordered the execution of the Deka Raja. A raft was made of plantain trees in the middle of which a stake was erected. The Raja was impaled on the stake and the raft floated down the river. His property was confiscated.[43] A brother, an uncle and two nephews of Haradatta were also put to death in this connection. This took place sometime towards the end of January and the beginning of February 1790.[44] Bishnunarayan, who was also known as Bairagi Kowanr, was appointed Deka Raja of Darrang, and Krishnanarayan was dismissed from Gauhati.[45]

Krishnanarayan plans revolt: Krishnanarayan was a youth of seventeen at the time of his father's execution. His understanding was reported to be of a degree below mediocrity.[46] If he had been left to himself or if the Ahom government had been as powerful as it was thirty years before he would have perhaps regarded the incident as a normal occurrence. But he was roused

42. Bolai Barbara had a grudge against Haradatta for having asked the Kamrupi officials to refuse to eat refreshments at a party given by the Barbara who was an *Ahamiya* or a man of Upper Assam, See *Kamarupar Puravritta* in S. K. Bhuyan's *Kamrupar Buranji,* p. 114.

43. J. P. Wade, *Account of Assam,* p. 245.

44. Welsh to Cornwallis, Jan. 13, Beng. Pol. Cons., Jan. 28, 1793. Krishnanarayan to Commissioner of Kooch Behar, Beng. Rev. Cons., July 29, 1791.

45. Krishnanarayan attributed his father's undoing to the machinations of Bishnunarayan. Gaurinath Singha afterwards informed Capt. Welsh that Krishnanarayan had, at the instigation of Haradatta, refused to accept the Deka-Rajaship offered to him after his father's execution.

46. Henry Douglas, Commissioner of Cooch Behar, to Cornwallis, July 14, Beng. Pol. Cons., Aug. 20, 1792, No. 15.

to energetic action by the persuasion of several experienced and aged leaders who entertained deep hatred of the Ahom government and who considered its destruction as the only means of their own preservation.

Krishnanarayan's chief instigator to rebellion was Haradatta Chaudhuri who has been described as his Dewan and again as "Zemindar of Darrang and servant of his [Krishnanarayan's] father." After the execution of his relatives for complicity in the rebellion of Hangsanarayan Deka Raja, Haradatta fled to Bengal with Phatik Hazarika and Bhotar Kowanr and kept himself in touch with Krishnanarayan. The prince would have entered into terms with the Ahom government, but Haradatta inspired him with dreams of sovereignty not only over Darrang but over the province of Kamrup both of which had formed part of the possessions of his ancestors. The selection of a prince to subserve the designs of political malcontents which had been so successfully employed by the Moamarias was now repeated by Haradatta and the other adherents of Krishnanarayan.

Krishnanarayan supported by Daniel Raush: Daniel Raush was at that time the principal merchant of Goalpara. After the abolition of Hugh Baillie's appointment Raush had purchased the entire stock of the Company's salt. In February 1790 he had entered into partnership with two other merchants, Thomas Cotters and Robert Brydie, to carry on the trade to Assam for which they had been granted a Perwanah by the Bengal Government. Sometime later Raush enterd into an agreement with the Assam agents at the Assam Choky, Rudram Barua and Chandram Barua, to furnish them with whatever quantity of salt they might require in return for Assam products.[47] The whole trade of Assam thus came through the Baruas' hands to Raush. This virtual monopoly was viewed with jealousy by other merchants, specially the Greeks led by Alexander Paniotty of Dacca and his two agents at Jugighopa, Alexander Kyriakos and Angelo Ducas. Raush's outstanding balances from Assam merchants came to 70,000 rupees. Of this amount the sum of rupees 22,000 was due from Rudram Barua with whom Raush had been trading since 1768 and whose debts to George Lear had formed the subject of Warren Hastings's letter to the Assam Raja in 1777. Raush could not recover any portion of his demands inspite of his repeated applications to the Assam government.[48]

47. Welsh to Cornwallis, Feb. 21, Beng. Pol. Cons., March 11, 1793, No. 15
48. Raush to Cornwallis, Sept. 17, Beng. Pol. Cons., Oct. 3, 1792, No. 18.

Krishnanarayan or rather his agents approached Raush for support to carry out their plans. The merchant visited Assam in the beginning of 1791. He promised to give Krishnanarayan possession of Darrang and Kamrup. Raush sent sepoys to Darrang and induced Krishnanarayan to go to Goalpara.[49] Raush also brought with him the two enemies of Krishnanarayan,—Bishnunarayan who had been appointed Deka Raja of Darrang and his brother Amritnarayan, as well as the warden of the Sonapur frontier Mandhan Barua who had been ill-used by the Buragohain. Bishnunarayan and Amritnarayan were kept in confinement by Raush from which they were released a few months later. Raush maintained Krishnanarayan at Goalpara for four months, March to June 1791, promising to reinstate him in his paternal inheritance. Raush then conducted Krishnanarayan to Cooch Behar where the prince obtained the support of the young Maharaja Harendranarayan who was his kinsman, being both descendants of Biswa Singha, the founder of the Narayan family.

Company's assistance solicited by Krishnanarayan: In July 1791 Krishnanarayan sent Lala Dhir Sing to Henry Douglas, Commissioner of Cooch Behar, asking for military assistance to recover possession of Darrang and Kamrup which he declared to be his "hereditary Rauj." He styled himself as "Raja of the Perganahs of Darrang and Kamrup appertaining to Assam." He alleges that Bishnunarayan, commonly known as Bairagi Kowanr, intriguing with "Gauri Sing, Raja of Assam" had killed Hangsanarayan sometime between January 11 and February 9, 1790, and dispossessed him of his Rajaship, and that the said Bairagi Kowanr became Raja instead. Krishnanarayan offered to pay to the East India Company a tribute of 5,001 Rajamohari rupees. The Commissioner did not hold out any encouragement to Krishnanarayan.[50]

The Supreme Board in their meeting of July 29, 1791, decided not to interfere in the disputes of Krishnanarayan, his relation Bishnunarayan and the king of Assam. They consequently refused to assist him with troops for the recovery of his Raj.[51] Government's decision was communicated to Krishnanarayan by John Lumsden, Collector of Rungpore.

49. Declaration of Krishnanarayanan before the Commissioner of Cooch Behar, Beng. Pol. Cons., June 8, 1792, No. 9.

50. Douglas to Bd. Rev., July 13, Beng. Rev. Cons., July 29, 1791, No. 19, forwarding Krishnanarayan's first petition.

51. Bd. Rev. Cons., Aug. 1, 1791.

Krishnanarayan was not the man to let the grass grow under his feet. Soon after the receipt of Government's reply he submitted a fresh petition on August 19, 1791, through Durjan Sing Jemadar and Phatik Saharia Barua[52] asking for permission to entertain sepoys on his own account, and for the issue of a Rahdari perwanah "of encouragement" so that no one might stop the sepoys on the way or at the ferries. He offered to pay the tribute previously proposed by him. He requested the Government to do whatever was for his advantage. "In this case," added Krishnanarayan, "I can take possession of my own country in the Company's name." He promised to provide for the payment of the tribute on his return to Assam.

The Collector of Rungpore refused to issue the perwanah asked for by Krishnanarayan, in the light of the Government's orders on the first petition. On August 26, 1791, the Collector forwarded the second petition to Government for being furnished with instructions for his guidance in the event of Krishnanarayan's endeavouring to raise troops in the Company's provinces or to entice adventurers from the upper parts of India into his service. Lumsden apprehended that Krishnanarayan's troops would make their way into Assam through the district of Rungpore.[53]

The Supreme Board in their meeting of September 9, 1791, resolved to adhere to their decision not to interfere in the affairs of Krishnanarayan. The Collector of Rungpore was instructed "neither to grant the Perwanah solicited by the Rajah [Krishnanarayan], nor to take measures to prevent him entertaining in his service persons residing in the Company's provinces"; the Collector was directed to "proceed against Krishnanarayan's agents or any persons in his employ should they excite disturbances or commit outrages within the Company's limits in the same manner as the Collector in his capacity as Magistrate would against other individuals who might be guilty of a breach of the peace."[54] Whatever might have been the intentions of the Government Lumsden understood by these orders, as he himself admitted afterwards, that he was "neither to assist or prevent Kissen Narain

52. Saharia Barua was the title applied to revenue administrators in Darrang, higher in rank to the Hazarikas of which Phatik was one. It was customary to call a Hazarika as Barua, though in official documents the real rank is always mentioned.

53. Lumsden to Bd. Rev., Aug. 26, 1791, forwarding Krishnanarayan's second petition, Beng. Rev. Cons., Sept. 9, 1791, Nos. 19 and 20.

54. Government to Board of Revenue, Sept. 9, 1791, Beng. Rev. Cons., same date, No. 21.

in raising such force as he might think proper as long as they acted peaceably within the Company's territories." Krishnanarayan then began to entertain men on his own account, and as his recruits conducted themselves peaceably the Collector of Rungpore took no notice of them.[55]

Burkendaz, Sannyasi and Fakir raiders: Krishnanarayan's recruiting campaign gained additional impetus from the presence in Rungpore and Cooch Behar of large hordes of vagabonds and dacoits who having or pursuing no means of subsistence maintained themselves and their families by the spoils of plunder. The Zemindars being weak and the Police Administration of the Company being not yet efficiently organised these freebooters carried on their ravages without much hindrance or opposition. The Zemindars entertained bodies of Burkendazes for protection, and in many instances they were sheltered for levying blackmail from neighbouring villages as the price of immunity from plunder. The local officers of the Company were even compelled to engage Burkendazes in their service to tide over any emergency.

The Burkendazes consisted of the cashiered soldiers of the Moslem armies, or troops disbanded by Zemindars, or ryots who were driven to plundering as a last resource for subsistence. They generally formed themselves into bands of Sannyasis and Fakirs; and under pretence of religious pilgrimages roamed about Bengal begging, stealing and plundering as they chose. Their depredations "unhinged the rural administration of Bengal," and became normal episodes in the life of the country.[56] "The Sannyasis are the stoutest and the most active men in India," wrote Warren Hastings to Josiah Du Pre, "many are merchants. They are all pilgrims and held by all castes of Gentoos [Hindus] in great veneration." Sometime later Hastings wrote to John Purling, Chairman of the Court of Directors, "We have been much troubled here by hordes of desperate adventurers called Sannyasis who have overrun the province in great numbers and committed great depredations."[57]

The Bengal district of Rungpore bordering on Nepal, Bhutan, Cooch Behar and Assam were peculiarly liable to be infested by banditti. There were tracts in the neighbourhood, such as Bhitur-

55. Lumsden to Charles Stuart, Member of Governor-General's Council, Feb. 15 and 29, Beng. Pol. Cons., March 16, 1792, Nos. 11 and 15.

56. W. W. Hunter, *The Annals of Rural Bengal*, Vol. I, pp. 70-72.

57. Hastings to Du Pre, March 9, 1773, to Purling, March 31, 1775, in Gleig's *Memoirs of Warren Hastings*. Vol. I, p. 267; also Bankimchandra Chatterji's *Anandamath* or *The Abbey of Bliss*, translated by N. C. Sen-Gupta, App. I.

bund and Sorooppore, and the 'no-man's land' lying south of the stations of Dinajpore and Rungpore which offered great facilities for refuge. The depredations of Bhawani Pathak and his female colleague Devi Chaudhurani, of Majnu Shah, Musa Shah and Cheragh Ali kept the Company's officers in the north-eastern districts of Bengal fully occupied during the fourth quarter of the eighteenth century. In 1787 Khagendranarayan, the Nazir Deo of Cooch Behar, with a force of 500 or 700 Sannyasis carried off Raja Harendranarayan, his mother and his grandmother and kept them in concealment in a house on the confines of Cooch Behar towards Bijni.[58] In June 1791 Lt. Purcell and the Sezawal of Rangamati were murdered by a gang of Burkendazes and Sikhs.[59] Bulchand Barua, a prominent Zemindar of Rangamati, had to leave Karaibari on account of the depredations of Majnu Shah.[60]

The Burkendazes, Sannyasis and Fakirs were equipped with horses, camels, elephants, rockets and jinjal pieces and arms of all kinds. A Burkendaz recruit would usually offer his service with a matchlock and a sword which relieved his employers of the necessity of supplying weapons. Some idea can be formed of the ravages of these freebooters from the following passage of a Bengali ballad dealing with the barbarities of Majnu Shah and his followers: "Majnu's march is well ordered like a king's. See how the standards and banners precede him. At every halting place a hundred guns are fired. What can the Bengalis do but flee? The peasant leaves his plough and cattle in the field. Women with hair and garments dishevelled rush from their houses. The Fakir scorns pots of brass. In his greed he breaks boxes, digs the loose earth and even rips open the pillows seeking for coins. The lady of gentle birth seeks the woods but the Fakirs quit their thieving to chase her. Like hawks on a pigeon they pounce on her and seek embraces."[61]

Assam was not free from the plundering raids of the Bengal Burkendazes. Owing to weakness of the government and the mutinous discontent of the chiefs Assam became in course of time the plundering preserve of the maruaders from Bengal. In June 1780 Warren Hastings had written to the king of Assam assuring

58. Glazier. *Rungpore.* ed. Firminger, pp. 37. 44.

59. Bd. Rev. Proceedings, July 1, 1791.

60. J. M. Ghosh, *Sannyasi and Fakir Raiders in Bengal*, p. 107; Bogra *District Gazetteer*, pp. 126-27.

61. Ghose, *Sannyasi Raiders*, p. 110. The Bengali text of the Ballad of Majnu or 'Majnur Kabita' is inserted in the appendix.

him that Hugh Baillie, the newly appointed Resident at Goalpara, would protect the Assamese from the depredations of one Rupa Sardar and other freebooters. During Baillie's residence at Goalpara from 1780 to 1783, and again from 1787 to 1790 we do not hear of any Burkendaz trouble in Assam. But after Baillie's withdrawal from Goalpara the Assam frontier became once more infested with banditti. The officer commanding at Jugighopa with only one company of sepoys was not able to check the entrance of Burkendazes into Assam.[62] The Sezawal of Rangamati was tempted to grant to every Burkendaz a free passage if he could obtain a bribe of half a rupee per Burkendaz. Besides, there were so many different routes to Assam through Bhutan and Bijni that it was difficult to effectively guard all the passes. "In short, my Lord," wrote Capt. Welsh to Lord Cornwallis, "this country [Assam] has been a receptacle for every vagabond who could bring a sword or a matchlock for these some years past, and a fine harvest it has been for them."[63]

Krishnanarayan occupies Darrang and North Gauhati: The Burkendaz rabble now rallied round the standard of Krishnanarayan. They consisted of Sikhs, Rajputs and all manner of men from Bengal to Lahore.[64] The force was augmented by Assamese recruits. Krishnanarayan's agents and captains were Phatik Barua of Darrang, Gaib Sing Barua of Bijni, Dhir Sing Jemadar of the Punjab, and Hari Sing Hazari of Rungpore. Haradatta played the role of Krishnanarayan's chief minister and adviser. The Burkendaz force consisted of about 3,000 men including 60 musketeers commanded by one Munder Khan, formerly a Subedar in the Company's service.

In December 1791 Krishnanarayan entered Assam with his army by way of Bhutan and Bijni. He easily took possession of Darrang. Having left a detachment to guard his conquests he marched towards Kamrup. Krishnanarayan and his Burkendazes gave out that they were fighting with the authority of the Bengal Government.

An attempt to prevent the influx of Burkendazes into Assam was made by Lt. Philip Crump of the 6th Battalion, Native Infantry, commanding the small party at Jugighopa. He wrote a letter to the Burkendazes in Darrang which induced 200 of them to return. In the first week of December 1791 about 500 Bhutias, sent by the

62. Douglas to Cornwallis, July 14, Beng. Pol. Cons., Aug. 20, 1792, No. 15.
63. Welsh to Cornwallis, Dec. 4, Beng. Pol. Cons., Dec. 17, 1792, No. 50.
64. Raush to Lumsden, May 7, Beng. Pol. Cons., June 8, 1792, No. 11.

Deva Raja of Bhutan to assist Krishnanarayan, had arrived in a village called Damamgong in the upper part of Bijni on which the ryots began to quit their homes. Lt. Crump sent a party of sepoys under a Subedar to give confidence to the alarmed villagers. Having heard that Krishnanarayan had been permitted by the Bengal Government to carry as many Burkendazes as he chose Lt. Crump desisted from taking more vigorous measures against them.[65]

The only noteworthy opposition offered by the Assamese was when in December 1791 some 4,000 or 5,000 of them surrounded 40 Burkendazes who had strayed too far from the main body. In making attempts to extricate themselves most of the Burkendazes were killed, and 15 were taken prisoners 10 of whom were impaled, and 5 maimed and sent to Goalpara and Jogighopa as a spectacle to deter the Burkendazes from going into Assam.[66] The Assam government, on hearing of Krishnanarayan's march towards Gauhati, opened negotiations with him for an amicable settlement. Krishnanarayan and Haradatta promised to compromise matters. They sent presents to Gaurinath who permitted them to come to Gauhati leaving their followers behind. It was agreed that Krishnanarayan would hold the Rajaship of Darrang, that he should consider himself as the subject of the Swargadeo and would even sacrifice his life in the cause of his liegelord. But instead of acting to their promises Krishnanarayan and Haradatta entered North Gauhati with the Burkendazes and plundered the villages and the house of the Paniphukan, the commander of the Ahom fleet.[67] In the battle that ensued Krishnanarayan was victorious with little loss, while the casualties on the royalist side included several principal officers. Krishnanarayan then encamped with his force at Aswakranta, on the north bank of the river Brahmaputra, at the site of the capital of Parikshitnarayan, brother of Dharmanarayan, the founder of the Darrang Raj family. This happened in February 1792.[68] The Burkendazes committed the most atrocious outrages upon the defenceless inhabitants and laid waste the country.

Bengal Government asked to recall Burkendazes : The Assam government not being in a position to drive away the Burkendazes

65. Crump to Lumsden, Jan. 25, Beng. Pol. Cons., March 16, 1792, No. 14.

66. Crump to Lumsden, March 6, Beng. Pol. Cons., Ap. 27, 1792, No. 21.

67. Letter from Bikaram Majumdar, Chandram and Rudram Duaria Baruas, Krishnanath Kandahar Barua, to Collector of Rungpore, Beng. Pol. Cons., Oct. 22, 1792, No. 21.

68. Lumsden to Charles Stuart, Feb. 15, Beng. Pol, Cons., March 16, 1792, No. 11.

and put a stop to their depredations deputed Krishnanath Gossain Kandahar Barua, and Rudram and Chandram Duaria Baruas to the Collector of Rungpore where they arrived in the first week of February 1792. The Baruas asked the Collector to issue a perwanah to the Sezawal of Rangamati directing him to recall the Burkendazes and others who had accompanied Krishnanarayan from Bengal. Lumsden, the Collector, in the light of the orders of the Government of September 9, 1791, did not consider himself warranted in acceding to the request of the Baruas. On February 12, 1792, the Baruas submitted a fresh petition asking the Collector to direct the Rangamati Sezawal and the Lieutenant Commanding at Jugighopa to send the Burkendazes to Bengal. On February 15 Lumsden forwarded the Barua's petitions to Charles Stuart, Senior Member of the Bengal Council, asking for instructions.[69] A fortnight later Lumsden wrote a letter to Neil Benjamin Edmonstone, Acting Persian Translator, narrating the circumstances which led him to take no notice of Krishnanarayan's levying troops in Bengal though he knew that it was done "with the avowed intention of asserting his right to the province of Darrang from which he had been expelled by the ruling power of Assam," adding that he did not think himself authorised to get the Burkendazes to quit Assam without fresh instructions from Government.[70]

Bengal Government's position examined: The Assam Baruas' petitions for the recall of the Burkendazes and the Rungpore Collector's request for specific instructions led the Supreme Board to review their position with regard to the recent developments in Assam. In his letter addressed to King Gaurinath Singha on July 23, 1787, Lord Cornwallis had declared the English Government's desire "for the preservation and improvement of that state of harmony and good neighbourhood which has so long subsisted between the countries of Bengal and Assam."[71] Government's refusal of aid to Krishnanarayan with which he had proposed to subvert the authority of the Assam Raja was consistent with the friendly professions of Lord Cornwallis. But by not preventing

69. Lumsden to Stuart, Feb. 15, Beng. Pol. Cons., March 16, 1792, No. 11. Charles Stuart was in charge of the administration as Lord Cornwallis, the Governor-General, was then at Seringapatam, engaged in operations against Tipu Sultan.

70. Lumsden to Edmonstone, Feb. 29, Beng. Pol. Cons., March 16, 1792, No. 15.

71. Cornwallis to Assam Raja, July 23, 1787, draft in Beng. Rev. Cons., July 18, 1787, reproduced in Beng. Pol. Cons., March 16, 1792, No. 16.

Krishnanarayan from recruiting troops in Bengal, the avowed purpose of which was the recovery of Darrang, the Bengal Government did indirectly help him to cause irruptions in Assam. The only condition imposed upon Krishnanarayan was that his men should conduct themselves peaceably within the Company's territories in default of which they would be treated like other individuals as guilty of a breach of the peace. The Collector of Rungpore, therefore, did not take any notice of Krishnanarayan's activities in Bengal.

The Darrang prince collected nearly 3,000 Burkendazes in Bengal, and most of them were armed with weapons provided by themselves. Armed bodies of Krishnanarayan's mercenaries must have met here and there in Rungpore and Cooch Behar before their departure for Assam; and Krishnanarayan's recruitment conducted on such a large scale could be construed as his open levying of troops. Either from a misconception of his duty or from the vagueness of Government's orders Lumsden did not disperse Krishnanarayan's Burkendazes which he could have done if he thought that Government had authorised him to do so. Acting on the same assumption Lumsden had refused to issue a perwanah to the Sezawal of Rangamati directing him to recall the Burkendazes. It was Lumsden's error of judgment or misreading of Government's intentions, combined with the lack of explicitness in the orders of September 9, 1791, which was responsible for the ingress of Burkendazes into Assam. It was admitted afterwards that "if care were taken to prevent armed men from assembling within the Company's territory the evil would in a great measure be prevented."[72] That the Bengal Government became conscious of some degree of responsibility for the depredations of Krishnanarayan's Burkendazes in Assam is proved by the series of remedial measures which they afterwards adopted, first, by issuing perwanahs for their recall, and on the failure of this measure, by the despatch of a detachment for their forcible expulsion from Assam.

The Supreme Board in the resolution adopted in their meeting of March 16, 1792, attributed a complete misunderstanding of their real intentions on the part of Lumsden. The Board observed "that they certainly did not mean by their order of the 9th September last to allow of the Dering Rajah's openly levying troops within the Company's territories for the avowed purpose of disturbing the

72. J. Long, *Selections from Unpublished Records of Government,* Vol. I, "Report relative to Assam in 1797," p. 553.

Rajah of Assam's Government; such a proceeding would have ill consisted with the friendly professions of Lord Cornwallis contained in his Lordship's letter to the Rajah of the 23rd of July 1787." The Collector of Rungpore was advised "that no open levies of the kind in question are to be allowed within the District under his charge, and that if any of the inhabitants should be induced by private agents to repair to the Dering Rajah and to serve him, that is a matter which is not incumbent on the Board to prevent."[73] But the mischief had been done already. Krishnanarayan's mercenaries had been supplementing their precarious wages by the spoils of plunder, and threatening to attack the Assamese monarch living at South Gauhati opposite to their own encampment at Aswakranta. The only way by which the Bengal Government could mitigate or undo the consequences of their passiveness and neutrality was to procure the return of the Burkendazes to Bengal by persuasion, intimidation or by force. But no such measure was adopted at this meeting of the Board, who were perhaps precluded from taking vigorous action owing to the absence of Lord Cornwallis at Seringapatam watching the conclusion of the definitive treaty with Tipu Sultan.[74]

Raush's negotiations with Krishnanarayan: In the same month the Assam Raja sent for Daniel Raush so that he might see for himself the distracted situation of the country and report on it to the Bengal Government. It was also expected that Raush, on the strength of his past services to Krishnanarayan, would be able to persuade that prince to desist from further hostilities with the Assam government which was now willing to cede to him Darrang with all the privileges enjoyed by his father and grandfather. It also transpired that the Assam Raja's people were afraid to approach Krishnanarayan's encampment. Raush went to Gauhati in April 1792 with the hope of realising his outstanding balances through the influence of the Assam Raja who, however, told him that the merchants would scarcely be able to pay him as long as the Bengal Burkendazes continued their depredations in Assam. Raush was accompanied by several boats loaded with merchandise consisting of salt, broadcloth, silk stuffs, jewellery, corals and looking glasses to the value of nearly half a lakh of rupees.[75] The

73. Beng. Pol. Cons., March 16, 1792.

74. On March 19, 1792, the hostage princes delivered the definitive treaty, confirmed by their father Tipu Sultan, into the hands of the British commander.

75. Raush at Gauhati to H. Douglas, July 16, Beng. Pol. Cons., Sept. 19, 1792, No. 14.

retention of Raush at Gauhati to exert his influence in procuring the intervention of the Company was a wise stroke of policy on the part of the Assam government.

On April 27 Raush met Krishnanarayan in the vicinity of North Gauhati where he came with his entire force of about 1,300 Burkendazes. Raush communicated to Krishnanarayan the Assam Raja's desire to come to terms. Krishnanarayan was willing to accept the Assam Raja's offer, but he was prevented from doing so by Hari Sing Hazari and Durjan Sing and other Jemadars of the Burkendazes whose plunder would naturally come to an end with the termination of hostilities. The Burkendazes objected to a compromise on the ground that they had received only one and a half month's wages within the last seven months. Their monthly wages amounted to more than 3,500 rupees, and they alleged that they had now about two lakhs of rupees due to them. They demanded that Krishnanarayan must pay them their balance before he could make peace with the Assam Raja. They further alleged that "he had brought them from Bengal with the permission of the Government," and that they would immediately go back to Bengal if the Assamese or Raush could shew them a perwanah from the Collector of Rungpore for their recall. Raush realised that Krishnanarayan was a virtual prisoner in the hands of the Burkendazes and had to yield to everything they desired.[76]

The Barphukan's letter to Collector of Rungpore: The Assam government's attempt to conciliate Krishnanarayan through the medium of Raush having failed Medhi Barphukan addressed a letter to the Collector of Rungpore on May 10, 1792, referring to the circumstances of Raush's visit to Gauhati. "The inhabitants of Bengal," wrote the Barphukan, "are ruining our country and we expect that you will interfere to put a stop to it. All the Bengal Burkendazes and Jemadars say that they came here with Krishnanarayan by the orders of the Company and that if they receive orders to return they will do so but not otherwise." The Barphukan's letter was accompanied by one from Raush who described his own experiences with Krishnanarayan and the Burkendazes. "Should they continue a few months longer in their depredations," wrote Raush, "the country here about must be ruined entirely, and the trade of Assam lost to the great detriment of Bengal and of every individual concerned in it."[77]

76. Raush to Lumsden, May 7, Beng. Pol. Cons., June 8, 1792, No. 11.

77. Raush to Lumsden, May 7, Medhi Barphukan to Lumsden, May 10, Beng. Pol. Cons., June 8, 1792, Nos. 11 and 12.

In forwarding the Barphukan's letter to Government the Collector of Rungpore confirmed the statements about the distracted condition of Assam from information collected independently by him. The government of Assam was so weak, said the Collector, that "it could not raise a force sufficient even to resist the banditti as that which now infects it." Meanwhile Lumsden had issued a perwanah to the Burkendazes warning them of the consequences of making "as false and groundless an assertion" that they had entered the Assam territories by order of Government. The Collector admitted his inability to go beyond the issuing of a perwanah by an apprehension that Krishnanarayan, if deserted by the Burkendazes, would fall a victim to the vengeance of the Assam Raja. He hoped to be furnished with specific instructions whether or not "he was to interfere any further in the business should the Burkendazes still continue in Assam."[78]

The Board in their meeting of June 8 approved of the perwanah issued by the Collector of Rungpore to the Burkendazes in the service of Krishnanarayan. They judged it necessary to remove any unfavourable impression which the mind of the Assam Raja might have received from the misrepresentation of the Burkendazes, and to disavow their conduct in a more explicit and direct manner. They therefore agreed to write a letter to the Assam Raja "assuring him in suitable terms of their [Burkendazes'] declaration being utterly untrue and unfounded and of our [Bengal Government's] sincere disposition to cultivate the strictest harmony with the Government of Assam." In the same meeting the Board resolved to instruct the Collector of Rungpore and the Commissioner of Cooch Behar to issue perwanahs directing the Burkendazes of Krishnanarayan "to quit the Assamese territories immediately on pain of being declared outlaws and of being dealt with accordingly." The Board did not see any reason why they should be restrained by any apprehension for the personal safety of Krishnanarayan. The letter to the Assam Raja was written by Charles Stuart who concluded it by declaring that it was "the sincere wish of the Bengal Government that Assam should always continue in a prosperous and flourishing condition."[79] Stuart's letter was forwarded to the Assam Raja by the Collector of Rungpore on June 18. The measures adopted by the Board in their meeting of June 8 marked the initiation of vigorous action on their part to stamp out the Burkendaz evil from Assam.

78. Lumsden to Cornwallis, May 19, Beng. Pol. Cons., June 8, 1792, No. 10.

79. Board's resolution, Beng. Pol. Cons., June 8, 1792, No. 17. Stuart to Assam Raja, June 12, Beng. Pol. Cons., June 15, 1792, No. 17.

On receipt of Government's orders the Collector of Rungpore sent a perwanah to the Assam government at Gauhati for transmission to the Burkendazes; and another was sent directly to them from Jugighopa. The Commissioner of Cooch Behar sent also a perwanah directly to the Burkendazes. On June 14, the Commissioner directed Lt. Lennon, Commanding at Jugighopa, to apprehend the ringleaders and disperse the rest by force if bodies of armed men would assemble within the Company's territories whether for the avowed purpose of entering into the service of Krishnanarayan or from any other motive. Lt. Lennon was informed that "though these people may not have committed any outrages, yet the act of assembling with arms is in itself illegal, as the peace of the country may thereby be endangered, and besides, the Governor-General in Council has been pleased to direct that troops shall not be openly levied in the Company's territories for the service of the Deringh Rajah."[80]

Raush's further negotiations with Krishnanarayan: In the meantime Raush had been carrying on negotiations with Krishnanarayan to come to a speedy and amicable settlement. On May 9, he, at the instance of the Assam government, proceeded with Gaurinath's vakils to Belkuchi, about 8 *coss* to the north-west of Gauhati, in the neighbourhood of Jikeri, Haradatta's village and stronghold. Raush had several interviews with Krishnanarayan who expressed his willingness to agree to the terms offered by the Assam Raja. But the Burkendazes would not allow him to do so and they declared publicly that they would conquer the whole of Assam by the force of arms. In the meantime a fresh band of 600 Burkendazes, led by Hazari Singh Jemadar and Baug Roy Jemadar had forcibly entered Assam by way of Jugighopa on or about June 12. All hopes of a settlement with Krishnanarayan became shattered when his Burkendazes, having heard of the coming of Hazari Singh's party, prevented him from entering into any correspondence with Raush and the Assam vakils.[81]

The conduct of the Burkendazes became gradually more and more violent. On June 24 the Rungpore Collector's perwanah was sent to them through Raush's Jemadar named Jam Singh and an Assamese messenger who were treated very roughly. The Burkendazes made Krishnanarayan write a letter to Raush that they were determined to drive him and the Assamese from that place. Next

80. Douglas to Cornwallis, July 3, with an extract of a letter to Lt. Lennon of June 14, Beng. Pol. Cons., July 18, 1792, No. 13.

81. Raush to Douglas, July 16, Beng. Pol. Cons., Sept. 19, 1792, No. 14.

day Raush sent a message to the Burkendazes that they were injuring themselves as well as Krishnanarayan and ruining the country by disobeying the Company's perwanah requiring them to quit Assam, and by not coming to an amicable settlement with Assam. To this Raush received no other answer than that he should go away with the Assam vakils, and that " they should pay no attention to the Company's perwanah not being under their authority, and that as they were not in the Company's territories they had nothing to do with the Bengal Government or with the Collector." This answer was given by the Burkendaz leader Hari Sing Hazari who kept the perwanah.[82]

On June 28 the Burkendazes took away an Assam Chowkidar to commence fresh hostilities. Then they came up to the Assamese at Belkuchi and told them that they would cut them all to pieces if they would not immediately leave that place. That very evening they were joined by the party under Hazari Sing and Baug Roy Jemadars.

Raush and Assam vakils attacked by Burkendazes: Raush, by supporting the Assam government, incurred the enmity of his former protege Krishnanarayan as well as of the Burkendazes and Sannyasis who now sought opportunities for revenge. About 3 o'clock in the afternoon of the 30th June, the Burkendazes came in three large bodies quite unexpectedly and attacked the boats of Raush and also of the Assamese. They fired on the boats with muskets and cannon, and four or five cannon balls went through Raush's pinnace when he was in it. Raush and the Assam officers including Krishnanath Gosain Kandahar Barua and Bandhuram Barua saved their lives by leaving the boats with all the effects to the mercy of the banditti. The fugitives reached Gauhati next morning.[83]

On June 25, 1792, Medhi Barphukan had addressed a letter to the Collector of Rungpore reporting the Burkendazes' refusal to obey the Company's perwanah requiring them to quit Assam. The Barphukan requested the despatch of a force to Assam "to return after having settled everything for its advantage." The Collector in forwarding the letter to Government asked for specific instructions respecting the measures to be taken to give effect to the sentence of outlawry passed against the Burkendazes in the service

82. Medhi Barphukan to Lumsden, June 25, Beng. Pol. Cons., July 18, 1792, No. 12.

83. Raush to Douglas, July 16, Beng. Pol. Cons., Sept. 19, 1792, No. 14.

of Krishnanarayan for disobedience to Government orders.[84] Lumsden's perwanah sent directly to the Burkendazes and made over to them on July 5 by two peons of Jugighopa Kutchery and a Harkarah of Raush also met with the same fate as well as the perwanah of Henry Douglas, Commissioner of Cooch Behar. The Commissioner was of opinion that the detachment at Jugighopa under the command of Lt. Lennon would be adequate for the purpose of expelling the Burkendazes from Assam. He was, however, not prepared to instruct Lt. Lennon to march into Assam without the express orders of the Governor-General.[85]

The Board in their meeting of July 18 ordered that the contumacy of Hari Sing Hazari manifested in his disregard of the Government's perwanah be punished by an immediate attachment of his property in Alipore in Bahirbund. The Collector of Rungpore was authorised to proceed in the same manner against other disobedient Burkendazes who possessed property within the limits of his jurisdiction. These resolutions were communicated to the Barphukan and Hari Sing Hazari. The latter was informed of Government's intention to rigidly execute the orders which would remain in force until himself and his adherents paid due obedience to the Collector's perwanah commanding them to quit the Assamese territories. These measures were regarded by the Board to be adequate for the present; and so they did not pass any orders on the request of the Barphukan or on the suggestion of the Commissioner of Cooch Behar.[86]

On July 14 Henry Douglas wrote another letter to Lord Cornwallis giving all available information on the situation in Assam. The Burkendazes had not only refused to obey the Commissioner's perwanah but had also roughly treated the messenger. The number of Burkendazes in Assam, according to the latest estimate of Douglas, was about three thousand. Hence, thought the Commissioner, that in the event of coercive measures being adopted the detachment stationed at Jugighopa consisting only of one company of sepoys would be inadequate to the service, and that it would be necessary to send five or six companies. The Commissioner then referred to the circumstances of Krishnanarayan's rebellion leading to his conquest of Darrang and attack on Kamrup. Krishnanarayan and the Assam Raja were both willing to make peace, but the Jemadars would not allow Krishnanarayan to do so foreseeing

84. Medhi Barphukan to Lumsden, June 25, Lumsden to Cornwallis, July 3, Beng. Pol. Cons., July 18, 1792, No. 12.
85. Douglas to Cornwallis, July 3, Beng. Pol. Cons., July 18, 1792, No. 13.
86. Beng. Pol. Cons., July 18, 1792, No. 12.

"that their great pay and still greater plunder must end with the war." "The trade of Bengal and Assam," said the Commissioner, "which was very considerable is now almost ruined by the disturbances in the latter country."[87]

Burkendazes' first arzy: On August 29 the Government received the reply of the Burkendazes, to the perwanah warning them of the consequences of their unfounded declaration that they had the orders of Government for going into Assam. The letter of the Burkendazes is a curious mixture of falsehood, flattery, defiance and evasiveness, and affords a glimpse of the peculiar mentality and logic of the criminal classes of India. The Burkendazes started by denying that they had made such a declaration. "We are servants of the Maharaja [Krishnanarayan]," they said, "we came from other countries and took service with him whereby we maintain our dependents. This is the obligation for the salt we eat—in whose service we ever enter we act according to his pleasure. We have not plundered the country of Assam under sanction of the Company's name. Having entered into the service of one government what business have we to assume the name of another? Had we, under the sanction of the Company's name, ravaged the country of Assam undoubtedly we should be punished." They alleged that Daniel Raush had thrown impediments in the way of their allowance by asking Krishnanarayan not to give them pay, and that their wages were stopped accordingly. About the attack made on the boats of Raush and the Assam vakils on June 30, 1792, the Burkendazes alleged the provocation to have been first given by Raush himself. According to their version Raush came that day at about 12 o'clock with 2,000 Assamese and 500 or 600 sepoys and attacked them when some were washing and some eating. They left their meals, made themselves ready and stood to oppose the force under Raush. They then addressed Raush,—"You are a European, why do you come thus hostilely against us?" Raush then ordered his men to open fire upon the Burkendazes by which many of the latter were killed or wounded. The sequal can be better told in the language of the Burkendazes, —"Upon this we also taking the name of the Thakurani [Kali] fired, and after one or two discharges all the Assamese and Sepoys were put to flight. Your Lordship [Governor-General] is ruler of the country. We are poor subjects."[88]

87. Douglas to Cornwallis, July 14, Beng. Pol. Cons., Aug. 20, 1792, No. 15.

88. "Arzie of the Russauladars, Zemmadars and Burkandauzes in the Service of Rajah Kishen Narain, Rajah of Dering," July 22, Beng. Pol. Cons., Sept., 10, 1792, No. 48.

Swargadeo Gaurinath Singha's petition for aid: In the meantime Gaurinath Singha, Raja of Assam, had written to Lord Cornwallis asking for the despatch of a battalion of sepoys to his assistance. This letter was received by the Government on August 9, and taken into consideration in the Board's meeting of September 10, 1792. The Raja referred to the circumstances of Krishnanarayan's revolt, and expressed his desire to reinstate the prince in the Rajaship of Darrang and cited Raush as a witness to his wishes. The Raja pointed out the devastation caused by the Burkendazes who had declared their intention of 'taking Assam by the sword.' Gaurinath requested Lord Cornwallis to recall the Burkendazes from Assam undertaking to pay for the troops who might be sent for that purpose.[89] The Assam Raja's letter was delivered to the Government at Fort William by his vakils Bikaram Majindar Barua, the Kanungo of Gauhati, Bishnunarayan, the nominal Raja of Darrang, Dattaram Khound and Bhaba Kataki.[90]

The Governor-General did not take any action on the petition of Gaurinath Singha waiting probably to see the effect of the orders of July 18 in pursuance of which the Collector of Rungpoor had attached the property of Hari Sing Hazari, Baug Roy, Durjan Sing, Mattoo Sing, Hurdy Roy, the only Burkendazes who were inhabitants of Rungpore. But their value being small this measure did not induce the Burkendazes to quit Assam. They continued to commit the greatest enormities and amassed plunder to a considerable extent. The prospect of partaking of the plunder of Assam operated on them more powerfully than the dread of anything they would be liable to suffer from their contempt of the Company's orders. They also surmised that no vigorous measure would be adopted to compel their obedience. In the meantime, fresh hordes of Burkendazes, hearing of the fortunes made by their compatriots, had entered into Assam through Bhutan, Bijni and other unfrequented routes. Krishnanarayan was able to inform the Collector of Rungpore that he had about 2,500 Jemadars and Burkendazes in his service in the perganahs of Darrang and Kamrup.[91]

On September 10, 1792, John Lumsden, Collector of Rungpore, wrote to Government describing the real situation in Assam

89. Assam Raja to Cornwallis, undated, Beng. Pol. Cons., Sept. 10, 1792, No. 49.

90. Gunabhiram Barua, *Assam Buranji*, p. 153; Robinson, *Descriptive Account of Assam*, p. 172; *Tungkhungia Buranji*, p. 131.

91. Krishnanarayan to Lumsden, Sept. 16, Beng. Pol. Cons., Oct. 26, 1792, No. 17.

and recommending compliance with the Raja's petition for military assistance. The Collector apprised the Government of the futility of pacific measures against the Burkendazes. He pointed out the extreme imbecility of the Assam government which could not oppose the Burkendazes when their numbers were far short of what they were at present. He referred to the total annihilation of Bengal's trade with Assam occasioned by the disturbances of the Burkendazes who, in his opinion, were not entitled to any more respectable appellation than robbers. "I do not think," concluded Lumsden, "It is to be expected that they [Assam government] will be able to free the country from them [Burkendazes] with any force they can themselves command while anything exists in it capable of exciting or gratifying their avarice."[92] In support of his recommendation to adopt coercive measures against the Burkendazes Lumsden enclosed three letters written by Daniel Raush from Gauhati.

In Raush's letter to Henry Douglas, Commissioner of Cooch Behar, dated July 16, 1792, he described the defiant attitude of the Burkendazes manifested on several occasions during his negotiations with Krishnanarayanan culminating in their attack upon his boats on June 30. He hoped the Governor-General would send a battalion of sepoys to expel the Burkendazes out of Assam, "otherwise," he added, "the Assam country will become an entire anarchy."[93]

In his second letter to Douglas, dated August 19, 1792, Raush referred to the Assam Raja's anxiety to receive a favourable answer from the Governor-General to his application for assistance of which the Raja was in great need as Krishnanarayan and his adherents with all the Bengal Burkendazes were close and daily threatening to take possession of South Gauhati, the temporary headquarters of the Assam government. Raush had wanted to leave Gauhati and go back to Goalpara, but the Assam Raja and all his Durbar entreated him to stay, otherwise they said they would be obliged with all the inhabitants to abandon the place and leave it to the mercy of the Burkendazes and go along with him to Goalpara.[94]

In his letter to Lumsden, Collector of Rungpore, dated September 5, 1792, Raush referred to the depredations of the Burkendazes and their daily threat to take possession of Gauhati, notwith-

92. Lumsden to Cornwallis, Sept. 10, 1792, Beng. Pol. Cons., Sept. 19, 1792, No. 13.

93. Raush to Douglas, July 16, Beng. Pol. Cons., Sept. 19, 1792, No. 14.

94. Raush to Douglas, Aug. 19, Beng. Pol. Cons., Sept. 19, 1792, No. 16.

standing their having received three perwanahs to quit Assam. The Raja and his ministers would not permit Raush to leave Gauhati before the arrival of an answer to their request for help. "And I trust and hope in God," wrote Daniel Raush, "that his Lordship will be pleased to comply with the Raja's application to assist him with a military force, or this country will unavoidably be subject to an anarchy which must be attended with the destruction of the trade very prejudicial to Bengal in general and the utter ruin of myself and my associates." Raush then pointed out the menace to the peace of the Company's territories on the borders of Bengal occasioned by the continuance of the troubles in Assam. The plunder of the Assam Choky being imminent, Goalpara, opposite to it, was therefore in danger of being robbed accompanied by the destruction of its inhabitants. In the opinion of Raush these were sufficient reasons to induce the Governor-General to comply with the Assam Raja's request to keep peace on the borders of Bengal and save his subjects from destruction.[95] Raush also wrote a letter to Messrs. Colvin, Bazette & Co. of Calcutta on behalf of the Assam Raja.[96]

On September 17, after his return to Goalpara, Raush addressed a letter directly to Lord Cornwallis recounting his own misfortunes in the Assam trade caused by the disturbances of the Burkendazes. He pointed out that the deputation of a small military force to the assistance of the Assam Raja would bring the country of Assam with the trade to its former flourishing state, prevent any further disturbance on the frontiers of Bengal, and "save Mr. Cotters, Mr. Brydie and myself from another ruin." He concluded by assuring the Governor-General that compliance with the Assam Raja's request "would be attended with great advantage to Bengal in general.[97]

The petition of the Assam Raja and the letters of Lumsden and Raush were sufficient to convince the Government of the gravity of the situation in Assam.

95. Raush to Lumsden, Sept. 5, Beng. Pol. Cons., Sept. 19, 1792, No. 15.

96. Robinson, *Descriptive Account of Assam*, p. 172.

97. Raush to Cornwallis, Sept. 17, Beng. Pol. Cons., Oct. 3, 1792, No. 18. This letter of Raush was received after the Board's decision on Sept., 19 to depute Capt. Welsh to Assam.

Appendix to Part III of Chapter VI

DANIEL RAUSH AND THE GREEK MERCHANTS

In his exertions for the Assam Raja in which his own interests were involved Daniel Raush created enemies in several quarters. After the withdrawal of the Company's monopoly of the Assam salt trade Raush had tried his utmost to repair his fortunes, but he was subjected to heavy losses "through the intrigues and unmerchantlike conduct of nine Greeks from Dacca with the Assam Baruas."[1] He had made heavy investments in the Assam trade and it was impossible for him, now advanced in age, to seek new fields for his commercial ventures. His outstanding balances from Assam merchants amounted to 70,000 rupees, and it was only after the restoration of stability and order in Assam that he could expect to recover his balances and reap the benefits of the Assam trade which he had obtained from the Baruas at the Assam Choky. To achieve this object he had conducted negotiations with Krishnanarayan for an amicable settlement, and on the failure of his attempts in that direction he wrote a number of letters to the authorities in Bengal for the despatch of a force to quell the Burkendaz freebooters. He had in the beginning encouraged Krishnanarayan in his attempt to recover possession of Darrang, and had taken him from Assam, given him shelter at Goalpara and conducted him to Cooch Behar. But by subsequently promoting the interests of the Assam Raja he incurred the enmity of Krishnanarayan and his chief adviser Haradatta and the Burkendazes. His boats were attacked and he had to fly for life leaving his vessels containing merchandise to the value of half a lakh of rupees. Krishnanarayan's sentiments found expression in his letter to Lumsden, where he said,—"Mr. Raush having come and joined the Assamese has in consequence thereof plundered and depredated the perganas of Darrang and Kamrup my country and they are now destroying it. Mr. Raush without rhyme or reason supports them [Assamese] and they have begun to oppress me."[2] Again wrote Krishnanarayan,—"In former days I used to call

1. Raush to Cornwallis, Sept. 17, Beng. Pol. Cons., Oct. 3, 1792, No. 18.
2. Krishnanarayan to Lumsden, Sept. 15, Beng. Pol. Cons., Nov. 26, 1792, No. 9.

Mr. Raush my father. He encouraged and then deceived me."[3] Neither Krishnanarayan, nor Haradatta, nor the Burkendazes could forgive Raush for deserting their cause however justifiable his motives might have been for thus transferring his political sympathies.[4]

In the field of commerce Raush had his enemies amongst the rival Greek merchants of whom he had become the eye-sore for again establishing himself at Goalpara with the virtual monopoly of the Assam trade. The number of Greek merchants dispersed in India did not exceed 50 or 55. Their chief was Constantino Parthenio who resided at Calcutta being deputed by the Patriarch of Constantinople for ministering to the several members of the Greek Apostolic Church of Asia. He erected the Greek church in Calcutta in 1780-81 with "the private munificence and bounty" of Warren Hastings who headed the subscription list with a donation of 2,000 rupees. The Supreme Board had granted to the Greeks the liberty of a free and uninterrupted trade in Sylhet. Parthenio in partnership with Govin Hamilton and other Greeks had engaged in the Sylhet trade speculating largely in the *chunam* or lime branch.[5] Robert Lindsay, the Company's Resident at Sylhet, was himself a *chunam* merchant. His salary and his emoluments were all paid in cowries for there was not a single rupee in the district. "But for this [*chunam*] traffic," wrote Lindsay to John Shore, Acting President of the Committee of Revenue, on September 9, 1783, "I would not purchase the necessaries of life in other parts of the country." In order to oust Lindsay from the *chunam* business the Greek merchants submitted repeated complaints to the Government alleging obstructions in their trade by Lindsay till he had to accommodate the matter with Parthenio. "But," wrote Lindsay, "he [Parthenio] and his partners are too unreasonable, and nothing will content them but my resigning the

3. Krishnanarayan to Ensign Thomas Wood, Jan. 30, Beng. Pol. Cons., Feb. 15, 1793, No. 17.

4. In connection with the sides taken by the French and the English in the conflict between the Peguans and the Burmese in 1754, Sir Arthur Phayre says,—"It is not to be wondered at that European traders, entirely dependent on the favour of the native rulers, should, when a struggle for empire was going on, be in perplexity as to the side they ought to take, nor is it surprising that the native authorities, seeing the fluctuating conduct of the Europeans, should accuse them of treachery."—*History of Burma*, 1883, p. 159.

5. Parthenio's three letters to Warren Hastings, in *Sylhet District Records*, Vol. I, pp. 145, 170, 178. The first and third letters are undated. The second is dated Oct. 22, 1783; and Firminger's note on p. 145-*n*.

business in their favour." Lindsay described the Greek merchants as "itinerant traders and people of the lowest classes."[6]

On Hugh Baillie's appointment to Goalpara in 1787 the Greek merchants, who had been employed by Lindsay in transporting his *chunam,* applied for the contract for carrying the Company's salt from Narayangunge to Goalpara. After Baillie's departure from that place in 1790 the Greeks attempted to obtain the monopoly of the Assam trade from the Baruas. Having failed to secure it they adopted the old device of ousting the successful rival by means of allegations and complaints. Rudram, one of the two Duaria Baruas or trade agents of the Assam government, owed rupees 22,000 to Raush and an equally large amount to Alexander Paniotty, a Greek merchant, who ordinarily lived at Dacca and conducted his Assam trade through his agent at Jugighopa named Alexander Kyriakos.[7] The latter offered to free Rudram from his debts on condition he undertook to make over the monopoly of the Assam trade to the Greeks if it would be wrested from the hands of Raush. The Greeks then attempted to bring to prominence certain actions of Raush which went against the interests of the Assam Raja and militated against the conditions on which he was trading at Goalpara under the protection of the Company's Government.

Advantage was taken of Raush's association with Krishnanarayan in the earlier part of 1791 when he had brought that prince from Assam together with Bishnunarayan, Amritnarayan and Mandhan Sonapuria Barua. On June 3, 1791, two letters were delivered to the Government of Bengal, one from the Raja of Assam and the other from Joyram Barua, the Raja's agent at Goalpara. They were brought by Bishnunarayan and Rammohan Ghose who introduced themselves as vakils of the Assam Raja. The letter from the Raja complained of a hostile incursion into Assam made by Raush wherein he plundered the district of Darrang from where he carried away Krishnanarayan as prisoner together with Mandhan Barua, put to death many of the inhabitants and possessed himself of plunder to a large extent. The Raja requested that the prisoners might be released and the plundered property be returned. Joyram Barua's letter,[8] besides confirming the Raja's representation, com-

6. R. Lindsay to John Shore, Sept. 9, 1783, in *Sylhet District Records,* Vol. I, pp. 164-65.

7. A Kyriakos was Paniotty's agent at Jugighopa from February 19, 1791, to October 14, 1791, and was succeeded by Angelo Ducas. They were both at Jugighopa on June 25, 1792, Beng. Pol. Cons., July 18, 1792, No. 10.

8. Joyram was perhaps one of the two Duaria Baruas in June 1791, the other being Rudram. Chandram succeeded Joyram in the beginning of 1792.

plained of the force used by Raush to obtain from him an agreement excluding all other merchants from the Assam trade. The Barua requested the Government to cancel the agreement so that he might be at liberty to deal with other merchants. The Collector of Rungpore was directed to make enquiries into the allegations, and Charles Stuart wrote assuring letters to the Assam Raja. In July 1791 Krishnanarayan was examined by the Commissioner of Cooch Behar when he admitted the circumstances of his being brought by Raush to Goalpara and Cooch Behar on promises of help. Krishnanarayan, however, declared that he was not a complainant against Raush.[9]

Krishnanarayan's entrance into Assam with the Burkendazes followed by his forcible occupation of Darrang and North Gauhati was used by Raush's enemies in instituting a second complaint against him. On February 16, 1792, a letter addressed to the Governor-General was received from Rudram and Chandram Duaria Baruas complaining that notwithstanding the reference of the petitions of June 1791 to the Collector of Rungpore he had not made any enquiry into the affair. They then added that Raush and Lt. Crump with 1700 or 1800 Burkendazes and a Subedar of the Company with 50 or 60 sepoys had entered the Assam territories plundering and committing devastations, that the Assamese had surrounded them, but considering that they were people belonging to the Company they were released.[10]

The Collector of Rungpore, at the instance of the Board, investigated into both the complaints. The Baruas refused to come to Rungpore to substantiate the charges before the Collector. They insisted on his coming to Jugighopa or to Goalpara where alone, in their opinion, proper enquiry could be made and witnesses produced. Mandhan Sonapuria Barua admitted that he had accompanied Raush to Goalpara of his own accord being afraid of being killed by the Buragohain who had put his wife and daughter in irons and robbed him of all his property.[11]

Lt. Crump denied the charges. "The villainous audacity of these poeple," said he, "I believe, is unprecedented. If these shameful falsities are admitted with impunity no officer will be able to perform his duty with any kind of satisfaction. Therefore I look

9. Abstract of correspondence between N. B. Edmonstone, Actng Persian Translator, and Lumsden, Beng. Pol. Cons., June 8, 1792, No. 9.

10. Beng. Pol. Cons., March 16, No. 12, and June 8, 1792, No. 9.

11. Mandhan Barua to Lumsden, undated, Beng. Pol. Cons., March 16, 1792, No. 13.

to Government for support and protection against such infamous aspersions." He pointed out that his name had been inserted at the instigation of Paniotty and Kyriakos with a view to give trouble and render his situation disagreeable.[12]

Daniel Raush characterised the Barua's representations "as nothing but fabricated falsities." He referred to Rudram's admission before two men of character that he had acted wrongly towards Raush in listening to the persuasions of Paniotty's agents to make such complaints without authority from the Assam Raja, and that the agents had promised them a great deal and performed nothing. Raush concluded his reply with an appeal to Government for satisfaction for the severe loss he had sustained since 1788 through the malicious manoeuvres of 'a certain enemy' and Paniotty and his agents.[13]

Some significant facts are revealed in the letters written in this connection by Paniotty and Kyriakos to the Assam Baruas and the Paniphukan, the admiral of the Ahom fleet, during the period from March 30, 1791, to March 24, 1792. They were written mainly to keep alive the Baruas' antagonism towards Raush, and to convince them of the exertions made by the Greek merchants at Calcutta on behalf of the Assam Raja to bring Krishnanarayan and Raush to punishment. The only reward which the Greeks wanted for their labours was the privilege of trading with the Baruas to the exclusion of other Bengal merchants if possible.

On March 30, 1791, Kyriakos wrote to the Paniphukan at Gauhati asking him to send a petition with two vakils stating the particulars of the oppressions and depredations committed by Raush. Kyriakos promised to have the complaints properly lodged before the Governor-General and to obtain redress in the matter. He concluded the letter by repeating his wishes to obtain the Assam Choky trade. Accordingly, Rudram and Chandram Baruas sent three letters of complaint with their agent Rammohan Ghose, one to the Governor-General, one to Hugh Baillie and the third to an unknown gentleman in Calcutta. Rammohan first proceeded to Dacca and then to Calcutta, and submitted the letters to the Government and the other two gentlemen. He waited in Calcutta till he received Government's reply to the Assam petition. He then

12. Crump to Lumsden, Jan. 25 and March 6, 1792, in Beng. Pol. Cons. of March 16, No. 14, and April 27, 1792, No. 21 respectively.

13. Raush to Lumsden, March 7, Beng. Pol. Cons., Ap. 27, 1792, No. 22. It is not known who this 'enemy' was,—probably Hugh Baillie.

proceeded to Dacca where he obtained some money from Paniotty. Hamilton and Paniotty wrote a letter to the Baruas on June 27, 1791, assuring them of the speedy settlement of their business at Calcutta. For further particulars of the transaction the Baruas were advised to ask Rammohan. On July 9, 1791, Kyriakos informed the Paniphukan that Raush had been personally exercising his influence at Calcutta to obtain for Krishnanarayan assistance in men and arms to take Assam, and that the Greeks would not permit it to be effected. The Paniphukan was assured that he would soon receive a letter of encouragement from Hugh Baillie and hear of Raush and Krishnanarayan being summoned to attend the Calcutta Adawlut. "Other people", wrote Kyriakos, "often expending 10 or 15 thousand rupees would be unable to obtain such business." He then concluded by saying that his masters would be more enthused in the matter if they heard of the Baruas' entering into business with the Greeks.

On September 4, 1791, Kyriakos entered into an agreement with Rudram and Chandram binding himself to obtain them ample justice within the space of two months "for the violences, robberies and murders committed by Raush in the Baruas' country," and that he would procure the release of the persons carried off by the Darrang Raja together with the effects of which they were plundered. Kyriakos's promise was based on the condition of his getting the Kandahar or Assam Choky trade. He bound the Baruas not to make friends with Raush within the two months. In March 1792 Paniotty despatched 3,000 maunds of salt to the Baruas for disposal in the Assam market.

Paniotty was examined by the Commissioner of Dacca on June 25, 1792, and Kyriakos by the Collector of Rungpore on September 28. It appeared that Kyriakos was the prime mover in the matter. At the end of his examination the Collector of Rungpore asked,—"Then it appears from your answers that you wrote all those letters for the purpose of procuring the trade of the Kandahar Choky." To this Kyriakos replied, "Exactly so. I wanted that I should trade as well as other people."[14]

The Board passed orders on the conduct of Alexander Kyriakos in their meeting of October 12, 1792. They concluded that Kyriakos had been a 'stirring agent' in the disputes in Goalpara and its neighbourhood and that he had encouraged complaints and misre-

14. The examination of Paniotty in Beng. Pol. Cons., July 18, 1792, Nos. 9 and 10; and that of Kyriakos in the Cons. of Oct. 12, 1792, No. 4, with abstracts of the letters.

presentations to the Government of Bengal, and fraudulently imposed on the Assam officers by promising to procure for them an order of the Government in return for the trade of the Kandahar Choky. Kyriakos's further presence at Jugighopa being considered undesirable the Governor-General directed the Collector of Rungpore to send him to Calcutta.[15]

From the resolution of the Board it is evident that they refrained from giving any opinion on the truth of the complaints. It comes out from the correspondence and examination of Paniotty and Kyriakos that they took advantage of the existing materials for complaint and merely promised to obtain speedy redress by exercising their influence at Calcutta. The Paniphukan was too responsible an officer to send the Baruas to Calcutta on a false or frivolous complaint against Raush. Krishnanarayan had himself admitted the encouragement given to him by Raush. In the past he was not totally innocent of violence against Assam and its officers. In 1779 Raush with Dow and Lear had set guards on the Assam Baruas for which they were warned by Charles Purling, Collector of Rungpore. In 1782 Raush was accused of having invaded Assam. The employment of Raush by the Assamese to mediate with Krishnanarayan on their behalf does not prove his innocence in the past. On the other hand it presupposes Raush's hold on Krishnanarayan in view of his previous service to that prince. "We resemble a loaded boat when sunk. What are we to do"? said the Assam Raja; and as such he would, in his emergency, take the help of Raush irrespective of any considerations of his past conduct. Though Raush refuted the accusation ascribing it to the jealousy of the Greek merchants he cannot be absolved of the part he played as a supporter of Krishnanarayan's designs against the Assam Raja in their initial stage. "If he [Raush] had not plundered in person", said Glazier, "he had by countenancing one Krishna Narayan, precipitated matters in Assam, and necessitated the occupation of Assam by British forces."[16]

15. Beng. Pol. Cons., Oct. 12, 1792, No. 4.
16. Glazier's *Rungpore*, ed. Firminger, p. 48.

CHAPTER VII

TENTATIVE INTERVENTION: CAPT. WELSH'S EXPEDITION

PART I

CORNWALLIS'S INTERVENTION IN ASSAM

Government's decision to depute Capt. Welsh: The petition of the Assam Raja and the recommendations of the Collector of Rungpore and of Raush produced the desired effect. On September 19, 1792, Lord Cornwallis informed the Collector of Government's intention to depute Capt. Thomas Welsh to Assam in order to acsertain the real situation of the Raja with regard to the Bengal Burkendazes. The Government proposed to judge from Welsh's report as to the possibility of terminating the disputes without force or whether it would be necessary to send a body of troops to the Assam Raja's assistance. Capt. Welsh was to be accompanied by a common escort for his own guard.[1]

On September 29 Lord Cornwallis issued orders directing three companies of sepoys, of 60 privates each, of the 16th Native Infantry with their European officers, and a detachment of the same strength from the 27th Native Infantry to proceed to Goalpara. A detachment of one Cossob and 10 Lascars from the artillery at the Presidency was to proceed with the three companies of the 16th N. I. from Barrackpore for taking care of the ammunition that would be sent for Assam service. Each company was furnished with a Sergeant Major, one Sarkar, one native doctor, and the usual number of smiths, firemen, hammermen, armourers, carpenters, sicklegurs, sailmakers, chucklers, bildars, lascars and doolies. Lt. Robert MacGregor was appointed Adjutant to the Detachment and Assistant to the Deputation, and Ensign Thomas Wood of the Corps of Engineers as Surveyor.[2] Dr. John Peter Wade who had served with Capt. Welsh in the Mahratta wars under General Goddard and attained some distinction by his medical treatises and knowledge of Persian was ordered to accompany the detachment

1. Members of Council to Lumsden, Sept. 19, Beng. Pol. Cons., Sept. 19, 1792, No. 17.

2. General Orders by Cornwallis, Sept. 29, Beng. Pol. Cons., Oct. 3, 1792, No. 17-A.

as Assistant Surgeon.[3] The whole detachment consisting of about 550 men were to wait at Goalpara where they would receive orders from Captain Welsh.

Objects of the Assam expedition: The objects which impelled Lord Cornwallis to send a deputation to Assam were stated in his minute delivered to the Board in their meeting of October 3, 1792. The application of the Raja of Assam was considered along with that of the Raja of Nepal who had solicited the Company's assistance against the invasion of the Emperor of China in revenge for the injuries which the Raja had done to the people of Tibet. "After considering the requests of the two Rajahs [of Nepal and Assam]", said Lord Cornwallis, "and the commercial advantages that Bengal may obtain by a friendly and open intercourse with both countries, it appears to me that it will be no less political than humane in us to interfere our good offices to establish peace and tranquillity in those quarters." In view of the friendly relations with the Emperor of China Lord Cornwallis held that it was only by conciliatory negotiations that assistance could be rendered to the Raja of Nepal in his present situation. The difficulty of transporting supplies to Nepal and to Tibet precluded the despatch of a military force for the relief of the Nepal Raja. The Governor-General therefore decided to send a friendly deputation to Nepal under Captain William Kirkpatrick.[4]

In the opinion of Lord Cornwallis there was not the same necessity for caution in the Company's interference in Assam; and as the disturbances there were "merely of an internal nature and principally occasioned by gangs of vagabonds belonging to Bengal" the Governor-General thought that his Government was "particularly called upon to make some exertions to quell them." He considered six companies of sepoys commanded by "an active and prudent officer" would be adequate for the purpose.

Lord Cornwallis pointed out the prevailing ignorance about the interior parts of Nepal and Assam which he ascribed to the reluctance of their Rajas to admit the English into their countries.

3. J. P. Wade's three medical books,—(1) *Select Evidences of a Successful Method of Treating Fever and Dysentery in Bengal*, London, 1791, dedicated to Warren Hastings; (2) *Paper on the Prevention and Treatment of the Disorders of Seamen and Soldiers in Bengal*, London, 1793, dedicated to the Court of Directors; (3) *Nature and Effects of Emetics, Purgatives, Mercurials and Low Diet in Disorders of Bengal and Similar Latitudes*, London, 1793, dedicated to his brother Charles Wade M.D.

4. For an account of Kirkpatrick's deputation to Nepal see his *Account of the Kingdom of Nepaul*, pub. in 1811.

Lord Cornwallis therefore directed "that no pains or attention should be spared to avail ourselves of so favourable an opportunity to obtain good surveys, and to acquire every information that may be possible both of the population and of the manners and customs, of trade and manufactures, and natural productions of countries with which it must ever be our interests to maintain the most friendly communication."[5] The Court of Directors were informed of the deputation of Capt. Welsh to Assam in the Bengal Government's despatch of October 14, 1792. Lord Cornwallis drew the attention of Henry Dundas, President of the Board of Control, to this measure in a private letter where he referred to the "favourable opportunities of sending persons to Nepaul and Assam."[6]

Capt. Welsh, the commander of the expedition: Capt. Welsh who was selected to command the Assam expedition was an officer of considerable military reputation. He had enjoyed the esteem and confidence of two successive Governors-General, Warren Hastings and Lord Cornwallis. "Welsh is an honourable and worthy fellow", wrote Lord Cornwallis to Henry Dundas, "and will do no wrong."[7]

Welsh who had joined the Bengal Army as a Cornet in 1769 first came into prominence by his gallantry in the Mahratta campaigns under General Goddard in 1779-1781. Lt. Welsh won a decisive victory over the Mahrattas led by Gunnes Punt in an engagement on May 17, 1780. In this connection General Goddard brought to the notice of the Bengal Government "the spirited and well-judged conduct of Lt. Welsh" and "the splendour of his action and the peaceful security which it has given to the new-acquired Pergunnahs."[8]

This was followed by the capture of Parneiro, a fort situated on a high hill. It was defended by a garrison of about 400 men, who finding Lt. Welsh determined to hold out, surrendered into the hands of the English. "This material piece of service", wrote General Goddard, "has completely eradicated every trace of Mahratta Power in this neighbourhood and destroyed even the most distant hope he could have of giving further disturbance to

5. Cornwallis's minute, Beng. Pol. Cons., Oct. 3, 1792, No. 17.

6. Cornwallis to Dundas, Oct. 15, 1792, Ross, *Cornwallis Correspondence*, Vol. II, p. 181.

7. Cornwallis to Dundas, Dec. 10, 1792, Ross, *Cornwallis Correspondence*, II, p. 186.

8. Philippart, *East India Military Calendar*, 1823, Vol. I, p. 72, General Goddard to Bengal Government, May 27, 1780.

our new possessions." Lt. Welsh then captured two inferior forts, Arzun Ghur and Under Ghur, the former being surrounded by a district yielding a revenue of one lakh of rupees. These acquisitions placed the English in entire possession of the sea-coast from Cambait to Dumaun comprehending a tract of nearly 150 square miles.[9]

In January 1781 Welsh was promoted to a Captaincy. In June 1784 Warren Hastings presented a sword to Capt. Welsh as 'a lasting testimony' of the Governor-General's esteem for his merit. "It is not of itself of any value", wrote Hastings to Welsh on this occasion, "but I flatter myself that there are many to whom such a pledge of the estimation in which I hold your character will at least prove of no disservice to it; especially if it is understood that you are known to me by no personal recommendation, nor by the habits of society, but only by public service."[10]

In 1789 Capt. Welsh was on leave in England.[11] This he had to do, according to the rules of his service, by resigning his commission in India.[12] In March 1790 Welsh asked the Court of Directors to make the necessary application to His Majesty's War Office for his commission as Captain in the Company's service on the Bengal establishment previous to his embarkation.[13] The Directors, in their despatch to the Bengal Government, dated April 28, 1790, recommended Capt. Welsh's reappointment to a command in the Cavalry on the Bengal establishment where "he had served so long with the approbation of his superiors," and to which rank he was entitled "by his gallantry and good conduct."[14]

After his return to India Welsh was reappointed to his rank in the Bengal Infantry. Soon after he was placed in charge of a detachment in the war with Tipu under the direct command of Lord Cornwallis. On December 23, 1791, Capt. Welsh, obtained possession of Ramgheri, a very important post on the direct road

9. Philippart, *East India Military Calendar*, I, pp. 72-73, General Goddard to Bengal Government, June 20, 1780.

10. Philippart, *East India Military Calendar*, I, p. 73. Hastings to Welsh, June 10, 1784.

11. Misc. Letters Received, 1789, Capt. Welsh to Court of Directors, Dec. 9, 1789.

12. *Shore's Letters*, ed. Furber, Introduction, p. 11.

13. Misc. Letters Received, 1790, Capt. Welsh's memorial to the Court of Directors, March 1, 1790.

14. Court's Letter to Bengal, Ap. 28, 1790, paragraph 9; also that of May 19, 1790, paragraph 2.

from Bangalore to Seringapatam.[15] Lord Cornwallis recorded in his General Orders of December 27, 1791, "that the complete success of the plan [reduction of Ramgheri and Sheriegheri] is primarily to be attributed to Capt. Welsh's judicious conduct, for which he [Governor-General] desires that he [Welsh] will accept of his warmest acknowledgements."[16]

At the end of the war with Tipu his second and third sons, Princes Abdul Khalic and Moaz Addeen, aged 10 and 8 respectively, were sent as hostages for the conclusion and fulfilment of the treaty. They arrived in Cornwallis's camp near Seringapatam on February 26, 1792.[17] On March 14, Capt. Welsh was appointed to command the guard of honour with the hostages on the departure of the guards sent with the princes by their father. Capt. Welsh encamped with the princes one mile in the rear of British headquarters.[18] Lord Cornwallis returned to Fort William in August 1792, and passed orders next month deputing Capt. Welsh to Assam.

Capt. Welsh's familiarity with Southern India words acquired during his service in the Mahratta and Mysore wars led to their occasional use in his letters to Government despatched from Assam. The Sannyasi raiders in Assam are called by him *Gossains,* the term applied to such freebooters among the Mahrattas.[19] Even the rebel chief Boragi Raja who was expelled by Welsh from Gauhati is called Burgi Raja and designated as a Gosain.[20] The name of the Assamese envoy Bhola Nath is transliterated by Welsh as 'Bousla Nauth'.[21] For boats he uses the word *Seringahs* which is a variant of the Tamil word *chelingo.*[22]

In March 1794 during his stay in Assam Captain Welsh was promoted to the rank of a Major. In January 1798 he was made

15. Lord Cornwallis to Sir John Kennaway, Dec. 24, 1791, *Cornwallis Correspondence*, II, p. 130.

16. Lord Cornwallis's General Orders, Camp Magri, Dec. 27, 1791, in *E.I.M.C.*, I, p. 74, where the reduction of another fort Sherie Ghery is mentioned. Ramgheri and Sherie Ghery or Shivanaghury were hill forts 13 miles west of Savandroog, *History of the Madras Army*, by Lt. Col. W. J. Wilson, Vol. II, pp. 218-19.

17. Cornwallis to Sir Charles Oakeley, Feb. 26, 1792. *Cornwallis Correspondence*, II, p. 151.

18. Malcolm, *Political History of India*, II, Appendix I, pp. xxi-xxii.

19. Beng. Pol. Cons., Dec. 17, 1792, No. 49; J. M. Ghose's *Sannyasi and Fakir Raiders in Bengal*, pp. 16-17.

20. Beng. Pol. Cons., Nov. 30, 1792, No. 31.

21. Beng. Pol. Cons., June 2, 1794, No. 23.

22. Beng. Pol. Cons., May 28, 1794, No. 28.

a Lt. Colonel. He was then in command of the 2nd Regiment of Native Cavalry in which capacity he earned the approbation of Sir James Craig and Lord Mornington, afterwards Marquis of Wellesley, specially for his services in connection with the formation of the Calcutta Militia Cavalry.[23] On Welsh's departure from India in 1799 the gentleman of the Corps presented him a sword "in grateful remembrance of the benefits they received from his attention to their discipline on their first formation."[24]

Welsh was appointed Colonel in May 1800 and placed on the retired list in August of the same year. In 1806 Col. Welsh was a candidate for a seat in the East India Direction. He died on April 11, 1822.[25]

Captain Welsh's march into Assam: Capt. Welsh arrived at Goalpara by boat on November 8, 1792, together with the detachment of the 27th N. I. from Berhampore under charge of Lt. George Dick. He waited at Goalpara for the arrival of the Barrackpore detachment under Lt. John Williams who had taken the route by Dacca. Welsh utilised the interval in collecting information about the affairs of Assam from Raush and from Bishnunarayan, the nominal Raja of Darrang, the latter being sent to Goalpara by the Assam Raja to conduct the detachment to Gauhati.

In the meantime the situation of the Assam Raja had become more critical and it appeared that his life was not safe at Gauhati; Krishnanarayan had consolidated his position at North Gauhati and threatened to attack the Raja's quarters on the opposite side of the river in league with Moamaria rebels. Gaurinath deputed Bikaram Majindar Barua, the Kanungo of Gauhati, to Kandahar Choky where in conjunction with the Baruas, Rudram, Chandram and Krishnanath, he submitted a petition to the Collector of Rungpore on October 13, urging upon the speedy compliance with his request for military assistance.[26]

The Burkendazes themselves had become more obstinate in their disobedience to Government orders. They as well as Krishnanarayan now petitioned the Government for withdrawal

23. Philippart's *E.I.M.C.*, I, pp. 71-75, Sir James Craig's Station Orders, Sept. 10, 1798, and Lord Mornington's Militia Orders, Dec. 21, 1798.

24. Philippart's *E.I.M.C.*, I, pp. 71-75, also Beng. Pub. Cons., Jan. 14, 1799, No. 46, Welsh's letter to G. H. Barlow, Secretary, Jan. 11, 1799, requesting for himself and family a passage home.

25. Philippart's *E.I.M.C.*, I. pp. 71-75.

26. From Bikaram, Rudram, Chandram and Krishnanath to Lumsden, received Oct. 13, Beng. Pol. Cons., Oct. 22, 1792, No. 21.

of the orders for the attachment of their property. Krishnanarayan represented that his interests would suffer by the departure of the Burkendazes. He promised to dismiss his mercenaries when his concerns would be finally adjusted. The Burkendazes asserted that they had entered into Krishnanarayan's service for the purpose of providing for their families who reside in the Company's provinces and for enabling themselves to pay their revenues, "Being in distressed circumstances", said the Burkendazes, "in our own country we have entered into service in another." They pointed out that they would prove themselves *Nimock-harams* or ungrateful if they left the Raja and that their houses would again be attached and they would be held culpable if Krishnanarayan complained to the Company of their desertion. The letters of Krishnanarayan and the Burkendazes were delivered by the former's Vakil Ramkishore Roy to the Collector of Rungpore on October 17 and were forwarded by Government in due course to Capt. Welsh.[27]

There now appeared in the neighbourhood of Gauhati a new leader named Hoidhan, a member of the Ahom Lukhurakhun clan. He had placed himself at the head of a few hundred fishermen of Pakariguri and Chelenghat and opposed the advances of the Burkendazes at several places. He then transferred his support secretly to Krishnanarayan maintaining at the same time a show of loyalty to the Assam Raja. Krishnanarayan emboldened by the assistance of his new allies threatened to attack Gauhati. At midnight on Thursday, November 8, 1792, Gaurinath despatched Pijali Kataki to Bishnunarayan, Bikaram, and the three Kandahar Baruas with a letter asking them to "entertain two, three or four hundred men more and send them to Gauhati with the utmost expedition, they travelling night and day", and to come with the Company's sepoys if they had arrived at Goalpara in the meantime. "We are reduced to greater distress in this place than heretofore", said the Raja, "we now resemble a loaded boat when sunk, what are we to do?" This letter was delivered by Bishnunarayan to Capt. Welsh on November 11, who realising the necessity for taking immediate steps to relieve the Raja proposed to proceed to Gauhati on the arrival of the rest of the detachment.[28]

27. Krishnanarayan to Lumsden, Sept. 18, Burkendazes to Lumsden, same date, Beng. Pol. Cons., Oct. 26, 1792, No. 17.

28. Welsh to Cornwallis, Nov. 12, Beng. Pol. Cons., Nov. 23, 1792, No. 14; Gaurinath's letter in No. 15.

Lt. Williams with the division from Barrackpore joined Capt. Welsh on November 15. On the next morning Capt. Welsh with the entire detachment of six companies started by boat from Gaolpara. Before he embarked into his boat he wrote to Lord Cornwallis,—"The detachment is now crossing the river to proceed to Gowhatty."[29]

Just before boarding his boat Capt. Welsh received Krishnanarayan's letter denying possession or molestation of any other country except Darrang and Kamrup which "had descended from generation to generation to him." The letter, originally addressed to Lumsden, was delivered to Welsh by Ramkishore Roy who had been authorised by Krishnanarayan to represent matters respecting the above perganahs and to act for him in everything else "excepting in the disposal of my [Krishnanarayan's] country and property." Ramkishore accompanied Capt. Welsh to Gauhati.[30]

The distress of Gaurinath at Gauhati thus compelled Welsh to leave Goalpara before he had completed his preparations for the march. He had not yet acquired any accurate information about the state of Assam. The sepoys were furnished with only 15 days' provisions. They were besides about two months in arrears as there was not a single rupee in the Rungpore Treasury; and Capt. Welsh with great difficulty procured 1,000 rupees at Goalpara to enable him "to proceed to save a kingdom."[31]

Capt. Welsh's march into Assam under the orders of the English Government and with the sanction of the Assam Raja constituted a landmark of the highest importance. Previously to this, forcible entries had been made by European traders into Assam; but they were repelled by the Assam government mainly by diplomacy. The aversion of the Assamese people towards strangers was a notorious fact. Now for the first time an authorised body of Englishmen equipped with the up-to-date methods of exploration and investigation entered into the territories of the Swargadeo and thereby broke the barriers which had sequestered Assam for centuries. The event was so significant that on the 16th November, the day of Capt. Welsh's march into Assam, Dr. John Peter Wade wrote to his friend Francis Fowke, living at Wimbledon in England,—"To-day we shall enter a kingdom

29. Welsh to Cornwallis, Nov. 16, Beng. Pol. Cons., Nov. 26, 1792, No. 8.

30. Krishnanarayan to Lumsden, Sept. 15, Beng. Pol. Cons., Nov. 26, 1792, No. 9.

31. Welsh to Lumsden, Dec. 2, Beng. Pol. Cons., Dec. 17, 1792, No. 46; Welsh to Cornwallis, Dec. 4, 1792, *ibid.*, No. 49.

scarcely if ever trodden by Euopeans before."[32] He wrote in the same vein a few years later,—" No Europeans have ever explored or probably ever will explore the province of Assam with the consent of the government of that country."[33]

Gaurinath's flight from Gauhati: In the meantime the events at Gauhati had turned from bad to worse. One Boragi had put himself at the head of Hoidhan's men, and on the pretext of getting assistance from Gaurinath to drive off Krishnanarayan approached the king's residence at South Gauhati and set fire to it. The Boragi then, with the support of Hoidhan, declared himself Raja. No body knew who this Boragi was, and Gaurinath himself admitted his ignorance of the pretender by saying that " the country is in such a state of anarchy and confusion that any man who can pick up 100 desperate fellows sets himself up for a Raja." But it is a fact that the Boragi Raja had been enjoying the shelter and support of Krishnanarayan. Gaurinath and his ministers had become so demoralised by this time that they were seized with terror at the sight of the negligible force of the Boragi Raja. Gaurinath procured a number of small boats and sailed down the Brahmaputra with some of his attendants leaving his family behind, at 2 o'clock in the morning of November 18. The Boragi Raja then occupied Gauhati. The inhabitants of the town began to desert their homes, but the Boragi Raja asked them not to disperse declaring that he was no other than " the nephew of the Swargadeo."[34]

Welsh meets Gaurinath near Nagarbera: On the morning of the 19th November, about three miles below Nagarbera Hill,[35] Capt. Welsh met the Assam boats containing the fugitive Gaurinath Singha. The Captain was not prepared for this sudden change of affairs in the situation of Assam ; and had this circumstance been known to him before his departure from Goalpara he would not have moved from that place without making the Government fully

32. J. P. Wade to Fowke, Nov. 16, 1792, Fowke Mss., India Office, European Mss., Vol. 22, letter No. 95.

33. J. P. Wade, *Geographical Sketch of Assam*, India Office Mss., printed in Martin's *Eastern India*, III, pp. 626-7.

34. Welsh to Cornwallis, Nov. 20, Beng. Pol. Cons., Nov. 30, 1792, No. 31 ; also letter of Nov. 27 in Beng. Pol. Cons., Dec. 17, 1792, No. 47 ; *Tungkhungia Buranji*, pp. 130-31, 179-80.

35. Nagarbera was the extreme limit of the Assam Raja's territories on the south bank of the river Brahmaputra, at a distance of 21 miles east from Goalpara, Lat. 26° 4′ N., Long. 91° 3′ E.

acquainted with it. But having advanced so far Welsh made up his mind to proceed to Gauhati with the utmost expedition. The Raja and his ministers assured Welsh that their friends would join them and their enemies retire on the appearance of the Company's troops at Gauhati. The combined fleet of the detachment and of the Assam Raja began their journey upstream. On the 21st Jainath Barbarua joined the Raja and assured Capt. Welsh that the vassal chiefs of Rani and Luki Duar would do everything in their power to assist their master Gaurinath and procure provisions for the detachment. The party reached Hatimura on the night of November 23. The villages on the south belonged to the Rani Raja who met Capt. Welsh next morning. "He is a fine-looking young man", wrote the Captain to Lord Cornwallis, "his village is full of people and his country beautiful. I am now perfectly easy in my mind having the command of the river with friends and provisions in my rear."[36]

Boragi Raja expelled and Gauhati occupied: On the 24th, at about eight miles from Gauhati a Barua informed Capt. Welsh that it would be possible to surprise the Boragi Raja at Gauhati by proceeding to that place by a circuitous route leading round the Kamakhya Hill. At 11 P.M., Capt. Welsh ordered five companies to parade leaving an officer with one company in charge of the Assam Raja and the boats. At the appointed hour, accompanied by Jainath Barbarua, Bishnunarayan and others of high rank, Capt. Welsh marched at the head of his troops by the route through Dharapur, Jhalukbari and Maligaon villages.[37]

The troops traversed a distance of seven or eight miles over a great deal of paddy till they got to the Kamakhya Hill which was surrounded by a wet ditch. They had to pass several Chokies in the narrow path leading round the hill. The guardsmen, being friends of the Assam Raja, permitted Welsh to proceed unmolested. The passes were so narrow that in the opinion of Welsh a dozen sepoys commanded by a Havildar might have defended against the whole detachment. After having passed Duar-garila, the last Choky at the foot of the Kamakhya Hill, Welsh expected some opposition from the post stationed at a gateway near the Bharalu stream with a wooden bridge over it from which place the town

36. Welsh's diary, Nov. 24, in his letter to Cornwallis, Nov. 27, Beng. Pol. Cons., Dec. 17, 1792, No. 47.

37. Ensign Wood's map of Gauhati and the surroundings, showing among other things, the march of the detachment under Welsh on the night of the 24th Nov. when he took possession of Gauhati, *List of Maps in the India Office Library*, 1878, p. 301.

commenced. This Choky met the troops with lighted torches, and as the sepoys approached they dropped the torches and ran off in all directions without making the least noise.

There was no noise on the part of the sepoys either, as Capt. Welsh was determined to make use of the bayonet only. He pushed on to the Boragi Raja's house which was about a mile and a half further on. Lt. Dick and Lt. MacGregor went in advance with a company and found the pretender and his associates performing some kind of religious ceremony. They offered some resistance in which Lt. Dick got a slight scratch above the eye and a sepoy was wounded with a spear. The rebels made off soon after leaving their women behind. The Boragi Raja made his escape and about 60 of his men were taken prisoners including his minister. The prisoners were delivered afterwards to Gaurinath with recommendations for lenity on such occasions.

The day was spent in encamping under fire from Krishnanarayan's Burkendazes from the other side of the river. The site selected for the encampment of the detachment was a square surrounded by a brick wall about six feet high, with a narrow wet ditch inside and out, with two gateways. This enclosure was situated within 100 yards of the river between the Duar-garila pass and the Bharalu stream. In the centre of the square was a large chopper or thatched building supported by wooden pillars sufficient to hold the entire detachment. There was also room enough in the square for the officers to pitch their tents, so that the whole formed a very convenient place for the use of the detachment.

Gaurinath re-enters Gauhati: Gaurinath Singha arrived with the boats in the evening of the 25th and entered Gauhati in great state. Thus within the space of a few hours the Assam Raja's enemies were routed and South Gauhati recovered. The Raja's precipitate flight from that town and his pompous re-entry seven days later showed that he was neither ashamed of cowardice nor of participation in the unaided triumphs of his allies.

The Boragi was captured afterwards. Under the orders of Gaurinath he was beheaded and the body transfixed to a spear. His lieutenant Hoidhan was strangled to death, and the other prisoners perished by similar punishments.

On the night of November 26 Gaurinath Singha attended by Jainath Barbarua paid a visit to Captain Welsh. The Raja expressed his gratitude for the assistance granted by the Governor-General. The Barbarua referred to the numerous enemies of the

Raja besides the Burkendazes, and enquired whether the force with Welsh would be sufficient for quelling them all. He suggested that the Burkendazes should first be asked to come to Gauhati and then sent to their provinces by promising to write to Government in their favour for restoring their property, which would be a certain way to get them out of the country; otherwise they would run away at the sight of the Company's troops and continue in Assam as the Raja's enemies. Gaurinath asked whether Krishnanarayan would be delivered to the Assam government if he came to Gauhati. Capt. Welsh assured the Raja and the Barbarua that he would write to the Governor-General if, after obtaining a thorough knowledge of the country, he thought more troops would be necessary. He promised to write to the Burkendazes to come to Gauhati and bring in Krishnanarayan also whom he would protect till he received instructions from Government. Capt. Welsh advised Gaurinath to adopt lenient measures against all enemies because his "Government detested every kind of harsh measures." He expressed his desire to do everything to support the Raja, and he "hoped soon to place Maharajah Surge Deo in his capital at Ghurgong [Gargaon]".[38]

Burkendazes expelled from North Gauhati: On November 27 Capt. Welsh sent a perwanah to the Jamadars of the Burkendazes, telling them that he had been sent by the Governor-General for their punishment as they had refused obedience to Government's repeated orders.[39] He asked the Jemadars to come to Gauhati with all their followers within ten days warning them of the severe punishment he would inflict in the event of their disobedience. To this perwanah the Burkendazes sent a prompt reply professing obedience and proposing to submit another petition to Capt. Welsh when all their 'brethren' or comrades would be collected. A letter from Krishnanarayan was also received expressing his satisfaction at the despatch of an 'Amin' or officer from Calcutta to settle his affairs.

Welsh sent a second perwanah to the Burkendazes asking them to carry out their professions of obedience, adding,—"I do not judge of men from their words; do you act as you have written." The Burkendazes wrote back that they would come to Gauhati

38. Welsh to Cornwallis, Nov. 27, Beng. Pol. Cons., Dec. 17, 1792, No. 47.

39. Their names were Durjan Sing, Munsa Ram, Hazari Sing, Hari Sing Hazari, Bang Roy, Dhir Singh, Gaib Sing Barua and Sebak Ram Duffadar, Beng. Pol. Cons., Dec. 17, 1792, No. 48.

when their 'brethren' living at a distance of two or three days' journey would arrive.[40]

It was not difficult for Capt. Welsh to see that Krishnanarayan and his Burkendazes were amusing him with vain promises, and he decided to act with vigour and determination. He was, however, "convinced that Kissna Narain had the strongest inclination to put himself under my [Welsh's] protection, but was prevented by the Jemadars, who had him entirely in their power and obliged him to act in the manner they conceived would best promote their interested views."[41]

Capt. Welsh had, on the day after his arrival at Gauhati, planned in his own mind to attack the Burkendazes. But he waited for the expiry of the time granted to them to offer their submission. Besides, the reluctance shown by the Assamese ministers in supplying the detachment with provisions made him indifferent about making an attempt on Krishnanarayan. In the meantime the Raja, cheered by a letter from Lord Cornwallis,[42] ordered the establishment of a *hat* or market at Gauhati which opened at 12 o'clock on December 1 with a plentiful supply of rice which was all purchased for the detachment. On the same day Raush's first boat arrived with 65 maunds of rice and other articles. On December 4 Welsh wrote to Lord Cornwallis to send a battalion of sepoys to join him at Gauhati and another for being posted at Bijni. Welsh also suggested that Raush should be asked to establish a magazine of grain for the detachment at Goalpara and another at Gauhati. Gaurinath had in his service about 90 Burkendazes who used to inform their friends and relations in Krishnanarayan's employ of the movements and designs of the Assam government. With the concurrence of the Raja Welsh seized them and sent them off to Goalpara and Rungpore.[43]

Having thus provided for future contingencies and purged the Raja's camp of the unreliable elements Capt. Welsh resolved to attack the Burkendazes in their strongholds at North Gauhati. Immediate action was necessary as a fresh band of 200 Burkendazes were coming from the Company's provinces by way of Bijni to join

40. Welsh's perwanahs to Burkendazes and their reply, and Krishnanarayan's letter and reply, Beng. Pol. Cons., Dec. 1, 1792, No. 48.

41. Welsh to Cornwallis, Jan. 1, Beng. Pol. Cons., Jan. 14, 1793, No. 21.

42. Cornwallis to Assam Raja, Nov. 12, Beng. Pol. Cons., Nov. 30, 1792, No. 30, assuring friendship and communicating the deputation of "Capt. Welsh, a gentleman much in my confidence."

43. Welsh to Cornwallis, Dec. 4, Beng. Pol. Cons., Dec. 17, 1792, No. 50.

Krishnanarayan, with the connivance of the Sezawals who passed them all for half a rupee each.

Krishnanarayan's Burkendazes were scattered in the whole area from Manikarneswar Hill at the mouth of the Barnadi which forms the eastern extremity of North Gauhati as well as of Kamrup, upto Sarai Hill where the present Amingaon station of the Assam Railways is situated. There were besides about 700 Burkendazes and a good number of Assamese posted at Aswakranta Hill which had a temple on its top. Krishnanarayan himself was strongly posted at a neighbouring hill with the greater part of his forces. There was a garrison at a third hill at a distance of three miles from Krishnanarayan's encampment, the whole length being covered with Chokies. Capt. Welsh's object was to get possession of Aswakranta Hill which would enable him to keep up a communication across the river and to take his own time to attack Krishnanarayan.

At 4 o'clock in the morning of December 6, 250 rank and file embarked at the foot of Sukreswar Hill in five boats with an officer with his division in each. At daybreak the detachment landed at Aswakranta without being discovered till very near the shore or any one knowing anything of the matter in Gauhati except those concerned. They met with little opposition in gaining the hill, but the enemy came in a body of about 3,000 men to dislodge the new occupants from Aswakranta. The cool and steady conduct of the British officers and their sepoys dispersed them in all directions. Lt. Williams had been given discretionary powers to act as circumstances might occur, and to push on to Krishnanarayan's post if he found a favourable opportunity. Having left a party in possession of the temple on Aswakranta Hill Lt. Williams marched towards Krishnanarayan's garrison and completely routed him from that place. The casualties on the British side were 2 Havildars and 2 sepoys wounded while 20 of the enemy were killed and 36 wounded; several were taken prisoners, and 40 guns were captured. In his despatch to Lord Cornwallis reporting on the engagements of this day Capt. Welsh expressed his indebtedness to "the good conduct of Lt. Williams and the officers and the cool and steady behaviour of the sepoys for this signal victory over superior numbers", to which he added, "the zeal and indefatigable support I experience from Lt. MacGregor on all occasions merits my warmest approbation."[44]

44. Welsh to Cornwallis, Dec. 7, Beng. Pol. Cons., Dec. 21, 1792, No. 19, and Ensign Wood's map of Gauhati and its surroundings.

On receiving the news of the expulsion of the Burkendazes from North Gauhati Lord Cornwallis wrote to Capt. Welsh conveying his satisfaction at the complete success which had attended his "judicious and spirited exertions." Lt. Williams, Lt. MacGregor and all the officers and soldiers were similarly thanked "for the zeal, attention and gallantry which they have manifested in the attack on Krishnanarayan and on every occasion since they entered the country of Assam."[45]

Burkendazes expelled from Kamrup and Darrang: After being driven off from North Gauhati Krishnanarayan with about 1,500 Burkendazes retreated to Haradatta's village Jikeri at a distance of 20 miles, where they were burning and destroying the country. People deserted their villages leaving their paddy-fields which had become ready for harvest. In order to give protection and confidence to the inhabitants and enable them to cut and bring in their crops of grain Capt. Welsh despatched Lt. Williams with 4 companies on December 22 with orders to dislodge the enemy from Jikeri. On the appearance of the detachment the Burkendazes showed some indications of making a stand; but on its approach they made off without allowing it to come within shot of them. Krishnanarayan then entrenched himself in a fort at Kalitakuchi in Darrang near the Bhutan boundary belonging to his cousin Samudranarayan.[46] On December 25 Lt. Williams detached Lt. Dick with one company towards Darrang, but on receiving intelligence that there were only 400 or 500 of the enemy at Kalitakuchi he marched himself against them with his three companies in the evening of the 26th and found the enemy drawn up to receive him. The enemy made a very good stand and wounded 11 sepoys. Of Krishnanarayan's troops about 100 were killed and wounded. They were then pursued by the detachment about 500 yards into Bhutan which was contrary to Capt. Welsh's instructions. When Lt. MacGregor found that they had proceeded so far without knowing the boundaries he wrote to the Bhutanese Jemadar apologising for the transgression and received a very polite answer. Lt. Williams returned to Jikeri on the 27th with the three companies and Lt. Dick remained posted at Rajabari some 20 miles from Jikeri. They both returned to Gauhati in the first week of January 1793.

45. Cornwallis to Welsh, Dec. 22, Beng. Pol. Cons., Dec. 24, 1792.

46. Ensign Wood's map of the route from Gauhati to Kalitakuchi, spelt 'Cooltakoosy' in contemporary records, and also the sketch in Beng. Pol Cons., Jan. 11, 1793, No. 23, p. 688, accompanying Welsh's letter to Cornwallis, Dec. 29, 1792.

After their reverses at Kalitakuchi most of the Burkendazes left Krishnanarayan and the Sannyasis were the only people who remained with him. Krishnanarayan and Haradatta both took shelter in Bhutan with the remnant of their forces. But the Bhutanese officers informed the two fugitive leaders that if they chose to remain there they must do so unattended by any force, and "not induce the English to enter their [Bhutan] country." Gaib Sing Barua, a relation of Krishnanarayan and a Sirdar of the Burkendazes, was accordingly dismissed with all his forces and they returned to Bijni. Krishnanarayan and Haradatta continued to reside at Kaliapani in Khalling Duar, one of the two border straths lying between Darrang and Bhutan proper.

Elated with his success Capt. Welsh wrote to Lord Cornwallis on the 1st January, 1793,—"The first object expected to be effected by the Detachment is now completed, *viz.*, to drive the Bengal Burkundosses out of Assam."[47] The information was only literally true. After being expelled from Assam the greater part of the Burkendazes, instead of returning to Bengal, took refuge in Bhutan and led sporadic incursions into the Assam plains. Krishnanarayan, in spite of the remonstrances of the Bhutanese government, entertained about 400 Burkendazes in his regular pay.

In the meantime Lord Cornwallis had written to Capt. Welsh asking him to inform the Assam Raja that as a preliminary to the detachment taking any further concern about him he must accommodate the differences with Krishnanarayan and restore him to the possession of the rights of his ancestors on condition that the prince should assist in restoring the Raja's authority in other parts of his dominions. "It is not consistent", continued the Governor-General, "with the political line of conduct which has been prescribed for the Company to attempt the conquest of a country from which we have received no injury, nor is it even the wish of this Government to acquire an influence in the internal management of the affairs of Assam." The Governor-General reminded Capt. Welsh of the necessity to confine the Company's temporary interference to the objects which were originally expected to be accomplished by the detachment, *viz., first,* to drive the Bengal banditti out of the country of Assam; and *secondly,* to endeavour by Welsh's presence and countenance to re-establish Gaurinath Singha in the exercise of his lawful authority.[48] Welsh wrote back that the second object could not be effected without interfering

47. Welsh to Cornwallis, Jan. 1, Beng. Pol. Cons., Jan. 14, 1793, No. 21.
48. Cornwallis to Welsh, Dec. 18, Beng. Pol. Cons., Dec. 21, 1792, No. 17.

with the internal management of the country, a measure which he did not think himself authorised to take without being empowered to do it by the Government.[49]

Measures against Gaurinath and his ministers: The difficulties met by Capt. Welsh in his efforts to strengthen the position of the Assam Raja originated principally from the imbecility of the Raja himself. "This poor debilitated man of a Rajah," said Welsh, "is not capable of transacting any business himself. He is either praying or washing; and when he is to be seen he is intoxicated with opium. His ministers are a set of villains all drawing different ways."[50] Gaurinath Singha, then only 27 years old, was reduced to such a state of debility and stupor by the excessive use of opium that he displayed total aversion to business, and was incapable of exerting himself to recover his lost authority. Capt. Welsh had to wait for days together to obtain an interview, and even then sometimes not without compulsion. He was surrounded by a set of crafty priests and dependants who imposed upon his credulity and flattered his vanity, and prevailed upon him to withhold his consent to any measure which would prove prejudicial to their interests though clearly beneficial to himself and his subjects. Welsh had to admit "how difficult it is to settle a country ostensibly governed by one who has absolutely lost the powers of reason."[51] Gaurinath's cruelty was equally abominable, and capital punishments were inflicted for very flimsy offences. "The Raja", said Welsh, "has always a number of executioners with him ready to despatch for their infamous purposes."[52] Capt. Welsh soon realised that the rapid decline of Gaurinath's authority and the universal discontent prevailing in the country were mainly due to the Raja's weakness and cruelty.

Such a monarch so notoriously capricious and devoid of any regard for his interest and character or the welfare of his subjects could easily be used by his ministers for the gratification of their own ends by artfully working on his vanity. They maintained professions of friendship towards the Raja, but engaged themselves secretly in actions which were avowedly prejudicial to the interests of the Raja and his government. Their chief aim was to keep the Raja in a state of subjection, and they opposed every measure proposed by Capt. Welsh if it tended to diminish their own powers.

49. Welsh to Cornwallis, Jan. 1, Beng. Pol. Cons., Jan. 14, 1793, No. 21.
50. Welsh to Cornwallis, Dec. 4, Beng. Pol. Cons., Dec. 17, 1792, No. 50.
51. Welsh to Cornwallis, July 1, Beng. Pol. Cons., July 15, 1793, No. 26.
52. Welsh to Cornwallis, Feb. 2, Beng. Pol. Cons., Feb. 15, 1793, No. 15.

Welsh suspected that without some sort of treachery amongst the ministers Krishnanarayan could never have got possession of North Gauhati.

Jainath Barbarua, the Raja's prime minister at Gauhati, was supposed to be the author of all the misfortunes of Gaurinath; and it was widely believed that he had instigated the Boragi Raja to come in at the head of a gang of thieves to kill his master for having sent to the Company for assistance.[53] Medhi Barphukan, the viceroy, who was in charge of Gauhati, was suspected to have allowed the enemies to enter it on both sides of the river.[54] Siring Choladhara Phukan, the lord chamberlain or private Dewan of the Raja as well as his foreign minister, supported Jainath Barbarua in his various nefarious deeds. The Phukan was nearly related to Purnananda Buragohain, the prime minister at Jorhat, and was suspected to be opposed to the Raja's restoration to the full possession of his authority which would consequently terminate that extensive influence exercised by the Buragohain only for the purpose of benefiting himself and his family.[55] The oppressions of the Swargadeo's ministers at Nowgong had roused the indignation of the inhabitants who came in a body to Gaurinath and demanded their dismissal. Medhi Barphukan and Jainath Barbarua were accordingly replaced by Haliram and Bhadari respectively; but the two dismissed officers were reinstated after nine days at the request of the original complainants.

Jainath Barbarua belonged to the Jalambata Bakatial family which first rose to power during the reign of Swargadeo Siva Singha, by the appointment of Rupchandra as Barbarua. The Barbarua was the head of the executive, civil and military, and was also the lord chief justice of the kingdom. He was besides the secretary of state for the middle provinces including Kaliabar and Nowgong.[56] The office of Barbarua had been confined to the members of the four Ahom clans Duara, Lahan, Sandikoi and Dihingia; and the selection of Rupchandra in contravention of the usages of the land created great discontent among the older Ahom nobles. The highhandedness of Rupchandra's son Kirtichandra which was directly responsible for the Moamaria revolt added to the unpopularity of the Bakatial family. Another Bakatial named Bhadrasen held the office of Barbarua in the reign of Swargadeo

53. Welsh to Cornwallis, Dec. 4, Beng. Pol. Cons., Dec. 17, 1792, No. 50.

54. Welsh to Cornwallis, Jan. 1, Beng. Pol. Cons., Jan. 14, 1793, No.21.

55. MacGregor to Welsh, Nov. 12, Beng. Pol. Cons., Dec. 16, 1793, No. 41.

56. Montgomery Martin, *Eastern India,* Vol. III, p. 613, and Robinson, *Descriptive Account of Assam,* pp. 190-1.

Lakshmi Singha, and was executed for conspiracy against the monarch. The appointment of Jainath, grandson of Kirtichandra, which restored the Bakatial family to power, was viewed with resentment by the older Ahom families and alienated their sympathy from the monarch. In the opinion of Capt. Welsh, which has received corroboration from all quarters, one of the sources of discontent and disaffection was "the supersession of the rights of the hereditary nobility by the appointment of Roop Sund [Rupchandra], and at a later period of Chiste Sund [Kirtichandra], the grandfather of Joinath to the high office of Burra Burrwah."[57] Lt. Robert MacGregor had come to the same conclusion after his conversations on the situation in Assam with Helimeli Solal Bargohain at Kaliabar,—"There seems to be no other objection to the Surge Deo's government than his injudicious selection of ministers in opposition to the wishes of those who from established custom had a right to make the selection.[58]

Soon after his arrival at Gauhati Capt. Welsh had seen the extreme helplessness of the Raja in the hands of his selfish and designing ministers. During the first few interviews with Capt. Welsh the Raja expressed his gratitude to the English Government for having given him his country again. He threw himself entirely and unequivocally into the arms of the Company and prayed for their assistance not only against Krishnanarayan but against all his enemies as far as his capital Rangpur. He promised to reimburse the Company for the expenses of the troops after he was put in full possession of the country. He addressed a letter to the Governor-General in appreciation of the Company's good disposition and the aid of Capt. Welsh "who gave me great comfort and encouragement, afforded me his support, and by the strength of the sword expelled my enemies, and reinstated me in my possession."[59] In the beginning the pitiable condition of the Raja had excited the sympathy of Capt. Welsh, but he soon found that he could not do anything to strengthen his position owing to the influence and obstruction of the corrupt and evilminded ministers. The most respectable and enlightened of the inhabitants declared it to be their opinion "that until every man in power about the

57. Welsh to Ed. Hay, Secy. to Government, Feb. 6, Beng. Pol. Cons., Feb. 24, 1794, No. 14; Mackenzie's *North-East Frontier of Bengal*, App. A., p. 381.

58. MacGregor to Welsh, Nov. 10, Beng. Pol. Cons., Dec. 16, 1793, No. 40.

59. Assam Raja to Cornwallis, undated, received by Government on Dec. 16, Beng. Pol. Cons., Dec. 28, 1792, No. 9.

Raja was dismissed and he was in some degree under the management of Capt. Welsh he would not be able to assert his own rights or exercise his lawful authority."[60]

Welsh then decided to purge the Raja's court of the sinister influences that had been working for the destruction of himself and his country. As Krishnanarayan was still holding out in his retreat in Bhutan Capt. Welsh thought it might be necessary to send a detachment or proceed himself to Darrang and Kamrup, in which case it would be improper to leave Medhi Barphukan in charge of Gauhati in view of his treacherous conduct in the past. With great difficulty Capt. Welsh carried his point with the Raja. Medhi Barphukan was dismissed, and Haliram of the Duara family was appointed in his place.[61] The new Barphukan understood his duties well, and appreciated and supported the measures of Capt. Welsh. But Haliram was an infirm old man, and unable from indisposition to pay that attention to business which the state of the country required.

In the second week of January 1793 Gaurinath went to pay a visit to his family at Rani, at a distance of 10 miles from Gauhati, promising to return within 6 or 7 days. The Raja had put to death 113 men since Welsh's arrival at Gauhati, and 24 men since Welsh had forbidden it. During the Raja's absence 6 prisoners were sent from Gauhati under his orders for being executed though they did not know the crime for which they were to suffer. Welsh sent an officer to bring all the prisoners who were in confinement at Gauhati. The officer returned with 70 men so much debilitated for want of food that two expired on the way and the rest were scarcely able to walk to Welsh's tent. Welsh examined the keepers who declared that they received orders from the Barbarua who had done nothing to relieve the prisoners though he had been frequently informed of their condition. Welsh concluded that the Raja's visit to Rani had been planned merely to give the Barbarua an opportunity of plundering the country and destroying the inhabitants without fear of discovery. The Barbarua was seized and kept in confinement. A few days later the Choladhara Phukan was also arrested for having acted in concert with the Barbarua. The latter had so much power in the country that the inhabitants lived in dread of his vengeance after the departure of the detachment from Assam. Welsh could scarcely persuade them to come

60. Welsh to Cornwallis, Jan. 1, Beng. Pol. Cons., Jan. 14, 1793, No. 21.

61. Haliram had held the office of Barphukan at Nowgong for three days, *Tungkhungia Buranji*, pp. 131-2.

forward with their complaints for redress to the Durbar which he had established for that purpose.

To give confidence Capt. Welsh issued a manifesto to the people of Assam enumerating the objects of the deputation and assuring them of his protection against the persecutions and oppressions of the ministers who had obtained an improper degree of influence "by rapine, perfidy and injustice to indulge their resentments or to gratify their avarice." He alluded to the punishments inflicted in the name of the king on innocent people and without a legal process or trial. "I know too", continued Welsh, "that your houses have been occasionally plundered, your effects confiscated, your women taken from you by force, and your brothers compelled to submit to bondage, and of all these matters I have had independent proofs." He promised to free the people from "the authors of these diabolical deeds," by requiring the Swargadeo to dismiss them. He referred to his invitation of the chiefs and principal men of Assam to concert measures for bringing about a reform in the civil government and for establishing the Raja's authority on more humane principles. He asked the people to come to the Durbar, held on Mondays, Wednesdays and Fridays, where he with the officers appointed by the Raja would hear their complaints and redress their grievances according to the laws of their country "which though they have been long dormant will now be revived and put in full force." Copies of the manifesto written in Assamese and Bengali were dispersed throughout the country and were also sent to the chiefs for making the contents known in their respective limits. Haliram Barphukan informed Capt. Welsh that the plan now adopted for the relief of the Raja and his country had been followed when Assam was in its most flourishing state.[62]

Soon after the issue of this manifesto Welsh received Lord Cornwallis's letter of January 15 authorising him to insist in very positive terms upon the Raja's dismissal of the Barbarua and other unreliable ministers and to appoint men of the best character in their places.[63]

Gaurinath continued in his country residence and would not return in spite of Welsh's repeated requests. Welsh had to inform the Raja that if he did not return soon the Barbarua and the Choladhara Phukan would be sent out of the country. The two

62. Welsh to Cornwallis Jan. 13, Beng. Pol. Cons., Jan. 28, 1793, Nos. 7 and 8.

63. Cornwallis to Welsh, Jan. 15, Beng. Pol. Cons., Jan. 17, 1793, No. 10.

officers were asked to be in readiness to set off for Jugighopa on February 2. The Raja returned to Gauhati on that day.

On his way to Gauhati Gaurinath had ordered one of his old servants to be mutilated for the offence of answering a simple question put to the Rani Raja by the Swargadeo. The Rani Raja laid his turban at Gaurinath's feet and requested him to mitigate the punishment but in vain. Capt. Welsh sent for the man and had him admitted into the detachment hospital. "He has been deprived of his ears as well as the cartilaginous part of his nose", reported the Surgeon Dr. John Peter Wade, "and both his eye-balls have been extracted."[64]

In the evening of the same day, February 2, Gaurinath Singha came to Capt. Welsh's tent and remained with him for nearly five hours. The interview was an event of great significance as it enabled Capt. Welsh to see for himself the Raja's real character. The Captain was schooled in the best traditions of the British army and British administration and of the enlightened institutions of Europe, and could ill brook the unbridled autocracy of an oriental despot. Raja Gaurinath was brought up in an atmosphere of adulation and flattery and had scarcely countenanced any opposition to his evil propensities, being bereft of the services of bold and patriotic advisers who alone could have checked his inhuman proceedings.

Capt. Welsh reminded Gaurinath of the unfortunate situation of the country brought about by his cruel conduct and the mismanagement of his ministers which had incensed the subjects against him. He advised the Raja to observe a different line of conduct and to dismiss his obnoxious ministers if he wanted to restore peace to his country and happiness to his people. The Raja in his reply "owned with a degree of exaltation that he had ordered the punishment inflicted on his servant, and that if he was deprived of the power of killing or mutilating his subjects at pleasure he would not wish to be a Raja." It was a privilege, said Gaurinath, enjoyed by his forefathers, and that he would rather resign his Raj than go without it. The Raja informed Capt. Welsh that he had been sent by the Governor-General to obey his orders and not to interfere in the management of Assam, and that he could summon 50,000 men to his assistance whenever he required them. Gaurinath ended by declaring to Capt. Welsh "that he owed the Company nothing." On the 3rd February Gaurinath summoned

64. Wade to Welsh, Feb. 3, Beng. Pol. Cons., Feb. 15, 1793, No. 16.

Bishnunarayan and the two Duaria Baruas and accused them of having sold Assam to the Company. The Raja gave orders to have the three put to death, and they requested Capt. Welsh for a guard of sepoys for their protection, "In fact, my Lord," wrote Welsh to Lord Cornwallis, "both his [Gaurinath's] words and actions are those of a mad man. He is constantly intoxicated with opium. History does not furnish an example of a more corrupt, cruel and despotic government than that which has existed in Assam for some years past."[65]

Welsh now realised the futility of his attempts to remove the disorders in Assam without putting any check on the cruelty and tyranny of the Raja by depriving him of his power to do harm. On February 4 Welsh issued orders restricting the Raja's attendants to 100 men by whom alone his orders would be obeyed. He forbade all people to hold any communication with the Raja and obey his orders until the meeting of the chiefs. Gauhati was henceforth to be managed by the Barphukan. Capt. Welsh posted guards round the Raja's compound to prevent access to him. A letter was written to the Raja setting forth the reasons for which such measures had to be adopted. "The tyranny and cruelty", wrote Capt. Welsh, "which you exercised and the misconduct of your ministers had justly incensed your subjects by whom you were driven from one extremity of your country to the other." A second manifesto was issued to the people of Assam describing the origin of the disorders in that country and acquainting them with the restraints imposed upon the Raja and the orders passed in that connection.[66]

Raja Gaurinath came gradually to his senses. On the night of February 7 he sent a message to Welsh expressing his willingness to dismiss the Barbarua and the Choladhara Phukan and to respect the administration of justice. Welsh took advantage of the Raja's penitent mood and sent a letter to him requiring him to agree to four articles, *first,* to dismiss all ministers who like the Barbarua and the Choladhara Phukan had acted treacherously towards him or who had oppressed the subjects; *secondly,* to pardon all rebellious subjects and enemies and to release from confinement all persons who might have committed offences against the government to which there seemed to have been sufficient provocation; *thirdly,* to refrain from inflicting punishment extending to death or mutila-

65. Welsh to Cornwallis, Feb. 4, Beng. Pol. Cons., Feb. 15, 1793, No. 15.

66. Welsh to Cornwallis, Feb. 4, Beng. Pol. Cons., Feb. 15, 1793, No. 15; letters to Assam Raja and the 2nd manifesto to the people of Assam in No. 17.

tion without giving culprits a fair trial and to prevent others from committing similar acts; *fourthly*, to summon the Rajas and chiefs in the districts round Gauhati and abide by the regulation made by them in concert with Capt. Welsh.

The letter was delivered to Gaurinath Singha on February 8 by Lt. MacGregor and was read and the different articles explained by one of the Baruas. Gaurinath listened with the greatest attention, and agreed to them without hesitation and ordered his seal and signature to be affixed to the document.[67]

On February 9 Jainath Barbarua and Siring Choladhara Phukan were publicly dismissed. They entered into a written agreement to have no communication with the Raja and not to interfere directly or indirectly with the government of Assam.

The Raja ordered Haliram Barphukan to act in concert with Welsh. He also issued summons to the chiefs to assemble at Gauhati. On February 10 Capt. Welsh wrote to Lord Cornwallis —"I have great reason to hope that everything now will go on smoothly and to your Lordship's satisfaction."[68]

Lord Cornwallis characterised Welsh's measures with regard to the Raja as "of a very strong nature;" but being confident that the Captain had acted with the purest motives of humanity the Governor-General considered them as highly deserving of his approbation. The Governor-General authorised Welsh to give a general assurance to the inhabitants that they would not be abandoned to the mercy of "so ferocious and sanguinary a tyrant" as Gaurinath.[69] This authority helped Welsh to rally all those who maintained a disposition to assist him in restoring peace to the country.

After this the Raja and Capt. Welsh came to a perfect understanding and the latter's work at Gauhati was made much easier. On April 4, Capt. Welsh was able to inform Lord Cornwallis, "The Rajah is perfectly tractable, and has been for sometime past under no restraint. The public Durbar meets once a week or oftener as business may require, and I meet with no opposition in my transaction here."[70]

Negotiations with Krishnanarayan: After having obtained the dismissal of the selfish and treacherous ministers of Gaurinath and being assured of the Raja's co-operation Capt. Welsh turned

67. The witnesses were Rudram Barua and Raghuram Barua.
68. Welsh to Cornwallis, Feb. 10, Beng. Pol. Cons., Feb. 22, 1793, No. 13.
69. Cornwallis to Welsh, Feb. 11, Beng. Pol. Cons., Feb. 22, 1793, No. 12.
70. Welsh to Cornwallis, Ap. 4, Beng. Pol. Cons., Ap. 22, 1793, No. 13.

his attention seriously to the conciliation of Krishnanarayan. After his father Hangsanarayan's execution in 1790 Gaurinath had intended to make him Raja, but on the advice of Haradatta Chaudhuri, Krishnanarayan fled from Assam assuming a rebellious attitude. During Krishnanarayan's occupation of North Kamrup the Assam Raja had promised, through Daniel Raush, to grant him the perganah of Darrang with all the privileges his father and grandfather had enjoyed to which he would have willingly agreed, but he was prevented by the Burkendazes to do so. Even after his expulsion to Bhutan Krishnanarayan had the strongest inclination to come to Gauhati, but was again prevented by the Burkendazes.

A week after his arrival at Gauhati Capt. Welsh had suggested to Gaurinath, the expediency of restoring Krishnanarayan. The Raja expressed his intention to try Krishnanarayan as a rebel and punish him accordingly. Welsh advised the Raja to convert Krishnanarayan into a friend by restoring him to his paternal inheritance, and to employ him in quelling the disturbances in other parts of the kingdom. The Raja was informed that he should inaugurate a policy of making as many friends as possible to counteract the activities of his many enemies amongst whom were included his wicked and intriguous ministers. Capt. Welsh pointed out to the Raja the propriety of having friends in the rear when he would proceed towards Upper Assam where he had so many enemies. The Raja adhered to his intention to try Krishnanarayan by the laws of the country alleging that it was not customary to confirm any person, who had rebelled against them, in the possession of which he had been deprived. On December 4, 1792, Capt. Welsh reported the circumstances to the Government of Bengal.[71]

On December 18 Lord Cornwallis wrote an emphatic note desiring the Assam Raja to compose his differences with Krishnanarayan and restore him to the quiet possession of his ancestral rights on condition that he would assist in re-establishing the Raja's authority in the other parts of his dominions. The Governor-General admitted that Krishnanarayan had "had no small provocation for revolt." He authorised Welsh to assure Krishnanarayan that if the Raja of Assam should in future disturb him in the possession of the ancient rights of his family the Bengal Government would in no shape take part against the Darrang Raja.[72]

71. Welsh to Cornwallis, Dec. 4, Beng. Pol. Cons., Dec. 17, 1792, No. 50.
72. Cornwallis to Welsh, Dec. 18, Beng. Pol. Cons., Dec. 21, 1792, No. 17.

Lord Cornwallis's intentions were comunicated to Gaurinath on January 3, 1793; and after a brief consultation with his ministers the Raja agreed to restore Krishnanarayan to the rights of his ancestors on the conditions recommended by the Governor-General. He accounted for his previous refusal by saying that he could not think of pardoning a rebellious subject while he remained in open arms against him, but now that he was driven out of Assam and his force disbanded he had great pleasure in conforming to the Governor-General's wishes. On the next day Capt. Welsh, as desired by Gaurinath, communicated the terms to Krishnanarayan. "My advice to you is", wrote the Captain "that you lose no time in making your appearance before Maharajah Surge Deo." Welsh's letter was delivered to Krishnanarayan by Ensign Wood who had been engaged in survey operations in the Darrang-Bhutan frontier.[73] A few days later Capt. Welsh, believing that the continuation of the enmity of Haradatta, "Zemindar of Dering and a faithful servant of Kissna Narain's family" would be equally injurious to the Raja, wrote a letter to him as well asking him to come with 'his master' Krishnanarayan.[74]

In a letter dated January 30, 1793, addressed to Ensign Wood, Krishnanarayan intimated his willingness to come to Capt. Welsh. He alluded to the conduct of Daniel Raush who "first encouraged and then deceived" him, and to the unprovoked attack made upon him by that merchant and the Assamese. "Yet, notwithstanding all this usage", wrote Krishnanarayan, "now that you are pleased to call me I will go to you." A letter was received at the same time from a Bhutanese officer, designated Karji Dowar, expressing his willingness to deliver Krishnanarayan on the assurance that he would not have to share the fate of his father Hangsanarayan Deka-Raja who had retired to the same place Kaliapani from whence the Assamese inveigled him forth and put him to death.[75]

Ensign Wood returned from the Bhutan frontier on February 23 and informed Capt. Welsh that neither Krishnanarayan nor Haradata was inclined to come to Gauhati fearing that their lives

73. Welsh to Cornwallis, Jan. 4, Beng. Pol. Cons., Jan. 17, 1793, No. 11; letter to Krishnanarayan in No. 12.

74. Welsh to Cornwallis, Jan. 13, Beng. Pol. Cons., Jan. 28, 1793, No. 7.

75. Welsh to Cornwallis, Feb. 4, Beng. Pol. Cons., Feb. 15, 1793, No. 15, with enclosures.

would not be safe when the Company's troops would be withdrawn from Assam leaving the Raja in absolute power. Capt. Welsh as a true administrator resolved to take decisive steps and to tell Krishnanarayan that he must either make his appearance at a fixed period or that Bishnunarayan and Hangsanarayan Burha-Raja would be confirmed in the Raj. A speedy settlement with Krishnanarayan was necessary as Welsh hoped to depend upon his exertions for supplies from Darrang.

On March 7, Capt. Welsh received a letter from "Jungpan Maha Rajah of Bekurar" [Benkar Soobah ?] referring to the friendship subsisting between the Deva Raja of Bhutan and the Company, which, in his opinion, should not be affected by the shelter given to Krishnanarayan, Haradatta and Bhotar Kownar, who had taken refuge in Bhutan being alarmed by the arrival of the Company's troops at Gauhati. Another letter was received from the Karji Dowar desiring to be informed of the reason "why the gentlemen [English] have joined their force to that of the Surge Deo and are now at Gwahatter". Capt. Welsh wrote to the Jungpan Maharaja commending his conduct for giving an asylum to the three fugitives if they had stood in need, and asking him to persuade Krishnanarayan to come to Gauhati.[76]

In the meantime Capt. Welsh received a petition from the inhabitants of Kamrup complaining of the depredations of a banditti from Bhutan. He despatched a company of sepoys to Jikeri with instructions to the officer to persuade Krishnanarayan and Haradata to come to Gauhati. C. A. Bruce, Commissioner of Cooch Behar, sent a Jemadar and ten Burkendazes with a letter from himself and another from Sarvananda Gosain, the Guru of the Cooch Behar Raja, asking Krishnanarayan to proceed to Gauhati.

On April 16 Krishnanarayan and Haradatta intimated their decision to come to Gauhati. The former repeated his desire to hold his country under the seal and protection of the Company and pay his tribute to them. "It was on this account", added Krishnanarayan, "that my father was put to death at Gwahatty by the Surge Deo." He concluded by claiming to hold possession of Kamrup in addition to Darrang. "There never was a distinction", said he, "between the Rauj-ship of Kamroop and Dering, both were held by one person, until the Assam Rajah possessing

76. Welsh to Cornwallis, March 11, Beng. Pol. Cons., March 22, 1793, No. 33, letter to Bekurar Raja in No. 34.

superior power, separated them and appropriated Kamroop to himself." Krishnanarayan informed Capt. Welsh that he had already sent people to repair his house in Darrang in which work he anticipated some interference from Bishnunarayan.

Haradatta's letter was less straightforward than that of Krishnanarayan. He alleged that the Na-Gosain and the Assamese people had plundered his property and removed his cattle and grain so that if he left Bhutan with his family he had no means to subsist even for ten days. Besides, Raush was in possession of his household. Haradatta warned Capt. Welsh to receive with caution the representations of his enemies. Lastly, said Haradatta, "You have obtained possession of the country of which Gwahatty is the capital: it is a country of considerable extent. Should you listen to the suggestions of the Beyragy Raja [Bishnunarayan] in managing it you will be deceiver. But this is a long story."[77]

To expedite business Capt. Welsh despatched Lt. MacGregor on April 21 to Kalitakuchi to conduct Krishnanarayan and Haradatta to Gauhati. But Krishnanarayan complained of being unwell and of his habitation not being furnished. Capt. Welsh directed Lt. MacGregor to proceed to Mangaldoi, the headquarter of the Darrang Raja, and hasten with the repairs.

Krishnanarayan's surrender at Gauhati: On May 20, 1793, at 4 in the afternoon, Krishnanarayan arrived at Gauhati accompanied by Haradatta's son and 400 Burkendazes.[78] Capt. Welsh paid him a visit immediately and assured him of his friendship and protection. Krishnanarayan impressed Welsh as "a mild and well-disposed young man." Welsh determined to dismiss the Burkendazes whose continued violence had made them a terror to the inhabitants of Darrang and their appearance there was expected to produce a very bad effect. Of the 400 Burkendazes 270 were in the regular pay of Krishnanarayan, the rest being recent additions to make an imposing retinue for the prince. A list was made and the arrears due to them were calculated which amounted to

77. Haradatta and Krishnanarayan to Welsh, April 16, Beng. Pol. Cons., May 1, 1793, No. 17.

78. Lt. Col. J. Johnstone is wrong when he says in his *Capt. Welsh's Expedition to Assam*, p. 27, that Krishnanarayan was accompanied by Haradatta, Raja of Luki Duar. There were *two* Haradattas, *1st.*, Haradatta Chaudhuri Bujarbarua of Jikeri, supporter of Krishnanarayan, and *2nd.*, Haradatta, Raja of Luki Duar, a vassal chief of the Ahom government. It was Haradatta Bujarbarua's son who arrived at Gauhati with Krishnanarayan on May, 20, 1793.

Rs. 5,782-4-4. The 270 Burkendazes were sent down to Rungpore under the escort of Lt. Robinett and a company of sepoys. On their arrival at Rungpore the Collector disarmed them, and dispersed them subsequently after having paid their arrears. Krishnanarayan gave a bond to reimburse the amount in six months at 12 per cent interest.[79] Krishnanarayan and Haradatta's son gave a present in money to Capt. Welsh which he accepted lest by refusal he would give offence to the prince.[80]

On May 24, Krishnanarayan took his oaths of allegiance to Swargadeo Gaurinath Singh and was formally installed in the Raj of Darrang. He pressed his claims to the Zemindary of Kamrup and solicited the privilege of paying a pecuniary compensation for the customary levy of men consisting of 6,000 *paiks* which the Darrang Raja had to furnish to the Barphukan at Gauhati for employment in the Ahom Raja's service as soldiers and labourers. Welsh proposed to examine Krishnanarayan's claims to Kamrup with the help of the papers in possession of the Darrang Raja and the Ahom king. The latter was not willing to receive the compensation in lieu of the customary levy of men.[81] The dispute was submitted to Lord Cornwallis who in his reply of June 10 recommended in emphatic terms that the Assam Raja should meet the reasonable demand of the Darrang Raja. "You will particularly inform the Swargadeo", wrote the Governor-General to Capt. Welsh, "that I never will support him in the oppressive levy of men, nor take any further concern in his favour if he should persevere in demanding it."[82]

Agreement among Darrang princes: On the recommendation of Capt. Welsh, the four princes of Darrang, Hangsanarayan I, Krishnanaryan, Bishnunarayan and Samudranarayan, entered into an agreement on June 8, 1793, with the object of terminating their family disputes and animosities and of uniting and supporting each other in their just claims to those districts formerly possessed by their ancestors, of part of which they had been forcibly deprived by the Raja of Assam. As regards the substitution of the levy of men by a pecuniary compensation Capt. Welsh insisted on the Assam Raja's acquiescence in the proposal, and incorporated the change in the agreement of the Darrang princes.

79. Welsh to Cornwallis, May 21, Beng. Pol. Cons., June 3, 1793, No. 9.

80. Welsh to Ed. Hay, Secy. to Governor-General, June 4, Beng. Pol. Cons. June 17, 1793, No. 9.

81. Welsh to Cornwallis, May 28, Beng. Pol. Cons., June 14, 1793, No. 11.

82. Cornwallis to Welsh, June 10, Beng. Pol. Cons., June 14, 1793, No. 13.

In the preamble to the agreement the princes declared their intention "to unite in one common bond of interest and amity, and not to consider the business of one as separate from that of the others." In the event of their obtaining the possession of Kamrup, Darrang and Kaliabar, they proposed to allot the government of Darrang and Kaliabar to Hangsanarayan and Krishnanarayan, and Kamrup to Bishnunarayan and Samudranarayan. The arrangement was based on the understanding that a descendant of Suryyanarayan and of Indranarayan would jointly govern the provinces in question.[83] It must be understood, however, that the rights to be exercised by the Darrang princes were those of a Zemindar or revenue collector. The Barphukan was the ruler or viceroy of Darrang, Kaliabar and Kamrup.

For Kamrup the joint Rajas engaged to pay to Capt. Welsh, on account of the Swargadeo, a land revenue corresponding to that which was collected when dissensions did not exist in the country,[84] and for Darrang and Kaliabar they proposed to pay the sum of rupees 58,000 if they were permitted to pay money in lieu of men. This sum was proposed to be raised as follows:—rupees 50,000, in lieu of men furnished by Darrang; rupees 2,000, by Sootia; from Chardwar and Kaliabar, rupees 3,000; and in lieu of customs on the trade between Darrang and Bhutan, rupees 3,000. To prevent disputes in future the princes fixed the line of succession as follows:—if there be a son, he will succeed to the partition of his father; if there be no son and there be a brother, the partition of the deceased will go to him; if there be two or three sons, the partition of the father will go to the eldest; if there be no sons and there be two or three brothers, the partition of the deceased will go to the eldest; if there should be neither sons or brothers, the partition of Samudranarayan will devolve on Krishnanarayan and *vice versa,* and the partition of Hangsanarayan on Bishnunarayan and *vice versa.*[85]

On June 15 Krishnanarayan left for his capital Mangaldoi to take possession of his Raj, and on his request Capt. Welsh ordered Lt. Burton with a company of sepoys to proceed with the new

83. Of the four, Hangsanarayan and Bishnunarayan were descendants of Suryyanarayan, and Krishnanarayan and Samudranarayan of Indranarayan. The two lines were thus represented in the government of the three provinces.

84. The land revenue of Kamrup, called 'Jaigiri Dhan', which was collected by the Chaudhuris amounted to rupees 80,000.

85. Welsh to Cornwallis, June 14, Beng. Pol. Cons., June 28, 1793, No. 39; the agreement in No. 40.

Raja. In July Bishnunarayan, joint Raja of Kamrup, was entrusted with the temporary charge of that district in view of the advanced age of Haliram Barphukan and his consequent incapacity to pay due attention to business.[86]

In the meantime Capt. Welsh investigated the claims of the ruling family of Darrang to the district of Kamrup. His first difficulty was to obtain the papers which would elucidate the claims. By special arrangement with the Commissioner of Cooch Behar, Capt. Welsh procured the presence of Bulchand Barua, Zemindar and Kanungo of Rangamati, whose ancestors had served as high revenue officials under the Muslim and Koch rulers of Kamrup. Bulchand came to Gauhati with old state papers likely to throw light on the complex problems of Kamrup history. Though the information supplied by Bulchand was avowed by Capt. Welsh to agree with that received from the Assamese yet it militates against the accepted facts of history. He says, for example, that the Muhammadans in conjunction with the Koch Rajas "managed the provinces from the vicinity of Ghurgong [Gargaon] westward during a period of 200 years." The longest period for which the Moguls ruled in any part of Assam was from 1639 to 1658, when they obtained possession of Kamrup after the treaty between Allah Yar Khan and Momai Tamuli Barbarua.[87] The only essential fact which could be deduced from Bulchand's account was that "Kamrup, in the time of Balit Narayan [Balinarayan, *alias* Dharmanarayan, founder of the Darrang family], was governed by the then Burra Fokun [Barphukan, Ahom viceroy in charge of Kamrup, Darrang and Kaliabar], under whose charge it had remained from the period of Joy Narain and Munsoor Khan's flight [1682 A.D.]"[88]

Chiefs invited to a conference at Gauhati: During the continuance of the negotiations with Krishnanarayan, Capt. Welsh had been attempting to hold a conference of the chiefs and principal men of Assam for the purpose of putting an end to their dissensions and concerting measures for the restoration of good government and the peace and tranquillity of the country. But it was unusual to expect the jarring factions to lay aside their differences and unite in evolving a common formula to prevent their country

86. Welsh to Cornwallis, July 1, Beng. Pol. Cons., July 15, 1793, No. 26.
87. Gait, *History of Assam*, pp. 118 and 127.
88. A descriptive genealogy of the Darrang Rajas and Bulchand's account of the Koch rulers of Darrang and Kamrup were enclosed with Capt. Welsh's letters to Lord Cornwallis dated May 28 and July 20, Beng. Pol. Cons., June 14, No. 11 and August 12, 1793, No. 8, respectively.

from being totally ruined. The only means which Welsh adopted to secure the attendance of the chiefs was an appeal to their sense of patriotism, but it failed to produce the desired effect.

The chiefs invited by Welsh were the vassal Rajas of the petty states situated in the present districts of Nowgong and Kamrup, and the principal officials and nobles who had any power or followers.[89] The Raja's title to sovereignty over these chiefs was founded on conquest or voluntary submission. The Swargadeo with the concurrence of the ministers could dismiss a chief and appoint his successor. The Rajas were judges in their own districts, and appeals from their decisions could be made to the king and the Barphukan. They had to attend the monarch with their complement of men when summoned to do so. They all paid an annual revenue to the Swargadeo, except the Raja of Rani.[90]

The refractory attitude of the Assam chiefs was brought to the notice of Lord Cornwallis by the Swargadeo so early as August 1792 when he said that half his Zemindars had rebelled and commenced hostilities against him.[91] Capt. Welsh on his arrival at Gauhati three months later found the Raja in no better predicament. Lord Cornwallis in his letter of December 28, 1792, authorised Capt. Welsh to convene a meeting of the chiefs and the men in power and authority for deliberating measures to compose the disorders.[92]

After the expulsion of the Burkendazes Capt. Welsh issued letters to the different chieftains and nobles asking them to repair to him at Gauhati. Capt. Welsh set forth the objects of his deputation to Assam, *viz.*, to expel the Bengal Burkendazes and to assist in re-establishing the Swargadeo in his lawful authority over all his dominions. The Governor-General, said Welsh, had furnished him with troops to effect the first object; and for the second he

89. These states are Rani, Beltola, Luki Duar, Barduar, Bholagaon, Mairapur, Pantan, Bangaon, Bagaduar, Dumaria, Neli, Gobha, Sohari, Dandua, Barepujia, Tapakuchia, Khaighoria, Panbari, Sora, Mayang, Dhing, Tetelia, Salmara, Garakhia, Baghara and Bhurbanda, See *Tungkhungia Buranji*, Introduction, p. xxviii, and Martin's *Eastern India*, Vol. III, pp. 619-22. Welsh's invitation was confined to the chiefs immediately near the districts of Gauhati.

90. Welsh to Ed. Hay, Feb. 6, Beng. Pol. Cons., Feb. 24, 1794, No. 14 with David Scott's additional observations in Bengal Secret and Pol. Cons., July 14, 1826, No. 2, and Mackenzie's *North-East Frontier of Bengal*, pp. 382-3.

91. Assam Raja to Cornwallis, undated, Beng. Pol. Cons., Sept. 10, 1792, No. 49.

92. Cornwallis to Welsh, Dec. 8, 1792, Charles Ross, *Cornwallis Correspondence*, Vol. II, pp. 186-7.

had been empowered "to endeavour by a friendly mediation to reconcile the contending parties throughout Assam and relieve the miseries of this distracted country." The first object, he continued, had been accomplished; but he found it impossible without the chiefs' aid to subdue the confusion and anarchy which prevailed in Assam. He assured the chiefs that the English Government had no intention to reduce to subjection any part of Assam. He referred to the proposal to dismiss the Barbarua and other ministers whose treachery and evil counsels had brought upon the king all his misfortunes. "From what I have said", added Welsh, "you will conclude I am your friend, the friend of the Surge Deo and that of your country." [93]

Purnananda Buragohain, the premier, who from his camp at Jorhat had been opposing the advance of the Moamarias replied that he could not afford to be absent from his headquarter.[94] Of the chiefs only the Rani Raja, Beltola Raja and Bishnunarayan expressed their readiness to obey the summons. Haradatta, Raja of Luki Duar, pleaded his inability to leave his state on the ground that the Raja of Barduar was meditating to surround and destroy him. He claimed to have possessed Barduar some time ago, and he asked Welsh to reinstate him in its possession. Haradatta had some arrears of tribute to the Assam Raja which he said "he would perhaps pay when convenient." The Dimarua Raja refused to admit the messengers into his capital as such an action would not be countenanced by his other two overlords, the Rajas of Khyrim and Jayantia. He met the messengers outside his state and told them that he would abide by whatever was agreed to by the Rajas of Darrang, Beltola and Rani. The Barpatra Gohain, one of the three principal ministers, advised Capt. Welsh to transact business with the Barbarua, Barphukan and other ministers who were at Gauhati, adding "I will hereafter join you." [95]

The real attitude of the chiefs found expression in the replies of Helimeli Solal Gohain, and his nephew the deposed Bargohain Bishnunarayan. "Both are men of excellent understanding and pleasant manners", wrote Lt. MacGregor of the two Gohains.[96]

93. Welsh to Cornwallis, Jan. 13, Beng. Pol. Cons., Jan. 28, 1793, No. 7; Welsh's letter to Assam chiefs in No. 9.

94. Welsh to Cornwallis, March 11, Beng. Pol. Cons., March 22, 1793, No. 33.

95. Welsh to Cornwallis, Feb. 21, Beng. Pol. Cons., March 11, 1793, No. 15, with enclosures containing the replies from the chiefs.

96. MacGregor at Kaliabar to Welsh, Nov. 11, Beng. Pol. Cons., Dec. 16, 1793, No. 41. Bishnunarayan was also known as Raj Bargohain.

The Solal Gohain was the governor of the territory, including the east end of the Majuli island, between the Brahmaputra and Kallang rivers. His jurisdiction extended to a portion of Charidwar. His headquarter was at Kaliabar where he maintained a considerable force with which he checked the conduct of the Bhutias, Miris and Dafalas when these mountaineers came down to levy blackmail from the border villages assigned to them for that purpose. The Solal Gohain was always selected from the family of the Bargohains; and Helimeli and Bishnunarayan both belonged to the Madurial branch of that family founded by the illustrious Bargohain Laithepena, father-in-law of King Gadadhar Singha. Helimeli was then living in dread of punishment from Gaurinath, and more specially from Jainath Barbarua who suspected him of having favoured the revolt of another Bairagi Raja, a Moamaria leader, in the neighbourhood of Biswanath.[97] Another promoter of the Bairagi Raja's rebellion was the Lahan Barbarua, commonly known as Baskatia or Panisilia Barbarua. Bishnunarayan had also shared the humiliation which had fallen to the lot of his uncle. He was deposed from the office of Bargohain for alleged complicity in the disloyal manoeuvres of Baskatia Barbarua. The two Gohains attributed their disgrace to the machinations of Jainath Barbarua who had interpreted their loyal actions in the darkest colours possible.

Bishnunarayan ex-Bargohain asked Capt. Welsh to send Jainath Barbarua to Kaliabar as a proof of his intenion to dismiss the king's evil advisers; or if the Captain refused to send the Barbarua to the Gohains for fear of retribution, "then send me", wrote Bishnunarayan, "100 or 120 sepoys from which I will know that you have acted from your own judgment in sending for me and not on the instigation of such bad men. Should you not therefore find it expedient to adopt either of these measures I cannot possibly attend you."

Helimeli Solal Gohain's reply was of the same tenor and purpose as that of his nephew. He recounted his services in suppressing the rebels and quieting the disorders which were all misinterpreted by the king's wicked counsellers. The Gohain had made a treaty with the Dafalas having paid rupees 28,000 and succeeded with their assistance in quelling the Moamarias under the Bairagi Raja of Biswanath who was killed, and his right arm and ears were sent to Gaurinath as a token of victory. The royalist chiefs then elected a Barbarua of the Lahan family and enlisted the support

97. See *ante*, Chapter VI, Part 2.

of the Miris. By their united exertions they succeeded in clearing the country of Majuli of all the enemies. The Lahan Barbarua then went to Nowgong to conduct the king to Rangpur but Gaurinath would not trust the Barbarua. In the meantime the men of Nowgong and Kharangi were leaving their villages on account of the continued oppressions of Gaurinath's officers. Helimeli and Bishnunarayan stepped in good time to save these people and to prevent their flight. But the ministers poisoned the ears of the king against the two Gohains who with their confederates swore at the temple of Biswanath that they would never go to the king until those evil advisers were sent to them ; at the same time they pledged that they would not injure the king. The Solal Gohain had become the virtual head of the Dafalas and the Miris who were not prepared to accompany him to Gauhati, nor was he allowed by his agreement to quit them. Helimeli asked Capt. Welsh to send Jainath Barbarua to Kaliabar or an escort of 100 or 120 sepoys. Then concluded Helimeli, "How should I otherwise know that they [Gaurinath's ministers] do not mean to kill me, and what confidence can I have unless you comply with my request ?"[98]

At the time of writing to Capt. Welsh the Barpatra Gohain, the Solal Gohain and the ex-Bargohain had not known of the dismissal of Jainath Barbarua and of the pardon granted by the Swargadeo to all his enemies. Capt. Welsh wrote to them again acquainting them with these circumstances. The Raja ordered the Barphukan to send official letters desiring the chiefs to meet Capt. Welsh at Gauhati without fear. But these assurances bore no fruit, and Capt. Welsh had to write to Lord Cornwallis on March 11,— "I do not think it will be possible, my Lord, to have a meeting with the principal people of the country until their confidence in us predominates over their fears and distrust of each other." The chiefs, continued Welsh, were, however, anxious to give their opinion privately and seemed to be much averse to declare it publicly. Welsh referred particularly to the disobedience of Haradatta, Raja of Luki Duar, who had unlawfully withheld payment of the Swargadeo's revenues which were by no means high or oppressive. Welsh had realised that without the aid of military force neither Haradatta Raja nor the other refractory Zemindars could be reduced to their obedience to the Swargadeo. Capt. Welsh asked the Governor-General for instructions whether he should give up the

98. Welsh to Cornwallis, Feb. 21, Beng. Pol. Cons., March 11, 1793, No. 15, letters from Bishnunarayan and Helmeli in enclosures, Nos. 6 and 7.

point or enforce the obedience of the chiefs by adopting compulsory measures.[99]

Before receiving Welsh's letter Lord Cornwallis had written to him hoping that time and conviction that the Company had no views of ambition or conquest in Assam would alone get the better of the distrust and apprehension which pervaded the minds of the discontented chiefs. The Governor-General instructed Welsh to remain with the detachment at Gauhati, prepared at any time to come down to Bengal if sickness or any other cause would render it necessary.[100]

In his reply to Capt. Welsh's letter of March 11, Lord Cornwallis reaffirmed his determination to adopt conciliatory measures alone for the restoration of peace in Assam. "However desirable it may be from considerations of policy and humanity to take such active means as our force enables us to adopt, in order to restore tranquillity, order and some degree of regular government in Assam, we must yet be careful not to suffer ourselves to be diverted even by the most benevolent motives from a strict obedience to the spirit of the Acts of the British Legislature, and from a steady perseverance in that system of moderation and peace which alone can convince the native powers that we have utterly abandoned all views of ambition and conquest, and that we are determined not to take the sword unless we should be called upon to resist insults and injuries that have been offered either to ourselves, or to such allies as are by Treaty entitled to our protection." Lord Cornwallis reaffirmed that the sole object of the Government in sending a military force into Assam was to relieve the Raja from the unprovoked invasions and depredations of the Burkendazes who were subjects of the Company. He allowed the detachment to continue in Assam after the accomplishment of the primary object in order that Capt. Welsh would be able to restore peace and order by conciliatory measures and mediations between the contending elements, and to establish a free commercial intercourse beneficial both to Assam and Bengal. The Governor-General hoped that the Assam chiefs would in course of time be convinced of the real character and intentions of the English Government. Capt. Welsh was instructed to undertake no military expedition without an absolute necessity, and to procure a meeting of the

99. Welsh to Cornwallis, March 11, Beng. Pol. Cons., March 22, 1793, No. 33.

100. Cornwallis to Welsh, March 18, Beng. Pol. Cons., March 18, 1793, No. 12.

chiefs by conciliatory methods.[101] After the installation of Krishnanarayan as Raja of Darrang Lord Cornwallis hoped that the kind treatment which that prince had received from Capt. Welsh would make a good impression on the minds of the other chiefs and enable him to establish peace in the western part of Assam.[102] The Governor-General made another gesture of good-will to the chiefs by recommending to the Swargadeo to relinquish the oppressive levy of men and to accept in lieu of it a pecuniary compensation.[103] But the inducements offered by Capt. Welsh and the assurances given by Swargadeo Gaurinath Singha failed to remove the diffidence and mistrust of the chiefs.

King Gaurinath became anxious to proceed to Rangpur against the Moamarias; but Capt. Welsh was unwilling to advance further before he settled the affairs of Western Assam, in which he was greatly obstructed by the continued defiance of the chiefs.

The reasons for the failure of the plan to hold a chiefs' conference are obvious. Most of the chiefs and nobles had taken part, directly or indirectly, in the commotions, or had refused to discharge their customary obligations to the Ahom government. They feared lest the invitations concealed some secret designs for their punishment. Though Capt. Welsh assured them of protection and Raja Gaurinath held out promises of pardon, the chiefs would trust in neither, for ignorance of the character of the Company, and of the real intention of the latter's interference in Assam on the one hand, and for their experience of the vindictiveness of the Assam Raja and his ministers on the other. Capt. Welsh had declared in his letter of invitation that he was a friend of the Swargadeo, and the chiefs could not naturally conceive that the Raja's British ally would support him in beneficent measures only and refrain from countenancing any acts of cruelty and injustice. The chiefs like all Assamese, were jealous of strangers and specially of Europeans, whom they designated under one name—*Bangal*; and the little knowledge which they had of Europeans was not very favourable, being gathered chiefly from the sporadic visitors to Assam as sailors and gunners in the several Mogul invasions and the merchants of the Goalpara frontier. The invitations would have been more effective if it were accompanied by some warning of the material injury which each chief was to suffer for disobedience. But Capt. Welsh was not authorized by his Government to enforce

101. Cornwallis to Welsh, Ap. 2, Beng. Pol. Cons., Ap. 5, 1793, No. 34.
102. Cornwallis to Welsh, June 3, Beng. Pol. Cons., June 3, 1793, No. 10.
103. Cornwallis to Welsh, April 19, Beng. Pol. Cons., Ap. 22, No. 14.

compliance with his request. Any compromise arrived at by the chiefs with the Assam Raja might besides be interpreted by their followers as a betrayal of the cause which had originally brought them together. Where obedience involved so many risks the appeal to patriotism could not get better of the fears and suspicions of the chiefs. The chiefs, however, expressed their willingness to give their candid opinions about the situation in Assam to Capt. Welsh in confidence. But they were in dread of retribution from the Swargadeo which their criticism of his measures would bring upon them; more specially as Capt. Welsh could not offer them any assurance of permanent protection. The capacity to sink their differences and jointly deliberate measures for the common good of the country demanded courage, sacrifice and a highly advanced form of patriotism which had yet to be born, unless the opposing elements could be fused for some common purpose under the leadership of an individual of outstanding personality.

The reluctance displayed by Gaurinath's vassals to come to him may be contrasted with the readiness with which the chiefs had responded to the summons of King Rudra Singha (1696-1714). The monarch had subdued the Rajas of Jayantia and Cachar after which he proposed to invade Bengal to avenge the humiliating overtures of its governor, Nawab Murshid Kuli Khān. In April 1714 the king proceeded from Rangpur to Gauhati where he completed his preparations to march into Bengal. "In a council of all the nobles", wrote Dr. J. P. Wade, "Swurge Deo now commanded the Burro Pokun to issue orders for the immediate attendance of the Dehrrung, Burdoorrea, Nohdooria, Pawntoneea, Balogoia, Ranee, Beltolia, Dimarooa, Tapakooseea, Pawnburreea, Kulla, Nelee, Gobah, Khozai, Gurukiea and Dehing Rajahs, who arrived shortly after with their respective quotas of men and presents for the King. Each of the chiefs performed the Khewa [*Seva*, homage] before the monarch."[104]

Barmels or grand conferences were a well-known feature of the Ahom administration. They were held in cases affecting the interests of the people at large, such as hostilities with foreign nations, appearance of a famine or an epidemic or the imposition of new taxes. All the officers of the state, from the Gohains to the Saikias or centurions were invited to take part in the deliberations of a *Barmel* and their joint decisions served as a decree of government.[105] The Gohains, Phukans, Rajkhowas and Baruas compo-

104. J. P. Wade, *Account of Assam*, ed. by B. Sharma, p. 130.
105. Maniram Dewan's Ms. *Assam Buranji*.

sing it were chiefly connected with the noble families, and the Hazarikas or chiliarchs and Saikias, being removable by the constituent *paiks,* represented the commonalty. After the expulsion of the Burmese from Assam in 1825 David Scott proposed to revive and properly organise the institution of the *Barmel,* "to be assembled at least once in two years and to have the right of petitioning the King for redress of grievances and for the punishment and removal of obnoxious officers of all ranks."[106]

It would have been more politic on the part of Capt. Welsh to resort to the existing machinery of a *Barmel* rather than summoning the chiefs to reaffirm—as they suspected—their allegiance to the imbecile and cruel monarch and answer for their past misdeeds. The feudal chiefs had profited by the disorders and were interested in their continuance. The *Barmel* would have at least placed at the disposal of Capt. Welsh the co-operation of a large number of trusted officials, inferior in rank, but easily amenable to reason and discipline as they had very little vested interest and practically no permanent following. The loyalty and example of these officials would have influenced the wavering section of the Assamese subjects.

Commercial arrangements with Assam: In spite of his preoccupation with active military measures and political negotiations Capt. Welsh had not lost sight of the commercial objects of his deputation to Assam. Since Hugh Baillie's first representation to the Court of Directors in 1771 the Company had been trying to place the commercial relations between Bengal and Assam on a proper footing. On his appointment to Goalpara in 1787 Baillie was asked to go to Assam and to form a treaty with its government or an agreement with the Assam merchants. But he failed to achieve any positive result owing to the disturbances in Assam which led ultimately to the abolition of his appointment at Goalpara. Advantage was now taken of the presence of a British officer in Assam in close contact with the Raja and his ministers who would be anxious to oblige him for the services rendered by the Company.

The East India Company was primarily a commercial concern and any opportunity to promote its mercantile views would be readily utilised. Lord Cornwallis had asked Capt. Welsh to en-

106. "Memorandum of terms upon which it is proposed to offer the government of Assam to a native prince," enclosure to David Scott's letter to Bengal Government, April 15, 1826, Beng. Sec. and Pol. Cons., July 14, 1826, No. 2.

quire into the trade and manufactures of Assam. The Governor-General admitted later that by allowing the detachment to continue in Assam after the expulsion of the Burkendazes he had hoped to restore internal peace and "to establish a free commercial intercourse that might be beneficial both to Assam and the Company's provinces." Capt. Welsh had aimed from the beginning to carry out the intentions of the Government. "The commerce of Assam", wrote he to the Governor-General, "has been the subject of my particular enquiry and appears to be an object deserving of the attention of Government."[107] While sailing up the Brahmaputra with the fugitive Assam Raja Welsh had witnessed the process of gold-washing on a bed of sand near Hatimura.[108] Soon after his arrival at Gauhati Welsh had written to the Governor-General of his confidence that with the restoration of peace and order in Assam "a new source of wealth and riches must flow to the Company."[109] He then asked the Government to despatch a few boat-loads of salt and opium which, he hoped, would pay the expense of the detachment. Welsh had found it difficult to collect rice at Gauhati without salt to barter for it and he had to take salt from Goalpara merchants at the rate of Rs. 7-4-11 pies per maund. On December 22, 1792, Lord Cornwallis proposed to send 40,000 maunds of salt for disposal at the Assam market.[110]

The trade of Assam and Bengal passed through the hands of the two Duaria Baruas who lived at Kandahar Choky, where all the imports and exports were received.[111] The Assamese merchants brought their products to the Choky, and bartered them for salt which they afterwards disposed of in different parts of their country. The Baruas collected the duties of 10 per cent upon all exports and imports on behalf of the Assam government. During the reign of Gaurinath Singhs the Baruas, who were the creatures of the ministers, not only collected the duties but by degrees monopolised the trade of Assam and Bengal. They paid rupees 90,000 per year to the Assam government of which the Raja received only 26,000, the remaining 64,000 being appropriated by the minis-

107. Welsh to Cornwallis, Feb. 21, Beng. Pol. Cons., March 11, 1793, No. 15.

108. Welsh to Cornwallis, Nov. 22, Beng. Pol. Cons., Dec. 3, 1792, No. 9.

109. Welsh to Cornwallis, Nov. 27, Beng. Pol. Cons., Dec. 17, 1792, No. 47.

110. Cornwallis to Welsh, Dec. 22, Beng. Pol. Cons., Dec. 24, 1792.

111. We hear of one Duaria Barua upto 1787; since 1792 there were three Baruas at the Assam Choky,—the Kandahar Barua vested with magisterial duties, and the two Duaria Baruas jointly holding the farm of Assam-Bengal trade, note by MacGregor and Welsh, Beng. Pol. Cons., Nov. 23, 1792, No. 15.

ters. At the time of Capt. Welsh's expedition Daniel Raush had obtained the virtual monopoly of the Assam trade as the Baruas had been bound by an agreement to receive all the salt from him. Capt. Welsh recommended to the Bengal Government that arrangements should be made for the regular collection of the Assam Raja's lawful duties, that the monopoly exercised by Raush should be abolished as it was "injurious to the Rajah, prejudicial to trade and oppressive to the inhabitants," and that the export of salt to Assam should be undertaken by the Government. Capt. Welsh believed that the exclusive privilege of selling salt in Assam, if exercised by the Company, would not only bring profits to the Company, but would also relieve the Assamese of the high price which they had to pay for salt at Gauhati, *viz.*, 10 rupees per maund; even then one seer of salt when purified yielded only 5 *chataks* or less than one-third of a seer. Welsh had hoped that the Company would be able to sell 100,000 maunds of salt in Assam when the country was settled.[112] On the basis of these proposals Dr. J. P. Wade informed his friend Francis Fowke,—"All the salt consumed in this kingdom [Assam] comes from Bengal. I am promised already a commission on salt to the amount of one and a half lack of rupees."[113]

On February 28, 1793, King Gaurinath Singha, on the recommendation of Capt. Welsh, "the representative at his court of the English Government", entered into on agreement with the object of establishing "a reciprocal and entire liberty of commerce between the subjects of Bengal and Assam for all singular goods and merchandizes." All imports were subject to a duty of 10 per cent. On salt the duty was to be reckoned on the supposed prime cost *viz.*, 400 rupees per 100 maunds; and on the invoice price in the case of broadcloths of Europe, the common cloths of Bengal, carpets, copper, lead, tin, tutanag, pearls, hardware, jewellery, spices and the various other goods imported into Assam. The duty of 10 per cent was to be levied on exports as well, reckoning the prices per maund as follows,—Muga-dhutis, rupees 95; Muga thread, rupees 70; elephants teeth, rupees 50; *cutna* lac, rupees 4; *chapra* and Jury lac, rupees 3½; munjit, rupees 4; cotton and pepper, not mentioned. Rice and every description of

112. Welsh to Cornwallis, Feb. 21 and 28, Beng. Pol. Cons., March 11, 1793, No. 15.

113. Wade to Fowke, Jan. 22, 1793. Fowke Mss., India Office Library, Vol. 28, letter No. 125.

grain were exempt from duties to provide against temporary scarcity in Bengal or Assam.

By the terms of the government two custom houses were to be established, one at Kandahar Choky and the other at Gauhati. The agents at the former place would collect the duties on all imports, and on all exports consisting of the produce of the country to the westward of Gauhati; those at Gauhati would collect the duties on all exports, the produce of the country parallel to it, north and south, and also of the country to the eastward as far as Nowgong. The remuneration of the agents was fixed at 12 per cent on their collections. Warlike implements and military stores were declared as contraband and liable to confiscation. According to the agreement no European merchant or adventurer of any description would be allowed to fix his residence in Assam without the permission of the English Government and that of the Swargadeo.

In recommending the new system of commerce for the ratification by the Government Welsh proposed that of the total probable collection of 90,000 rupees at Kandahar Choky the sum of 26,000 rupees should be paid as before to the Assam Raja, and the balance be appropriated to defray the expenses of the detachment serving in Assam, to be supplemented by the pecuniary compensations to be paid by the Rajas and Zemindars in lieu of men.[114]

However well-conceived the commercial arrangements might have been their success depended largely on the establishment of peace in Assam. The Governor-General was therefore unwilling to publish the treaty as the Assam government was not in a position to give protection to the merchants, nor was the Bengal Government sure of the continuance of its troops in Assam. Lord Cornwallis apprehended that the publication of the treaty might encourage the merchants to think that they would receive the protection of the English Government and would therefore be "induced to embark too large a capital and enter too deeply in commercial transactions to be carried on in a country [Assam] with which it cannot be certain that we shall have a lasting connection and which it may not be in our power to extricate from its present anarchy as I do not see that, according to the spirit of the Act of Parliament, we can take any other steps to re-establish the authority of Surge Deo except those of friendly mediation." The

114. Welsh to Cornwallis, Feb. 28, Beng. Pol. Cons., March 11, 1793, No. 17. The agreement is in No. 18; and also in Sir C. U. Aitchison's *Collection of Treaties, Engagements and Sanads*, 1931, Vol. XII, pp. 112-115.

Governor-General proposed instead to issue a general notification to the effect that all boats might pass freely to and from Assam paying the duties, and that the merchants should apply to Capt. Welsh for information regarding the distance to which the boats could proceed up the river with safety. The Governor-General decided to place the management of the Kandahar Choky under the Company with a view to secure the collections and to give protection to the merchants. The Commissioner of Cooch Behar was appointed to take charge of the Kandahar Choky and to act with Capt. Welsh in making the collections.[115]

The new measures began to operate in full force. In February 1794 Welsh was able to inform the Government that the iniquitous monopoly had been abolished. The Kandahar Choky remained in charge of the Commissioner of Cooch Behar till October 1794.

Retirement of Lord Cornwallis: There was a lull in the activities of the detachment during the rains of the year 1793. The season was quite unsuitable for military operations, for the floods and inundations and the strong currents of the Brahmaputra and the other rivers made transport of troops and provisions a very difficult matter. Unless proper precautions were taken a foreign army in Assam was bound to share the fate of the Moguls under Nawab Mir Jumla. "The rain was fearful", wrote Shihabuddin Talish, the chronicler of Mir Jumla's expedition, "the men soon suffered from severe fever and the casualties became numerous. A similar case never happened before in the history of Dihli. Here were 12,000 horse and numerous infantry locked in for six months, prevented by the rains from continuing operations, and yet scarcely attacked by the enemies that surrounded them. Nor did during this time provisions arrive. The Amirs turned their eyes longingly to Dihli, and the soldiers yearned for their wives and children." [116]

Early in March 1793 Lord Cornwallis had advised Capt. Welsh to lay in a plentiful stock of provisions, make the best accommodation for the troops, and secure a sufficient number of boats to enable the detachment to come down to Bengal in case of sickness or any other cause. In accordance with Welsh's requisition for more troops three companies had arrived on February 8, followed by five companies from the 16th N.I. which arrived on April 21

115. Cornwallis to Welsh, April 19, Beng. Pol. Cons., April 22, 1793, No. 14.
116. H. Blochmann, *Koch Bihar and Assam*, in *J.A.S.B.*, 1872, pp. 86, 91.

under the charge of Lt. Menur. Two companies from the 30th N.I. were returned to join their corps at Dacca. Welsh collected six months' provisions for the whole detachment now consisting of 12 companies, and stored them in separate granaries on both sides of the river, kept in readiness a sufficient number of boats, and repaired a building for the accommodation of the five new companies. The sepoys had erected huts for themselves. The market at Gauhati which met twice a week afforded abundance of rice. During the three months, August to October, Capt. Welsh entered into a long correspondence with the Commissioner of Cooch Behar and the Government in order to fix the average exchange of the Narayani rupees, *i.e.*, the coins issued from the mint of the Rajas of Cooch Behar, who always affixed the word *Narayan* after their first name. Seeing that the Commissioner of Cooch Behar and Capt. Welsh could not come to an agreement respecting the valuation of the Narayani rupees the Government of Bengal instructed the former not to issue any more coins of that specie to Capt. Welsh, but to advance the amount of the latter's pay abstracts in Sicca rupees.[117]

Through the exertions of Capt. Welsh great improvements were effected in the situation in Assam during the short period of seven months since his arrival at Gauhati. The Bengal marauders were expelled, the rebellious prince Krishnanarayan was converted into a friendly vassal of the Swargadeo, negotiations were conducted for inducing the other refractory chiefs to return to their allegiance, the Assam Raja was liberated from the influence of his corrupt and intriguing ministers, and himself purged of those cruel propensities which had brought ruin to himself and his country, and facilities for beneficial trade between Assam and the Company's provinces were established for the first time after the repeated failures of the preceding two decades. These results were achieved against enormous odds, such as the unknown character of the country and its people, the supineness of the Raja, the opposition of the ministers and the necessity for strict adherence to the neutrality clause of Pitt's India Act of 1784 which required Capt. Welsh to restore the peace of Assam by unarmed mediation.

But to Assam's great misfortune Lord Cornwallis whose intervention had effected these improvements retired from office towards the end of October 1793, and was succeeded by Sir John Shore, who by his temperament, conviction and past associations, was an

117. Govt. to Welsh, Oct. 25, Beng. Pol. Cons., Nov. 1, 1793, No. 55.

avowed advocate of the pacific system of forbearance and neutrality in the affairs of the native powers of India. Lord Cornwallis's deputation of Capt. Welsh to Assam at the head of an armed force was an act of bold statesmanship. The Act of 1784 had restricted the Company from interfering in the disputes of native powers. The expulsion of the Burkendazes which was declared to be the primary object of the expedition would necessarily involve some interference in the quarrels of the Assam Raja and his refractory chieftain Krishnanarayan neither of whom had offered any provocation to the Company. The expulsion of the Burkendazes was essentially the look-out of the Assam government; and the critics of the Company's Government in India could construe Cornwallis's action as one of aggression, "of ambition and conquest." The trial of Warren Hastings was then going on in full swing; and the Governor-General would not venture to do things which had the remotest resemblance to the condemned measures of his predecessor. But Lord Cornwallis's position was different from that of an ordinary Governor-General. He was the personal friend of Henry Dundas, President of the Board of Control, and of William Pitt, the Prime Minister, and enjoyed the support and confidence of the Court of Directors; besides, he was vested with extraordinary legal powers by the Act of 1786. This privileged position combined with his characteristic boldness enabled him to launch measures which could be interpreted as decided departures from the pacific system of neutrality recommended by the Act of Parliament.

That Lord Cornwallis anticipated some criticism of his intervention in Assam can be inferred from what he wrote to Henry Dundas on December 10, 1792,—"As Mr. Francis, or some such candid person, may represent our interference in the affairs of Assam as a continuation of our spirit of ambition and conquest, and as a cruel interruption of the tranquillity which that happy nation has hitherto enjoyed, I send you a copy of a letter which I have received from Capt. Welsh, containing a full narrative of what has passed, and of the state of the country as far as it has come to his knowledge." Lord Cornwallis assured Dundas that "Welsh is an honourable and worthy fellow, and will do no wrong."[118]

118. Charles Ross, *Cornwallis Correspondence,* Vol. II, p. 186. Lord Cornwallis refers to Welsh's letter of Nov. 27, Beng. Pol. Cons., Dec. 17, 1792, No. 47. The substance of the letter, in Ross's words, "is to describe the wretched state of the country [Assam], torn to pieces by contending factions, which gave full scope to the horrors which barbarians always inflict upon the inhabitants of the state which is the scene of their struggles for power."

In spite of his confidence in Welsh's moderation Lord Cornwallis reminded him constantly of his defined limits. Even the disturbances of the Burkendazes were to be composed by Welsh's "mediation and without bloodshed". "It would be more agreeable to me", wrote Lord Cornwallis to Capt. Welsh, "that you could obtain the submission of the Burkendazes by conciliation". Welsh was empowered "to act with the utmost vigour without exposing the detachment to the risk of meeting with a check" only when the Burkendazes had shown a design to amuse him and gain time by insincere negotiations.[119] He was instructed to endeavour to compose the civil feuds of Assam by the "amicable interposition of our good offices."[120] Lord Cornwallis repeatedly declared that he was not empowered to attempt to conquer Assam from which the Company had received no injury nor to acquire an influence in its internal management.[121] He wrote again that he would by no means permit the employment of the Company's troops to restore Gaurinath to the Raj,[122] and that Welsh should undertake no military expedition without an absolute necessity.[123] Welsh was reminded that the Government should not be "diverted even by the most benevolent motives from a strict obedience to the spirit of the Acts of the British Legislature."[124]

Lord Cornwallis would not have launched the enterprise if he had not seen in the invitation of the Assam Raja an opportunity to accomplish certain political objects. The Company had long been endeavouring to place its commercial relations with Assam on a regular basis and to acquire knowledge of its economic resources and the customs of its inhabitants. Lord Cornwallis had charged Hugh Baillie with the mission to collect information on these points on his appointment to Goalpara. But Baillie's letters did not go further than his immediate concerns. After the conclusion of the commercial treaty between the company and the Nawab Vizier of Oudh in 1788 Lord Cornwallis expected "from the adoption of such liberal plans to see new channels of wealth and commerce opened with the neighbouring countries of Nepaul, Tibet and Assam."[125]

119. Cornwallis to Welsh, Nov. 26, Beng. Pol. Cons., Nov. 26, 1792, No. 6.

120. Cornwallis to Welsh, Dec. 28, 1792, Ross, *Cornwallis Correspondence*, Vol. II, p. 187.

121. Cornwallis to Welsh, Dec. 18, Beng. Pol. Cons., Dec. 21, 1792, No. 17.

122. Cornwallis to Welsh, Jan. 15, Beng. Pol. Cons., Jan. 17, 1793, No. 10.

123. Cornwallis to Welsh, Ap. 2, Beng. Pol. Cons., Ap. 5, 1793, No. 34.

124. Cornwallis to Welsh, Ap. 2, Beng. Pol. Cons., Ap. 5, 1793, No. 34.

125. W. S. Seton-Karr, *Selections from Calcutta Gazette*, Vol. I, p. 262, Aug. 21, 1788.

The expedition to Assam supplied the opportunity for acquiring first-hand knowledge of that country and for adopting measures to regulate its trade with Bengal. It will be seen that the Court of Directors approved of the measures taken by Lord Cornwallis with regard to Assam as an exception to the general line of policy drawn for the guidance of the Government of India, such measures being warranted by the peculiar circumstances of the case.[126]

126, Court's Letter to Bengal, June 5, 1795.

PART II

Shore's Withdrawal of Troops from Assam

Lt. Williams and Lt. MacGregor at Kaliabar: Sir John Shore assumed the reins of office on October 28, 1793. He had arrived in Calcutta in the preceding March, and devoted the interval "in acquiring the most accurate information on the affairs of every Department."[1] Pacific from the outset it was possibly during this period that he formulated his Assam policy to which he gave expression soon after the commencement of his administration. What Capt. Welsh achieved meanwhile in Assam was owing to the delay on the part of the Government for preparing the ground for passing orders recalling the detachment.

On the appearance of the dry season Capt. Welsh, unaware of the new Governor-General's intentions, commenced his measures for the accomplishment of the two remaining objects, *viz.*, to meet the chiefs and to concert measures with them for the establishment of good government in Assam, and to restore Gaurinath Singha to his Raj. According to the instructions of the Government he was to effect these objects by friendly mediation. In the beginning of November 1793 Lt. Williams and Lt. J. A. Irwin were sent with a detachment to Kaliabar, 120 miles up the river Brahmaputra. Lt. MacGregor accompanied the party in his capacity as Assistant to the Deputation. Lt. Williams, the Officer Commanding, was directed to consult Lt. MacGregor and to attend to his requisitions on all occasions. The two officers were made fully acquainted with the instructions defining the objects of the expedition which Welsh had received from the Governor-General from time to time. The object of sending the detachment to Kaliabar was merely to give confidence to the inhabitants in general and encourage a free commercial intercourse. Lt. MacGregor was specially entrusted with the task of procuring a meeting of the chiefs with Capt. Welsh at Kaliabar or at Gauhati. The party arrived at Kaliabar on November 6, 1793.

Kaliabar was the headquarter of the Solal Gohain, and during the occasional occupation of Gauhati by the Moguls Kaliabar had

1. H. Furber: *The Private Record of an Indian Governor-Generalship,* letters of Sir John Shore to Henry Dundas, 1793-98, p. 26.

also been the headquarter of the Barphukan. Behind it lay the fertile district of that name inhabited by a numerous gentry. The fort of Simalugarh, whose impregnable character has been described with such animation and vividness by the authors of the *Fathiyah-i-Ibriyah* and *Maasirul-Umara*, was situated on the river bank at Kaliabar.[2] During the disorders at the Ahom capital between 1671 and 1681 the ambitious and intriguous Barphukan, named Laluk Sola, acting in collusion with Sultan Azamtara, governor of Bengal, had surrendered Gauhati to that prince's deputy Nawab Mansur Khan. Laluk Sola then proceeded to the capital, placed the boy-king Sulikpha on the throne and assumed virtual sovereign power. The nobles and chiefs met at Kaliabar and deliberated measures to remove the prevailing confusion and anarchy. The choice fell upon Prince Gadapani, who was likely to settle the disorders, establish a strong government and expel the Moguls from Gauhati. The chiefs then proceeded to the capital and placed Gadapani on the throne who justified the expectations of his supporters. Kaliabar, lying between Gauhati and the Ahom capital, thus served as the rallying point of the Ahoms where they matured schemes of rehabilitation.

Lt. MacGregor's first meeting with Helimeli Solal Gohain took place on November 8 at a distance of six miles from the fleet. The Gohain was attended by a numerous armed retinue, but Lt. MacGregor proceeded alone to the place of meeting. The Gohain promised to do everything in his power to promote the designs of Capt. Welsh and furnish supplies for the troops. He could not speak freely to Lt. MacGregor as he was surrounded by men of adverse parties and interests. Next day the Solal Gohain's Dewan and a confidential servant of Bishnunarayan ex-Bargohain met Lt. MacGregor. They conveyed their masters' willingness to offer co-operation to Capt. Welsh in suppressing the feuds provided the influence of the Barbarua and other obnoxious ministers would not again become predominant. Lt. MacGregor realised from the conversation of the two messengers that the government of Gaurinath Singha was rendered odious by his injudicious selection of ministers in suppression of the rights of the ancient nobility to make the selection.[3]

2. Mir Jumla, after a siege of six days, entered Simalugarh, *Simlahgar* as it is called in Persian chronicles, on February 26, 1662, "and was astonished to see the strength of the fortifications",—H. Blochmann, translation of *Fathiyah-i-Ibriyah* in *J.A.S.B.*, 1872, p. 72. See also *Maasirul-Umara*, tr. H. Beveridge, Bibliotheca Indica, *A.S.B.*, Vol. I, pp. 498-99.

3. MacGregor to Welsh, Nov. 10, Beng. Pol. Cons., Dec. 16, 1793, No. 40.

Lt. MacGregor met the Solal Gohain again on November 11, and Bishnunarayan ex-Bargohain the day after. They both promised by touching their images and *Sastras* or scriptures to exert themselves to the utmost of their abilities in promoting the restoration of peace. They demanded from Lt. MacGregor a similar testimony of the good intentions of the English Government and of his own personal friendship for them. Lt. MacGregor made the asseveration required of him by touching a book which for that purpose he had carried with him. The Solal Gohain informed Lt. MacGregor that the ceremony of dismissal had deprived the Barbarua and the Choladhara Phukan of the power of doing mischief at Gauhati; that the Barbarua's influence still continued in the territories formerly governed by him where his son had been raising contribution from the chiefs; and that the Choladhara Phukan was interested in debarring the Raja from regaining his influence which would consequently cripple that of the Phukan's relative Purnananda Buragohain. Bishnunarayan's grievance was his deprivation of the *Dola*,[4] the insignia of his position, through the instrumentality of the Barbarua. Lt. MacGregor recommended that Gaurinath Singha should pardon Helimeli and Bishnunarayan and restore the *Dola* to the latter, and deal with the Barbarua and and the Choladhara Phukan more severely.[5]

In his negotiations Lt. MacGregor obtained special help from a man sent by Krishnanarayan to go to the Gohains to tell them of the justice, equity and benefit which his master had received from the British officers in Assam. Lt. MacGregor proposed to leave for Jorhat on November 18 attended by a Subedar and 44 rank and file and Ensign Wood. On the 16th he despatched letters to Purnananda Buragohain, and to Pitambar Mahajan, the spiritual leader of the Moamarias at Rangpur. In his letter to the prime minister Lt. MacGregor expatiated upon the desire of Capt. Welsh and himself to restore peace and order in Assam in concert with the chiefs and nobles. He assured the Buragohain of his anxiety to cultivate the latter's friendship "whom everybody speaks in the language of commendation." In his letter to Pitambar Lt. MacGregor reminded him of the warfare subsisting between the Assam

4. The *Dola* was the Assamese litter, sedan or palanquin, having no wooden cover, and containing only an oval-shaped hollow boat-like seat with a curved or straight ridge-pole. The senior ministers, Buragohain, Bargohain and Barpatra-Gohain and the frontier governors enjoyed the use of a distinctive *Dola* during the continuance of their office.

5. MacGregor to Welsh, Nov. 12, Beng. Pol. Cons., Dec. 16, 1793, No. 41.

Raja's people and the Moamarias which was prejudicial to both parties. He assured the Mahajan of Capt. Welsh's determination not to attend to the interested reports of the Swargadeo or of any other man. The Mahajan was advised to repair to Kaliabar to meet Capt. Welsh who would explain the intentions of the Company with regard to Assam and grant amnesty, on behalf of the Swargadeo, to all offenders. "In acting otherwise", said Lt. MacGregor, "the blame of the consequences will be imputable to yourself alone."[6] In the meantime Helimeli and Bishnunarayan received letters from the Assam Raja pardoning their offences and reinstating them in their former offices. They were exhorted to act in concert with the Buragohain in suppressing the Moamarias so that the Raja might return to Rangpur during November or December.[7]

The only chief who could not be persuaded to come to Kaliabar was Sindhura Hazarika living at Nowgong at a distance of about 32 miles from the detachment camp. He was an officer of the Raja commanding 1,000 *paiks*, but taking advantage of the prevailing confusion, and specially of the defection of the Nowgong people, he had asserted his independence and became the leader of a faction. He had led the mob who demanded the dismissal of the officers for their oppressions during the Raja's stay at Nowgong, and had later compelled the Raja to flee from his camp at Khutarmur and return to Gauhati.

On November 15, 1793, Lt. MacGregor sent a Naick named Deen Dyal and 4 sepoys to seize Sindhura and bring him to Kaliabar. The party was accompanied by several guides who undertook to point out the residence of Sindhura. Deen Dyal arrived at Nowgong on the same night. He then crossed a stream and came upon the dwelling-place of Sindhura. A man came out, and the Naick informed him of Lt. MacGregor's orders to take Sindhura to Kaliabar, adding that if he declined to accompany the sepoys of his own accord he would be obliged to apply force. The man went in with the message. Shortly afterwards 1,000 men issued out of Sindhura's premises and compound armed with bows and knives. They declared that the Naick and his party were thieves, that Lt. MacGregor had no authority to force Sindhura from his residence and that he would not go. They demanded the immediate departure of the Naick threatening to throw him into the

6. MacGregor to Purnananda Buragohain and to Pitambar Mahajan, Nov. 16, Beng. Pol. Cons., Dec. 16, 1793, No. 41.

7. Gaurinath to Purnananda Buragohain, Helimeli Solal Gobain and Bishnunarayan ex-Bargohain, Nov. 18, Beng. Pol. Cons., Dec. 16, 1793.

stream on refusal. In the meantime another 1,000 men gathered on the scene. The Naick did not consider it advisable to commence hostilities with his small party consisting of only 4 men believing that it was not Lt. MacGregor's intentions to oppose force under such circumstances. He left Sindhura's place and returned to Kaliabar on the night of the 16th.

Lt. MacGregor accused Deen Dyal of neglect of duty in not making use of arms to enforce the execution of positive orders he had received from his superior. On November 18 a court martial consisting of one Subedar and two Jemadars was held under the orders of Lt. Williams, and on the requisition of Lt. MacGregor. Deen Dyal was convicted of a breach of the 2nd Article of the 15th Section of the Articles of War, and sentenced to be reduced to the ranks for the space of one month.[8] Lt. Irwin who superintended the proceedings of the court martial dissented from their verdict, but he had to record the sentence "much against his inclination."[9]

Capt. Welsh disapproved of the decision of the detachment and ordered the restoration of Deen Dyal to his rank as Naick. In communicating his orders to Lt. Williams Capt. Welsh observed that Deen Dyal had acted with caution in not attempting to oppose with 4 men 1,000 armed men, adding that "a different conduct in him would not only have been attended with inevitable destruction to his party, but would have defeated my object in sending up the detachment which was to promote peace and not to commence hostilities." Lt. Williams was taken to task for having detached a party on MacGregor's requisition without knowing the objects on which they were to be employed. Capt. Welsh reiterated his instruction to Lt. Williams that he should make use of no military force but with the utmost caution and when the exigency of the service absolutely required it.[10]

Capt. Welsh wrote to Lt. MacGregor at the same time permitting him to proceed to Jorhat with a personal guard, and expressing his inability to extend any detachment beyond Kaliabar. Lt. MacGregor was asked to desist from the adoption of harsh measures which might tend to weaken the confidence of the inhabitants in the lenity and moderation of the English Government.[11]

8. Williams to Welsh, Nov. 23, 1793, Beng. Pol. Cons., January 6, 1794, No. 14.

9. Irwin to Welsh, Dec. 6, 1793, Beng. Pol. Cons., Jan. 6, 1794, No. 17.

10. Welsh to Williams, Nov. 28, 1793, Beng. Pol. Cons., Jan. 6, 1794, No. 15.

11. Welsh to MacGregor, Nov. 28, 1793, Beng. Pol. Cons., Jan. 6, 1794, No. 15.

But the departure of Lt. MacGregor to Jorhat was prevented by an unforeseen development in his relations with Capt. Welsh. Lt. MacGregor had made a requisition to Lt. Williams for a small party of sepoys which was refused. On demanding the reasons, Capt. Welsh's instructions authorising Lt. Williams not only to dispute but to refuse compliance with Lt. MacGregor's requisition, were shown to the latter. In his letter of December 6, 1793, Lt. MacGregor informed Capt. Welsh of his inability to serve in a situation where he was not at liberty to carry out the intentions of the Government. He also disclaimed the reprehension which fell to his lot in Capt. Welsh's disapprobation of the proceedings of the court martial as he believed that the prosecution of Deen Dyal Naick was perfectly correct.[12]

Capt. Welsh expressed his displeasure at Lt. MacGregor's "unmilitary conduct in having presumed to comment upon the strictures he [Welsh] thought proper to make on the proceedings of the Court Martial held on Deen Dyal Naick."[13] With regard to Lt. MacGregor's expression of his inability to act with efficacy in his civil capacity as Assistant to the Deputation, Capt. Welsh suspended him from that position and recalled him to Gauhati.[14] Lt. Burton was appointed to succeed Lt. MacGregor. The suspension of Lt. MacGregor was approved by the Supreme Board in their meeting of January 6, 1794.[15]

Sir John Shore's first minute: On the same day when Lt. MacGregor's suspension was confirmed by the Board Sir John Shore delivered in his first minute on the affairs of Assam. The Governor-General pointed out that after the accomplishment of the first object of the Company's interference, *viz.*, the expulsion of the Burkendazes, the continuance of the detachment was permitted with the hope of establishing peace and order which would react favourably on the trade between Bengal and Assam. Though a year had passed after the expulsion of the Bengal marauders the Governor-General did not see any prospect of the establishment of peace in Assam. The obstacles, in the opinion of Sir John Shore,

12. MacGregor to Welsh, Dec. 6, 1793, Beng. Pol. Cons., Jan. 6, 1794, No. 18.

13. Welsh to MacGregor, Dec. 13, 1793, Beng. Pol. Cons., Jan. 6, 1794, No. 19.

14. Welsh to MacGregor, Dec. 13, 1793, Beng. Pol. Cons., Jan. 6, 1794, No. 20.

15. Secy. to Govt. to Welsh, Jan. 6, 1794, Beng. Pol. Cons., same date, No. 23.

came mainly from the imbecility and cruely of the Raja, the suspicions and animosities of the chiefs and the tyranny and profligacy of the ministers, though some of the chiefs had acknowledged their submission to the Raja and the wicked counsellors had been removed. It would appear inconsistent with the humane object of the Company's interference, thought the Governor-General, to leave the subjects at the mercy of the despotic monarch Gaurinath Singha without control or protection; and hence Capt. Welsh had been instructed to persuade the principal people of Assam to assemble and concert the establishment of some form of government in their country. But it was obvious to the Governor-General that no convention had yet been assembled, and that there was no possibility of one taking place soon. The advantages that would accrue to the Company from its interference in Assam were, in the opinion of Sir John Shore, *first*, the acquisition of Assam, and *secondly*, unrestrained commercial intercourse when the tranquillity of the country would be restored. The first, declared the Governor-General, was interdicted by the Act of Parliament from which he did not consider himself authorised to deviate; the second object had been partially achieved by the commercial arrangements made with the Swargadeo, though they were not confirmed by the Government lest the merchants should embark too heavily in their transaction during the unsettled condition of Assam.

To Sir John Shore the Company's interference in Assam appeared to be undefined as far as its ultimate object and duration were concerned. He therefore asked Capt. Welsh to supply information on the following points to enable the Government to determine on the 'mode, propriety and extent' of the continuance of that interference:—

1. The form of government that existed in Assam before the arrival of the detachment;

2. The extent to which the Raja's influence had been re-established, and whether any of his subjects still refused submission, if so their names, quality, force and situation, and also the measures that would be necessary to secure their obedience to the Raja's authority and the time required for carrying out those measures;

3. Whether there was any probability of the chiefs meeting soon to concert a form of government;

4. Whether there were persons of sufficient ability, weight and authority to take the place of the dismissed ministers;

5. Krishnanarayan's attitude and conduct towards the Swargadeo after his admission to the Raj of Darrang, and the probability of his assistance, if required, in supporting the Swargadeo;

6. The reasons for the Raja's delay in proceeding to his capital Rangpur;

7. Whether the commercial regulations settled between Capt. Welsh and the Raja were in full force, and if so, with what benefit; and whether any alterations were necessary for the improvement of the commercial intercourse between the two states;

8. Whether from the knowledge of the Raja's character he could be expected to observe the commercial stipulations after the return of the detachment;

9. Whether, in the event of the detachment being recalled, the government of Assam would be so regulated as to admit of a beneficial commercial intercourse between the two states, and to what extent and in what articles the commerce might be carried on. Welsh was also asked to supply information on the productions and actual commerce of Assam;

10. How far the pecuniary compensation to be made by the vassal Rajas in lieu of men has been carried into effect, and to what extent the money paid in consequence of such commutation has contributed to defray the expenses of the detachment;

11. The expenses of the detachment employed in Assam over and above the ordinary expenses and any means by which the expenses might be defrayed;

12. What more was proper to be done for the arrangement of the affairs of Assam, considering that arrangement as concluded by the establishment of the Swargadeo's authority, combined with the general assurances which Welsh was authorised to make in conformity with the instructions of Lord Cornwallis;

13. The consequences of recalling the detachment from Assam without further measures or interference on the part of the English Government.

The recommendations of the Governor-General were accepted by the Board and a letter was written to Capt. Welsh by the Secretary to the Government,—the first occasion when a letter was addressed to the commander of the Assam expedition by a secretary instead of the Governor-General.[16] The Board asked Capt. Welsh to furnish some account of Sindhura Hazarika and the

16. Secy. to Govt. to Welsh, Jan. 6, 1794, Beng. Pol. Cons., same date, No. 23.

offence he had committed to render his seizure necessary, their curiosity being probably excited by the similarity between the name of the Assamese rebel leader and that of the Mahratta chieftain Mahadaji Sindhia.[17]

One reading between the lines can trace in Sir John Shore's queries his intention to recall the detachment from Assam which becomes explicit in what he wrote in a private letter to Henry Dundas on January 10, 1794, four days after he had delivered in his minute: "I know not whether the Assam Business has attracted your Attention; I confess for my own Part, that I sincerely regret this Government ever interfered in it, and my present wish is to extricate ourselves from prosecuting our Interposition, as speedily as possible, without discredit, and if it can be effected, with some commercial Benefit. I have proposed a number of Queries to Captain Welsh comanding the detachment in that Country, in the hopes of bringing the Business to an issue: no inference must be drawn as to the Conduct I mean to pursue, which is perfectly open, notwithstanding any apparent Indication in the Queries."[18]

In the despatch to the Court of Directors of January 17, the Governor-General recounted the work achieved by Capt. Welsh in Assam and referred to the queries made to that officer and to the Government and the "anxious expectations for the limitation of its [of Company's interference] duration."

Capt. Welsh and Raja Gaurinath at Kaliabar: In the meantime Capt. Welsh, without any knowledge of the deliberations at Calcutta, had gone on steadily with the prosecution of the objects of his mission in Assam. On being convinced of the pernicious influence still exercised by the dismissed Barbarua and the Choladhara Phukan he sent them both to Rungpore in Bengal. He requested M. Leslie, Judge of that district, to treat the two Assam nobles with respect, and to advance them rupees 300 per month for their expenses. Capt. Welsh specified that the dismissed officers were not to be kept in confinement and that they should only be prohibited from corresponding or having any communication with

17. The name of this Assamese chief is spelt in the original records as 'Sindiah Hazare.' The Mahratta chieftain's name is also spelt in Shore's correspondence as 'Sindiah', *vide Shore's Letters,* Furber, pp. 39, 40, 48, 62, 89, 111, 140-147. Mahadaji died on February 12, 1794. A pair of Assam hawks had been presented to him by Lord Cornwallis in 1787, *Rungpore District Records,* Vol. VI, No. 151, p. 154.

18. Shore to Dundas, January 10, 1794, *Shore's Letters,* Furber, p. 35.

the people of Assam.[19] The good effects of their removal from Assam were soon felt: the Swargadeo finding it impossible to procure their interested advice began to pay more attention to that of Capt. Welsh.[20]

Bishnunarayan who was in temporary charge of Kamrup agreed to pay annually from February 1, 1794, the sum of rupees 51,000 towards the expenses of the detachment. Sivadatta Chetia, who had been meanwhile appointed Barphukan on the death of Haliram, agreed to raise 300,000 rupees from his provisions for the Swargadeo's treasury, part of which would be used for the payment of the Company's troops. Krishnanarayan and Hangsanarayan, joint-Rajas of Darrang, had paid rupees 10,000 out of the sum of rupees 50,000 which they had originally agreed to pay for the expenses of the detachment. Krishnanarayan had also discharged his debt to the Company on account of the Burkendazes. The Rajas of Darrang had supplied grain to Capt. Welsh and promised to furnish him in future with any quantity of rice that he might require.

After thus restoring the whole of Lower Assam upto Kandahar Choky to order and tranquillity Capt. Welsh proposed to quit Gauhati in the company of the Assam Raja to place the latter on the throne at his capital Rangpur. But he could not leave Gauhati before the third week of January 1794 the delay being due to several reasons. The ministers at Gauhati were unwilling to go to Upper Assam where their influence would be overshadowed by that of the prime minister Purnananda Buragohain. They therefore contrived to awaken the Raja's fears by representing to him the dangers of returning to the capital. Purnananda Buragohain was also not in favour of the Raja's proceeding to Upper Assam as the numerous officers about his person at Gauhati, having grants of land and feudal vassals, then employed by the Buragohain for other purposes, would demand their restitution.[21]

Another reason for the delay was the Raja's ill-health and domestic misfortunes of both of which Capt. Welsh was fully aware. There was discord in the Raja's household. Two of his wives, the one a daughter of Helimeli Phukan, and the other a

19. Welsh to M. Leslie, Nov. 30, Beng. Pol. Cons., Dec. 16, 1793.

20. Welsh to Shore, Jan. 17, Beng. Pol. Cons., Feb. 3, 1794, No. 6.

21. Lt. MacGregor was of opinion that "both his [the Buragohain's] interest and vanity is concerned in desiring to avert these claims", letter to Capt. Welsh, Feb. 19, Beng. Pol. Cons., May 28, 1794, No. 31. The produce of these lands was evidently used for feeding the large multitude whom the Buragohain had given shelter within the enclosures of Jorhat, see *Tungkhungia Buranji*, pp. 119-120.

daughter of a former Buragohain, had been treated very cruelly by the superior Rani; and from an apprehension that they would be murdered they left the Raja's house and proceeded to Cooch Behar to seek the protection of the English Government. C. A. Bruce, the Commissioner of Cooch Behar furnished them with a house and a guard of 4 peons and advanced 50 rupees to procure their necessaries. The two Ranis lived in retirement in Bengal though in constant dread of being taken away by the Assamese.[22]

Another Rani who was much beloved by the Raja, died on December 5, 1793. Her body was cremated in conformity with Brahmanical customs, and the thumb was buried in a mound to satisfy the requirements of the Ahom priestly code. The Brahmans and Gosains were invited to the *Sraddha* ceremony at the end of a month and given 7 to 20 rupees each and their share of all other things, utensils etc. In the absence of a Barbarua the Barphukan officiated as the master of the ceremonies on this occasion.[23]

At the end of the period of mourning Raja Gaurinath made preparations to proceed to Upper Assam. On January 17, 1794, Gaurinath in the company of Capt. Welsh and the remainder of the 16th Battalion left Gauhati by boat to Kaliabar. Before his departure Capt. Welsh wrote a letter to Sir John Shore announcing the event and regretting the absence of an encouraging tone in the correspondence of the Government after the retirement of Lord Cornwallis. "I quit Gauhati", wrote Welsh, "with the most sanguine expectation of being enabled completely to fulfil the intentions of Government, but it would have been a source of additional satisfaction to me had I received your approbation of the measures I have lately adopted."[24]

The party reached Mangaldoi on January 20. Lt. MacGregor had in the meantime submitted his apology to Capt. Welsh for his "intemperance" in writing the letter in question, and was reinstated in the duties of his civil station. About January 27 Capt. Welsh received Government's letter of the 6th with the queries to which he proposed to send an answer on his arrival at Kaliabar.

22. C. A. Bruce to Shore, Dec. 5, Beng. Pol. Cons., Dec. 16, 1793. In 1796 the Ranis were granted a pension of 100 rupees by the English Government. The younger Rani died in 1799; and the older, named Kamaleswari, continued to live in Bengal. In 1806 Kamaleswari planned to regain possession of Assam by force of arms, see Chapter VIII, Part I, *post*.

23. Welsh to Shore, Dec. 8, Beng. Pol. Cons., Dec. 20, 1793, No. 17. The ceremonies are vividly described by Dr. J. P. Wade in his *Geographical Sketch of Assam*, India Office Ms.

24. Welsh to Shore, Jan. 17, Beng. Pol. Cons., Feb. 3, 1794, No. 6.

The first act of Capt. Welsh at Kaliabar which he reached on January 31 was the despatch of Lt. MacGregor and Ensign Wood on February 3 for acquiring accurate information respecting the country to the east of Kaliabar. Capt. Welsh then held a meeting with Bishnunarayan Bargohain, Helimeli Solal Gohain and Sivadatta Barphukan who recommended the restoration of the ancient form of government, the appointment of Panisilia of the Lahan family as Barbarua,[25] and of two princes kept in concealment by the Gohains as Tipam and Charing Rajas. The two princes were to be vested with executive authority to relieve the monarch from the lesser cares and assist him in the greater cares of government. They were to be declared to be the next in succession to the throne. The appointments were to take place at a full meeting of the government which was possible only when the Buragohain would meet the Raja.

Gratified with the exertions of Capt. Welsh Swargadeo Gaurinath Singha had a private interview with him on February 10, where he expatiated upon the help he had received from the British Government, his inability and disinclination to transact business and the mistake committed by him in entrusting the administration to ministers. The Raja expressed his desire to place his affairs in the care of Capt. Welsh hoping that the latter would act for his benefit in concert with his ministers. Gaurinath Singha begged that he and Capt. Welsh might exchange swords as a token of the friendship which must in future subsist between them. The Raja evinced his anxiety to do everything in his power to promote the commercial intercourse between Bengal and Assam.[26]

Capt. Welsh's statement on Assam affairs: While at Kaliabar Capt. Welsh submitted his answers to the queries of Sir John Shore. Though concise in form his observations throw much light on the political and economic condition of Assam of the period preceding the occupation of the country by the British. Capt. Welsh received the special commendation of the Government for the clearness and accuracy of his replies.[27]

The information supplied by Capt. Welsh can be grouped under five different heads,—the form of government in Assam, the sources of the prevailing discontent, the results achieved by the Company's

25. This Panisilia or Lahan Barbarua is more popularly known as Baskatia Barbarua; his personal name is unknown.

26. Welsh to Shore, Feb. 12, Beng. Pol. Cons., Feb. 24, 1794, No. 15.

27. Secy. to Govt. to Welsh, March 19, 1794, Beng. Pol. Cons., same date, No. 20.

interference and the measures proposed, the commerce of Assam, and the probable consequences of the recall of the detachment.

The dominion of Assam was vested by right of conquest in the descendants of Sukapha, the original conqueror, and of his principal associates. The monarchy was partly hereditary and partly elective. The power of the monarch was limited by the necessity to obtain the consent of the aristocracy in all important matters such as conferment of honours, titles and offices, declaration of war or peace and decisions on foreign affairs. The king's order was necessary to execute sentence of death in a form by which the criminal's blood might be shed. Coins were struck in the king's name and his person was sacred. The aristocracy or *Patra-Mantri* was composed of Buragohain, Bargohain, Barpatra-Gohain, Barphukan and Barbarua. The three Gohains were known as *Patras*, and the Barphukan and the Barbarua as *Mantris*. The concurrence of the Gohains was necessary in all important affairs, such as proclamation or deposal of a sovereign. Provinces were allotted to the three Gohains where they exercised the independent rights of sovereignty. The Barbarua commanded forces, received the revenues and administered the justice of the upper and middle provinces from Sadiya to Kaliabar and also Darrang with the exception of the Gohains' districts. The Barphukan's jurisdiction commenced at Kaliabar and Darrang and extended to the confines of Bengal at Nagarbera on the south bank and Kandahar on the north. The two *Mantris* had each the command of 12,000 men. The establishment was composed of the officers who superintended the various arts, trades, sources of revenue and supplies to the king's household and the government stores. The Nyaya-Sodha Phukan received appeals from the decisions of the lower courts. One man in every unit of four had to serve the state by rotation, and in cases of emergency two or even three men had to serve simultaneously. Twenty men were commanded by a Bara, 100 by a Saikia, 1,000 by a Hazarika, 3,000 by a Rajkhowa and 6,000 by a Phukan. The constituent *paiks* could demand the dismissal of their Baras and Saikias. A Barua was the head of a department, or a deputy when it was presided over by a Phukan.

In the opinion of Capt. Welsh the prevailing discontent was due to the following sources,—the supersession of Mohanmala Barjana Gohain by his younger brother Rajeswar Singha through the intrigues of Kirtichandra Barbarua; the supersession of the rights of the hereditary nobility by the appointment of Rupchandra and Kirtichandra to the office of Barbarua; the secret machinations of Gohains, the general struggle for power under a weak monarch and the discontent of the people culminating in the Moamaria insurrections; the execution of Astabhujdeva, the Guru of the Moamarias and of his son; the depravity, caprice and cruelty of Gaurinath Singha and the oppressions of his ministers; the execution of Bailung Bargohain and of his five sons, and the mutilation of Sibram Barbarua and other nobles; and the division of the men of consequence in opposite interests, united only by sentiments against the wicked favourites of Gaurinath.

The result of the Company's intervention in Assam was mainly seen in the restoration of the Assam Raja to some degree of authority. Krishnanarayan behaved with proper submission to the Swargadeo inspired by a desire to meet the wishes of Capt. Welsh. The chiefs outwardly professed obedience to the Raja's authority but were inclined to act independently of it. To obtain their obedience more decided interference on the part of the Company was necessary. Welsh hoped to see the union of the chiefs to concert measures for the restoration of peace when they would be convinced of their protection by the Company from the tyranny of the Assam Raja, and the impossibility of prosecuting their ambitious designs. The period required for the submission of the chiefs would depend upon adventious circumstances. Capt. Welsh proposed to appoint capable ministers in his arrival at the capital in consultation with the three Gohains whose concurrence was necessary. The extra expense of the detachment in Assam would amount to rupees 113,872 per annum, of which the sum of rupees 102,600 would be paid as follows,—rupees 50,000 by the joint-Rajas of Darrang, rupees 1,600 by the Beltola Raja, and rupees 51,000 by Bishnunarayan from Kamrup.[28] The Assam Raja had promised to pay the arrears on his arrival at Rangpur; and to arrange for the payment of the entire expense of the detachment amounting to about three lakhs per year. In the opinion of Capt. Welsh there were abundant resources in Assam from which this sum could be raised.

Welsh reported that the commercial regulations settled in the treaty of February 28, 1793, were in full force, that the iniquitous monopoly had been abolished and Arcot rupees 12,012-2-9 had been received as part of the collections at the Kandahar Choky. From a knowledge of the Raja's character and the views of many

28. These arrangements made before Feb. 6 were altered in the agreement of Feb. 12. The Beltola Raja agreed, according to the second arrangement, to pay rupees 2,500, while the sum of 80,000 was to be raised from Kamrup instead of 51,000.

individuals whose interests were affected by the arrangements made with him Capt. Welsh foresaw that none of the stipulations would be observed after the withdrawal of the detachment and the control of the English Government. "Commerce would again be suppressed by the confusion prevalent in the country and the monopoly would revive in its pristine vigour." Welsh then enumerated the imports and exports of Assam. The former were mentioned under four heads based on the countries from which they came, *viz.*, the eastern confines of Sadiya, the northern confines inhabited by the Miris, Duflas and Bhutanese, from the southern confines or the Naga or Garo hills, and from the western confines of Bengal. The exports were classified into two main groups, *viz.*, the produce of the other confines and the produce of Assam. The latter were again treated under three heads of vegetable, mineral and animal productions. Of the first Capt. Welsh mentioned sugarcane, pepper vine, poppy 'growing in luxuriance in most of the Lower Provinces', indigo, mustard seed, tobacco, betelnut, ginger and rice. The mineral productions were gold obtained by washing the sands of Brahmaputra and other streams flowing from the mountains on the north and the south, iron and saltpetre. The animal productions consisted of lac, muga silk, elephant's tusk, rhinoceros's horn, buffalo's hide and deer's skins; of these muga silk was described as a most valuable and extensive article of export.[29] Welsh pointed out that the navigable streams which intersected Assam in every direction, specially in the season of the rains, offered great facilities for commercial intercourse.

In the opinion of Capt. Welsh, supported by that of the Raja and the most respectable natives of Assam, the consequences of recalling the detachment and the cessation of British influence would be highly disastrous to the country. The chiefs and the principal officers would revive their contest for power and influence producing the same confusion, devastation and massacre from which the country had been rescued by the intervention of the Company. Krishnanarayan would invite the Burkendazes to protect him from the vengeance of the Assam Raja. The wicked ministers would be restored to their offices. Commerce would be at a standstill owing to the prevailing confusion and would pass once more into the

29. David Scott added the following observation on Welsh's note on muga silk—"This is an article of great value and importance, and which will probably prove a useful material in many of the mixed stuffs manufactured in England from its superior strength and durability to silk."—Bengal Secret and Pol. Cons., July 14, 1826, No. 2.

hands of the monopolists. The monarch would be compelled to abandon his kingdom and seek asylum in foreign territories.[30] The events of the three subsequent decades justified the predictions of Capt. Welsh.

Arrangements for the payment of the detachment: In order that the services of the Company's troops in Assam might not be a burden on the finances of the Government Capt. Welsh made regular arrangements for the payment of the expenses by the Assam Raja. On February 12, 1794, at the instance of Capt. Welsh, Sivadatta Barphukan entered into an agreement with the Swargadeo for the annual payment of the sum of rupees 150,000 to be appropriated towards defraying the expenses of the detachment. The sum was to be raised partly from the usual taxes and partly from the pecuniary compensations payable by the chiefs in lieu of men. The Barphukan had represented the necessity of his being supported by the Company's troops in the exercise of his authority as he was to dispense with the services of men furnished by the chiefs of the districts under his jurisdiction. The sums to be collected by the Barphukan from the different districts for the year 1794 including the supposed collection from the Kandahar Choky were as follows,—Dimarua, rupees 5,000; Kamrup, 80,000; Darrang, 50,000; Beltola, 2,500; Rani, 6,000; Naduar, 15,000; Chatgurriah, 2,000; Sootia, 2,000; Charduar, 6,000; Ghiladhari, 3,000; Mayang Panbari, 400; Dhing, 2,000; Satrajiah, 1,000; Panchrajiah and Bebejia, 1,000; Nowgong, 2,000; Kharangi, 2,000; Chundorriah, 400; Dooria, 400; Kandahar Choky collections, 20,000, producing a total amount of rupees 200,700, of which the sum of rupees 150,000 was to be paid towards the expense of the Company's troops, leaving rupees 50,700 for the Swargadeo. The agreement was attested by the Khargharia Phukan, Krishnanath Goswami, Rudram Barua and Bikaram Majumdar. Capt. Welsh presented to Sivadatta Barphukan a *nuzur* in the name of the English Government on the ground that the Barphukan had expected it and that it was the custom of the country to give one on the signature of any agree-

30. Capt. Welsh's letter of Feb. 6, 1794, containing his answers, is inserted in Beng. Pol. Cons., Feb. 17, 1794, No. 20. In 1826 the queries with Welsh's answers were forwarded to David Scott for additional observations in the light of the events between 1794 and 1825. The whole is recorded in Beng. Secret and Pol. Cons., July 14, 1826, No. 2, from where Sir Alexander Mackenzie obtained the text of Appendix A inserted on pp. 377-394 of his *North-Eastern Frontier of Bengal.*

ment of importance.[31] The new Barbarua when appointed was to enter into a similar agreement for the remaining sum of rupees 150,000. Sir John Shore did not approve of Capt. Welsh's presentation of a *nuzur* to the Barphukan, "which", said the Governor-General, "from a regard to the dignity of this Government he [Welsh] ought to have avoided".[32]

On February 23 Capt. Welsh received a letter frcm Lt. MacGregor at Dergaon containing an account of his engagements with the Moamarias and asking for a reinforcement. Two companies were despatched from Kaliabar to MacGregor's relief on the 24th. On the following day Capt. Welsh himself proceeded to Dergaon leaving Lt. Burton with one company to guard the grain depot at Kaliabar.

Lt. MacGregor's encounter with the Moamarias: The circumstances which compelled Capt. Welsh to proceed in haste to Upper Assam arose out of the overzealous character of one of his subordinate officers. Lt. Robert MacGregor was a bold and energetic soldier, but his zeal for adventure sometimes exceeded its limits causing embarrassments to his superiors. He was perfectly amenable to discipline and reason when he acted under the immediate eye of his commanding officer, but he could not keep himself under proper restraint when left alone to act for himself. It was illustrated in the case of Deen Dayal Naick who was punished for not having opposed the numerous followers of the rebel chief Sindhura Hazarika.

On February 3, 1794, Lt. MacGregor had left for Deragon, at a distance of 75 miles to the east, in the company of Ensign Wood. He was given a personal guard composed of the Subedar Feyzand Ali, 3 Havildars, 3 Naicks and 44 sepoys. The duties entrusted to Lt. MacGregor, as specified in Capt. Welsh's instructions of February 2, were to proceed to Jorhat, the residence of the prime minister Purnananda Buragohain, at a distance of 19 miles to the east of Dergaon, to procure information relative to the nature and progress of the dissensions prevailing in Upper Assam, to select a spot of ground in the vicinity of Jorhat for the encampment of

31. Welsh to Shore, Feb. 12, Beng. Pol. Cons., Feb. 24, 1794, No. 15. The agreement is inserted in full in S. K. Bhuyan's *Early British Relations with Assam*, pp. 66-67, from a copy supplied in 1928 by the Imperial Record Department, Calcutta.

32. Shore's minute and Secy.'s letter to Welsh, March 19, 1794, Beng. Pol. Cons., same date, Nos. 16 and 20.

the battalion, to procure grain for the detachment for six months and to erect *golahs* for the storing of the provisions.[33]

Lt. MacGregor and his party arrived at Dergaon on February 11. He examined several sites for the encampment of the detachment but they were all reported to be inundated in the wet season. On February 14 Lt. MacGregor and Ensign Wood proceeded to Jorhat with a party of 24 sepoys and met Purnananda Buragohain in his fortified encampment. The conversations continued till next day. The prime minister promised to furnish 1,500 maunds of rice for the detachment. With regard to *dal, ghee,* oil and tobacco, which Lt. MacGregor requisitioned for the Bengal sepoys, the Buragohain declared they were luxuries which even the better sort of people among the Assamese could not afford themselves since the trouble commenced. The rice was to be raised from the locality of Kaziranga at a distance of 49 miles to the west of Jorhat; and at the instance of the Buragohain Lt. MacGregor sent one Naick and four sepoys to give confidence to the inhabitants of Kaziranga. Lt. MacGregor's arrival at Jorhat with a small force encouraged the fugitives to come back to their villages. MacGregor and Wood finally selected an elevated spot on the bank of the Dichoi river in the neighbourhood of the Buragohain's encampment.

During his stay at Jorhat Lt. MacGregor had an opportunity to study the situation in Upper Assam. He observed that the indiscriminate massacre of men, women and children which the Moamarias had committed on all those who were not favourable to their cause had created a general terror in the minds of the loyalists preventing the latter from openly co-operating with the Buragohain. "In the field", said MacGregor, "he [Buragohain] found himself unsupported, and it was only behind his bamboo fence that he looked for safety." Of the inhabitants many joined the successful Moamarias for safety and ultimate advantage, and many betook themselves to the neighbouring hills and many were carried off by the Duflas. According to Lt. MacGregor "in the space between Kolliabar and Joar Hat it would be difficult perhaps to find three hundred persons." Lt. MacGregor also noticed the general defection of the people and the encouragement which the Moamarias had received from the principal chiefs in the beginning of their muti-

33. MacGregor to Sir Robert Abercromby, Commander-in-Chief of the King's and Company's Forces in India, June 26, Beng. Pol. Cons., June 30, 1794, No. 34.

nious career. "The Moahmariahs", said MacGregor, "were for political purposes held out as a bugbear to the Surga Deo and his Government. They were encouraged in their rebellion by most of the principal chiefs in the first stage. But when they began to encroach too far on the privileges of the Boorah Gohain and some others of the Chiefs they thought it was then time to oppose their progress. It was then too late. The successful ravages of this factious and daily increasing rabble had inspired them with a spirit of enterprize which had entirely abandoned their adversaries. On this subject it is no incurious circumstance to observe that there is hardly a cadet of any good family in Assam, who is not bound to the interests of the Moahmariahs, while his father, mother, brother, uncle or cousin is engaged in that of the Surge Deo." Lt. MacGregor was astonished at the timidity of the Buragohain's adherents and the entire annihilation of the affections usually dependant on the ties of kindred so that none of them was willing to carry a letter from him to the Raja or Guru of the Moamarias although several confessed they had their near relations in the camp of the rebels.

Lt. MecGregor was of opinion that in view of the obdurate character of the Moamarias the language of negotiation alone would be of no avail and that it would be ultimately necessary to use coercive measures. Moderation; he believed, was precarious unless provided with the means of acting in a dictatorial capacity. He thought that he would be able to expel the Moamarias from Rangpur with only three companies of sepoys provided with ammunition and two months' provisions. He further suggested that the poverty of the country would not permit bringing such a number of people from Kaliabar as must attend Capt. Welsh and the Assam Raja.[34]

While at Jorhat Lt. MacGregor heard of the recent depredations of the Moamarias. The Hirkara despatched by him to ascertain the facts came back and reported that the Moamarias had killed one person and cut off the hand of a woman for not being able to supply information respecting the Company's troops. Lt. MacGregor left Jorhat on the morning of the 17th and reached his boats at Dergaon by 3 P.M. At 9 that evening MacGregor received a message from the Buragohain entreating his return to Jorhat. It was not possible for MacGregor to comply with the Buragohain's request in view of Capt. Welsh's wishes to desist

34. MacGregor to Welsh, Feb. 19, first letter, Beng. Pol. Cons., May 28, 1794, No. 31.

from harsh measures. On the morning of the 18th Lt. MacGregor fearing "that the already depressed spirit of himself [Buragohain] and his adherents should fall entirely under the daring efforts of their enemy", despatched the Subedar with 20 rank and file to assist in the defence of the Buragohain's fort should it be assailed, but on no account to proceed further against the Moamarias. Two hours after the departure of the Subedar's party Lt. MacGregor received another message from the Buragohain to which he replied that the Subedar with his troops would be able to defend the Jorhat fort and that the few men remaining at Dergaon were necessary for protecting the boats.[35]

At 7 P.M. on the 19th Lt. MacGregor and Ensign Wood left Dergaon for Jorhat with one Havildar, one Naick and 14 sepoys. One reason assigned by Lt. MacGregor for this sudden resolution was his apprehension of the Subedar acting improperly notwithstanding the orders he was given.[36] The two officers travelled incessantly the whole night in heavy rain till 4 o'clock in the morning when they approached so near the encampment of the Moamarias, four miles west of Jorhat, that they could distinctly hear their sentinels challenging. The party abandoned the main road and proceeded by a circuitous route till they arrived at Jorhat at 8 A.M. with two sepoys and a few servants. The Moamarias had meanwhile burnt all the houses in the vicinity.

By 9 A.M. on the 20th the Moamarias extended themselves between the main road and the route followed by Lt. MacGregor who now became extremely anxious for the 12 sepoys and the Havildar and the Naick left behind. Lt. MacGregor took out the Subedar's party of 20 rank and file and drew up, with their right flank covered by a bund. The Moamarias numbering 2,000 ignored the presence of the Assamese and Manipuri forces and charged the few sepoys of the Company. The onset was tumultuous and irregular and the Moamarias fought with the confidence inspired by their superior numbers and their uninterrupted successes. The sepoys behaved with courage and coolness, and fired singly and only when the necessity and the objects were pointed out by the two officers. This had its desired effect, and in a short time the sepoys and the troops of the Buragohain were enabled to advance and clear the plain. This initial success was attained without any

35. MacGregor to Welsh, Feb. 19, 1794, first letter, *ibid.*

36. MacGregor to Welsh, Feb. 19, second letter, written immediately before departure for Jorhat, Beng. Pol. Cons., May 28, 1794, No. 33. MacGregor assured Capt. Welsh "of his discretion on this occasion."

injury to the sepoys. At the close of the encounter Lt. MacGregor and Ensign Wood repaired to take some refreshment.

In this interval the enemy under the cover of the jungle moved to their right; and watching their motions the Subedar moved to his left. At about 1 P.M. Lt. MacGregor proceeded on horseback within a short distance of the enemy's situation and discovered a secure spot which he directed his party to occupy. The Moamarias desiring to prevent the sepoys occupying that place advanced quickly and saluted them with a shower of arrows from a distance of 120 paces. The sepoys began a quick fire the effects of which did not make much impression on the enemy at first; but in the course of ten minutes, seeing considerable diminution of their numbers the Moamarias deserted the field in great precipitation. Lt. MacGregor did not consider it advisable to pursue the enemy so feebly supported as he was by the Buragohain's troops. After keeping possession of the field for some time MacGregor marched his troops back to their quarters. In this engagement only 4 sepoys were wounded, while the enemy lost not less than 80 men. The party left in the rear joined Lt. MacGregor in the evening with the loss of a Naick and a sepoy who were both killed by the Moamarias.

In his report on the encounter with the Moamarias Lt. MacGregor admitted the necessity of avoiding "a reconnoitre with this [Moamaria] people, aware as I am of the instructions you have received from Government to abstain from coercive measures." He pointed out the circumstances which compelled him to act in the manner he had done considering the provocations offered and the objects which the Government had in view. "These objects," said MacGregor, "I am now firmly persuaded never could, nor can be effected without humbling the spirit of this cruel and obdurate people." He, however, assured Capt. Welsh that until the arrival of the reinforcement from Kaliabar he would be very careful of his men and ammunition nor go beyond 300 yards from the Buragohain's fort. He suggested the necessity of medical assistance in the event of further engagements with the Moamarias.[37] In the Assamese account of the encounter the provocation is attributed to the Moamarias: "In *Saka* 1715 [January, 1794 A.D.]", wrote Srinath Barbarua in 1804, "the Swargadeo, accompanied by the Captain [Welsh] proceeded upstream and arrived at Kaliabar. From there he despatched the two Sahibs, Mihnagar Saheb [Lt.

37. MacGregor to Welsh, Feb. 21, Beng. Pol. Cons., March 14, No. 28.

MacGregor] and the Chota Saheb [Junior Sahib, *i.e.*, Ensign Wood] with a detachment of sepoys, to the camp of the Buragohain who had been fighting with the Moamarias at Dichoi [Jorhat] for full seven years. The Moamarias then attacked the fort of the Dangaria [Buragohain], but fortunately the Sahebs had now joined the Mahamantri Buragohain at Dichoi. The Dangaria engaged the sepoys in the fight and it resulted in his victory."[38]

Lt. MacGregor's defeat of the Moamarias produced the desired moral effect upon them. They were astonished that 20 men should have stood against an army who had successfully attacked thousands. They showed themselves again on the 21st, but on the appearance of Lt. MacGregor and his small party they took to their heels and retreated towards Rangpur. From his experience of those few days Lt. MacGregor wrote to Capt. Welsh,—"If my existence was to be the forefeit of a failure I should not hesitate with three companies to proceed with confidence against Rangpore [Rangpur] and Ghurgong [Gargaon]".[39]

But Capt. Welsh considered Lt. MacGregor's attack on the Moamarias as a distinct violation of the instructions given to him at the time of sending him to Dergaon and Jorhat. Capt. Welsh had contemplated to conciliate the Moamarias but Lt. MacGregor's almost unprovoked attack on them defeated his plan of obtaining their submission by pacific overtures. "I regret extremely", wrote Capt. Welsh to Sir John Shore, "it [MacGregor's encounter with the Moamarias] should have occasioned, as it may probably involve me in hostilities which I am so anxious and have been so particularly directed to avoid."[40] Lt. MacGregor had been asked to collect accurate information about the districts round Jorhat and Rangpur, and in no part of the instructions was he authorised to commence hostilities with the Moamarias. Besides, military measures were prohibited by the Governor-General of which MacGregor had full information. The 44 sepoys detached with MacGregor were meant for his personal guard and not intended for employment on military purposes except in cases of urgent necessity. The night march to Jorhat, the loss of the Naick and the sepoy, the death of more than 80 Moamarias and the exposure of the small party to the increased provocation of the rebels were caused by Lt. MacGregor's precipitancy.

38. *Tungkhungia Buranji*, p. 132.
39. MacGregor to Welsh, Feb. 26, Beng. Pol. Cons., May 28, 1794, No. 35.
40. Welsh to Shore, March 9, Beng. Pol. Cons., March 27, 1794, No. 22,

At 11 o'clock on the night of the 23rd February Capt. Welsh received Lt. MacGregor's letter of the 21st, reporting on the engagements of the previous day. On the morning of the 24th. Capt. Welsh despatched two companies in advance to Jorhat and decided to proceed himself with the Assam Raja on the 26th.

The conduct of Lt. MacGregor, which involved a second offence within the course of two months, was reported to the Commander-in-Chief Sir Robert Abercromby. Capt. Welsh expressed his disapprobation of "Lt. MacGregor having employed, in the manner he related, a party sent with him merely as a personal guard."[41] The Board in their meeting of April 14, supported Capt. Welsh and recorded their own disapprobation of "the impudence and impolicy" of Lt. MacGregor's conduct, and ordered his removal from the detachment in Assam and directed him to join his corps at Berhampore. The Board also abolished the appointment held by Lt. MacGregor as Assistant to the Deputation.[42]

Lt. MacGregor's defence is embodied in his letter to Capt. Welsh and in his subsequent memorial to Sir Robert Abercromby. In his letter of February 22, which was written in anticipation of Capt. Welsh's disapprobation, Lt. MacGregor detailed the circumstances which had come to his knowledge after the occurrences of the 20th. The Moamarias had bound the Naick and the sepoy with cords before killing them, had captured Ensign Wood's horse and wounded his *Syce* or groom. These were, in the opinion of Lt. MacGregor, sufficient reasons for having treated the Moamarias as enemies, to whose fury and vengeance the Buragohain and his adherents would have fallen sacrifices had not their advance been checked. The Moamarias had planned to march to Dergaon to attack the sepoys and then move on to Kaliabar. From these circumstances Lt. MacGregor believed that his action, instead of militating against the instruction of Government to avoid coercive measures, was greatly conducive to the prosecution of the objects of establishing the Swargadeo in his authority and restoring peace to the country.[43] In his letter of March 1 Lt. MacGregor declared that he had acted "under the statutory reflection of having saved the lives of thousands by hazarding that of a few."[44] In his letter of May 14, written at the Ahom capital Rangpur, MacGregor requested that Government would require his presence at Calcutta

41. Welsh to Lt. Col. P. Murray, Adjutant-General, Feb. 24, Beng. Pol. Cons., March 14, 1794, No. 27.

42. Board's resolution, Ap. 14, 1794, Beng. Pol. Cons., No. 24.

43. MacGregor to Welsh, Feb. 22, Beng. Pol. Cons., May 28, 1794, No. 33.

44. MacGregor to Welsh, March 1, Beng. Pol. Cons., May 28, 1794, No. 36.

where he would be able to prove that he had in the first instance executed Capt. Welsh's orders and eventually acted from the "purest motives of humanity and self-defence." After considering these representations of Lt. MacGregor the Board confirmed their disapprobation and orders of recall passed previously in their meeting of April 14.[45]

Lt. MacGregor returned to Berhampore in the last week of May. On June 26 he submitted a memorial to Sir Robert Abercromby narrating all the circumstances connected with his deputation to Dergaon and Jorhat, and his actions on February 20, emphasizing on the plea of self-defence. "I had no alternative," asserted Lt. MacGregor, "but either to suffer the minister [Buragohain] with whom I was sent to concert measures for the advancement of the public service, and his people to be murdered, the grain intended for Capt. Welsh's detachment to be plundered or destroyed, and my own party and myself to be cut to pieces, or to chastise the aggressors." The Board in their meeting of June 30 once more upheld their disapprobation and order of recall.[46]

Gaurinath Singha restored to Rangpur: Capt. Welsh reached Dergaon on March 8, 1794, with the Swargadeo and the 16th Battalion. The country through which he passed was in the most devastated state though it showed traces of cultivation and thick population.[47] On the 10th Capt. Welsh wrote a letter to Pitambar Mahajan, and other Moamaria chiefs asking them for assistance in restoring peace and order, "in effecting which", said Welsh, "it is by no means my wish to adopt harsh or coercive measures unless you oppose me in the prosecution of these laudable designs." But it was found difficult to convey this letter to the destination.[48]

From Dergaon Capt. Welsh proceeded to Sonari Noi at a distance of about 18 miles from the capital Rangpur. On the 17th he sent Lt. J. A. Irwin by land with two companies to proceed

45. MacGregor to Welsh, May 14, Beng. Pol. Cons., May 28, 1794, No. 30; Board's resolution in No. 37.

46. MacGregor to Sir Robert Abercromby, June 26, Beng. Pol. Cons., June 30, 1794, No. 34.

47. Welsh to Shore, March 9, Beng. Pol. Cons., March 27, 1794, No. 22. "The distance between Kulyabar and Ghargaon is well cultivated; everywhere are houses, gardens and orchards. Along the sides of the road there are high bamboo shrubs. There are many wild and cultivated flowers, and behind the bamboos, as far as the hills, there are fields and gardens."—H. Blochmann, *Koch Bihar and Koch Hajo*, *J.A.S.B.*, 1872, tr. of *Fathiyah-i-Ibriyah*, chronicle of Mir Jumla's invasion of Assam, 1662-63.

48. Welsh to Pitambar, March 10, Beng. Pol. Cons., March 27, 1794, No. 23.

towards Rangpur, then in occupation of the Moamarias, and to endeavour to forward the letter to the Moamaria chiefs. Lt. Irwin was authorised, in the event of any indication of hostility from the Moamarias, to march forward and take possession of the capital provided his force was equal to the undertaking. Lt. Irwin had proceeded about 8 miles when he was furiously attacked and surrounded by a large body of men armed with matchlocks, bows and spears, while some had remained concealed in the jungle with *jinjals.*[49] Lt. Irwin pushed on with his force defeating the Moamarias in several skirmishes, and took his post at the stone bridge at Namdang, the western extremity of the town of Rangpur at a distance of about 4 miles from the Raja's palace. The rebels suffered heavy losses; their chief was dangerously wounded; while on the side of the Company's troops there were 50 wounded, mostly by arrows.

On receiving information of Lt. Irwin's encounter Capt. Welsh marched from Sonari Noi with two companies and joined him at daybreak on the 18th. After having made the necessary preparation for storming the capital in case of his meeting with resistance Capt. Welsh proceeded to Rangpur and took possession of the capital, the enemy having evacuated it a few hours before his arrival leaving large quantities of grain, cattle, household furniture and treasure. Orders were issued forbidding the sepoys and the camp-followers to go to the villages in search of plunder or to conceal articles of value found in the capital. On the 19th Capt. Welsh detached a company to escort Gaurinath Singha to Rangpur. The Raja arrived on the 21st with the Buragohain, Bargohain, Barphukan and the newly appointed Barbarua. The Barpatra Gohain was on his way to Rangpur and on his arrival would be completed the whole assembly of the Ahom *Patra-Mantri.*[50]

Rangpur as Welsh saw it was about 20 miles in extent with an enclosure or *Killah* in the centre of the town. The country round the capital was in the highest state of cultivation. The occupation of Rangpur gave particular satisfaction to Capt. Welsh and his colleagues. Immediately after that event he wrote with exultation to the Adjutant-General to inform the Commander-in-Chief "that I have taken possession of Rungpore."[51] Lt. MacGregor with his characteristic enthusiasm wrote in an independent

49. *Jinjals* were wall pieces carrying small balls varying from half a pound to 2 or 3 pounds in weight.

50. Welsh to Murray, March 21, Beng. Pol. Cons., April 7, 1794, No. 42.

51. Welsh to Murray, March 18, Beng. Pol. Cons., April 7, 1794, No. 40.

letter to the Government,—"I do not know whether Captain Welsh has had leisure to inform the Governor-General that he is now in possession of the capital of Assam, and I were negligent did I omit to mention a circumstance that will give Government so much pleasure."[52]

A Durbar was held on the 21st where Capt. Welsh asked the Raja whether he needed any longer the assistance of the Company's troops now that he was restored to his throne. The Swargadeo and his ministers expressed their unanimous opinion that the country would relapse into confusion and anarchy without the support of the Company. At the instance of Capt. Welsh they promised to pardon the rebels if they returned to their allegiance to the Swargadeo, and Welsh became the guarantor of that promise. Letters to that effect were despatched to the Moamarias who were now posted in the villages round Sibsagar on the opposite bank of the Dikhow river, which they frequently attempted to cross with an intention to set fire to the houses in the capital.[53] The major portion of the Moamarias retreated to their stronghold at Bengmara to plan fresh schemes of retaliation. On March 26 Swargadeo Gaurinath Singha and his *Patra-Mantri* despatched letters to the Governor-General referring to the occupation of Rangpur through Capt. Welsh's "spirited conduct and the good behaviour of the Sepoys" and requesting the continuance of the detachment in Assam.[54]

Property captured at Rangpur: The goods left by the Moamarias on their precipitous flight from Rangpur were claimed by the detachment as prize property on the ground that they had taken by storm the outworks of the capital situated on the Namdang bridge from where the town commenced and where the Moamarias in their last stand were repulsed by Lt. Irwin. The post at Namdang was the only defensible one about Rangpur, and Capt. Welsh was of opinion that Lt. Irwin could have occupied the capital on the 17th as easily as it was done on the following day. Agents were appointed for the captured property consisting of Lt. J. Williams, Lt. T. C. Wroughton, Lt. J. A. Irwin, Lt. R. Eyton,

52. MacGregor to H. Cornish, Secy. to Govt., March 19, Beng. Pol. Cons., April 7, 1794, No. 39.

53. Welsh to Shore, March 22, Beng. Pol. Cons., April 7, 1794, No. 41.

54. King Gaurinath, Purnananda Buragohain, Bishnunarayan Bargohain, Panisilia Barbarua and Sivadatta Barphukan to Governor-General, March 26, received at Calcutta on Ap. 12, Beng. Pol. Cons., June 2, 1794, No. 22.

Lt. G. Welsh, Lt. R. MacGregor, Dr. J. P. Wade, and Ensign T. Wood. The value of the goods was estimated as follows:—

A. Specie, 36 gold mohurs, each valued at 11 Rajamohury rupees	..	Rs. 396- 0-0
B. Specie, silver Rajamohury rupees	..	Rs. 25,200- 0-0
C. Gold bullion, 6020 *Phalas* or plates at rupees 8 each	..	Rs. 48,160- 0-0
D. Silver bullion, 21673 *Phalas* at 9 annas each		Rs. 14,722- 5-0
E. Amount from sales of sundry articles	..	Rs. 10,325-14-0
F. Probable amount of articles unsold	..	Rs. 6,000- 0-0
Total	..	Rs. 104,804- 3-0

Besides the above there were numerous heads of cattle and a large quantity of grain of which no just estimate could be formed by the agents.[55]

On March 21, Lt. Williams, on behalf of the officers of the detachment, asked Capt. Welsh to represent to the Swargadeo about their claims to the captured property, which in their opinion were founded on " the usages and laws of war and the frequent and recent decisions of Courts of Law ". They held that the articles in question were " by no means the subject of future donations but the immediate, indisputable and inviolable property of the captors." [56]

The Raja and his ministers in appreciation of the gallant exertions of the troops admitted the claims of the captors regretting at the same time that the prize captured was inadequate for rewarding their services. On the 23rd, Capt. Welsh requested the Commander-in-Chief to obtain the sanction of the Government for the division of the prize property.[57] Lt. MacGregor claimed the share of a Captain on the ground that the allowances granted to him by the Government as Assistant to the Deputation were those of a Captain. To this claim the agents replied that Lt. MacGregor was entitled only to the share of a Lieutenant as Adjutant to the Detachment. On the 26th March, Lt. MacGregor asked Capt. Welsh to submit his claims to Government expressing his intention " in the last resort to have recourse to law."[58]

55. Welsh to Murray, Ap. 5, Beng. Pol. Cons., Ap. 25, No. 23; also Cons. of May 28, 1794, No. 29.

56. Williams to Welsh, March 21, Beng. Pol. Cons., May 28, 1794, No. 29.

57. Welsh to Murray, March 23, Beng. Pol. Cons., May 28, 1794, No. 29.

58. MacGregor to the Agents for the captured property, March 26, Beng. Pol. Cons., Ap. 14, 1794, No. 22.

Sir John Shore's minute on the proceedings in connection with the claims of the detachment to the property captured at Rangpur, delivered to the Board on April 14, were in strict conformity with the rectitude of conduct which he himself possessed and which he demanded so rigorously from his officers. Sir John Shore was not prepared to accept that Rangpur had been taken by storm as Capt. Welsh had found it evacuated on his approach. The Governor-General held that the property found at Rangpur either belonged to the Raja or to his subjects, and as Capt. Welsh had proceeded to Rangpur for the express purpose of re-establishing the Raja in the possession of his legal authority over his capital "the appropriation of the property found there is contrary to every maxim of policy and justice, disreputable to the character of this Government, and calculated to excite a distrust of the equitable assurances made in its name and by its authority." Capt. Welsh was directed to suspend the distribution of the property if it had not already taken place, and to replace it in the situation in which it was found on his arrival at Rangpur. Sir John Shore assumed that the proceedings respecting the captured property had taken place without the knowledge and authority of Capt. Welsh; but he waited for Welsh's explanation before passing judgment on his conduct. Lt. MacGregor's conduct in proposing to appeal to law in case his claim was not admitted by Government was considered by the Governor-General as "very disrespectful and censurable." It was at this meeting of the Board that orders were passed recalling MacGregor from Assam.[59]

In the meantime, the demands of the officers for an immediate distribution of the captured property being insistent, Capt. Welsh had on March 28 ordered the apportionment of the whole conformable to the customary rules, without receiving the sanction of the Government for which he had applied. The reason assigned for this irregularity was, in Capt. Welsh's own words, "consideration of the situation we were then in, thinking it advisable that it should be at the risk of individuals rather than at that of the public."[60]

With regard to the grain and cattle the agents for the captured property demanded from the Raja a pecuniary compensation of one lakh of rupees payable at a specific period. They complained of the diminution of the goods owing to their frequent depredations by the Raja's men. A part of the grain had to be distributed to

59. Shore's minute, Beng. Pol. Cons., Ap. 14, 1794, No. 24.
60. Welsh to Murray, April 16, Beng. Pol. Cons., May 28, 1794, No. 29.

the cultivators to sow the land which had already been tilled. As regards the cattle it transpired that a large proportion had been plundered by the Moamarias from the neighbouring villages and their owners thought it a fitting opportunity to regain what was once their property. The prime minister at last agreed to pay rupees 12,530 in the course of the next three months estimating the value of the remaining property as follows:

35,000 *toplas* or bags of paddy at 20 *toplas* per rupee	Rs.	1,750
820 buffaloes at 5 rupees each ..	Rs.	4,100
890 cows at 2 rupees each ..	Rs.	1,780
100 Seringahs[61] at 30 rupees each ..	Rs.	3,000
100 „ „ 12 „ „ ..	Rs.	1,200
100 „ „ 7 „ „ ..	Rs.	700
Total ..	Rs.	12,530

The Buragohain's offer was not acceptable to the agents who now proposed to refer the matter to the Government of Bengal. The idea was not supported by Capt. Welsh who considered the prize "as the voluntary gift of the Swargadeo." On April 18 Capt. Welsh was able to inform the Commander-in-Chief that after securing a sufficient quantity of grain for the use of the detachment the remainder and the cattle in question had been given up to the Swargadeo for the benefit of the inhabitants of Assam.[62]

On receiving the full account of the transactions the Board in their meeting of May 28, 1794, censured the action of Capt. Welsh in permitting the division of the captured property. The Government was not prepared to consider the possession of Rangpur as coming in any respect within the description of a capture by storm. The consent of the Assam Raja had, in the Board's opinion, no validity under the particular situation in which it was given. This consideration, it was held, should have precluded Capt. Welsh from making any application to the Raja for his consent, but "should even have prevented his [Welsh's] acceptance of it had it been voluntarily given." The Board then pointed out that Capt. Welsh

61. 889 Seringahs or boats were found at Rangpur of which 589 belonged to the ryots and were consequently returned to the owners. Boats had been kept in readiness by the Moamarias on the Dikhow at Rangpur. *Seringah* is probably a variant of the South Indian word *Chellengo,* a boat, *vide* Hobson-Jobson. Chelengi is a sort of Assamese boat used for express service.

62. Welsh to Murray, Ap. 18, Beng. Pol. Cons., May 28, 1794, No. 29.

had not considered the right of Government to a proportion to which it would be entitled if the property had been admitted as prize property, and that he ought to have waited for Government's orders for which he had applied. The Governor-General expressed his conviction of "the extreme impropriety which had accompanied the whole transaction." The Government's strictures on Capt. Welsh for his action respecting the captured property were however, accompanied by its "approbation of the general tenor of his former conduct on his present service." In the same meeting of the Board Lt. MacGregor was acquitted of any intentional disrespect in the communication to appeal eventually to a court of law, though the orders for his recall to Berhampore were once more upheld.[63]

Recrudescence of Burkendaz troubles: The expulsion of the Burkendazes as effected by Capt. Welsh offered only a temporary relief to the inhabitants, for within a few months they assembled again in the frontier districts of Bengal and made plans to enter Assam. In February 1794 the Burkendazes declared their intention of attacking Cooch Behar and its treasury on a certain day, and in the beginning of March a gang of about 3,000 Burkendazes posted themselves within six *coss* from Cooch Behar. Lt. Sloane was asked by the Magistrate of Rungpore to take up a position in or near Cooch Behar "till reinforced or relieved or the Fakirs move off towards Assam which is their avowed route." On March 9, the Commissioner of Cooch Behar reported of the Burkendazes' intention of entering into Assam by the low countries of Bhutan. They were commanded by Phatik Barua, Hazari Singh, Jogangiri and Cherag Ali Fakir. The two former were reported by the Commissioner to be under some Assam chiefs.[64]

Having heard of the intended invasion of Assam by the banditti Capt. Welsh despatched Lt. William Cresswell to join Lt. George Dick at Gauhati who had remained there in charge of the Company's magazine and *golah*. On the 19th March, the day after Capt. Welsh's occupation of the Ahom capital Rangpur, the

63. Resolution of Governor-General in Council, Beng. Pol. Cons., May 28, 1794, No. 37. According to Srinath, the captured property consisted of 400,000 pieces of gold ornaments, 400,000 pieces of silver ornaments, gold to the value of 20,000,000 rupees, 2,000 boats, one tusker, one she-elephant and 4,000 guns, *Tungkhungia Buranji*, p. 134. According to Dutiram, Welsh was permitted by Gaurinath to ransack the subterranean vaults where treasures had been hidden since the time of Rudra Singha, *Asamar Padya-Buranji*, pp. 112-13, 288-89.

64. J. M. Ghose, *Sannyasi and Fakir Raiders in Bengal*, p. 121.

Burkendazes consisting of Sannyasis and Fakirs entered into Assam in three divisions commanded by Russeldar Hazari Sing, Kanak Sing and Jogangiri Bairagi. The chief commander was one Dyan Gir Bairagi, and Phatik Barua was with him. The party that entered Assam numbered 2,500 and many more were on their march from the westward to join their comrades in Assam. Their chief destination was reported to be Darrang the Rajas of which prepared to flee into the jungles. The feeble garrison of the Company stationed at Jugighopa could not resist the march of the Burkendazes, and Lt. Sloane had been ordered back to Tajpore. On their entrance into Assam the Burkendazes plundered every village in the neighbourhood, and the task of opposing their advance fell upon Lt. Dick who had at his disposal only two companies and a half including the detachment ordered from Goalpara under Lt. Robinet. Besides, there was no Surgeon at Gauhati.

On March 24 Lt. Dick pursued the Burkendazes to their post at Rowmari on the Barnadi. After a series of skirmishes they retreated in several directions to Bhutan. About 14 Sannyasis and Sikhs were killed and one Sannyasi was taken prisoner. Phatik Barua and his new-made Raja Pedloor fled before the Company's troops being followed by Lt. Cresswell for about two hours, at the end of which the chase had to be given up owing to the exhaustion of the sepoys. The two officers returned to Gauhati on the 25th. It was, however, realised that no permanent benefit was likely to be produced by the flight of the Burkendazes into Bhutan as they were sure to come back to Assam after some time. Lt. Dick was of opinion that Assam could be protected from the depredations of the Burkendazes only if they were caught or expelled, and prevented from returning by the co-operation of a considerable force in the frontiers of Assam, Bijni, Cooch Behar and Bhutan.[65] Simultaneously with the depredations in Assam, Sannyasis and Fakirs had also been committing ravages in the Bengal districts of Rajshahi, Dinajpur and Purnea.[66]

The Burkendazes under Hazari Singh having entered Kamrup from Bhutan, Lt. Dick in the company of Lt. Cresswell, Lt. Cruttenden and Lt. Robinet crossed the Brahmaputra to Amingaon on the 12th April, and posted his troops from where he moved to Kulahi. He arrived at that place next day at 8 A.M. The Burkendazes crossed the Bolli river and made towards the camp of Lt. Dick

65. Dick to Welsh, March 26 and 27, enclosures to Capt. Welsh's letter to Murray, April 10, Beng. Pol. Cons., April 28, 1794, No. 8

66. Ghose, *Sannyasi and Fakir Raiders in Bengal*, pp. 114-120.

who now advanced in four divisions till they came within 100 yards of the enemy. After the exchange of a few shots the Burkendazes went into the jungle and began to annoy the sepoys. Lt. Dick then detached parties to scour the jungles on every side, and himself advanced with Lt. Cruttenden towards a large section of the enemy and compelled them to retire across the Bolli river. In this way the four officers continued contending with the Burkendazes scouring the jungles and defeating different parties which endeavoured to advance upon the sepoys, till 3-30 in the afternoon. Lt. Cresswell was wounded in the beginning of the action in his stomach, but continued gallantly in that condition to command his division. The party reached North Gauhati in the morning of the 14th, where Lt. Cresswell was sent up to Nasirabad in a light boat, doubly manned, in the care of Sergeant Luck and two sepoys. In the afternoon the 12 sepoys who had been severely wounded were sent up to the same place for medical assistance.

It transpired that the Burkendazes under Hazari Sing, Kanak Singh and Jogangiri, numbering about 2,000, were in the pay and under the command of Phatik Barua. They were recruited from the country west of Benares. About one thousand of them were equipped with matchlocks. Lt. Dick was of opinion that their reverses on the 13th April would not induce the Burkendazes to quit the country, and that they would continue on the borders of Assam and infest the district in the vicinity by periodic incursions He considered his small force to be inadequate against such superior numbers.[67]

Lt. Cresswell died of his wounds in his boat on the same day that he was sent down from North Gauhati. He was buried at Goalpara, and a monument—one of the very few to commemorate the valour and sacrifice of the pioneering band of Englishmen—was afterwards erected over his grave bearing the following inscription :

"Sacred to the memory of Lt. William Cresswell, who died on the 14th of April, 1794, of a wound he received when gallantly exercising himself in the action of the 13th, AEtat XXVII. This monument has been erected as a tribute of friendship by three of his brother officers,[68] who most sincerely regret the untimely misfortune which has deprived them of an invaluable friend, his

67. Dick to Welsh, April 15, Beng. Pol. Cons., May 19, 1794, No. 28.
68. The three were probably Lieutenants Dick, Cruttenden and Robinet.

country of a brave and deserving officer, and the world of a worthy member of society."[69]

Recall of the detachment: Just when Capt. Welsh and his detachment were making good progress in bringing order into the existing chaos Sir John Shore penned the fateful minute to give effect to his intention to terminate the Company's interference in Assam.[70] Capt. Welsh's letters of February 6 and 12 where he pointed out the precarious character of the Assam Raja's influence and the necessity of employing the Company's troops to restore the Raja to his authority led the Governor-General to formulate definite propositions respecting the detachment in Assam.[71] In his opinion the interposition of the English Government in the affairs of Assam had been "already protracted beyond the probable limits of an intended temporary interference." The Governor-General declared his intention to expressly defined objects of the Company's continued interposition and to fix precise limits for its duration on the ground that indefinite enterprises in Assam would require an additional force to support them leading to embarrassments of a graver nature than those which impeded the immediate recall of the detachment. He submitted the obligation, to a certain degree, to continue the troops in Assam in view of the assurances of protection given to its people by Capt. Welsh on the authority of Government. This humane intention was conceived by the Governor-General to be inconsistent with the Company's attempts to re-establish the authority of the Assam Raja Gaurinath Singha who had been found to be tyrannical, vicious and inefficient, and whose expulsion, if it ever took place through the resolutions of the Assam chiefs, the Governor-General was not disposed to prevent by the employment of the Company's troops. Sir John Shore was not inclined to oppose Gaurinath's enjoyment of his sovereignty if the people of Assam were willing to admit it. "But I," said he, "object to any further attempt to establish it by our interference." The Governor-General was, however, prepared to give all protection to Gaurinath and his private property as long as the troops remained in Assam, and to afford him an asylum in Bengal if the Raja chose to leave Assam after the withdrawal of the detachment.

69. *Bengal: Past and Present*, Vol. III, pp. 368-70.

70. Shore's minute, March 19, 1794, Beng. Pol. Cons., March 19, 1794, No. 16.

71. Welsh to Ed. Hay, Secy. to Govt., Feb. 6 and 12, Beng. Pol. Cons., Feb. 24, 1794, Nos. 14 and 15 respectively.

The Governor-General was of opinion that the establishment of Gaurinath in his authority was entirely a matter for the determination of the inhabitants of Assam; and for this purpose he was willing to provide all possible facilities to enable the chiefs to concert measures for the establishment of a regular government in their country. Capt. Welsh was authorised to publish a proclamation to the chiefs and inhabitants of Assam explaining the resolutions of Government, and advising the chiefs to meet under the protection and security offered to them by the presence of the Company's troops. Capt. Welsh was particularly enjoined to give equal protection to Gaurinath and the chiefs and to refrain from influencing their decisions. The Governor-General did not see any objection to Capt. Welsh giving his opinion if it was solicited by the congress of chiefs in their collective capacity, supposing it assembled. The Governor-General permitted the detachment to remain in Assam for three months to enable the chiefs to effect their union during that period. "If they [chiefs] should renounce the offered mediation", said Sir John Shore, "they must submit to be left to the consequences." From a knowledge of their character and the limited terms under which the Company's mediation was offered Sir John Shore doubted the possibility of the chiefs meeting to concert measures. Besides, the chiefs had considered Capt. Welsh as being specially deputed by the Government to support Gaurinath's authority or to establish that of the Company. The Governor-General was not prepared at the same time to use force to compel the chiefs to adopt any particular form of government or to effect their union. "Compulsion must be succeeded by succeeding violence", said the Governor-General, "which would intail the necessity of perpetual interference, and we should thus in fact attain the object which has been constantly disavowed and which I disclaim,—the subjection of Assam to the control of the Company."

The recall of the detachment, it was thought, might be harmful to the Company for two reasons, that it might be attended with disgrace and that it might affect the trade of Bengal. The first contingency was, in Shore's opinion, obviated by the notification of the period assigned for the continuance of the detachment. As regards the second, Capt. Welsh was directed to enter into commercial stipulations if the chiefs could unite in establishing a regular government in Assam. This might lead to the necessity of posting a representative of the Company in Assam, which the Governor-General proposed to take up when it would arise. Capt. Welsh had informed the Governor-General that the trade was not very considerable under the injudicious restraints imposed by the Assamese government, and that it had been further reduced by the anarchy and desolation. He had further suggested the possibility of rendering that trade beneficial to Bengal in time under the influence of the British Government. But Sir John Shore was not prepared to authorise that control over Assam by which alone the necessary influence could be exercised.

Sir John Shore's minute was accompanied by the draft of a proclamation addressed to the Sirdars and inhabitants of Assam and also of definite proposals to give effect to his recommendations. On March 19, 1794,—the day after Capt. Welsh's occupation of the Ahom capital Rangpur—which fatefully synchronised with the entrance of a fresh band of 2,500 Burkendazes into Assam, the Board took into consideration the Governor-General's minute on the detachment in Assam, and concurred entirely in the opinion expressed there. Capt. Welsh was accordingly directed to commence his march from Assam on or before the 1st July, to desist from undertaking all military operations, to withdraw all control that he might have exercised over the internal government of Assam, and to consider the commercial and financial stipulations of February 28, 1793, and February 12, 1794, to be in full force as long as the detachment remained in Assam. He was also furnished with instructions regarding all the points arising from the Governor-General's minute.

Previously to the decision arrived at by the Board on March 19 the Governor-General had received two petitions, one from the Assam Raja, and the other jointly from the two dismissed officers Jainath Barbarua and Siring Choladhara Phukan.[72] The two letters contained a number of complaints against Capt. Welsh alleging highhanded interference in the affairs of the Assam government. The Raja's letter concluded with a request to prohibit other merchants to trade in salt except Daniel Raush who in the words of the petition, "will provide as much salt as is wanted, and with whom formerly my [Assam Raja's] people used to carry on a traffic in salt at Kandahar Choky." The Raja also solicited the restoration of the two officers who had been deported to the Bengal district of Rungpore. The Governor-General could at once see that the complaints were inspired by people whose interests had been injured by the authority temporarily exercised by Capt.

72. The two letters, undated, were received by Government on Feb. 1, and March 5 respectively. Another letter from the two officers, dated Dec. 27, 1793, was entered in Beng. Pol. Cons., of March 31, 1794, No. 34.

Welsh. Sir John Shore, however, declared,—"From the perusal of these papers I deduce an additional argument in favour of the propositions which I have submitted to the Board." It transpired afterwards that the Raja's letter had been written by the dismissed Barbarua and Choladhara Phukan who had clandestinely obtained possession of the Raja's seal. Sivadatta Chetia Barphukan, writing to the Governor-General in June, 1794, on behalf of the Raja characterished the complaints as "extremely false."[73]

It will be seen that the orders of Sir John Shore recalling the detachment from Assam were based on no other consideration than his desire to comform strictly to the policy of neutrality enjoined in Clause 34 of the India Act of 1784 which was repeated as Clause 42 in the Charter Act of 1793. Sir John Shore regretted that the Bengal Government had ever interfered in the affairs of Assam and he had made up his mind to recall the detachment as we know from his letter to Henry Dundas, President of the Board of Control.[74] The reasons which he adduced in his minute of March 19 clearly showed that no circumstance however favourable to the reputation of the Government and the commerce of the Company's provinces would induce the pacific Governor-General to depart from the principle prescribed for him by the authorities in England. Lord Cornwallis was equally conscious of the restrictions imposed upon him by Parliamentary legislation; but the large-heartedness which distinguished his character and the courage and foresight which animated his political measures actuated him to launch and maintain the expedition for the relief of the neighbouring kingdom of Assam. This difference in the Assam policy of the two Governors-General was reflected in their respective relations with the other native powers of India, followed no doubt by different results respecting the power and prestige of the Company's administration in India. A historian writing of the period when Sir John Shore took charge of the Supreme Government says,—"The English Government had at no period been so strong in actual military force and resources."[75] To this may be contrasted what the same historian says about the period at which Sir John Shore left India,—"A period of six years' peace, instead of having added to the strength, or improved the security of the British dominions in India, had placed them in a situation of comparative

73. Sivadatta Barphukan to Shore, June 18, Beng. Pol. Cons., Aug. 1, 1794, No. 21.

74. Shore to Dundas, Jan. 10, 1794, in *Shore's Letters*, Furber, p. 35.

75. Sir John Malcolm, *Political History of India*, Vol. I, p. 118.

danger. Though the British strength was not lessened, the power and resources of the other states of India had increased. The confidence and attachment of our allies were much shaken, if not destroyed; and the presumption and hostile disposition of the principal native powers in India too clearly showed, that it was to a principle of weakness, or of selfish policy, and not of moderation, that they ascribed the course which had been pursued by the British Government."[76]

The orders of recall which were received by Capt. Welsh at Rangpur on April 21 caused great disappointment in the Assam camp. Neither Capt. Welsh nor his officers had ever thought that they would have to quit Assam before the completion of their mission. In his replies to the Governor-General's queries Welsh had enumerated in very forcible language the disastrous consequences of the withdrawal of the detachment hoping this consideration would induce the Government to sanction its continuance in Assam. The officers had under the same impression commenced building houses at Rangpur. Dr. John Peter Wade had informed his friend Francis Fowke in England of the possibility of his getting the commission of the Assam salt trade bringing him an annual profit of one lakh of rupees.[77] As the orders were imperative Capt. Welsh had no other alternative but to write back that he would attend particularly to the directions conveyed to him by the Governor-General in Council.[78] He, however tried his utmost to induce the Government to rescind their orders of recall. For this purpose he brought to the notice of the Government the favourable change that had taken place in the affairs of Assam since his communications of February 6 and 12 on which the orders had been based. He informed the Government that the ministers and Sirdars had meanwhile evinced an earnest desire to co-operate with him in establishing peace and order in the country and had rendered all possible assistance to him in carrying out his objects, that the Moamarias had expressed their inclination to return to their allegiance to the Swargadeo who had offered them pardon. The Swargadeo had informed Capt. Welsh that the appearance of a small force at the Moamaria headquarter Bengmara would give confidence to the wavering section of the rebels and induce them

76. Malcolm, *Political History of India*, Vol. I, pp. 192-3.

77. Wade to Fowke, Jan. 22, 1793, Fowke Mss., India Office Library, Vol. 28, letter No. 125.

78. Welsh to Ed. Hay, Secy. to Govt., Ap. 21, Beng. Pol. Cons., May 12, 1794, No. 1.

to come in and receive their pardon.[79] Welsh believed that the change in the situation of Assam warranted a deviation from the orders of March 19. Pending further orders from Government he proposed to stay at Rangpur. Welsh concluded his letter by an expression of regret that Government had not deemed it proper to give him discretionary instructions.

A few days later Capt. Welsh explained the intentions of the Bengal Government to the Assam Raja and his ministers in full Durbar. The following conversation was reported by him to Government in his letter of April 25, to add strength to his own proposition that the detachment should continue in Assam:

Members of the Assam government: "Were these resolutions adopted by Government after the receipt of our letters of the 26th ultimo?"

Capt. Welsh: "No, they were answers to letters of the 6th and 12th February which I had occasion to write from Kaliabar."

Members of the Assam government: "When your Government receive our letters requesting their further support, and when they know from you that the Burkendazes are in our lower provinces and the Moamarias still unsubdued they certainly will not at this critical period withdraw their assistance."

Welsh: "As circumstances have undergone a considerable change since this resolution was adopted by Government, which was probably done in consequence of my representation of the difficulty of effecting the union of the chiefs and the impossibility of establishing peace and order without it, I am induced to hope that the joint representation of the Raja and his ministers will be complied with."

Members of the Assam government: "What do you desire us to do, and what can we say more to ensure the attention of Government to our instructions?"

Welsh: "Represent the present state of affairs in Assam, express your sentiments freely and use your utmost endeavour to prevail upon the Moamarias to return to their duty. I am restricted from employing the Company's troops in any other manner than to afford protection to the Raja and his ministers. My Government seems not to have been informed of the late irruption of the Burkendazes. However, I will venture to use coercive measures with

79. For this purpose Welsh despatched three companies of sepoys to Bengmara a few hours before he received Government's letter of March 19, but they were immediately recalled as Govt. had prohibited military measures.

them if necessary to prevent their depredations in the lower provinces."[80]

In the same letter where he communicated the sentiments of the Assam Durbar Capt. Welsh mentioned additional circumstances to show that the establishment of the Raja in his authority was now almost completed. The members of the government were now united and the Barphukan had returned to Gauhati to take charge of Lower Assam. The reduction of the Moamarias was, in Welsh's opinion, an easy matter as they had, by their repeated acts of cruelty, made themselves obnoxious to the inhabitants. The families who had taken refuge in the hills and the lower provinces were returning to their old villages in consequence of the assurances of protection which Welsh had given on the authority of the Government.

He pointed out to Government the extreme difficulty of transporting the detachment to Bengal during the months of June, July, August and September, owing to the dangerous state of the Brahmaputra and the inclemency of the weather. It was equally impossible to proceed by land for the floods and inundations. He therefore recommended that the detachment should not move from Assam before October 1. The Raja despatched an embassy to the Governor-General with letters from himself and his ministers repeating their original request to permit Capt. Welsh to remain in Assam with his troops or post some other commander with two or three battalions to restore the country to peace and order.[81]

After despatching his final recommendations Capt. Welsh did all he could to improve the Raja's position at Rangpur on the assumption and make-believe that the Government would be persuaded, in view of the altered situation in Assam, to revise their orders of recall.

On the 3rd May a party of the Moamarias encamped at Sibsagar crossed the river Dikhow and set fire to several houses and granaries in the town of Rangpur. Capt. Welsh had on the first alarm marched out the 16th Battalion for the protection of the capital and at the sight of the troops the Moamarias recrossed the Dikhow and fled to their camps. The Moamarias repeated their

80. Welsh to Ed. Hay, April 25, Beng. Pol. Cons., May 12, 1794, No. 2.

81. Gaurinath, Purnananda Buragohain, Bishnunarayan Bargohain, Panisilia Barbarua, Sivadatta Barphukan, Ap. 26, to Shore, Beng. Pol. Cons., June 2, 1794, Nos. 22-23. The Vakils were Bikaram, Bholanath, Tanusyam and Baloram.

82. Welsh to Murray, May 6, Beng. Pol. Cons., May 28, 1794, No. 26.

annoyances on the next day retreating again on the appearance of the sepoys. At 2 A.M. on the 5th of May, Capt. Welsh crossed the Dikhow and proceeded towards the enemy's encampments at Sibsagar. But they had previously moved off to a different direction. Capt. Welsh despatched at the same time conciliatory letters to the Moamarias but they proved of no avail.[82]

The encroachments of the Moamarias now became a matter of frequent occurrence. At 10 a.m. on May 12, Capt. Welsh, at the head of 250 sepoys, crossed over to Sibsagar and reached within half-an-hour the vicinity of the Moamaria camp. The rebels advanced to meet the sepoys to a distance of 40 yards and began to discharge their arrows and matchlock pieces. The sepoys, undaunted by these preliminary greetings of the Moamarias, continued to advance in different parties, and within half-an-hour succeeded in completely routing the enemy who crossed over the Darika river and fled to a considerable distance from their encampment. Capt. Welsh returned to Rangpur after having set fire to the huts of the rebels. Their number was estimated at 6,000 with 4,000 fighting men. The skirmishes of May 3, 4 and 12 convinced the Moamarias of the superiority of the Company's troops; and expecting that they would now more readily listen to conciliatory proposals Capt. Welsh persuaded the Assam government to repeat them to the Moamarias. Even these petty skirmishes with the rebels had to be justified by Capt. Welsh by saying that they had to be undertaken as the constant inroads of the Moamarias had endangered the safety of the detachment under his command and that of the members of the Assam government whom he was instructed to protect. The encounter on the 12th May was described as being necessary to give him some respite to make the arrangements preparatory to his departure.[83]

According to Assamese traditions Capt. Welsh's last encounter with the Moamarias was a severe and decisive one. The Moamarias were led by their Rangpur Raja Bharath Singha reinforced by a contingent despatched to his aid by the Bengmara chief Sarvananda under Godha Barbarua. The battle took place at Sibsagar on the road called Dhai Ali near the site of the lines occupied by the Assam Light Infantry from 1840 to 1843.[84] Gaurinath watched

83. Welsh to Murray, May 13, Beng. Pol. Cons., June 2, 1794, No. 21.

84. Lt. Col. Sir James Johnstone, *Capt. Welsh's Expedition to Assam*, 1912, p. 44.

the engagement from the Ranghar near his palace enclosure.[85] He was terrified lest the Moamarias after having beaten the troops would advance towards the capital and massacre all its inhabitants. One lady who was at Ranghar in the company of the Raja assured him of the victorious return of Capt. Welsh.[86] The poet Visweswar Vaidyadhipa describes the battle of Sibsagar with epical vigour: "The contest was a terrible one and the smoke from the British guns clouded the sky, and the earth was littered with corpses like palm fruits at the end of a tempest. Bharathi lost a finger and he fled from the battlefield with Godha and the remnant of his force."[87] Capt. Welsh was for obvious reasons compelled to inform the Government that the encounter was a light skirmish.

On the day that Welsh finally repulsed the Moamarias from their strongholds in the vicinity of Rangpur the Board took into consideration his recommendations as well as the petitions of the Raja and his ministers for continuance of the troops in Assam. But the Government, even in view of the altered circumstances in Assam, were not willing to admit any departure from the principles on which their orders of recall had been founded. Capt. Welsh was therefore directed to consider those orders to be in full force.[88] Thus the recommendations of the man on the spot and of others who were the best judges of the situation were superseded by the contrary views of Government, based not on the merits of the interference but on their stubborn desire to withdraw it in strict conformity to the principles laid down by the authorities at Home.

Return of the detachment: Capt. Welsh left Rangpur by boat on the morning of May 25 with the 16th Battalion without waiting for Government's reply to his letter of April 25 and the petitions of the Assam Raja and his ministers. Gaurinath and the

85. *Ranghar*, a two-storeyed masonry building near the ruins of the Ahom Raja's palace at Rangpur, still in good condition. It was used as a pavilion from where the Rajas and their court watched amusements in the surrounding fields.

86. The metrical chronicles of Assam written by Dutiram Hazarika and Visweswar Vaidyadhipa, as well as the Ahom chronicle translated by the late Golapchandra Barua, state that Capt. Welsh was accompanied by a Bibi in his Assam expedition. Srinath Barbarua, the author of the *Tungkhungia Buranji*, is silent on this point, and also the Company's records of the period.

87. *Asamar Padya-Buranji*, or a metrical chronicle of Assam, edited by S. K. Bhuyan, pp. 224-5, 300.

88. Government's orders of May 12 confirming their decisions of March 19 were received by Capt. Welsh at 8 A.M. on May 29, 1794, when he was nearing Gauhati on his return journey to Bengal, Beng. Pol. Cons., May 12, No. 2, and June 13, 1794, Nos. 10 and 11.

prime minister Purnananda Buragohain left Rangpur for Jorhat on the day following leaving the Bargohain, Barpatra Gohain and the newly appointed Barbarua of the Lahan family in charge of the affairs at the capital. The inhabitants fled from Rangpur and those who could procure boats accompanied the detachment to the lower provinces.[89] Capt. Welsh as well as the members of the Assam government entertained a faint hope that on his arrival at Gauhati he would receive the Board's orders permitting him to remain in Assam. But the orders of the 12th May which reached Capt. Welsh on the 29th of the same month belied his expectations as well as those of his Assam friends.

Capt. Welsh stayed at Gauhati for the whole month of June, where he was deluged by petitions from the Assam Durbar and from Bengal merchants asking for the continuance of the battalion or of a part of it in Assam.[90] In one of his letters the Raja wrote to the Governor-General in imploring terms as follows:—"Please order the inhabitants here to repair to you. As the cows and Brahmans of this country have found safety in your assistance it is not proper for you now to sacrifice our lives and property."[91] Several petitions were sent by the Raja directly to Calcutta, to which he received the following reply from Sir John Shore,—"I am sorry I cannot admit of the further continuance of Capt. Welsh and the Sepoys in your country agreeably to your request, as the occurrences render it indispensably necessary that they should return within the Company's territories without delay."[92]

Robert Brydie who had entered into a partnership with Raush and Cotters represented the loss the Bengal merchants would have to suffer after the departure of the troops from Assam. The Governor-General allowed the merchants who had paid the prescribed import duty to the Company's officers at the Kandahar Choky to receive back the amount upon such parts of the goods which they would return to Bengal.[93]

Dr. J. P. Wade represented the necessity of protecting the property of his friend Horsely spread over several parts of Assam.

89. Welsh to Ed. Hay, May 25, Beng. Pol. Cons., June 13, 1794, No. 7.

90. The reason for this long halt at Gauhati is not known. Capt. Welsh might have been waiting for the Commander-in-Chief's orders respecting the disposition of the 16th Battalion or for Government's revision of the orders of recall in view of the merchants' representations and the subsequent petitions of the Raja.

91. Assam Raja to Shore, May 15, Beng. Pol. Cons., June 13, 1794, No. 12.

92. Shore to Assam Raja, June 30, Beng. Pol. Cons., July 25, 1794, No. 38.

93. Brydie to Welsh, June 19, Beng. Pol. Cons., June 30, 1794, No. 33.

Angelo Ducas, the Greek merchant, who relying on the terms of the commercial treaty of 1793 had imported considerable Bengal merchandise into Assam, pointed out the dangers to which his property would be exposed after Capt. Welsh's return. Krishnachandra and Nilmony Ganguli, Gomastahs of a merchant named Aditya Pal, referred to the precarious condition of their property in Kaliabar, Darrang and the capital of Assam, part of which had already been plundered at Gauhati and Kaliabar. To these petitions the Government replied expressing their inability to continue the Company's troops in Assam. Capt. Welsh was, however authorised to station a sufficient guard at Goalpara for two months for the protection of the Bengal merchants' property.[94]

In the meantime the depredations of the Fakirs and Sannyasis had caused great alarm in the Bengal districts of Purnea, Dinajpore and Rungpore, and the ryots in many places had left their homes with their families leaving their effects in charge of the Thanadars. On June 20, 1794, the Governor-General requested the Commander-in-Chief to station the detachment under Capt. Welsh in Dinajpore and Rungpore as might seem suitable.[95] On July 1, Capt. Welsh left Gauhati and arrived at Goalpara two days later.

The Darrang Rajas Bishnunarayan and Hangsanarayan I accompanied Capt. Welsh to Bengal. On July 5 Capt. Welsh proceeded with the 16th Battalion to Rungpore under orders received meanwhile from the Commander-in-Chief. The Company's officers who had been posted at Kandahar Choky to collect the duties were withdrawn and its management made over to the representatives of the Assam government. The Dawk which had been established between Goalpara and Rungpore for the use of Capt. Welsh's detachment was maintained to carry mails three times a week to enable the Commissioner of Cooch Behar to receive and report to Government the accounts from Assam and for the benefit of the merchants of Goalpara and Jugighopa.

The withdrawal of the detachment from Assam was followed by the recurrence of the disorders from which it had been rescued through the humane policy of Lord Cornwallis and the exertions of Captain Welsh. The Moamarias renewed their guerilla warfare in Eastern Assam and the Burkendazes their depredations in

94. Wade to Welsh, June 22; A. Ducas to Welsh, June 20; Aditya Pal's Gomostahs to Welsh, June 21, in Beng. Pol. Cons., July 7, 1794, Nos. 21-23.

95. Ghose, *Sannyasi and Fakir Raiders in Bengal*, pp. 122-3.

Darrang and Kamrup. Sivadatta Barphukan leagued with Helimeli Solal Gohain and Haradatta Chaudhuri, and with the help of the Burkendazes commanded by Hazari Sing, set up the son of one Bapi Gohain, a boy of 13 years, as Raja at Gauhati. The Barphukan used the Swargadeo's seal, which was in his possession by virtue of his office, in unauthorised correspondence with the officers of the Company.[96] The Barphukan appointed Rudram Barua as Duaria Barua at the Kandahar Choky after having confined the Swargadeo's nominee Krishnanath Gosain. The pretender despatched messengers to the Governor-General communicating his elevation to the throne and the deposal of "the senseless idiot Gaurinath who had wantonly destroyed three or four score men of rank and murdered the father of Krishnanarayan Jemindar with a hatchet."[97] He promised to do ample justice to the Bengal merchants on their making a representation to him. His letter was accompanied by a present of a bag of musk and two rhinoceros's horns. The Barphukan executed several men of rank at Gauhati including Bolai Barkaith who had in 1790 conducted the expedition against Hangsanarayan II and Haradatta Chaudhuri. The loyalist officers of Gauhati, who had refused to accept the new Raja, procured the arrest of the Barphukan by Hazari Sing by paying him a reward of rupees ten thousand. The Barphukan was sent up to Jorhat where he was executed. Helimeli Solal Gohain was similarly captured and killed near Kaliabar. Haradatta retreated once more to Bhutan where he planned fresh schemes of revolt.

Hazari Sing continued to dictate affairs at Gauhati. He received 60,000 rupees from Badanchandra for appointing him Barphukan at Gauhati. Soon after another Burkendaz leader named Jogangiri occupied Gauhati after having expelled Badanchandra.[98] On receiving the report of the commotions in Assam the Governor-General reiterated his old decision "that under the system which he has adopted relative to the country he cannot exercise any interference in that country." He authorised the Commissioner of Cooch Behar to grant protection to Raja Gaurinath and his family and his immediate dependants when it would be

96. Raush to Shore, Aug. 19, Commissioner of Cooch Behar to Shore, Aug. 24; Beng. Pol. Cons., Sept. 8, 1794, Nos. 27 and 30, respectively.

97. From the "present Raja of Assam" to Shore, Nov. 28, 1794. The pretender's name is not known. He is described as the son of Bapi Gohain and the grandson of Swargadeo Rajeswar Singha. Beng. Pol. Cons., March 30, 1795, No. 17.

98. *Tungkhungia Buranji*, pp. 135-139.

sought.[99] At the same time Sir John Shore wrote a letter to Gaurinath and his ministers reminding them of his inability to render any assistance. "It is more in your power than in mine", said the Governor-General, "to effect the object by evincing a disposition to settle with the various chiefs their several disputes upon principles of equity by establishing order in the administration of your affairs and by observing a mild and conciliatory conduct towards the inhabitants of your country. The necessity of military aid will be superseded and the prosperity of your territories be secured upon the only permanent basis, the attachment of your subjects." [100]

The return of the detachment to Bengal was reported by the Governor-General to the Court of Directors in his despatch of August 18, 1794.[101] The subsequent commotions in Assam were communicated in the next despatch, dated May 12, 1795. "We are not now much interested", wrote the Governor-General, "in the affairs of Assam having withdrawn all interference whatever in them on the recall of Capt. Welsh's Battalion." [102]

The Directors in their letter of June 5, 1795, approved of the Bengal Government's original intervention in the disputes between the Raja of Assam and Krishnanarayan. "Although we wish you not to depart", wrote the Directors, "from the general line of policy that has been drawn for your guidance for avoiding any interference in the disputes with the country powers, we nevertheless think, under the circumstances stated, that you were justified in the part you have taken in the disagreement between the Rajah of Assam and the Rajah of Deringh." The Directors had hoped that from the amicable settlement between Krishnanarayan and his sovereign the country would be restored to tranquillity and the commercial arrangements made by Capt. Welsh would be carried into execution. "But", concluded the Directors, "we are sorry to find by your subsequent despatch of the 18th August that the detachment commanded by that officer was returned within the Company's districts without having effected the purposes of its march." [103]

99. C. A. Bruce to Shore, July 26, Beng. Pol. Cons., Aug. 8, 1794, No. 15.

100. Shore to Assam Raja Gaurinath, and to his Barphukan, Buragohain, Barpatra Gohain and the Barbarua, Aug. 7, Beng. Pol. Cons., Sept. 15, 1794, No. 30.

101. Bengal Letter to Court, Pol. Dept., Aug. 18, 1794, paras 52 and 53.

102. Bengal Letter to Court, May 12, 1795, para 48.

103. Court's Letter to Bengal, June 5, 1795.

Sir John Shore's policy of non-intervention with special reference to Assam: The recall of the detachment from Assam was a shortsighted action on the part of Sir John Shore. The great majority of contemporaries viewed it with disapproval. The Assam Raja considered the measure to be a contradiction of the assurances of protection given to him and his subjects by the Bengal Government. Capt. Welsh chafed under it though as a soldier and a servant of the Company he could not give free expression to his disappointment and resentment. The Bengal merchants, both European and Indian, were seized with panic at the sudden withdrawal of the protection afforded by the detachment. The Court of Directors, taking a detached view of the subject, regretted the action of Sir John Shore in recalling the troops before they had accomplished the objects of their march. All writers on the subject, William Robinson, Lt.-Col. Sir James Johnstone, Sir Edward Gait and Lt.-Col. L. W. Shakespeare, have pointed out the disastrous consequences of the recall which might have been averted if Sir John Shore had acted with a little understanding and vigour.[104]

The circumstances were highly favourable to the continuance of the detachment in Assam. The restrictive clause in the Act of 1784, as repeated in that of 1793, aimed at preventing aggression and interference of the type attributed to Warren Hastings's measures against the Rohillas. Even within limitations of the clause the Company's Government in India had ample scope to prosecute their legitimate ends. In Assam, the interference was a clear case of non-aggression. The detachment went to Assam on the express invitation of its sovereign. The expedition had been initiated by Lord Cornwallis, and nobody could have blamed Sir John Shore if he had prosecuted his predecessors's measure to its logical conclusion. The Court of Directors had been kept constantly informed of the activities of the detachment in Assam; and Lord Cornwallis had frequently written to Henry Dundas, President of the Board of Control, on the subject.[105] Not a word of disapproval was ever uttered by the authorities at Home. With the progress of the troubles in Europe Dundas himself was "becoming more and more sympathetic to a policy of aggrandisement

104. Robinson, *Descriptive Account of Assam,* p. 174; Johnstone, *Captain Welsh's Expedition to Assam,* p. 40; Gait, *History of Assam,* pp. 211-12; Shakespeare, *History of Upper Assam,* pp. 56-57.

105. Cornwallis to Dundas, Oct. 15 and Dec. 10, 1792, and Jan. 25 and March 24, 1793, Ross, *Cornwallis Correspondence,* Vol. II, pp. 181, 186, 205 and 219 respectively.

in India."[106] The entrance of a fresh band of 2,500 Burkendazes into Assam in March 1794 would have justified the continuance of the Company's troops in that country as the expulsion of those marauders had been accepted as incumbent upon the Government of Bengal. The co-operation of the Assam Raja and his ministers had increased with their appreciation of the motives underlying the Company's mediation. Capt. Welsh who had in his campaigns under General Goddard won success against the power of the Mahratta leaders could have easily crushed the undisciplined Moamaria rabble fighting with primitive weapons. The commercial arrangements with Assam were being given a fair trial, and would have proved highly beneficial to Bengal when peace had been restored to the Swargadeo's kingdom. The Assam government had undertaken to defray all the expenses of the detachment which amounted to three lakhs of rupees. They had already entered into an agreement to pay 1½ lakhs from the revenues of Lower Assam, and were prepared to draw up another agreement for the payment of the balance. By permitting the detachment to complete its mission in Assam the Bengal Government would have secured a prosperous and powerful neighbour, attached to its interests, and serving as a barrier against the expanding and aggressive Burman Empire.

The arguments advanced by Sir John Shore to justify the withdrawal of the force from Assam fail to convince us of the necessity of that action unless we assume the principle of neutrality behind which he usually sheltered himself. His professed desire of protecting the Assamese people from the tyranny of Gaurinath Singha by refusing to strengthen his authority failed in the very object which he wanted to attain. The reduction of the Raja's authority was followed by the perpetuation of the disorders, by the renewal of the oppressions of the ministers and the chiefs and of the ravages of the Burkendazes and Moamarias which inaugurated a reign of terror in Assam greatly increasing the misery of its inhabitants. The submission of the refractory chiefs, thought Sir John Shore, could only be obtained by the employment of force which would lead to reciprocal violence; but the chiefs in Assam were not like the powerful members of the Mahratta confederacy with whom he always dreaded a conflict. The Assam chiefs were petty vassal lords and Zemindars with disorganised and

106. *Shore's Letters*, Furber, Introduction, p. 7, and also Furber's *Henry Dundas*, pp. 128-9.

ill-equipped followings. Many of them had already returned to their allegiance to the Swargadeo who, when fully restored to his authority, could have maintained his power. Sir John Shore knew very well of the spirit of jealousy and ambition which animated the Indian chiefs, and of the 'incapacity of Indians for acting together'.[107] He therefore foresaw the improbability of the Assam chiefs meeting together to concert measures for the good government of their country. The instructions given to Capt. Welsh to promote such a meeting were issued in full cognizance of the fact that no such union was likely to be effected, and they were therefore unnecessary.

It is evident that Sir John Shore, from his assumption of office in October 1793, was opposed to the Company's interference in Assam, and he had made up his mind early in January 1794 "to extricate ourselves from prosecuting our interposition, as speedily as possible, without discredit, and if it can be effected, with some commercial benefit."[108]

Sir John Shore's Assam policy was the offshoot of his cautious, overprudent and pacific temperament which manifested itself in his strict adherence to the principle of neutrality and non-interference. "I have ever been disposed", he declared, "to adhere as literally as possible to the strictest interpretation of the restrictive clause in the Act of Parliament against entering into hostilities."[109] In formulating his principles of action as Governor-General he had decided "that war should be avoided as the bane of our interests, a conclusion deducible also upon other grounds, and sanctioned by the Legislative of Great Britain."[110] Acting on this principle Shore left the Nizam to his fate when he sought the Company's support against the Mahrattas and Tipu Sultan, to which he considered himself entitled according to the terms of the Treaty of Paungal of July 1790. Some of the reasons advanced by Sir John Shore in withholding his support to the Nizam merit particular notice as they elucidate his measure towards Assam. The evils resulting from the subversion of "the tottering fabric of

107. P. E. Roberts, *History of India to the End of the East India Company*, 1916, p. 241; Shore's *Political Reflections on the State of Hindustan*, in App. A, *Shore's Letters*, Furber, p. 147.

108. Shore to Dundas, Jan. 10, 1794, *Shore's Letters*, Furber, p. 35.

109. Shore's minute of Feb. 18, 1795, inserted in App. II in Malcolm, *Political History of India*, Vol. II, p. lxv.

110. Shore's *Political Reflections*, in App. A, *Shore's Letters*, Furber, pp. 146-7.

the Nizam's government', thought Shore, "would be much weaker than the ruin of a long-protracted war".[111] About the loss of prestige or political consequences in the estimation of the native powers from any breach of faith with the Nizam, Sir John Shore believed "it cannot be placed in competition with the greater evils attending a war with Tippoo and the Mahrattas."[112] In the case of Assam, Sir John Shore was not disinclined to see the subversion of the government of Gaurinath Singha "who is deficient in every good quality which belongs to a sovereign, and possesses every vice which is a disgrace to human nature."[113] The Government of Bengal had, besides, no treaty obligation to support the Raja in any emergency. The discredit arising from the withdrawal of the troops from Assam after proceeding so far would be confined to an obscure corner of north-east India and would not reach the ears of the chiefs or inhabitants of other parts of India with whom the Government had more intimate political relations. So in Assam Sir John Shore could act even more freely in pursuing his policy of non-intervention than he could in regard to the powers of Northern and Southern India.

Sir John Shore's timidity and the consequent "slavish observance of neutrality"[114] sprang principally from his inexperience and dread of war, and to some extent from the peculiar circumstances of the Company's administration at that time. He was a scholar, a man of strong religious principles, and experienced mainly in revenue administration. He lacked that vigour and energy of action which alone would have qualified him to deal efficiently with the complicated political problems of India. His abhorrence of war was aggrevated by his insufficient knowledge of military matters and his want of confidence in the abilities of the Commander-in-Chief Sir Robert Abercromby and his officers. "I am bound by duty to mention to you", wrote Shore to Henry Dundas, "that I deem his [Abercromby's] abilities totally inadequate to the station of Commander-in-Chief.....I am sorry to add, that amongst the Colonels of this Establishment, and the Case is I fear the general throughout India, I know not one equal to the conduct of a war, and if the Mahrattas or Tippoo were to attack us we should be in a deplorable condition."[115] The position was

111. Shore to H. Dundas, Aug. 21, 1794, *Shore's Letters*, Furber, p. 56.

112. Shore's minute, Feb. 18, 1795, Malcolm, *Political History of India*, Vol. II, App. II, p. lvi.

113. Shore's minute, Beng. Pol. Cons., March 19, 1794.

114. P. E. Roberts, *History of India*, p. 241.

115. Shore to Dundas, Dec. 31, 1794, *Shore's Letters*, Furber, p. 60.

rendered more difficult by the bitter discontent of the Company's officers occasioned by the delay of the Home authorities in redressing their grievances.[116]

The results of Sir John Shore's policy of neutrality were felt in the Deccan for a prolonged period. The Nizam was forced by the Mahrattas to conclude a humiliating treaty. He dismissed the English battalions and augmented his army under the direction of French commanders. Tipu partly succeeded in obtaining the support of the Afghan king and made considerable progress in effecting an offensive and defensive alliance with the French Republic. The prestige of the Company was undermined while the resources and strength of its enemies were greatly increased.

In Assam, the effect of the withdrawal of the Company's influence was first perceived in the heavy losses sustained by the English and Indian merchants of Bengal. They could not obtain payment of their balances from Assamese traders in spite of the repeated demands upon the Swargadeo made by the Bengal Government on their behalf. Early in 1796 Daniel Raush was murdered by the Burkendazes in Darrang which he visited to claim liquidation of his debts.

But the effect was more perceptible in the wider scope which Shore's conduct permitted to the ambitious designs of the Burmese monarch. The Moamarias allied themselves with the Singhphos and sent repeated requests to the king of Ava for assistance. Parties of Burmese were twice brought into Assam, but they were bribed and bought over through the influence and diplomacy of Purnananda Buragohain.[117] In 1797 an Ahom prince presented his daughter to Bodawpaya, king of Burma, and requested that monarch for troops to seize the throne of Assam by expelling the successful rival Kamaleswar Singha. Bodawpaya arranged to send an army of 20,000 soldiers to invade Assam, and after its subjugation to march to Bengal if possible. Capt. Hiram Cox, the Company's envoy at Amarapura, warned the Burmese ministers of the consequences of such action and told them that Assam was tributary to the English and under their protection. On hearing Capt. Cox's representations Bodawpaya recalled the troops.[118]

116. J. C. Marshman, *A History of India*, Vol. II, p. 65; *Shore's Letters*, Furber, Introduction, pp. 9-16.

117. Capt. S. O. Hannay, *Account of the Moa Morah Sect*, *J.A.S.B.*, 1838, p. 673.

118. Capt. Cox, *Journal of a Residence in the Burman Empire*, pp. 138-9; and Cox to Shore, Nov. 27, 1797, Beng. Pol. Cons., March 2, 1798, No. 5.

He was, however, indignant with the English for having thus anticipated his plans. Cox was censured by Shore for his misrepresentation though it averted rupture with the Burmese.[119]

Sir John Shore did not attach much importance to the Burmese menace to the Company's possessions. In 1794 the Governor of Pegu, a province of the Burman Empire, sent a detachment to the Company's district of Chittagong claiming the restitution of certain Burmese who had taken shelter there. "The Pegu Government is powerful," said Sir John Shore, "but it can never send any army of consequence into the Company's territories and the invaders, I trust, will soon be repulsed."[120] From that time onwards Burmese agents frequented the districts of Northern India taking plans and collecting information about the resources of the Company's possessions. In 1817 the Burmese invaded Assam, and laid claim next year to Chittagong, Dacca, Murshidabad and Cossimbazar. In 1822 the Burmese became masters of Assam, and the whole of the eastern districts of Bengal were threatened by them. "Government will now begin to feel", wrote David Scott, "the inconvenience of the line of conduct imposed upon them by the Act of Parliament."[121] As a result of Scott's representations the Government decided ultimately to dislodge the Burmese from their commanding position on the Brahmaputra.

A little courage, foresight and generosity on the part of Sir John Shore would have averted the thirty years of devastation which Assam suffered at the hands of the Moamarias, Burkendazes and the Burmese.

119. A. Aspinall, *English Relations with Burma*, in *Bengal: Past and Present*, Vol. XL, pp. 118-19.

120. Shore to Dundas, March 10, 1794, *Shore's Letters*, Furber, p. 50.

121. Scott to George Swinton, July 10, Beng. Pol. Cons., July 26, 1822, No. 51.

APPENDIX TO PART II OF CHAPTER VII

Dr. John Peter Wade

Captain Welsh's expedition brought to Assam an Englishman of varied and brilliant attainments,—an industrious physician, an indefatigable historical investigator, a keen student of literature, a close observer of men and society, a warm-hearted friend, a bold critic and a humanist. He was Dr. John Peter Wade, Assistant Surgeon to the expedition.

In her memorial to the Marquis Wellesley, Governor-General of India, dated 27th January 1803, the widow Mrs. Rachel Wade truly delineated the character, disposition and pursuits of her deceased husband when she said,—

"That, possessing an Active and Cultivated mind, and the laudable ambition of being useful in his station to his Country and to Mankind, his time was unremittingly devoted to the practice and studies of his profession, or the Pursuits of General Literature; and that several valuable Treatises on the Diseases of most general occurrence in this Country, an History of Assam for which he had favourable means of collecting materials when Surgeon to the Embassy to that Kingdom, and many smaller pieces of Natural History and Botany, presented at different times to Government and to the Asiatic Society, remain in evidence of the extent and useful direction of his labours.

"That, as instrumental to these Pursuits, he had also acquired a very extensive knowledge of the Languages of this country, which as your Memorialist had gratefully understood, and believes, had suggested to Your Excellency, nearly at the time of his death as mode [a mode] of conferring on him a mark of Your Excellency's Patronage and Favour, and at the same time, of rendering his acquirements in that way of Public Utility."[1]

Dr. Walter Ross Munro, an eminent medical officer of the Bengal establishment who knew Dr. Wade very intimately, wrote in the same vein while communicating the sad news of his death to his relatives in Britain,—

1. Mrs. Rachel Wade to the Marquis Wellesley, dated Calcutta, Jan. 27, 1803, Beng. Military Cons., 1803, India Office Library, Range 20, vol. 44. Shortly before his death Dr. Wade was appointed by the Marquis Wellesley as a teacher at the College of Fort William in Bengal.

"There were few men whom I loved, none I honoured more than him, for I know few whose principles were more pure, or whose hearts were more benevolent. His talents, far above the ordinary level, were unfortunately exerted on an unnatural as well as on an unprofitable theatre; and the distance at which his military duties placed him from Calcutta, removed him from the observation of those who could have appreciated and rewarded his merit. But the public at last noticed them, and Government had just given him an appointment in the College which would have gradually led to every other object he wished for when his Death blacked [blasted] all our hopes."[2]

Our chief interest in Dr. Wade lies in the books that he wrote on the history and geography of Assam. They represent the earliest attempts to collect and disseminate information about Assam the paucity of which had caused great regret amongst the officers and merchants of the East India Company. But, unfortunately, none of Wade's compilations saw the light of day during his lifetime, though portions of his *Geographical Sketch of Assam* were inserted in historical publications of the early nineteenth century.[3] We are also interested in Wade as a man who struggled against odds in the uninterrupted pursuit of his cherished ideals.

John Peter Wade was born in the year 1762. One of his brothers, Charles Wade, M.D., was a physician at Lisbon; and another, Joseph Wade, was described by John Peter as "doing nothing." Joseph however used to attend to John Peter's interests in London during the latter's residence in India.[4]

John Peter was educated in Medicine at Edinburgh University where he obtained the degree of M.D. The licence to practise in Medicine was granted to him by the king of Portugal, obviously through the intervention of his brother Charles. John Peter came

2. Dr. Walter Ross Munro to Francis Fowke, dated Calcutta, Dec. 4, 1802, in Fowke Manuscripts, India Office Library, vol. 30, letter No. 11. In a letter to his father-in-law John Carruthers, Dr. Munro wrote, "Mr. Wade died just at a time when his merits, too long overlooked, began to be effectually noticed by Government", quoted by John Carruthers in his letter to F. Fowke, from Edinburgh, June 24, 1803, Fowke MSS., 39-12.

3. *Asiatic Annual Register* for 1805; Montgomery Martin, *Eastern India*, 1838, vol. III, pp. 637-640; there are two references in Charles Stewart's *History of Bengal*, Bangabasi edition, Calcutta, 1910, pp. 67, 317, footnotes; Government Gazette, 1825; *Asiatic Journal* for October 1824.

4. Dedication in Wade's *Nature and Effects of Emetics*, etc.; letter from J. P. Wade to F. Fowke, undated, and from Joseph Wade to Francis Fowke, July 10, 1788, Fowke MSS., 30-55, 29-55.

to India in the Portuguese vessel "Arabida." It was perhaps for his early Portuguese associations that John Peter betrayed an un-English twist in his manners. He once wrote to his friend Francis Fowke that Mrs. Wade "values anything of yours to a degree that, considering I am a Portuguese, ought to make me very jealous."[5]

On his arrival in India Wade was first appointed Assistant Surgeon to the Bombay detachment under General Thomas Goddard during the First Mahratta War.[6] This appointment was made on February 25, 1782, and it was officially confirmed on November 4, 1782. During this early period of his medical career Wade was placed in charge of two large hospitals at Kalyan, containing about two hundred patients, "under the pressure of the worst complaints." He felt "his recent arrival in the country, and consequent inexperience and ignorance of the language must have rendered him very inadequate to any independent Medical duty."[7]

About the year 1784, Wade was at Benares where Francis Fowke had been Resident of the Company since 1775. Francis and his father Joseph Fowke took an active part in the controversies of the period, and supported Philip Francis in his opposition to Warren Hastings. Francis Fowke made a large fortune by his trade in opium, boats and diamonds. His father, after having served as third-in-council at Fort St. George, had settled at Benares as a diamond merchant. Francis Fowke as Benares Resident had constantly given protection to Raja Chait Sing by which action he incurred the displeasure of Warren Hastings who suspected him as "a screen between the Raja and the Government of the Company." In one of the articles of charges in the impeachment of Warren Hastings, Burke alluded to Hastings's opposition to the continuance of Francis Fowke as Resident of Benares, even though the appointment had been made under the express orders of the Court of Directors. Hastings was accused of throwing upon Francis Fowke, "the person appointed by the Company, several strong but unspecified reflections and aspersions, contrary to the duty he owed to the Company, and to the justice he owed to all its servants."[8]

5. J. P. Wade to F. Fowke, about Nov. 1795, Fowke MSS., 22-179.

6. A short sketch of J. P. Wade's career is given in the "Roll of the Indian Medical Service, 1615-1930", by Lt.-Col. D. G. Crawford, Bengal Medical Service, London, 1930, p. 28.

7. J. P. Wade to F. Fowke, dated Chunar, July 10, 1788, Fowke MSS., 29-55.

8. *The Works of Edmund Burke,* pub. George Bell, London, 1894, vol. IV, pp. 147, 279.

Joseph and Francis Fowke were joined as co-defendants in the trial of Maharaja Nandakumar for a conspiracy against Warren Hastings. The Fowkes were also friends of Dr. Samuel Johnson. The Doctor spoke of Joseph Fowke as " a scholar and an agreeable man," and a letter from Johnson to his brother, dated 11th July 1776, is preserved in Boswell's life. His son Francis was a scholar and commanded an elegant style of writing. His essay on the *Veena* was published in the first volume of the *Asiatick Researches.* He was one of the founders of the Asiatic Society of Bengal.[9] He left India for good in 1786, and his father in 1787. Before he left India, Francis Fowke presented his writing desk to his friend John Peter Wade.

After return to England, Francis first settled at Wimbledon and then at Worthing. Subsequently he purchased property in Radnorshire. He helped his friends with money, not always with any prospect of return. Fowke's purse as well as his influence with the Court of Directors were availed of by John Peter Wade whenever he fell in any difficulty or embarrassment. It was surmised in Fowke's intimate circles that he would some day return to India as a Member of the Supreme Council.[10]

John Peter Wade and Francis Fowke developed a strong mutual attachment, and Wade referred throughout his life to the happy days passed together at Benares. This attachment continued even after Fowke's final departure from India. Wade kept up a correspondence with Fowke and acquainted him with what was happening in India, specially about their mutual friends such as Sir William Jones and Lady Jones, Captain Michael Symes, Charles and Francis Gladwin, and Sir Charles Blunt. In a letter, dated 1st February 1789, Wade wrote about Lady Jones and her learned husband, —" Lady Jones is more agreeable than she appeared at Benares, and Sir Billy has grown much less professorial in his conversation. They are incomparably the best company to which I had access in Calcutta. He has just published the first volume of the Society's researches. Your paper on the Veen has a conspicuous place in it." [11]

9. Raja Rajendralal Mitra, *Centenary Review of the Asiatic Society of Bengal,* 1784-1883, Calcutta, 1885, Part I, pp. 3, 134.

10. "You will be greatly pleased with its appearance [Chowringhee, Calcutta] when you come out in the Supreme Council. I really doubt whether that office would prove a bribe to you to return",—Wade to F. Fowke, from Sunderbands, Feb. 1, 1789, Fowke MSS., 29-72.

11. J. P. Wade to F. Fowke, dated Sunderbands, Feb. 1, 1789, Fowke MSS., 29-72.

In the same letter Dr. Wade referred to a satire on himself by John Lewis Chauvet in the form of an epic poem entitled *The Wadead* of which the author intended to print about a hundred copies for the entertainment of friends. "It is really an excellent piece of humour," wrote Wade to Fowke, "and will certainly excite your visibility at the expense of your friend the hero. You will think I possess a large share of cunning or vanity to affect a pleasure in his performance; the former might prompt me to join the laugh in order to escape it; while the latter might induce me to suppose that no powers of Satire could render such a respectable personage as oneself the object of ridicule. The poem turns altogether on my fondness for argument. I really have benefited by the hint, and do avoid arguments with more care than formerly." Our principal sources of information about the personal details of John Peter Wade's life are the letters which he wrote to Francis Fowke. They are preserved in the India Office collection known as "Fowke MSS.", and are described in the *Catalogue of European Manuscripts in the India Office Library,* Vol. II, Part II.

During the years 1787-1790, Wade had served at several places, —Benares, Chunar, Barasat and Sunderbands.

Wade had been applying himself wholeheartedly to his work; but he received a great shock to find himself degraded by having forty junior men placed above him. Owing to the gradual abandonment of services in the Company's ships, on the part of medical officers, for services on land, it became difficult for the Company to run their ships properly. The Court of Directors, therefore, passed an order on 16-3-1784 removing from service 24 Assistant Surgeons who had been appointed between 1-1-1782 and 10-3-1783. Wade was not included in this list though he was appointed during this period. The Directors proposed to send from England a sufficient number of new Assistant Surgeons for the above 24 vacancies and other casualties.

But curiously enough, the Governor-General in the Secret and Military Department passed orders on the 27th June, 1788, to the effect that the new Assistant Surgeons, appointed under the Court's General Letter dated 16-3-1784, "should rank before all the Gentlemen who were appointed in the Country between the 1st of January 1782 and the 10th March 1783, whether their names are specified in the letter or not, it being evidently the spirit of the order to disapprove of all appointments made within that period."[12] As a

12. Extract from Court's General Letter to Bengal, March 16, 1784, appended to Wade's letter to F. Fowke, July 10, 1788, Fowke MSS., 29-55.

result Wade found himself degraded to about 40 Assistant Surgeons below his official rank. "Never was any order," wrote Wade to Francis Fowke, "so unjust, so mortifying, and so damning to my prospect. Had I been on the spot my supersession would never have taken place." [13]

Wade moved heaven and earth to get the wrong redressed. He interviewed Lord Cornwallis who acknowledged the peculiarity of the case but expressed his inability to countermand his own order. Wade addressed petitions to the Court of Directors, and sought the mediation of Francis Fowke by sending letters to him by sea as well as by land.

About the same time Dr. Wade was removed from Benares, and he was disappointed in not obtaining the post of Deputy Surveyorship. His monthly income which had been Rs. 600 a month came down to half the amount on his removal from Benares. All his efforts for obtaining official preferments were opposed at head-quarter, and "what is still stranger, by a private influence in Calcutta." Wade, filled with resentment, interviewed Lord Cornwallis, but unfortunately the Assistant Surgeon's conduct on this occasion was "something very like insult"; and Wade had to admit that owing to the displeasure which he occasioned "his prospects were ruined as far as they were in the power of the Great offended Lord."

Wade was far from being a sycophant, and he expressed his opinion candidly and fearlessly about Lord Cornwallis. In one place he said,—"The whole elasticity of Lord Cornwallis's soul, the primum mobile of every action is derived from an inordinate love of fame......His manners are conciliating beyond expectation, even to those whom he dislikes. He is a perfect Chesterfield in his refusals. He is economical and generous, and is what the world calls,—the best man in the world." [14] Sometime later Wade thus poohpoohed the idea of erecting a memorial to Lord Cornwallis,—"They say Scindia means to attack the Nizam, and there is talk of raising a statue to Lord Cornwallis by subscription, he is so much loved here. I will subscribe myself if they agree that the statue shall be without a head." [15]

13. J. P. Wade to F. Fowke, dated Calcutta, Jan. 10, 1788, letter by sea, Fowke MSS., 29-50.

14. J. P. Wade to F. Fowke, dated Sunderbands, Feb. 1, 1789, Fowke MSS., 29-72.

15. J. P. Wade to F. Fowke, dated Madras, Aug. 26, 1792, Fowke MSS., 28-124.

Wade's disappointment in official matters has nevertheless a silver lining in the cloud. He decided to make it up by additional industry so that he might obtain the approbation of the public, and ultimately compel the Government to recognise his merit and ability. To use his own words he made a resolution "to become an industrious man and to make money." [16]

Wade was engaged during the time in compiling a number of medical treatises on the proper methods of treatment of patients suffering from tropical diseases. In 1787, he submitted to Government the outlines of treatise on fever.[17] He recommended the evacuating system as a primary step in the treatment of tropical disorders. Dr. Munro agreed with Wade that "the evacuating system must be allowed to be the basis of all sound practice in the disorders of our climates." [18] The outlines on fever were elaborated into a three-volume book entitled "Select Evidences of a Successful Method of Treating Fever and Dysentery in Bengal." Wade compiled two other medical books entitled "Nature and Effects of Emetics, Purgatives, Mercurials and Low Diet in Disorders of Bengal and Similar Latitudes", and "Paper on the Prevention and Treatment of the Disorders of Seamen and Soldiers in Bengal."

In 1790, Wade returned to England to arrange for the publication of his books, and to get himself married. He lived for sometime at Tunbridge Wells which he described as "being convenient for the correction of the proof-sheets of my book." Boswell's *Life of Johnson* was published about that time, and Wade wrote to Fowke on the 4th July 1791,—"I have received lately the greatest pleasure from the perusal of Boswell's Life of Johnson. Read it as soon as you can. Bossy however is himself very silly occasionally, but Johnson's gold is everywhere scattered amongst his farthings."[19]

In October 1791, Wade published his first book *Select Evidences.* Its dedication to Warren Hastings was described by the author as "the conferment of a smaller portion of the celebrity on a character already loved and revered throughout India." The trial of

16. J. P. Wade to F. Fowke, dated Purnea, April 4, 1799, Fowke MSS., 22-103.

17. J. P. Wade's letter, Chunar, July 9, 1787, Public Department Records, O.C., July 18, 1788, No. 18.

18. Testimonial of Dr. Ross Munro, Nov. 1, 1795, Home Misc. Series, vol. 85, pp. 957-975.

19. J. P. Wade to F. Fowke, dated Tunbridge Wells, England, July 4, 1791, Fowke MSS., 28-109 and 28-115.

Warren Hastings was then going on in full swing; and his friends were collecting evidence of his popularity in India, and Wade's complimentary words were calculated to lessen the rigour of the impeachment. Wade's second book *Nature and Effects of Emetics* was published in 1793, and was dedicated to his brother Charles Wade, M.D., who was a physician at Lisbon. His third book *Disorders of Seamen and Soldiers in Bengal* was published in 1793, and was dedicated to the Court of Directors.

During his stay in England Wade seized the opportunity of placing his case before the Court of Directors, and organised some support in his favour; but here also, as in India, he found the doors of justice closed against him. "This Court of Abominables", wrote Wade, "have made me somewhat grave lately. They will not even let my case come before them although at least fifteen of them had promised me and my friends to do their best; yet, when one Director more sincerely my friend than the rest, mustered the force, he found he could only get the support of eight of them. The De'il take the fellows. I must only make it up with additional industry."[20]

Wade's matrimonial project had proceeded side by side with his activities in the publication line and his efforts to regain his lost rank. He had met Miss Rachel Carruthers, daughter of John Carruthers of the Tax Office at Edinburgh. In November 1791 Wade was in a position to write to his friend Fowke,—"The Ladies here are extremely beautiful and very unaffected. One of them has seized my fancy in an uncommon manner. Had I fortune to remain at home, I think, I might succeed. But though I am determined to endeavour to make some impression during my short stay here, yet she is a girl of the first connection of this place with some accomplishments, and with every advantage which Fortune can give; though, like most Scots girls of every rank, she has no fortune of her own. You will naturally think, I have not much chance, however, 'Neck or nothing'—'None but the brave deserves the Fair', and so forth. You will think me the most impudent dog alive to dream at all of marriage with my very limited means. These are fine castles in the air. They may possibly be realised, for her parents who know I am not rich see my attentions, and do not discourage them. Her brother is my oldest intimate."[21] The marriage was celebrated at Edinburgh on Monday, 12th December 1791, and Wade wrote immediately to Fowke,—"Ten thousand thanks

20. J. P. Wade to F. Fowke, about Aug. 1791, Fowke MSS., 30-60.

21. J. P. Wade to F. Fowke, dated Edinburgh, from No. 5, George's Street, Nov. 7, 1791, Fowke MSS., 28-113.

for all your kindness. I am just going to step into the Chaise. The indissoluble knot has been tied this moment."[22]

Towards the end of December Wade left his wife at Edinburgh and came to London to complete his preparations for return to India. He had already settled with his wife £150 per year to be paid for the time being by Fowke during his absence in India. Wade obtained from Fowke introductions to several influential gentlemen in Calcutta including William Cowper, Member of the Supreme Board.[23] He persisted in his efforts to have his case brought before the Court, but to no purpose, which compelled him to write,—"The d-d Directors, or rather the Chairman, will not so much as permit my business to come before the Court at all, so that I am disappointed but not much chagrined. I must only work doubly hard to make up for the want of my rank."[24] In April 1792 Wade embarked for India and arrived at Madras on the 25th August. During the voyage he worked hard at Arithmetic and in Persian, and considered himself "passable in both."[25]

On his return to Bengal Wade proposed to set up a practice in Calcutta, which idea he had to abandon in view of a new opportunity that just occurred to him. The Government of Bengal was planning to send a military expedition to Assam to suppress the Burkendazes, subjects of the Company, whose ravages had disturbed the peace and security of the Assamese people. Captain Thomas Welsh was appointed to command the expedition.

Dr. Wade was persuaded by his friends to accept the post of Assistant Surgeon to Captain Welsh's detachment. As a shrewd man Wade embraced this opportunity of re-establishing himself in the good opinion of the Government which he thought he had lost for his bold and repeated protests against the loss of his official rank. He also thought he would be able to recoup his fortune by business in diamonds or some other trade.

On the 1st October 1792 Wade wrote to his friend Fowke,—"I have every reason to think I shall succeed well in practice in Calcutta at last. I did not mean to quit Calcutta on any account but to remain and prosecute that object with unremitting attention.

22. J. P. Wade to F. Fowke, dated Edinburgh, Dec. 12, 1791, Fowke MSS., 30-85.

23. J. P. Wade to F. Fowke, Jan. 27, 1792, Fowke MSS., 30-13.

24. J. P. Wade to Fowke, from No. 75 Wimpole Street, London, about Feb. 1792, Fowke MSS., 21-38.

25. J. P. Wade to F. Fowke, from Madras, Aug. 26, 1792, Fowke MSS., 28-124.

However my friends have insisted on my taking the office of D'r, Naturalist, etc., to an Embassy which sets off after tomorrow for Assam. They insist that it is a great thing for me; and will prove handsome in point of emolument. But I think it would have been more prudent to remain here in pursuit of my ultimate object,—Calcutta practice. One good effect it certainly must produce.—I shall not be transmitted down as an *obnoxious man* from Governor to Governor, for by this appointment it seems that I am not entirely out of favour with the Lord. I have not attended to Botany or other parts of Natural History since I left the university, but I mean to make amends for my negligence hitherto, and acquit myself as well as incessant industry, the Rudiment of knowledge in those branches of science, books and other aids will enable me to do. It seems I am also to be useful as a person pretty well acquainted with Persian language. I am glad I studied this particularly during my voyage. It is possible I may do something in the Diamond business in that part of the world; but it is not very probable. At present I have not a moment left for anything but preparations for this expedition, which, to say the truth, is creditable enough; tho' I would rather stay where I am. I shall not have it in my power even to write to Mrs. Wade till my return; God knows when that may be; perhaps one, perhaps two years. My letters of introduction to the people here have had every effect I wish them to have, and more than I expected. This trip to Europe has altogether, I think, been the most fortunate business in the world for me."[26] Wade's additional salary while employed in Assam was fixed at Rs. 100 per month; he was also given an extra deputation allowance of Rs. 104, and boat allowances of Rs. 80 per month.[27] This sum of Rs. 284 was in addition to his basic pay of Rs. 300.

On November 16, 1792, Captain Welsh's detachment left Goalpara and entered into Assam waters. This gave an occasion to Wade to write to Fowke on the very same day,—"Today we shall enter a kingdom scarcely if ever trodden by Europeans before,.... Prospects open. Assam is not a country for Diamonds, but it is for Gold dust, and what is much better, for trade, I think I shall do well in it, but of this more presently." [28]

26. J. P. Wade to F. Fowke, dated Calcutta, Oct. 1, 1792, Fowke MSS., 28-122.

27. Mackenzie, *North-East Frontier of Bengal*, 1884, p. 391.

28. J. P. Wade to F. Fowke, from Goalpara, Nov. 16, 1792, Fowke MSS., 22-95.

Owing to the incursions of the Moamaria rebels King Gaurinath Singha had been living at Gauhati with his principal officers and nobles. Captain Welsh conducted negotiations for enacting a commercial treaty between the East India Company and the Assam government. The main article of trade was salt of which Assam imported annually from Bengal about 100,000 maunds. Several Indian and European merchants were engaged in this salt trade, and the Company had also tried to conduct the trade as an exclusive monopoly.[29] During the progress of the negotiations Wade arranged to obtain a commission on salt, and he wrote to Fowke from Gauhati on the 22nd January 1793,—" I have written only one letter to you from Assam, and I have so much to do that I have scarcely a moment to write another tho' you know I like to write long letters to my intimates. For the present my diamond prospects are at a stand; as this country is not well favourable for that business; but I have the pleasure to tell you that another source of profit is likely to be opened to me very soon. All the salt consumed in this populous and extensive kingdom comes from Bengal. I am promised already a commission on salt to the amount of one and a half lakh of rupees. This will lead to still better things, so that in reality, without being very sanguine, my prospects, I may say, are pretty good at present. Everything however depends on our permanent residence in this country, which, tho' probable, is by no means certain as yet."[30]

Dr. Wade stayed at Gauhati with the detachment from November 1792 to January 1794. He came in daily contact with members of the Assam government which gave him an opportunity to see the working of the Ahom system of administration and to judge the character of the Assamese. King Gaurinath Singha's cruelty was illustrated in the mutilation of a man for a very trivial offence, and Wade reported on 'this horrid spectacle' as follows,—" I have examined the mutilated Assamese who was yesterday received into the Hospital. He has been deprived of his ears as well as the car-

29. This monopoly was first given to David Killican in 1780, but it was annulled by the Court of Directors; Hugh Baillie exercised this monopoly on the Company's behalf from 1787 to 1789, but he had to close down the Goalpara Factory on account of civil strifes in Assam, Beng. Rev. Cons., July 25, 1780; Court's Letter to Bengal, July 12, 1782; Beng. Rev. Cons., July 18, 1787, and Dec. 9, 1789.

30. J. P. Wade to F. Fowke, from Gauhati, Jan. 22, 1793, Fowke MSS., 28-125.

tilaginous part of his nose, and both his eyeballs have been forcibly extracted."[31]

Dr. Wade's rectitude of conduct as a servant of the Company came out in his refusal to take charge of the business of a merchant named Mr. T. Horsely. In reply to Governor-General's permission to take charge of Horsely's affairs in Assam, Wade wrote to Sub-Secretary Mr. C. Shakespeare,—"I am extremely sorry that Mr. Horsely, unauthorised by me, should have made this application to the Government. I disclaim every wishes of a commercial concern since it has proved incompatible with the views of Government. I decline the permission with respectful thanks. I have not at any time received, nor shall I on any account receive the slightest emolument from that prohibited source."[32]

Wade accompanied the detachment in its march to the Ahom capital Rangpur which had been in occupation of the Moamaria insurgents. On the morning of 18th March 1794, Captain Welsh occupied the fort of Rangpur already evacuated by the enemy, and took possession of the property left behind in the fort and in the houses of the Moamaria chiefs. The value of the property which included gold and silver specie and bullion was estimated at Rs. 1,05,000. Dr. Wade was one of the Prize Agents for the disposal of the property captured at Rangpur, and it was apportioned according to customary rules. The value of Dr. Wade's share of the captured property is not known but some inference can be made from his subsequent admission that "this trip to Assam, altho' it has enabled me to save a large sum has completely ruined my views of getting established in Calcutta."[33] Captain Michael Symes also described Wade's visit to Assam as "an excursion that has not been unprofitable to him."[34]

Captain Welsh was doing good service to the Assam Raja. Gaurinath was reinstated on the throne at Assam's permanent capital Rangpur, and the resistance of the Moamarias was reduced to a great extent. But the pacific Governor-General Sir John Shore did not like to continue the vigorous policy of his predecessor

31. J. P. Wade to Capt. Welsh, Gauhati, Feb. 3, 1793, Beng. Pol. Cons., Feb. 15, 1793, No. 16.

32. J. P. Wade to Sub-Secretary C. Shakespeare, from Gauhati, Jan. 13, 1794, Beng. Pol. Cons., Jan. 27, 1794, No. 26. This extract represents the official version of Wade's views on his participation in trade: his real sentiments come out in his private letters to F. Fowke.

33. J. P. Wade to F. Fowke, from Purnea, Oct. 17, 1794, Fowke MSS., 28-128

34. Michael Symes to F. Fowke, about 1795, Fowke MSS., 22-166, A. 52

Lord Cornwallis. He issued orders for the withdrawal of the detachment from Assam. Welsh accordingly returned with his troops to Gauhati on the 30th May 1794, and to Goalpara on the 3rd July.

The recall of the detachment created a panic amongst the merchants who had been hoping for a stable trade under the protection of the Company's forces. Dr. Wade informed Captain Welsh of the precarious situation of his friend Mr. Horsely's affairs, though he asked the Captain "not to entertain the slightest suspicion that I take a prohibited interest in his concerns." "He has much property", wrote Wade on the 22nd June 1794 while he was at Gauhati, "to the eastward as well as at this place [Gauhati]. I believe my apprehensions agree with your sentiments that all Bengal property in this country will be exposed to the danger of being plundered after your departure, and that it will not be possible to re-export any considerable portion of Mr. Horsley's property from this country before the 1st of the ensuing month."[35]

After his return from Assam Dr. Wade planned to make some investment in indigo, and being appointed to Purnea he was "employed in looking out for a proper spot for indigo works" in partnership with a connection of a Judge named Mr. Hannay. The district of Purnea was particularly well calculated for indigo works, and Wade ultimately succeeded in obtaining a number of shares in that business.[36] In 1799 Wade was in a position to inform Fowke that his indigo speculations enabled him "to clear a large sum this last season."[37]

Wade now thought of bringing his wife to India. He wrote to Fowke from Purnea on the 17th October 1794,—"I am preparing the Surgeon's bungalow here for my little Scotch woman whom I expect by the first ships of the next season. I shall have a good house ready to receive my wife and a little sum over and above all expenses."[38]

Mrs. Wade had been living at Edinburgh with her parents. She maintained a correspondence with Francis Fowke mostly on family matters, and in regard to her progress in music for which he himself had considerable reputation. She became a god-mother

35. J. P. Wade to Capt. Welsh, from Gauhati, June 22, 1794.

36. J. P. Wade to F. Fowke, from Purnea, Oct. 17, 1794, Fowke MSS., 28-128.

37. J. P. Wade to F. Fowke, from Purnea, April 18, 1799, Fowke MSS., 22-103.

38. J. P. Wade to F. Fowke, from Purnea, Oct. 17, 1794, Fowke MSS., 28-128.

exceeding the number of sixty or seventy Bengal subjects which form his mighty army, would scarcely venture to oppose a single company of sepoys armed with the name of Surgi Deo. It is necessary to distinguish between the man and his title. Gowrinath is a tyrant they fear; but every rank of subjects holds the race and the lawful authority of Surgi Deo in a degree of veneration, scarcely to be paralleled in history. The Boora-Gohaign himself affects to rule his districts in the name of Surgi Deo, and we may truly believe that the meanest peasant would be gratified by Surgi Deo's restoration to his throne and capital if he were promised a permanent protection against the tyranny of Gowrinath and his ministers. In a former part of this narrative we have described the extreme dislike of the people of Bossa-Doyungh to the Boora-Gohaign. The character of the man authorises us to believe that his Government cannot be more popular among the inhabitants who reside nearer his person. If he might dare to oppose, he must assuredly experience a general defection of all, except his personal adherents and connections. But we cannot possibly suppose the Gohaign to be destitute of common sense or.........".—*Unfinished.*

The subject-matter of the above piece is the contest waged by Jai Singha, Raja of Manipur, and his son Madhuchandra, who had come to Assam at the invitation of the government of that country to render assistance in the suppression of the Moamaria disturbances.[51] The piece is also valuable for the indication it gives of what critical contemporaries thought of Purnananda Buragahain's character and disposition. Many however think that Purnananda was a great statesman whose patriotic measures were commonly misunderstood or misrepresented.[52] The language of the piece is *journalese*, and it approaches the sonorous rhythm of Gibbon and other English prose-writers of the eighteenth century. The piece is also interesting for the example it affords of the symmetry and vigour into which the raw materials of Assamese chronicles can be shaped by the artistic handling of a constructive historian.

But, what happened to the manuscript of Wade's history of King Gaurinath Singha? The shawls which were sent from India by the same ship were received in England in due time in the beginning of 1797. It is unexplainable why Francis Fowke did not write a line about the manuscript for five long years. As Wade

51. S. K. Bhuyan, *Tungkhungia Buranji*, English translation, pp. 126-8.

52. S. K. Bhuyan, *Tungkhungia Buranji*, Assamese version, Introduction, pp. xiv-xv.

here begin to think my advertisement was a mere stage-effect to serve some temporary purpose, and I am anxious to convince them that there is something real in my promise.....Let me once more urge you to publish the Memoirs, and to favour me with a line ".[48]

The same note of regret was sounded in Wade's dedicatory preamble to his *Account of Assam,* addressed to Lieutenant-Colonel Kirkpatrick, dated Kishengunge in Bengal, 20th March 1800,—" The most curious and interesting circumstances relative to Assam are exhibited at some length in the continuation of this history, containing the reign of late monarch Surgi Deo Gowrinath Sing. I have compiled the Memoirs of his reign from authentic documents, and despatched the book to Europe for publication in the month of April 1796 with the approbation of Lord Teignmouth, but I have not as yet received any account of it, and not having retained a copy I am deprived of the pleasure of sending it to you ".[49] So late as July 4, 1802, Wade referred to the same regrettable event in the epistolary introduction to his *Geographical Sketch of Assam,*—" I regret that the Europe press has not yet enabled me to offer you a copy of the History of Maha Rajah Surgi Deo, late Monarch of Assam ".[50]

The only evidence of the style and treatment of this book has fortunately been preserved for us in a few stray leaves bound with the India Office manuscript of the *Geographical Sketch of Assam.* As a precious fragment of a constructive and critical history of the reign of an Assamese king written by a contemporary western scholar, who was a spectator of some of the most important events of the reign, we reproduce below an extract from the piece:—

Wade's prophetic remarks.—" Before we take our final leave of the Moamarias we may venture to prophesy that the mere name of the British Government will, at any time, prove sufficient to repress the overt resistance of the Boora-Gohaign or the Moamarias, although every kind of secret counteraction may be expected from those who derive advantage from the destruction and desolation of the country. The miserable band of cowardly and undisciplined peasants amounting perhaps to six or seven hundred men, armed with awkward weapons which they dare not and cannot use, the small body of unwilling and unpaid burkendazes not

48. J. P. Wade to F. Fowke, April 1799, Fowke MSS., 22-167.

49. J. P. Wade to Lt.-Col. Kirkpatrick, prefixed to *Account of Assam,* dated Kishengunge, March 20, 1800.

50. Letter prefixed to Wade's *Geographical Sketch of Assam,* dated July 4, 1802.

do I permit myself to have ".[44] He considered his opportunities to be unique as "no Europeans have ever explored, or probably ever will explore the province of Assam with the consent of the Government of that country".[45]

The first book compiled by Wade was the history of the reign of King Gaurinath Singha whom the author had met almost daily from November 1792 to May 1794. Wade collected materials from the Raja's officers and nobles, and from the records in possession of the court chroniclers. Gaurinath Singha died in August 1795. In April 1796, Wade sent the manuscript of his "Memoirs of the Reign of the late Monarch Surgi Deo Gowrinath Sing" to Fowke with the approbation of Sir John Shore, for printing and publication. He did not even keep a copy. Captain Colebrooke, Surveyor-General, furnished to Wade at the instance of the Governor-General, a copy of Ensign Wood's map of Assam for being prefixed to the history.[46] Wade perhaps sent the book by the boat *Earl of Wycombe*, along with the testimonials to justify his restoration to his original rank, and the packet containing the latter was received by the Court of Directors on the 18th February 1797.[47] Wade announced the publication in some periodicals of the time. But the book never saw the light of day. The non-publication of this book was a matter of lifelong regret to its industrious compiler.

In April 1799, Wade wrote to Fowke,—"And now, let me entreat you to give me some account of my other offspring of the literary mind, I mean the "Memoirs of the Reign of Surgi Deo Gowrinath Sing, late Monarch of Assam". I am very partial to that little production, and wish anxiously to see it in print. I sent it Home to you in April 1796, and here we are in April 1799, and not a line have I received acknowledging the receipt of it, though some shawls sent by the same ship were delivered safely two years ago. Let me urge you in favour of your old friend to exert yourself for a few days in order to correct and prepare that little work for the press, and to favour it with a preface in your own elegant and judicious style. Pray, gratify me as soon as you can, for people

44. J. P. Wade to F. Fowke, from Goalpara, Nov. 16, 1792, Fowke MSS., 22-95.

45. J. P. Wade's *Geographical Sketch of Assam*, introductory chapter dealing with the sources of information about Assam.

46. Wade's *Geographical Sketch of Assam*, introductory chapter.

47. Endorsement at the bottom of Wade's letter to Court, dated Berhampore, April 8, 1796, runs as follows,—"Berhampore 8th April 1796 Asst. Surgeon J. P. Wade to the Court of Directors. Recd. per Earl of Wycombe 18 Feb. 1797", Home Misc. Series, Vol. 85, pp. 957-975.

to one of Fowke's daughters. In November 1793, Mrs. Wade sent to Fowke "a piece of Scotch manufactory for a vest". She used to receive occasional monetary help from Fowke in addition to the yearly allowance settled on her.[39] In October 1794 Wade was restored to his rank "except two steps", and was subsequently promoted to a full Surgeonship.[40] In April 1796 Wade submitted to the Court a number of testimonials from his superior officers "as proofs that you have not conferred the valuable indulgence [restoration to his original rank] on a person altogether unworthy of your favour".[41]

On 17th July 1795, Mrs. Rachel Wade and her sister embarked at Ryde for India, and arrived in Bengal in the middle of February 1796 "in safety but not without frights and troubles". The ship *Triton* by which the two sisters travelled was captured by about a dozen of 'desperate democrats'. The Captain, one Mr. Burnyeat, "who had shown the kindest attention on all occasions to the fair emigrants", died at his post. The ladies were transferred to the ransomed ship *Diana* and brought to Ganjam.[42]

So, by the beginning of 1796, the Wades were well settled in Purnea, and the indefatigable Surgeon-scholar could now work upon the materials he had collected in Assam. Miss Carruthers was married to Dr. Munro who was very much older than his bride. Dr. Wade wrote about his new brother-in-law,—"The mistress [Miss Carruthers] before mentioned to you had married an old Surgeon, after refusing some young civilians. Munro is his name. If anything could compensate for want of youth in a young girl he has everything in his favour, being one of the noblest fellows in existence".[43]

The desire to compile some books on Assam was entertained by Wade before his entry into Assam. In the letter to Fowke from Goalpara, dated the 16th November 1792, Wade had written,—"I fag hard in every way to get a little credit by accounts of a country entirely unknown and to get money. Not a single moment's leisure

39. Mrs. Rachel Wade to F. Fowke, Edinburgh, Nov. 18, 1793, and John Carruthers to same, Edinburgh, Aug. 14, 1804, Fowke MSS., 30-131, 30-13.

40. J. P. Wade to F. Fowke, about Nov. 1795, Fowke MSS., 22-179.

41. J. P. Wade to Court of Directors, from Berhampore, forwarding his testimonials, April 8, 1796, Home Misc. Series, vol. 85, pp. 957-975.

42. J. P. Wade to F. Fowke, about Feb. 1796, Fowke MSS., 22-179.

43. J. P. Wade to F. Fowke, possibly from Purnea, April 1799, Fowke MSS., 22-167.

did not keep a copy the prospect of its publication was dashed for ever. Fowke perhaps lost the manuscript, or mislaid it irrecoverably, or it was destroyed through the negligence of some dependant or menial. Anyway, the tragedy of the loss of "Gowrinath Sing" has its lamentable parallel in the destruction of the first volume of Thomas Carlyle's *French Revolution*, through the negligence of John Stuart Mill. "I learnt from Mill this fact", wrote Carlyle in a letter dated 23rd March 1835, "that my poor Manuscript, all except some four scattered leaves, was *annihilated*: He had left it out (too carelessly); it had been taken for waste paper: and so five months of as tough labour as I could remember of, were gone like a whiff of smoke.—There never in my life had come upon me any other *accident* of much moment; but this I could not but feel to be a hard one. The thing was lost, and perhaps worse; for I had not only forgotten all the structure of it, but the spirit it was written with was past.......Mill, whom I had to comfort and speak peace to, remained injudiciously enough till almost midnight".[53] The next morning Carlyle began the work afresh with courage and resolution, and in another seven months of hard work he completed the volume. Wade could have done the same thing if he had kept copious and ample notes, but he was living in expectation of seeing the book in print. Francis Fowke was living at a distance of four or five months' voyage, and the author breathed his last before he could contact his friend, make search for the manuscript or re-create the book by fresh labour as in the case of the historian of the French Revolution. But that was not to be. One lesson which every author should learn from this regrettable event is that no manuscript should ever leave his hand of which a copy has not been kept, or sufficient notes preserved to permit an opportunity for its resuscitation.

Wade's second book *An Account of Assam* is mainly a translation of two Buranjis or chronicles, one written in Assamese, and the other in the Ahom language.[54] The Assamese manuscript was presented by Wade to Captain Welsh; and the Ahom manuscript, written in cotton cloth, to Lord Teignmouth.

53. Thomas Carlyle's letter to Dr. Carlyle, March 23, 1835; cf. also letters to his mother, March 23, 1835; and to Emerson, May 13, 1835, referred to in "Selections from Carlyle's *French Revolution*", edited by S. B. Hemingway and C. Seymour, Oxford University Press, 1948, pp. xvii-xviii.

54. The manuscript of Wade's translation has been described in the *Catalogue of European Manuscripts in the India Office Library*, vol. II, part II, pp. 697-700.

The Ahom Buranji used by Wade was known as *Roo-poot*, literally, a book of knowledge; and was compiled by one Manohar, head of the Ahom priestly clan of Bailungs, under the orders of King Siva Singha. They were communicated to the historiographer in the following significant words,—"That the histories of the King's predecessors should be compiled, the succession of the Ahom monarchs mentioned in details, and the book should be called *Roopoot*; that the history should contain only the names and transactions of the Swurgeedeos".[55]

Wade's translation was submitted to Colonel William Kirkpatrick with a dedicatory letter dated March 20, 1800. The book is described as "a small part of my literary labours during a residence of eighteen months in Assam", and the dedication as the outcome of the author's desire to interest the good-will of the Colonel "in favour of the uninterrupted exertion of professional and literary industry which (excuse the humble boast of Industry) has pervaded every period of my life, since my first entrance into this service".

The book begins with a description of the seniormost officers of the Ahom government known as Phukans, which title, Wade correctly surmised, did not have any connection with the language of Hindusthan. "It is probably derived", wrote Wade, "from the language of Sookaphah, and the eastern conquerors of Assam who entered the extensive valley from the mountains of Nara". The Phukans were next in respectability and rank to the Gohains. They were divided into two categories, the military Phukans and the civil Phukans. The author then describes the functions of the whole body of Phukans belonging to both the establishments at Rangpur and at Gauhati. The real account of Assam commences after the enumeration of the Phukans

Wade was not satisfied by merely translating the original Assamese documents. Here and there he has adopted the interpretative method with the help of the information acquired during his stay in Assam. The following passage in Wade's book describing the functions of the Phukans could never occur in any Assamese chronicle of those days,—"In some respects to Fokuns resemble the judges of Israel. They not only command the armies and administer the justice of the Kingdom, but also have a principal share in the public councils. Their opinions are received on

55. J. P. Wade's *Account of Assam*, edited by Srijut Benudhar Sharma, 1927, pp. 1-2.

all affairs of importance in the presence of the Monarch. This privilege is however confined to a declaration of their sentiments, for they possess not an effective vote like the Gohaigns. Yet the opinion of an eloquent man frequently influences the decrees of the Gohaigns. Eloquence is therefore in high estimation at court, and leads to fame and honours under the government, not in any degree democratic".

The first part of Wade's *Account of Assam* deals with the Ahom monarchs from the earliest times up to the reign of Lakshmi Singha, 1769-1780. It contains an exhaustive treatment of the reign of King Rudra Singha and of his colossal preparations to invade Bengal for the purpose of including the Ganges within the Ahom dominions. The scheme however fell through owing to the sudden death of the royal dreamer. The death-bed injunction of the mighty monarch bespeaks his ambition and wisdom, and prophetically hints at the causes which led to the dismemberment of the Ahom kingdom,—

"Take your seats. Remain in friendship. You will thus become monarchs in your turns, nothing will succeed if you are inimical to one another. If any attempts are made to place you at variance, and many will be made, listen not to suggestions of that kind, but remain united. I had formerly two brothers [we were formerly two brothers], but listening to the suggestions of enemies, I drove away the younger [Lechai Namrupia Raja]. I now perceive my error; continue therefore in friendship, and all your pursuits will succeed; if you prove enemies, nothing. Old and young, you shall be Kings successively. I have subdued the countries that surrounded my dominions. I proposed the reduction of the provinces contiguous to the Coroteea river: but my design must perish with me, for who will be found capable to pursue my plans?"

Dr. Wade has given us a novel, though curious, interpretation of the origin of the word *Asam* or *Ahom*. The consort of the king of the Naras, who constituted the parent-stock of the Ahoms, was bearing a child through Indra, the god of the gods. The child was to have the resemblance of his divine progenitor, and was destined to rule the earth. The celestial paramour visited the queen in a dream, and asked her not to receive the embraces of her royal husband till the birth of the child. She asked Indra if he intended to come to her again on which the god replied,—"*Ahim, Ahim,*" literally meaning,—"I will come, I will come". The word *Ahom* or *Asam* is supposed to originate from this *Ahim*. The child in question was known as *Swarga-narayan,* and became the royal ancestor of the Ahoms. *Swarga-narayan* or *Swargadeo* became in fact the common title of all the Ahom monarchs indicating their divine origin.

The second part of the book is devoted entirely to the origin and history of Kamrup from the earliest times down to the period of Captain Welsh's expedition. The reigns of the descendants of Biswa Singha in Cooch Behar and Darrang have been detailed elaborately. The account is brought down to Krishnanarayan, who as claimant to the Rajaship of Darrang, had revolted against the Ahom government with the help of Bengal Burkendazes. Reference is also made to the insurrection of the Moamarias in Darrang, and of Haradatta in Kamrup.

This second part aimed at furnishing the background of Welsh's expedition for the expulsion of the Burkendazes from Assam, and it concludes with the following preroration,—"Sometime after Krisnanarain and Hurdutt made their appearance in Camroop at the head of a large body of Burkundazes who took possession of Dehrrung and Camroop. Krisnanarain was again proclaimed Rajah but the Swarge Deo claimed and obtained the assistance of the Bengal Government to expel the Burkundazes who were subjects of Bengal. The Records of Government [East India Company] contain the transaction in that quarter from the period at which this History terminates".

In fact, Wade's history of the reign of Gaurinath Singha is described in the dedicatory letter as a continuation of this *Account of Assam.*

The third part deals with the wars between Assam and Bengal, including the expeditions sent to Assam at the instance of the Emperors of Delhi. It ends with the final defeat of the Moguls in the battle of Itakhuli in 1682 when the forces under the Delhi Fauzadar Mansur Khan were completely defeated, and he "abandoned a great quantity of valuable plunder to the victors".

By far the most important of the compilations of Dr. Wade is his *Geographical Sketch of Assam.*[56] Some portion of it was published in "The Asiatic Annual Register" of 1805. A portion has also been inserted in the third volume of Montgomery Martin's "Eastern India". Wade revisited Assam in 1798 in connection with the compilation of this book. The manuscript was among the papers

56. The manuscript of Wade's *Geographical Sketch of Assam* was borrowed by the Government of Assam in 1927. The book has been edited by the present author and published as a serial in the *Assam Review*, Silchar, vols. I and II, Dec. 1928 to Aug. 1929, under the title *Assam in the Eighteenth Century*.

deposited by Sir John Malcolm in the library of the East India House in 1827, and it is now in the Record Department of the India Office. In 1814, the London firm of Arrowsmith published a map of Assam from the information contained in Buchanan-Hamilton's accounts, and Ensign Wood's surveys, and in Wade's *Geographical Sketch.*[57] A copy of this map is also in the India Office Library.

The book deals with the divisions and districts of Assam as grouped for administrative purpose by the Ahom government. The natural products and manufactures of the country are mentioned *en passant.* The author also alludes to the religious institutions and social customs of the people. The chapters on the river system and vegetable products of Assam are contributions of permanent importance.

The dedicatory letter attached to the manuscript is undated, while a copy of the same found in another volume of India Office records bears the date July 4, 1802.[58] The letter begins,—" Permit me to send you a few sheets on the Geography of a Country entirely unexplored by Europeans before the late Deputation, which I had the pleasure to attend. These pages are chiefly translations from original documents in the Assamese language; but partly derived from the information of intelligent natives and partly from my own observation ". The letter is addressed to Sir John Malcolm.

The plan of the book has been set forth in the prefatory pages; but the author deviated from this plan in the actual compilation. The *first* part was to contain an account of the divisions of the kingdom,—Uttarkul, Dakshikul, Majuli, Upper Assam and Lower Assam. The *second* part was to comprise an account of the rivers of Assam, grouped under three heads,—rivers flowing from the northern mountains; river flowing from the southern mountains; and the Brahmaputra and its branches. The *third* part was to deal with the western, northern, southern and eastern confines of Assam and the neighbouring nations. The first two parts are now available in the original manuscript, and they have also been reproduced in Martin's " Eastern India "

There is no trace of the third part except a few disjointed notes on the Mikirs and the Manipuris. This omission has, however

57. S. K. Bhuyan, Buchanan-Hamilton's *Account of Assam,* 1809-1814, pub. by Department of Historical and Antiquarian Studies in Assam, where frequent references are made to Arrowsmith's map of Assam. A copy of the map is in the India Office Library, and several reproductions have been prepared for the above Department by Messrs. R. B. Fleming of Bloomsbury, London.

58. Home Misc. Series, vol. 736, pp. 78-84.

been compensated by the inclusion of notes on sundry topics, which did not find place in the original plan, the most important being the author's dissertation on the natural history of Assam, being notes on "Vegetables collected October 6", which contained accounts of endi and muga silk-worms. Under this head of nondescript matter can be included the author's account of the death and burial of King Gaurinath Singha's consort; the ordination of Gosains; anecdotes of Kabir Gosain, who is described as "a Muhammadan much reverenced by all the Hindoo who sing the hymns of his composition", during whose residence at Hazo "a temple was formed by God"; route from Bengal to Ava through Assam; itinerary of Captain Welsh's expedition to Assam, 1792; princes of the southern provinces; Chokies or military and commercial outposts; Turner's description of Bhutan and Tibet; and translation of a portion of the story relating to the origin of the name *Nilakantha*. The last few leaves of the manuscript contain, as we have said before, a fragmentary portion of the author's history of Gaurinath Singha.

Dr. Wade begins his book by mentioning his sources of information, Turner, D'Anville, Du Halde, Glanius, Chevalier, Rennell and Vansittart, besides the materials received from his Pandit and the Assamese documents. Kamrup and Darrang are then described with the necessary particulars of all the contiguous tracts. The jurisdictions of the Ahom officers are stated in precise terms besides the principal trades and the customs of the people.

Of the miscellaneous information supplied by Wade, that about a Muslim priest offering worship on behalf of the Ahom monarchs deserves reproduction:—

"A Mussleman of the name of Newas was Gooroo-general of his persuasion in Assam, from about the time of Roodur Singha. He had numerous attendants dressed in the high Mussleman dress. He resided at or near the capital and frequented the durbar; and the Swargadeos used to despatch him to pray at Hadjoo after the Mussleman fashion for their prosperity. He was usually succeeded by his nearest relations. He and his family disappeared on Swargadeo's flight (during the Moamaria disturbances). The latter has had no pooja since at Hadjoo. He was indulged with the privilege of riding on horseback, but not in palki-dolah. Three or four priests always remained in attendance at the palace. The moment the king came forth to take the air, they called down the blessing of god on him with elevated hands. Whenever the Surgee sent this man to perform pooja for him at Mokam-Hadjoo, he always sent considerable presents to the temple, but they had no regular establishment from the kings".

Hadira Choky or Kandhar Choky, so important in the commercial relations between Assam and Bengal, is thus described by Wade :—

" After passing Gualparah at a considerable distance, the views of the houses on the projecting hill are truly picturesque, and would afford an elegant view to the painter. On the northern bank is established the custom house of Assam called the Kondhar-Choky, whence in the season of innundation the king's officers are compelled to retire to the Phoolora Hill considerably inland, known principally for the former cutcha temple of Boora-Gohain dedicated to the god Siva. The temple has gone to ruin since the Moamaria flight. The inhabitants retired to Bengal and the priests into Camroop ; for, neither the Kondhar Burrowah who superintended the commerce with Bengal, contributed one mite to their support of the establishment nor to the protection of the inhabitants ; and the hill became a wilderness. A Linga or phallus miraculously made its appearance on the spot spontaneously, and consecrated the hill, out of the memory of men, to the worship of Siva. It was not however under the royal protection at any time. The traders who visited the Choky were its support."

Wade's remarks on the possibility of a Burmese invasion of Bengal through Assam are significant in the light of subsequent events,—" there are several routes from Assam to Ava, of which the Burmans might with some facility take advantage to enter Bengal, having by the conquest of Munipoor and the capital of the Cosaree country approached very near to Assam in that quarter."

Dr. Wade contemplated to write a fourth book on Assam as we learn from the dedicatory letter prefixed to his *Geographical Sketch*,—" Should these communications prove acceptable, I shall hope in a short time to present you with some account of the civil, military and ecclesiastical Government of that country which you will probably find more interesting than a dull geographical detail."[59]

Incessant literary labours in connection with his researches on Assam marked the closing years of Wade's life. The "credit" which he had hoped to derive from his investigations came to him in some measure, and his friends acknowledged his labours though

59. Letter prefixed to Wade's *Geographical Sketch of Assam*, Home Misc. Series, vol. 736, pp. 78-84.

they did not know what exactly he was doing. Captain Michael Symes, author of *Account of an Embassy to the Kingdom of Ava,* informed Francis Fowke that "Peter Wade [is] about to publish his travels into Assam, an excursion that has not been unprofitable to him; he is appointed to Purnea where he means to become an extensive Indigo planter."[60]

Wade's scholarship and attainments were known to his intimate friends but it took some time for the Government to be acquainted with them and to recognise them. This delay was considered to be due to the fact that he served at places situated at a distance from Calcutta, which in consequence "removed him from the observation of those who could have appreciated and rewarded his merit."[61]

But the public began gradually to know Wade. In 1797 he became a Fellow of the Asiatic Society of Bengal; and he submitted to that society several specimens of Natural History and Botany. The Marquis Wellesley, in appreciation of Wade's scholarship and linguistic attainments, gave him an appointment in the College of Fort William. This appointment was expected to give Wade full facilities for pursuing his literary labours. But all the prospects of a brilliant future which would have as well reflected on the dissemination of knowledge about Assam were destroyed by his death at Calcutta on the 14th October 1802 "by one of those remitting fevers which are so fatal in this country, and to which, notwithstanding his utmost caution he was peculiarly subject."[62] His remains were buried in the North Park Street Cemetery, Calcutta.

By his will Wade had appointed Francis Fowke, Maitland and Dr. Ross Munro as his executors.[63] He left no property except a few shares of some indigo factories at Purnea. All his savings were sunk in payment of the security of Rs. 40,000 for his brother-in-law Captain Carruthers who had died at Midnapore on 27th November, 1801. The widow was left with three children, and they would be entitled to a meagre provision from the Military Orphan Fund. The family were also to get some relief from provision in the second

60. Capt. Michael Symes to F. Fowke, about 1795, Fowke MSS., 22-166.

61. Dr. W. Ross Munro to F. Fowke, from Calcutta, Dec. 4, 1802, Fowke MSS., 39-11.

62. Dr. Munro to F. Fowke, from Calcutta, Dec. 4, 1802, Fowke MSS., 39-11.

63. Maitland was probably Peter Maitland whose permission to proceed to Assam for the purpose of trade was solicited by Mr. Horsely in his letter to Government, dated Calcutta, March 27, 1793, Public Department Records, O. C., March 29, 1793, No. 29.

class of the Laudable Insurance on Lives in Calcutta to which Wade had contributed. Mrs. Wade was permitted to draw her share from the pension allowed to a Surgeon's widow from the date of decease of her husband.[64] On January 27th, 1803, she applied to the Marquis Wellesley for "affording her an essential relief in her actual circumstances." The Governor-General expressed his inability to grant her any assistance to procure accommodation for her and her children to England; but he expressed "a favourable sense of the merits and services of her late husband, and that he will take an early opportunity of recommending her and her family to the notice of the Hon'ble Court of Directors." Mrs. Wade and her children took their passage to Europe by the ship *Lady Burgess,* Captain Swinton, and arrived in Edinburgh about the middle of 1803. About a year later Mrs. Wade was granted a compassionate pension from Lord Clive's Fund.[65]

Here ends the story of a man who was animated throughout his life by a zeal to obtain eminence in his profession, and to introduce to his countrymen the land of Assam, a virtual *terra incognita* in those days.

64. Orders of the Supreme Board at Fort William, Beng. Military Cons., Dec. 11, 1802, No. 7.

65. Court's Military Despatches to Bengal, June 20, 1804, and July 12, 1805. Also John Carruthers to F. Fowke, from Edinburgh, June 24, 1803, Fowke MSS., 30-12; Court's letter to Bengal, June 10, 1801 to Dec. 23, 1806, vol. 40, p. 526, and vol. 43, p. 450.

Chapter VIII

NON-INTERVENTION AND ITS ABANDONMENT

PART I

Repeated Applications for Assistance

Company's Assam policy, 1794-1823: The relations of the Company with Assam for the thirty years after the departure of Captain Welsh arose mainly out of the petitions made by its Government for assistance in arms and troops, and those made by private individuals to promote their designs to establish their claims or recover their lost possessions. The Company rendered help to the Assam government as far as it was consistent with the necessity for adherence to the restrictions imposed by the Act of 1784; and as regards the requests of individuals they were summarily rejected as the Government was not willing to be a party to the spread of commotions in Assam or to the subversion of the lawful authority of the Swargadeo. Towards the end of the period the Government vigilantly watched the progress of events in Assam as they tended to disturb the peace of the Bengal frontier.

During the stay of Captain Welsh's detachment in Assam its people had seen that a handful of troops commanded by British officers had produced changes which they had not been able to effect for years together. Having realised the superiority of the discipline and organisation of the Company's army, the Assam government made repeated requests to the Governor-General for English officers and for assistance in arms, accoutrements and sepoys. At the same time the Assam government trained its troops on the lines of the Company's sepoys.

In asking for help the Assamese were led by their confidence in the justice and benevolence of the English Government. This is seen in the explanation they suggested for the withdrawal of the detachment. The Assamese were unaware of the real intentions of Sir John Shore or of the policy of non-intervention. They believed it was the imbecility and untrustworthiness of Raja Gaurinath Singha which had provoked the displeasure of the Governor-General as manifested in the sudden recall of Capt. Welsh before the completion of his mission. "You were kindly pleased," wrote Gaurinath's successor Kamaleswar to the Governor-General in

1796, "from a wish to restore the country [Assam] to tranquillity, to depute Captain Welsh hither. But, before the disputes could be properly settled, being given to understand that no reliance could be placed on our words and engagements you were incensed against us and removed Captain Welsh." Kamaleswar's ministers wrote in the same vein,—"The Swargadeo Maharaja Gaurinath first drew down your displeasure upon us, but as he is now no more, remit your displeasure, and reflect on your former kindness."[1]

The Government on the other hand rigorously pursued a policy of neutrality and non-interference. All appeals for troops were uniformly refused, though requests for arms and ammunition were acceded to on most occasions when made by the Assam government. "I am prevented," said Sir John Shore, "from affording you the aid you solicit [a party of sepoys with an English officer] by impediments which is out of my power to obviate."[2]

Sir Alured Clarke, during the absence of the Marquess Wellesley in the war with Tipu, dismissed similar requests of the Assam Raja saying,—"The laws and regulations of this Government preclude the possibility of compliance with them."[3] Wellesley complied with the Assam Raja's application for the supply of arms, but dismissed the request for troops without assigning any reason for his refusal.

In the meantime Shore's policy of non-intervention was abandoned by his successors. The Government had to fight in self-defence, if not in aggression. But in Assam the policy of neutrality was rigidly followed even when it ceased to be a dominating factor in the Company's political activities in India. The case of Assam was quite different from that of other native states. Its troubles did not for a long time extend, or threaten to extend, beyond the limits of its frontier; and the Company's Assam policy of quiescence was not likely to produce any repercussions on its relations with the principal powers of Northern and Southern India. There was thus no immediate danger to the Company in pursuing that policy towards Assam. Sir John Shore's assertion in 1795, "We

1. Assam Raja and ministers to Shore, Feb. 7, Beng. Pol. Cons., July 29, 1796, No. 13. Srinath probably refers to Shore's displeasure when he says—"The Barasaheb [Governor-General] despatched a letter to the Captain [Welsh] not to stay any longer in Assam. He also wrote *many other things* in that letter. The Captain having received that note resolved to return." *Tungkhungia Buranji*, p. 134.

2. Shore to Assam Raja, Oct. 31, Beng. Pol. Cons., Nov. 4, 1796, No. 55.

3. Clarke to Assam Raja, May 3, Beng. Pol. Cons., May 3, 1799, No. 8.

are not now much interested in the affairs of Assam, having withdrawn all interference in them on the recall of Captain Welsh's Battalion,"[4] provides the key to the Company's Assam policy in the pre-Burmese period. It was upheld by Lord Hastings when he refused assistance to Swargadeo Chandrakanta Singha in 1815 though the latter offered an annual tribute of 1½ lakh of rupees. "While the domestic feuds of that Government [Assam]," said the Governor-General, "are not of a nature to affect the tranquillity of the Company's Provinces we are necessarily precluded from any interference in its internal affairs. Our policy is merely to attend to the concerns of our own Government and not to interfere into those of other states, even although the greatest advantage be offered as the price of our interference".[5] It was only when the Burmese occupied Assam and threatened the peace of the neighbouring districts of Bengal that the Government sent an army to expel the invaders from their newly acquired possessions.

In refusing active military assistance to the Assam Raja the Government reminded him of the necessity to suppress the troubles by his own exertions without depending upon the aid of any exterior agency. "It is more in your power than in mine," said Sir John Shore, "to effect the object [restoring peace to Assam] by evincing a disposition to settle with the various chiefs their several disputes upon principles of equity."[6] With regard to the oppressions committed by individuals who entered Assam for purposes of trade Sir Alured Clarke, the acting Governor-General, wrote to the Swargadeo—"You must be sensible that it is not in the power of this Government to put a stop to such practices, it being a point which appertains exclusively to the internal administration of your country."[7]

It must be pointed out that the Assam government displayed their recuperative power to an amazing extent. The central authority was strengthened by the maintenance of an army of trained troops; the vassal chiefs were reduced; the Moamarias were practically quelled; the Burkendazes driven off; and the rebellion in Kamrup suppressed. The country returned to its normal order, and the capital Rangpur was almost restored to its former prosperity. The king paid visits to the monasteries, and performed the

4. Bengal Letter to Court, May 12, 1795.
5. Swinton to Scott, Dec. 8, Beng. Pol. Cons., Dec. 8, 1815, No. 54.
6. Shore to Assam Raja, Sept. 15, Beng. Pol. Cons., Sept. 15, 1794, No. 30.
7. Clarke to Assam Raja, March 23, Beng. Pol. Cons., March 23, 1798, No. 6.

usual round of festivities; and jugglers were imported from Bengal and they entertained the king and the courtiers as well as the ladies of the royal harem.[8] The change was partly effected with the arms and ammunition supplied by the Company. "Through the influence of your Lordship's kindness," wrote the Assam Raja to the Governor-General in 1806, "this country enjoys a certain degree of tranquillity."[9] Sir George Barlow in a letter to the Assam Raja referred to "the disturbances having been happily composed and perfect tranquillity being again restored in the Kingdom of Assam."[10]

But the peace was of a temporary character. The man through whose patriotic endeavour the change had taken place was the prime minister Purnananda Buragohain. He had stemmed the tide of Moamaria advances, and had kept up a show of government in Upper Assam when Gaurinath and his nobles had taken shelter in Gauhati and the neighbouring districts. On the return of the Ahom monarch to the capital Purnananda adopted vigorous means to suppress the disorders. The measures of a patriotic minister acting in a dictatorial capacity in degenerate times are bound to encroach upon hereditary interests. His actions will impose burdens upon the subjects which will be manipulated by short-sighted and designing rivals to excite animosity against him. Purnananda's motives were misunderstood and misrepresented, and conspiracies were set on foot to murder him, which when detected drove the authors to seek foreign aid to accomplish their original object. The Burmese came, saw and conquered. The government of Assam which had survived the depredations of the Moamarias, the Burkendazes and the Singphos succumbed finally to the consequences of internal jealousies.

Bishnunarayan's proposal to become Company's tributary: We have seen that the Darrang prince Bishnunarayan, Zemindar of Kamrup, had accompanied Captain Welsh to Bengal. On August 24, 1794, he submitted a petition to Sir John Shore for being vested with the government of Kamrup under the Company on the same footing and authority as the Raja of Cooch Behar. He offered to pay an annual tribute of 135,000 rupees.

Bishnunarayan had an interview with the Governor-General on October 1. Sir John Shore elicited information from Bishnunarayan on the origin of the Moamaria rebellion, the extent to

8. *Tungkhungia Buranji*, pp. 149, 177-8.

9. Assam Raja to Governor-General, Nov. 3, 1805, Beng. Sec. and Pol. Cons., July 17, 1806, No. 110.

10. Barlow to Assam Raja, Sept. 27, Beng. Pol. Cons., Oct. 2, 1806 No. 18.

which the Assam Raja's authority was exercised after the withdrawal of the Company's troops, and the claims of the Darrang Raja to the government of Kamrup. Bishnunarayan expatiated upon the savage disposition of Gaurinath Singha and the cruelties practised by him upon his subjects and his near relatives by maiming and killing them for the smallest fault. The Swargadeo, said Bishnunarayan, stood alone and unsupported, and the ministers exercised their authority without any regard to their monarch. Kamrup was represented by Bishnunarayan as being under the Darrang princes till the reign of Gaurinath's grandfather Rudra Singha (1696-1714).[11]

During Bishnunarayan's stay at Calcutta the Governor-General had received a communication from the Assam Raja complaining of the delinquency of that Darrang prince, his failure to pay the revenue for three years and his active participation in the intrigues against his master. The Governor-General was asked to order Bishnunarayan to return to Assam and attend to his responsibilities.[12]

The matter was taken up by the Board in their meeting of October 3, when they affirmed their adherence to the decision, made in the case of Krishnanarayan three years ago, not to interfere in the disputes between the Darrang prince and the Assam Raja.[13]

Defeat of Hazari Sing's Burkendazes: Two Hindustani sepoys, Dina and Phakirchand, belonging to the detachment of Captain Welsh, had been induced by heavy bribes to remain in Assam. They were employed in the training of the Assamese recruits on the lines of the Company's troops. For want of guns the soldiers had to be instructed with the help of bamboo clubs and shoulder-pieces in their hands.[14]

Soon after Captain Welsh's departure from Assam, Gaurinath despatched Bikaram Majumdar Barua to the Governor-General communicating his intention "to arm part of his subjects for the defence and protection of the whole" and regretting his want of European arms and accoutrements to give the troops the respect and consequence so conducive to success. The Raja requested

11. Substance of a conversation between Shore and Bishnunarayan on Oct. 1, Bishnunarayan to Shore, Aug. 23, 1794, Beng. Pub. Cons., Oct. 3, 1794, Nos. 18 and 19.

12. Assam Raja to Shore, Aug. 10, Beng. Pol. Cons., Sept. 26, 1794, No. 20.

13. Beng. Pub. Cons., Oct. 3, 1794, No. 19.

14. *Tungkhungia Buranji*, pp. 134-5.

the Governor-General to supply him with 300 or 500 stand of arms with a proportionate quantity of gunpowder. Another embassy led by Bishnuram Kataki, Datta Bairagi and Devanath soon followed that of Bikaram. Assuming that assistance in troops could not be obtained the envoys applied for the delivery of 300 muskets with their bayonets, 4 maunds of balls, 2 maunds of flints and 200 cartridge boxes.[15]

Sir John Shore allowed the Assam Vakils to purchase 300 stand of arms with their appurtenances. They deposited rupees 6,098 with the Persian Secretary Neil Benjamin Edmonstone as the price of the articles supplied. Hazari Sing was then in Kamrup with his Burkendaz followers, and another up-country leader named Jogangiri was in occupation of Gauhati. To protect the arms from being intercepted by the Burkendazes the Assam Vakils entertained three companies of sepoys in Bengal and placed them under the command of one Niamutulla Subedar. They proceeded from Goalpara towards Gauhati on April 26, 1795.

Hazari Sing attacked the Assam Raja's sepoys and an engagement took place at Gauhati on May 30. Hazari Sing was shot through the breast and drowned in attempting to reach his boat. Nine hundred of his followers were drowned or killed in the engagement. The Assamese then occupied Gauhati, and the Barphukan Badanchandra returned to that place from his retreat at Kajali. Niamutulla remained with the Barphukan at Gauhati.

The major portion of the arms and troops was sent up to Jorhat. Purnananda armed the Assamese soldiers with the new weapons, and gave them regular uniform consisting of red jackets and caps. The Assam Raja thanked Sir John Shore for having granted the 300 stand of arms. "On receipt of them," said he, "I entertained some Sepoys and continued to arrange some points immediately necessary, but I am unable to eradicate other evils."[16] Flint guns were first introduced in Assam since the consignment of arms supplied in 1795 by Sir John Shore.[17]

Accession of Kamaleswar Singha: Swargadeo Gaurinath Singha died of dysentery on August 4, 1795, leaving a daughter named Jayanti Aideo and no male issue. Purnananda Buragohain who had been in attendance on the monarch in his dying moments

15. Bikaram to Shore, undated, Beng. Pol. Cons., Sept. 8, 1794, No. 25; and Assam Raja's Vakils to Govt., undated, Beng. Pol. Cons., Sept. 26, 1794, No. 20.

16. Assam Raja to Shore, Feb. 7, Beng. Pol. Cons., July 29, 1796, No. 13.

17. *Tungkhungia Buranji*, pp. 135, 139.

concealed the event for three days utilizing the interval in the selection of a successor, and in killing the Baskatia Barbarua who had behaved inimically towards the premier and the late sovereign.[18]

The question of appointing a new Raja presented great difficulties. Between the years 1714 and 1795 the throne had been occupied by the sons and grandson of Swargadeo Rudra Singha. The princes of Rudra Singha's line had almost all been mutilated by Lakshmi Singha or his son Gaurinath, and were therefore disqualified for the throne. Bijoy Barmura Gohain, great-grandson of Rudra Singha and grandson of Rajeswar Singha, was a capable and energetic prince; but Bijoy and his son Brajanath had also their ears cut off by Lakshmi Singha about the year 1775.

There was the Charing Raja Kadam Dighala Gohain, grandson of Rudra Singha's brother Lechai Namrupia Raja. Dighala had displayed considerable gallantry in the operations against the Moamarias. But he was disqualified for succession owing to the mutilation of an eye. With the concurrence of the other ministers Purnananda placed Dighala's young son Kinaram on the throne. The new king assumed the name Kamaleswar Singha. The actual authority in the state was wielded by Purnananda Buragohain. The Charing Raja and his wife Numali Rajmao, as guardians of the king, exercised some influence on the deliberations of the prime minister.

The selection of Kamaleswar Singha was unpopular for several reasons. It was believed that as Lechai Namrupia Raja had rebelled against his brother Rudra Singha and had been blinded in consequence, his descendants were permanently debarred from elevation to the throne. To this disqualification was added the supposed illegitimacy of Ayursut Gohain, the father of Dighala Gohain. Buchanan-Hamilton writing in 1809 pointed out another reason for the unpopularity of Kamaleswar's succession; he and his forefathers were disciples of the Sudra Mahantas of Sologuri, whereas the five monarchs preceding Kamaleswar had Brahmans as their Gurus.[19]

Kamaleswar's elevation gave rise to a supposition in many quarters that in selecting him Purnananda Buragohain was actuated

18. Scott's *Historical Notes* in Beng. Sec. and Pol. Cons., July 14, 1826, No. 2, and Robinson's *Descriptive Account of Assam*, p. 175. Srinath says that Baskatia Barbarua was executed as the result of a trial held after Kamaleswar's accession, *Tungkhungia Buranji*, p. 140.

19. Martin's *Eastern India*, Vol. III, p. 608.

by a desire to perpetuate his own authority in the person of a prince who, owing to his defective title, would have always to depend upon the support of the prime minister's party. But it must be pointed out at this stage that David Scott who very carefully examined the relative claims of the Ahom princes admitted that in view of the absence of an eligible candidate "the Buragohain did not perhaps exceed the powers vested in his predecessors when he appointed Kamaleswar to the royal dignity."[20] The illegitimacy of Kamaleswar's ancestors was not confirmed by Scott's enquiries. The same difficulty of finding a suitable prince was experienced by the British Government in 1826-1832 when it proposed to set up a native administration in Upper Assam. The eventual appointment of Purandar Singha to nominal authority as a tributary prince had to be accompanied by a number of carefully drawn-up safeguards to ensure good government.[21]

Haradatta's rebellion and murder of Raush: Soon after the installation of Kamaleswar Singha one Bhadrakanta of the Sandikoi family, commonly known as Bhadari, was appointed Barbarua. His nephew Gendhela Rajkhowa, *alias* Kalia-bhomora, undertaking to pay the arrears due to the Hindustani sepoys, was appointed Barphukan, and Badanchandra was recalled from Gauhati. The new Barphukan was a very efficient and patriotic officer, and had served with conspicuous bravery against the Moamarias.

On his arrival at Gauhati Kalia-bhomora Barphukan found Haradatta Bujarbarua and his brother Biradatta arrayed against the Ahom government with a large force of Hindustanis and Sikhs. These merceneries were called *Dumdumiyas* or *Dundias,* probably because the Sikhs had their headquarters at the Gurudwar Dumdumé at Dhubri, which had been founded by the ninth Sikh Guru Teg Bahadur in 1669 during his visit to Assam with his patron Raja Ram Singha, son of Mirza Raja Jai Singha of Amber.

Haradatta is said to have been secretly aided by the Rajas of Cooch Behar and Bijni who wanted to see a member of their own family restored to the government of Kamrup. Arrangements were made for the marriage of Haradatta's daughter Padma Kumari to a prince of Cooch Behar. Haradatta succeeded in occupying a large part of North Kamrup. But the two brothers made themselves obnoxious to the people of Kamrup by their overbearing temper and heavy exactions. The Barphukan, aided by the

20. Scott to Swinton, Ap. 15, Beng. Sec. and Pol. Cons., July 14, 1826, No. 2.

21. See Chapter X, *post*.

disaffected nobles of Kamrup, defeated Haradatta's party. Haradatta was captured and put to death. His brother and his son had their eyes extracted and were then sent up to Jorhat.[22]

Haradatta's Burkendazes continued to commit depredations in the villages opposite Gauhati under their own leaders Baju Sing and Alu Sing, and threatened to cross over to the south bank. Fresh parties of these marauders began to arrive from Bengal. The Barphukan raised an army of Hindustani sepoys reinforced by levies from the neighbouring vassal chieftains.

In February 1796 Kamaleswar Singha and his ministers applied to Sir John Shore for a party of sepoys under an English officer and 500 muskets. The Assam government proposed that the English officer, in the event of one being deputed, would be put in command of all the existing sepoys as the Assamese captains had found it difficult to keep them in subjection. The petition, which was delivered by Bandhuram Majumdar, Devanath Sarma and Tanusyam Das, was accompanied by the present of a pair of elephants to the Governor-General.[23] Sir John Shore ordered the supply of 200 muskets, with powder and shot in proportion, to the Assam Vakils. The Governor-General expressed his regret at his inability to comply with the Raja's request for troops and an English officer "for impediments which it was not in his power to obviate."[24]

The Assam Raja sent a number of petitions asking the Bengal Government to prevent the incursions of Burkendazes. A detachment of sepoys was accordingly stationed at Jugighopa who succeeded in dispersing the banditti assembled on the Bengal frontier for the purpose of entering and plundering Assam. Similar orders were issued to the Commissioner of Cooch Behar and the Magistrates of Rungpore and Dinajpore.[25]

Kalia-bhomora Barphukan succeeded finally in expelling the Burkendazes from Kamrup and restoring both banks of the river to quiet and peace. For these services he received special distinctions from the monarch, and the title of "Pratap-ballabh", literally, "one whose friend is valour." He was also given the lands of Haradatta which had been confiscated to the state.[26]

22. *Tungkhungia Buranji*, p. 141.
23. Assam Raja to Shore Feb. 7, Beng. Pol. Cons., July 29, 1796, No. 13.
24. Shore to Assam Raja, Oct. 31, Beng. Pol. Cons., Nov. 4, 1796, No. 55.
25. Clarke to Assam Raja, March 23, Beng. Pol. Cons., March 23, 1798, No. 6.
26. Copper-plate grant of Kamaleswar Singha, *Saka* 1722 or A.D. 1800 in favour of Pratapballabh Barphukan, in possession of the writer.

Pratapballabh Barphukan realised that the association of the East India Company was the only possible remedy for counteracting the grave situation into which his country had been plunged. He submitted formal proposals to the prime minister requesting him to negotiate with the Governor-General to extend to Assam the protection of the Company's arms. Purnananda had firm faith in his own capacity, and thought that he would be able to restore his country to peace and orderly government without the intervention of any exterior power. The Barphukan's proposals were therefore shelved as being pessimistic and premature.[27]

One of the first acts of the Dumdumiyas had been the murder of the Goalpara merchant Daniel Raush in January 1796. He had paid a visit to Darrang with several boats loaded with merchandise to demand adjustment of his claims, specially in connection with the loss suffered by him at the hands of Krishnanarayan's Burkendazes on June 30, 1792. Large hordes of Fakirs and Burkendazes were in 1795 and 1796 engaged in plundering the villages in Darrang causing great alarm to its Raja. Amongst the Dumdumiyas there must have been many persons who had served under Krishnanarayan in 1791-1793 and whose attitude towards Raush was avowedly hostile. The officers of the Assam Raja, in view of the commotions in Darrang and the existing animosity of the Burkendazes towards Raush, had asked him not to go there leaving their protection. Raush refused to listen to the warnings, and proceeded by land to Darrang where he was murdered by a party of Fakirs, his papers destroyed and his effects looted. It cannot be ascertained to what extent Raush's old enemy Krishnanarayan or any other Darrang prince was responsible for his murder. The Marquess of Wellesley held that Raush had been murdered by the Raja of Darrang into whose country he had proceeded on the invitation of the Raja for the settlement of his balances.[28] This view was also held by the Court of Directors and successive Governors-General, and the local administrators in Assam up to Colonel Jenkins. The Ahom government attributed the murder to the turbulent Burkendazes into whose hands Raush had strayed ignoring the warning of the Assamese officers.[29] At the time of

27. Gunabhiram, *Assam Buranji*, p. 175.

28. Wellesley to Assam Raja, Nov. 20, 1802, Beng. Pol. Cons., May 2, 1805, No. 97.

29. Assam Raja to Gov.-Gen., recd. Jan. 15, Beng. Sec. and Pol. Cons., July 17, 1806, No. 110; same to same, recd. May 26, Beng. Pol. Cons., July 9, 1807, No. 40.

his death. Raush's outstanding claims on the Assamese amounted to nearly three lakhs of rupees.

Sir John Shore's interest in Assam: In spite of his disinclination to afford active military assistance, Sir John Shore continued to take an interest in Assam and to help the Raja and private individuals whenever practicable. He adopted measures to prevent the entrance of Bengal Burkendazes into Assam. Bengal merchants used to send their goods to Assam under escorts of Burkendazes, and under the pretence of accompanying Bengal merchandise large numbers of nondescript people used to travel to and from Assam. To stop this, Sir John Shore issued orders requiring all persons desirous of sending escorts of Burkendazes and other armed men into Assam to apply for passports from the Commissioner of Cooch Behar specifying in their applications the number of the escort, the goods under their charge, and the destination of the goods. The local officials were asked not to allow armed men to pass into Assam from the Company's provinces without such passports.[30] A detachment of sepoys was stationed at Jugighopa to disperse Burkendazes assembled on the frontier for the purpose of entering Assam. The benefits of these measures were admitted by Purnananda Burgohain in a letter to the Governor-General,—"Through the kindness of the English gentlemen Rajah Surgi Deo together with all the inhabitants of this country remain in perfect security, since through their assistance all the turbulent people on the side of Gawahatteh [Gauhati] have withdrawn their hands from plunder and devastation."[31] Sir John Shore supplied the Assam Raja with arms and accoutrements on two occasions, and the suppression of the troubles caused by Hazari Sing and Haradatta was partially due to that assistance.

The most benevolent act of Sir John Shore was the financial help he granted to Gaurinath Singha's two widows who had been residing at Chilmari in Rungpore since December 1793. After the death of Gaurinath Singha the senior widow Kamaleswari Devi went to Calcutta and petitioned to the Governor-General for help. "In consequence of the dissensions which prevailed in the country of Assam I proceeded to Calcutta," said Kamaleswari, "and presenting my respects to the Governor-General. I distinguished him

30. Board's resolution, Beng. Pol. Cons., Dec. 19, 1794, No. 41; *Calcutta Gazette*, Jan. 1, 1795.

31. Purnananda Buragohain to Gov.-Gen., recd. Feb. 21, Beng. Pol. Cons., April 15, 1799, No. 6.

with the title of father, and threw myself under the shadow of his influence and protection." In April 1796 Sir John Shore granted the two ladies a pension of 100 rupees per month. A sum of 500 rupees was given to Kamaleswari Devi to defray the expenses of her journey from Calcutta to Chilmari.[32]

Sir John Shore retained possession of a manuscript chronicle or *Buranji* of Assam, written on cotton cloth in the Ahom language, which had been obtained by Dr. J. P. Wade during his stay in Assam in 1792-94. Shore encouraged Dr. Wade to publish his "Memoirs of the Reign of Surgi Deo Gowrinath Sing", and the author accordingly sent the manuscript in April 1796 to his friend in England, Francis Fowke, for printing.[33]

Wellesley imprisons Niamutulla and Padum Kowanr : The Earl of Mornington, afterwards Marquis Wellesley, assumed charge of the Governor-General's office in May 1798, and from that time the Company's Government acted with greater energy and vigour in its relations with the native states, and this change was reflected in the few occasions when it had to deal with Assam. Sometime in 1798 Niamutulla Subedar, a commander of the Assam government's troops, fled into Bengal, and having placed himself at the head of a gang of freebooters plundered Goalpara and Jugighopa, and robbed Lakshminarayan Brahmachari, the agent of the Assam government at the Kandahar Choky, of a large sum of money and everything that was valuable. Niamutulla had taken into his protection an Assamese named Padum on whom he conferred the title of "Rajkowanr" or prince. Padum entered Assam, plundered the people and then fled into Bengal.

Niamutulla presented his protege to the Bengal Government to which Padum preferred a complaint against the Assam Raja. After making enquiries Lord Mornington concluded that Niamutulla and Padum were avowed enemies of the Assam government, and threw them both into prison. "The knowledge of this", wrote the Assam Raja to the Governor-General, "has afforded me unbounded satisfaction." Purnananda Buragohain wrote in this connection to the Persian Secretary,—"Being then convinced that they [Niamutulla and Padum] were inimical to us he [Governor-General] directed them both to be imprisoned. The knowledge of

32, Rani Kamaleswari to Governor-General, recd. Feb. 10, Beng. Pol. Cons., June 26, 1800, Nos. 155-157 ; same to same recd., July 28, Cons., Aug. 14, 1806, No. 26.

33. Wade, *Account of Assam,* ed. B. Sharma, p. ii; Wade's letter to Fowke, Ap. 1799, *Fowke Mss.* India Office Records, Vol. 22, letter No. 167.

this circumstance has offered all the inhabitants of this quarter the most lively satisfaction."[34]

Wellesley supplies arms to the Assam government: In the beginning of 1799 the Assam Raja and his ministers were able to inform the Government at Calcutta of the establishment of peace in Lower Assam brought about mainly through the exertions of Pratapballabh Barphukan and the restrictions imposed on the entrance of Burkendazes as escorts of Bengal goods. But a new element now entered into the disorders of Assam. The Singphos living on the eastern confines of Assam, acting in league with the Moamarias, made frequent inroads, laid waste the country and carried off numerous inhabitants into slavery. The Assam Raja applied to the Governor-General for a supply of 500 new muskets. Referring to the 300 stand of arms supplied by Sir John Shore the Raja said that the muskets had been worn out and the powder expended.

The war with Tipu had commenced and Lord Wellesley was absent in the Deccan. As there was only a small quantity of musketry in the Company's arsenal at Fort William, Sir Alured Clarke, the Senior Member of Council, considered it to be a sufficient reason to decline a compliance with the Assam Raja's application independent of other objections. One A. Davidson of Calcutta who had received rupees 5,000 from the Assam Vakils to pay for the arms was refused permission by the Board to purchase them.[35]

In June 1802 the Assam Raja sent an embassy to Lord Wellesley, headed by Baloram Khangia Phukan, asking for the supply of 800 stand of new arms with ammunition and five companies of sepoys under an English officer. Alluding to the benefits derived from the arms supplied by Sir John Shore on two previous occasions the Raja said that these aids had preserved him from the evil machinations of his enemies. "From that period," continued the Raja, "the plunderers of this country having been intimidated, my country has been permitted to enjoy in some small degree peace and tranquillity." The Raja then referred to the fresh irruptions of the Moamarias at Bengmara against whom he had despatched five companies of sepoys armed with the old muskets supplied by the Company. The Moamarias made a surprise attack upon the

34. Assam Raja and Purnananda Buragohain to Wellesley, recd. Feb. 21, Beng. Pol. Cons., Ap. 15, 1799, Nos. 5-7.

35. Davidson to Govt. Ap. 10, Beng. Pub. Cons., Ap. 12, 1799, No. 25; Govt's. resolution, Beng. Pol. Cons., Ap. 15, 1799, No. 7.

sepoys, defeated and despoiled them of all their arms and carried the whole away, "so that", said the Raja, "I am now left without a single musket." The Raja's letter was accompanied by one from Pratapballabh Barphukan who concluded by saying,—"We have the fullest confidence in the British Government, what more shall I represent?" Lord Wellesley issued orders to supply the Assam Raja with 800 stand of serviceable repaired arms with an equal number of bayonets, scabbards, belts and cartridge-boxes, 40,000 ball cartridges and 1,600 spare flints.[36] The help rendered by the Government on this occasion was remembered by the Assamese for a long time and was frequently alluded to in the correspondence of the subsequent period.

The arms supplied by Lord Wellesley enabled Purnananda Buragohain to equip and maintain an army of 14 companies of 50 sepoys in each, mostly Hindustanis. The force was placed under the command of Captain Chandra Gohain, a relation of Purnananda, with Baloram Khangia Phukan as Junior Captain. The strength of the army was subsequently raised to 18 companies. The Subedars and Jamadars were appointed from among the Hindustanis, and the captaincies were conferred on Assamese officers of the rank of Barua, Rajkhowa and Phukan. Smaller detachments aided by irregulars were stationed at Gauhati, Sadiya and other important places. In 1806 the Raja was able to inform the Governor-General,—"Through your Lordship's kindness the turbulent are expelled from my country and it enjoys a certain degree of tranquillity." The Raja in stating his preference for new arms informed the Governor-General of the absence of men in his country who were skilled in repairing muskets of the description supplied by the Company.[37]

Accession of Chandrakanta Singha: The remaining years of Kamaleswar's reign were passed in comparative peace. Bharath Singha, the Raja of the Moamarias, had been killed in an engagement with the Ahom forces. The religious leader of the Moamarias, Pitambar Mahajan, had died in prison. The Moamaria chief at Bengmara had offered his submission and become a vassal of the Ahoms with the title of Barsenapati. The Singphos, the Khamptis and the Duflas were kept in check by the timely measures of

36. Assam Raja and Purnananda Buragohain to Wellesley, June 20, 1802 and Board's resolution, March 31, 1803, Beng. Pol. Cons., March 31, 1803, Nos. 71-73.

37. Assam Raja to Governor-General, Nov. 3, 1805, Beng. Sec. and Pol. Cons., July 17, 1806, No. 110.

Purnananda Buragohain. Several parties of Burmese who had arrived on the frontier of Assam at the invitation of the Moamarias and the Singphos were dismissed by Purnananda by kind words and presents. The fugitives who had taken shelter in the neighbouring provinces were encouraged to come back to their respective villages and resume their old pursuits. As has been pointed out by Sir Edward Gait the credit was due not to Kamaleswar but to his able and energetic minister Purnananda.[38] In spite of the calumny and vilification to which he has been subjected in the hands of many contemporary and posthumous writers, no one who has an opportunity of closely studying the events of the period can fail to be impressed with the manner in which Purnananda conceaselessly endeavoured to bring order out of anarchy and confusion, strengthen the central authority and make it felt even in the extremities of the kingdom.

Kamaleswar Singha died of smallpox on January 17, 1811, and was succeeded by his brother Chandrakanta, aged 16. The king being a minor Purnananda continued to wield the reins of Government as before.

Claims of Raush's estate: One circumstance which had induced Lord Wellesley to comply so readily with the Assam Raja's request was the possibility of an adjustment of the claims of Raush's estate. His letter to the Assam Raja communicating his decision to supply the arms contained also a narration of the circumstances of Raush's murder and the attempts made previously by Government for the liquidation of his debts; and it ended with a request to settle the demands. The person who was entrusted with the delivery of the arms to the Assam Raja was also furnished with all the documents and accounts necessary to establish the justice of the demands.

No subject arising out of the relations of the Assamese and English merchants in the eighteenth century led to such frequent and prolonged correspondence between the Government of the East India Company and that of Assam as the attempt to obtain payment of the balances due to Daniel Raush. It was initiated by his executors soon after his death in 1796, revived by his widow in 1801, and by his son-in-law in 1813, and continued by his children till 1835 when Assam had passed into the hands of the British. All those connected with the Company's administration, from the Collector of Rungpore to the Board of Control, moved in the matter

38. Gait, *History of Assam*, p. 223.

of obtaining satisfaction of the demand till the new Government of Assam deemed it inexpedient to pursue the subject any further in view of the lapse of time, the absence of documents relating to the claims, and the want of accounts, combined with the poverty of the then Darrang Raja Bijoynarayan who had been held responsible for the debts of his predecessors of 1796.

The debts due to Raush's estate amounted to nearly three lakhs of rupees, and included the expenses incurred by him in paying the troops which he had once procured from Dacca for the Assam Raja, the value of the property plundered by Krishnanarayan's Burkendazes on June 30, 1792, and by the Dumdumiyas at the time of his murder in Darrang, together with the balances due from Assamese merchants.

The executors to Raush's will appointed Bernard MacCullum their agent for the adjustment of the accounts of the estate. In April 1796 MacCullum was permitted by Sir John Shore to reside at Goalpara for purposes of trade as well as for the recovery of all debts and balances due to Raush's estate. The Governor-General wrote a letter to the Assam Raja asking him to assist MacCullum to realise the debts. The Raja assured the Governor-General that the accounts would be duly examined and adjusted.[39] MacCullum accordingly despatched a man to Assam with all the accounts and vouchers, who during his residence of two years in that country failed to induce the persons concerned to enter into an examination of the accounts.[40]

Mrs. Martha Raush who had been in England for the education of her two eldest daughters returned to India in May 1801 in the hope of recovering her husband's debts. In August 1801 she submitted a petition to Lord Wellesley to adopt measures "to obtain some remuneration from the [Company's] Government as Mr. Raush lost his life while living under its protection." After this Mrs. Raush met some Assamese Vakils who assured her of a reasonable satisfaction of her demands by the Assam government. In October 1802 Mrs. Raush applied to Lord Wellesley to recommend the case to the Assam Raja, agreeing to accept a reasonable compromise of her claims without exacting the whole. It was at

39. Shore to Assam Raja Ap. 29, Beng. Pol. Cons., June 10, 1796, No. 43; Barlow to Assam Raja, Sept. 27, Cons., Oct. 2, 1806, No. 18.

40. Wellesley to Assam Raja, Nov. 20, 1802, Beng. Pol. Cons., May 2, 1805, No. 97.

this time that Lord Wellesley received the Assam Raja's application for arms submitted by Baloram Khangia Phukan.[41]

Kamal Lochan Nandi, the person entrusted with the delivery of the arms to the Assam Raja and the accounts and documents to establish the claims of Raush's estate, arrived at Jorhat in the middle of 1803, and he stayed there till October 1804. No final adjustment could be effected as the debtors offered various excuses, though the Raja admitted some of the claims to be just on the basis of the documents produced by Kamal Lochan and examined by Purnananda Buragohain. The Raja ordered the payment of 10,032 rupees to Kamal Lochan in settlement of the pecuniary loan made by Raush for the payment of the troops procured from Dacca. The Raja pointed out the discrepancies between the accounts submitted by Raush in 1792-93, MacCullum in 1796 and by Kamal Lochan in 1803-4. "I therefore cannot accept the present account", wrote the Assam Raja to Lord Wellesley, "your letter also contains no detailed statement of these claims. For these reasons I am rather perplexed."[42]

Kamal Lochan left Jorhat towards the end of 1804. On January 16, 1805, two days after his arrival at the Assam Choky the post was attacked by a party of 150 armed men led by Mirza Ghulam Ali Beg, a cashiered servant of the Assam government. They killed two persons and carried away considerable property consisting of the balances realised by Kamal Lochan on behalf of Raush's estate, and the papers in his possession as well as the presents sent by the Assam Raja to the Governor-General. Ghulam Ali Beg retired to the Bhutan and Bijni frontier where he was said to have acquired a kind of sovereignty over 16 villages on the eastern bank of the Manas river. The sum of rupees 1,600 was recovered from twelve of his followers who were apprehended three months later. Pratapballabh Barphukan reported the details to Marquis Wellesley and so did Kamalnarayan Duaria Barua in his *arzi* to the Magistrate of Rungpore.[43]

41. Mrs. Raush to Wellesley, Aug. 4, 1801; Ap. 16, 1802; Oct. 7, 1802; in Beng. Pol. Cons., May 2, 1805, Nos. 94-96.

42. Assam Raja to Governor-General, Nov. 3, 1805, Beng. Sec. and Pol. Cons., July 17, 1806, No. 110; Barlow to Assam Raja, Sept. 27, Beng. Pol. Cons., Oct. 2, No. 18.

43. J. Wordsworth, Magt. of Rungpore to Govt., Feb. 7, Beng. Jud. Cons., Feb. 28, 1805, Nos. 10-11; same to same, Dec. 6, 1805, Beng. Jud. Cons., Jan. 16, 1806, No. 21.

In 1805 the two Darrang Rajas Krishnanarayan and Hoy-narayan were called to Jorhat to answer for charges of neglect of duty. Krishnanarayan had been sent against the Kacharis; but instead of fighting he leagued with Bijoy Barmura Gohain and returned to Darrang. Another charge raised against him was the murder of Raush. The two princes were deposed on September 17, 1805, and Samudranarayan placed on the *musnud of* Darrang.[44]

The letter of the Assam Raja sent with Kamal Lochan was received at Fort William in January 1806. In September Sir George Barlow wrote to the Raja reminding him of the assistance he had received from the Company and Raush's services to the Assam government. The Governor-General communicated the executors' willingness to accept 50,000 rupees as a compromise on account of the balances due to Raush's estate and of the plunder of his property. The Assam Raja pleaded his inability to liquidate the demands owing to Kamal Lochan's failure to produce satisfactory accounts and vouchers, the protests made by the alleged debtors and the distracted state of the country. "The principal Raja of Darang is dead," wrote the Swargadeo, "many of the others also are dead, and those who are still living are poor and helpless. I now hope that the country will not in future be exposed to distress and desolation on account of the money claimed as due to the estate of Mr. Raush." The Assam Raja informed Sir George Barlow of Mrs. Raush's willingness to grant a discharge on the receipt of only 20,000 rupees. The Government at Calcutta did not take further action till it received reminders from the Court of Directors.[45]

Mrs. Raush returned to England in 1809 when she addressed a petition to the Court of Directors on the subject of the claims. The Directors in their letter to Bengal, dated April 21, 1809, asked the Governor-General to write again to the Assam Raja. The Court proposed to authorise the Governor-General to adopt vigorous language in the demand for the payment of the dues by inserting the following instruction,—"Your application to the Raja will of course be enforced by such arguments and persuasion as you may think will induce him to take effectual measures for

44. *Tungkhungia Buranji*, p. 178; Assam Govt. Records, letter from Major Hamilton Vetch, Magt. of Darrang, Ap. 30, 1838. The two Darrang Rajas died shortly after their deposal.

45. Assam Raja to Gov.-Gen., recd. May 26, Beng. Pol. Cons., July 9, 1807, No. 40.

securing a compliance with the demand." The paragraph was however expunged by the Board of Control.[46]

In the meantime Raush's eldest daughter Charlotte Mary had been married to Henry Droz, Chief of the Cossimbazar Factory. In January 1813 Droz as a relative and as agent for Mrs. Raush asked the Governor-General to request the Directors to grant a compensation to his mother-in-law. In February 1813 Lord Minto addressed a letter to the Assam Raja referring to the obligations on the Raja's part to compel his officers and servants to satisfy the claimants at least to the extent of 50,000. The peons who carried Lord Minto's letter to Assam had to wait at Jorhat for about nine months. This delay gave rise to reports of their confinement at the Assam capital. Lord Hastings, who had assumed charge in October 1813, was unwilling to believe "that the Rajah of Assam can have been guilty of so gross an insult towards the British Government as that of placing its messengers in confinement." The Assam Raja's reply arrived at Fort William on February 3, 1814, where he referred to the death or flight of many of the debtors and the extreme poverty of the rest. "Your Lordship demands 50,000 rupees," said the Assam Raja, "but they [debtors] are not able to pay even 25 rupees."[47]

The Governor-General now abandoned all hope of success of any further application to the Assam Raja. "The circumstances of the case," Henry Droz was informed by the Government on April 9, 1814, "are not of a nature to warrant the interference of Government in any other form than that of employing the language of representation and remonstrance which experience has proved to be utterly unavailing. A regard for the honour and dignity of Government will not permit the Governor-General in Council to comply with any further solicitation to address the Rajah again on this subject."[48]

The Court of Directors, however, granted Mrs. Raush an annuity of £100 from March 1, 1816, which she enjoyed till her death in 1830, when it was claimed by her widowed daughter, Mrs. Droz who afterwards married Colonel Marmaduke Browne.[49]

46. Beng. Letter to Court, Ap. 21, 1809.

47. Assam Raja to Gov.-Gen., recd. Feb. 3, Beng. Pol. Cons., Ap. 29, 1814, No. 51.

48. Persian Secretary to H. Droz, Ap. 9, Beng. Pol. Cons., Ap. 29, 1814, No. 52.

49. Board's Collection, No. 317 of 1832, 51540-1149.

Prince Brajanath's bid for the Assam throne: On the failure of the Governor-General's representations to the Assam Raja for the payment of Raush's debts, Prince Brajanath Gohain, a claimant to the Assam throne, came forward to discharge the whole of the above debts, if the British Government would vouchsafe its aid, dethrone Chandrakanta Singha and place him in possession of Assam.[50]

Brajanath was the son of Bijoy Barmura Gohain, and grandson of Ratneswar Tipamia Gohain, and great-grandson of King Rajeswar Singha [1751-69]. Barmura Gohain had been implicated in the conspiracies of 1775 for which he was punished with the removal of an eye, and his second ear, the first having been cut on a previous occasion. The punishment was extended to his son Brajanath, then only five or six years old, who had an ear slit.

On the death of Gaurinath Singha in 1795 Barmura Gohain, whose claims to succession, but for his mutilation, were superior to those of Kamaleswar, had attempted to seize the throne. But being repulsed by Purnananda Buragohain Barmura fled with his family to Cachar and then to Manipur. From the latter place he made overtures to the Burmese Government by offering his daughter to King Bodawpaya. An army was equipped at Amarapura for being despatched to Assam, but the expedition was abandoned on the representation of Captain Cox that Assam was tributary to the Company. Barmura then organised a confederacy of the Moamarias, the fugitives from Assam, and the Kacharis and instigated them to wage war against the Ahom government. He was joined by Krishnanarayan Darrang Raja who had been sent against him by the Swargadeo. On the defeat of the confederate forces by Purnananda, Barmura continued to live at Khaspur, the capital of Cachar. The Assam Raja made several applications to the Cachar Raja for Barmura's extradition but without any success.[51]

Brajanath took shelter in Bengal where he tried to obtain assistance from the Company and other parties to invade Assam and re-establish his claims. Brajanath's son Durganath was adopted by the two widows of Gaurinath Singha who had been living in retirement at Chilmari with a pension of rupees 100 from the British Government. On the death of the younger Rani in 1799 the Governor-General fixed the surviving widow Kamaleswari

50. J. Digby, Collector of Rungpore to Govt., Jan. 1. Beng. Pol. Cons., Feb. 4, 1814, No. 72.

51. *Tungkhungia Buranji*, p. 175.

Devi's pension at rupees 80 per month to enable her to maintain Durganath.[52]

In April 1806, Kamaleswari proceeded to Calcutta with Brajanath and applied to Government for assistance to expel Purnananda Buragohain and place Brajanath in the Raj, promising to pay a tribute equal to one-fourth of the total revenue of Assam. Kamaleswari alluded to the conduct of Purnananda who, on the death of Gaurinath Singha, "instead of placing Brijnaut Sing Gohain Deuta [Brajanath], the grandson of my husband's own brother, on the Rauj of his inheritance, treacherously elevated another person [Kamaleswar] and himself assumed the uncontrolled direction of public affairs and is still in power." She further alleged that her husband Gaurinath Singha had nominated Brajanath his successor, and that she had taken up his cause being sensible of the justice of his claims. To Kamaleswari's petition the Government replied by expressing its inability to afford any means of assistance as it possessed no authority over the kingdom of Assam to decide the justice or injustice of any person's claim to the Raj.[53]

On July 7, 1806, Rani Kamaleswari submitted another application where she declared,—"It is now my wish to raise a body of troops and regain possession of my country by force of arms." She asked the Governor-General to direct the officers stationed at Rungpore and Goalpara not to oppose or molest her passage through those districts. Anticipating Government's refusal to her request Kamaleswari submitted another petition on July 28 to authorise Brajanath to levy a body of troops or grant him an allowance for the maintenance of himself and his dependants. She expressed her inability to provide for Brajanath as the allowance she received from the British Government was not sufficient for her own support. She then requested for monetary help to return to Chilmari reminding the Government of Sir John Shore's grant of rupees 500 for the same purpose ten years ago.[54]

Nothing came out of Kamaleswari's efforts to place Brajanath on the throne of Assam. In 1809 he was in Calcutta soliciting assistance from the Company.[55] On Kamaleswari's death in 1812

52. Kamaleswari Devi to Wellesley, recd. Feb. 10, Beng. Pol. Cons., June 26, 1800, No. 155.

53. Kamaleswari Devi to Governor-General, recd. May 20, Beng. Sec. and Pol. Cons., July 17, 1806, No. 111.

54. Kamaleswari to Gov.-Gen. recd. July 7 and 28, Beng. Pol. Cons., Aug. 14, 1806, No. 19.

55. Martin's *Eastern India*, Vol. III, p. 606.

a continuation of the pension of 50 rupees was authorised to her adopted son Durganath. Brajanath had no means of subsistence except the precarious bounty of persons who pitied his distress; he is said to have been assisted among others by the Rajas of Burdwan and Cooch Behar.[56]

Failing in his attempt to obtain the aid of the British Government Brajanath turned his attention to other quarters. He met Raja Rung Bahadur, king of Nepal, at Benares, who promised to help him to carry out his designs. Brajanath accompanied Rung Bahadur to Nepal where he entered into a stipulation to pay an annual tribute of 3 lakhs of rupees on condition that the Nepal Raja would place him on the throne of Assam. Rung Bahadur procured the orders of the Emperor of China directing the Bhutias to permit the Nepal army to proceed through their country to Assam. But the death of Rung Bahadur and the outbreak of hostilities between the Nepalese and the British in 1814 put an end to the scheme of Brajanath.[57]

Early in January 1814, Brajanath was again in Bengal. He informed J. Digby, Collector of Rungpore, of his intention to pay up the whole of Raush's Assam debts if the British Government placed him in possession of the throne. Digby was almost inclined to support Brajanath's proposal and he informed the Government that the "usurper's" force amounted to 14 companies consisting each of about 50 undisciplined and ill-armed sepoys.[58]

In the meantime Brajanath obtained the help of Raja Harendranarayan of Cooch Behar who had married the sister of that Ahom prince. Brajanath was also assisted by Robert Bruce, a native of India, who owned a factory at Jugighopa.[59] Some of the officers and favourites of the Raja were employed in raising men for Brajanath in Cooch Behar, Rungpore and Mymensing; and Bruce despatched some of his Burkendazes to Murshidabad for the same purpose. On March 12, 1814, Brajanath applied to David Scott, Magistrate of Rungpore, for a passport to enter Assam with an

56. *An Account of the Burman Empire and Assam,* 1839, p. 116.

57. E. G. Glazier, *Further Notes on Rungpore Records,* 1876, p. 29. G. does not give the name of the Ahom prince: but considering the circumstances he could be no other than Brajanath, the only claimant who made such persistent efforts from outside Assam.

58. Digby to John Monckton, Persian Secy., Jan. 1, Beng. Pol. Cons., Feb. 4, 1814, No. 72.

59. R. Bruce in a letter to David Scott stated that he was a native of India. He appeared before Scott on Ap. 25, Beng. Pol. Cons., Ap. 29, 1814, Nos. 24, 59.

armed force of about 150 or 200 men. To this Brajanath received a reply in the negative on April 1.[60]

Norman Macleod, who had been appointed Commissioner of Cooch Behar in 1813 with enlarged powers in view of the imbecility of the Raja and the corruptions of his officials, had received reports of Harendranarayan's secret manouvres to promote the designs of his brother-in-law Brajanath. Macleod had also received reports circulated by Brajanath's adherents that their cause was countenanced by the British Government. Macleod was aware of the "deception formerly practised by British subjects [Krishnanarayan's Burkendazes etc.] unduly taking a part in the intestine commotions of Assam and which occasioned to Government the utmost vexation and very considerable expense." In his report Macleod described Harendranarayan's support of Brajanath as a violation of his agreement with the British Government according to which the Raja was precluded from forming political connection with any foreign power or chief.

Among other objections to the Raja's supporting Brajanath, Macleod pointed out,—"The most important of these is, that the present ruler of Assam [Chandrakanta Singha], whatever be the merits of the title by which he is now seated on the throne of the country, is recognised by the English Government as the Surge Deo Raja of the Assam State; and in that character, is connected with the Honourable Company by relation of amity and friendship. The giving any aid or countenance therefore to an enterprise, such as that of Bryjnauth Coonwur, of which the declared and immediate object is the forcible deposition of the said Rajah from his sovereignty, is little short of partial hostility against the British Government which is politically a friend of that prince." Macleod foresaw that Harendranarayan by espousing the cause of Brajanath might bring down the vengeance of the Assam government which might despatch a force through Bhutan to invade Cooch Behar which the British were bound by treaty to protect. The Government directed the Commissioner to warn Raja Harendranarayan against aiding and abetting the designs of Brajanath. The Magistrate of Rungpore was asked to place under restraint the persons of Brajanath and his principal adherents.[61]

In the third week of April Brajanath voluntarily made his appearance before David Scott when he was taken into custody.

60. Scott to J. Adam, Secy., Ap. 18, Beng. Pol. Cons., Ap. 29, 1814, No. 23.

61. Macleod to Adam, March 19, Adam to Macleod and Scott, Ap. 1, Beng. Pol. Cons., Ap. 1, 1814, Nos. 50-52.

His followers dispersed upon receiving orders to that effect. Three of Brajanath's principal adherents were arrested, and bail was taken from Bruce for his appearance on April 25. Bruce admitted having given to Brajanath a few Sarkars and other people and also some money in support of himself and his followers as it was the practice of merchants to relieve the wants of emigrants of rank who might be recalled to power in their country. Bruce was let off with a warning as well as Brajanath whose subsequent conduct had been found to be satisfactory.[62]

Brajanath continued to live at Chilmari. A pension was afterwards granted to him by the British Government which he enjoyed till circumstances induced him to quit the Company's territories.

Conspiracy against Purnananda Buragohain: The allegation made by Rani Kamaleswari Devi that Purnananda "had himself assumed the uncontrolled direction of public affairs" indicated the attitude of interested people towards that minister. The strong hand with which the Buragohain had suppressed the disorders, and the inability of the monarch, by virtue of his age, to take part in the affairs of the state, had led to reports of Purnananda's assumption of absolute powers, which were exaggerated by his enemies and rivals who were prevented by his vigilance from continuing their practices of doubftul loyalty. On his appointment as prime minister in 1784 he inherited the effects of the previous troubles one of which was the absence of a properly qualified person to sit on the throne. Gaurinath Singha's death in 1795 without leaving a son made matters difficult for Purnananda and his colleagues. The selection fell upon Kamaleswar Singha, who though a child, was at least untarnished by a disqualifying scar.

Having assumed the inevitability of Kamaleswar's succession, it follows that some one had to act for him and supervise and conduct the responsible duties of administration. The Buragohain was the officer who by custom was vested with supreme executive authority under such circumstances. All important letters were written and grants made in the name of the monarch; and the premier never made any attempt to eclipse the king or obscure his name. On the restoration of peace the Buragohain took the king round to the principal localities in the districts near the capital to give confidence to the inhabitants and recreate their respect for Ahom monarchy which had been greatly impaired by Gaurinath's imbecility and cruelty. In a country where the nobles had dis-

62. Adam to Scott, May 13, Beng. Pol. Cons., May 13, 1814, No. 60.

played their incapacity for concerted action, where revenge provided a stronger incentive for combination than the well-being of the state, it was only natural that Purnananda's actions should be misjudged and his character depicted in the darkest colours. It is worthy of note that whereas Badanchandra brought an army from outside to punish Purnananda, his paternal uncle Srinath Duara Barbarua described the prime minister as a great patriot. "Day and night", wrote Srinath, "he thought of the best means of restoring peace and order in the country and prayed to God for the same. During that period of affliction and misery the Mahamantri Buragohain Dangaria [Purnananda] protected the people like a mother-bird guarding her nestlings under her wings."[63]

If Purnananda had to adopt drastic measures now and then they were warranted by the exigency of the situation. Captain Welsh had realised the futility of the language of persuasion and moderation in his dealings with Gaurinath and his "unscrupulous ministers." The Raja had to be placed in virtual restraint, and his advisers dismissed and deported to Bengal. Welsh's measures were characterised by Lord Cornwallis as strong, but were justified on the ground that they were necessary. The banished ministers levelled a number of accusations against Captain Welsh. No harm could be done to him as the complaints were examined by the Government in the light of the motives which had inspired them and the character of the persons who had made them. In the case of Purnananda there was no impartial tribunal or authority to judge his conduct and afford him protection from the machinations of his enemies.

The opposition to Purnananda Buragohain came to a head when Chandrakanta's favourites launched a conspiracy to seize and murder him and invest the boy-king with full executive authority. In 1802 a similar conspiracy organised by one Panimua, a member of the fraternity of night-worshippers, and directed towards the annihilation of the king and his premier had been promptly detected and suppressed.[64]

The leader of the conspirasy of 1814 was one Satram, the son of a royal poultry-keeper named Bhut. The Buragohain had selected him for his handsome and intelligent looks to be the companion of Chandrakanta. Satram worked his way into the heart of the king and an inseparable friendship grew up between the

63. *Tungkhungia Buranji*, pp. 119-120.
64. *Tungkhungia Buranji*, pp. 169, 199.

two. They used to sleep and eat together; and the king used to have Satram seated by his side in the audience chamber, and the obeisance paid to the monarch was shared in by his plebeian friend, a practice which greatly exasperated the ministers and courtiers. Through the influence of Chandrakanta Satram was appointed Charingia Phukan, or the officer who administered the affairs of the Charing Raja. The garments which the nobles presented to the monarch were freely worn in public by Satram. In trying to check these indulgences on the part of the monarch the Buragohain incurred the animosity of Satram who began to poison the ears of his royal friend against the premier.

On account of the depletion of the royal treasury owing to the long-continued disturbances the Buragohain had to exercise strict control over the state finance. He had withheld the coronation ceremony of Kamaleswar and Chandrakanta and thereby saved four lakhs of rupees in each case. No ruler was considered a full-fledged sovereign unless he was crowned; no coins could be struck in his name; and his name would not be included in the list of those to whom offerings were made in the rituals of the Ahom priests. Satram interpreted this economic measure of the prime minister as a denial of sovereignty to Chandrakanta. The boy-king, while permitted to live in comfort and affluence, was not allowed to draw money freely from the state treasury, a circumstance which was used by Satram in widening the breach between the king and his premier. At the age of eighteen, Chandrakanta, against the advice of Purnananda Buragohain, had married his maid Padmavati, coming from a family very much inferior in rank to those from which royal consorts were by custom selected. Chandrakanta is said to have had an umbrage against the Buragohain for not showing Padmavati the honour due to a queen.

Chandrakanta had for a long time withheld his consent to Satram's proposal to form a plot for the undoing of the Buragohain. Dighala Gohain had died in 1799, and the widowed queen-mother Numali Rajmao warned her son against countenancing Satram's designs directed towards the destruction of Purnananda through whose influence he and his brother had been elevated to the throne. Chandrakanta had himself seen the futility of a plot against the Buragohain who had the support of the army and which was commanded by his relative Captain Chandrā Gohain. But Chandrakanta could not long resist the machinations of Satram and ultimately gave tacit consent to the latter's proposal.

Satram gradually widened the circle of his supporters, and the two principal ones were Jagadhar Charingia Barua and Gurudatta Chaliha. The three succeeded in enlisting the sympathy of Badanchandra, who had been reappointed Barphukan at Gauhati on the death of Pratapballabh Barphukan.[65] Badanchandra was made to believe that Purnananda was his arch-enemy and that he was engaged in discovering means to destroy the Barphukan. The conspirators procured the despatch of a letter from the Barphukan's daughter Pijou Gabharu who had been married to a son of Purnananda. Several officers of the court secretly supported the conspiracy of Satram.

The Buragohain was informed of the plot by Juhan Sing, brother of Balavanta Sing. These two Rajputs of Bhojpur had been stationed within the enclosures of the palace to act as body-guards to the king. Juhan Sing submitted to Purnananda the names of 97 persons concerned in the conspiracy. Seizing an opportune moment when most of the conspirators were closeted with the monarch or near about the precints of the palace, the Buragohain assembled the eighteen companies of sepoys under his command, who together with a number of Bairagis and Sannyasis surrounded the palace. Purnananda then repaired to the *Barchora*, or council chamber, attended by a body of armed men consisting mainly of his relatives, and convened a council of state to which he summoned the Bargohain, Barpatra Gohain and Barbarua, and others. On the arrival of the nobles Purnananda Buragohain unfolded to them the purpose of the meeting, stating his mortification to see such a design meditated against him, after he had, for so long a time, been assiduously striving to promote the welfare of the country. The officers pleaded complete ignorance of the plot of which they had now heard for the first time.

The Buragohain then sent his two sons Biswanath and Jagannath and his cousin Captain Chandrā Gohain, with two representatives of the opposite party, to explain the matter to the king and learn his sentiments upon it. Chandrakanta pleaded entire ignorance of the conspiracy and this was proclaimed by order of the Buragohain to the assembly at the Barchora. The prime minister then turned to the audience and asked their opinion regarding the measures to be adopted against the conspirators who had plotted his destruction. All present dreading that an answer

65. Pratapballabh Barphukan died at Gauhati on Nov. 20, 1810, see S. K. Bhuyan, *Deodhai Assam Buranji*, 1932, p. 159.

unfavourable to the Buragohain's wishes would only bring down his resentment upon themselves, and knowing that he had the military at hand to enforce his pleasure declared with one accord that the conspirators deserved to be brought to condign punishment.

The Buragohain sent his sons with a guard to arrest the conspirators, a good number being in the vicinity of the court which had already been invested with guards. Satram who had taken shelter in the palace was, after long protests by the king, made over to the Buragohain's emissaries with a request from the monarch that his life should be spared. Of the 97 offenders 77 were put to death; and the remaining 20 were on account of their youth let off with dismissal and mutilation. Satram was banished to the hills where he was killed by some Nagas. The trial and execution of the conspirators which lasted for nearly a year created a sensation throughout Assam. This event is known in Assam as "Satram Bhutar Putekar Khabar", or the news of Satram, son of Bhut.[66]

Badanchandra's flight from Gauhati: It was revealed during the course of the trial that the conspirators had received encouragement from Badanchandra. This offence, added to the accusations of oppressive behaviour and gross exactions, led the Buragohain to decide upon Badanchandra's apprehension and punishment. A Brahman official, named Maheswar Parvatia Phukan, was sent with an escort to Gauhati, to arrest Badanchandra and bring him up to Jorhat for trial. Maheswar arrived at Gauhati in the evening of October 18, 1815.[67] The Barphukan, not knowing the real object of Maheswar's mission, received him with the courtesy usually shown to deputies from the metropolis. The Parvatia Phukan retired to his camp for the night and made preparations to arrest the Barphukan at the viceregal residence early at dawn.

In the meantime an express courier despatched by Pijou Gabharu delivered a letter to Badanchandra in which she informed her father of the real object of Maheswar's deputation. Badanchandra collected whatever treasures he could, and fled from Gauhati at midnight in a swift boat. He was accompanied by his three sons Janmi, Piali and Numali, and two Hindustanis, Uday

66. Maniram Dewan's Ms. *Assam Buranji*; Scott's Historical Notes, Beng. Sec. and Pol. Cons., July, 14, 1826, No. 2; Gunabhiram Barua, *Assam Buranji*, pp .176-81.

67. This is the date given in Chandrakanta's letter to Scott, Beng. Pol. Cons., March 30, 1816, No. 49. Gunabhiram has 9 *Aswin*, 1737 *Saka*, or Sept. 24, 1815, *Assam Buranji*, p. 183.

Sing Subedar and his brother Krishnaram Havildar. Uday Sing had served in the Assam Raja's army but had been discharged for his faithless conduct; and Krishnaram had been accused of stealing some silver and gold ornaments belonging to the Assam Raja for which he had been detained in prison for some months by David Scott, Magistrate of Rungpore.[68]

After some escapades with his pursuers, Maheswar Phukan and Parasuram Duaria Barua, Badanchandra reached Rungpore and made his appearance before David Scott in the first week of November 1815.

Badanchandra in Bengal: Badanchandra told David Scott that he had been deputed by Swargadeo Chandrakanta Singha to implore the assistance of the British Government to reduce to obedience the prime minister Purnananda Buragohain "who keeps the Raja in confinement and continues to exercise in a most despotic manner the authority he acquired during the minority of his sovereign." On being asked by Scott to reduce to writing the proposal he had been authorised to make, Badanchandra submitted to the Magistrate two letters, both from Chandrakanta, one addressed to himself asking him to procure the aid of the Company, and the other addressed to the British Government with the same object. The second letter was signed "Chanderkant Sing Surge Deo, by the pen of Buddin Chunder Burra Phookin Dewarah." Both letters bore evidence of being written under the stress of emotion and excitement.[69]

In the first letter Chandrakanta referred to the occurrences at Jorhat. "The Buragohain," said the Raja, "has by degrees cut off all my people, and I now see no prospect of my own safety." Badanchandra was asked to reduce the powers of the Buragohain and re-establish the authority of the sovereign. If Badanchandra could not do it himself he was enjoined to procure the aid of the Magistrate of Rungpore and the Governor-General at Calcutta. Badanchandra was authorised to tell the British everything relative to Purnananda Buragohain and to explain "how he has poisoned my predecessor Gowree Nath and my father and brother,

68. Scott to Adam, Feb. 21, and enclosures, Beng. Pol. Cons., March 30, 1816, Nos. 48-A to 49.

69. First letter, Chandrakanta to Badanchandra, Sept. 12, 1815; second letter, Chandrakanta to Government, Nov. 12, 1815; Scott to Adam, Nov. 15, 1815, Beng. Pol. Cons., Dec. 8, 1815, Nos. 52, 53-A, and 53-B. The second letter was written by Badanchandra for Chandrakanta and hence bore the date of its submission to Scott.

and killed my servants, and placed his creatures around me night and day, and how he has taken into his own hands the Seals of the Raj." Chandrakanta asked Badanchandra to return with six or seven companies of sepoys with their officers and undertook to pay all the expense. "If the British," said Chandrakanta, "will not consent to this, offer them a tribute of a lac of rupees. If that will not do, offer one and a half. By whatever means the enemy may be destroyed adopt them and return." Considering the possibility of his being put to death by the Buragohain in the meantime, Chandrakanta made the following provision for his succession, "A Kowanr [prince] of our house resides down the river, bring him back and re-establish our authority in this country.'[70] Badanchandra was enjoined to observe strict secrecy in his mission.

The second letter contained a repetition of the charges against the Buragohain, and a confirmation of Chandrakanta's offer to pay a tribute to the Company retaining the internal management of the country in his own hands. He also promised to remove the iniquitous duties levied from Bengal merchants at the Assam Choky and to restore the rates introduced by Captain Welsh and H. A. Bruce in 1793-94.

On November 15, 1815, David Scott forwarded the letters of Chandrakanta without offering any comment. The matter was taken up by the Board in their meeting of December 8 where it was decided not to interfere in the internal affairs of Assam, the reasons advanced being the absence of any agreement binding the Company's Government to support the Assam Raja, and the unlikelihood of the domestic feuds of Assam affecting the tranquillity of the Company's provinces. The Magistrate was advised to manifest a suitable degree of attention to Badanchandra and to dismiss him with expressions of civility and assurances of friendship of the Government towards the state of Assam. Scott was further asked to collect from Badanchandra information regarding the Government of Assam, its resources, and its relations and intercourse with the neighbouring countries.[71]

Badanchandra left Rungpore in the beginning of December 1815 having obtained from the Magistrate a *dustak* or permit and a Burkendaz. He then proceeded towards Murshidabad counting upon the help of Jagat Seth the famous firm of bankers at that place. Badanchandra took up his abode at Meerpoor where, at

70. Perhaps by this Chandrakanta meant Brajanath's sons living at Chilmari. They were among the few unscarred princes.

71. Adam to Scott, Dec. 8, Beng. Pol. Cons., Dec. 8, 1815, No. 54.

the request of Krishnaram Havildar, the Daroga of Thanah Bhumineah stationed two Burkendazes to protect the fugitive's house. The emissaries of Purnananda Buragohain had been following the footsteps of Badanchandra. In the meantime a Sannyasi leader named Siddhi Gir Gosain, living in Zeeagun, received a letter from Purnananda Buragohain stating the circumstances of Badanchandra's flight, and alleging that he had absconded after having squandered large sums of money belonging to the Assam Raja and mismanaged the Raja's affairs. Siddhi Gir Gosain, acting as Badanchandra alleged "by order of the old Gohaeen", sent one night about 25 armed Burkendazes who apparelled like a gang of assassins broke into Badanchandra's house at Meerpoor, and plundered it of all the effects including jewels, valuables and necessaries.[72] Badanchandra, claiming the protection of the laws and customs of the British Government, demanded of the Burkendazes why they had entered his house at that time at night. Without giving any reply the Burkendazes asked Badanchandra to get up and accompany them to appear before the Judge at Calcapore, warning him that if he made any delay they would, agreeably to the Judge's order, put him to death. Badanchandra was greatly alarmed, and prepared to go with the Burkendazes who put him and his two[73] young children and Uday Sing into two palanquins. The Burkendazes forcibly took away the swords from Badanchandra and Uday Sing, and under pretence of their being required to appear before the Judge at Calcapore carried the four to Bhagavangolah, where they were detained in a house belonging to Siddhi Gir Gosain. Krishnaram acquainted the Daroga of Thanah Bhumineah of all the circumstances who despatched four Burkendazes and a Jemadar after Badanchandra. On the following day the Jamadar took Badanchandra, his two sons and Uday Sing, from the hands of Siddhi Gir Gosain's Burkendazes, and sent them back to Meerpoor. The Daroga acting in collusion with the Gosain made no report to the Magistrate of Murshidabad. On the other hand two Burkendazes of the Bhumineah Thanah and two in the service of the Gosain were set over Badanchandra and his attendants.

From Meerpoor Badanchandra proceeded to Calcutta where on February 16, 1816, he submitted a petition to Government com-

72. This happened sometime between December 12 and 17, 1815.

73. Badanchandra's third son Numali who had accompanied his father in the flight from Gauhati perhaps died before the party reached Meerpoor.

plaining against the conduct of Siddhi Gir Gosain. The Magistrate of Murshidabad had in the meantime received letters from Chandrakanta Singha and Purnananda Buragohain alleging defalcation of public funds by Badanchandra and desertion of his charge. "All this is false," said Badanchandra in his petition of February 16,—"for if I had clandestinely absconded from Gooahuttee after squandering the money entrusted to me, is it conceivable that the Raja should have charged me with a letter under his own seal? Moreover, if I had abused my trust and absconded from Gooahuttee in the manner alleged, why should I have repaired to the Capital [Calcutta] of the country? Is it not likely, that I should in that case rather have concealed myself in some obscure situation?"[74]

W. Loch, the Magistrate of Murshidabad, having learnt that Badanchandra had left for Calcutta sent a Roobekary to the Magistrates of the Suburbs of Calcutta, of the City of Calcutta, and of the 24 Perganas, to ascertain and watch the movements of the fugitive.[75]

The Magistrate of Rungpore had also received two letters from Chandrakanta, both dated November 21, 1815, and one from Parasuram Duaria Barua, dated December, 6, with requests to induce the Barphukan to return to Assam with the money combined with assurances of pardon for any offence he might have committed.[76]

Badanchandra's case was taken up by the Board on March 30, 1816, when he was at Calcutta. Government's decision not to interfere in the domestic feuds of Assam arrived at in the meeting of December 8, 1815, had been meanwhile communicated to Badanchandra. The charges preferred by the Assam Raja against Badanchandra were considered to be too vague to induce the Government to authorise the seizure of the Barphukan. The whole transaction appeared to the Governor-General in Council to be an affair of intrigue between two opposite parties in the government of Assam, in which the Company had no concern. Badanchandra was informed that he need not be under any apprehension regarding his personal safety. He was advised to prefer a complaint in

74. Badanchandra to John Monckton, Persian Secy. to Govt., recd., Feb. 16, Beng. Pol. Cons., March 20, 1816, No. 50.

75. Loch to Monckton, Jan. 16. Beng. Pol. Cons., March 20, 1816, No. 51.

76. Assam Raja to Scott, Nov. 21, 1815, two letters; Parasuram Deva Sarma to Scott, Dec. 6, 1815; Beng. Pol. Cons., March 30, 1816, No. 49.

the regular way to the Magistrate of Murshidabad against the party who had seized and confined him at Meerpoor.[77]

Having failed to obtain the assistance of the British Government in his project to reduce the power of Purnananda Buragohain Badanchandra turned to other quarters for the same.

David Scott: David Scott who conducted Government's relations with Assam at this period in his capacity as Magistrate of Rungpore, was an officer of extraordinary ability of whom it has been said: "Had the scene of his life's labours been in the North-West or Central India, where the great problem of Empire was then being worked out, instead of amid the obscure jungles of Assam, he would occupy a place in history by the side of Malcolm, Elphinstone and Metcalfe."[78]. He witnessed the beginnings of the convulsions in Assam which led to the establishment of the Burmese as its supreme rulers. Their expulsion was practically the result of his far-sighted policy. After the occupation of Assam by the British he, almost single-handed, tried to confer upon the people the benefit of peace and security of which they had been deprived for nearly half a century. From 1814 when he first held charge of the Bengal district of Rungpore till his death at Cherapoonji in 1831 the destiny of the Assamese people was in a great measure influenced by the opinions and decisions of David Scott.

Born near Montrose in Scotland in 1786 David Scott was appointed a Writer in the Bengal establishment of the season 1800.[79] After three years of training in the College of Fort William where he attained proficiency in Persian and Hindi, Scott was appointed Assistant to the Collector of Goruckpore, and then acted as Judge and Magistrate to Purnea. In the latter capacity he succeeded in suppressing the gang robberies prevailing in the Morung border of the district. In 1812 he served as Collector of Midnapore and then of Tipperah. In December 1813 he was appointed Judge and Magistrate of Rungpore which was then exposed to the outrages of the tribes living on the frontier, in many cases provoked by the illegal exactions of the local Zemindars.

These disturbances and the relations with the independent chiefs in the territories bordering on Rungpore having required

77. Adam to Scott and to Loch, March 30, Beng. Pol. Cons., March 30, 1816, Nos. 52-53.

78. Mackenzie, *North-East Frontier of Bengal,* p. 5-n.

79. D. Scott was the second son of Archibald Scott of Usan and Dunninald, the family seats, near Montrose,—*Memoir of the late David Scott, Esq.,* 1832, Preface, p. ix.

special attention Scott was appointed in September 1816 Commissioner in Cooch Behar and Joint Magistrate of Rungpore. As Commissioner he became the channel for conducting, on the part of the British Government, all business of a political nature with Bhutan, Assam and other independent states and chieftains on the northern and eastern frontier of Rungpore. In his capacity of Joint Magistrate of Rungpore he was directed to take under his special charge the Thanas of Dhubri, Nageswari, Goalpara and Karaibari with a view to guard against the commission of further outrages by the Garo mountaineers. The appointment of a special officer to govern the above tract which belonged to the district of Rungpore marked the formation of a new unit of administration which was for some time known as North-Eastern Parts of Rungpore, and afterwards as Goalpara which name has continued till now. Scott with tact and conciliation, accompanied by the use of force when necessary, succeeded in inducing the Garos to abstain from the excesses they had been committing in the Company's territory. As a result, the corps raised for service on the Garo frontier was considerably reduced; and Government informed the Directors of "the uninterrupted repose and freedom from outrage which those tracts of country [frontier perganahs of Rungpore and Mymensing] have, with one or two exceptions, enjoyed."[80]

Scott pointed out the necessity of introducing in the district under his charge a modified judicial procedure excluding the Regulations of the Bengal law courts and enabling him to settle all disputed points in conformity to general rules and instructions to be furnished for his guidance by Government and fashioned with reference to the peculiar customs and prejudices of the people. Scott's proposal was accepted by Government, and the three Thanas of Goalpara, Dhubri and Karaibari were separated from Rungpore and placed in charge of an officer denominated Civil Commissioner of the North-Eastern Parts of Rungpore. In December 1821 the General Regulations were declared not to extend to that tract. Special instructions were prepared for its administration and were embodied in Regulation X of 1822.[81] On January 1, 1822, Scott had been appointed to the new office with which he combined the Commissionership of Cooch Behar. In the new situation Scott received a salary of 40,000 rupees per year including all travelling and other personal charges.

80. Bengal Letter to Court, Feb. 8, 1822.

81. This Regulation is reproduced in Mackenzie's *North-East Frontier* pp. 250-54; see also Criminal Judicial Cons., Dec. 28, 1821, No. 100.

In the same year Assam was conquered by the Burmese, and their aggressive spirit as manifested in their outrages committed in British districts, was viewed as a source of insecurity to the frontier of Bengal. Government had foreseen that a rupture with the Burmese was inevitable, and it was therefore thought necessary that the conduct of the political relations and negotiations should be committed to "an officer of approved talents, judgment and experience." On November 14, 1823, David Scott was appointed, in addition to his existing charge, Agent to the Governor-General on the North-Eastern Frontier on a consolidated pay of rupees 52,000 per year. His duties as Agent were thus defined in the Governor-General's minute to the Board: "He should exercise a general control and superintendence over our political relations and intercourse with the petty states in that quarter, including Sikkhim, Bootan, Tibet, Cooch Behar, Bijnee, Assam, Cachar, Manipur and Jyntia, and other independent states."[82] This office with the same designation continued till 1874 when Assam was separated from Bengal and constituted into a Chief Commissionership.

82. See sketch of Scott's career prepared in March 1831 by Thomas Fisher, Searcher of the E. I. C's Records, series *Personal Records*, India Office, Vol. XIX, pp. 27-61; and Captain Adam White's *Memoir of the late David Scott*, pub. in 1832; and *East India Company's Bengal Civil Servants*, by H. T. Prinsep and R. C. Doss, 1844, p. 332.

Part II

The Burmese Invasions of Assam

Badanchandra in Burma: While in Calcutta Badanchandra became acquainted with the agents of the Burmese government whom he accompanied on their return to Amarapura, the capital of Burma. Badanchandra appeared before the Burmese monarch Bodawpaya and asked for military aid to establish King Chandrakanta in authority which, he alleged, had been usurped by the premier Purnananda Buragohain.[1] The response made by Bodawpaya to Badanchandra's request for help can be imagined from the character of that monarch and the spirit of aggrandisement which had animated the Burmese government during the six preceding decades.

In the year 1752 a great leader appeared in Burma in the person of Alaungpaya. In 1754 he liberated the Burmese from the yoke of the Talaings and three years afterwards completely subdued Pegu. In the contest between the two kingdom the French and the English had given their support to whoever appeared at the moment to be the stronger party, as on the favour of the final victor they mainly depended for their commercial success. Their duplicity and fluctuating conduct so exasperated Alaungpaya that he resolved to put to death the principal Europeans on both sides.[2] In 1756 he killed the French agent at Syriam as well as the captain and officers of the French ship which had arrived from Pondicherry with military stores for the Talaing rebels. Three years later, on a similar suspicion of selling arms to the Talaings the whole of the Company's servants including eight Englishmen and about a hundred Indians were massacred at Negrais.[3] "The impression of ill faith," wrote a British officer, "on the part of the

1. The exact nature of Badanchandra's application to the Burmese king is known from the following passage in Mingimaha Tilwa's letter to David Scott,—"Under the Golden Soles of his Royal Feet came the chief of Gwahatty and represented that Chandaganda, the lawful sovereign of that place, had by force been divested of his royal power by Pooya Coonhay [Buragohain] with indignity,"—Scott to Swinton, Nov. 28, 1821, Beng. Pol. Cons., Jan. 11, 1822, Nos. 22-23.

2. Sir Arthur P. Phayre, *History of Burma*, 1883, p. 159-60, and Capt. W. White, *Political History of the Extraordinary Events which led to the Burmese War*, 1827, pp. 2-3.

3. G. E. Harvey, *History of Burma*, 1925, p. 240.

European factories long survived the reign of Alam-praw, and took deep root in the mind of the Burmese."[4] They considered all white people as belonging to one class, and could not make any distinction between the English, the French, the Dutch and the Portuguese.[5]

Alaungpaya died in 1760 while returning from an unsuccessful expedition in Siam. The spirit of conquest which dominated Alaungpaya was inherited by his successors on the throne of Ava. His son Naungdawgyi (1760-63) refused reparation for the murder of the British subjects at Negrais. Naungdawgyi's brother Hsinbyushin (1763-76) conducted a fresh war against Siam and captured its capital Ayuthia. The Raja of Manipur planned an invasion of Burma to recover his lost possessions, and applied to the English who, angry at the Negrais massacre, gave a promise of help.[6] In January 1763 six companies of sepoys were sent from Chittagong under Henry Verelst, but they had to be recalled as they suffered much from continuous rain and from disease.[7]

Some years later the Burmese army invaded Manipur whose ruler Raja Jai Singha fled to Assam and appealed for help to the reigning sovereign Swargadeo Rajeswar Singha to whom the Raja gave his daughter Kuranganayani in marriage. An army sent from Assam under the command of Harnath Phukan, father of Badanchandra, had to return owing to heavy causalties among the troops from starvation and disease. Some years later a second expedition was despatched from Assam which remained at Manipur until Jai Singha with his Naga levies expelled the usurper whom the Burmese had placed on the throne.

In 1767 the Burmese army occupied Ayuthia after a siege of fourteen months. Hsinbyushin then busied himself in a war with the Chinese, who decimated by malarious fever were easily overpowered by the Burmese, and before the close of the year 1769 peace was established by a convention signed at Bhamo.[8] In an expedition to Manipur the Burmese army advanced on Cachar

4. White, *Burmese War*, pp. 2-3. Capt. White was for some time at Chittagong, attached to the 2nd Battalion 15th Bengal Native Infantry, p. 11.

5. Harvey, *Burma*, pp. 258-9. A Persian named Agha Muhammad was considered by the Burmese as being related to the English for his fair skin and red beard, H. H. Wilson's *Documents Illustrative of the Burmese War*, 1827, p. 239.

6. Harvey, *Burma*, p. 297.

7. Gait, *History of Assam*, p. 271.

8. Harvey, *Burma*, pp. 251-8; John Nisbet, *Burma under British Rule and before*, 1901, Vol. I, p. 8.

and Jayantia and returned to Ava with a large number of prisoners. Hsinbyushin's subsequent expeditions to Siam and Manipur were not so successful. The Siamese leader Paya Tek reoccupied Ayuthia and founded the capital Bangkok. Hsinbyushin transferred his capital to Ava, though Rangoon with a fine sea-port would have been a much better place as it would have facilitated contacts with the outside world and modified the medieval Burmese government's ambition "to build pagodas, to collect daughters from tributary chiefs and to sally forth on slave raids, to make war for white elephants."[9] Hsinbyushin's son Singu Min (1776-82) was mainly preoccupied with wars in Manipur whose ruler Raja Jai Singha made repeated attempts from his base in Cachar to oust the Burmese nominee.

The spirit of conquest and aggrandisement was more predominant with Hsinbyushin's successor Bodawpaya (1782-1819), the seniormost surviving son of Alaungpaya. Bodawpaya commenced his reign by the massacre of a large number of people, including many monks, who were suspected of having favoured a plot to depose him. He removed his capital from Ava which had witnessed so much bloodshed to a new site further up the river Irrawady. Here he built Amarapura, "the city of the immortals," and entered into possession of it in May 1783. In 1784 Bodawpaya conquered Arakan which had remained independent for the past 600 years and which had inspired every powerful Burmese monarch with the hope of resuming its domination. The spoils of victory included a great gun 30 feet long and of 11 inches calibre, and the great Mahamuni image cast by Chanda Suriya in about 150 A.D. which had long been coveted by the Burmese.

The conquest of Arakan increased the political pretensions of the Burmese and led to continual misunderstanding with the English who possessed the district of Chitagong, contiguous to Arakan and separated from it by the river Naaf. In 1785 Bodawpaya led an expedition to Siam, but not being able to overcome the heroic defence of the Siamese he had to retreat to Rangoon. His martial ardour having thus received a severe check he determined to erect a pagoda at Mengun, a few miles above the capital, bigger than any in existence. Villagers were forced to leave their agricultural pursuits to work on the construction of the pagoda. The Arakanese who had been subjected to cruel oppressions and severe exactions at the hands of Burmese officers were further

9. Harvey, *Burma*, p. 249.

exasperated by being forced in thousands to labour at Mengun. Their chiefs, maintained a guerilla resistance for several years, and thousands of Mughs or Arakanese abandoned their country and took refuge in Chittagong where they were permitted to settle in unoccupied land. Three Arakanese chiefs who had led the insurrections against the Burmese were compelled to fly across the border. In 1794 a Burmese army of 5000 soldiers led by Nandakyazo crossed the Naaf, entrenched themselves in British territory and demanded the surrender of the three fugitives who were charged with rebellion, robbery and murder. Major-General Erskine was sent by Sir John Shore to oppose this aggression. After some negotiations the three delinquents were delivered to the Burmese general; two of them were put to death by the most cruel torture, and the third again effected his escape to British territory.[10]

The forbearance shown by the British Government in not punishing the Burmese for their aggression followed by the surrender of the three fugitives was construed at Amarapura as an act of cowardice. Captain Hiram Cox who was deputed to Burma by Sir John Shore in 1797 had to return having accomplished nothing, and having been subjected to all kinds of indignities. Captain Cox realised from his conversations with the Burmese officials that they were intending to claim the restitution of Chittagong, Luckipore, Dacca, and the whole of Cossimbazar, which in their opinion had formerly belonged to Arakan.[11]

Towards the end of 1798 not less than 10,000 Mughs entered the British territories having been driven from their homes by the tyranny and oppression of the Burmese officers. This body was followed by another still more numerous. It was believed that two-thirds of the Mughs of Arakan had forsaken the province. The Burmese followed the fugitives into Chittagong and maintained a petty warfare with British troops for several weeks. The Burmese commander wrote a letter to the Magistrate of Chittagong in which he observed,—" If you, regarding former amity, will deliver up all the refugees, friendship and concord will continue to subsist. Our disagreement is only about the refugees. If you will keep the Arrakanese in your country the cord of friendship will be broken."[12] After sometime the Burmese retired to their own bounds. The

10. Phayre, *Burma*, pp. 220-21, and Sir John Malcolm, *Political History of India*, 1826, Vol. I, p. 549.

11. Cox, *Burman Empire*, p. 300.

12. Malcolm, *India*, I, p. 552.

Government at Calcutta resolved to assign to the refugees waste lands in Chittagong. Captain Cox was appointed to select a site for the Mugh emigrants and supervise their settlement, and the place was named after him, Cox's Bazaar.

The Mughs from their new home in Chittagong and other scattered settlements in that district renewed their incursions into Arakan; and demands for their unconditional surrender were frequently made by the Burmese governor of Arakan, accompanied by threats of invasion if the requisition was not immediately complied with. Lord Wellesley, being engrossed in counteracting the designs of Tipu Sultan and his French supporters, and a threatened invasion of India by Zeman Shah of Afghanistan was prevented from dealing effectually with Burmese aggression. After the defeat and death of Tipu Sultan there sprang other eventualities like the preparations for an expedition to the Isle of France, the departure of troops to Egypt and the apprehension of disagreement with the Mahratta powers which precluded the idea of a war being undertaken against the Burmese.[13] Capt. Symes was for a second time deputed to Burma in 1802, but had to return without accomplishing his purpose and having been subjected like Cox to indignities. Canning who was at the Burmese court in 1809 ascertained that Bodawpaya had long entertained the project of conquering the provinces of Chittagong and Dacca. The British embassies instead of obtaining the good-will of the Burmese monarch only served to confirm his notions of self-importance.

In 1811 the Mughs in Chittagong led by Nga Chin Pyan, commonly known as Kingberring, entered Arakan and attacked Burmese detachments. Kingberring repeated his predatory attacks on Arakan, and the British authorities in Chittagong, with their limited military resources, could not restrain him from his activities. The result was that Burmese troops entered frequently into British territory in pursuit of the marauders, and much complaint and recrimination took place between the officers on the two frontiers. In 1812 the viceroy of Pegu received orders from the king of Burma to hold Captain Canning as a hostage for the delivery of the Arakanese rebels. This design was frustrated by Canning's escape on board the Company's cruiser *Malabar*.

In 1813 rumours were afloat that the Burmese were making active and extensive preparations for the invasion of British India. The Magistrate of Chittagong reported to the Government of a

13. Phayre, *Burma*, p. 222.

plan supposed to have been formed by the Burmese for uniting the principal states of India in a confederacy against the British.[14] It was believed that Burmese agents had proceeded or were on their way to Poona and Lahore to effect the union. One Burmese sent by Bodawpaya to Benares for the professed purpose of collecting Sanskrit books was said to have spent his time in secret intrigues of a character hostile to the British Government.[15] However unpracticable might be these designs to form political alliance with the powers of Hindustan they at least show the inveterate hostility cherished by the Burmese towards the English.

The Burmese entertained no friendly disposition towards the Assam government which had once frustrated their designs in Manipur. Purnananda Buragohain had also helped a refractory Shan chief of Hukong with a few companies of sepoys.[16] The Singphos, the Khamptis and the Moamarias had sought the assistance of the Burmese in their hostilities against the Ahoms. Parties of Burmese had twice entered Assam, but the prime minister Purnananda Buragohain contrived to send them back with bribes and presents.[17]

In 1796 an Ahom prince, described as the brother of the reigning king, sent messengers to Amarapura to supplicate Bodawpaya's assistance in gaining possession of the throne of Assam to which he claimed to have superior rights.[18] The prince promised to become a vassal of the Burmese monarch and forward the latter's views on Bengal. His representations were promoted at the Burmese court by the Malabar Shabunder.[19] King Bodawpaya had sent early in 1797 an advanced army of 20,000 men to clear the

14. Bengal Letter to Court, June 24, 1813, Parl. Papers, Discussions with the Burmese Government, 1812-24, printed by order of the House of Commons, May 30, 1825, p. 87.

15. Malcolm, *India*, I, pp. 558-9; Phayre, *Burma*, pp. 224-6; Nisbet, *Burma*, I, p. 17; Alleyne Ireland, *The Province of Burma*, Boston and New York, 1907, Vol. I, p. 26.

16. G. C. Barua, *Ahom Buranji*, pp. 575-6.

17. *J. A. S. B.*, August 1838, p. 673.

18. Cox, who mentions the fact in his *Burman Empire*, p. 70, does not give the name. He was most probably Bijoy Barmura Gohain, father of Brajanath. Being defeated by Purnananda in 1795 Barmura took shelter in Cachar and Manipur. From Manipur he possibly sent overtures to Burma.

19. *Shabunder*, in the ports to the eastward of Calcutta, was a situation similar to that of master-attendant in English harbours. The intrigues of the Moslem, Malabar and other factions in Amarapura in exciting the Burmese against the English have been noted in particular by Cox, *Burman Empire*, p. 301.

roads in the route to Assam and intended to follow it up by a much larger force. There was great excitement in the city, and all the way up the river Irrawady was alarmed with the din and preparations for war. Captain Cox, who was then at Amarapura, foresaw that the invasion of Assam by Burma would disturb the peace of Bengal and ultimately embroil the English into hostilities. Cox therefore told the Amarapura ministers that Assam was "tributary to the English and under their protection, and that it was not more than three years since our troops had settled the country, and placed the present rajah on the throne."[20] Bodawpaya recalled the troops after receiving Cox's warning of the probable consequences. The king was, however, offended with the English who according to Cox's bluff had already become masters of Assam.

In June 1797 a daughter of the Ahom prince, intended for the harem of Bodawpaya, arrived at Amarapura. On June 26 the princess was escorted in a procession to the court by the queen-mother accompanied by spearmen, musketeers, musicians, and Burmese and Assamese priests. The princess soon became a favourite of the doting monarch then 53 years old. The Assamese party at the court availed themselves of her influence to induce Bodawpaya to take up their cause and "break with the English."[21] In August 1797 Bodawpaya renewed his intention to place the father of his Assamese consort on the Assam throne and through him carry out his cherished designs against the British. The British agent's repeated warnings in very strong language dissuaded the monarch from sending an expedition to Assam. But Captain Cox, from the intimate knowledge of the character of the Burmese and of their political ambition at that time, was convinced that their resolution to desist from interference in Assam was only temporary, and that it would be taken up whenever favourable opportunities would present themselves. "Deficient in judgment to see the whole of their danger," predicted Cox in this connection, "and elated with their success against the barbarous borderers of their country, yet alarmed at my steadiness and candour, they have recourse to procrastination, the refuge of weak minds; hoping, perhaps, for some turn in the scale of politics, that may

20. Cox, *Burman Empire,* p. 138-9; his despatch of 27th Nov. 1797 in Beng. Pol. Cons., March 2, 1798, No. 5.

21. Cox, *Burman Empire,* pp. 277, 301.

afford them an opportunity of gratifying their ambition without incurring the risk of our enmity.'"[22]

Such a turn of events occurred in 1816 when Badanchandra, the fugitive Ahom viceroy of Gauhati, appealed to the Burmese king for military assistance, on behalf of King Chandrakanta Singha. It is believed that another Assamese consort of Bodawpaya, belonging to the same Duara family as Badanchandra, interceded on his behalf describing him as her own brother and the virtual master of Assam.[23] Bodawpaya saw in Badanchandra's request an opportunity to push on to Assam which was contiguous to British territory; and being assured of the support of Chandrakanta, the *dejure* ruler of Assam and of his viceroy, Bodawpaya resolved to avail himself of it. In execution of his plan to establish his influence over the states lying between Burma and British India he had in 1813 set Marjit Singha, son of Jai Singha, on the throne of Manipur after having dispossessed his elder brother Chaurajit Singha. Marjit acknowledged his dependence on the Burmese king and ceded the Kabaw Valley to his protector. The prospect of obtaining the allegiance of the Assam Raja by suppressing his prime minister was not a thing to be abandoned by the ambitious monarch Bodawpaya. He therefore commanded the chiefs of Mogaung, Bhamo and Moying, three principalities lying between Assam and Ava, to proceed against the Buragohain, each with 5,000 soldiers.[24] "Our sovereign," wrote the Burmese commander Mingimaha Tilwa, "with that compassion which marks his character, deeming the claim of Chanda Ganda Sing to be just, and in compliance with the petition presented by his agent for His Majesty's protection, ordered that the rebels should be put out of power, and the rightful owner placed on the throne, feeling at all times an aversion to support usurped authority. Chanda Ganda Sing, having on investigation been discovered to possess every title to his pretensions, the Governors of Mogoun, Bamo and Moying, each with 5,000 soldiers, were despatched against Pooya Coonhay [Buragohain]."[25]

First invasion: alliance with Chandrakanta: Early in 1817 the Burmese army crossed the Patkai Hills and arrived in Namrup within the territories of the Assam Raja. The Buragohain sent a

22. Cox, *Burman Empire*, entry against Aug. 6, 1797, p. 330.

23. *Barphukanar Git*, or ballad of Badanchandra, edited by the present writer.

24. Ramri Raja to Gov.-Gen., received June 8, 1818, Wilson, *Documents*.

25. Tilwa to Scott, Beng. Pol. Cons., Jan. 11, 1822, No. 23.

force of sepoys against the invaders under two Rajkhowas but it was repulsed at Ghiladhari. At this critical juncture Purnananda Buragohain became ill of diabetes and breathed his last, or as some say, he committed suicide by licking diamonds.

Chandrakanta immediately appointed Purnananda's eldest son Ruchinath as Buragohain, and the two other sons Biswanath and Jagannath as Naosalia Phukan and Dhekial Phukan respectively. A fresh army was equipped to resist the invaders who had meanwhile advanced to Dihing. The Assamese army proceeded to the same place and erected a stockade in the vicinity of the Burmese camp. Badanchandra Barphukan and the Burmese commanders declared their intention not to fight the Assamese. Badanchandra then gave out that he was espousing the cause of Prince Garbhe Singha, whom he described as the son of Gaurinath Singha. He invited the Assamese commanders to a parley to fix the terms of truce. Believing in the assurance of Badanchandra the commanders proceeded to his camp where they were seized and tied with ropes. The Burmese then attacked the Assamese stockade and compelled the soldiers to offer their submission. After this the Barphukan commenced his march towards the capital Jorhat.[26]

Ruchinath Buragohain fearing the vengeance of Badanchandra advised the king to leave Jorhat and go down to Gauhati. This the monarch refused to do which made Ruchinath think that Chandrakanta had been at the root of Badanchandra's visit to Burma and therefore he (the Raja) apprehended no mischief from Badanchandra or the Burmese. Ruchinath collected his valuables and proceeded in a boat to Gauhati with all the members of his family just when Badanchandra reached Jhanji, 18 miles to the east of Jorhat.

The queen-mother Numali Rajmao sent a few officers to welcome Badanchandra. He stationed the Burmese force outside the fortifications of Jorhat and proceeded to the palace enclosures with three trusted companions. Badanchandra made his obeisance to Chandrakanta and in tears narrated his adventures since his departure from Assam. The king and his mother accorded a warm reception to Badanchandra who reciprocated it by promises of loyalty. This happened in the middle of March 1817.

Badanchandra then offered to administer the affairs of state as Purnananda had done before. Chandrakanta appointed him his prime minister with a new designation *Mantri Phukan*. Badan-

26. Maniram's Ms. *Assam Buranji*.

chandra elevated the supporters of the monarch and of himself to power, and punished those who had been instrumental in the executions following the conspiracy of Satram. The historian Srinath Barbarua, uncle of Badanchandra, who had supported Purnananda throughout, was dismissed from office and was replaced by one Dhani Rajkhowa, and one Nirbhaynarayan was appointed Bargohain. Maheswar Parvatia Phukan who had been deputed in October 1815 to seize Badanchandra at Gauhati had both his eyes extracted though a sum of rupees 7,000 had been accepted from him for preserving at least one. Eight other Phukans and Baruas, all Brahmans, underwent the same punishment. Eight men were executed by various forms of torture.

A *Barmel* or conference of the nobles and officers was then held to devise means for procuring the peaceful return of the Burmese. They resolved to send to the Burmese monarch a sum of rupees one lakh as well as a princess. According to this resolution Hemo Aideo, daughter of the Ahom prince Baga Kowanr, was made over to the Burmese commanders being represented as Chandrakanta's own sister. The princess was given a rich dowry consisting of ornaments and a large retinue of Brahmans and attendants. Her brothers Biswanath Tipam Raja and Dhaniram Gohain accompanied her to Burma. Suitable presents were given to the Burmese captains and 50 elephants to their king. The Burmese retired from the neighbourhood of Jorhat in April 1817.

In whatever light Chandrakanta and his new prime minister might have represented this friendship with the Burmese a large section of the Assamese including Ruchinath Buragohain understood that the king, by offering a subsidy, a princess and elephants had become tributary to the Burmese sovereign. It was in this light that the Burmese themselves considered Chandrakanta's position on the Assam musnud, as according to their customs the presentation of a princess was tantamount to the acceptance of allegiance. "The rights of Chanda Ganda," wrote Mingimaha Tilwa, "were restored and he was placed on the throne. Chanda Ganda, being thus under obligation to our sovereign declared himself a slave in common with other subjects."[27]

Chandrakanta deposed and Purandar proclaimed king: Badanchandra governed the country with zeal and efficiency. But the nobles began gradually to realise the worth of Purnananda Buragohain and the magnitude of Badanchandra's treachery in bringing

27. Tilwa to Scott, Beng. Pol. Cons., Jan. 11, 1822, No. 23.

a foreign army to Assam and reducing the kingdom to Burmese vassalage. A conspiracy against Badanchandra was set on foot under the leadership of Numali Rajmao, Dhani Barbarua and Nirbhaynarayan Bargohain. Rupsing Subedar and Rahman Khan Jamadar were appointed to carry out their purposes into execution. The two sepoys approached the Barphukan one morning when he was rubbing his hands with clay after performing his ablutions on the riverside. When questioned as to the object of their visit, they replied that it was customary for servants to come to pay respects to their masters and to persons of authority and eminence. Thus disarmed of all suspicion the Barphukan continued busy in the water when Rupsing dealt him a cut over the neck with his sabre which felled him to the ground. The Jamadar followed up the stroke and the minister breathed his last imprecating curses on the king, his country and the assassins.

After the murder of Badanchandra Chandrakanta sent messages to Ruchinath Buragohain asking him to return to Jorhat and resume charge of the administration. But Ruchinath could not forgive the monarch for having set up Badanchandra against his father Purnananda and for having entered into a humiliating alliance with the Burmese.

After his flight from Jorhat Ruchinath had proceeded to Gauhati where he remained with a considerable force. The female part of the family was sent down to Jugighopa under the escort of his brother Jagannath Dhekial Phukan. The Phukan, at the instance of Ruchinath, proceeded to Rungpore to invite Prince Purandar, then ten years old, to return to Assam and take upon himself the government of the country. He was then living at Chilmari with his father Brajanath Kowanr, both receiving pensions from the British Government. Purandar was prevented from going to Gauhati by his father who resolved to try his fortunes once more in spite of his disqualification for succession by the mutilation of an ear. For the time being Jagannath and Ruchinath had to waive their objections to Brajanath's pretensions as his co-operation was expected to be more effective than that of his minor son.

Towards the end of May 1817 Jagannath Dhekial Phukan appeared before David Scott, Magistrate of Rungpore, with an application for military assistance, and in the event of its refusal, for permission to purchase and transport to Assam 700 stand of fire-arms. A few days later Brajanath himself interviewed Scott and explained that personally he would have preferred to pass the remainder of his life in Bengal, but that he found difficulties in the matter of his children who could intermarry only with certain families resident in Assam. Brajanath expressed his intention to avail himself of Ruchinath Buragohain's offer of support and to return to Assam to assert his claims to the throne. The Board in their meeting of May 31 permitted Brajanath to proceed to Assam in prosecution of the views held out to him by the Buragohain. The Government in conformity to its determination to abstain from any interference in Assam restricted Brajanath from taking with him any armed force from the Company's territories, and from purchasing fire-arms within the Company's provinces.[28]

As the Board's orders were directed against the assembling of armed men within British territories or entering Assam otherwise than singly, David Scott instructed the Police officers not to offer any molestation to individuals proceeding with arms to join Brajanath's headquarters established within Assam, of which a considerable portion had been in the possession of Ruchinath Buragohain. By this indulgence Scott hoped to rid the district of Rungpore of many soldiers of fortune and disorderly persons who had formerly served in Assam and who now possessed no regular means of livelihood nor had any prospect of finding employment in British territories.[29]

Brajanath proceeded to Gauhati where he spent some months in organising and equipping his force of Hindustanis and local levies. It is said that failing to obtain the assistance of the Company Brajanath dressed up a native sepoy in the full regimentals of an English officer to encourage people to think that British aid had been obtained.[30] Brajanath and Ruchinath then marched towards Jorhat. Their force consisting of four companies was commanded by Jagannath Dhekial Phukan. On their approach Chandrakanta fled to Rangpur leaving Luku Deka-phukan in charge of Jorhat. The Deka-phukan's force was easily repulsed and Ruchinath Buragohain entered Jorhat early in February 1818.

Chandrakanta, on assurances of allegiance and fealty on the part of Ruchinath Buragohain and his brothers, ventured upon visiting Jorhat where for ten days he was treated with all becoming attention and respect. The Buragohain had in the meantime sent for Purandar as the elevation of his father Brajanath to the throne was out of the question in view of his old disqualifi-

28. Scott to Adam, May 20, Adam to Scott, May 31, Beng. Pol. Cons., May 31, 1817, Nos. 91-92.

29. Scott to Swinton, Aug. 7, Beng. Pol. Cons., Sept. 16, 1820, No. 95.

30. *Asamar Padya-Buranji*, ed. S. K. Bhuyan, pp. 42, 303.

cation. On February 20, Chandrakanta was deposed and sent as a prisoner to Taratali, a notoriously unhealthy place to the south-east of Jorhat. On the same day Purandar was acclaimed as sovereign. A few days later Chandrakanta was visited by Biswanath, who caused the slicing of the ex-monarch's right ear. Biswanath was appointed Marangikhowa Gohain by Purandar.

The year 1818 is important for two reasons: it witnessed the increase of the boastfulness of the Burmese government following the reduction of the Assam king to vassalage, and also saw the release of the Company's forces from the theatres of operation in India making it possible for the Government to employ its military resources in the counteraction of the designs of any eventual enemy. In April 1817, before the return of the Assam expedition to Burma, the governor of Ramri, in demanding the surrender of the Arakanese, had referred to the king of Assam as living in amity with the sovereign of Ava. After having heard of the reduction of Chandrakanta the same governor of Ramri wrote to the Governor-General in June 1818 referring to the success of the Burmese arms in Assam, and claiming Ramoo, Chittagong, Murshidabad and Dacca. "The Governor-General" the letter concluded, "representing the English Company, should surrender these dominions, and pay the collections therefrom to our sovereign. If this is refused, I shall represent it to His Majesty. Generals with powerful forces will be despatched, both by sea and land, and I shall myself come for the purpose of storming, capturing and destroying the whole of the English possessions which I shall afterwards offer to my sovereign."[31]

In the same year 1818 the East India Company attained the highest degree of stability as a ruling power. On the termination of the Nepal War, 1814-16, the Gurkha chieftains became friendly though independent neighbours. In 1817 the Pindaris were crushed; and the different Mahratta powers, Sindhia, Holkar and Nagpur, were humbled; the Peshwaship was abolished, and the last incumbent Baji Rao became a pensioner of the British Government; and the Sikh ruler stood firm in alliance with the British. All the important chiefs of India had by this time entered into treaty relations with the English.[32]

Being relieved of his anxieties with the Mahrattas Lord Hastings, the Governor-General of India, could now pay more attention to the Burmese. The reply to the Ramri Raja's letter was

31. Ramri Raja's letter to Gov.-Gen., Wilson, *Documents*, No. 6.
32. H. H. Dodwell, *India*, Vol. I, pp. 81-2.

firm and determined. The Governor-General informed the governor of Pegu that in his opinion the Ramri Raja's communication was a piece of forgery engineered by the evil-minded counsellers of the Burmese monarch to plunge him into a calamitous war or to serve some unworthy purpose of their own.[33] The Burmese king in the meantime had heard of the defeat of the Mahrattas who were supposed to be his secret allies; and so instead of carrying out his threat to invade Bengal he availed himself of the excuses suggested by Lord Hastings and kept quiet, and did not answer the Governor-General at all.[34]

Second invasion: Chandrakanta reinstated: The friends of the murdered Barphukan fearing for their lives fled to Burma and informed the Amarapura court of the recent happenings in Assam. King Bodawpaya's Assamese consort who had interceded on behalf of Badanchandra now urged the monarch to despatch an army to Assam to avenge the murder of her kinsman. To her request were added the solicitations of Hemo Aideo whose "brother" Chandrakanta had been deposed and maimed by Ruchinath's followers. King Bodawpaya despatched an army of 20,000 men to Assam, under the command of Kee-Wooumingee, commonly known as Kiamingi or Alumingi Bargohain. It is believed that the Burmese army was guided on this occasion by an Assamese named Patalang Senapati, *alias* Momai Barua, who had been long resident in Burma.

Kiamingi's force entered Assam in January 1819. Jagannath Dhekial Phukan advanced from Jorhat at the head of 18 companies of sepoys and with 200 *jinjals* and 8 guns of large calibre. On February 15, 1819, an engagement took place at Phulpanichiga, near Jhanji, in which the Burmese lost 300 or 400 men. They then retreated a short distance leaving the Dhekial Phukan in possession of the field. Instead of following up his victory the Dhekial Phukan retraced his steps to Jorhat where he raised an alarm giving a frightful description of the overwhelming force of the Burmese urging on his companions to fly from that place and proceed towards the western districts. Ruchinath Buragohain and Purandar Singha took from the royal treasury all the property it contained and sailed down to Gauhati with their families and

33. Lord Hastings to Viceroy of Pegu, June 22, 1818, Wilson, *Documents*, No. 7.

34. Harvey, *Burma*, p. 293, Sir John Malcolm, *Political History of India*, Vol. I, p. 575.

adherents. Brajanath had in the meantime died a natural death in March 1818.

Janmi, son of Badanchandra, was sent with a guard to Taratali to bring Chandrakanta who was conducted to Rangpur and placed on the throne on March 7, 1819. In the middle of April Kiamingi returned to Ava leaving the affairs at Rangpur in charge of Mingimaha Tilwa and his two lieutenants Sajati Phukan and Patalang Senapati, with a force of 2,000 men composed partly of Doanias or naturalised Burmese, and Singphos.

Mingimaha Tilwa despatched Patalang and another commander named Seik Phukan to seize Purandar and Ruchinath. Having defeated a detachment of the Buragohain's force at Nowgong the Burmese troops proceeded to Gauhati where they arrived on June 11, 1819. The Burmese were fired at by the Buragohain's men with a couple of guns which sank two of their boats. The Burmese afterwards effected a landing and approached the town by the eastern entrance. Finding that they were surrounded Purandar and Ruchinath fled to the Assam Choky, opposite Goalpara, where they arrived on June 17. Having left a party at Gauhati Patalang and Seik Phukan pursued Purandar and Ruchinath to their last retreat wherein they again withdrew to Chilmari. Being forbidden to take warlike stores into the Company's territories Ruchinath left a large quantity of arms and accoutrements, including 400 muskets and 8 or 9 maunds of gunpowder at Goalpara, in charge of the Jamadar of Sebundies.[35]

The second Burmese invasion of Assam resulted in the re-establishment of the authority of Chandrakanta Singha and the expulsion of his enemies Purandar and Ruchinath. Chandrakanta arranged to send a princess again to the Burmese monarch as a fresh token of his allegiance. The selection fell this time on Upama Aideo, whose parentage is unknown.

During the absence of Patalang Senapati in Lower Assam the Burmese commanders Sajati Phukan and Baju Phaya put to death the leading nobles and officials who had formerly supported Purandar and Ruchinath. Dhani Barbarua and Nirbhaynarayan Bargohain both suffered death at Rangpur, the former by having his belly ripped open and the latter by decapitation. Patalang was appointed Barbarua. On January 27, 1820, Mingimaha Tilwa and Sajati Phukan left Rangpur and returned to Ava, taking with them

35. Scott to Swinton, Sept. 26, Beng. Pol. Cons., Oct. 7, 1820, No. 53; Purandar Singha to Lord Hastings, recd. Feb. 11, Cons., May 12, 1821, No. 84; Scott to Swinton, May 19, Cons., June 16, 1821, No. 70.

the princess Upama Aideo. The Changrung Phukan and Parvatia Phukan accompanied her to Amarapura at the head of the escort supplied by Chandrakanta.[36]

In June 1820 Patalang Barbarua married Chandrakanta's sister Majiu Aideo who had been wrested from her husband Biswanath Marangikhowa in view of the animosity between the two families. Patalang became from that moment the ruler in the ascendant, everything being subjected to his control, and Chandrakanta was reduced to a mere cipher.

This Patalang Barbarua was originally an Assamese and had his home in Namrup. He had been deputed by Purnananda Buragohain to the Singpho country to recover the Assamese captives and refugees. Having failed to subdue the refractory Singphos Patalang proposed to coerce them with the help of a Burmese force for which purpose he visited Burma. Bodawpaya having discovered his abilities despatched him against the Arakanese. Having attained some success in his enterprise Patalang was rewarded with the governorship of a place in Arakan. He was brought from his charge to accompany Kiamingi to Assam. Though officially subordinate to the Burmese government Patalang was naturally sympathetic towards his Assamese countrymen. In the early stage of the second invasion he had stopped the barbarities committed by the Burmese by procuring the intervention of Kiamingi Bargohain. By long association with the Burmese Patalang had imbibed their gasconading spirit. At the war-council held after Chandrakanta's reinstatement to devise means to resist the possible manoeuvres of Ruchinath, Patalang is reported to have delivered the following oration,—"Don't be afraid, I shall take the field myself. If the real Firingis come to fight, and if the Bargis [Mahrattas] sharpen their swords, I possess the necessary courage to defeat them all. Even if the enemy receive the support of the gods I am sure of putting them to flight and of preserving the independence of my country."[37]

The influence which Badanchandra and Patalang had upon the Burmese enabled them to check the barbarities of the invaders which so often attended their foreign expeditions. It was only

36. Beng. Sec. and Pol. Cons., July 22, 1825, No. 7; it contains a journal of the route *via* Mogaung and Bhamo to Amarapura kept by an Assamese who accompanied the princess.

37. *Asamar Padya-Buranji*, pp. 305-6, where Patalang figures as Momai Barua, *Momai* literally means maternal uncle; Patalang was in relationship a maternal uncle of Chandrakanta.

after the withdrawal of the control of Badanchandra and Patalang that the Burmese relapsed into their old cruelties. On their departure from Jorhat in April 1817 they had behaved peacefully for some distance; but after having crossed the Dikhow river they plundered the villages and carried off numerous captives of both sexes to Burma. During Patalang's absence in Lower Assam the Burmese committed the most horrible atrocities upon people who were suspected to have sympathy for Chandrakanta's enemies. In spite of the intervention of Badanchandra and Patalang the first two Burmese invasions gave the Assamese a foretaste of the miseries that were in store for them.

Purandar and Ruchinath at Calcutta: Purandar Singha and Ruchinath Buragohain stayed at Chilmari till October 1819. They had been accompanied by 10 or 15 thousand Assamese of respectability all flying for refuge in British territories.

In August 1819, Purandar Singha, submitted a petition to David Scott, addressed to the Governor-General, asking for help to repel his enemies, and proposing to pay in return a money tribute or make over a portion of Assam. He also undertook to pay the expenses of the troops that might be employed by Government in effecting his restoration to authority. "From England to India there is no other asylum to which I can refer for refuge save that of the Honourable Company, who is the virtuous cherisher of our rights and at once the glory and asylum of the world." He proposed in spite of his ill-health, to proceed to Calcutta to see the Governor-General leaving his family and dependants at Chilmari.[38]

In October 1819, Purandar Singha submitted another petition repeating his former proposition to become a tributary of the Company "in the way in which engagements are entered into with the Rajas of Hindoostan for their permanent continuance in authority over their respective territories in pursuance of which they pass time in ease." He promised to pay an annual tribute of one lakh of rupees of his own coinage together with another lakh as Nuzzeranah, as well as the expense of the troops.[39] In November 1819, Purandar Singha proceeded to Calcutta where he lived in Chitpore.

On December 27, 1819, Ruchinath Buragohain, who had gone to Calcutta with 500 attendants, submitted two petitions to the

38. Purandar Singha to Lord Hastings, recd. Sept. 4, 1819, Beng. Pol. Cons., July 29, 1820, No. 79.

39. Purandar Singha to Lord Hastings, recd. Nov. 1, 1819, Beng. Pol. Cons., July 29, 1820, No. 80.

Governor-General describing the affairs of Assam, with a request to inform the Burmese government of the defective title of Chandrakanta. He further asked for a supply of 2,000 muskets "to preserve the country of Assam to us." "Whoever also among the sons of the Surga Deb's family," said Ruchinath, "shall be found fit for the throne I will procure his being installed in the seat of authority with the regular ceremonies." Ruchinath expatiated upon the supreme character of the Buragohain's authority in Assam. "I, the Buragohain," observed Ruchinath, "am supreme over the country and its affairs. My possession is but a small portion; still I am master of the government of one kingdom." Referring to the three Gohains, who in Ruchinath's opinion were the offspring of the Swargadeo's family, he said,—"I am Buragohain, supreme in the province and over them."

Ruchinath then referred to the powers of the three Gohains to instal a prince on the throne and to remove him if he acted illegally. During the interval between the deposal or death of one prince and the installation of his successor the Buragohain alone, alleged Ruchinath, possessed the authority to carry on the duties of the Raja. Such an eventuality occurred on the death of Gaurinath Singha who left no male issue, nor was there any prince qualified for succession; for this reason, said Ruchinath, "my late father maintained the authority over the Assam country for a period of 26 [22, 1795-1817] years." About Kamaleswar and Chandrakanta who had both been elevated to the throne by Purnananda, Ruchinath pointed out that they could not be made full-fledged sovereigns. Their ancestor Lechai Namrupia Raja had rebelled against his brother King Rudra Singha in consequence of which the descendants of the former had been debarred from succession. In proof of this permanent disqualification Ruchinath referred to the fact that no coin had been struck in either Kamaleswar or Chandrakanta's name, and that no coronation ceremony had been performed in the case of either. The friction between Chandrakanta and Purnananda came to a head, observed Ruchinath, when the monarch pressed for his right to be crowned and the minister refused to do it. On the return of the Burmese, Ruchinath and Brajanath, "with the assistance of the Magistrate [Scott]", collected a force and punished Chandrakanta.[40] As

40. This assistance was the indulgence shown by Scott in permitting individuals to proceed with arms to join Brajanath's headquarters in Assam. Scott took exception to this statement of Ruchinath and explained the circumstances in which the permission had been given, Scott to Sainton, Aug. 7, Beng. Pol. Cons., Sept. 16, 1820, No. 95.

Brajanath was disqualified by mutilation, continued Ruchinath, his son Purandar was placed on the throne whereupon the Burmese came once more to Assam and reinstated Chandrakanta. The reason assigned by Ruchinath for the Burma Raja's interest in Chandrakanta's elevation was the long-standing friendship between the sovereigns of the two kingdoms, though Chandrakanta had no claim to the title of a monarch. Ruchinath concluded his memorial by saying,—"Nothing improper has yet been done by us in the province of Assam, else what prohibition has there been to myself taking the name of Raja, I being supreme in the district ?"[41]

Purnananda Buragohain had placed the two minors Kamaleswar and Chandrakanta on the throne for want of better candidates and was obliged to take upon himself the responsibilities of government. This arrangement which had been necessitated by the exigency of the moment was interpreted by Ruchinath as evidence of the Buragohain's vested right to supreme authority, the delegation of that authority to a monarch being a matter of choice on the part of the Buragohain. This curious doctrine enunciated by Ruchinath Buragohain was pointed out by Lord Hastings to the Court of Directors,—"He should remark that there is some confusion and obscurity in the petitions presented by the Bura Goheyn [Ruchinath]; he sometimes represented himself as the adherent and supporter of Poorunder Singh, and at other times seemed to state the supreme authority as being vested in his own person, owing to the default of legal heirs to the Raj."[42]

Ruchinath Buragohain's claim to supreme authority was contradicted by Malbhog Bargohain who was also in attendance upon Purandar Singha at Calcutta. This noble had been appointed Bargohain in February 1818, but had been dismissed by Chandrakanta a year later. He submitted two petitions to the Governor-General requesting interviews for himself and Purandar Singha. After having alluded to the "treacherous conduct" of Ruchinath, Malbhog characterised the Buragohain's claim to the authority over Assam as an "impudent assertion." "Three of us among the Maharaja's ministers," observed Malbhog, "myself with the Barpatra Gohain and the Buragohain, are all engaged in the public service of the said Maharajah. If the Buragohain can be chief over Assam, then why not all the others of the Maharaja's ministers become chiefs also ?" Malbhog Bargohain requested the

41. Ruchinath to Gov.-Gen., recd. Dec. 27, 1819, Beng. Pol. Cons., July 29, 1820, Nos. 81 and 82.

42. Bengal Letter to Court, Sept. 12, 1823, paragraph 93.

Governor-General to issue a precept to David Scott for an investigation of the claim and of the frauds practised by Ruchinath.[43]

Government's reply to the petitions of the Assam chiefs was in consonance with its policy of non-interference in the internal dissensions of foreign states, and its consequent disinclination to pronounce on disputed titles. Purandar Singha and Ruchinath Buragohain were informed that in view of Government's resolution to maintain relations of friendship with the reigning prince, it could not take cognizance of the disputes between the petitioners and Chandrakanta Singha, the latter being established on the *musnud* of Assam. The Governor-General, however, assured Purandar and Ruchinath that they would not be denied the asylum they had sought within the Company's territories so long as they continued to conduct themselves in a peaceable manner and conform to the orders of the Government.[44]

Chandrakanta's petitions against Purandar and Ruchinath: Between November 1819 and June 1820 Chandrakanta submitted several petitions to Lord Hastings for the seizure of Purandar Singha and Ruchinath Buragohain, and the latter's brothers Biswanath Marangikhowa and Jagannath Dhekial Phukan, with their property and effects which he claimed to be the property of the state.[45] Chandrakanta alleged that the fugitives had plundered the royal stores at Rangpur and Gauhati of all the property of the state consisting of cash, jewels, ornaments and other articles, amounting to 35 lakhs of rupees.[46] He described at length the treacherous conduct of Ruchinath and his brothers, and asked the Governor-General to seize them or send them to Assam or punish them as Government would on enquiry think fit. In November 1819 Chandrakanta sent with his messenger 15 Burmese soldiers

43. Malbhog Bargohain to Lord Hastings, Jan. 29, and March 17, Beng. Pol. Cons., July 29, 1820, Nos. 83 and 84.

44. Swinton to Purandar and Ruchinath, July 20, Beng. Pol. Cons., July 29, 1820, No. 85.

45. Chandrakanta's letters were received at Calcutta on Nov. 8, 1819, and March 13 and June 14, 1820. The first letter was presented by the Raja's Vakil Mahodar Khaund Barua who also submitted a separate petition detailing the circumstances of Ruchinath's treachery; the second by the Darrang Raja and Hansraj Sing; and the third by Mahodar and Hansraj, Beng. Pol. Cons., July 29, 1820, Nos. 90 to 94.

46. Colonel Jenkins testifying to the poverty of Chandrakanta's son Ghanakanta said,—"All the royal property of the Rajas was carried off by Purandar Singha's branch of the family; and Ghanakanta's branch only obtained their personal jewels," letter to Government, September 17, 1858, in Assam Secretariat Records.

to conduct the Buragohain to Asam in the event of his being delivered by the Governor-General.

Important revelations are made in the letters of Chandrakanta about the events in Assam of that period. Tinged though they are by Chandrakanta's resentment at the Buragohain's defection they are significant as coming from practically the last Ahom sovereign of Assam.—Chandrakanta acknowledged the services of Captain Welsh who suppressed the Moamarias and re-established Gaurinath Singha. Purnananda by various artifices brought over the troops of the government under his own influence, and committed acts of treachery and ingratitude against his sovereign. Purnananda accused several persons in Chandrakanta's service; hanged and impaled some and deprived others of their eyesight. "I despatched the Barphukan Badanchandra," said Chandrakanta, "to inform your Lordship [Lord Hastings] of all these particulars but he receiving no orders from your Lordship was helpless and proceeded to the Burmese country."[47] Purnananda died when Badanchandra reached Bagariguri Choky with his Burmese army. Chandrakanta overlooked the treacherous conduct of Purnananda, and appointed the deceased's eldest son Ruchinath as Buragohain, the second son Biswanath as Naosalia Phukan,[48] and the third son Jagannath as Dhekial Phukan. Chandrakanta kept Ruchinath in the royal presence so that no harm could be done to him by Badanchandra. After the retirement of the Burmese troops Ruchinath acted so wickedly and rebelliously to the detriment of Chandrakanta's peace and honour "that the like conduct has never yet been acted towards a master in these strange times, nay, nor even been witnessed." Notwithstanding Chandrakanta's kind treatment Ruchinath proceeded to Gauhati, invited Brajanath and set up his son Purandar on the throne, and placed Chandrakanta in confinement after causing him many troubles and hardships. Ruchinath put to death many of Chandrakanta's adherents, and after greatly annoying Brajanath ruined him as well. The Burma Raja hearing of Chandrakanta's deposal sent an army of 30,000 men. Ruchinath, unable to cope with that force fled with all the property of the state which he had plundered at Rangpur and Gauhati. "What an ungrateful wretch," said Chandrakanta "did this Buragohain

47. This admission on the part of Chandrakanta sets at rest the doubts hitherto existing as to whether Badanchandra's applications for help against Purnananda were made of his own accord or at the instance of his master.

48. Biswanath is better known as Marangikhowa, the office conferred upon him by Purandar Singha in 1818.

[Ruchinath] prove himself. Be pleased to seize that ungrateful person and send all the property to me here."[49]

Lord Hastings's reply to Chandrakanta's representation was in the same tenor as that addressed to Purandar and Ruchinath. The Governor-General, however, expressed his desire to maintain friendly relations with Chandrakanta as the reigning prince of Assam, and pay every attention to his wishes as long as a compliance with them was not at variance with the established usage and policy of the British Government. With regard to Chandrakanta's request for the apprehension and surrender or punishment of the heads of the defeated party Lord Hastings declared his inability to meet his wishes on the ground that "it is not the practice of the British Government to deny an asylum to persons of that description so long as they conduct themselves in a quiet and peaceable manner."[50]

Mingimaha Meula Mengong, a Burmese minister who afterwards became Governor of Pegu,[51] also addressed a letter to the Governor-General demanding the extradition of Purandar, Ruchinath and their principal followers for the purpose of being conducted to Arakan. Meula Mengong concluded his letter by pointing out that Arakan, Ramoo, Cheduba and Pegu were countries of great commercial intercourse and that the enemies of the Burmese government should never be countenanced by the Governor-General. Lord Hastings's reply to Meula Mengong's letter was couched in amicable terms. With regard to the surrender of the Assamese refugees the Governor-General referred Meula Mengong to Chandrakanta from whom letters had been received on the same subject.[52]

Third invasion: Chandrakanta's flight: Towards the end of 1820 the Burmese relaxed their domineering influence in Assam. They regarded raiding as conquest, and when they obtained a wife for their monarch and some tribute they considered that conquest to be complete, upon which they would leave their tributaries

49. Chandrakanta Singha to Lord Hastings Nov. 8, 1819, Beng. Pol. Cons., July 29, 1820, No. 90.

50. Swinton to Chandrakanta, July 20, Beng. Pol. Cons., July 29, 1820, No. 95.

51. Mengong to Lord Amherst, recd. March 17, 1824, Wilson, *Documents*, No. 31.

52. Mengong to Lord Hastings, undated, and Swinton to Mengong, July 20, Beng. Pol. Cons., July 29, Nos. 3, 86-87.

alone.[53] At the time of Mingimahs Tilwa's departure the Burmese army in Assam consisted of only 1,000 men, mostly Doanias and Singphos, tribes living on the immediate border of Assam. Burmese interests were left in the hands of Patalang Senapati who had espoused the Assamese cause, married Chandrakanta's sister and accepted office under him. His Burmese compatriot Sajati Phukan had also returned to Burma with Tilwa. Either through the influence of Patalang Barbarua or Chandrakanta, or through the anxiety of the Doanias and Singphos to return to their normal agricultural pursuits in their own native villages, the number of the Burmese force in Assam in the beginning of 1821 did not exceed 100.[54] But the Burmese used to come occasionally to Assam in large bodies for the purpose of plundering the country and carrying off the cattle and women.

Emboldened by the slackness of the Burmese and the support of Patalang Barbarua Chandrakanta now tried to shake off the yoke of the king of Ava. Patalang was despatched to Dighalighat on the river Buri-Dihing, lying on the Burmese route to Assam, where he proceeded with his wife Majiu Aideo. The place had a fine dockyard, in the vicinity of which Patalang constructed a fort to oppose the entrance of the Burmese into Assam. Dighalighat was thenceforth known as Jaipur, or the city of victory.[55]

Chandrakanta sent proposals to Ruchinath and the refugees of consequence for their return with a view to effect a general union for the purpose of repelling the Burmese in the event of a fresh invasion. In the meantime Purandar Singha having failed to obtain assistance from the British Government had collected troops in the Bhutan territory to invade Assam. Purandar's force was to be commanded by Robert Bruce, who had been receiving a pension from the Government for having been formerly in the Mahratta army. Ruchinath continued to live at Calcutta till June 1821. In view of Purandar Singha's preparation to invade Assam which would cause the marching of his troops to the frontier of that country the Government permitted the retention of a party of the Rungpore Local Battalion at Goalpara or Jugighopa.[56]

53. Harvey, *Burma*, pp. 293, 299.

54. Scott to Swinton, Feb. 6, Beng. Pol. Cons., March 19, 1821, No. 111.

55. Lt. R. Wilcox who visited Jaipur in 1825 described the fort as "a square of 350 yards, with a dry ditch of 6 feet deep, the earth from which is thrown up in the form of a wall or bank 6 feet high," *Asiatick Researches*, Vol. XVII, p. 323.

56. Scott to Swinton, Feb. 6, Beng. Pol. Cons., March 10, 1821, Nos. 111-112; and Scott to Swinton, Feb. 25, Cons., March 24, 1821, No. 51.

The old King Bodawpaya who had been responsible for the first and second invasions of Assam died in May 1819, and was succeeded by his grandson Bagyidaw. The new monarch was a man of mild disposition; but there was a strong party at the court, led by the queen and her brother, who thirsted for fresh victories.[57] His commanders, elated by the success of the Burmese arms in Manipur and Assam were anxious to annex fresh trophies; and Bagyidaw had ultimately to yield to the clamours of the war party, and countenance schemes of conquest in which the Burmese were guided by a jealousy of the British and overwhelming confidence in their own prowess.

As a result of the invasions of 1817 and 1819 the Burmese had established a partial hold on Assam, and the Swargadeo had accepted some degree of subordination to his Burmese allies. After the accession of Bagyidaw the government of Ava became anxious to make its authority in Assam more effectual by annexing it to the Burmese dominions. In the same year Bagyidaw had ordered one Gibson to construct a map of Burma together with the adjacent countries of India, Siam and Cochin China. The king on seeing the map remarked,—"you have assigned to the English too much territory." The king is reported to have observed in this connection that Assam would be a desirable acquisition to the Burmese.[58]

The coronation of Bagyidaw had been celebrated with an unusual degree of splendour when all the umbrella-bearing chiefs had been summoned personally to do homage to the new sovereign. Marjit Sing, the Burmese nominee on the throne of Manipur, failed to appear at the installation of the king who now determined to depose him. In the campaigning season of 1819 Mingimaha Bandula led an army into Manipur; Marjit fled to Cachar, and Bandula returned to Burma leaving a garrison at the capital Imphal and taking with him a large portion of the population of Manipur. One Shubal was placed on the Manipur *guddi* by the Burmese. In Cachar the rival Manipuri brothers Marjit, Chaurajit and Gambhir Sing became reconciled for some time, and established their authority in that country after having turned out the rightful Raja Govindachandra who fled to British territory.

57. Phayre, *Burma*, p. 230; Harvey, *Burma*, p. 304.

58. Rev. Dr. Adoniram Judson's deposition, Wilson, *Documents*, No. 174 (c), pp. 231-32.

he devised and matured schemes to measure his strength with Burmese.[63]

During Chandrakanta's residence in British territ October 1821 Mingimaha Tilwa had addressed a letter Scott demanding the surrender of that prince and oth refugees. "We learn", said Tilwa, "that Chanda C sheltering himself in some of the British dominions. great states we must keep in view that what is both. He has acted contrary to the tenets of his established law of his country. If he and h applied to you for protection it will be of fu render them." A letter was also written commander Raja Chydung of the country said,—"Our country is larger than Ben powerful. If you do not deliver up Chand the case may prove like that of stale fi be sweetened for a time by the force of to stink if left standing. Ours is a great emp will act with propriety so as to preserve peace."[64]

These letters after some misadventure were receive towards the end of November, and a translation was made the assistance of Jagannath Dhekial Phukan, brother of Ruchinath Chandrakanta had by that time returned to the Assam Choky. David Scott informed Tilwa of the custom of the British Government not to deliver up political refugees, adding that Chandrakanta was not in the Company's territory. "Understanding this," concluded Scott, "you regulate your conduct so as to preserve the existing amity between the two countries."[65]

Company's Assam Policy in 1821-1822: In the meantime a change had taken place in Government's policy towards Assam in view of the possibility of Burmese authority being effectively and permanently established in that country. Jogeswar Singha who had been set up by the Burmese was king only in name; and the actual power was wielded by the Burmese commander Mingimaha Tilwa.

63. Scott to Swinton, Sept. 26, Beng. Pol. Cons., Oct. 13, No. 24; Scott to Swinton, Sept. 30, Cons., Oct. 27, 1821, No. 69; Scott's *Historical Notes*, Beng. Sec. and Pol. Cons., July 14, 1826, No. 2.

64. Tilwa and Chydung to Scott, undated, Beng. Pol. Cons., Jan. 11, 1822, Nos. 23-24.

65. Scott to Tilwa and Chydung, undated, Beng. Pol. Cons., Jan. 11, 1822, No. 24.

The change of attitude on the part of the Government was first manifested in its decision on the application made by Purandar and Ruchinath for the restoration of the arms left by them in deposit at Chilmari in 1819 before their departure for Calcutta. Ruchinath who was at Calcutta till 1821 further applied for leave to purchase arms from the arsenal at Fort William. Both the applicants expressed their wish to return to Assam with their followers. On May 5, 1821, Government forwarded their petitions to David Scott with a request for information regarding the existing state of Assam and for his opinion as to the course to be pursued in regard to the proposal of Purandar and Ruchinath to return to Assam to try their fortune whether jointly or independently.[66] Scott took the opportunity of pointing out that the interests of the British Government would be best consulted by permitting the Assam refugees to obtain the necessary means for the expulsion of the Burmese.

It was ascertained that the Burmese force in Assam did not exceed 300 or 400 men. Scott, however, anticipated that the force would soon be strengthened by fresh reinforcements, and that the Burmese government, actuated as it was by the spirit of conquest, would soon establish its complete authority in Assam. The presence of the turbulent Burmese in place of the peaceful Assamese in the neighbourhood of Rungpore would necessitate the stationing of a considerable British force in that unhealthy frontier. The Burmese had already made themselves obnoxious to all classes of people in Assam by the cruelties practised by them and the devastation of property that had taken place since they first entered Assam. "All that seems necessary," said Scott in his despatch of May 19, 1821, "to enable either Poorunder Sing or the Boorah Gohayn to re-establish their authority is a supply of fire-arms."[67] He foresaw the objections to furnishing them with muskets from the arsenal at Fort William, but he was aware of none to permitting them to transport arms obtained by private purchase.

Chandrakanta Singha who was then at Gauhati had also applied for the restoration of the Chilmari arms to himself. Scott, fearing that he would soon be expelled from Assam by the Burmese, urged the Government to speedily comply with Chandrakanta's request or grant him permission to transport such arms as he could procure by private purchase.

66. Swinton to Scott, May 5, Beng. Pol. Cons., May 12, 1821, No. 88.
67. Scott to Swinton, May 19, Beng. Pol. Cons., June 16, 1821, No. 69.

In the light of Scott's recommendation Government permitted Purandar and Ruchinath to return to Assam with such partisans, natives of Assam, as might collect round them, and to export privately purchased arms to equip their adherents. As the arms at Chilmari had been left by Ruchinath with the Jamadar of the Sebundies at Goalpara his claim to have them restored was considered as superior to that of Purandar. Ruchinath was given a rahdari pass for himself and 200 armed followers; and about the middle of June 1821 he proceeded from Calcutta to Rungpore by the route of Murshidabad, Rajshahi and Sirajgunj.[68] Purandar Singha had already left Calcutta, after which he collected a force in Bhutan which was defeated by Chandrakanta's troops on May 25, 1821.

In permitting Purandar Singha and Ruchinath Buragohain to return to Assam with their partisans and carry arms across the frontier Government did not explicitly admit the ground on which Scott's recommendation had been based, that its interests would be best served by permitting the Assam refugees to obtain the necessary means for the expulsion of the Burmese. Government was mainly actuated by its reluctance to impose any restraint upon individuals which might eventually operate inequitably. It would be unjust to either Purandar Singha or Ruchinath Buragohain, thought the Government, to prevent his repairing to his adherents prepared to receive him within the territory of Assam. The position of the two refugees was considered to be distinct from the rule, which the Government invariably maintained, of not permitting armed bodies to be assembled within the Company's territory for the invasion of a neighbouring state. Assam was at that time, June 1821, in such a condition of anarchy and confusion that no party or individual possessed sufficient authority to be considered as exercising the executive functions of government.

In the light of Government's orders Scott issued the following instructions to the Officer Commanding a detachment of the Rungpore Local Battalion at Goalpara—that no molestation whatsoever was to be offered to the transport of arms, ammunition and other military stores into Assam; that natives of Assam were at liberty to return to their country with arms either singly or in a body; and that Hindustani or other armed men who were not natives of Assam could go into that country only singly.[69]

68. Prinsep to Scott, June 9, Beng. Pol. Cons., June 16, 1821, No. 71.
69. Scott to Prinsep, Dec. 23, 1821, Beng. Pol. Cons., Jan. 26, 1822, No. 77

The decision of the Government read with the recommendations of David Scott helps one to realise that in view of the peculiar situation in Assam Government was obliged to admit again a partial relinquishment of the policy of neutrality. In 1792 Captain Welsh had been deputed to Assam on the invitation of its ruler, Government's inducement being the prospect of improvement in the trade of Bengal in consequence of the establishment of peace in Assam which the expedition was expected to effect, and the collection of information about the extent and resources of Assam of which very little was known. In 1821 the Company's relations with Burma were strained but not declaredly hostile. To provide facilities to Assamese chiefs to enable them to attack and expel the Burmese was a case of positive intervention, though it might be justified on the ground of its being necessary for the tranquillity of the frontier districts.

Chandrakanta's successes against the Burmese: Chandrakanta continued to hold out against the Burmese from his camp at the Assam Choky. There were three circumstances favourable to his cause at that time; his rival Purandar Singha had been defeated by his troops and the commander Robert Bruce had accepted service under him; Government was now prepared to assist the Assam chiefs to expel the Burmese by granting permission to export fire-arms; and the number of Burmese in Assam was comparatively small.

Towards the end of October 1821 Chandrakanta applied through his agent Robert Bruce at Jugighopa "to avail himself of the permission granted by Government to the different contending parties to transport gunpowder and military stores to Assam." Scott in view of the urgency of the case gave a certificate to Bruce's messenger that he had the permission of Government to transport the arms and gunpowder to Assam. Bruce was able to purchase 300 muskets and 90 maunds of gunpowder for Chandrakanta.[70]

With these arms Chandrakanta equipped his adherents, marched against the Burmese, and defeated them in several skirmishes. By December 10, 1821, Chandrakanta succeeded in pitching his camp in the neighbourhood of Gauhati.[71]

The Burmese garrison at Sarai Choky, near the present Amingaon Railway Station, was attacked by a detachment of

70. Scott to Swinton, Nov. 3, and Swinton to Scott, Nov. 30, Beng. Pol. Cons., Dec. 8, 1821, Nos. 81-82.

71. Scott to Swinton, Dec. 10, Beng. Pol. Cons., Dec. 29, 1821, No. 62.

The change of attitude on the part of the Government was first manifested in its decision on the application made by Purandar and Ruchinath for the restoration of the arms left by them in deposit at Chilmari in 1819 before their departure for Calcutta. Ruchinath who was at Calcutta till 1821 further applied for leave to purchase arms from the arsenal at Fort William. Both the applicants expressed their wish to return to Assam with their followers. On May 5, 1821, Government forwarded their petitions to David Scott with a request for information regarding the existing state of Assam and for his opinion as to the course to be pursued in regard to the proposal of Purandar and Ruchinath to return to Assam to try their fortune whether jointly or independently.[66] Scott took the opportunity of pointing out that the interests of the British Government would be best consulted by permitting the Assam refugees to obtain the necessary means for the expulsion of the Burmese.

It was ascertained that the Burmese force in Assam did not exceed 300 or 400 men. Scott, however, anticipated that the force would soon be strengthened by fresh reinforcements, and that the Burmese government, actuated as it was by the spirit of conquest, would soon establish its complete authority in Assam. The presence of the turbulent Burmese in place of the peaceful Assamese in the neighbourhood of Rungpore would necessitate the stationing of a considerable British force in that unhealthy frontier. The Burmese had already made themselves obnoxious to all classes of people in Assam by the cruelties practised by them and the devastation of property that had taken place since they first entered Assam. "All that seems necessary," said Scott in his despatch of May 19, 1821, "to enable either Poorunder Sing or the Boorah Gohayn to re-establish their authority is a supply of fire-arms."[67] He foresaw the objections to furnishing them with muskets from the arsenal at Fort William, but he was aware of none to permitting them to transport arms obtained by private purchase.

Chandrakanta Singha who was then at Gauhati had also applied for the restoration of the Chilmari arms to himself. Scott, fearing that he would soon be expelled from Assam by the Burmese, urged the Government to speedily comply with Chandrakanta's request or grant him permission to transport such arms as he could procure by private purchase.

66. Swinton to Scott, May 5, Beng. Pol. Cons., May 12, 1821, No. 88.
67. Scott to Swinton, May 19, Beng. Pol. Cons., June 16, 1821, No. 69.

he devised and matured schemes to measure his strength with the Burmese.[63]

During Chandrakanta's residence in British territories in October 1821 Mingimaha Tilwa had addressed a letter to David Scott demanding the surrender of that prince and other principal refugees. "We learn", said Tilwa, "that Chanda Ganda is now sheltering himself in some of the British dominions. Between two great states we must keep in view that what is advantageous to both. He has acted contrary to the tenets of his religion and the established law of his country. If he and his ministers have applied to you for protection it will be of future benefit to surrender them." A letter was also written by another Burmese commander Raja Chydung of the country of Meeung where he said,—"Our country is larger than Bengal, our Rajah is very powerful. If you do not deliver up Chandrakanta who is a criminal the case may prove like that of stale fish which, although it may be sweetened for a time by the force of spiceries, will soon begin to stink if left standing. Ours is a great empire, so is yours. You will act with propriety so as to preserve peace."[64]

These letters after some misadventure were received by Scott towards the end of November, and a translation was made with the assistance of Jagannath Dhekial Phukan, brother of Ruchinath. Chandrakanta had by that time returned to the Assam Choky. David Scott informed Tilwa of the custom of the British Government not to deliver up political refugees, adding that Chandrakanta was not in the Company's territory. "Understanding this," concluded Scott, "you regulate your conduct so as to preserve the existing amity between the two countries."[65]

Company's Assam Policy in 1821-1822: In the meantime a change had taken place in Government's policy towards Assam in view of the possibility of Burmese authority being effectively and permanently established in that country. Jogeswar Singha who had been set up by the Burmese was king only in name; and the actual power was wielded by the Burmese commander Mingimaha Tilwa.

63. Scott to Swinton, Sept. 26, Beng. Pol. Cons., Oct. 13, No. 24; Scott to Swinton, Sept. 30, Cons., Oct. 27, 1821, No. 69; Scott's *Historical Notes*, Beng. Sec. and Pol. Cons., July 14, 1826, No. 2.

64. Tilwa and Chydung to Scott, undated, Beng. Pol. Cons., Jan. 11, 1822, Nos. 23-24.

65. Scott to Tilwa and Chydung, undated, Beng. Pol. Cons., Jan. 11, 1822, No. 24.

to dispel his apprehension by an assurance that presents would be delivered to him. To this Chandrakanta replied that he could not place any confidence in the Burmese to be induced to risk the consequences of a meeting as they had put his Barbarua to death and killed his people. Chandrakanta's refusal highly exasperated Mingimaha Tilwa and he put to death a large number of Assamese including several high officials. Chandrakanta retaliated these atrocities by killing Yegoon Kyodoo and his companions who formed the deputation.[60]

Mingimaha Tilwa losing all hope of Chandrakanta's return declared him to be deposed, and set up Punyadhar, a brother of Hemo Aideo, on the throne of Assam. The new Raja assumed the name Jogeswar Singha. It was represented that Jogeswar's elevation was due to the insistence of his sister who had become a favourite of Bagyidaw.[61]

Chandrakanta remained posted at Gauhati for some months. In May 1821 Purandar Singha entered Assam with troops from the Bhutan territory on the northern part of Bijni to expel Chandrakanta from Gauhati. Purandar's troops, commanded by Robert Bruce, were attacked on May 25 by a party detached by Chandrakanta and dispersed. Bruce was taken prisoner and sent to Gauhati.[62]

Chandrakanta maintained his position at Gauhati till the beginning of September 1821. The Burmese then sent a powerful force against him, and on their reaching Rahachoky, 56 miles east of Gauhati, Chandrakanta fled with his adherents to the Assam Choky, opposite Goalpara, where he arrived on September 23. Two Burmese commanders Seik Phukan and Makhan Phukan pursued Chandrakanta to the Assam Choky, and on their arrival in the neighbourhood he crossed over to Goalpara. In order to deprive his pursuers of any pretext to commit excesses on the borders David Scott required Chandrakanta to proceed to some distance down the river. The Assamese troops left at the Assam Choky repulsed the attacks of the Burmese whereupon the latter returned their steps to Gauhati. Towards the end of October Chandrakanta returned to the Assam Choky, where single-handed

60. David Scott's Historical Notes in Beng. Sec. and Pol. Cons., July 14, 1826, No. 2.

61. Scott to Govt., May 7, Beng. Pol. Cons., May 26, 1821, No. 39; Scott to Prinsep, Dec. 23, 1821, Cons., Jan. 26, 1822, No. 77.

62. Scott to Swinton, June 1, Beng. Pol. Cons., June 16, 1821, No. 70.

After re-establishing their authority in Manipur the Burmese now turned their attention to Assam. In February 1821, Mingimaha Tilwa and Sajati Phukan returned to Assam with a force of 500 men bringing with them valuable presents from King Bagyidaw to Chandrakanta. The object of sending the presents was obviously to strengthen the friendship between the rulers, specially as Bagyidaw had newly succeeded to the throne of Ava. The Burmese avowed that "His Majesty Bagyidaw pitying the condition of Chanda Ganda ordered these presents."[59] If this statement be true the Burmese king was possibly actuated by the impoverishment of Chandrakanta after the plunder of the Assam royal jewels by Purandar and Ruchinath.

On approaching Jaipur Mingimaha Tilwa witnessed the preparations made by Patalang Barbarua. Tilwa exhibited the royal presents to Patalang and asked him not to interfere with the march of the Burmese to Jorhat. The Barbarua, during a friendly conversation, was suddenly seized by Sajati Phukan and knocked down to the floor after which he was severely assaulted and then beheaded. Patalang's soldiers deserted the garrison, and his widow Majiu Aideo who alone remained at the fort was outraged by the Burmese in a most inhuman manner.

Chandrakanta at the Assam Choky: Mingimaha Tilwa then sent Majiu Aideo to her brother Chandrakanta to assure him of the protection of the Burmese and of their determination to re-establish his old influence. Majiu Aideo advised the monarch to place no faith in these promises alleging they would undoubtedly end in his destruction. Chandrakanta took her advice, and leaving a force under Kalibar Matak Buragohain to protect the capital, fled with his sister to Gauhati where they arrived on March 14, 1821. The Burmese had in the meantime occupied Jorhat after having repulsed the Assamese force. They then committed the most cruel atrocities upon the people.

Tilwa despatched the Barpatra Gohain to ask Chandrakanta to return, but without success. He then sent a Burmese deputation under Yegoun Kyodoo to invite Chandrakanta to a conference and

59. These presents were,—one umbrella, a sword, a pair of shoes set with precious stones, a cap and covering for the ears set with precious stones, these four articles "which are usually possessed by Kings," were valued at one lakh of rupees each; and also a belt made of fine golden cords, bangles, an armlet, rings and 'net Sah' (?), Butti and Tea boxes, dresses,—'each article worth a lakh of rupees'—Tilwa to Scott, Beng. Pol. Cons., Jan. 11, 1822, No. 23.

Chandrakanta commanded by Bhola Paniphukan, Gopal Sing and Jadir Buksh Subedar, but the royal force was repulsed with the loss of 20 men among whom was the Subedar. Meanwhile a body of 200 or 300 Burmese attacked Chandrakanta's position at Palasbari, 14 miles west of Gauhati, where he was entrenched with about 1,400 men. The Burmese were driven back and compelled to retreat to Khanamukh, 7 miles from Gauhati. A desultory conflict continued for about a week at the end of which the Burmese force commanded by the Deka-Raja, son of Tilwa, retired from Gauhati which was occupied by the royal troops.[72] On December 23, 1821, Scott reported to Government that Chandrakanta was in possession of all that part of Assam which bordered upon the Company's territories and that he had arrived at Gauhati after defeating the Burmese troops.[73]

On receiving this report Lord Hastings instructed Scott to prohibit the refugees from returning to Assam with armed followers except under Chandrakanta's sanction. The recognition of Chandrakanta's authority by the Government was represented by Jogeswar Singha's Barbarua as an act of active support on the part of Scott. "One Chandrakanta," wrote the Barbarua, "is again marauding the country with the countenance of Mr. Burke [Bruce] and Mr. Scott."[74]

On November 19, 1821, Ruchinath Buragohain had requested Government's permission to proceed to Assam to join Chandrakanta with a force consisting of natives of Hindustan. Scott refused compliance unless he received a letter to that intent directly from Chandrakanta. A few days later Ruchinath interviewed Scott at Rungpore and repeated his request. The Magistrate suspected that Ruchinath's design was to join Chandrakanta apparently in amity, and after having cut him off to go over to the new Raja Jogeswar Singha. But it so happened that Ruchinath was soon prevented from carrying out his treacherous schemes or from otherwise interfering in the affairs of Assam, thus leaving Chandrakanta in the field without an enemy except the usurpers from Burma. The eight Assamese messengers, in charge of the letters of Tilwa and Raja Chydung, had visited Ruchinath at Chilmari to deliver him a verbal message. Ruchinath fearing the

72. Scott's Historical Notes, Beng. Sec. and Pol. Cons., July 14, 1826, No. 2.

73. Beng. Pol. Cons., Jan. 26, 1822, No. 77.

74. Barbarua Rajmantri to Gov.-Gen., recd. Feb. 23, Beng. Pol. Cons., March 16, 1822, No. 99.

exposure of his duplicity had seized the letters, detained the messengers, employed them in tracking his boats to Rungpore and confined them subsequently in the hold of a vessel. Scott had learnt of the interception of the letters from a spy kept by him in Ruchinath's camp, and the story was confirmed by the investigations of a police officer. Under instructions from Government Scott in January 1822 placed Ruchinath Buragohain under restraint in his boat at Rungpore. It was proposed to deliver him to Chandrakanta but Government refused to sanction the proposal on the ground that it would be tantamount to condemning him to death.[75]

After being defeated by Chandrakanta the Deka-Raja retreated to Jorhat. Jogeswar Singha had meanwhile proceeded to the Burmese court to receive confirmation of his appointment as Raja of Assam.[76] Chandrakanta halted at Gauhati to recruit his finances and consolidate his influence over the Chaudhuris or landlords of Kamrup. It is possible that if Chandrakanta, instead of halting at Gauhati, had pursued the Deka-Raja to Jorhat he could have taken the capital. Judging from the difficulty which the Burmese had met in obtaining any advantage over the troops of Chandrakanta their military strength in Assam at that time appeared to be very contemptible. He marched from Gauhati in the beginning of March 1822, and arrived at Mahgarh Ghat, near Jorhat, on the 15th. Soon afterwards Biswanath Marangikhowa and Jagannath Dhekial Phukan entered Assam from Bhutan and defeated a party sent against them by Chandrakanta.[77]

Bandula conquers Assam: In the meantime, having heard of the reverses of the Burmese in Assam King Bagyidaw deputed Mingimaha Bandula, the greatest of all Burmese generals, to properly establish Jogeswar Singha on the *musnud* and effect the final expulsion of Chandrakanta. Accompanied by an army, supposed

75. Scott to W. B. Bayley, Chief Secy. to Govt., Nov. 28, 1821, Swinton to Scott, Jan. 11, 1822, Beng. Pol. Cons., Jan. 11, 1822, Nos. 22, 25; Scott to Swinton, Ap. 1, Swinton to Scott, May 17, Beng. Pol. Cons., May 17, 1822, Nos. 79-80; Judicial Dept. Proceedings of May 30th, Beng. Pol. Cons., June 14, 1822, No. 48; Scott to Swinton, Aug. 17, Beng. Pol. Cons., Sept. 6, 1822, No. 16. Ruchinath was under house-arrest on Aug. 7, 1822; his subsequent career is not known.

76. It was possibly on this occasion when another relation of Jogeswar was presented to Bagyidaw's harem where she was known as "Atau Meengh Terirenei", Scott to Swinton, May 12, Beng. Sec. and Pol. Cons., June 25, 1830, No. 4.

77. Scott to Swinton, June 1, Beng. Pol. Cons., June 14, 1822, No. 47.

to consist of 20,000 fighting men, Bandula arrived at Rangpur on April 8, 1822. He then proceeded to Jorhat, and on April 17 attacked Chandrakanta's force at Mahgarh on a field called Kaliani Pathar. In the engagement that followed Chandrakanta is said to have displayed distinguished bravery, and to have slain five of the enemy with his own hand. His Sikh and Hindustani mercenaries fought gallantly for a long time, but they fell short of ammunition, and were defeated with heavy losses.[78]

Chandrakanta left the place with his nobles and proceeded by boat to Gauhati where he halted for more than a month. Learning that the Burmese were on the move towards him he considered it prudent to withdraw himself and his family to a greater distance from the enemy. He in consequence left Gauhati, and arrived at the Assam Choky with his family and the greatest part of his army on June 3, 1822. Soon after his arrival at the Choky he was attacked by the Burmese, but he succeeded in repelling them. Jagannath Dhekial Phukan visited Chandrakanta at the Assam Choky on June 17 with a view to join him with the troops the Phukan had collected in Bhutan. From the enmity existing between the two parties it seemed doubtful whether they could ever act cordially together.[79]

Gauhati was soon occupied by Mingimaha Bandula. From there he despatched a large force under Mingimaha Tilwa to the Assam Choky. An engagement took place at the Choky at 4·55 on the morning of June 21, 1822. This is how this fateful contest is described by Lt. A. Davidson who listened to the rumbling of the guns from his camp at Goalpara on the opposite side of the river: "The engagement continued brisk for the space of three minutes, when it was evident that one of the parties had received a check. After a few minutes the firing again commenced in a very faint manner, and in about ten minutes, from the number of boats that left Assam Choky, it was evident that they had received a defeat. The Burmese then proceeded to the Candahar Choky [Assam Choky] of which they took possession without resistance."[80]

78. Gunabhiram Barua estimates the loss on Chandrakanta's side to be about 1,500 men, *Assam Buranji*, p. 200, which view is accepted by Gait in his *History of Assam*, p. 230. David Scott in his *Historical Notes* states 200 men to have fallen on either side. In his letter to Govt., of July 10, 1822, Scott observed that "Chandrakanta perhaps never had more than 5 or 6 hundred men decently armed," Beng. Pol. Cons., July 26, 1822, No. 49.

79. Scott to Prinsep, June 25, Beng. Pol. Cons., July 5, 1822, No. 99.

80. Davidson to Scott, June 21, Beng. Pol. Cons., July 5, 1822, No. 104.

After his defeat Chandrakanta proceeded to Jugighopa in Company's territory. On June 23 the Burmese threatened to go during night to Jugighopa and seize the fugitive Raja. Lt. A. Davidson, Officer Commanding at Goalpara, despatched a sepahi to Jugighopa with orders to open Chandrakanta's boats from the *ghat* and send him to Chilmari.

Chandrakanta's defeat at the hands of the Burmese on June 21 marked the extinction of Ahom authority in Assam. "The struggle in Assam may be considered at an end," David Scott had written to Government on June 14. On the 26th he wrote,—"Chandrakanta's force has been completely dispersed, and it is not known what has become of him."[81]

Towards the end of June Mingimaha Tilwa, the chief commanding at the Assam Choky, was declared Raja of Assam. On July 11, 1822, David Scott informed the Governor-General,—"The Burmese having obtained complete mastery of Assam and a person of that nation having been appointed to the supreme authority, the country may now be considered as a Province of the Burman Empire."[82]

Settlement of Assamese refugees at Singimari: The Assamese refugees in Rungpore presented a problem almost similar to that of the Arakanese who had towards the end of the eighteenth century fled into the British district of Chittagong to escape from the oppressions of the Burmese. In the year 1819 several thousands of Assamese had taken shelter in Rungpore, and were deterred from returning to their country by the continuance of disturbances there and the dread excited by the excesses committed by the Burmese. The troubles of the subsequent period, 1819-22, had caused the influx of fresh bands of Assamese into Bengal. Chandrakanta is said to have been accompanied by one to two thousand Assamese when he entered Bengal after his final defeat at the Assam Choky. Most of the Assamese were rich people, and the Zemindars knowing that they would not settle for good in Bengal extorted from them as much money as they possibly could. The emigrants had to pay for a hut on the sandbanks or on the sides of the river as much rent as was realised from a garden and a house in the populous towns of Jugiphopa and Goalpara. These unreasonable demands on the part of the Bengal landholders dissuaded the Assamese from applying themselves to agricultural

81. Scott to Swinton, June 14, Scott to Prinsep, June 26, Beng. Pol. Cons., July 5, 1822, Nos. 97, 102.

82. Scott to Prinsep, July 11, Beng. Pol. Cons., July 26, 1822, No. 50.

pursuits, and they lived upon the capital which they had brought with them.

In May 1822 Scott suggested the expediency of offering the Assamese refugees a settlement under the immediate protection of Government upon the estate of Singimari in Rungpore which was remote from the frontier, and which contained a sufficient quantity of waste land to settle more than 200 families. He proposed to take from the Zemindar of Singimari a lease of the lands meant for the refugees for a period of about five years at a rent of 523 rupees per year. Before the expiration of that period Scott hoped the new settlers would be firmly established and be able to pay the perganah rates of rent. Scott's plan to settle the Assamese refugees at Singimari was approved by Government, and he was authorised to carry the arrangement into effect.[83] On the expulsion of the Burmese from Assam in 1825 the Shans who refused to go back to their country were settled at Singimari, and they supplied recruits to the Sebundy corps formed by Scott.

Burmese menace to British territory: The conquest of Assam by the Burmese increased the embarrassments and anxieties of the Government. Scott pointed out that a warlike and comparatively speaking powerful government was now substituted in the place of the feeble administration that had hitherto ruled Assam. The attention of the Government was first directed to the strengthening of the defence of the Rungpore frontier maintaining at the same time relations of friendship with the new neighbours.

The Burmese had given a forecast of their future dealings by plundering and destroying a number of villages in Habraghat perganah in Rungpore in November 1821. After the conquest of Assam they evinced a persistent haughtiness of tone in their communications, and contrived to use Assam as a base for operations in execution of their general design to expel the English from the frontier districts of Bengal, and if possible from India.

From Jugighopa Chandrakanta proceeded to Rangamati. For some time his movements were unknown to the British authorities, though possibly he was somewhere in Rangamati, Chilmari or Singi mari. Government had anticipated the eventual flight of the Assam Raja into Company's territories, and had issued instructions on the subject to the officers posted on the frontier. In 1794, in view of the disturbed condition of Assam Sir John Shore had

83. Scott to Swinton, May 8, Swinton to Scott, May 31, Beng. Pol. Cons., May 31, 1822, Nos. 44-45.

thought it probable that the Raja might be compelled to seek refuge in Bengal for himself and his immediate dependents. The Commissioner of Cooch Behar was accordingly authorised to afford him an asylum if it was sought. This proposal was approved by the Court of Directors.[84]

In December 1821 the Officer Commanding at Goalpara had received instructions from David Scott to give protection to Chandrakanta in the event of his being driven into Bengal by his adversaries. Chandrakanta's troops were to be asked to deliver up their arms with the exception of twelve men for a personal guard. That officer was also ordered to repel by force any attempt made by the Burmese to seize Chandrakanta or his followers in Bengal, but without pursuing the attackers into Assam. It was also resolved that Chandrakanta should be prohibited from going further down the Brahmaputra than Chilmari. These instructions were approved by Government in January 1822.[85]

On June 19, 1822, two days before the final defeat of Chandrakanta, some messengers despatched by the Burmese Sirdar informed Lt. Davidson that they had received orders from their general to follow Chandrakanta wherever he went and take him by force of arms, and that their army consisted of 18,000 fighting men and was commanded by 40 Rajas.[86] After Chandrakanta's defeat on June 21, Mingimaha Tilwa who had been in occupation of the Assam Choky at the head of about 7,000 men, sent a letter to David Scott demanding the apprehension and surrender of Chandrakanta. "If he is not taken," said Tilwa, "we wish without delay to follow him and seize him." Similar demands were made by two Burmese chiefs who had met Lt. Davidson on June 22, accompanied by a Portuguese interpreter named Charley.[87]

These threats of the Burmese caused considerable anxiety to Scott and Davidson. The detachment at Goalpara amounted to only 55 sepoys fit for duty. Opposite the river at the Assam Choky Tilwa was posted with an army of 7,000 soldiers, while Bandula was in the rear at Gauhati at the head of 10,000 Burmese. The speed of Burmese war-canoes was well-known. Reinforcements from the Company's headquarters at Teteliya would not arrive in

84. Bengal Letter to Court, Aug. 18, 1794; Court's Letter to Bengal, June 5, 1795.

85. Scott to H. T. Prinsep, Persian Secy. to Govt., Dec. 23, 1821, Prinsep to Scott, Jan. 11, Beng. Pol. Cons., Jan. 26, 1822, Nos. 77-78.

86. Davidson to Scott, June, 20, Beng. Pol. Cons., July 5, 1822, No. 103.

87. Davidson to Scott, June 24, July 13, 1822, No. 51.

less than six weeks from the time of making application for it; besides, the march of troops from Teteliya with guns at that season of the year appeared to be scarcely practicable. "I consider this place," wrote Lt. Davidson on June 23, "in great danger in case of an attack from the Burmese." He urged on the speedy despatch of at least one battalion and 2 or 3 six-pounders to Goalpara. He repeated his requisition two days later saying that the Burmese were planning to follow Chandrakanta and attack Goalpara as soon as they would receive a reinforcement from Gauhati. In his desperation Davidson asked Scott to detach at least a few troops to impress upon the Burmese that he had reinforcements at hand.[88]

In the meantime stray parties of the Burmese had committed robberies in the frontier villages of Rungpore and in the presence of British troops on one occasion. Some Burmese had carried off one 300-maund boat and 5 canoes from the Company's island near Goalpara and made 7 prisoners at that place. They had also captured 70 more boats besides a woman in Company's territory. Hearing of these outrages on the part of the Burmese all the native merchants left Goalpara, and no boat or boatman could be procured at that place. Davidson's establishment was reduced to three men.

On June 27, Jagannath Dhekial Phukan, then living at Paglatek, near Jugighopa, sent a letter to Davidson offering his assistance and requesting permission to engage the Burmese should they go so far down the river. Lt. Davidson refused the proffered help of the Phukan. The arms in his possession and in that of his brother Biswanath Marangikhowa were confiscated, and they were both removed to Chilmari. They were informed that if they again proceeded to Bhutan or elsewhere for the purpose of creating disturbance in Assam they would not be given an asylum within the Company's territories. Their eldest brother Ruchinath was in confinement at Rungpore as a state prisoner.[89]

The inadequacy of the British troops on the frontier compelled Scott and Davidson to treat with the Burmese in a conciliatory manner. Davidson received the Burmese, who occasionally interviewed him on the subject of Chandrakanta's surrender, with great cordiality. On one occasion he treated them with Hindustani sweetmeats; and on another, having nothing suitable to give in return for the presents he had received from Tilwa and Bandula,

88. Davidson to Scott, June 25 and 28, July 1, Scott to Swinton, July 8, 10 and 11, Beng. Pol. Cons., July 26, 1822, Nos. 48-50.

89. Scott to Swinton, July 11, Beng. Pol. Cons., July 26, 1822, Nos. 50-2.

he parted with a gold watch and chain valued at rupees 500 and a pair of European fox-hounds of the same price. This display of friendliness eased the situation to some extent.[90]

Scott was however convinced that the Burmese had not abandoned their intention of ultimately executing their threat to follow the refugees into Bengal. He realised that with the small party at Goalpara Lt. Davidson would not be able to protect so extensive a frontier, nor to oppose the progress of the Burmese down the Brahmaputra as far as Mymensing or Dacca and their subsequent return in safety to Assam. Scott therefore instructed Davidson to concentrate his efforts on the defence of Goalpara and the protection of the country below that place. The outpost at Mergram was withdrawn and that at Kamarpota was reduced to 1 Havildar, 1 Naick and 12 sepoys.[91]

Measures re: the defence of the Eastern Frontier: In a private letter of July 10, 1822, addressed to George Swinton, Political Secretary to Government, Scott described the danger threatening the Eastern Frontier of Bengal in consequence of the change of rulers in Assam. "Government will now begin to feel", said Scott, "the inconvenience of the line of conduct imposed upon them by the Act of Parliament, and will have to keep a much larger force in this quarter than would have sufficed in 1816, in six months to establish the Assam government on its former footing." He pointed out that the whole of Dacca, Mymensing, Rungpore and Natore districts were at the mercy of the Burmese who possessed the upper part of the Brahmaputra. If the Burmese planned to invade these districts, "5,000 men", said Scott, "would be insufficient to prevent them for re-acting on water, in their war-boats, the part of Pindaris in the South of India." Scott then alluded to the claims made by the Burmese to Dacca and to Captain Cox's representation to the Burmese government in 1797 of Assam being a tributary of the English Government. "It does not require much insight into Asiatic politics," said Scott, "to enable me to predict that they [Burmese] will not neglect the first opportunity of asserting their claims under the encouragement of being allowed quietly to possess themselves of a country that we not long ago declared to be a dependency of ours."

In Scott's opinion Government, from its experience with the Burmese in the mountainous tract bordering on Chittagong and

90. Davidson to Scott, June 23, Beng. Pol. Cons., July 13, 1822, No. 51; Davidson to Scott, Sept. 8, Cons., Nov. 14, 1822, No. 11.

91. Scott to Davidson, June 25, Beng. Pol. Cons., July 5, 1822, No. 101.

Tipperah, was justified to some extent in regarding them not sufficiently powerful to disturb the British possessions in the east. But the situation, he observed, was now completely changed owing to the occupation of the Brahmaputra Valley by the Burmese whence they could sail down and sack Dacca and the adjoining districts. The superior discipline of the British troops, pointed out Scott, would not be of very great help in a warfare which would have to be conducted during half the year in boats. It was well known that the Burmese prowling about in India for the past twenty years upon pretence of collecting king-fishers' feathers were acquainted with every creek and rivulet between Chittagong and Hardwar. Scott even anticipated that the Burmese might be provided with arms, officers and artillery men by the Russians "in the not impossible event of a war with them in the northward."[92]

On July 11 Scott wrote an official letter to Government requesting to be provided with 3 guard-boats to be employed for protecting the navigation of the river near the boundary between Assam and the Company's territories. He also pointed out the necessity of equipping a few gunboats adapted to the navigation of the Brahmaputra. He suggested that the permanent cantonment on the Assam frontier should be situated somewhere between Dhubri and Chilmari to avoid exposure to the noxious influence of the climate of the borders.[93]

To give forewarning to the frontier station of any unexpected irruption of the Burmese on the Assam borders Scott proposed to establish a chain of beacons on the tops of certain hills. Government was not in favour of this proposal as extensive alarm might be needlessly created if any hill-top were mischievously or inadvertently set on fire.[94]

That Scott and Davidson were not mistaken in their fears regarding an eventual attack of the Burmese is proved by the subsequent confession of some Burmese commanders in Assam who declared "that in 1822, Mengee Maha Silwa [Tilwa], at the head of an army of 20,000 men, deliberately meditated the plunder of Goalparah, and the adjacent country." That the Burmese desisted from such an attack was represented by them as an act of forbearance.[95]

92. Scott to Swinton, July 10, Beng. Pol. Cons., July 26, 1822, No. 51.

93. Scott to Swinton, July 11, Beng. Pol. Cons., July 26, 1822, No. 50.

94. Scott to Swinton, Aug. 15; Swinton to Scott, Sept. 27, Beng. Pol. Cons., Sept. 27, 1822, Nos. 66, 69.

95. Bengal Letter to Court, Dec. 23, 1825, A. White, *David Scott*, p. 78, A. 69

The forcible manner in which Scott explained the situation compelled Government to adopt precautionary measures for the defence of the Eastern Frontier. Government admitted the exposure of the inhabitants of Bengal along the Eastern Frontier to violence and plunder by the Burmese troops in Assam whose number was considerable and who could not be suppressed under the restraint of strict discipline. The whole frontier was placed under the special command of a Lieutenant-Colonel assisted by a Brigade Major. The river Teesta was considered to be the western boundary of his command, which would include the frontier of Rungpore, Dacca, Sylhet and Tipperah. The troops in Chittagong were left under a separate command. Government resolved to send a number of row-boats of the largest size armed with a 12-pounder carronade in the bow of each, and with 5 Golundauzes for each boat. These boats would be commanded by a subaltern of artillery and employed on the Brahmaputra. This flotilla was intended as an experiment to be withdrawn or increased according to circumstances. The corps to be employed in the frontier was to be composed of the Legion then in service in Orissa,[96] and the Sylhet Provincial. The new corps was to be designated as Rungpore Local Battalion, the headquarters of which would be stationed at Chilmari or such other central position as might be selected afterwards.[97]

Demands for extradition of Assam refugees: On July 9, 1822, a Burmese Vakil named Yagoung Yabo Noratha arrived at Rungpore to proceed to Calcutta for the purpose of laying before the Government representations respecting Chandrakanta and other refugees. Desiring to allow the unhealthy season of the year to pass over in negotiations and hoping in the meanwhile that the Burmese army would disperse for want of food, Scott sent up Noratha to Calcutta attended by a Chaprasi. The Vakil had evinced great curiosity about the roads, rivers and military resources of Bengal, and the Chaprasi was directed to watch his conduct. Noratha arrived at Calcutta in the last week of July and submitted two letters addressed by Mingimaha Bandula and Mingimaha Tilwa.[98]

96. This Legion was known as the Cuttack Legion, and was raised in 1817 in consequence of the disturbances in Cuttack. It consisted originally of 2 troops of cavalry, with 2 small guns, and 3 companies of infantry.

97. Govt.'s resolution, Military Dept., Beng. Pol. Cons., Aug. 9, 1822, No. 56.

98. Scott to Swinton, July 8 and 10, Beng. Pol. Cons., July 26, 1822, Nos. 48 and 51.

Bandula alluded in his letter to the treachery of Chandrakanta and his subsequent flight to Bengal. "A great intercourse of gold and silver, of purchase and sale," said Bandula, "subsist between the British and Burmese countries, and as he [Chandrakanta] entered the British dominions our troops with their commanders were withdrawn." In demanding the surrender of Chandrakanta Bandula reminded the Governor-General that from the Raja's extradition "the two great states will hereafter derive much advantage." Tilwa wrote in the same vein as his chief Bandula, and added the names of Biswanath Marangikhowa, Jagannath Dhekial Phukan and their principal compatriots in the list of refugees whose surrender was desired.[99] On September 2, Noratha submitted a third letter, supposed to be from Tilwa, repeating the demand. The writer adverted to the advantages of commercial intercourse between Bengal and the Burmese Empire. "Should the gentlemen of the Company need anything in Assam Wezalu," said Tilwa this time, "make me acquainted with it."[100]

Lord Hastings's reply to the letters of Mingimaha Bandula and Tilwa was conciliatory but firm. The Governor-General expressed his desire to promote the relations of friendship which had long subsisted between British India and Burma. He expected the Burmese generals and their subordinates to exert themselves in maintaining friendly relations with the British authorities on the frontier. The surrender of refugees, observed Lord Hastings, was contrary to the usages of all nations and specially of the British Government. "The British Government," said the Governor-General, "would have been guilty of a gross breach of the rules of hospitality had it refused to shelter Chandrakanta and his followers when they entered the Company's territory and threw themselves on our protection." At the same time Lord Hastings assured the Burmese generals that the British Government would not interfere in the measures which they proposed to adopt in regard to the rulers of Assam and the occupation of their country, and also that it would not permit the Assamese refugees to disturb the tranquillity of Assam which had been annexed by conquest to the Burmese dominions. Any such attempts, said the Governor-General, made by the refugees from their asylum in the Company's territories, would be instantly repressed, and if repeated, would entitle them to the certain forfeiture of British protection. Mingi-

99. Bandula and Tilwa to Lord Hastings, undated, Beng. Pol. Cons., Sept. 6, 1822, No. 20-21.

100. Tilwa to Lord Hastings, Sept. 27, 1822, No. 71.

maha Bandula and Mingimaha Tilwa were asked to restrain their troops from any further commission of excesses within British boundary. Repetitions of such aggressions, said the Governor-General, would be met immediately as an act of positive hostility and the Burmese authorities in Assam would be held responsible for the consequences. In conclusion the Governor-General adverted to the conduct of the Burmese authorities in Arakan in seizing and confining British subjects employed in catching elephants in Chittagong district.[101]

To give effect to the views of the Governor-General David Scott was instructed to ask the Assamese refugees to refrain from all attempts to disturb the peace of the frontier under pain of being delivered up to the Burmese. Chandrakanta's whereabouts being still unknown to Government, the instructions provided that on his appearance in Rungpore he should be compelled to abstain from collecting any body of armed followers and to withdraw to distance from the frontier.[102]

Assam chiefs invited to return: In the meantime there was seen a definite change in the attitude and movements of the Burmese owing to the reduction of their number by sickness and mortality, and the scarcity of food grains. Three hundred men and six captains of Bandula are reported to have died of cholera. Towards the end of July 1822 the Burmese troops retired from the frontier with the exception of a small guard at the Assam Choky. On August 1, Bandula left Gauhati for Rangpur; and Tilwa remained posted at Gauhati with only 1,000 men and no large boats. Bandula had more soldiers with him than necessary; and as he found difficulty in providing them with food he scattered them in the villages where they committed the most horrid atrocities upon the inhabitants. Bandula thought of taking his army back to Burma, if possible, through Assam, Bengal and Arakan.[103]

Before leaving Assam Bandula proposed to place its affairs on a proper footing. He declared his intention to remove Jogeswar Singha, the nominal Raja of Assam, from his office on account of his incapacity to govern. Bandula sent through Robert Bruce who had been employed by the Burmese for the management of the

101. Lord Hastings to Tilwa, Oct. 11, to Bandula Nov. 23, Beng. Pol. Cons., Oct. 11, 1822, No. 53, and Dec. 7, 1822, No. 64.

102. Swinton to Scott, Oct. 11, Beng. Pol. Cons., Oct. 11, 1822, No. 54.

103. Scott to Swinton, July 23, Beng. Pol. Cons., Aug. 16; Davidson to Scott, July 18, Cons., Sept. 6, Nos. 13-15; Davidson to Scott, Aug. 8, Cons., Sept. 20, 1822, No. 81.

custom house at the Assam Choky an invitation to Purandar Singha to confer on the subject of reinstating him in the government of Assam as a dependent of the king of Ava. On Purandar Singha applying for permission to proceed to Jugighopa for the above purpose Scott warned him of the danger he ran of treachery on the part of the Burmese. The negotiations between Purandar Singha and the Burmese were carried on till September, but they failed ultimately, the ex-Raja requiring terms which the Burmese were not inclined to grant.[104]

In October 1822 Purandar Singha submitted a petition to the Governor-General to be taken under the "fostering guardianship" of the British Government, "in the same way as are the Rajahs of Hindustan who benefiting by its aid and support are allowed to conduct the internal affairs of their own countries." He offered to pay an annual tribute of 3 lakhs and to defray the expenses of the troops which would have to be employed to recover Assam from the Burmese. Purandar Singha was informed through David Scott that his request could not be complied with as it was the practice and policy of the Government not to interfere in the affairs of Assam.[105]

During the continuance of the negotiations with Purandar Singha, Bandula and Tilwa had sent a message, through Lt. Davidson, to the Assam nobles Ruchinath and his two brothers Biswanath and Jagannath, inviting them to a conference at Goalpara in order to make arrangements for their return to Assam. The Burmese officers who had been deputed to Lt. Davidson with the message told him that Bandula intended to place some Assam chief on the throne though they could not say upon whom the selection would fall until they knew the fitness of the respective chiefs for that station. They further stated that "Assam is to remain dependent upon the King of Ava in the same manner as the Kingdom of Oude is at present dependent upon the British Government." Lt. Davidson shrewdly inferred from his conversations with the Burmese deputies that their plan was to make prisoners of the nobles and that they had no intention to give the government of the Assam country to an Assam chief.[106] Nothing is known of the result of these overtures with the three nobles; they obviously failed owing

104. Scott to Swinton, Aug. 6, Beng. Pol. Cons., Sept. 6, 1822, No. 12.

105. Purandar Singha to Lord Hastings, undated, A. Stirling to Scott, Nov. 9, Beng. Pol. Cons., Nov. 14, 1822, Nos. 39-40.

106. Davidson to Scott, Aug. 16, Beng. Pol. Cons., Sept. 6, 1822, No. 17.

probably to Ruchinath's confinement as a state prisoner at Rungpore from where he sent petitions to the Burmese to be allowed to return to Assam in response to which a Burmese officer was sent to escort him to Gauhati.[107]

The Burmese claim an island near Goalpara: Towards the end of August 1822, the Burmese resumed their haughty demeanour. Emboldened by the arrival of an additional force of 500 men at the Assam Choky the chiefs demanded the removal of the British flag from an island near Goalpara. A bamboo with the British flag had been erected at the time of the arrival of the Burmese at the Choky in June to distinguish the island from the Assam dominions. Lt. Davidson having refused to comply with the peremptory demand of the Burmese they threw down the bamboo. "The island is not worth a pie to the Company," said Lt. Davidson, but neither he nor Scott was prepared to give up an inch of British territory, nor to yield to such summary mode of settlement. Scott proposed to re-establish the landmark on the arrival of the gunboats at Goalpara. The incident was pointed out by Scott as a forecast of what was to be expected in future from neighbours like the Burmese.[108] A year later the Burmese massacred a small British outpost at Shahpuri Island, at the mouth of the river Naaf, in prosecution of their claim to its jurisdiction. These disputes over valueless sandbanks or islands were believed by all who were well acquainted with Burmese temperament at that time to have been got up to cover vaster designs of war and invasion.[109]

In October 1822 the Burmese, under the pretence of a boundary dispute, marched their troops into Bhutan. But the real motive for the expedition was believed to be the acquisition of certain gold mines in Bhutan, and the punishment of the Bhutanese officers for harbouring Assamese refugees. Mingimaha Bandula was himself encamped in Kamrup with 4,000 soldiers and 200 to 300 boats directing the operations against the Bhutias.[110]

Company's Assam policy in 1822-1823: As we have seen Lord Hastings in his reply to Mingimaha Bandula and Mingimaha Tilwa had, in view of the existing friendship with Burma, undertaken to restrain the Assamese refugees in Bengal from collecting

107. Davidson to Scott, Aug. 25, Beng. Pol. Cons., Sept. 27, 1822, No. 68.

108. Scott to Swinton, Sept. 2, Davidson to Scott, Aug. 25, Beng. Pol. Cons., Sept. 27, 1822, Nos. 67-68.

109. T. C. Robertson, *Political Incidents of the Burmese War*, 1853, p. 12.

110. Scott to Swinton, Oct. 29, Beng. Pol. Cons., Nov. 9, 1822, No. 42.

troops to invade Assam which was then a dependency of the king of Ava. David Scott was directed to carry out the intentions of the Government. The permission granted to the Assam chiefs in 1821 to transport arms and armed men across the frontier had been justified on the ground of there being no regular government in Assam at that time. The Burmese had all along complained that the Mugh refugees in Chittagong were assisted by the British in making incursions into Arakan; and Government was naturally anxious to avoid giving an opportunity to the Burmese to entertain suspicions in respect of the Assamese refugees. Whatever provocation the British Government might have received from the Burmese it was bound till the declaration of hostilities to maintain an attitude of friendliness and to abstain from giving occasions for complaint or retaliation.

Scott had warned the Assamese refugees not to recruit or assemble troops in the Company's territory. Chandrakanta then living in Paglatak in Goalpara seeing no prospect of regaining his throne with the help of arms made overtures to the Burmese commander at the Assam Choky. He was then in possession of a quantity of military stores including 200 maunds of gunpowder. They were attached under orders of Government and retained in deposit at Rungpore with the exception of the gunpowder which was destroyed.[111] In the meantime the Burmese promised to restore the Raj to Chandrakanta. Relying on this assurance, Chandrakanta deserted his Phukans and Baruas in February 1823 and proceeded to the Assam Choky where he surrendered himself to the Burmese chief stationed at that place. The Burmese conducted him to the capital Rangpur and kept him in confinement granting some allowance for his maintenance.[112] The credit which Chandrakanta had acquired by his patriotic exertions in 1821-22 and which had cost him two or three lakhs of rupees,[113] was bedimmed by this voluntary surrender to his enemies. This circumstance was pointed out by Scott in 1826 in submitting proposals

111. The arms in possession of Chandrakanta were: 51 guns, large and small; 61 Pahlangis; 88 muskets; 25 broken muskets; 18 Hindustani muskets; 5 broken Hindustani muskets; 49 bayonets; 22 swords etc.; 38 barrels of muskets; and 200 maunds of gunpowder,—Scott to Swinton, March 17. Beng. Pol. Cons., Ap. 11, 1823, Nos. 77-78.

112. Gunabhiram Barua, *Assam Buranji*, p. 202.

113. "With a view to protect this country I fought with the Burmese troops which cost me 2 or 3 lakhs of rupees, but owing to my evil destiny I was defeated,"—Chandrakanta in his memorial to Lord William Bentinck, Beng. Pol. Cons., May 30, 1833, No. 116.

for elevating one of the ex-Rajas to the government of a portion of Assam when he said,—"Chandrakanta's connection with the Burmese, his extreme imbecility of mind, and his indecision and aptitude to be misled, so particularly exemplified in the act of surrendering himself to the Burmese after fighting with them and flying into our territories, may be considered as objections to his elevation."[114]

After the surrender of Chandrakanta a number of Assamese refugees residing in the villages bordering on Assam made incessant efforts to recruit and assemble troops, in spite of the precautions of Scott. They were encouraged by the organised opposition offered by the Moamarias and other Assamese tribes, who unable to bear the tyranny of the Burmese, had united together and attacked the invaders on several occasions, and succeeded in recovering the upper part of Assam and cutting off the communications with Burma. Of the Assamese leaders who opposed the Burmese in Upper Assam the names of Matibar Barsenapati, head of the Moamarias, and Hao Sagar-Bara, head of the Baskatias on the north bank, come out prominently; and the leaders who made their last effort to recover the independence of their country from their refuge in Bengal were the Dihingia Phukan, the Siring Barbarua, the Gandhia Gohain and Lakhi Bara.

The Assamese refugees carried on their preparations by assembling men in the jungles round Goalpara. As many of the emigrants possessed considerable wealth they easily purchased the connivance of the police officers and the Zemindari *Amlahs*. One of the Assamese leaders actually offered a bribe of rupees 21,000 to Lt. Davidson; and it was reported that the Subedar commanding the post at Goalpara and the police officers had been given money and valuables to the amount of rupees four or five thousand. The leaders succeeded in collecting a considerable force in Bhutan and Rungpore which was commanded by the nephew of the Dihingia Phukan. To prevent the Assamese refugees from making preparations to invade Assam Government issued a notification giving them liberty to quit the Company's territory; and those who remained were to be removed to the interior and required to enter into an engagement, under a suitable penalty, not to proceed further up the river without the Magistrate's permission. The

114. Scott to Swinton, Ap. 15, Beng. Sec. and Pol. Cons., July 14, 1826, No. 2.

refugees named above were accordingly removed to Chilmari under Section 2 of Regulation 11 of 1812.[115]

In their despatch of July 31, 1823, the Government at Calcutta wrote to the Court of Directors,—"Our continued refusal to interfere in the affairs of Assam has by no means prevented the troubled and distracted state of that country from proving a source of embarrassment to the Government." It was also pointed out that the Burmese nation had, by the possession of Assam, come in contact with British territories at another and most inconvenient point, a situation made more dangerous by their acquisition of the command of the upper part of the Brahmaputra.

Events so developed in the Eastern Frontier and elsewhere that the policy of studied neutrality which Government had observed in its relations with Assam had to be soon abandoned. In November 1823 Government desired Scott to be prepared to encourage the disposition on the part of the Assamese to expel the Burmese from their country should the contemplated contingency arise.[116]

Burmese reign of terror: Mingimaha Bandula remained in Assam for some months to consolidate the conquest. Jogeswar Singha was still the nominal Raja of Assam in which office he had received confirmation by presenting to King Bagyidaw a female relation who was known in the Burmese court as Atau Meengh Terirenei Barkowanri.[117] The general direction of affairs was in the hands of Mingimaha Tilwa. The existing machinery of government was not disturbed, and the officials continued to be appointed from amongst the Assamese. The Buragohainship was held successively by Kalibar, Rupeswar and Kaliman; one Pijali became Barpatra Gohain, and Kotal's son Bargohain; the office of Barbarua was held in turn by Jabar Khampti, Badanchandra's son Piali, Bali Sandikoi and Bhadrachandra Sandikoi; Bagadamara and the same Piali became Barphukan.[118]

115. Scott to Swinton, June 3, Beng. Pol. Cons., June 13, 1823, No. 93; Scott to Swinton, June 15, Cons., June 27, 1823, No. 58.

116. Swinton to Scott, Nov. 14, Beng. Sec. and Pol. Cons., Nov. 14, 1823, No. 17.

117. One Dhutoowa Gohain, a relation of Jogeswar, had accompanied her to Burma; Dhutoowa became Governor of Menda Tin Myoo. Dhutoowa's son Gadadhar returned to Assam in 1830, Scott to Swinton, June 12, Beng. Sec. and Pol. Cons., June 25, 1830, No. 4.

118. Harakanta Barua, Assam Buranji, p. 94.

The weight of Burmese domination was felt in the arbitrary taxes imposed upon all classes of people and the manner in which the money was realised. Personal service in lieu of revenue which had been the general custom in Assam was abolished by the Burmese. The usual rate for commutation of personal service by money payment which was 3 rupees per *paik* was now doubled. The revenue collectors were allowed as before their allotted share of *paiks* as commission or salary. The *paiks* attached to temples had also to pay capitation tax at the rate of 6 rupees. The only relaxation was made in the case of the Pandits and Maulavis attached to the court who had to pay 2 rupees each, though like the temple *paiks* they had enjoyed complete exemption under the Ahoms. The Ahom priests, Deodhais and Bailungs, and the Hindu Gosains, as well as princes of the blood royal, were made to contribute sums fixed arbitrarily by the Burmese. In addition, the Burmese collected whatever gold they could lay their hands on.

The hardships of the arbitrary exactions can be understood from a few examples. The Barbarua had 6,015 *paiks* under him, of which losses by desertion and death came up to 969; and 918 men were appropriated by the Barbarua as commission which he had to share with his subordinate officials. He had thus to pay 24,768 rupees for 4,128 *paiks*. Under the old system the Barbarua had to pay only for a very few *paiks* who were permitted to commute their liability to personal service by pecuniary payment. The Barphukan had similarly to pay 47,790 rupees for 7,965 crown *paiks* in actual service; the Choladhara Phukan, 19,090 rupees; Bacha Rajkhowa, 16,668 rupees; and Khargharia Phukan, 16,308 rupees. The total number of *paiks* liable to pay the poll tax of 6 rupees was estimated by the Burmese at 89,850, of which 12,749 were runaways, and 12,546 engaged in the services of the revenue collectors. The total amount realised as *paik* revenue came up to 447,940 rupees as follows:—

From *paiks* liable to personal service	..	Rs. 405,930
„ temple lands, newly taxed	..	„ 18,666
„ courtiers, Pandits, Maulavis	..	„ 1,272
„ followers of Gosains	..	„ 11,447
„ arbitrary impositions	..	„ 10,625

plus 260 rupees weight of gold.[119]

119. Scott to Swinton, May 25, Beng. Sec. and Pol. Cons., July 7, 1826, No. 35.

The collections were made only once and during the year 1822, and it is believed that the Assamese accountants bribed the Burmese supervisors who accepted 25 per cent of the collections, so that Bandula received only a little more than a lakh of rupees.[120]

The Assamese were not accustomed to pay revenue in cash, and coins were not much in circulation. Parties of Burmese used to accompany the revenue collectors and to torture the poor ryots till they were compelled to deliver whatever they possessed. The collectors themselves were not spared. It was in the matter of revenue collection that the cruelties of the Burmese spread to the remotest villages of Assam.

Mingimaha Bandula returned to Burma towards the end of 1822 to play his destined role in the preparations for the conflict with the English. The affairs of Assam continued to remain in charge of Mingimaha Tilwa who was assisted by Sajati Phukan.

According to Burmese custom a provincial pro-consul had to appear before his monarch at the end of every three years. Tilwa who had left Burma at the end of 1820 now became impatient to return to Ava to pay his triennial homage. Fearing that the journey by the old route across the Patkai Hills might be intercepted by the insurgent tribes, Tilwa, in June 1823, asked for Government's permission to return *via* Rungpore, Dacca, Chittagong Ramoo and Arakan, with his suite consisting of 300 armed followers, 2,150 muskets, and a large number of Assamese slaves of both sexes. He promised to return in 12 months. The reasons assigned by Tilwa were his old age, the obstruction of mountains and rivers in the other route and the commencement of the rains. Government refused to meet Tilwa's request till compensation amounting to rupees 21,998 for the villages plundered by the Burmese in Habraghat and Doopguri had been paid. Even if a pass were granted to Tilwa, Government ordered that his suite was to be restricted to a small guard of 20 or 30 men, and that the bringing of slaves to British territory could never be countenanced.[121]

Failing in his project to return to Burma through Bengal Tilwa left Jorhat in September 1823 and proceeded through the Patkai Hills. In all likelihood he followed the route by which the Burmese had effected their last invasion of Assam and which lay through a depression of the Patkai range where its height is only about 2,500 feet above the sea.[122] Mingimaha Tilwa came again

120. Maniram's Ms. *Assam Buranji.*
121. Swinton to Scott, June 27, Beng. Pol. Cons., June 27, 1823, No. 61.

to the forefront in 1824 when at the head of 12 Rajas he commanded an army in Pegu in the operations against the British.[123]

Tilwa was succeeded in Assam by the Raja of Mogaung, Mingimaha Nund Kroden, generally known as the Burha Raja to distinguish him from his son the Deka Raja.[124] The Burma Raja's lieutenant was Moonkoong Aloonapoo, better known as Sham Phukan, who having lived long in Assam resented his supersession by the new governor.

The atrocities committed by the Burmese in Assam have passed into the common traditions of the people, and have been confirmed by the recorded versions of sufferers and eye-witnesses, and of those who had come in contact with them. The Burmese soldier was supplied with provisions only for a few days, and for the rest he had to forage in the villages. While in a foreign land they let loose their passions without any restraint. The commanders were incapable of checking the excesses of their followers, and even where they could they would not interfere as indulgences of that nature served as inducements to the Burmese to join an expeditionary force. The Burmese incursions in Manipur are said to have depopulated the country and removed all traces of Manipuri civilisation. The ravages of Bodawpaya and his predecessors had reduced parts of Siam into a desert; for years the fields round Tavoy were white with human bones. To escape from Burmese oppressions the greater part of the population of Arakan had deserted their country and taken shelter in British territory "where taxation was reasonable, and a man could go to bed at night without wondering whether his throat would be cut in the morning by order of some official."[125] It is believed that these oppressions and barbarities were committed out of deliberate policy to produce terror in the minds of foreigners so that they might abstain from provoking the wrath and vengeance of the Burmese.

The first outburst of Burmese outrages in Assam was seen when on their return in April 1817 they plundered the border villages and carried off women and slaves to their country. In

122. Col. W. F. B. Laurie, *Our Burmese Wars and Relations with Burma*, 1880, p. 75.

123. Wilson, *Documents*, Nos. 84-5, 102.

124. The Mogaung Raja was called by the Assamese Nara Raja, and belonged to the same family as the Ahom princes. Mungrimungram, so famous in Ahom history, was the ancient capital of the Mogaung or Pong kingdom, see Pemberton, *Eastern Frontier*, pp. 110-111.

125. Harvey, *Burma*, pp. 289-90.

1819-1821 they robbed, mutilated and killed all people who were suspected to have sympathy for Purandar Singha and Ruchinath Buragohain. The outrages were repeated with greater severity after the flight of Chandrakanta from Upper Assam and during the scarcity of provisions in 1822. But the most terrible atrocities were committed in their final retreat from Assam following their defeat by the British forces in 1825. They drove off before them all the young people they could get hold of. David Scott estimated the number of Assamese captives carried off into Ava to be 30,000.

The exact nature of the Burmese outrages can be understood from the following description by Maniram Dewan (1806-1858) who was an eye-witness: "Thefts were comparatively rare under the rule of the Burmese as they punished every thief by decapitation. In attacking the house of a rich man they would tie him with ropes and then set fire to his body. It was dangerous for a beautiful woman to meet a Burmese even in the public road. Brahmans were made to carry loads of beef, pork and wine. The Gosains were robbed of all their possessions. Fathers of damsels whom the Burmese took to wives rose speedily to affluence and power.[126]

A similar account is given by another author who received his information from Purandar Singha: "A number of men and women would be shut up in a house which would be set fire to afterwards. Youthful virgins were forced to become their wives. The people fled to distant parts of the country where they were plundered and killed by the Dafalas and other wild tribes. Villagers were robbed of their property and were subjected to inhuman tortures in the event of their inability to produce their money. The fathers of beautiful maidens had great credit with the Burmese; they would be readily admitted into their fold; and they would dress themselves as Burmese and commit excesses upon their own countrymen. The people taking shelter in forests did not fare better and babies in arms died for want of milk due to the starvation and death of their mothers. The Burmese dishonoured all women they came across in the roads and thoroughfares. The ugly and unattractive ones were left to the mercy of fate while their more beautiful sisters enjoyed the continued patronage of the Shan invaders. Daughters were molested in presence of their parents and wives before their husbands." [127]

126. Maniram Dewan's Ms. *Assam Buranji.*
127. *Asamar Padya-Buranji*, ed. S. K. Bhuyan, pp. 295-6, Analysis.

Major John Butler who came to Assam in 1837 and met many survivors of the Burmese rule recorded the story of a massacre committed in 1819-20 on the bank of the Kalang river. After having decapitated 50 persons in one day, the Burmese placed a large number of men, women and children on a bamboo platform inside a house erected of bamboo and thatch. They then set fire to the fuel placed round the building. In a few minutes 200 persons were consumed in the flames. "All who were suspected of being inimical to the reign of terror, were seized and bound by Burmese executioners, who cut off the lobes of the poor victims' ears and choice portions of the body, such as the points of the shoulders, and actually ate the raw flesh before the living sufferers. They then inhumanly inflicted, with a sword, deep but not mortal gashes on the body, that the mutilated might die slowly, and finally closed the tragedy by disembowelling the wretched victims."[128]

The conquest of Assam stimulated the warmindedness of the Burmese. It was triumphantly proclaimed in the Burmese epistles to the Government while enumerating the achievements and possessions of the king of Ava. For the first time the Burmese had a footing in the soil of India, and acquired sovereignty over a Hindu population whose co-religionists had been conquered by the English. The Burmese now considered themselves superior to the Hindus; and equal if not superior to the English.

Purnananda Buragohain had maintained eighteen companies of sepoys, dressed, equipped and disciplined like the soldiers of the Company's army. In their contest with the Assam chiefs the Burmese had encountered these imitation sepoys; and the ease with which they defeated the first men clad in red led the Burmese to think lightly of the wearers of the British uniform.[129]

The small detachments posted on the British frontiers adjoining Arakan and Assam were not calculated to convey a just impression of the real strength of the British army. The detachments were composed not of stalwarts from Upper India, but of men recruited mainly from the adjacent districts. The number of sepoys was just sufficient to protect British subjects from the hillmen in the neighbourhood. The Burmese had no opportunity to see the triumphs of the British in the wars with the great powers of Hindustan.

128. Major John Butler, *Travels and Adventures in the Province of Assam*, 1855, pp. 247-9.

129. Robertson, *Burmese War*, pp. 2-13.

Assam placed in the hands of the Burmese new facilities and resources which could be used in any future conflict with the British. It provided a suitable base from where they could proceed by water to Bengal and by land to Cachar and Manipur. Assam could, besides, supply soldiers and provisions to enable them to maintain their hostilities for any length of time. The effect of the conquest of Assam on the political schemes of the Burmese is conveyed in the suggestion of Mingimaha Bandula "that the English were mere merchants and such indifferent soldiers that it was unnecessary to send proper Burmese troops, and Assamese levies would suffice to conquer Bengal."[130]

Burmese aggressions in Chittagong, Cachar and Jayantia: After Bandula's triumphs in Assam the Burmese assumed a more aggressive attitude in their dealings with the English. The people, specially under the influence of the war-faction at the court, became impatient for hostilities. From the end of 1822 to the beginning of 1824 the actions of the Burmese were marked by an intention to offer studied affront to the English, inspired by their deeprooted conviction that in the event of hostilities victory was bound to come to "the invincible and virtuous arms of the sovereign monarch of the universe, King of all Kings, Lord of the seas and of White Elephants."[131]

Fresh troubles arose again on the Chittagong frontier when in February 1822 a party of elephant hunters in the Company's employ were attacked by a Burmese force, and six of the hunters carried off to Arakan where they were imprisoned and threatened with death unless they paid a ransom. The place where the *Kheddah* operations had been conducted being undoubtedly within the Company's territory Government wrote to the Raja of Arakan and the court of Ava, but no notice was taken of either representation. Some of the prisoners were released, and some died in captivity. In January 1823 the Burmese demanded duty from some Mughs who were British subjects proceeding in their boat laden with rice down the Naaf estuary. On their refusal the Burmese fired on the Mughs killing the steersman.

Reports were meanwhile received of the assemblage of Burmese troops on their side of the Naaf for the purpose of destroying the villages in the British territory. The military guard at the Tek

130. Harvey, *Burma*, p. 303.

131. Conventional epithets applied to the king of Burma, Scott to Swinton, Aug. 6, Beng. Pol. Cons., Sept. 6, 1822, No. 12.

Naaf was raised from 20 to 50 men, and a small outpost was stationed at the adjacent island of Shahpuri. A Burmese officer asked the Magistrate of Chittagong to withdraw the outpost at Shahpuri which he claimed to be a possession of the king of Ava. The demand was repeated by the Raja of Arakan. Government informed the Burmese authorities of its right to the island, and suggested that the claim should be examined by representatives of the two states. On the night of September 24, 1823, 1000 Burmese commanded by the Raja of Ramri attacked the British outpost at Shahpuri, killed 3 of the sepoys and wounded 4 others. On October 17, 1823, Lord Amherst, the new Governor-General, addressed a letter to the Burmese Government, recapitulating the past occurrences, attributing the outrage at Shahpuri to the local Burmese officers of Arakan and reaffirming the desire of the British to continue the existing relations of friendship. On October 29 a letter was received from the Raja of Arakan saying that Shahpuri was never under the authority of the English. "If you want tranquillity", added the Raja, "be quiet, but if you rebuild a stockade at Shelnma-bu [Shahpuri], I will cause to be taken, by the force of arms, the cities of Dacca and Moorshedabad, which originally belonged to the great Arrakan Rajah, whose Chokies and pagodas were there."[132]

In November 1823 the troops of the Government occupied Shahpuri. Two companies were stationed there for the protection of the island as well as a number of gunboats at the mouth of the Naaf. Two months later the outpost had to be withdrawn on account of the unhealthiness of the island whereupon the Company's pilot schooner *Sophia* was ordered to join the gunboats off the island to serve in some degree as a substitute for the troops placed.

In the meantime Government having received information that the Burmese were collecting troops in Assam, Manipur and Arakan to attack the different exposed parts, made arrangements, as a measure of precaution, for the immediate reinforcement of the small force on the North-East Frontier. Five companies of the Champaran Light Infantry were ordered to proceed to Rungpore, and five companies of the 1st Battalion 10th Native Infantry to advance upon Sylhet, and five companies of the 23rd N. I. to proceed to Jamalpore. The Commander-in-Chief Sir Edward Paget then studied the whole situation with the object of providing for the defence of the frontier as well as for offensive operations should war with Burma become inevitable.

132. Wilson's *Documents*, Nos. 21-22.

Early in January 1824 Mingimaha Bandula arrived in Arakan, as its new governor, at the head of 6,000 men and 2 commissioners, bringing with him positive orders to dislodge the English from Shahpuri. On January 20, Chew, commander of the *Sophia*, and Ross of the gunboats, with their crew were enticed ashore by the Burmese commissioners and sent as captives to Arakan. It was reported that Arakan was to be made a base for operations against the British, and that Bandula was soon to be joined by a fresh army of 20,000 men.[133]

Shortly afterwards the Burmese commissioners planted the flag of Ava on the island stealthily at night. Chew, Ross and their crew were released on February 23 under the orders of Bandula but no apology or explanation was offered for their detention. These acts were considered by the British as an obstinate determination of the Burmese government to establish their claim on the island even at the risk of precipitating a war with the English; and they were confirmed in their opinion by the aggressive proceedings of the Burmese in Assam, Manipur, Cachar and Jayantia.

It has been stated that after Bandula's invasion of Manipur in 1819 the country was ruled by one Shubal, the nominee of the Burmese. The Manipuri prince Marjit Sing had fled to Cachar where he and his brothers Chaurajit and Gambhir Sing established their authority and expelled the legitimate ruler Govinda Chandra who fled to British territory. A struggle for supremacy then ensued between the three brothers disturbing the peace of the adjacent district of Sylhet; and renewed applications were made by them and by Govinda Chandra for the intervention of the Company; but they were not acceded to as the situation in the frontier was not at that time supposed to be fraught with so much danger. Govinda Chandra being unsuccessful in interesting the British Government in his behalf appealed to Burma to aid him in the recovery of Cachar. The request was readily accepted, and preparations were made to despatch two armies, one by way of Burma and the other by way of Assam, to place Govinda Chandra on the throne and expel Marjit, Chaurajit and Gambhir Sing.[134]

On June 19, 1823, the Governor-General in Council, knowing fully that the Burmese had never made any claim to Cachar or to any right of influence in its affairs, had adopted a resolution to take the country under British protection on the usual condition

133. T. C. Robertson, *Burmese War*, pp. 24-25.

134. Wilson's *Documents*, Nos. 13 and 21 (C).

of political dependence. This measure was considered to be necessary in view of the occurrences of the preceding months. One of the passes from Ava to the Company's possessions lay through Manipur and Cachar, and the occupation of the latter was necessary for the defence of that pass. The dissensions in Cachar had disturbed the tranquillity of Sylhet, and the appeals of the four princes for assistance had caused considerable trouble and embarrassment to the local authorities. The occupation of Cachar by the British would give the opportunity to appease the dissensions. The conquest of Assam by the Burmese and the stationing of a force there made the acquisition of control over Cachar a matter of comparative importance.

The right of the Manipuri princes to transfer Cachar being questionable Government opened negotiations with Govinda Chandra, the legitimate heir, whereupon he abandoned his alliance with Burma. Government induced Marjit, Churajit and Gambhir Sing to accept pensions and the command of some Manipuri forces on the frontier. When the arrangements for defining the terms with Govinda Chandra were in progress Government learnt that the Burmese commander in Assam was preparing to despatch an army to invade and conquer Cachar in response to Govinda Chandra's invitation made previously to the promise given by the British to take him under their protection. David Scott wrote letters of remonstrance to Mingimaha Nund Kroden, the Burmese governor of Assam, briefly apprising him of Government's views and measures regarding Cachar and asking him to desist from any interference with that state.[135]

Jayantia bordering on Sylhet had been recognised as a British dependency since its restoration to the Raja's family in 1774. It was also in subordinate alliance with the Ahom government, paying an annual tribute which had, however, been suspended since the disturbances in King Gaurinath Singha's reign. The Burmese, as successors to the Ahom rulers of Assam, called upon the Jayantia Raja to acknowledge submission and allegiance to the king of Ava, to renew the payment of tribute and repair forthwith to the Burmese headquarters. The British determined to protect Jayantia from the Burmese. When pressed to enter into a treaty of

135. Wilson's *Documents*, No. 21 (A).

alliance with the British the Jayantia Raja declined to do so until, as he said, necessity for such a measure might prove more urgent.[136]

Towards the end of December 1823 a Burmese force consisting of about 4,000 Burmese and Assamese marched from Assam under the command of Nund Kroden, crossed into the plains at the foot of the Bhurteker Pass, and stockaded themselves in the village of Bikrampore in Cachar, 45 miles to the east of Sylhet. A stronger force advanced from Manipur and defeated the irregular troops under Gambhir Sing who had proceeded to oppose their march. A third force were crossing the Mulagul Pass into Jayantia.

To prevent these Burmese forces uniting or otherwise strengthening their position the British troops stationed on the Sylhet frontier were concentrated at Jatrapore from where Major Newton marched on the morning of January 17, 1824, for the purpose of expelling the Burmese from the stockade at Bikrampore. The attack was made in two divisions. The southern face of the stockade was assaulted by Captain Johnstone, and the enemy's line in the villages at the foot of the hills was attacked by Captain Bowe. The latter was immediately successful. The greater part of the enemy supposed to have come from Assam fled to the hills at the first fire. Captain Bowe then wheeled his force to the attack of the stockade which was vigorously resisting Captain Johnstone; and in a short time it was carried by assault by the united exertions of both parties. Major Newton then retired to Budderpore, 8 miles from Jatrapore. The Burmese then advanced to Jatrapore, near which they effected a junction of the two divisions from Assam and Manipur, and threw a bridge over the Surma river on both sides of which they erected stockades. Their united force amounted to about 6,000 of which 4,000 were Assamese and Kacharis. The Burmese had also a force of about 2,000 at Kilakandi. The manner in which the Burmese concerted the junction of the armies after marching from distant points was considered as evidence of their sagacity and discretion. David Scott arrived at Budderpore from Sylhet to maintain a more direct communication with the Burmese authorities.[137]

Mingimaha Nund Kroden in a letter to Scott declared that he had received orders from Ava to place Govinda Chandra on the

136. Wilson's *Documents,* Nos. 22 (a) and 23 (c). The engagements with Raja Govinda Chandra of Cachar and Raja Ram Singh of Jayantia were concluded on March 6 and 10, 1824, respectively.

137. Scott to Swinton, Feb. 6, Beng. Sec. and Pol. Cons., Feb. 13, 1824, No. 15.

throne of Cachar and to imprison Chaurajit, Marjit and Gambhir Sing who had taken shelter in British territories. He demanded the surrender of the three brothers and other Manipuri refugees. "If they receive protection," wrote Nund Kroden, "know that the orders of the most fortunate Sovereign are that without reference to any country, they must be pursued and apprehended." Scott in his reply of January 23 reminded Kroden that Cachar was under British protection, and called upon him to withdraw the forces to the places from which they came, adding that on refusal British troops would enter Assam and Cachar to effect their expulsion. In his letter of February 2 addressed to the Burmese commander in Cachar, Scott said,—"Hitherto you have experienced the advantages of being at peace with us; now, if you insist upon war you will also taste its bitter fruits."[138] To this letter no reply was received.

Soon afterwards a series of engagements took place with the Burmese on the frontier of Sylhet. The stockades on the bank of the Surma were captured by Captain Johnstone on February 13. The Burmese forces then divided themselves into two divisions; the portion which had advanced from Assam retreated to the Bhurtekar Pass, and the division from Manipur fell back to a place called Dudpati. The stockades at Bhurtekar Pass were occupied by Lt.-Col. H. Bowen on February 18. The Burmese division supposed to consist of 2000 Burmese and 3000 Assamese fled towards the passes into Assam. The attack made on the Burmese stockades at Dudpati on February 21 being repulsed it was renewed a week later after the arrival of a reinforcement under Lt. Col. Innes. The Burmese unwilling to try conclusions with a stronger force abandoned the post and retreated into Manipur. Thus by the end of February 1824 Cachar was relieved of the presence of the enemy. The British troops were withdrawn from Cachar for difficulties of supplies with the exception of a small detachment. For some months nothing of importance occurred on the Sylhet frontier.

Abandonment of non-intervention: On January 9, 1824, Lord Amherst had written to the Secret Committee of the Court of Directors,—"We have uniformly declined to listen to any overtures from the Assamese for assistance in their struggle with the Burmese for the independence of their country, and we will persevere in the same course unless some fresh act of aggression, on

138. Wilson's *Documents*, No. 22 (c) and (d).

the part of the Burman government itself, shall compel us to resort to arms."[139] The events of January and February proved beyond doubt that the security of the frontier could not be ensured unless the Burmese were made to feel the consequence of provoking the British Government.

Scott in his despatch of February 6, written from his camp at Budderpore to Lt. Col. Macmorine, Commanding on the Eastern Frontier, clearly explained the situation in that quarter. He amplified his views in a private letter of the same date addressed to George Swinton, Political Secretary. Scott pointed out to Col. Macmorine the three possible routes by which a Burmese army could enter Bengal: the first from Manipur by Tipperah and Cachar; the second from Assam by Cachar and Jayantia; and the third from Assam by the Brahmaputra in their war-boats. The first route which lay through impenetrable jungle in any season of the year could be defended by the inhabitants of Tipperah if provided with fire-arms. One battalion of sepoys stationed at Sylhet with detachments at Budderpore and Dumduma would be sufficient for the defence of that district.

The third possibility, *viz.* invasion from Assam by the Brahmaputra, was considered by Scott to be the most serious source of danger. "I must confess," said he, "that after mature reflection on this subject during the course of several years I am unable to devise any effectual and readily practicable means of meeting it, other than that of expelling the Burmese from the upper part of the river." It would be difficult, observed Scott, to overtake the Burmese war-boats once they passed the flotilla at Goalpara which they could do with very little loss in the daytime and still less danger at night. The Burmese canoes, narrow and long, each with 40 to 100 paddles rowed by the soldiers themselves, moved with great velocity, at the rate of 8 to 10 miles per hour, while the speed of the British gunboats was not more than 4 to 5 miles. The chief object of the Burmese being plunder and devastation, they would be joined in their expedition by their Assamese subjects, and, their countrymen and Mughs in Bengal.[140]

Scott assured the Government, through Swinton, of the offer of aid by the Assamese whose hostility towards their conquerors had been kept down by the fear of massacre of their wives and

139. Wilson's *Documents*, No. 23.

140. Scott to Macmorine, Feb. 6, Beng. Sec. and Pol. Cons., Feb. 13, 1824, No. 16.

children. It would be possible, observed Scott, to make arrangements for bringing the Singphos, Khamptis and other tribes to British interest, and to cut off Burmese reinforcements to Assam. The advance of the British troops, he pointed out, would give to the Government the whole means which Assam then afforded to the Burmese for the annoyance of the British. Scott urged the expediency of occupying the country up to Gauhati, if not up to Rangpur the capital of Assam, to prevent its falling again into Burmese hands. The climate of Gauhati was healthier than that of Goalpara in which opinion Scott was supported by Colonel Wood who had accompanied Captain Welsh in 1792-94 as Surveyor.[141] Scott also pointed out that the occupation of Gauhati would enable the Government to establish a route by which troops could march from Sylhet to Gauhati in 7 or 8 days and letters carried in 3 or 4 days.[142]

Whatever hesitation Government might have entertained was now dispelled by the clear exposition of the situation given by Scott in his letters to Colonel Macmorine and Swinton. "The arguments and observations", Government wrote to Scott on February 13, "which you have now submitted seem to establish satisfactorily the expediency of our advancing to Gowahatty and occupying the country between that place and Goalpara even as a measure of defensive policy." The Government authorised Scott to carry the proposed movement into execution within a month, and an adequate and respectable force was ordered to assemble at Goalpara by that time. It was also suggested that the inhabitants of the tract which the Government proposed to occupy should be called upon to rise in its support and that a distinct pledge of being released from the Burmese yoke should be given to them.[143]

On February 16 the Commander-in-Chief Sir Edward Paget communicated his opinion to the Government "that the insolence and encroaching disposition of the Burmese have now assumed such a decided character as to call for the adoption of the most powerful measures on our part to punish and humble that spirit.[144]

141. In connection with the projected advance of British troops into Assam Col. Wood was asked by Govt. to submit information about the climate and topography of that country, Home Misc. Series, Vol. 662, No. 16.

142. Scott to Swinton, Feb. 6, Beng. Sec. and Pol. Cons., Feb. 13, 1824, No. 15.

143. Swinton to Scott, Feb. 13, Beng. Sec. and Pol. Cons., Feb. 13, 1824, No. 17.

144. Wilson's *Documents*, No. 25.

The plan of campaign, which had been meanwhile decided, included the formation of three brigades, each composed of 3,000 men, to be placed at Chittagong, Jamalpore and Goalpara with a corps of reserve at Dinajpore, and an efficient flotilla on the Brahmaputra towards Assam and in the vicinity of Dacca.

On February 24 the Governor-General in Council published a declaration addressed to the government of Ava and to the princes and peoples of India setting forth the ground on which the British Government was compelled to resort to hostilities. It was followed by a public proclamation on March 5. The relations of peace and friendship between the East India Company and the state of Ava, declared the Governor-General, had been strained by the latter's acts of provocation and aggression, placing the two countries on the brink of hostilities, averted only by the moderation and forbearance of the British power. The Burmese, continued Lord Amherst, elated by their conquest of Assam had offered studied insult, menace and defiance to the British power; they had laid a false claim to the island of Shahpuri, and their official communications had been singularly boastful and insolent, and their interference in Cachar, Manipur and Jayantia had been unwarranted. The officers and crew of the Company's armed vessel *Sophia,* the Governor-General pointed out, had been released but no apology or explanation had been offered. For the wanton violation of the relations of friendship, Lord Amherst affirmed, he had ordered the advance of the force assembled at Goalpara into the territory of Assam to dislodge the enemy from their commanding position on the Brahmaputra, but was ready even yet to listen to pacific overtures on the part of the Burmese government.[145]

Within a short time after the declaration of war the force ordered to march into Assam was assembled at Goalpara, and on March 13, 1824, the troops moved forward from that place under the command of Lt.-Col. George Macmorine.

The advance of British troops into Assam marked the termination of the policy of neutrality which Government had uniformly followed in its relations with that country for the past thirty years, 1794-1823, with some small modification in 1821-22. The intervention of 1824 was warranted by the aggressiveness of the Burmese which had increased since their conquest of Assam two years before.

145. Wilson's *Documents,* Nos. 29-30.

Captain Welsh had pointed out the disastrous consequences of the withdrawal of British troops from Assam. For a numer of years after his departure the Assam government had made repeated application for arms and troops. Rajas Chandrakanta and Purandar Singha had at different times offered to become tributary to the Company. Similar applications for assistance were made by Bishnunarayan Darrang Raja, Kamaleswari Devi, Brajanath and Ruchinath Buragohain. There were thus many occasions when Government could have intervened to adjust the affairs of Assam, and restore it to peace and order, or otherwise afford assistance to the inhabitants to do so. That any such aid would have been used to advantage by the Assamese can be inferred from the results of the occasional supply of arms or grant of permission to transport military stores across the frontier. Sir John Shore's supply of 300 stand of arms enabled the Assam government to expel the Burkendaz bandittis from the districts round Gauhati. With Lord Wellesley's grant of 800 stand of arms Purnananda Buragohain maintained tranquillity in the kingdom for many years. Chandrakanta being permitted to carry to Assam 300 muskets and 90 maunds of gunpowder recovered a large portion of his possessions from the Burmese. The refusal of Government to interfere in the affairs of Assam had led Chandrakanta's agent Badanchandra to seek the aid of the Burmese who thereby acquired an authority fraught with danger to the safety of the outlying districts of Bengal. The Government thus gave to an enemy advantages which it might have used for itself had it acted with foresight.

Non-intervention had been tried in other parts of India, and it had proved to be an impediment in pursuing measures of political utility. The British Government invariably emerged into power and eminence whenever a farsighted Governor-General acted, as circumstances arose, with initiative, promptness and vigour.

One reason for Government's inaction in Assam is to be sought in its lack of sufficient knowledge of the politics of the countries beyond the North-Eastern Frontier of Bengal. The Company's Government was an interested and watchful observer of the interplay of ambition and rivalry of the powers of Northern and Southern India, and of the designs of remote European powers and of neighbours on India's frontier. It was not conceivable that any danger could ever emanate from an old-fashioned race like the Burmese. The sinister experiences of the British envoys at the Burmese court, and the boastful demands made by the government of Ava for the surrender of a number of Bengal districts, were viewed with comical interest rather than with any serious apprehension of future hostilities. So late as November 1823 the Adjutant-General informed the Government "that the Commander-in-Chief can hardly persuade himself that if we place our frontier in even a tolerable state of defence, any very serious attempt will be made by the Burmese to pass it."[146] In January 1824 when information about Bandula's preparations in Arakan to invade British territory was forwarded to Calcutta by T. C. Robertson, the Commissioner of Chittagong, it was received with indifference and partial distrust. "If I was not positively scolded," wrote Robertson, "for troubling Government with silly tales, I was greatly admonished to beware putting too much faith in the reports of my messengers."[147]

That Government was persuaded ultimately to take up arms was owing principally to the forcible manner in which David Scott exposed the dangers along the whole line of the Company's North-East Frontier, in his official communications to Calcutta, and in his private letters to his friend George Swinton, Political Secretary. The situation on the Chittagong frontier was examined in the light of the developments in Assam and Cachar, and Government at once decided that the Burmese should no longer be permitted to remain in authority in Assam or meddle with the affairs of Cachar. David Scott may be rightly considered to be the author of the proposal to send troops into Assam. He was vested with the power of directing the advance of the force assembled at Goalpara for that purpose.

Another reason for Government's inaction against Burma may be found in its preoccupation in Northern India and the Deccan. Lord Wellesley's career was practically spent in eliminating the further possibilities of French intervention. Lord Minto was concerned with the establishment of British influence in Persia, Afghanistan and Sind, and with expelling the French from Java, Mauritius and Bourbon. The Gurkhas, the Pindaris and the Mahrattas kept Lord Hastings fully occupied. When Lord Amherst assumed charge on August 1, 1823, he found the Company's Government of India in the highest possible state of security and power owing to the policy of his three predecessors which enabled him to turn his attention seriously to Burma.

146. Wilson's *Documents*, No. 24.

147. Robertson, *Burmese War*, p. 25.

CHAPTER IX

EXPULSION OF THE BURMESE

Plan of operations: The plan of operations determined by the Government was partly defensive and partly offensive. The Burmese had established themselves in Assam and Manipur, and had commenced hostilities to obtain possession of Cachar and Jayantia. Burmese troops had made hostile incursions into Chittagong from Arakan. In view of the difficulty of supplies and the long distances to be traversed over hills, forests and swamps, it was considered impracticable to penetrate into Ava through any of the above border territories. The course of operations on the Eastern Frontier was therefore to be confined to the expulsion of the Burmese from the British territories and the re-establishment of the states which they had overrun and conquered. The Commander-in-Chief was not prepared to recommend any other military attempt upon the internal dominions of the king of Ava from the Eastern Frontier "as instead of armies, fortresses and cities, he is led to believe that we shall find nothing but jungle, pestilence and famine." The only effectual means by which the Government proposed to compel the Burmese to treat was by an attack from sea on the vulnerable parts of their maritime province.[1]

The measures which the Government decided on adopting were, therefore, *first*, the expulsion of the Burmese from the territory they had recently annexed in Assam; *secondly*, to maintain a defensive attitude for the present on the Sylhet and Chittagong frontiers, merely strengthening the forces there, so as to prevent any further incursions from the Burmese forces in Manipur and Arakan; *thirdly*, to despatch an expedition by sea to subdue the maritime provinces of Ava, and, if possible, penetrate to the capital by the line of the Irravadi river.[2]

The brigade destined for Assam was composed of the following units and placed under the command of Lt. Col. George Macmorine of the 2nd Battalion, 21st Bengal Native Infantry, —a detachment of artillery with six 6-pounders, a detachment of irregular horse,

1. Letter from Adjutant-General to Govt., Nov. 24, 1823, H. H. Wilson, *Documents Illustrative of the Burmese War*, 1827, No. 24.

2. G. W. de Rhe-Philipe, *Narrative of the First Burmese War*, 1905, p. 35,

seven companies of the 2nd Battalion 23rd Bengal Native Infantry, six companies of the Rungpore Light Infantry, the Dinajpore Local Infantry and a wing of the Champaran Light Infantry, and a gunboat flotilla on the Brahmaputra. Information about the climate of Assam and the facilities for conveyance and supplies had been furnished to Government by Lt. Col. Wood who had accompanied Captain Welsh as Surveyor in 1792-94.[3]

Occupation of Gauhati: The major portion of the force under Colonel Macmorine moved from Goalpara by land on March 13, 1824, the guns being carried on elephants. The route lay along both banks of the Brahmaputra through forests and reeds, intersected at intervals by streams and swamps rendering the march extremely difficult and slow. Five companies of the 23rd Native Infantry under Lt.-Col. Arthur Richards proceeded up by water from Goalpara.

On March 27, Colonel Macmorine arrived at Palasbari, 14 miles west of Gauhati. An advanced party under Captain Sneyd came upon a number of Burmese, who being closely pursued took to flight and hid themselves in the huts of the villagers. From Palasbari Colonel Macmorine moved on to Pandunath, 5 miles west of Gauhati. Here he learnt that on the previous night the Burmese had evacuated Duar-garila, the fortified western entrance to Gauhati, as well as the stockades and outposts in and near that town. The reports were confirmed by the reconnaissance party who also learnt that the Burmese had retreated towards Rahachoky, 56 miles east of Gauhati, to join their comrades.

On the night of March 27-28 incessant roar of cannon-firing from the Burmese stockades at Gauhati had been heard at Pandunath. On March 28 the British troops entered and occupied Gauhati where they saw the effects of the cruelties committed by the Burmese before their departure. In a stockade a dead body was found with the head cut off and otherwise dreadfully mutilated. Fourteen Assamese chiefs had been killed by the Burmese on suspicion of their intention to come over to the British. Some 100 or 150 residents of Gauhati including several Marwari and Bengali merchants were killed on this occasion by the Burmese. The Raja of Luki Duar and several other chiefs were carried away as captives.[4]

3. Wood to Swinton, Feb. 11, 1824, Home Misc. Series, Vol. 662, No. 16, pp. 215-9.

4. Extracts from the Govt. Gazette, Wilson's *Documents*, No. 32.

The Raja of Darrang and several petty chiefs came to Gauhati and accepted the protection of the British. Reports were received by Colonel Macmorine that several Assamese tribes had assembled to cut up the Burmese and prevent their passage to Burma.

Proclamation to the Assamese: During the course of the preparation for war Government had framed the text of a proclamation to the people of Assam stating the causes of the hostilities and the reasons for which it could not so long interfere in the affairs of that country in spite of its regret at witnessing their miseries at the hands of the Burmese. 300 lithographic impressions in Assamese were made of the proclamation "the people in general being unable to read the printed character."[5] Scott being at Sylhet, Captain Davidson was ordered to accompany the troops to Assam and distribute copies of the proclamation under the instructions to be given by Colonel Macmorine. They were accordingly distributed after British troops had entered the territory of Assam. "Inhabitants of Assam!" the proclamation began, "It is well known to you that some years ago the Burmese invaded your territory, and that they had since dethroned the Rajah, plundered the country, slaughtered Brahmins, and women, and cows, defiled your temples, and committed the most barbarous outrages of every kind, so that vast numbers of your countrymen have been forced to seek refuge in our dominions, where they have never ceased to implore our assistance." The circumstances leading to the war were then briefly enumerated, concluding with the mention of the advance of British troops into Assam. The people were then exhorted to avenge their wrongs,—"The wished-for opportunity of relieving yourselves from the hands of your oppressors has now arrived. Come forward, therefore, without fear for the present or the future. Fail not, where you have an opportunity to wreak your vengeance on the remnant of those who have caused you so many calamities. We are not led into your country by the thirst of conquest; but are forced, in our own defence, to deprive our enemy of the means of annoying us. You may, therefore rest assured, that we will never consent to depart until we exclude our foe from Assam, and re-establish in that country a government

5. Scott to Swinton, Feb. 10. Beng. Sec. and Pol. Cons., Feb. 20, 1824, No. 7. The Assamese written script was considerably different from the corresponding Bengali, and still more from Bengali printed character. Assamese printed types had not possibly been set up in 1824.

adapted to your wants, and calculated to promote the happiness of all classes."[6]

The Burmese retreat to Moramukh: On the occupation of Gauhati by British troops the Burmese had retreated to Rahachoky, Nowgong and Kaliabar. They soon left their stockades in those places and retired to Moramukh in Upper Assam, 70 miles higher up from Rahachoky. Scott who had been at Sylhet marched to Gauhati across Jayantia with an escort of three companies of the 23rd N. I. commanded by Captain Horsburgh. On April 15, 1824, Scott arrived at Nowgong, one of the largest towns in Assam and extending for about 12 miles on both banks of the river Kalang, and containing about 4000 families. The inhabitants of the villages through which Scott passed expressed great satisfaction at the arrival of British troops. On April 17 Scott proceeded to Gauhati leaving Captain Horsburgh at Nowgong with instructions to clean that locality of the Burmese stragglers. Scott arrived at Gauhati on April 28.

Towards the end of the month the Burmese finding that no steps were taken to pursue them began to move towards their old encampment at Kaliabar and its neighbourhood. Having collected accurate information about the roads and the position of the enemy Colonel Macmorine despatched Colonel Richards to Kaliabar, to give protection to the inhabitants and to prevent the return of the Burmese to that quarter.

On his arrival at Kaliabar Colonel Richards found that a party of Burmese had appeared in a neighbouring village called Hatbar. Sometime later they evacuated their stockade at Hatbar and retreated to Rangaligarh at a distance of about 20 miles to the east. On Colonel Richards advancing with a small party to demolish the stockade he learnt of the return of about 60 Burmese to the place. On May 17, Lt. Richardson of the 2nd Battalion, 21st N. I., was sent to surprise the enemy with a *risala* of cavalry and a company of infantry. The Burmese were attacked by the infantry and forced to retire in the direction where the cavalry had been posted. The latter fell upon the enemy and killed 20 of them including a Phukan or Commander. Captain Horsburgh was stationed at Hatbar with 4 companies and the *risala* of cavalry.

On May 24 the Burmese advanced from Rangaligarh towards Hatbar and came within 300 yards of Captain Horsburgh's stockade. Their progress was checked by the picket under Lt. Jones till the

6. Wilson's *Documents*, No. 32; Home Misc. Series, Vol. 662, pp. 173-5, 373-4; Beng. Sec. and Pol. Cons., Feb. 20, 1824, No. 7.

rest of the men could be got under arms. The enemy had planted a number of *jinjals* in the jungle to the right of the road. The picket was ordered to proceed along the bank of the Kalang river. On the approach of Captain Horsburgh the enemy fled through the jungle leaving their *jinjals* behind. Meanwhile Lt. Jones with the horsemen cut off the retreat of about 200 Burmese, of whom 40 were killed by the *sowars*, a number were drowned and several were sabred or shot in the water. After their defeat the Burmese abandoned Rangaligarh and retired to Moramukh. In the meantime a party of Burmese had been defeated by Captain Wallace near Biswanath on the north bank.

The Burmese had erected at Moramukh a very large stockade on an open plain near a river. It was considered to be their chief rallying point and was commanded by Mingimaha Nund Kroden, governor of Assam, with a force of 1000. At Rangpur the Burmese had a force of 1000, and at Jorhat 100.[7]

Brigadier Macmorine died of cholera at Gauhati on May 30, and the command of the troops devolved on Colonel Richards. The rains now set in and further operations became impracticable. David Scott urged the continuance of the corps at Kaliabar or Rahachoky, and had even asked Major Cooper to proceed from Mangaldoi to Rahachoky to oppose the Burmese who might come down from Manipur and Cachar. Colonel Richards could not act upon Scott's suggestion, as the river Kalang, being narrow and winding, would not permit the swift passage of the fleet of boats extending to one mile and a half; and there was no other suitable place except Gauhati. Besides, the undefended condition of Gauhati might induce the enemy to attack it in which case the safety of the Company's provinces would be jeopardised. Colonel Richards returned with his force to the original headquarters in July.[8]

The result of the first campaign in Assam was decidedly favourable. British authority was established over Western Assam from Gauhati to Goalpara giving satisfaction to its chiefs and inhabitants who came forward with offers of aid against their common enemy. It was believed that if Colonel Richards had advanced soon after the occupation of Gauhati a greater portion of Assam could have been cleared of the enemy, their number and their equipment being in no way formidable. Captain Horsburgh had

7. Wilson, *Documents*, No. 32.

8. Scott to Swinton, July 10, Bengal Sec. and Pol. Cons., July 23, 1824, Nos. 9-10.

asserted that the 3 companies under him were adequate to repel the attack of the whole Burmese army then in Assam.[9]

Provisional administration in Western Assam: One of the reasons assigned by Sir John Shore for withdrawing Captain Welsh's detachment was the unwillingness of Government to occupy Assam which, it was anticipated, would be the inevitable result of any attempt made by the Company to adjust its affairs. In deciding upon the advance of British troops into Assam in 1824 Government had foreseen the same eventuality; and had, in the light of the existing circumstances, defined its policy respecting the future disposal of the province. "Although by our expulsion of the Burmese from the territory of Assam," wrote Swinton to Scott, "the country would of right become ours by conquest the Governor-General in Council does not contemplate the permanent annexation of any part of it to British dominions."[10] Scott had pointed out that during the continuance of the approaching hostilities with Burma a declaration on the subject of setting up a native prince in Assam would be premature and impolitic as it would discourage the people who had lost all confidence in their chiefs, "their imbecility, cowardice, and treacherous principles having been so fully developed in the last contest as to remain no longer concealed even to the meanest peasant."[11] He suggested that Government should retain possession of the south bank as far as Rahachoky on the Cachar frontier, and that Kamrup on the north bank should be made over to one of the Darrang princes who were always discontented with the Ahom rulers. Government accepted Scott's recommendation, and decided to retain possession of the tract on the south bank pending "the general settlement to be made with the tributary government proposed to be established in Assam." The degree of encouragement to be given to the Darrang Raja was left to the discretion of Scott. These proposals had been made previous to the declaration of war with Burma.

After the occupation of Gauhati by Colonel Macmorine arrangements were set on foot to administer the country from Goalpara to Gauhati, generally known as Western or Lower Assam, as distinguished from Eastern or Upper Assam where the Burmese were still in power. The chiefs of Western Assam, whom Captain

9. Scott to Swinton, Ap. 16, Beng. Sec. and Pol. Cons., May 7, 1824, No. 7.

10. Swinton to Scott, Feb. 20, Bengal Secret and Pol. Cons., Feb. 20, 1824, No. 15.

11. Scott to Swinton, Feb. 10, Beng. Sec. and Pol. Cons., Feb. 20, 1824, No. 7.

Welsh could not persuade to meet him, now proceeded of their own accord to Gauhati to see David Scott and his assistant Captain Davidson, and expressed their satisfaction at the expulsion of the Burmese and the establishment of British authority in that country.[12] The willing submission of the Assam chiefs and their offer of co-operation rendered the task of setting up an administration comparatively easy.

The occupation of Gauhati was immediately followed by a proclamation that strict punishment would be inflicted upon all offenders. The measures inaugurated by the Government for the administration of Western Assam proceeded on the consideration that it was an "enemy's country" and in military possession of the British. It was, therefore, not subject to the ordinary operation of civil and criminal justice administered in the British territories. Martial law being declared its administration was entrusted to the Officer Commanding Colonel Macmorine, and after his death to his successor Colonel Richards. As Western Assam had not yet attained the degree of tranquillity to admit of regular administration of justice, punishment of offences was left in the hands of the Officer Commanding.

The respective duties of the Political Agent and the Officer Commanding were precisely defined. Scott was vested with the general arrangement and control of all transactions and negotiations with the friendly native chiefs and with the Burmese as well when required. The collection of revenue was entrusted to Scott and his assistant Captain Davidson. They were however not authorised to call in the aid of the military power to enforce the collections.[13]

Scott's establishment was now considerably increased. He was provided with 7 interpreters and 12 messengers speaking Lepcha, Bhutia, Tibetan, Burmese, Manipuri, Khasi, Kachari, and Assamese languages. He had newswriters in Sikhim, Jayantia and Cachar. The staff representing the states with which the Agent had to carry on correspondence or diplomatic negotiations were placed under one Siddon, an uncovenanted officer of recognised linguistic attainments. Major R. Bayldon, Brigade Major, in his capacity as Deputy Post Master, supervised the Dawk for the conveyance of despatches between Kaliabar in Assam and Mymensing in Bengal, and maintained for that purpose 30 boats, some of which were furnished by the Assamese.

12. Scott to Swinton, May 12, Beng. Sec. and Pol. Cons., May 28, 1824, No. 19.

13. Swinton to Scott, July 2, Beng. Sec. and Pol. Cons., July 2, 1824, No. 16.

It was in the sphere of revenue collection that the labours of David Scott, as the first British administrator of Assam, were mainly exerted. In this matter he was influenced by several considerations. No innovation could be introduced in view of the temporary character of the occupation of the country by the British. Besides, the revenue system of Assam was highly complicated, admitting of many local and individual variations; and Scott with his limited staff had no other alternative but to carry on the old arrangements with native assistants. The assessment was to be as light as possible to allow the ryots to recover from the effects of the preceding disorders and to induce the refugees to return and settle in their former lands.

The basis of the old revenue system in Assam was the liability of every adult male to work for the benefit of the state for 3 or 4 months in the year, in lieu of tax on a limited quantity of land. Field-labourers were employed as soldiers, and in peace times in building and repairing roads and bridges, and in excavating tanks or similar works of public utility. These labourers were called *Kari-paiks,* from the word *Kar* meaning an arrow, as they were originally organised for military duties. Exemption from personal service was allowed when a *Kari-paik* was vested with some office, in which case his name was removed from the *Kari* rolls and registered with the Chamuas, the next higher order of subjects. Artisans, smiths, weavers, oil-makers, gold-gatherers, brass-workers etc., enjoyed their share of lands for their homestead and farm free of tax and without any liability to personal service on condition of supplying to the royal household and public stores certain quantities of the articles produced by them. Commutation or payment in money in lieu of personal service or payment in kind was permitted only to persons of superior birth or caste. This system enabled the Government to command the services of practically all the able-bodied men of the country. The numerous highways and tanks which we see in Assam are the products of the mass employment of the *paiks.*[14] The officers of the government were remunerated by allotments of *paiks* in lieu of salary. The *paiks* thus employed were called *Likchows.*

14. The Assamese *paik* system resembled to some extent the *Corvee* system in France according to which villagers had to do unpaid labour on the public roads. In towns the townsmen obtained exemption from personal work by supplying carts, draught animals, etc.—*Encyclopaedia Britannica,* 14th edition, under *Corvee.*

Each *paik* was given 2 *puras* (2½ acres) of first-class cultivable land free of rent. No direct impost was levied on his homestead and garden.[15] If he cultivated lands in excess of two puras he had to pay one rupee per *pura* of the additional land. If his services were not required, he paid a commutation tax at the same rate even for his original two *puras*. Four and sometimes three *paiks* formed a squad, called *got*, one of whom had to work for the government for 3 or 4 months, being replaced by another member of the *got* for the same period. Thus all the members of a *got* were employed in public work by rotation during the course of the year. The absentee member's fields were cultivated by his home-keeping comrades. The *paiks* were grouped into *khels* according to the nature of their duties, each *khel* ranging generally from 3,000 to 6,000 men. At the head of a *khel* was a Phukan or a Barua, who was assisted by a number of subordinates called Hazarikars, Saikias and Baras. This system is known as the *khel* system.

As payment of land revenue in cash was not universal in Assam, its annual collections were disproportionate to its population and its size. Numerous temples, religious institutions and individuals were exempted in perpetuity from the payment of land revenue, either wholly or partially. To increase the collections a poll tax in different forms was introduced in the beginning of the 19th century. In Kamrup Chandrakanta instituted a house-tax upon all subjects whether liable to pay land revenue or not. This tax was continued by the Burmese and came to be known as *Kharika-tana*[16] Its equivalent in Nowgong and Upper Assam was the *Gao-dhan* or body-tax, at the rate of one rupee per *paik*. In Darrang a hearth-tax of one rupee was imposed upon every family or person, cooking separately.[17]

Western Assam or the territory first occupied by the British troops comprised Kamrup, Darrang, Naduar, Dimarua, Rani and Beltola. Scott carefully studied the revenue system of Western Assam under the Ahoms and during its temporary occupation by the Moguls in 1663-67 and 1679-82, with the help of the papers in

15. F. Jenkins, *Report on the Revenue Administration of Assam*, 1849-50, in Selections from the Records of the Bengal Government, No. XI, 1853, p. 58.

16. It literally means the drawing out of a *Kharika* or a slender stick of the size of a knitting needle. The Burmese deposited at the headquarter a bundle of the specified number of such sticks against every collector, each stick representing a household from which he was to realise the tax.

17, Jenkins, *Revenue Administration of Assam*, 1849-50. p. 61.

possession of the Majumdar Barua who had held the office of Kanungo in the preceding regime. Scott had before him the register compiled on the survey of Assam during the reign of Siva Singha in 1742-43.[18] The papers supplied by the Majumdar Barua gave him particulars of a settlement made " 78 years ago ", i.e. in 1746, in the reign of Siva Singha's successor, Pramatta Singha (1744-51).[19] Scott, in the settlement of Kamrup, followed the assessment made in the latter survey.

The population of Western Assam was, during the first few years of British rule, about 350,000, of which some 18 to 19 thousand were obliged to temporary or permanent servitude of some form or other. There were about 11,000 adult male slaves debarred from the right of redeeming themselves or their posterity. There were about 4,000 bondsmen who, in consideration of receiving a specific sum, had mortgaged their labours for seven, fourteen or twenty years. There was another class of labourers who had voluntarily placed themselves under the protection of influential men working upon the latter's estates like absolute slaves from whom they differed in so far as they were at liberty to depart when they pleased.[20]

The revenue administration of Western Assam was to a great extent different from that of Eastern Assam. Kamrup followed the perganah system introduced by the Moguls which was confirmed by the Ahom King Chakradhwaj Singha (1863-70). The *khel* system was also partially introduced and mixed with the perganah system. For fiscal purposes Kamrup was divided into 26 perganahs each under a Chaudhuri who received as remuneration a certain portion of the lands under his management. Of the 220,520 *puras* of cultivable lands in Kamrup about half was alienated for religious and other purposes. Of the 16,512 *paiks* only one-fourth were in the direct service of the state, the rest being employed in the temples or in the fields of the officers and state proteges.[21] The *paiks* in

18. The register was complete as regards Kamrup. Two copies sealed by Scott were deposited, one in his own office and the other in that of the Collector of Kamrup. Mills's *Report on Assam*, 1854.

19. Pramatta Singha initiated settlement operations in Kamrup and made arrangements for the maintenance of records of rights, *Tungkhungia Buranji*, p. 49.

20. Parliamentary Papers, 1841, Vol. 28, p. 402; letter from Capt. A. White, Magistrate of Kamrup, to David Scott, August 9, 1830.

21. Scott to Swinton, May 12, Beng. Sec. and Pol. Cons., May 28, 1824, No. 19.

Kamrup had long been in the habit of paying pecuniary compensation in lieu of personal service. Scott continued the commutation system together with the house-tax introduced by Chandrakanta Singha. In his opinion the *Kharika-tana* tended to equalise the burden of tax from which many persons were exempted.[22] The lands granted by the Ahom Rajas to temples, religious institutions and pious and meritorious persons were known as *Nisf-Khiraj* or half-revenue-paying estates, as distinguished from Khiraj or full-revenue-paying estates. In course of time these lands were held revenue-free, and the owners called themselves *Lakhirajdars,* denoting total exemption from payment of revenue. Lakhiraj lands were classified under several heads,—*Debottar* lands granted for the maintenance of temples, *Brahmottar* lands for that of Brahmans, and *Dharmottar* lands granted for religious and charitable purposes, such as for reading the *Bhagavat,* performing the *Nama-Kirtan* [religious music and recital] and feeding pilgrims. Scott found that Assam Rajas had occasionally imposed a tax on Lakhiraj lands at five annas per *pura.* He continued this tax at the old rate and subsequently increased it to 7 or 8 annas a *pura* by introducing a tax known as Police Baragoni.[23]

The sources of revenue in the beginning of British administration in Kamrup were therefore,—the poll tax of rupees 2 on the state *paiks,,* the tax on the unalienated lands, the tax on Lakhiraj lands and the house-tax. Of the 26 perganahs Scott concluded settlements with 19; the remaining 7 being mere waste was managed by a Sejawal.

The assessment of Darrang was comparatively simple, and was made on the basis of the 21,500 *paiks,* one-fourth of which the Raja had to send to the Barphukan for employment in public work. The assessment of Rani, Beltola and Dimarua was made on what the Rajas voluntarily offered; and the same procedure was probably adopted in the case of the Rajas of Naduar.

The rates introduced by Scott in 1824 are not known. He considered the assessment to be very light, not amounting to one-fourth of the rates of land levied by the Zemindars in Goalpara

22. The *Kharika-tana* was realised in early British period at four rates on a valuation of the cattle of the farmers, *viz.,* rupees 3 for 1st class, 2 for 2nd, 1 for 3rd and 12 annas for the lowest class. Jenkins, *Revenue Administration of Assam,* 1849-50, p. 61.

23. *Sir Wm. Ward's Note on the Land Revenue System of Assam,* 1896, p. 69. This note was inserted as introduction to Gait's *Assam Land Revenue Manual,* 1896.

thana. The rates could not be higher than what he adopted finally in Kamrup before his death in 1831, viz., 8 annas per *pura* (1¼ acre) of *rupit* or first-class land, 4 annas per pura of *baritali* or homestead and garden land, and 2 annas per pura of *faringati* or land used for dry cultivation.[24]

The revenue demands for the first six months of the Bengali year 1231, April 12, 1824, to October 15, 1824, and the collections made, stood as follows ;[25]

Mahals.		*Malguzars.*		*Demands.*	*Collections.*
Darrang	..	Raja Bijoynarayan	..	Rs. 21,000	12,831
Assessed perganahs in Kamrup	..	The Chaudhuris	..	„ 34,150	21,532
Unsettled Mahals	..	Sezawal	..	„ 2,188	2,188
Naduar	..	The Rajas	..	„ 6,180	2,633
Dimarua, Rani, Beltola	..	The Rajas	..	„ 6,174	5,084
Brahmottar lands	..	The proprietors	..	„ 5,090	3,294
Devalay lands	..	The managers	..	„ 1,462	693
		Total in Narayani	..	Rs. 76,244	48,255

The land revenue of Western Assam for the entire Bengali year 1231, and for the subsequent two years 1232 and 1233 was respectively, rupees 171,824, 247,683 and 300,383.[26]

The above figures prove that the establishment of security produced a remarkably rapid improvement in the condition of the people.

Dissensions among the Burmese: Mingimaha Nund Kroden, the Burmese governor of Assam, was the Raja of Mogaung, a Shan state in Upper Burma in Myitkyina district, and a tributary to the king of Ava. He belonged to an ancient dynasty which had once ruled in the great Tai Kingdom of Pong now contracted into the

24. Kamrup Chaudhuris' petition, May 26, 1853, in Mills's *Report.* The terms are explained in Gait, *History of Assam,* p. 294, and *Assam Land Revenue Manual,* 1896, Introduction by Sir William Ward, pp. 79-80.

25. Scott to Swinton, Feb. 28, Beng. Sec. and Pol. Cons., April 5, 1825, No. 28.

26. Home Misc. Series, Vol. 671, pp. 816-17, The land revenue of Western Assam (Kamrup and Darrang) was in 1849-50 Rs. 444,531, Jenkins, *Rev. Adm. of Assam,* 1849-50, p. 52,

small principality of Mogaung. Sham Phukan, second in command to the Mogaung Raja in Assam, was a principal chief of Munkang, another Shan state to the north of Mogaung. Two and a half centuries of Burmese exactions, oppressions and misrule had reduced the Shan states to the lowest stage of calamity, and their relations with the government of Ava were far from being friendly.[27] During the Chinese wars in the reign of the Burmese king Hsinbyushin (1763-76) several of the Shan dependencies, including Mogaung, had co-operated with the enemies of their masters.[28]

Hoping that Mogaung Raja and Sham Phukan would be capable by their influence of performing essential service to the British Government David Scott sent messengers with letters suggesting that the war had offered an opportunity to the conquered Shan states to throw off the yoke of the Burmese. He promised to offer aid to the Shan chiefs to regain their independence and avenge themselves of the many injuries suffered at the hands of the Burmese. One Khangia Barua, an Assamese refugee, was placed in charge of the negotiations with the Shan chiefs and nobles serving in Assam. The latter sent a message to the Khangia Barua expressing their willingness to come to terms with the British. The Barua was also informed that either the Mogaung Raja or his son would soon come from their headquarters in Upper Assam to settle the preliminaries. Sham Phukan, who described himself as a subordinate agent of the Raja of Munkang, sent express horsemen to his chief for a decisive answer respecting the aid offered by the British Government.[29]

In the meantime a quarrel broke out between the Mogaung Raja and Sham Phukan and their respective adherents. Sham Phukan was the head of the *Purani Mans* or that section of the Burmese in Assam who had lived long in the country and had participated in the operations resulting in its conquest. They claimed the continuance of certain privileges which the governor of Assam, in his anxiety to free the administration of corrupt practices, was unwilling to concede. Each *Purani Man* of consequence used to have three or four wives and ten or twelve Doanias or naturalised Burmese. Sham Phukan and his followers being ordered by the

27. Rev. W. W. Cochrane's historical introduction in Mrs. L. Milne's *Shans at Home*, 1910, p. 29.

28. Harvey, *History of Burma*, 1925, p. 221.

29. Scott to Sham Phukan and Bagli Phukan, Sham Phukan to Scott, Wilson's *Documents*, Nos. 92-D and E; Scott to Swinton, Oct. 16, Beng. Sec. and Pol. Cons., October 29, 1824, No. 25.

Mogaung Raja to proceed to Dikraimukh left their wives and servants at the Burmese headquarters at Jorhat and Moramukh. During the absence of their masters the Doanias plundered the neighbouring villages of which complaints were made to the Burmese minister Peyanda Seik who ordered the reduction of each *Purani Man's* establishment to one wife and one Doania. This curtailment, subsequently approved by the Mogaung Raja, caused grave discontent and resentment amongst Sham Phukan's followers. Afterwards the wife of a *Purani Man* was seized under the orders of the governor for alleged indecorous behaviour in public and outrageously assaulted in the presence of the court.[30] The Mogaung Raja also put to death Sham Phukan's wife by drowning.[31]

On receiving reports of these proceedings the *Purani Mans* with their leaders Sham Phukan, Bagli Phukan and Nebaru Phukan, deserted their stockade at Dikraimukh and proceeded to the headquarters. A battle ensued between the adherents of the Mogaung Raja and those of Sham Phukan with heavy casualties on both sides. The former being discomfited left Moramukh and fled towards Nowgong to escape to Manipur by way of Cachar through the route he had traversed last year. His son the Deka-Raja fled by the route of Barphàlang Hills, sixty miles below Rangpur. Sham Phukan then proceeded with his men to Jorhat where he declared himself joint-Raja with Jogeswar Singha. The Mogaung Raja cleared the passage to Manipur over the hills inhabited by the Nagas in which work he employed the Rengmas and the Lhotas.

In the beginning of October 1824 the Mogaung Raja's followers scattered themselves in the villages round Rahachoky and Nowgong, pillaged the country and levied contributions from the people. They took possession of Kalita, Athgaon and Dhing. Ligira Phukan and Sooti Phukan were posted with 20 Doanias at Kerji in Athgaon, while 1,500 Doanias were stationed at Kampur and 500 Burmese at Rahachoky. A party of 140 men proceeded to Cachar. Another party plundered the outlying villages of Jayantia which had meanwhile become a British dependency. The Burmese prepared rafts to plunder the villages of the two petty states Gobha and Khola. The Mogaung Raja fixed his headquarters at Khagarijan on the site of the present town of Nowgong.

30. Maniram Dewan's Ms. *Assam Buranji*.

31. Scott to Swinton, October 16, Beng. Sec. and Pol. Cons., October 29, 1824, Nos. 25-26.

One of the principal adherents of the Raja was an Assamese named Nijapi who had joined the Burmese with 50 muskets obtained by him from Scott the previous April to assist the men of Nowgong to defend themselves. The depredations of the Burmese compelled the villagers to leave their homes.[32]

The Burmese retreat to Rangpur: The British troops remained in their camp at Gauhati till the middle of October. Colonel Richards was directed by Government to clear Assam of the Burmese in the ensuing campaign.[33] His force amounted to 3,000 men; and the total strength of the Burmese troops in Assam, scattered in different places, was supposed not to exceed that number. Colonel Richards had realised the necessity of marching the troops in the interior; and Scott having heard of the outrages committed by the Mogaung Raja's followers had shown considerable impatience to resume the operations to prevent the Burmese from recruiting their finances by levying contributories in Nowgong and elsewhere. But a forward movement was not practicable at an earlier period owing to the necessity of recourse to water-conveyance.[34]

It was not till the middle of October that Colonel Richards could despatch forces to repossess the country west of Kaliabar. Major Waters with a flotilla and a part of the Dinapur Battalion proceeded to Rahachoky and Nowgong by the Kalang river; and Major Cooper along the Brahmaputra with a detachment of the Champaran Light Infantry to Kaliabar.

On his way Major Cooper heard of the presence of 60 Burmese belonging to the Mogaung Raja at Dickari in Charduar on the north bank. They were commanded by Kakati and Hilli Phukans. A party of 40 sepoys was despatched in 3 police row-boats under Lt. Watson who surprised the enemy at Dickari and killed 6 Burmese including Kakati Phukan, took Hilli Phukan and several Burmese of both sexes prisoners. The Burmese released on this occasion two native Christians Henry Collins and Frederick Swain formerly in the employ of Robert Bruce at Jugighopa. Major Cooper reached Kaliabar on October 30 and found the post un-

32. Scott to Swinton, Oct. 17, Beng. Sec. and Pol. Cons., October 29, 1824, Nos. 27-28.

33. Wilson, *Historical Sketch of the Burmese War*, prefixed to the *Documents*, p. 44.

34. Scott to Swinton, Oct. 16, Beng. Sec. and Pol. Cons., Oct. 29, 1824, No. 25.

occupied by the enemy who were reported to have been principally collected at Nowgong.[35]

About the same time Major Waters who had proceeded by the river Kalang succeeded in expelling the Burmese from their stations at Athgaon and Rahachoky. He had arrived at Marikalang on the road between Jagi and Rahachoky on October 27 where he learnt of the presence of 250 Burmese at Athgaon. Major Waters with a detachment of 100 Light Infantry from the Dinajpore Battalion reached their position on the morning of October 28 after a fatiguing march of 7 hours. In the attack a number of genuine Burmese were killed, but the survivors could not be overtaken in their retreat as it lay through heavy ground and grass jungle. Major Waters was of opinion that if he had a party of cavalry with the detachment not a single man could have escaped. On November 1 two parties, one led by Lt. James Bryan Neufville of the Quarter-Master General's Department, and the other by Major Waters, surprised the enemy in their posts on the Kalang near Rahachoky. Lt. Neufville having pushed on for some time came upon the enemy's chief guard all of whom were either bayonetted or shot. On receiving alarm the main body of the Burmese rushed out of their houses only to be received by the party under Major Waters with great loss. The remainder were pursued nearly 2 miles and many killed and wounded in the jungles. A party of 60 Burmese having returned to Athgaon was ambushed by Major Waters and fled in confusion towards Nowgong after having half their number killed.

The Burmese had concentrated their strength at a distance of about 19 miles from Rahachoky under the command of the Mogaung Raja. Having heard of the reverses at Rahachoky the Mogaung Raja and his followers had moved to another station with the intention of crossing the hills to Manipur. On November 4, Major Waters pursued the fugitives for 25 miles, all covered in one march, at the end of which he bivouacked for the night. Having resumed the march next morning he came upon an empty stockade where he learnt that the enemy had proceeded too far to render a pursuit profitable. The British troops captured 20 iron guns, several boxes of powder, 3 war-boats and the state boat of the Mogaung Raja. The Raja's force was supposed to amount to 1,300 in all, of whom 500 were Burmans. It was not definitely known whether the

35. Major G. Cooper to Captain Bayldon, Brigade Major, Oct. 31, 1824, in Rhe-Philipe's *Narrative*, p. 254; also Wilson's *Documents*, No. 87 (b).

Mogaung Raja would attempt to cross the hills or skirt them in order to return to Moramukh or Jorhat. Major Waters took post at Nowgong leaving a Subedar's party and the gunboats at Rahachoky.[36] The whole area from Rahachoky to Kaliabar was thus cleared of the enemy within a fortnight of the commencement of the winter campaign.

The headquarters of the British troops were removed to Kaliabar on December 27, considerable time being taken in tracking the heavy boats against the current of the Brahmaputra. The people evinced a friendly disposition and there was no enemy to offer opposition. From Kaliabar Colonel Richards proceeded to Moramukh where he arrived on January 6, 1825, with the flotilla of gunboats and the main part of his brigade consisting of the 46th[37] and 47th Regiments, the Dinajpore Local Battalion, the Rungpore Light Infantry and a detachment of artillery.

Soon after his arrival at Moramukh Colonel Richards detached a company from the 46th Regiment under Lt. Jones against a Burmese party who had been reported to be stationed 3 miles off on the road to Jorhat. The enemy were on the move except about 10 stragglers who were pursued but without effect. The want of a small party of cavalry was felt this time as on several previous occasions.

Colonel Richards estimated the strength of the enemy to be between 6 and 8 thousand men of every description under Sham Phukan who was stationed at Jorhat. The Mogaung Raja and his son had in the meantime returned to Upper Assam in the hope of effecting a reconciliation, but they were both murdered by Sham Phukan's adherents. Parties of Burmese being posted at different places in the districts surrounding Jorhat and Rangpur Colonel Richards sent detachments to the different stations of the enemy.

Captain Macleod, commanding the Rungpore Light Infantry, was directed to proceed with 200 men of his corps to Kacharihat to dislodge a party of Burmese there who, if allowed to remain, would be able to command the road between Kaliabar and Moramukh and cut off the supplies. Captain Macleod was further instructed to send, after having expelled the enemy from Kacharihat, an officer and 100 men to Kaliani to surprise the enemy there. Lt. N. Jones of the 57th N. I. proceeded with a company from his corps to Dhodar Ali on the direct road to Jorhat to intercept the

36. Waters to Richards, Oct. 29, Nov. 3 and 6, 1824, Wilson's *Documents*, Nos. 87, (c), (d) and (e).

37. Formerly the 2nd Battalion, 23rd N. I.

fugitives from Kacharihat. Lt. Hopper of the 57th N. I. marched with a patrol of a company from that regiment towards Dergaon. Having learnt subsequently that there were 400 Burmese at Dergaon Colonel Richards despatched Captain Martin, commanding the 57th N. I., with a complete company from his corps to reinforce Lt. Hopper and to make the attack. Captain Waldron marched with 150 men of the 46th N. I. to attack a Burmese party of 120 men at Deoguru.

Captain Martin accompanied by Lt. Neufville reached the vicinity of Dergaon at midnight of January 10. They marched towards the enemy's stockade by making a detour to the right to avoid two advanced posts. But the enemy had learnt from their scouts of the advance of the troops who were now challenged by both outposts and their approach communicated by signal lights from the Chokies. The detachment moved on rapidly and entered the stockade as the last of the fugitives were quitting it on the opposite side. They were pursued to the jungle, and six men were killed and seven taken. After having destroyed the stockade Captain Martin returned to camp on January 13.[38]

Captain Waldron's party on arriving at Deoguru was informed that the enemy numbering about 100 or 120 had moved to a stockade at a distance of some 16 or 17 miles. Captain Waldron proceeded by road and then crossed the Dhansiri about a mile below the Burmese stockade which he reached at sunrise. A fog having enabled the party to come up unperceived the enemy were completely surprised, and about 20 men were killed including a Phukan or a person of rank. The remnant of the Burmese fled towards Kacharihat, which had meanwhile been occupied by Captain Macleod. These successes were accomplished within the course of four days, January 9 to 13, 1825.

The Burmese being thus expelled from their different outlying stations concentrated themselves at Jorhat. A proposal for an armistice was received meanwhile from Sham Phukan, but it was not found expedient to treat with the enemy at that stage.[39] The Burmese abandoning the hope of success in defending Jorhat set fire to their encampments at that place and retreated to Rangpur, the capital of Assam. Colonel Richards advanced in the direction

38. Martin to Bayldon, Brig. Major, Jan. 10, 1825, Wilson's *Documents*, No. 89 (B).

39. Scott to Swinton, Jan. 17, Beng. Sec. and Pol. Cons., Feb. 4, 1825, No. 25.

of Jorhat on January 17 with the intention of marching towards Rangpur.

Occupation of Rangpur by British troops: On January 25 Colonel Richards arrived at Gaurisagar eight miles to the west of Rangpur. The Dikhow being too shallow to admit the passage of big boats they were left at the mouth of the river, and the guns and ammunition were carried to Gaurisagar by land conveyance. A detachment of the Rungpore Light Infantry was sent under Captain Macleod to Namdang river over which there is an old masonry bridge on the high road to the capital. A considerable force of the Burmese attacked the advanced post at Namdang which was steadily defended by the British troops. On hearing the firing Colonel Richards moved to the support of Captain Macleod with two companies of the 57th Regiment and the Dinajpore Local Battalion. The enemy spread themselves to the right and left in a very heavy jungle, and those in the immediate front of the British troops kept up a sharp fire of *jinjals* and muskets. Colonel Richards ordered the party on the bridge to cease firing. Thinking the sepoys were meditating a retreat the enemy gained confidence and began to show themselves boldly. Colonel Richards gave them half an hour to collect at the expiration of which Captain Macleod charged the enemy's position with the Rungpore Light Infantry, and the Volunteer Cavalry under Lt. James Brooke.[40] The enemy fled after fighting for some time but were overtaken. In this charge 69 men of the Burmese force were killed amongst whom were 3 Phukans mounted on horseback.

Being repulsed at Namdang the Burmese retired to Rangpur in the vicinity of which they had erected a large stockade across the road with the entrenched tank Jaisagar on the left while the right was within gun-shot of the fort. The stockade was defended by more than 200 men and a number of guns. Two howitzers and two 12-pounder carronades having arrived in the meantime Colonel Richards advanced towards Rangpur at daybreak on January 29. The British force was saluted by a heavy fire from the stockade which brought down half of the leading division causing a momentary check. Colonel Richards then ordered a couple of shells and a round or two of grape to be thrown in, and Captain Macleod prepared to assault the stockade with the right wing of the 57th

40. Lt. James Brooke (1803-68) went home in consequence of his wound and afterwards retired from service. Latterly he became well-known as Sir James Brooke, K. C. B., Raja of Sarawak. He was Governor of the British settlement of Labuan in Borneo from 1847-1856.

Regiment assisted by a detachment of the 46th. This was done in a very gallant manner, and the enemy fled at the moment the troops began to scale and break down the stockade. Colonel Richards being slightly wounded Major Waters assumed the command till the former's return in a *dooly* or litter in about twenty minutes. Soon afterwards the two temples on the right and left of the stockade were occupied by which means the south side of the fort was invested and the enemy driven in at all points. Colonel Richards ordered two more guns from the fleet and arranged for mounting a battery. In the course of the day the troops fired a few rounds of shells, carcasses and round shots at the fort to give the enemy a specimen of the means of annoyance. Lt. Brooke was very severely wounded at the first advance to the stockade. The firing from the fort continued the whole night. On the morning of the 30th January the enemy came out in small parties and attacked the pickets but were compelled to retire.[41]

About 10 o'clock a flag of truce was seen coming from the fort, and with it appeared a Ceylonese monk, named Dharmadhar Brahmachari, the Rajguru or chief priest of the Shan and Burmese commanders in Assam. He was sent by Sham and Bagli Phukans, the leaders of the party willing to stipulate for terms. The opposite faction who were more numerous and powerful were bent on continuation of hostilities and threatened their pacific comrades with destruction.

Through the mediation of the Rajguru the preliminary terms for the cessation of hostilities and the surrender of the fort were settled on the first day of truce. Such of the Burmese who favoured continuance of war were permitted to return to their country provided they took the directest route, committed no ravages on the road and carried away none of the inhabitants then in their possession. The party numbering about 9,000 including 2,000 fighting men prepared to evacuate the fort on the morning of the 31st January and the rest were ready to surrender.

The various terms of capitulation were agreed upon in a conference with the leaders of the pacific party, Sham Phukan, Seik Phukan and Nebaru Phukan. The Phukans agreed that they and their followers would deliver up their arms and warlike stores of all descriptions, and would give possession of the fort as soon as the evacuating party should quit it. Colonel Richards permitted Sham Phukan and his followers to remain unmolested in their

41. Col. Richards's despatches of January 27, 29 and Feb. 2, 1825, Wilson's *Documents*, Nos. 90, 91(b) and 92(c)

present situation with their wives and property until the arrival of David Scott or instructions from him respecting their final destination. He also promised not to deliver them to the king of Ava should he make such a stipulation at the conclusion of the war.

These points being settled the Burmese Phukans expressed their willingness to surrender without delay, and Major Waters was directed to proceed with a party to take charge. The British troops at Rangpur had soon "the satisfaction of seeing His Majesty's colours flying on the top of the palace in the inner fort under a salute from the battery in camp." "By the acquisition of Rungpore," wrote Colonel Richards, "I may now consider myself in entire possession of Assam." The ex-Rajas Chandrakanta and Jogeswar were in the British camp on that memorable day.

The ordnance and military stores surrendered to the British force consisted of 22 brass guns with one 12-pounder, 943 iron guns including one 40-pounder, 332 muskets, 226 swords, 228 spears and several thousand iron balls and a considerable quantity of gunpowder.[42]

The peaceful evacuation of the fort of Rangpur followed by its immediate surrender conferred decided advantages on the British force. Colonel Richards had to depend for supplies on the fleet at a distance of 20 miles. The enemy could have held out for sometime as the fort was in a favourable situation being surrounded by deep swamps and jungle and a ditch, while on its gates and walls more than 200 pieces of ordnance were mounted ready for service. Even if Colonel Richards had succeeded in carrying the fort by assault he would have found it difficult, with his inadequate means, to prevent the escape of the greater part of the garrison or to pursue the fugitives. From the easy occupation of Rangpur which was centrally situated operations could now be conducted from that base against any future disturbance in Eastern Assam.[43]

Final expulsion of the Burmese: The fall of Rangpur practically completed the conquest of Assam for the enemy held no other fortified position in the province. But some time had to elapse before the country could be brought to perfect order. The Singphos, the most formidable of the Assam hill tribes, taking advantage of the anarchy and confusion, made frequent inroads into the districts up to the neighbourhood of Rangpur, devastating the villages and carrying off the inhabitants into slavery. The Singphos were

42. Col. Richards's despatch, Feb. 2, 1825, Wilson's *Documents*, No. 92(c).
43. *Ibid.*

notorious in those days for their total abstention from manual labour, and they depended upon the service of slaves for their very subsistence.[44] They were sometimes joined in their incursions by stray bodies of Burmese lurking in the frontier for opportunities of plunder.

Colonel Richards having heard of the presence of a party of Singpho marauders in a village on the Dalang Nandi, at a distance of 7 miles from Rangpur, despatched Captain Martin at the head of the mounted cavalry and 105 rank and file. The Singphos received intelligence of the advance of the British detachment, and left their stockade dividing themselves into three parties. Captain Martin pushed on the cavalry in pursuit of one party who were soon overtaken and dispersed. He came upon another body of about 30 armed men with several Burmese women amongst them. They threw down their arms and were secured for future investigation. Captain Martin in passing through a village in Kudulpara saw stocks in every hut for confining the villagers, and he rescued a few. Captains Chapman and Waldron were also sent against the Singphos, but the latter had fled prior to the arrival of the British parties. "Their [Singphos'] ravages in this quarter," wrote Colonel Richards, "seem to have been unusually barbarous and cruel; whole villages have been burnt to the ground and their inhabitants carried off into slavery."[45]

The final operations against the Singphos and the Burmese were prosecuted by Lt. Neufville in May and June 1825 from his camps on the Noa Dihing river in the country round Sadiya. After the expulsion of the Singpho raiders from the vicinity of Rangpur negotiations were conducted with the chiefs to bring them over to the British cause. Assurances were held out to the four Singpho *Gams* or chiefs of Bisa, Duffa, Luttora and Lattao that they would be allowed to retain possession of their lands if only they would give up the Assamese slaves and booty. The Singphos showed some inclination to enter into terms as they counted upon the British for protection against the Burmese. But no tangible progress could be made in the negotiations as the Singphos were stubbornly opposed to the restoration of the captives and plunder.[46]

Early in May a body of Burmese newly arrived from Mogaung pushed on an advanced party of 60 with 3 mounted chiefs to a

44. Mackenzie, *North-East Frontier*, p. 64.

45. Colonel Richards's despatch of Feb. 8, 1825, G. W. de Rhe-Philipe's *Narrative*, pp. 273-5.

46. Mackenzie, *North-East Frontier*, pp. 63-5.

village within an accessible distance from Lt. Neufville's post. On May 7 Lt. Neufville accompanied by Ensign Bogle left for the Burmese position where they arrived next morning. On being charged by the troops the Burmese immediately fled in the greatest confusion. The 3 Burmese chiefs sent a message to Lt. Neufville desiring him to return to Rangpur and quit Assam with the whole force. To this Lt. Neufville sent the following reply, "I have received your communication. If, my friends, you want us to quit the country of Assam, you had better come, and turn us out."[47]

In June several parties of Burmese appeared in the Singpho country in the cantons Bisa and Duffa. The Singphos, seeing that no measures were taken by the British to protect them against the Burmese made over the stockades to the latter, though at the same time they sent messages to Lt. Neufville wishing to be rid of the Burmese. On June 5, Lt. Neufville commenced his progress up the Noa Dihing river in covered canoes and rafts. On reaching Duffa he learnt that a body of Burmese of about 200 foot and 50 horse had taken post in a stockade in the vicinity. Lt. Kerr brought up his men to the assault, and they commenced firing upon the trenches. They were soon deserted by the enemy who pressed for escape through the gate at the opposite face. Without cavalry the enemy could not be pursued and they were soon lost sight of in the jungle.

The Burmese then concentrated themselves at Bisa, and as their works were reported to be very strong Lt. Neufville proposed to carry them by a night surprise. He marched towards Bisa on the afternoon of June 11. The enemy were now joined by the fugitives from Duffa, and the whole force was accommodated in a number of stockades belonging to the chief of Bisa with whom the Burmese had been acting in concert. On the approach of Lt. Neufville the enemy withdrew from an open spot into the stockade behind and were followed up by the troops. They then retreated from the first into the second stockade; and similarly they abandoned successively their five formidable defences without attempting a stand. Lt. Neufville's men advanced with their bayonets, and not a single shot had to be fired. On quitting their last stockade the enemy took to precipitate flight.

On the morning of June 13 Ensign Bogle with 80 men pressed upon the rear of the fugitives as far as the villages of Ninko and Kesson to the first pass in order to confirm their confusion and to

47. Wilson, *Documents*, Nos. 94 (a and b).

cover the escape of the Assamese captives. From the top of the first pass Ensign Bogle saw the extreme rear of the enemy soon clearing the second. Their flight was in great panic as was known from the gilt umbrellas, silver swords and other insignias of the chiefs abandoned on the route.[48]

The Singpho chiefs dreading the consequences of their conduct in harbouring the Burmese fled to the hills. Their houses were destroyed, and Lt. Neufville rescued on this occasion about 3,000 Assamese captives. Soon after Lt. Neufville with the aid of the Barsenapati, Khamptis and the Miris entered into the other Singpho villages to release the Assamese captives. Lt. Neufville's operations resulted in the submission of the Bisa Gaum and other Singpho chiefs in September 1825. David Scott visited Sadiya next year when 36 Singpho chiefs entered into an engagement acknowledging their submission to the British Government, and agreeing not to side with the Burmese or any other people to commit any aggression whatever, and to set at liberty any Assamese people whom they might seize.[49] Lt. Neufville released altogether 6,000 Assamese captives from the Singphos. The loss was severely felt by the Singphos, and as indirect compensation Scott proposed to create a trade between Assam and the Upper Irrawady which should pass through the hand of the Singphos. But effect could not be given to this project as Scott's hands were full.[50]

Operations in Cachar and Manipur : The occupation of Cachar and Manipur was much more easily effected than that of Assam, for after obtaining some victories in the engagements with the forces under Colonel Innes and Gambhir Sing in June and July 1824, the Burmese gradually retreated from their stockaded positions and ultimately withdrew themselves from that quarter. As the resources of the government of Ava were fully employed in the defence of Arakan and Irrawady no reinforcements could be sent to the support of its troops engaged in hostilities outside the Burmese borders.

In October 1824 Colonel Innes, commanding the Sylhet frontier, received reports that the Burmese army in Cachar posted at Tilain and Dudpati were retiring towards Manipur. It was confirmed by the reconnaissance party sent under Captain Hawes and Lt. Fisher.

48. Neufville to Brigade Major Martin, June 15, 1825, Wilson's *Documents*, No. 95.

49. Sir C. U. Aitchison, *Treaties, Engagements and Sanads*, 1931, Vol. XII, pp. 119-20.

50. Mackenzie, *North-East Frontier*, p. 64.

Towards the end of the month Colonel Innes proceeded towards the posts formerly occupied by the Burmese at Tilain and Dudpati, and directed the defences at those places to be destroyed. Captain Lister was posted at Tilain, and Raja Gambhir Sing at Dudpati with his Manipuri force armed by the British Government. On October 30 Colonel Innes was able to inform the Government that Cachar was entirely vacated by the enemy as far as Banskandy on the direct route to Manipur.[51]

In December 1824 a design was formed of marching a considerable force towards Ava by way of Cachar and Manipur on the assumption that if the Burmese could penetrate the jungles to invade Cachar British troops could do the same in the opposite direction. With this object an army of about 7,000 men was assembled at Sylhet early in January 1825 under Brigadier-General Shuldham, Commanding Eastern Frontier. The supplies were to be conveyed on camels, bullocks and elephants. 1,000 large and 4,000 ordinary bullocks were collected for that purpose. A road was constructed by the pioneers from Badarpur to Banskandy, and General Shuldham then advanced towards Dudpati with the artillery and the 3rd Brigade. An advanced party under Captain Dudgeon and Raja Gambhir Sing was sent to cover the pioneers who were engaged in opening a pathway from Banskandy to the banks of the Jiri Nulla, a distance of about 40 miles. The country from Banskandy to Manipur was a continuous range of thickly wooded hills, the base of the one touching the foot of the others, or separated by swollen mountain streams. The soil itself was soft and alluvial, and converted by a slight shower into a plashy mire. In carrying supplies to the pioneers and the advanced guard, several hundred bullocks and a large number of camels perished. Many elephants were lost on account of the exertions they had to make in proceeding through the mire.

General Shuldham spent about a month in moving his force from Dudpati to Banskandy, his advance being impeded by frequent torrents of rain rendering the road almost impassable. On reaching Banskandy the Brigadier-General examined the condition of the road to Jiri and found that it would not permit the sending of supplies on to the advanced guard either on camels, bullocks, elephants or men. After examining the position more closely General Shuldham was convinced of the impractibility of penetrat-

51. Innes to Adjutant-General, Oct. 25 and 30, 1824, Wilson's *Documents*, Nos. 96 and 97.

ing into Ava through Manipur. The scheme was abandoned and the force broken up and the headquarters removed to Dacca. A force under Brigadier-General Donkin was posted at Sylhet, and two corps of Native Infantry with the Sylhet Local Corps and the Manipur levy were left in Cachar.[52]

It had been ascertained that the Burmese in Manipur were not at all formidable. On the return of General Shuldham's force Raja Gambhir Sing proposed to recover Manipur with the help of his own levy formed of 500 Kacharis and Manipuris armed by the British Government. This being permitted Lt. Richard Boileau Pemberton volunteered to accompany the Raja for the additional purpose of obtaining some accurate information regarding the different passes into the country, its resources and the strength of the enemy. The force reached Banskandy on May 23, 1825. The difficulties experienced by General Shuldham in moving his large army did not prove insurmountable to Gambhir Sing's small force of hillmen. It advanced through constant rain and suffered all sorts of privations without the slightest appearance of dissatisfaction. On June 10 Gambhir Sing's force encountered the Burmese pickets stationed 12 miles in advance of the capital of Manipur; a large portion of the enemy was killed and some taken. On June 11 it was learnt that the enemy had evacuated the stockade in the town of which Raja Gambhir Sing and Lt. Pemberton took possession on the following day. The Burmese halted for some time at Undro, about 10 miles distant. Raja Gambhir Sing and Lt. Pemberton advanced to Undro, but after proceeding for six miles they learnt that the enemy had retreated from their last camp and altogether left the district. The two then returned to Sylhet leaving in Manipur a force consisting of 300 foot and 20 horse armed with muskets received from the British Government; to this force was added a contingent of 700 Manipuris armed in their own way. This force of 1020 men was considered sufficient to cope with any fresh invasion by the small parties of Burmese who might be still on the confines of Manipur.[53]

Treaty of Yandabo: The operations in Chittagong commenced with the attempt of Captain Noton to hold on to Ramoo at the head of only 1,000 soldiers, while the invading army despatched from Arakan by Mingimaha Bandula numbered 8,000. In the

52. Shuldham to Adjutant-General, Dec. 1824 and Jan. 21, Feb. 24 and 26, March 11 and 23, 1825, Wilson's *Documents*, Nos. 98 to 103.

53. Lt. R. B. Pemberton, to Quarter-Master General of the Army, June 14, 1825, Wilson's *Documents*, No. 104(b).

action that took place on May 17, 1824, the sepoys seized with panic at the sight of Bandula's cavalry threw away their arms and fled in spite of the exertions of the officers to preserve order. In the retreat Captain Noton and five other officers were killed, and 250 sepoys killed and wounded. The Ramoo disaster caused great alarm in Dacca, Chittagong and even in Calcutta. In the last place the European inhabitants formed themselves into a militia, and the crews of the Company's ships were landed to assist in the defence of the city. Some native troops stationed at Barrackpore made public avowal of their dread of the Burmese to whom they attributed supernatural powers.

The victory was, however, fruitless to the Burmese as they did not advance beyond Ramoo; and Bandula being recalled soon after to Ava the enemy abandoned the posts they had occupied in Chittagong and retired into Arakan.[54] An expeditionary force commanded by Brigadier-General Morrison was assembled in January 1825 in the vicinity of Cox's Bazaar.

The army reached Tek Naaf on the 1st February, and after a series of operations in forests and hills succeeded in capturing the capital of Arakan on April 1. The whole country was occupied by the end of the month.

The main theatre of war was, however, Rangoon and the valley of the Irrawady. In spite of the difficulties occasioned by an imperfect knowledge of the country, and its unhealthiness combined with the initial underestimation of the enemy's strength, the British army succeeded within the course of 20 months in pitching its camp within four marches of the capital and dictating terms to the government of Ava.

Sir Archibald Campbell, the commander of the oversea expedition, occupied Rangoon unopposed on May 11, 1824, and repulsed the attacks made afterwards on that city by Mingimaha Bandula who had been despatched from Ava at the head of 60,000 men including the troops recalled from Assam and Arakan. The stockades at Kokine which had been occupied by 20,000 men commanded in chief by Mingimaha Tilwa ex-governor of Assam, were captured by the British in December. In the meantime Cheduba and Negrais as well as Tavoy, Mergui and Martaban, were occupied by the British troops.

In February 1825 General Campbell marched north at the head of two columns, one proceeding by land and the other by the

54. *Frontier and Overseas Expeditions from India*, Simla, 1907, Vol. V, pp. 12-13, and 44.

Irrawady. The Burmese were occupying a strongly fortified position at Danabyu, 60 miles north-east of Rangoon, under the immediate command of Bandula. On April 1, 1825, Bandula was killed by a rocket, and with his death all resistance practically collapsed, for none of the other Burmese commanders possessed the military skill and leadership of that great general.

The British army continued to march onward and occupied Prome where they went into cantonment for the rainy season. In September, Burmese deputies arrived at Prome to ask for an armistice which they obtained. The terms proposed by the British included non-interference of the Burmese in the affairs of Assam, Manipur and Cachar. The negotiations having failed General Campbell detached forces to dislodge the enemy at several advanced positions to the north and the country round Prome. The enemy being completely dispersed the British resumed their advance on Ava in the beginning of December, 1825.

On the 26th, General Campbell received proposals from the Burmese to terminate hostilities, peace being advocated by the majority of the counsellers and relations of the king of Ava. In the conference that was held in a boat moored in the centre of a river between Malun and Patanaga, about 50 miles north of Prome, General Campbell, T. C. Robertson and Sir James Brisbane discussed the terms of the proposed treaty with the Burmese envoys. Mingimaha Tilwa was in the Burmese delegation on this occasion. The treaty was signed by the two parties on January 2 and 3, 1826, and armistice was agreed until the 18th to enable the envoys to obtain the necessary ratification. As the ratified treaty did not arrive in time, and as the Burmese did not show genuine indications of friendliness, General Compbell continued his march after having attacked and occupied Malun, where both the English and Burmese copies of the treaty, signed and sealed as they had been at the meeting, were found in the house of Prince Menciabu, half-brother of the king, which at once proved that the documents had never been forwarded to the king.

On January 31, The British army was met by Dr. Price, an American missionary, and an Englishman named Sandford, who had been sent on parole to communicate the king's sincere wishes for peace and to ascertain the terms. The two gentlemen were further authorised to tell the English commander that it was Mingimaha Bandula and not the king who had originated the war.[55]

55. T. C. Robertson, *Political Incidents of the Burmese War*, 1853, pp. 197-8.

General Campbell renewed the terms settled at Malun and promised to halt at Pagan-Myo for twelve days till the return of the delegates from the capital. The king resolved upon a last attempt to repel the invading British army, collected a force, by means of large bounties, and called it "Retrievers of the King's Glory." They were attacked by the British on February 9, and routed with great slaughter.

General Campbell continued his march and was met again at Yandabo, distant 45 miles from the capital, by Price and Sandford, accompanied this time by two Burmese ministers, and the British prisoners. The delegates delivered 25 lakhs of rupees, the first instalment of the indemnity of one crore demanded by the British. The terms offered at Malun were agreed upon. The Burmese ministers being authorised to accept whatever terms the British might propose, peace was signed on February 24, 1826.[56]

By Article 2 of the Treaty of Yandabo the king of Ava renounced all claims upon, and agreed to abstain from all interference with, the principality of Assam and its dependencies, and also with the contiguous states of Cachar and Jayantia. With regard to Manipur it was stipulated that should Gambhir Sing desire to return to that country, he should be recognised by the king of Ava as Raja thereof. The king also ceded to the British the conquered provinces of Arakan, Yeh, Tavoy, Mergui and Tenassirim.[57]

56. Col. W. F. B. Laurie, *Our Burmese Wars and Relations with Burma*, 1880, pp. 21-60; Lt. F. G. Cardew, *The Services of the Bengal Native Army*, 1903, pp. 146-53; Frontier and Overseas Expeditions from India, 1907, Vol. V, pp. 15-71.

57. Sir C. U. Aitchison, *Treaties, Engagements and Sanads*, 1931, Vol. XII, pp. 230-233.

CHAPTER X

ADMINISTRATIVE BEGINNINGS IN ASSAM

Plan of administration: As we have seen, Government had been in possession of Assam before the Treaty of Yandabo, and measures for its administration were being adopted in the course of its conquest. Gauhati was occupied by Colonel Macmorine in March 1824, and Rangpur by Colonel Richards in January next year. The letter which conveyed the congratulations of Government to Colonel Richards and his force was accompanied by general instructions "for the temporary administration of Assam pending the final decision of the Government regarding the disposal of the country."[1] Government had originally intended to establish a tributary government in Assam,[2] and after its conquest it was engaged in determining whether the whole province or a portion should be restored, and to which prince the restoration was to be made. Till a decision was arrived at and given effect to in 1833, the old native system was continued. Any modification that was introduced by the British authorities was intended to remove either glaring abuses or inconvenient practices, and did not alter the fundamental characteristics and forms of the older administration.

The Assamese system of government had preserved its traditional form, well suited to the peculiar conditions of its society and people. But the manner in which it had been administered during the last few decades, had rendered it odious to the inhabitants, specially when directed by the Moamaria rebels or the Burmese invaders. To revive the efficiency of the Assamese system and make it productive of good to the inhabitants was among the principal preoccupations of the first British administrators.

To undo the effects of the civil wars and the Burmese reign of terror which had dislocated the normal life of the people was another task before the new rulers of Assam. Almost every family had some tale of suffering, of being driven to hide in the jungle, of a brother or a sister killed, mutilated, assaulted or carried off,

1. Swinton to Scott, Ap. 5, Beng. Sec. and Pol. Cons., April 5, 1825, No. 25.

2. Scott to Swinton, May 12, Beng. Pol. Cons., May 28, 1824, No. 19.

or of property plundered. "When therefore we assumed the charge of Assam," wrote Lt.-Col. Francis Jenkins, Commissioner of Assam, 1834-61, "nothing could possibly be more unpromising than the state of the country. The small remnant of the people had been so harassed and oppressed by the long civil and internal wars that had followed the accession of Rajah Gaurinath Singh in 1780 down to 1826, that they had almost given up cultivation, and lived on jungle roots and plants, and famine and pestilence carried off thousands that had escaped the sword and captivity."[3]

In such a situation the Assamese hailed the advent of the British as a god-send. A contemporary Assamese ballad recording, in an unsophisticated manner, the sufferings of the people under the oppressive domination of the Burmese, says,—"The hearts of the people became glad at the coming of the English."[4] We have besides the testimony of two very critical Assamese, Maniram Dewan and Anandaram Dhekial Phukan, the first of whom was a youth during the Burmese rule, and the other was born four years after the Treaty of Yandaboo. "In the month of *Magh* 1746 *Saka*, [January 1825]," wrote Maniram, "the Sarkar Bahadur [British Government], having vanquished the Burmese, occupied the *Killa* of Rangpur, and brought the whole country of Assam under their subjection. As the reward of this pious action in rescuing the people of Assam from the sea of Burmese troubles, may God continue their uninterrupted and undiminished sovereignty till the end of a *Kalpa* [4,320,000,000 years], and make them as vigorous and powerful as the Lord of *Amravati* [paradise, i.e. Indra] and ever-glorious like Priyavrata Raja."[5] Anandaram Dhekial Phukan, the first Assamese gentleman to be educated on western lines, wrote in the same vein,—"Our countrymen hailed the day on which British supremacy was proclaimed in the Province of Assam, and entertained sanguine expectations of peace

3. Jenkins to A. J. M. Mills, May 23, 1853, in Mills's *Report on Assam*, 1854, Appendix B.

4. This ballad, known as *Barphukanar Git*, was orally circulated for nearly 100 years, and was first published by the present writer in 1924. See *J. R. A. S.*, Oct. 1925, for Lt. Col. P. R. T. Gurdon's review.

5. Ms. Assam Buranji, written in 1838 A.D. Maniram Dewan (1806-58) was executed in February 1858 for complicity in the attempt to set up Kandarpeswar Singha, grandson of Purandar Singha as Raja of Assam, see Sir Fred. Halliday's *Mutinies as they affected the Lower Provinces of Bengal*, 1858, p. 83. Priyavrata Raja is a mythical king, son of Brahma, and according to some, of Manu.

and happiness from the rule of Britain. For several years antecedent to the annexation, the Province groaned under the oppression and lawless tyranny of the Burmese, whose barbarous and inhuman policy depopulated the country and destroyed more than one-half of the population, which had already been thinned by intestine commotions and repeated civil wars."[6]

The difficulties which often beset the path of new rulers in establishing their authority were therefore not experienced in Assam. The masses looked upon the new connection with feelings of gratitude. The officers and nobles of the older regime willingly co-operated, whenever their services were required, in working their own system of administration under the superintendence of the British rulers.

Appointment of Commissioners: The first step taken by Government was the appointment of David Scott and Colonel Richards as Commissioners, the former to be in charge of Western Assam and the latter of Eastern Assam with headquarters at Gauhati and Rangpur respectively. Scott was declared to be the Senior Commissioner; and as Agent to the Governor-General he was authorised to negotiate with the Assamese and other friendly races, and even with the Burmese when required. The two Commissioners were independent in their jurisdiction, but were expected to act conjointly when together. The Commissioners were empowered to decide all civil disputes, and to administer criminal justice where they could pass sentence of 5 stripes and imprisonment with or without hard labour, and transportation for life. The Commissioners were not authorised to inflict capital punishment. The process of commitment by a lower magistrate was dispensed with, and the Commissioners were permitted to take up criminal cases directly and pass sentence. They were also empowered to introduce a police system and set up jails in each division.[7] Western and Eastern Assam were known from that time as *Senior Khanda* and *Junior Khanda* respectively.

In December 1825 Colonel Richards resigned his appointment as Junior Commissioner and was succeeded by Colonel Cooper who was also the commander of the troops in Assam. On Scott's request for European assistants Captain Adam White of the 59th Regiment, and author of "Considerations on the State of British

6. *Observations on the Administration of the Province of Assam*, in Mills's Report.

7. Swinton to Scott, Ap. 5, Beng. Sec. and Pol. Cons., April 5, 1825, No. 24.

India", was appointed in December 1825 to assist him at Gauhati.[8] In March 1828 Government decided to withdraw the regular troops from Eastern Assam and place that division under civil management, and Lt. Neufville, who had distinguished himself in the operations against the Singphos and had remained in political charge of Sadiya, was appointed Junior Commissioner to administer Eastern Assam and command the troops embodied for the defence of that part of the province. On Captain Neufville's death in July 1830 Captain White was appointed to Upper Assam, but he could join his new duties only on October 1, 1831, Lt. James Matthie having officiated in the interval. Captain Davidson, Assistant to David Scott, remained in Judicial and Revenue charge of the North-East Parts of Rungpore with headquarters at Goalpara.

Measures for defence and security: Soon after the occupation of Assam arrangements were made for its defence, specially with regard to the possibility of incursions by the Burmese, and the Singphos and other hostile and predatory tribes. Biswanath was selected for the headquarter of the British troops. Fieldworks were to be thrown up at Jorhat, Barhat and Sadiya. Colonel Richards suggested the maintenance of a few steam boats in Assam for towing up supplies, stores and troops.[9] Both he and Scott urged the construction of a road across the hills between Sylhet and Gauhati, and work was begun in 1827 from Cherapoonji *via* Nungklao, 20 miles west of Shillong. Tirut Sing, the Siem or chief of Nungklao, and other Khasi chiefs gave their consent to the construction of the road through their territories after a great deal of hesitation. The road was fairly complete by the beginning of 1829. A few bungalows were erected at Nungklao which Scott proposed to develop as a sanitarium for the province. Lt. Bedingfield and Lt. Burlton were at that time at Nungklao for the benefit of their health with a small guard of the Assam Light Infantry. On April 4, 1829, a party of 500 Khasis, being alarmed by reports that they would soon be subjected to taxation, made a sudden attack on the British party at Nungklao killing Lt. Bedingfield on the spot. Lt. Burlton with 50 or 60 followers was killed the next day while retreating towards Assam. David Scott who was on his way from Nungklao to Cherapoonji was invited by the Khasis to pass the night in a village inimical to the British alliance. His

8 Swinton to Scott, Dec. 16, Beng. Sec. and Pol. Cons., Dec. 16, 1825, Nos. 25 and 27.

9. Richards to Scott, Oct. 7, 1825, Beng. Sec. and Pol. Cons., Jan. 6, 1826, No. 43.

suspicions being roused Scott pushed on rapidly to a safer place, where he passed the night and thus saved his life. A desultory conflict was maintained with the Khasis for two years until at length tranquillity was restored in 1832.[10] The road, known as "Brigg's Trace," was rarely used, and was practically abandoned when Shillong, the present capital and sanitarium of Assam, came into being.[11]

The British force which had been employed in the operations of 1824 and 1825 remained in the province till 1828 when Government passed orders for their withdrawal leaving in Assam only the Rungpore Light Infantry. This regiment had been raised at Cuttack in 1817 as an irregular force by Captain S. Fraser and was known as Cuttack Legion. In 1823 it was formed into a regular corps and transferred to Rungpore in Bengal when it was renamed "The Rungpore Light Infantry." In 1827 after three years of service in Assam it was known as the 1st Assam Light Infantry and had its headquarters at Biswanath.

In 1828 the A. L. Infantry was strengthened by the addition of two companies from the Sylhet Local Corps. Its strength finally rose to about a thousand men consisting mainly of Gurkhas and Hindustanis. In 1829 the commandant of the force was Captain J. B. Neufville; and Lts. A. Charlton and James Matthie were Second in Command and Adjutant respectively. Another battalion raised in 1835 at Sadiya was known as the "Assam Sebundy Corps (Irregulars)." In 1843 it was brought on to the strength of the Bengal army and renamed "2nd Assam Light Infantry."[12]

In addition to the regular troops there was in Assam a semi-military "Levy" or militia body trained in an elementary fashion. It was under the civil Government and officered by Civil Police officials. The first unit of this force was organised in 1835 and called the "Cachar Levy." Another was raised three years afterwards and known as the "Jorhat Militia." These two forces had to perform arduous duties in connection with the defence of the Eastern Frontier from the Brahmaputra river to Cachar supported by strong detachments of troops at Nowgong and Silchar. The other parts of the Eastern Frontier were guarded by troops and the armed

10. Major White, *Memoir of David Scott*, pp. 40-42; Cardew, *Services of the Bengal Native Army*, p. 157; Gait, *History of Assam*, p. 302.

11. Colonel L. W. Shakespear, *History of the Assam Rifles*, p. 12.

12. The two regiments, 1st and 2nd A. L. I. are now known respectively as 6th and 2/8th Goorkha Rifles.

Civil Police. The Cachar Levy formed the first unit of the force which is now known as the Assam Rifles.[13]

Divisions of Assam: The two divisions Western Assam and Eastern Assam require some explanation at this stage, for their limits, never rigidly defined, underwest considerable fluctuations in the early years of British rule. Western Assam extended in Scott's time from Goalpara to Biswanath; it was thus equivalent to the present districts of Kamrup, Nowgong and the greater portion of Darrang. Biswanath was selected for its comparative healthiness as the headquarter of the British troops, and a few detachments were stationed there in 1825. The terms "Western Assam" and "Eastern Assam" were gradually dropped in official correspondence, and were replaced by "Lower Assam" and "Upper Assam," respectively.

Eastern Assam, according to the division of Scott, covered roughly the present districts of Sibsagar, Lakhimpur, a small portion of Darrang, and the Sadiya Frontier Tract. It thus included three minor tracts of considerable political importance, *viz.*, the territories occupied by the Moamarias, the Khamptis and Singphos; and as they were managed at first from the British station of Sadiya they were generally known as the Sadiya country, and the name "Upper Assam" came to be strictly applied to the intervening districts between Lower Assam and the Sadiya country.[14]

The Matak country or the tract occupied by the Moamarias lay between the Brahmaputra and the Buri-Dihing and extended as far as Sadiya. Its ruler was called the Barsenapàti, whose independence had been acknowledged by Purnananda Buragohain and survived the Burmese troubles. In May 1826, Matibar Barsenąpati entered into an engagement with David Scott in which he promised to furnish 280 *paiks* to the British Government. He was allowed to dispose of petty criminal cases in his jurisdiction, but was required to send up serious cases to the British courts with the results of his investigation. The district round Sadiya had been in the occupation of the Khamptis since 1794 when they expelled the Ahom governor and established their own chief in his stead. The Khampti chief Chow Salam Sadiyakhowa Gohain

13. Colonel L. W. Shakespeare, *Assam Rifles*, pp. 7-9.

14. Between the years 1828 and 1833 we find the term "Central Assam" being occasionally used for "Upper Assam" in order to exclude the Sadiya country from its limits. At present the district of Lakhimpur includes the Matak country and excludes Sadiya; the name "Central Assam" is applied to the districts of Nowgong and Darrang.

undertook to maintain a force of 200 men armed by the British. The Singpho country lay to the east of Matak and was bounded on the north by the Lohit river and on the south by the Patkai range. As we have seen the Singpho chiefs acknowledged their subjection to the British Government and promised to be friendly and peaceful neighbours.[15] The Moamarias returned to their old agricultural pursuits and gave no trouble to the British Government; but the Khamptis and the Singphos gradually became impatient of restraint and relapsed into their old predatory habits.[16]

The population of Lower Assam was roughly estimated at 350,000,[17] and of Upper Assam at 300,000.[18] The revenue at first expected from the former was 4 to 6 lakhs of rupees exclusive of customs, abkari and Khedas,[19] but later Scott lowered the figure to 300,000 rupees.[20] The revenue to be derived from Upper Assam was estimated at 180,000 rupees including custom duties, rent of salt wells and fisheries.[21]

Restoration of an Ahom prince: Government, as I have said, could not arrive at a final decision with regard to the future disposal of Assam till November 1832 owing mainly to the difficulty in finding an efficient Assamese prince to rule over the country, interposed between British territories and the wild tribes of the extreme eastern confines of Assam. Throughout the discussions Scott advocated the retention of Western Assam under direct British control, and the restoration of Eastern Assam, with the exception of the Sadiya country, to a native prince on a tributary basis.[22] In Scott's opinion the revenues of Western Assam were necessary for the expenses of the troops to defend the province.

15. For Scott's engagements with the Matak, Khampti and Singpho chiefs, see Aitchison's *Treaties*, 1931, Vol. XII, pp. 119-22.

16. Mackenzie, *North-East Frontier of Bengal*, pp. 57-60, 65-71.

17. Capt. White to Scott, Aug. 9, 1830, Parliamentary Papers, 1841, No. 28, p. 401.

18. Scott to Swinton, Ap. 15, Beng. Sec. and Pol. Cons., July 14, 1826, No. 2.

19. Scott to Swinton, Feb. 28, Beng. Sec. and Pol. Cons., Ap. 5, 1825, No. 27.

20. Scott to Swinton, Feb. 2, Beng. Sec. and Pol. Cons., March 7, 1828, No. 4.

21. Scott to Swinton, Ap. 15, Beng. Sec. and Pol. Cons., July 14, 1826, No. 2.

22. The limits of the area to be made over to a native prince were —from Biswanath to Dihang river on the north bank, and Solal Choky to Buri-Dihing and Barhat on the south,—Scott to Swinton, Feb. 2, Beng. Sec. and Pol. Cons., March 7, 1828, No. 4.

The inhabitants of Western Assam being conquered by the Ahoms only in recent times and being thus ruled by strangers would not be so averse to the introduction of foreign authority as would be the people of Eastern Assam. Besides, he believed, that the permanent annexation of Western Assam would be welcomed by the greater portion of the people "who had always been treated by Surgy Deo and the insolent aristocracy of Upper Assam as a conquered people upon whom all sorts of indignities might with impunity be heaped."[23] The restoration of Eastern Assam, was in Scott's opinion, desirable as Ahom princes and nobles would be discontented at the establishment of foreign authority and the diminution of their own. He further apprehended that the annexation of the entire province would have a bad appearance in the eyes of the neighbouring nations. He recommended the exclusion of the Moamarias, Khamptis and Singphos from the jurisdiction of the proposed tributary prince, as they had been in open rebellion against the Ahom rulers for the last 40 years and would thus be a source of continuous trouble in view of their old animosity.[24]

However, since Government had intended not to annex any part of Assam permanently, Scott submitted a scheme for the establishment of a native prince to rule over the whole territory of Assam, although he argued it would be wiser to retain Western Assam. The prince should be required to pay an annual subsidy of 2 lakhs for protection. Measures should be adopted to provide a constitutional check upon the internal administration, such as the formal recognition of the powers of the *Patra-Mantri* or the council of the three Gohains, the Barbarua and the Barphukan, and the revival of the *Barmel* or the conference of the officers of the realm as far down as the grade of Saikias or centurions. At first no member of the *Patra-Mantri* should be appointed or removed without the sanction of the British Government. The *Barmel* should be assembled at least once in two years, and vested with the right of petitioning the king for the redress of grievances and for the punishment and removal of obnoxious officers of all ranks. Scott then entered into an examination of the titles of Chandrakanta Singha and Purandar Singha for nomination to the rulership of Assam. Purandar Singha's claim to the succession taken by itself was superior in view of his descent from King Rajeswar Singha

23. Scott to Swinton, Feb. 28, Beng. Sec. and Pol. Cons., Ap. 5, 1825, No. 27, The settlement of Ahoms in Kamrup was discountenanced by the Ahom government, Cons., March 7, 1828, No. 4.

24. Beng. Sec. and Pol. Cons., March 7, 1828, No. 4.

(1751-69), son of King Rudra Singha (1696-1714); whereas Chandrakanta was descended from Lechai Namrupia Raja, who had been blinded by his brother Rudra Singha for treason. But Chandrakanta's brother Kamaleswar Singha having been raised to the throne in 1795 before the birth of Purandar Singha, the former's claim was held to be superior to that of Purandar; and besides Kamaleswar had ruled for 15 years and Chandrakanta for 9 years. The arguments in favour of Purandar Singha were that he had more ability and general information than Chandrakanta, and being possessed of considerable wealth he was more able to support his dignity and give his people breathing time than a starving king. But there was an objection to the elevation of either of these two claimants, *viz.*, that all men of consequence who belonged to the party of the unsuccessful rival would be obliged to quit Assam for fear of vengeance. Scott therefore proposed two alternatives, *first*, the elevation of Chandrakanta to be succeeded by Purandar and his heirs, in view of the superior claims of the line of Rudra Singha; *secondly*, free election of a sovereign from all the eligible princes of full age, including Chandrakanta and Purandar, by an assembly of all the nobles and officers as far down as the grade of Hazarika.[25]

Early in February 1828 Scott once more submitted his opinions on the management and disposal of Assam. He pointed out the advantages of retaining possession of Lower Assam and restoring Upper Assam to an Assamese prince. On March 7, 1828, Government in concurrence with one of these recommendations, declared Lower Assam to be permanently annexed to the British possessions. But it was opposed to the restoration of Upper Assam on the ground that the imbecility, weakness and rapacity of the Assam prince would lead to the oppression of the ryots, and that collisions with the eastern tribes would involve Government in embarrassments with the latter. Besides, it considered that it would gain financially by retaining Upper Assam, even after making liberal provision for Chandrakanta, and other princes and ministers, for little more than a nominal increase in the military and civil establishments would be necessary. Scott's arguments were met by saying that Government was not pledged by any declaration or engagement to restore any part of Assam to native authority if it were not otherwise expedient and desirable. The opinion of other states was considered by Government to be immaterial as long as its arrangements were just. As regards the discontent of the influ-

25. Scott to Swinton, Ap. 15, Beng. Sec. and Pol. Cons., July 14, 1826, No. 2.

ential classes, Government thought, it could be easily obviated by giving them employment in high offices.[26]

The discussions were resumed in 1831 in the light of the events of the intervening period. After the first wave of enthusiasm for the new connection had subsided signs of discontent began to manifest themselves. "The inhabitants of Upper Assam," wrote Scott, "are far from being reconciled to our rule, and it may be expected that the higher classes will continue to cherish hopes and engage in schemes for the re-establishment of the ancient form of government under a native prince." Sadiya had not been completely pacified, and Captain Neufville, Political Agent in Upper Assam, had to be constantly present there leaving the affairs of the headquarter at Jorhat under a junior officer. In the meantime a few companies of troops were withdrawn from Upper Assam, and reports were circulated that the entire force would soon return to Bengal. Taking advantage of these circumstances an Ahom prince named Gomdhar assumed the insignia of royalty, styled himself Swargadeo, addressed letters to the ex-functionaries asking them to acknowledge him, and actually occasioned resistance to revenue officers and plundered several houses. Timely intimation being received the pretender's followers were attacked and defeated by Lt. Rutherford on October 29, 1828. Gomdhar escaped to the jungles, but he came in and surrendered twelve days later.[27]

Early in 1830 reports were received of hostile preparations among the Singphos and Khamptis aided by their brethren residing beyond the frontier. Almost at the same time another Assamese prince named Gadadhar, disguised as a Khampti priest, had been secretly attempting to win over the troops and assassinate the European officers in Upper Assam. He described himself as an agent of the Burmese monarch who, he said, was preparing troops to invade Assam next year.[28] In March 1830 the Khamptis and the Singphos invaded the plains and set out for Sadiya. Captain Neufville, however, succeeded in dispersing them. With regard to the proposed invasion by the Burmese, arrangements were made to repel such an attack; and Raja Gambhir Singh of Manipur was asked to hold his troops in readiness to march across to Sadiya.[29]

26. Swinton to Scott, March 7, Beng. Sec. and Pol. Cons., March 7, 1828, No. 8.

27. Scott to Swinton, March 14, 1829, Beng. Sec. and Pol. Cons., March 12, 1830, No. 15.

28. Scott to Swinton, June 12, Beng. Sec. and Pol. Cons., June 25, 1830, No. 4.

29. Mackenzie, *North-East Frontier*, pp. 65-6.

A rebellion in a more determined and violent form had meanwhile been organised by Piali Barphukan, son of Badanchandra, with the assistance of some nobles who had been convicted in Gomdhar's trial but had succeeded in escaping from prison. The Ahom prince who was proposed for elevation to the throne was one Rupchand Kowanr. The leaders addressed letters to the chiefs of the Moamarias, Khamptis, Nagas, Dafals, Manipuris, Garos and Khasias. They seduced the second son and a few disaffected subjects of the Moamaria chief contrary to the latter's orders. The letter addressed to the Khampti chief was made over to Captain Neufville who instantly arrested the messenger. In the meantime the rebels, well armed, marched to Rangpur and burnt down the sepahis' lines; but having failed to carry out their project of attacking the guard retreated to Geleki where they were captured by a detachment with some armed levies.[30]

The events of 1828 and 1830 convinced Scott of the deeprooted discontent of the Ahom nobles and of the insecurity of the Sadiya frontier. His anxiety was aggravated by the death in July 1830 of Captain Neufville whose vigour, enterprise and high reputation among border tribes had been mainly responsible for the prompt suppression of disorders before they could become serious. On May 18, 1831, Scott wrote to Government urging the appointment of a duly qualified officer to reside constantly at Sadiya with two companies of Light Infantry and 20 horse who with the militia maintained by the Barsenapati, Sadiyakhowa Gohain and Bisa Gaum would place at the officer's disposal a force of 800 men. Scott pointed out again the advisability of restoring Upper Assam to a native prince by which measure alone he hoped the plots and intrigues would come to an end. This proposition had been very strongly supported by Captain Neufville who compared the position of the future Assam Raja with that of the *faineant* king of Delhi. "In both cases," said Neufville, "we rescue a prince utterly unable to maintain himself or his throne from foreign thraldom and domestic treason, and in both the acquired territories remain dependent upon our political and military protection."[31]

Assam affairs were discussed by the Board on June 10, 1831, in the absence of the Governor-General, Lord William Bentinck. Sir Charles Metcalfe, Vice-President of the Council, was opposed to the restoration of Upper Assam to a native prince on the ground

30. Scott to Swinton, Aug. 7. Beng. Pol. Cons., Sept. 24, 1830, No. 76.
31. Scott to Swinton, May 18, 1831; Neufville to Scott, Ap. 29, 1830, in Beng. Sec. and Pol. Cons., June 10, 1831, Nos. 50 and 58.

that it would interpose a foreign government between Lower Assam and the unproductive and isolated territory of Sadiya. He was, however, prepared to waive his objection if some means could be devised to get rid of Sadiya without mischief. For this purpose Metcalfe suggested three alternatives: that the defence of Sadiya should be made over to the proposed native government; or if it was considered incapable for the charge some arrangements should be made with the Sadiya chiefs who furnished militia to the British Government, preventing at the same time the possibility of any collision between them and the Assamese ruler of Upper Assam; or if neither the Assamese prince nor the chiefs were capable of the defence of Sadiya, Metcalfe proposed to make it over to Raja Gambhir Singh of Manipur.[32]

In July 1831 Lord William Bentinck expressed his inclination to restore Upper Assam to a native prince. He admitted that the old native system was miserably defective, but the fact that the ancient government continued for six centuries indicated that there must be something intrinsically good in the constitution. On August 4, sixteen days before his death, Scott recorded his decided opinion "that the transfer of Central Assam to a native prince offers such superior prospects of tranquillity as compared with the arrangement now existing as would outweigh the objections."[33]

In October 1832 Lord William Bentinck passed formal orders that Upper Assam should be restored to Purandar Singha and that Sadiya must be maintained as a British post and well fortified. The Governor-General was not inclined to give Raja Gambhir Singha a footing in Sadiya. To obviate Metcalfe's principal objection Lord William Bentinck ordered that the headquarters of the Assam Light Infantry should be established at Jorhat, the proposed capital of Purandar Singha, who would be required to relinquish a space of two square *coss* for troops and cantonment.[34]

T. C. Robertson who had on April 25, 1832, received charge of the duties of Agent to the Governor-General from William Cracroft, the temporary incumbent, held several interviews with Purandar Singha, and reported that he saw no reason, from that prince's "outward appearance and manners, to doubt of his fitness

32. Swinton to Scott, June 10, Beng. Sec. and Pol. Cons., June 10, 1831, No. 59.

33. W. H. Macnaghten, Secy. to Governor-General, to Swinton, July 18, and Scott to Swinton, Cherapoonji, Aug. 4, Beng. Pol. Cons., Sept. 2, 1831, Nos. 2 and 3.

34. Macnaghten to Swinton, Oct. 14, Beng. Pol. Cons., Nov. 5, 1832, No. 4.

for the dignity, for which all unite in prefering him to his only rival Chandrakant."[35]

On March 2, 1833, Purandar Singha entered into an engagement with the British Government in which he undertook to pay an annual tribute of 50,000 rupees. He promised to abstain from the former practices of cutting off ears and noses. He further bound himself not to permit women to become *Sati,* though there was no necessity for this provision in Assam as in its recorded history there is only one instance of *Sati, viz.,* that of a concubine of Kumar Bhaskaravarma, king of Kamarupa, and friend and ally of Emperor Harshavardhana.[36] By the terms of the treaty Purandar Singha was to exercise no power over the Moamaria country of the Barsenapati. The Government reserved the right of transferring Upper Assam to another ruler or to take it into its own immediate occupation in the case of mal-administration on the part of Purandar Singha.[37]

On April 24, 1833, Purandar Singha was formally installed as Raja of Upper Assam by Major Adam White, Political Agent. Due obeisance was paid to him by the nobles and other influential people. The troops were paraded in front of the palace and a salute of 19 guns fired on the occasion.[38]

Revenue administration: The work of the administrative organisation had gone on apace unhampered by the discussions in progress regarding the final disposal of the province. Soon after the Treaty of Yandaboo Scott had laid down the principle on which the administration was to be conducted in Lower and Upper Assam. The administration of Upper Assam was to conform to the old native system in view of the likelihood of its eventual transfer to a native prince; and that of Lower Assam was to be assimilated more to the system in vogue in Bengal to which it had a very great resemblance as that part of Assam had been under the Mahammadans for some time; besides, there was the possibility of retaining Lower Assam under direct British control.[39]

The administration of Lower Assam had been actually commenced in the year 1824-25. Settlements had been made with the

35. Robertson to Swinton, Jan. 18, Beng. Pol. Cons., Feb. 4, 1833, No. 113.

36. Damodara Gupta's *Kuttanimatam,* Kavyamala, Part III, p. 77, verse 549, Nirnaysagar Press, Bombay, 1887.

37. Aitchison's *Treaties,* 1931, Vol. XII, pp. 135-7.

38. White to Robertson, Ap. 24, Beng. Pol. Cons., May 30, 1833, No. 112.

39. Scott to Swinton, May 25, Beng. Sec. and Pol. Cons., July 7, 1826, No. 31.

Chaudhuris, Rajas, and managers and proprietors of lakheraj lands;[40] and the collections showed a decided increase in the subsequent years. In 1826 the Revenue and Judicial Departments were placed under a native Sheristadar in conformity with the practice in Bengal districts.

In Upper Assam the management of the revenues was placed in charge of Janardan Barbarua, a person of rank and substance, and connected by marriage with Gaurinath Singha, while the Judicial Department was under Lambodar Barphukan, a man of talents, character and considerable wealth. The Barphukan was a brother-in-law of Chandrakanta Singha. The Barbarua was paid, as in the previous regime, in lands and *paiks*; but the Barphukan received 300 rupees per mensem. Most of the old revenue officers were re-appointed, and under their supervision an enumeration of the *paiks* was held. The three Assamese commissioners placed in charge of the work were paid 1000 rupees each. Considerable help was obtained from a rent-roll of the *paiks* prepared by the Burmese in 1822, showing the allotments under each officer together with the revenue payable by him.[41]

The old *khel* and *perganah* systems were retained. The liability of the *paiks* to render personal service was abolished, except when allowances were made to princes and ex-functionaries by allotting them a specific number of *paiks* or *likchows.* Some of the officers and clerks in the establishments of the two Commissioners applied to be remunerated by grants of *paiks* in lieu of salary in cash. About 700 *paiks* were allotted to these nobles and officials. From the rest of the *paiks* a poll-tax of rupees three was realised as revenue for the farm, homestead and garden. This tax was collected by the old staff of the *khel.* The Chaudhuris and the junior officers of the *khels* were elected by the ryots, a system partially in existence before.

Several difficulties arose in the collection of the poll-tax. There was an insufficiency of currency in Assam. The people grew and made what they needed, and there was very little necessity for using money. The ryots were unaccustomed to the payment of taxes, and it soon became unpopular. Many of the *paiks* on being relieved from the necessity of labouring for a certain number of months for the benefit of the state gave themselves up to idleness;

40. See *ante*, Chapter IX, Section *Provisional Administration in Western Assam.*

41. Scott to Swinton, May 25, Beng. Sec. and Pol. Cons., July 7, 1826, Nos. 34-35.

and being unable to pay the tax deserted the country and settled in Bhutan and Cachar where the taxation was very nominal.[42] Another difficulty was the distribution of the *paiks* in scattered localities. In the earlier times the *paiks* of a particular *khel* resided together; but gradually they were dispersed in several parts of a district or the province, *e.g.*, the *Naosalias* or boat-builders, and *Hiloidaris* or musketeers, had to be stationed at different places to meet local exigencies. Some liberty of movement was allowed when personal service was commuted for pecuniary payment. So when Assam was occupied by the British very few *khels* were found together in any body; and the *paiks* of many *khels* were frequently mixed up together in the same villages, each party or family paying their taxes to different collecting officers, who had to travel throughout the province in pursuit of stray *paiks*.[43]

In Kamrup too the *perganahs* were not all districts comprised in one locality or a compact area within one boundary, but some of the perganahs had *taluks* scattered throughout the whole division. Another difficulty arose from the concealment of *paiks*. Slaves were not taxed; and the self-sale of male adults as slaves was not permitted as it meant loss of revenue to the state. In consequence of the exemption of slaves from taxation, and the liability of every free man to personal service and capitation tax, many *paiks* were content to be called slaves, and concealed themselves among the slaves of families who could give them protection. There was no difference in the treatment accorded to slaves and other agricultural labourers; on the other hand, slaves being permanent and hereditary possessions, were more endeared to the family than the *paiks* whose services could be commanded only during the tenure of office. There were about 3 or 4 thousand paik-slaves in Western Assam alone. Scott instituted an enquiry into the titles by which slaves were held with the result that 12,000 persons were restored to the ranks of the paiks.[44]

The realisation of the revenue in Upper Assam was more difficult than in Lower Assam. In the latter division the people had been generally accustomed to cash payments in lieu of personal service. In the very first year 1824-25 the actual collections in Lower Assam came up to more than two-thirds of the original demand. But in

42. Scott to A. Stirling, Ap. 26, Beng. Sec. and Pol. Cons., June 27, 1828, No. 115.

43. Jenkins, *Revenue Administration of Assam*, 1849-50, p. 58.

44. Jenkins, *Revenue Administration of Assam*, 1849-50, p. 62.

Upper Assam the collections for the first three years averaged one-third of the estimated receipts,—[45]

Year		Estimated Receipts	Actual Collections
1825-26	..	rupees 139,616	28,057
1826-27	..	„ 145,832	46,072
1827-28	..	„ 143,267	38,835

The ryots had abundance of grain, but very little cash. The Kheldars were in many cases incapable of keeping accounts of their receipts and balances, as they had not been accustomed to that system. At the same time many Kheldars, long habituated to indolence and slackness, did not pay in the money collected by them on account of the state. Colonel Cooper, who was in charge of Upper Assam for the first three years, granted remissions liberally in order to conciliate the Kheldars who constituted the nobility of the land. This leniency was in the opinion of Scott a necessary policy as he thought that the realisation of revenue was " a matter of secondary importance which could not be put in competition with the superior consideration of conciliating the good-will of the most influential classes in society.[46]

Colonel Cooper's successor Captain Neufville effected improvements in every branch of the administration of Upper Assam. Tahsildars were appointed to collect the revenue on the North Bank. They were mostly Bengalis or Assamese clerks of inferior rank. The ryots were permitted to pay their revenue in kind consisting of marketable and non-perishable articles, such as gold, ivory, muga silk, munjit and cotton cloth. There was visible improvement in the collections during the two years of Neufville's administration, averaging three-fifths of the original demands,[47]—

Year		Estimated Receipts	Actual Collections
1828-29	..	rupees 153,835	78,452
1829-30	..	„ 155,232	100,000

The vigorous steps adopted by Captain Neufville to realise the revenue and to improve the administration of justice and police,

45. Scott to Swinton, May 18, Beng. Pol. Cons., June 10, 1831, Nos. 50-51.
46. Scott to Swinton, May 18, Beng. Pol. Cons., June 10, 1831, No. 50.
47. Scott to Swinton, May 18, Beng. Pol. Cons., June 10, 1831, No. 51.

which could be done only by appointing foreigners and capable men of inferior rank, produced discontent amongst the higher classes. Scott pointed out the incompatibility of native customs with the principles of British administration. He recommended a thorough overhauling of the revenue system in Upper Assam if in future it came under direct British control.

During the life-time of Scott no alteration was made in the revenue system for it was not decided whether Government would retain the whole or any part of Assam. It was after the installation of Purandar Singha as tributary Raja of Upper Assam in April 1833 that Government adopted measures for the revision of the revenue system of Lower Assam which was then retained directly under British control. The districts of Nowgong and Darrang were each divided into a number of fiscal units, called *mauzas*, thus abolishing the machinery of the *khel* system. The *perganahs* of Kamrup were entirely remodelled and made into compact blocks each being given well-defined boundaries. The residents in a *mauza* paid the dues to the revenue collector who was variously known as Mauzadar, Bishaya, Chaudhuri, Kakati or Patgiri.[48] Arrangements were made to introduce an assessment based on the area under cultivation; by 1836-37 the poll-tax was abolished in Nowgong and Darrang divisions; and in 1938-39 the *Kharika-tana* tax,[49] of which Scott had been in favour, was abolished in Kamrup. In 1837, the assessment per *pura* stood as follows: *Rupit,* 1st class Rs. 1-4, 2nd class Re. 1-0; *Baritali,* Rs. 1-4; *Baotali,* 1st class Re. 1, 2nd class, annas 12; *Faringati,* 1st class annas 10, 2nd class annas 6.[50]

Changes in the revenue system of Upper Assam could be introduced only in 1838 when it was resumed by Government on the failure of Purandar Singha to pay his tribute. The *khel* system was abolished forthwith, and assessments were fixed from 1839-40 on the area under cultivation at the rate of one rupee per *pura* of *rupit* land, and eight annas for all other lands.[51]

Judicial administration: Under the Ahoms minor civil and criminal disputes were decided by *panchayats* presided over by Chaudhuris and *khel* officers. In cases of official indiscipline the officers could themselves inflict minor corporal punishment. The *panchayats* were known in Assam as *mels.* Important cases were

48. Gait, *History of Assam,* pp. 293-4.

49. For *Kharika-tana tax,* see *ante,* Chap. IX, Section *Provisional Administration in Western Assam.*

50. John M'Cosh, *Topography of Assam,* p. 123

51. Jenkins, *Revenue Administration of Assam,* 1849-50, p. 67.

tried at the Barphukan's court at Gauhati and at the king's court at the capital. The Barbarua was the highest judicial officer of the government to whom all appeals lay. Brahman Pundits conversant with the laws of the country were attached to the principal courts. Capital punishments requiring shedding of blood could be inflicted by the orders of the monarch alone.[52]

Scott continued the *mel* system, and the other ancient forms of judicial administration. He instituted a *panchayat* composed of the local gentry in every populous *perganah* and village. Minor breaches of peace as well as civil cases up to rupees 100 were referred to the Chaudhuris and Kheldars. Towards the end of 1826 three civil courts were established at Gauhati. The lowest of the three courts was vested with the powers of *Munsifs* in Bengal provinces ; the second with those of *Sudder Ameens* for the purpose of hearing original suits and deciding appeals from the first tribunal ; and the third and the highest court was vested with the same powers as the second, but with the additional authority to decide criminal cases of minor consequence and to receive appeals from the Rajas, Chaudhuris and other Malguzers. The first court at Gauhati was presided over by a Rajkhowa, the second by Ghinai Barphukan and the third by Bapuram Barphukan. To each of the four courts were attached Pandits and three paid assessors in each.[53]

As we have seen martial law had been declared in Lower Assam after its occupation by British troops in March 1824. It was extended next year to Upper Assam and Sadiya. On the assumption of the civil management of Assam in March 1928 martial law was withdrawn from the province. During the four years 1824-28 no native court-martial which alone was competent to try capital offences had ever assembled in Assam, with the result that towards the end of the period there were 34 murder cases still pending, and 94 suspects in jail and 20 on bail.

In these circumstances Scott recommended that Assam should be placed under the jurisdiction of the Nizamat Adawlat, and the native courts empowered to try all criminal cases including capital offences. From his experience during the year 1827 Scott was convinced of the ability of the Assamese judges. In the tribunals, Scott pointed out, the ablest man no doubt dominated, but his

52. Capital punishment was inflicted in Assam in various ways. See Mackenzie, North-East Frontier, p. 378 ; Martin, Eastern India, III, p. 612.

53. Scott to Swinton, Dec. 30, 1826, Beng. Sec. and Pol. Cons., Feb. 16, 1827, No. 2.

extreme views were always checked by his colleagues. The orders passed by them were, in Scott's opinion, correct in essentials and agreeable to the custom of Assam. Scott strengthened his recommendation by pointing out that only 50 decrees were appealed against out of a total of 756. About the corruptibility of the judges Scott observed that in view of their previous official habits "it was extremely difficult or rather impossible to substitute all at once a system of purity for one of gross corruption." He then asserted an opinion of considerable forensic interest,—"According to my experience in this quarter there is less reason to hesitate about coming to a decided opinion as to the guilt or innocence of a person accused of murder, than there is in forming an equally satisfactory judgment in cases of the magnitude where the parties have stronger reasons for endeavouring to disguise the truth." The judges in Scott's courts had held similar appointments under the Ahoms; and he believed that their appointments had not only given them subsistence but had rendered their talents and local knowledge available in the service of the state.[54]

In May 1828 Government sanctioned the establishment of the 4 native civil courts which it characterised as "a novel and interesting experiment." Scott was directed to require the courts to submit their decisions for his confirmation. With regard to the administration of criminal justice Government decided to utilise the tribunals and institutions which Scott had "so judiciously revived." In the opinion of Government this measure had nothing at variance with that in other newly conquered territories excepting "the extensive resort to the agency and instrumentality of the natives themselves in the administration of justice." The extension of the jurisdiction of the Nizamat Adawlat was regarded by Government as premature and inexpedient in the existing state of Assam. Government authorised Captain White, Scott's Assistant in Western Assam, and Captain Neufville, Political Agent in Upper Assam, to apprehend criminals and exercise the functions of Magistrates. All criminals were to be tried by the native courts, according to the rules in force in Bengal, presided over by Captain White or Captain Neufville. Sentences beyond three years could not be passed by these courts; and right of appeal to Scott was always open. Serious offences were to be sent up by the Magistrates to Scott with their opinions. Scott was authorised to

54. Scott to Swinton, March 29, Beng. Sec. and Pol. Cons., May 2, 1828, No. 11.

pass sentence of death and carry it out without reference to Government.[55]

The legal position of the province of Assam comprising at that time the Assam districts of Kamrup, Darrang and Nowgong, and the Bengal district of Goalpara, was defined by Act II of 1835, by which the functionaries were placed under the control and superintendence of the Sudder Dewanny Adawlat and Nizamut Adawlat in civil and criminal cases, and under the Sudder Board of Revenue in matters of fiscal administration. It was also enacted that such control and superintendence were to be exercised in conformity with the instructions received from the Governor-General in Council.[56] In 1837 rules were framed for regulation of judicial procedure and were known as the Assam Code. These rules were merely extracts from the Bengal Regulations of all that was considered necessary at that time for the proper administration of Assam. No provision was however made for revenue administration beyond directing that officers were to conform, as nearly as the circumstances of the province would permit, to the provisions of the Bengal Regulations. Goalpara which is included in the Permanent Settlement continued to remain under those Regulations in revenue matters. On the resumption of Upper Assam in 1838 Act II of 1835 was extended to that tract as well. Sadiya and the Moamaria country were placed within the operation of that Act in 1842. The Assam Code was regarded as repealed on the extension of the Civil and Criminal Procedure Codes to Assam in 1860 and 1861, and the passing of the Penal Code in 1862. In revenue matters the province was administered as before according to the spirit of the Regulations.[57]

The system of administration followed in Assam from 1824 to 1860 was similar to that of the non-regulation districts. It appears that no specific declaration was made to the effect that the Bengal Regulations would not apply to Assam, though such a declaration had been made in the case of Goalpara when it was separated from Rungpore and formed into a new district in 1822 with Scott as Civil Commissioner.[58] The non-regulation system grew up in Assam by

55. A. Stirling to Scott, May 2, Beng. Sec. and Pol. Cons., May 2, 1828, No. 13.

56. The Act was passed on Jan. 12, 1835, and was applicable to Arakan and Tenasserim as well. The provisions of this Act were extended to Khasi Hills and Cachar by Act VI of 1835.

57. Sir William Ward's *Note on the Assam Land Revenue System*, 1896, pp. 53-6.

58. See *ante*, Chap. VIII, Section "David Scott."

necessity and by practice, the backwardness of the inhabitants and the proximity of the hill tribes being almost the same as in Goalpara. Besides, the province being administered by Scott who retained his old jurisdiction over Goalpara the system automatically extended further east to the area newly placed under his control.

Under this system Assam escaped from the elaborate processes of the Bengal law courts. Even the indispensable formalities which had to be observed under the Assam Code proved too troublesome and complicated for the people. Under the former government complaints were generally heard *viva voce,* and parties concerned could obtain redress within a fortnight or week, or even sooner. " Under the present judical system of the province " wrote Anandaram Dhekial Phukan in 1853, " a party, how trivial soever may be the nature of his complaint, can never obtain relief without submitting to a vexatious and harassing course of procedure, extending from at least six months to an unlimited length of time." He, however, admitted the wisdom shown by Government in preventing " the mischiefs of introducing in full the Regulation law of procedure among a simple and ignorant people."[59] The practice of taking written depositions had appeared to Purandar Singha as an obstacle in the speedy adjustment of disputes. " It was our custom," said the ex-king of Assam, " to hear all complaints *viva voce*, afterwards to summon the party complained against; and if his statement proved unsatisfactory, prompt punishment ensued, without further delay for witnesses; whilst the European gentlemen take down the complainant's deposition, and that of his witnesses, summon the defendant and take down his statement, then call for his witnesses; ere they arrive a couple of months elapse, and the Judge forgets everything, and is completely at the mercy of the *amlahs,* who read what they please to him; and after all the trial may be made over to the Circuit Judge." To justify the practice of writing down depositions Scott replied,—" Swurgo Deo [Lord of heaven, title of Assam kings], you are of celestical origin, and can recollect everything. We are earth-born, and when we go to dinner, forget what we have heard in the course of the day; therefore we write down what we hear."[60]

To encourage people to approach the courts for the satisfaction of their grievances Scott simplified the procedure for institu-

59. A. Dhekial Phukan, *Report on the Administration of Assam,* in Mills's *Report on Assam,* App. J.

60. A. White, *Memoir of David Scott,* pp. 58-59; Purandar Singha's statement is given by White in indirect narration.

ting complaints. A large box was placed in the Kutchery to receive all petitions and no tax was imposed on them, whereas in Bengal eight annas had to be paid on each petition.[61]

As in other non-regulation districts all authority, judicial and executive, was concentrated in Assam in the Political Agents and their assistants who were judges, magistrates and revenue collectors, and some of them took the field when necessary. In judicial and revenue administration the old system was followed for many years, and the agency employed in the previous regime retained as far as practicable, though in revenue matters this arrangement proved to be a source of material inconvenience. The officers who conducted the civil administration were mostly men from the army, a practice which lingered till the twenties of this century.

Police: The Police force in Assam was divided into the armed Civil Police and the ordinary Civil Police. The former was employed in protection of jails and treasuries, and for guards and escorts, and the latter for judicial and administrative purposes. At first Police Stations were established only in the big towns like Gauhati, Rangpur and Jorhat. Police work in the interior was left in the hands of the Rajas, Chaudhuris and Kheldars. In the event of frequency of offences in any particular locality attended by the failure of the revenue collectors to discover and secure a due proportion of the criminals, Scott deputed Police officers to the spot, and the expense of the establishment was levied by an additional cess upon the inhabitants of the disturbed district. The Darrang Raja Bijoynarayan rendered great assistance in the Police Department. On three several occasions he had proceeded with a small party of Sebundy Sepahis having received information of the approach of dacoits, and killed five Bhutanese robbers on the spot and secured a considerable number. This action of the Raja led to a diminution of dacoities in that quarter. Scott presented him with an elephant and a *Khelat* of the total value of 500 rupees, and granted him a regular allowance for maintaining a Police establishment.[62] The system of entrusting Police duties to the local revenue collectors proved unsatisfactory. Felony was suppressed or compromised by the aggrieved parties and the witnesses for the dread of being summoned in evidence. Police control was therefore soon extended to the neighbourhood of Sadar stations.[63]

61. A. White, *Memoir of David Scott*, p. 16.

62. Scott to Swinton, Dec. 30, 1826, Beng. Sec. and Pol. Cons., Feb. 16, 1827, No. 2.

63. Neufville to Scott, Ap. 29, 1830, Beng. Pol. Cons., June 10, 1831, No. 58.

Education, agriculture, etc.: The multifarious duties which engaged the attention of Scott did not allow him time to perfect the arrangements for the establishment of educational facilities in Assam. He however obtained from Government a provision for establishing 12 or 15 schools in Lower Assam. A few schools were opened by some Europeans at Gauhati and the work was reported to be successful. In view of the special needs of Assam Scott considered carpentry and husbandry as more appropriate pursuits than knowledge of letters. He urged Government to provide facilities for instruction in the useful arts as soon as possible without waiting for their slow introduction by chance or in the ordinary progress of events.[64] He paid special attention to improvement in the production of muga silk, the staple commodity of Assam, and suggested a scheme for the extended cultivation of the mulberry food-plant. He brought some men from Rungpore in Bengal to teach the Assamese better methods of preparing and spinning the muga silk. He tried his best to improve the breed of cattle; and distributed potatoes and other useful vegetables.[65]

Scott was very keen on introducing missionary activities in Assam, and on his representation a branch of the Serampore Mission was established at Gauhati with James Rae, a native of Dumfries.[66] Scott himself used to distribute copies of the New Testament translated into Assamese by Dr. Carey, and published in 1811. He was, however, of opinion that rude tribes were more likely to profit by the teachings of the Gospels than Hindus and Muhammadans in whose hearts religious notions are ingrained from childhood. He wrote to his agent in London to send one or more missionaries to work among the Garo mountaineers.[67] A school was eventually established in the Garo hills with one Henley as teacher who was selected for his medical knowledge and which he was expected to impart to the Garo youths. Another teacher, one Fenwick, was appointed in 1827 to instruct the pupils in husbandry and the arts.[68]

In 1836 Rae was joined at Gauhati by William Robinson, and after his arrival several schools were opened and Rae was able to

64. Scott to Swinton, May 18, Beng. Pol. Cons., June 10, 1831, No. 50.

65. A. White, *Memoir of David Scott*, p. 26; Scott to Swinton, Ap. 17, Beng. Pol. Cons., May 7, 1830, No. 51.

66. *Calcutta Christian Observer*, Vol. IV, 1835, p. 408.

67. Scott to W. B. Bayley, Secy. to Govt., Ap. 27, 1825, in Mackenzie's *North-East Frontier*, pp. 253-4 *n*.

68. Scott's letters to Fenwick, March 7 and Aug. 18, 1827, in Appendix to White's *Memoir*, pp. 138-143.

make extended tours in the interior. He had soon to retire from Assam owing, it is alleged, to the profligacy of some of the new converts and lack of reinforcement.[69] Robinson continued in Assam as a school teacher and afterwards as Inspector of Schools. In response to the representations of Major Jenkins, the then Commissioner of Assam, Nathan Brown and O. T. Cutter of the American Baptist Mission, arrived at Sadiya in March 1836 to take up missionary work in Assam.[70]

Another object on which Scott set his heart was the establishment of a sanitarium in the Khasi hills. At first he selected Nungklao, but it was found unhealthy and consequently abandoned for Cherapoonji where Scott passed most of his time. In 1864 Shillong at an altitude of about 6,000 feet was selected as the site of the provincial capital.

Death of David Scott: Scott died at Cherapoonji on August 20, 1831, agd 45. His loss was mourned by all sections of the Assamese who called him their father. He had piloted the Government's relations and transactions in Assam during a very momentous period, and his measures and decisions affected the vital interests of the people. But no Assamese entertained any grievance against him, and his memory is still held in very high esteem among the inhabitants. By mixing freely with the people he was able to appreciate their wants and understand their viewpoints and the real spirit of their institutions which were being gradually modified. In fact no Assamese could have more efficiently championed the cause of his country than did Scott in his numerous representations to the Government.

This aspect of his official career comes out clearly in his report on slavery in Assam and in his recommendation for ameliorating the condition of the Assamese nobles who had lost their old privileges by the change of government. His views on slavery, as far as Assam was concerned, were not in accord with those of the reformers who advocated its abolition on philanthropic grounds. Scott had seen that slaves were treated in Assam like adopted children. "The servile classes," said he "are in general treated by their masters with a degree of consideration, familiarity and kindness, of which few examples are to be found in the intercourse between English masters and their hired servants." He held that slavery was interwoven with the whole frame of Assamese society

69. Rev. Dr. V. H. Sword, *Baptists in Assam*, 1836-1936, pp. 38-39.
70. *Calcutta Christian Observer*, Vol. IV, p. 413.

and that it was essential to the comfort and honour of the families of the higher classes. He further pointed out that European states with armies, navies and colonies furnished receptacles for those who are incompetent to manage their own affairs. "The people in Assam," he observed, "have none of the resources. The thriftless poor must starve or fill the jails."[71] During a temporary famine in 1825 Scott had permitted the *paiks* to sell themselves as slaves or bondsmen. This measure was approved by the Calcutta Council, but was condemned by the Court of Directors who held that slavery in every form was peculiarly revolting to the moral feelings of Englishmen.[72] In fact, it was the only censure passed on Scott during his whole official career.

One principal reason of his recommending the restoration of Upper Assam to a native prince was the opportunity which the nobles would get for employment. With the same object he appointed native officers in the Judicial and Revenue Departments. He regretted that he could not appoint more Assamese in the ministerial establishment in Lower Assam owing to their ignorance of the Company's system of district administration. He recommended the appointment of an Assamese as Assistant to the European officer in civil charge of Lower Assam with the full powers of a European Mofussil Magistrate. Effect was given to this proposal after Scott's death by the appointment of Haliram Dhekial Phukan as Assistant Magistrate at Gauhati.[73] In suggesting the replacement of the Kheldars in Upper Assam by Tahsildars for collection of revenue he proposed to continue the allotment of *paiks* made to the former in return for conducting petty judicial cases in the interior. Scott granted pensions and allowances to the Ahom princes and ex-functionaries in lands, *paiks* or cash.

As a servant of the Company Scott was held in very high esteem by the Government of India and the Court of Directors. "Tried skill and activity,"[74] "Firm, frank and direct proceedings,"[75] "conciliatory spirit and sound discretion,"[76] "zeal and intelligence,"[77] "temper, judgment and local knowledge,"[78]—are

71. Scott to Swinton, Oct. 10, 1830, Parliamentary Papers, 1841, No. 28, App. VI, No. 5, p. 402.

72. Court's Letter to Bengal, March 10, 1830.

73. Swinton to William Cracroft, March 19, Beng. Pol. Cons., March, 19, 1832, Nos. 81-2.

74. Beng. Letter to Court, Nov. 29, 1814.

75. Court's Letter to Bengal, Dec. 13, 1820.

76. *Ibid.*

77. Secret Letter from Bengal, Nov. 21, 1822.

78. Beng. Letter to Court, Oct. 24, 1817.

some of the expressions used by them in commending his services at different times. Scott's services to the Government and the people have been aptly summarised in the epitaph on his tomb at Cherrapoonji erected by order of the Supreme Council,—"By his demise the Government has been deprived of a most zealous, able and intelligent servant, whose loss it deeply laments, while his name will be held in grateful remembrance and veneration by the native population, to whom he was justly endeared by his impartial dispensation of justice, his kind and conciliatory manners, and his constant and unwearied endeavours to promote their happiness and welfare."

Scott's task would have been unusually arduous even in normal times. Whether as Commissioner or Agent to the Governor-General on the North-East Frontier he had to deal with a variety of races of different social, economic and political traditions. The extensive territories in his charge were but imperfectly known. There were besides the difficulties of communication combined with the inadequacy of European assistants. The Burmese war and the consequent pacification and settlement of Assam imposed on Scott duties of a responsible, many-sided and undefined character. It was his vigilance, versatility and industry which enabled him to lay a secure foundation for the orderly government of the country. The secret of his greatness was his mental vigour and a very eminent degree of conscientiousness. Whether it was the defence of the Eastern Frontier, or the cultivation of the mulberry plant, he expressed his opinions like an expert and in a clear and forcible manner, compelling the Government to pay proper attention. The abandonment of non-intervention in Assam, and the restoration of Upper Assam, of which Government was not much in favour at first, were mainly the result of Scott's representations. His conscientiousness is shown in the last words which he spoke from his death-bed to his attendants,—"I wish you, gentlemen, to bear witness to Government, that I am no longer able to conduct the affairs of the country."[79] His last important despatch on Assam, in 49 paragraphs, was written on May 18, 1831, in the midst of acute physical agony of which he wrote to a friend on June 2,—"I have been very unwell for the last month, and I am afraid my disorder [chronic disease of the heart] is now going

79. White's *Memoir of David Scott*, App. 43, pp. 136-7. The gentlemen present were Lt. Col. Watson, Dr. Rhodes and Lt. Day.

to progress in good earnest. I can neither breathe, sleep nor eat, being affected by frequent sickness at the stomach."[80]

A man of Scott's talents, judgment and moral qualities would have risen to fame in any sphere of the Company's administration, but having had to serve on the little known Eastern Frontier he has been consigned to obscurity and oblivion. At the same time, local administrators like David Scott of Assam and Augustus Cleveland of Bhagalpur have contributed as much to the rearing of the great fabric of British administration in India as those who have formulated its policy or laid down instructions from a distance.[81]

80. Scott to Lt. Vetch, June 2, 1831, in White's *Memoir*, App. 30.

81. A. Cleveland (1755-1784), Judge and Magistrate of Bhagalpur, reclaimed the marauding tribesmen living between that district and Burdwan, see Bishop Heber's *Journal*, Vol. I, Ch. 9; and Warren Hastings, *Memoirs Relative to the State of India*, 1786, London, pp. 132-33.

Appendices to Chapter X

A. DISCOVERY OF THE TEA PLANT

The tea plant was discovered in Assam in 1823 by Robert Bruce, merchant and soldier of fortune, during his visit to Rangpur, where he was imprisoned by the Burmese. Robert Bruce learnt from a Singpho chief that the tea plant was growing wild on the hills. The chief undertook to furnish him with some plants in return for an equivalent. Robert's brother Charles Alexander Bruce who had commanded a division of gunboats during the Burmese war, and later resided at Sadiya as a trade agent and a Local Lieutenant, obtained from the Singpho chief several hundred plants and a considerable quantity of the seed. The specimens were forwarded by Scott to the Superintendent of the Botanical Gardens at Calcutta, and they were pronounced to be of the same family but not of the same species as the China plant. Later, through the investigations of Major Jenkins and Lt. Charlton it was proved that the tea shrub is indigenous in Assam. Tea nurseries were established by Government in Upper Assam, and C. A. Bruce, who had been in charge, was able in 1837 to send to the Tea Committee a consignment of 46 boxes of Assam tea.[1] The discovery of the tea plant in Assam enabled the Company in India to develop a trade which China had hitherto monopolised, and as such it was declared by the Tea Committee " to be by far the most important and valuable that has ever been made on matters connected with the agricultural or commercial resources of this Empire."[2]

The Board of Control and the Court of Directors however decided that the cultivation of the plant and the manufacture of tea in Assam should be left in private hands. The Assam Company was accordingly formed in England in February 1839 with a capital of £500,000. In 1841 it was expected that about 120,000 lbs. of tea would be exported from Assam.[3]

1. Gait, *History of Assam*, Chapter XVIII, and Robinson, *Descriptive Account of Assam*, pp. 127-45. The Tea Committee was nominated by Government in 1834 for effecting the introduction of tea into the Company's territories.

2. India Revenue Consultations, Jan. 28, 1835, No. 6.

3. Robinson, *Descriptive Account of Assam*, p. 144.

B. Survey and Exploration

The occupation of Assam offered the long-sought opportunities of exploration which could not be undertaken so long owing to the unwillingness of the old government to admit strangers. The Government at Calcutta now resolved to take full advantage of 'the opportunities so suddenly and unexpectedly opened of pushing our investigations beyond those barriers which the well or ill-founded jealousy of our Eastern neighbours had hitherto opposed to us, and which we had till then [October 1824] no immediate hope of surmounting."[4]

In 1765 Major James Rennell had traversed the area where Bengal districts ended and Assam began, "but", he wrote with regret, "I was not allowed to proceed further."[5] Ensign Wood who accompanied Captain Welsh in 1792-94 surveyed the country only up to Rangpur, the capital, and prepared several maps of the different parts of the Brahmaputra and of Gauhati and the Darrang frontier. He left the space beyond Rangpur a blank.[6] Dr. John Peter Wade compiled a geography of Assam based on information obtained from his own observations and from the reports of the Assamese.[7] Dr. Francis Buchanan-Hamilton experienced the same difficulty as Rennell. He collected whatever information he could from natives whom he met at Rungpore in Bengal. He prepared a map of Assam which was published in London by Arrowsmith in 1816.[8]

In October 1824 Major J. Blacker, Surveyor-General, first suggested the deputation of a number of Surveyors to the Eastern Frontier "to acquire geographical and physical knowledge of a tract of country which may be termed *terra incognita*."[9] David

4. Lt. R. Wilcox, *Assam and the Neighbouring Countries* in *Asiatick Researches*, Vol. XVII, p. 315.

5. Rennell's *Memoir of a Map of Hindustan*, 1793, p. 298.

6. For Wood's maps see *List of Maps in the India Office Library*, 1878, pp. 117, 301.

7. The Ms. of Wade's *Geography* is in India Office Library. It was partially pub. in *Asiatic Annual Register*, 1805, and Martin's *Eastern India*, III, pp. 626-59. The whole, edited by S. K. Bhuyan, was published in *Assam Review* for 1928 and 1929.

8. Buchanan-Hamilton's *Account of Assam* was pub. in *Annals of Oriental Literature*, 1820, pp. 193-278; partially reproduced in Martin's *Eastern India*, III, pp. 600-25, 660-81.

9. Major Blacker, Surveyor-Gen. to Govt., Ap. 22, Beng. Sec. and Pol. Cons., May 14, 1824, No. 26.

Scott who took great interest in the progress of geographical discovery in Assam specified the areas which ought to be visited by the Surveyors. Their task was of great difficulty owing to the inhospitality of the tribesmen and the want of proper conveyances. Captain Bedford and Lt. Wilcox were particularly instructed to consider the Brahmaputra as the object of their investigation. Lt. Burlton and Colonel Wilford interested themselves in tracing the source of that mighty river. Captain Neufville explored, in the course of his military operations, the country occupied by the Singphos and their neighbours. Investigations were carried up to Brahmakunda, the traditional fountain-head of the Brahmaputra, the Hukong Valley and the neighbourhood of Tibet. Within the course of five or six years the tribes of the Eastern Frontier,—Khamptis, Barkhamptis, Singphos, Abors, Duflas, and Mishmis—visited by the Surveyors, who also explored the numerous rivers in that region. The results of their investigations were mostly published in the *Asiatick Researches* and the *Government Gazette*, and some have been reproduced in the appendix to Horace Hayman Wilson's *Documents Illustrative of the Burmese War*, published in 1827.

In 1832 Lord William Bentinck appointed Captain Jenkins and Lt. Pemberton to survey the North-East Frontier including Cachar, Manipur and the Khasi Hills. Their reports, highly commended by the Governor-General and the Directors, never saw the light of day. Some valuable information is, however, contained in Pemberton's *Report on the Eastern Frontier of British India*, published in 1835.

Chapter XI

CONCLUSION

The occupation of Assam forms an interesting episode in the expansion of British dominion in India. The conquest was unpremeditated, and in a way it was forced upon the British who had for many years deliberately refused to assume any control over the affairs of Assam though such assumption was within easy reach of accomplishment. The Company had throughout respected the integrity of Assam as an independent territory, and had uniformly discountenanced any move that tended to disturb the authority of the Swargadeo Raja of Assam. The incorporation of Assam within the Company's dominions was the result of circumstances which had been produced neither by the conquerors nor by the conquered but by their common enemy, the Burmese. A singular feature of the conquest is the absence of any preceding conflict between the Assamese and their new rulers, so that when the British occupied the country the inhabitants entertained no acrimony or bitterness which is generally occasioned by remembrance of past enmity.

Assam was outside the orbit of the Company's political interests. On the decline of Mogul authority there was a regular scramble for power among the native princes of Northern and Southern India. The rise of the British was viewed with jealousy by the Indian chiefs who were consequently urged " to continual efforts, secret or avowed, to destroy the English Government, and to expel every individual of that nation from India."[1] The English were in constant collision with the native powers until the year 1818 when, partly by military successes and partly by diplomatic alliances, the Company established its virtual supremacy in India. The Ahom rulers of Assam had been enjoying uninterrupted sovereignty since the beginning of the thirteenth century. The Moguls had ruled in Lower Assam by dispossessing the Ahoms only on three different occasions extending to a total period of 27 years.[2] The indepen-

1. Sir John Malcolm, *Political History of India,* 1826, Vol. II, p. 61.

2. The Moguls ruled in Lower Assam, with capital at Gauhati or Hajo, from 1638 to 1658, 1663 to 1667, and lastly from 1679 to 1682, *vide* Sir Edward Gait, *A History of Assam,* 2nd ed., pp. 118, 127, 139, 153-4, 164 and 167. Upto 1612 Lower Assam was ruled by Koch princes. During 1612 to 1638 the

dence of Assam was of separate origin and growth, and was not derived from the decaying authority of the Moguls. Assam did not therefore become jealous of the English who were gradually stepping into the place of the Moguls. It did not entertain any fear from the English to induce it to throw obstructions in their way; neither did the English consider Assam as a possible source of danger to render its suppression desirable, or of strength to make its alliance necessary. The position would have been quite different if King Rudra Singha had succeeded in carrying out his scheme of conquering Bengal in which case the government of Assam would have been brought into closer contact with the vital interests of the East India Company.[3] As Assam was situated at the end of the eighteenth century and the beginning of the nineteenth the Company's attitude towards it was one of general amity usually existing between neighbouring states. Any desire on the part of the Company to promote the relations of friendship was actuated only by the possibilities of a beneficial commercial intercourse. It can be asserted that upto the period preceding the Burmese war the Company had never for a moment conceived any idea of conquering Assam either for economic advantage or for prestige.

The friendship of the Assam government being of no political consequence to the Company it uniformly followed a policy of non-intervention. It was within the power of the Governor-General to deviate from this policy if he so desired, as did Lord Wellesley and Lord Hastings in their relations with the Deccan chiefs; but no exigency to justify such a deviation ever arose with regard to Assam. In deciding on the Assam government's applications for arms and troops the Company was perfectly at liberty to act as it chose, owing to the absence of treaty obligation and of any necessity on the part of the Company to help the Assam government to obtain some positive advantage for itself. The occasional help rendered by the Company was an act of benevolence, actuated by the consideration that the restoration of peace in Assam might lead to the improvement of the trade of Bengal with that country.

From the departure of Captain Welsh in 1794 upto the Burmese conquest the Assam government solely depended for weapons

Moguls fought for the possession of Lower Assam first with the Koches, and latterly with the Ahoms, *vide ante*, Chapter VI, Part III, Sections "The Dynasty of Koch rulers" and "Dharmanarayan appointed Raja of Darrang."

3. "He had no possible chance, even less than the Burmese",—Sir Edward Gait's marginal comment, July 1938.

upon purchases made in Calcutta, either from the Company's arsenal at Fort William or from private dealers. As no arms could be carried to Assam without the permission of the Bengal Government the latter's decisions on this subject reacted upon the military strength of Assam. Its smithies and gunpowder factories ceased to exist during the period of trouble for want of workers and of supplies. The existing stock had been either used up in the war with or seized by the Moamarias. The few matchlocks which were deposited at the public stores were unserviceable and out of date. So the Assam government had no other alternative but to apply to the Company for the supply if fire-arms and for permission to carry them across the frontier. Compliance with such requests was dictated by the Company's own military arrangements, by conditions prevailing in Bengal or by its relationship with the power against whom the Assam Raja intended to use the arms. No importation of arms was possible from China and Burma, and so Bengal was the only place from where the Assam government could procure them. Assam was thus dependent on the Company for its most essential supply.

A government continually dependent on the precarious supply of arms from a foreign country cannot long maintain its position specially when it is confronted by unending distractions to counteract which arms are a matter of daily necessity. The strength of the army is in such a case limited by the facilities for its equipment. The prime minister Purnananda Buragohain had less than a thousand soldiers under his command, and that he succeeded with this small force to maintain some sort of peace in the country was almost a miracle.

During the Mogul wars of Assam the smithies and the gunpowder factories worked day and night under the direct supervision of the monarch. The civil government was intact, and officers and men performed their allotted duties. But during the troubles in the reigns of Gaurinath, Kamaleswar and Chandrakanta, the working units were considerably reduced. The iron ore remained unworked and so local gun-making was out of the question. The ingredients necessary for preparing gunpowder were not available. Saltpetre used to be supplied by the subjects of Darrang who ceased to do so from the reign of Gaurinath Singha. In fact the normal functioning of the administrative machinery became increasingly difficult since the flight of that monarch from the capital Rangpur in 1788. That the government lingered for some time was owing to the partial but substantial relief afforded by Capt. Welsh's detachment, the occasional supply of fire-arms by the Company and the patriotic exertions of Purnananda Buragohain.

The preservation of independence imposes upon the state a two-fold burden: it must be able to keep its subjects under proper control and protect the country from the attacks of foreign enemies. Purnananda achieved the first object, and by diplomacy was able to ward off the invasion of the Burmese. But that nation had rejuvenated itself by its political enterprises against the neighbouring states carried on since the time of Alaungpaya (1752-1760). It was in incessant search of opportunities for expansion and aggrandisement. The collapsing state of Assam presented a fitting field for the ambitions of the Burmese, and having brought that country under subjugation they turned to the realisation of their designs against the British. In the contest that followed the victory went naturally to the stronger side, and Assam passed in consequence from the temporary occupation of the Burmese to the permanent possession of the British.

The Company's Government, though it was kept fully informed of the developments in Assam, could not foresee the logic of events in that country. Assam was not strong enough to be an effectual ally of the Company; but it was weak enough to allure a powerful and designing neighbour who could use it as a base for operations against the English. Failure to see this contingency caused the Company the expensive war with Burma, and the loss of half the population of Assam attended by the endless destruction of property.

The prolonged non-intervention of the Company was due to its inability to realise the dangers that would in time emanate from Assam on account of the instability of its government. The abandonment of this passiveness was the result of David Scott's forceful exposition of the situation on the Eastern Frontier, but Government continued for some time under the influence of the old pacific policy. Before launching war on Burma it proposed to make a declaration on the subject of setting up a native prince in Assam from which course it was only dissuaded by David Scott who advocated the retention of Lower Assam. Soon after the occupation of Assam, troubles broke out in the territory round Sadiya which convinced the Government for the first time of the necessity of establishing in that province a strong government as a kind of glacis in advance of its administrative border-line. It was about the year 1830 that Government first realised the consequences of having a feeble administration in Assam. Even at the present time the importance of the Eastern Frontier has not been properly understood in all its implications. The comparative neglect in which Assam has languished as contrasted with the prominence given to its counterpart in the north-west of India has been a subject of common complaint. With the experience of a century the Government of Assam pointed out to the Simon Commission in 1928,—"the time may soon come when that Frontier [North-East] will become no less, if it is not more, important for the defence of India than the North-West Frontier."[4]

The Assamese in their turn paid dearly for their mistakes. They neglected the lesson that the fortunes of individuals are inseparable from those of the state. They directed their energies to the humiliation or destruction of their personal foes without foreseeing that such revenge would ultimately recoil upon themselves. A large section of the Ahom subjects co-operated with the Moamaria rebels. The Burkendazes and the Burmese were both introduced by Assamese chiefs. Many Assamese joined the Burmese in their plundering excursions. The devastation of the country was thus largely due to the suicidal policy of the Assamese themselves. Those who were well-intentioned were misrepresented and thwarted at every stage so that selfishness became more profitable and secure than public service making it impossible to offer organised resistance to the invaders. The task of defence and protection was the special responsibility of the Ahom rulers, and as their authority had already collapsed the inhabitants, long unaccustomed to the exercise of arms, became an easy prey to the rapacity of the Burmese. Nothing speaks more eloquently of the helplessness of the Assamese than the indifference with which they had to observe their properties plundered, their sanctuaries violated and their brothers and sisters assaulted, killed or carried off into slavery.

The causes which led to the disintegration of Ahom authority in Assam have been enumerated in a previous part of this book.[5] The Ahoms living long in the Brahmaputra Valley lost the martial ardour which had enabled them to conquer the country and to maintain their power in the face of constant conflicts with the neighbouring tribes and the periodic invasions of the Moguls. Re-

4. Quoted in Sir George Dunbar's *Frontiers*, London, 1932, pp. vii, 75. My observations on the comparative neglect of the North-East Frontier were penned in 1938, before World War II during which Assam suddenly sprang into limelight.

5. *Ante*, Chap. VI, Part II, Section "General survey of the Moamaria disturbances".

inforcements from their Shan homeland beyond the Patkai Hills having ceased the dependence of the Ahoms upon the conquered races gradually increased leading to their adoption of the language, customs and lastly the religion of their subjects, accompanied by the establishment of a free social intercourse between the two. The Ahoms thus became one with the governed imbibing the latter's habits and losing their own superior traits which had helped them to maintain their domination. The subjects in their turn regarded he Ahoms as their natural political leaders and their government as a native institution.

But this assimilation of the conquers with the conquered and the consequent identification of their interests affected the efficiency of the administration. The adoption of rigorous measures against refractory subjects become difficult as the Ahom officers commissioned to carry out those measures hesitated to strike against their fellow-citizens, co-religionists, neighbours and comrades. In many cases the Ahoms themselves became champions of the rebels' cause, partly from the belief that it was just, and partly from the opportunity which co-operation with the rebels offered for the realisation of their own ends. The methods of the Ahoms ceased to be mysterious; and their tactics could now be easily anticipated and prepared against.

The adoption of a new religion by the Ahoms changed their outlook on life and human relations; and politics which had been their absorbing passion in the preceding ages now became less important than before, if not subordinate to their newly acquired religious interests. That the Ahoms succeeded in maintaining their authority in Assam for six hundred years, 1228 to 1822, in spite of the strong influences of their physical and cultural environments, is a record of which any race can be proud. Admiration for this long continuance of Ahom rule was a strong reason for Bentinck to restore Purandar Singha in 1833. "Tho' an old Government of 500 [600] years standing", said Bentinck, "the condition of the province and of its population at the time of the Burmese and of the British conquest sufficiently shows that the institutions which existed must have been miserably defective with no inherent disposition to improvement, and it may be a question whether their restoration would not perpetuate ignorance and barbarism rather than tend to the advancement of the country in civilisation and happiness. Their continuance at the same time for a period of time almost without example in History would seem to indicate something intrinsically good in the original constitution and at all events that it is deeply rooted in the feelings of the people."[6]

The Ahom cult which was an offshoot of the traditions of the great Tai race was militaristic in tone. Khunlung and Khumlai, the reputed progenitors of the Shan rulers of Assam, Burma and Siam, were believed to have been sent down by their grandfather Lengdan who was probably some chief of Yunan but was afterwards vested with the attributes of divinity.[7] The two princes were furnished with the insignias of royalty consisting of a magic sword, a pair of drums, an embroidered cloth and a golden idol called Somdeo ;[8] and the following instructions, intended to ensure strong and good government, were delivered to Khunlung and Khunlai by Lengdan and his court-prophet Jasingpha. "I advise you", said Lengdan, "to rule wisely. You should try to get the hearts of people by sweet words. When you may be in war with a neighbouring tribe you must inform me by beating the drums. I shall send down eight lakhs of gods who will cut down all the enemies to pieces. You must always be alert in carrying out state duties. At the end of a year you must wash and sharpen the sword. You will never be overcome or defeated by others. I give you this sword which you must place in the middle of your council hall. If a person commits a crime don't kill him without a fair trial." To this Jasingpha added,—"We wish you to govern the earth with prudence."[9] These instructions were recorded in the Ahom chronicles and read out and explained to the princes and nobles from time to time, and the development of Ahom polity closely followed the traditional advice believed to have been given by Lengdan and Jasingpha.

The descendants of Khunlung and Khunlai founded several states, the leading ones being Mung-mau and its dependencies of Mogaung, Mungkang, Monyin and Momiet. In the beginning of the thirteenth century Sukapha, a Shan chief, quarrelled with his

6. H. T. Prinsep, Secretary to the Governor-General, Simla, to G. Swinton, Chief Secretary to the Government, Fort William, July 18, 1831, Beng. Pol. Cons., Sept. 2, 1831, No. 2.

7. Ney Elias, *History of the Shans*, pp. 2, 13 ; Rev. W. W. Cochrane's Hisotrical Introduction to Mrs. Leslie Milne's *Shans at Home*, p. 19-n ; D. G. E. Hall, *Early European Intercourse with Burma*, p. 16.

8. This idol was in possession of the Ahom kings till 1819 when a nephew of the fugitive Purandar Singha is said to have sold it to some one in Calcutta, Ney Elias, *History of the Shans*, p. 14, *n;* also *J.R.A.S.*, 1913, p. 253.

9. Extract from G. C. Barua's *Ahom Buranji*, pp. 11-17.

brother, crossed the Patkai at the head of 9,000 men and established his authority in the valley of the Dikhow. Sukapha and his descendants subjugated the Morans, Kacharis and the Nagas. After the overthrow of the Bhuyans and the Chutiyas in the reign of Suhungmung Dihingia Raja, Ahom authority was firmly established in the whole of Eastern Assam. The Ahoms came into collision with the Moguls and the Koches; the Ahoms seeking expansion westward and the two latter eastward. By the year 1658 the Ahoms were able to extend their western boundary to the Manas river which they maintained with very small interruptions till the end of their rule. Natural disadvantages played an important part in the reverses of the foreign invaders, but they alone would not have conferred sovereignty on the Ahoms for such a long period without an efficient military organisation and gallantry in arms.

All Ahom institutions, religious, social and political, were designed to make the rulers good soldiers and good governors. All distinctions and honours were confined to meritorious services in war, for success in subduing predatory tribesmen, in defeating enemies, or in conducting diplomatic negotiations. The Ahom religious ceremonies in which kings and nobles had to take part were mostly celebrated on the successful termination of hostilities. In crowning a monarch the Ahom priest reminded him of his great ancestors since the time of Lengdan, his son Thenkham, and his grandsons Khunlung and Khunlai. The reading of passages from the chronicles recounting the deeds of the ancestors of the bride and the bridegroom formed a principal feature of Ahom marriages. In the wedding of a princess the son-in-law was informed that the honour of royal kinship was conferred on him in recognition of the services of his ancestors and in anticipation of similar exertions on his own part. Land-grants to Ahoms were made for no other consideration than eminent services to the state. The system of chronicling events, too, served as an incentive to the Ahoms to the performance of heroic deeds which alone would perpetuate their names in the annals of their race and entitle their descendants to high honour and responsibility. The installation of a new officer was invariably accompanied by a few remarks from the monarch and his ministers alluding to the services of his ancestors and the continued loyalty of his family. The attainment of distinction by meritorious service to the state was thus the principal passion of the Ahoms.

According to the rules of the Ahom government it was obligatory on the part of every male adult to perform state service for three or four months in the year. Conscription was thus in the very blood of the administrative system, making it possible to mobilise the required number of men already trained, within a short time, and if necessary the reserves could be called upon to come forward. As the home-keeping adults were bound by law to carry on the cultivation and other affairs of their absent comrades no dislocation was caused in the normal life of the inhabitants, and supplies were secured. By rendering obligatory service every subject was made to take an interest in the affairs of the state; and the peasants being made to work for their co-villagers, and indirectly for the state, developed some degree of civic consciousness and a sense of public duty. This feature was also noticed by Lord William Bentinck who said,—"The people [of Assam] are stated to have an hereditary attachment to the institutions handed down to them, and not the indifference as to who might be their governors which is the common feeling in Hindoostan."[10]

The practical sagacity of the Ahoms was displayed in the manner in which they provided for reducing every branch of useful knowledge to writing. They had official manuals on the training of elephants, horses and hawks, on civil and military engineering, on the duties and insignias of officers, on the order of precedence in the court, and on the administration of justice. The maintenance of official chronicles of events as they actually took place, based mainly on the despatches of governors, commanders and ambassadors, and the recorded proceedings of the king and his ministers, distinguished the Ahoms from the races of India. In their zeal for increasing the efficiency of their government the Ahoms deputed agents to various parts of India to observe the manners and customs of the people, and the methods of administration as well as the current political movements. Every diplomatic agent who visited a foreign court had to submit to the government a written account of what he had seen or heard, and what he had acquired from books during his residence abroad.[11] Assamese chronicles contain frequent references, brief or detailed, to the personages and events of India; while independent chronicles of Muslim India, commonly known as *Padshah-Buranjis*, from

10. Prinsep to Swinton, July 18, 1831, Beng. Pol. Cons., Sept. 2, 1831, No. 2.

11. The three chronicles *Kachari Buranji, Jayantia Buranji* and *Tripura Buranji*, ed. S. K. Bhuyan, and pub. by the Dept. of Historical and Antiquarian Studies, Assam, are the results of this practice.

Kutbuddin to Aurangzib and even of later periods, were compiled under the auspices of the Ahom government.[12]

The eclecticism observed in the recording of facts in the *Padshah-Buranjis* shows on what lines the Ahom rulers sought knowledge. Considerable prominence is given to the war-methods of India. In one place, for example, it is noted how Sher Khan was instructed by his unknown hostess not to fall upon the centre of Humayun's troops but to round them up gradually from one corner,[13] and how he learnt from his spies that Humayun's camp might be surprised towards the closing hours of the night. In another place it is mentioned that the fugitive Emperor Humayun was taken to task by Shah Tahmasp, king of Persia, for losing the support of his subjects as manifested in his discomfiture at the hands of Sher Khan. "At least a hundred thousand men would be found", said Shah Tahmasp, "who would have willingly sacrificed their lives for you if you had asked them to do so. During your Padshahate you must have regarded the gratification of your desires and pleasures as of supreme importance without investigating the weal and woe of your subjects. The minds of the people therefore became disaffected towards you on the slightest provocation."[14] We read how Man Singha's ultimatum to the refractory Afghan ruler of Gaur conveyed his determination to commence hostilities as well as a covert invitation to open peace overtures. It is also recorded how a designing Padshah despatched warlike spies and soldiers to settle in Secunderabad as peaceful merchants and citizens, and how with their help he ultimately effected the subjugation of that country.[15]

The Ahoms regulated their war-measures against the Moguls in the light of the events in Northern India and the Deccan. King Chakradhwaj Singha who had been planning to expel the Moguls

12. S. K. Bhuyan, *New Lights on Mogul India from Assamese Sources*, pub. in *Islamic Culture*, Hyderabad, Deccan, 1928-1929, *Annals of the Delhi Badshahate*, pub. in the same, 1933-4, and also *Padshah-Buranji*, Assamese text, pub. 1934. *Annals of the Delhi Badshahate*, D.H.A.S., Gauhati, 1947.

13. The story of acquiring the correct method of military operations from the analogy of a dishful of rice is attributed to Timurlane, with precisely the same details. Manucci, *Storia do Mogor*, tr. Irvine, Vol. I, pp. 99-100.

14. S. K. Bhuyan, *Delhi Badshahate*, *Islamic Culture*, Jan. 1933. That such a conversation took place is known also from the *Massiru-l-Umara*, "Shah Tahmasp in conversation with Humayun discussed the question in India, and the loss of sovereignty," tr. H. Beveridge, Vol. I, p. 125; See also Manucci, *Storia*, tr. Irvine, Vol. I, pp. 114-5.

15. S. K. Bhuyan, *Delhi Badshahate*, *Islamic Culture*, April, 1933.

from Lower Assam expedited his preparations on receiving intelligence of Shivaji's successes. "We are making preparations according to our might," wrote Chakradhwaj to the Raja of Cooch Behar, "and hope you will do the same. When fire and wind combine they take no time to clear the forests by burning the trees and the grasses. You have informed me that war has commenced between Shewa [Shivaji] and the Moghuls, and that Shewa having defeated the Moguls has pushed them back to a distance of twenty days' march; that Daud Khan has fallen and Dilel Khan has been wounded, and that the Badshah has moved from Delhi to Agra. Because the Moguls have humiliated us once does it follow that we should make no attempt to throw off this position of subordination to them?"[16]

Another factor which accounted for the success of the Ahoms in continuing their rule in Assam for so long a period was their immunity from the prejudices of the Hindu caste-men. Their anti-caste tendencies come out in their conception of the Satya-yuga or the Golden Age. "Love was the order of the day", wrote an Ahom prime minister in his chronicle, "men used to take food in the same dish like sons of the same mother; nobody entertained any jealousy or hatred towards any other person."[17] To the Ahoms all subjects were equal. All superior offices were the exclusive privilege of the rulers, and a Baruaship which was the highest office to which a non-Ahom could ordinarily aspire was conferred on Hindus and Muslims alike. The Ahoms admitted the Barahis, a Kachari tribe, as their cooks which no Hindu ruler would ever have thought of doing. It was this freedom from the fear of pollution which endeared Ahom rule to the original non-Hindu settlers. The Barahis are reported to have said,—"These Ahoms have by contrivance made us their slaves; still we do not feel aggrieved at our subjection. On the other hand we feel happy if we can associate with and work for them."[18] The Mikirs, a rude tribe, living in the outlying hills of Nowgong, were visited by a party of Ahom soldiers on reconnaissance duty. The hillmen deserted their homes at the sight of the Ahom force, and the latter lived on the food obtained in the deserted houses. The old and decrepit frontiermen who had been left behind became extremely pleased to

16. Chakradhwaj Singha to Prananarayan, c. Feb. 7, 1666, Ms. Assamese historical letters. S. K. Bhuyan, *Lachit Barphukan*, 1947, pp. 24-25.

17. *Assam Buranji*, by Atan Buragohain, prime minister, 1662-1679, in S. K. Bhuyan, *Deodhai Asam Buranji*, pp. xi, 88.

18. *Assam Buranji*, by H. K. Barua, ed. S. K. Bhuyan, p. 12.

see that the Ahoms had eaten their food, from which they concluded that the rulers were of the same caste as themselves. They procured the return of the fugitives, and twenty-four families of Mikirs and Lalungs migrated to Assam to live under the beneficent rule of the Ahoms.[19] In addition to the Ahom and Brahman priests the monarchs entertained at their court Muslim priests. One of them, wrote John Peter Wade, "resided at or near the capital and frequented the Durbar, and the Swargadeos used to despatch him to pray at Hajo after the Mussleman fashion for their prosperity. He was usually succeeded by his nearest relations."[20]

Not being imbued with the prejudices of the Hindu caste system the Ahom rulers were sometimes surprised at the distinctions made in society between one class of their subjects and another. But in their dealings with the subjects they maintained strict neutrality and never forced their ideas upon the Hindu inhabitants. In this religious tolerance the Ahoms were governed by the considerations which had been pointed out to the first Muhammadan conqueror of India by the priest of Pithor Raja and which were recorded in their own chronicles. "O! Padshah, you are yourself acquainted with all laws and traditions," said the priest, "God has created the nations of the earth in separate groups, each different from the other; and He has not provided uniform customs and religions for all. If the different castes and creeds are protected God will protect you also, and you will be able to remain at Delhi without any trouble or fear."[21]

The Ahoms knew how to exploit superstitions for political advantage. In their war with Cooch Behar during the reign of Khora Raja the Ahoms dressed up their soldiers as Brahmans and mounted them on cows at the sight of which the devout Hindu monarch Naranarayan and his general Chilarai left the field as slaughter of an Ahom soldier would mean a double sin.[22] The enthusiasm created by Rudra Singha for his preparations against the Moguls was mainly derived from his declaration that his object in conquering Bengal was to make the sacred Ganges flow within his territories so that his subjects might bathe there in security and peace.[23]

19. S. K. Bhuyan, *Deodhai Asam Buranji*, pp. xiii, 122.

20. J. P. Wade, *Geographical Sketch of Assam*, India Office Ms., also S. K Bhuyan, *An Early Historian of the East India Company*, Proceedings of the Indian Historical Records Commission, 1929, Gwalior Session.

21. S. K. Bhuyan, *Delhi Badshahate*, *Islamic Culture*, Jan. 1933.

22. J. P. Wade, *Account of Assam*, p. 198.

23. Gunabhiram Barua, *Assam Buranji*, 1876, p. 128.

The Brahmans in order to conciliate the Ahom rulers circulated myths attributing to them a divine origin. According to these myths Lengdan became Indra, the great god of paradise, who as a punishment for having carried on dalliance with his wife Sachi in the vicinity of Vasistha's hermitage was changed into a Daitya or demon, but was subsequently redeemed from his degradation by the birth of a son through a mortal maiden. This son became the progenitor of the Ahom kings and was known as Swarga-narayan.[24] Another account which was embodied in a new chapter of the *Mahabharata*, entitled *Stri-parva*, connected the birth of the first Ahom ruler with the war between the Kauravas and the Pandavas.[25] The Brahmanical accounts of the Ahom rulers avoided detail and abounded in high-sounding generalities. This is what we read about Rudra Singha,—"After his [Gadadhar Singha's] death in 1618 [1696 A.D.] his son Rudra Singha sat on the throne. He was endowed with superior powers, strength and enterprise; and he was rare among sovereigns and distinguished from the rest by his gifts and the honour and fame which he acquired. In his previous birth he was a Brahman; he had offered penances at Manikut Parvat [at Hajo] in the guise of a Sannyasi praying for the sovereignty of Saumarpith [Eastern Assam]. He invaded and conquered the Hiramba [Cachar] country in 1628 *saka;* and in the following year he subjugated Jayantidesa. He died in 1636 *saka* in Kamrup whither he had proceeded with the object of invading the territories of the *Yavanas* [Muhammadans]."[26] But no attempt was made to show how Rudra Singha showed his superior power and how he effected the subjugation of Cachar and Jayantia. For the actual facts one has to turn to the officially compiled chronicles which are well-known for their precision and fulness of details.[27]

The conversion of the Ahoms to Hinduism falls into two distinct stages. From Jayadhwaj Singha to Ratnadhwaj Singha Lora Raja, 1648-1681, the monarchs and the nobles were all followers of the Vaisnava faith. Its preachers did not interfere with the converts of the ruling class in the discharge of their legitimate duties, and Vaisnavism in fact did not produce any change in their

24. S. K. Bhuyan, *Deodhai Asam Buranji*, pp. xxxi-xxxiv, 196-208.
25. J. P. Wade, *Account of Assam*, pp. 2-15.
26. S. K. Bhuyan, *Deodhai Asam Buranji*, pp. xxxii, 200.
27. Detailed accounts of Rudra Singha's Cachar and Jayantia wars are recorded in the chronicles *Kachari Buranji* and *Jayantia Buranji*, ed. S. K. Bhuyan.

temperament or habits. The greatest triumphs over the Moguls were achieved during this period. Gadadhar Singha, a powerful monarch, but a gourmand specially notorious for his indulgence in food forbidden to Hindus,[28] argued that a non-flesh-eating creed like Vaisnavism would soon reduce the vigour of the Ahoms. He further entertained misgivings from the unbounded authority possessed by the Vaisnava preachers over his subjects. He therefore dissolved the Vaisnava monasteries and killed or banished the chief leaders. He was in practice a follower of the more vigorous Sakta faith into which, however, he did not accept formal initiation. Rudra Singha's religious views were negative, though towards the end of his regime he is said to have evinced Sakta tendencies. His sons Siva Singha, Pramatta Singha, Rajeswar Singha and Lakshmi Singha, and his grandson Gaurinath Singha were devoted followers and energetic patrons of Saktaism. The effects of Hinduisation became clearer during this period. Sakta priests frequented the court, and Sakta sacrifices were performed in the monarch's household. Siva Singha used to spend most of his time in Sakta worship, and he prided himself on the belief that he had been blessed with a vision of the goddess Durga.[29] The monarch's voluntary retirement from state duties to avert the impending dethronement which had been predicted by priests and astrologers, and the humiliation of the heads of the Vaisnava monasteries by his queen, showed that in their fanatic zeal for religion the Ahoms had become indifferent to the political consequences of their actions. In adopting Saktaism the Ahoms abandoned their traditional lines of conduct and belief. Having adopted the new creed, they were drawn deeper and deeper into its intricate meshes from which they found it impossible to retreat. They did what their Sakta advisers or their new tenets required them to do without considering the effects of their actions upon the stability of their government.

In playing the role of patrons of Brahmans, the Ahom sovereigns encouraged learning and scholarship. This patronage would have been an ornament if along with it they had maintained their original military character. Such patronage now became the criterion of excellence as rulers and individuals to which gallantry

28. It is said that Gadadhar Singha's desire to taste human flesh was destroyed by the ministers who contrived to give him a dish of that flesh deliberately made bitter.

29. Gunabhiram Barua, *Assam Buranji*, 1876, p. 132. A similar vision was also claimed on behalf of Rajeswar Singha.

in arms became gradually subordinated. In a chronicle compiled by an Ahom official special mention is made of the fact that King Gaurinath Singha was a devoted benefactor of Brahmans,[30] whereas in earlier records prominence is given to achievements in the battle-field and the organisation of the state.

The incompatibility of Sakta worship with the demands upon an official's time was pointed out by the Barpatra Gohain of Lakshmi Singha's reign. The orthodox Ahom priests, too, foresaw the disastrous consequences of the adoption of Saktaism by the rulers and the nobles. But their protest was a cry in the wilderness. The process of absorption went on apace till, to quote the words of an Assamese historian, " the Ahoms gave up the manly and arm-strong character of the Kshatriyas, and imbibed the lip-strong traits of the Brahmans."[31] The repeated discomfiture of the royalist forces at the hands of the Moamaria rebels was attributed by the Ahoms to the preordination of the gods, an attitude of mind which precluded the idea of facing the realities of the situation.[32]

Hinduisation and the consequent relaxation of character made the Ahoms much less active and vigorous. The dash and gallantry which had helped them to conquer Assam were now replaced by hesitancy and speculation. Hinduism looks at things from the idealistic point of view, while political conduct can never neglect expediency, and cannot always be determined by stereotyped convention or a rigid moral standard. Ahom nobles who were despatched against the insurgent Moamarias led by disaffected but popular princes began to wonder whether it was right for them to kill their neighbours and kinsmen. The same hesitation had attacked the mind of the Pandava hero Arjuna when he confronted his Kaurava kinsmen in the field of Kurukshetra from which mood he had to be liberated by Sri Krishna by expounding the nothingness of this life and the meaninglessness of human relationship. It is the excessive insistence on the superiority of the soul over the body, of the spirit over matter, of peace over warfare, wherein lies the supreme merit of Hinduism as a religion and its greatest handicap as an active political creed. India has made many a captor captive, but has not devised means to avert the initial captivity. It is in the reconciliation of the two extremes that the influence of the modern age has been mainly felt in India.

30. *Tungkhungia Buranji*, p. 91.
31. Gunabhiram Barua, *Assam Buranji*, p. 138.
32. *Tungkhungia Buranji*, O.U.P., pp. 110–11.

If the Ahoms with their Tai upbringing had retained their military character and had not lost their individuality by an attempt to emulate foreign ideals not germane to their traditions, or if they had maintained a proper balance between the softening tendencies of their new faith and the vigorous demands of their old militaristic cult, they could have perhaps exerted some influence on the political life of India. They were a race whom the Moguls could not overthrow. The vigour which they still commanded in the beginning of the eighteenth century made many Hindu and even Rajput rulers look upon Assam as a power which might save them from humiliation at the hands of the Moguls. To Rudra Singha's invitation to join a Hindu confederacy under his lead the Rajas of Hindusthan are said to have replied,—"Under the rule of the Moguls we have been subjected to endless harassments, and many have lost their religion. We have to pay obeisance to the Moguls and it has become gradually unbearable. We have heard of the great renown of the Swargadeo Raja of Assam, and we shall have no hesitation in saluting him."[33] But having failed to retain their racial individuality, whether from the uncontrollable effects of their physical environments or of their voluntary adoption of a foreign culture, the Ahoms, like the other conquerors of India, became in course of time mere nonentities. Here on a little scale was enacted what had happened in the main theatres of political upheaval in India. "India was made by nature", says a historian, "to be the home of empires; transcient as all military domination must be, but, when shattered by internal dissension or foreign invasion, always tending to be replaced by another of a like nature."[34]

The new conquerors in the case of Assam were the Burmese who belonged to the same stock as the Ahoms, but who had succeeded in retaining their primitive vigour. Nowhere is the irresistible influence of the surroundings better illustrated than the conquest of Assam by the Burmese Shans from the hands of their own tribesmen who had gained mastery over the kingdom six hundred years before.

33. Maniram Dewan's Ms. *Assam Buranji;* Rudra Singha's attempt to form a Hindu confederacy is described in *Tripura Buranji,* ed. S. K. Bhuyan, p. x, 1. See also J. P. Wade, *Account of Assam,* pp. 130-32. The list of Rajas varies in different chronicles. Gunabhiram Barua states that Rudra Singha established friendly relations with the Rajas of Amritsar, Kashmir, the ruler of Bundelkhand, and the Nawabs of Oude and Bengal, *Assam Buranji,* p. 123.

34. H. H. Dodwell, *India,* Part I, pp. 4-5.

In view of the perpetual absorption of conquerors in the conquered soil the Directors of the East India Company at first discountenanced Europeans from possessing and cultivating lands in India. This prohibition was founded originally on political grounds, though an examination of the causes operating in the decay of empires in India dictated its continuance. But for this regulation Englishmen would have shared the fate of their political forerunners, or India would have witnessed the singular spectacle of the settlers of a ruling race emancipating themselves from the control of the mother country or co-operating with the governed in wresting political privileges from it.

The Ahoms had also realised the consequences of the settlement of rulers in a conquered territory. " The settlement of Ahoms in Lower Assam ", said David Scott, " was discountenanced by the Ahom Government as British subjects are excluded from the possession of lands in India." [35] But the mischief had already begun in Upper Assam which the Ahoms regarded as their home country, and it soon permeated Lower Assam. On the other hand the anti-settlement orders created mutual distrust and thus intensified the estrangement between the Ahoms and their subjects in Lower Assam which in its turn led to complications and troubles which those orders were calculated to avert.

35. Scott to Swinton, Feb. 2, Beng. Sec. and Pol. Cons., March 7, 1828, No. 4. The parallel was probably suggested to Scott by his assistant Capt. Adam White who had vigorously advocated European colonisation in India in his book *Considerations on the State of British India*, Edinburgh, 1822, Chapter I, pp. 1-25.

BIBLIOGRAPHY

BIBLIOGRAPHICAL WORKS, REFERENCE BOOKS, ETC.

A. ORIGINAL MATERIALS:

(1) Unpublished—

(a) English

(b) Assamese

(2) Published—

(a) English

(b) Assamese

(3) Travels and other contemporary publications.

B. SECONDARY WORKS:

(1) English

(2) Assamese.

BIBLIOGRAPHICAL WORKS, REFERENCE BOOKS, ETC.

BELL, A. G. List of occasional articles relating to Assam and the countries adjoining, to be found in the journals and books in the Shillong Government Library. Shillong, 1905.

Bengal obituary, a record to perpetuate the memory of the departed worth. By Holmes and Co., Calcutta, 1848.

BUCKLAND, C. E. A dictionary of Indian biography. London, 1906.

CAMPBELL, FRANK. Index-catalogue of Indian official publications in the Library, British Museum. London, 1900.

CORDIER, HENRI. Bibliotheca Indo-Sinica, Premiere partie: Birmanie et Assam. Leiden, 1908. Reprint from T'oung Pao, Vols. IV to IX, 1903-1908.

CRAWFORD, D. G. Roll of the Indian Medical Service, 1615-1930. London, 1930.

DODWELL, EDWARD, AND MILES, JAMES SAMUEL. Alphabetical list of the officers of the Indian Army, 1760-1837. London, 1838.

—Alphabetical list of the Medical officers of the Indian Army 1764-1838. London, 1839.

—Alphabetical list of the E. I. C.'s Bengal Civil Servants, 1780-1838. London, 1839.

GAIT, SIR EDWARD. List of writings relating to Assam, in *Report on the Progress of Historical Research in Assam*, pp. 30-68. Shillong, 1897.

Glossary of vernacular terms used in official correspondence in the province of Assam. Shillong, 1879.

HAMILTON, WALTER. East Indian Gazetteer. London, 1815, 1828.

HODSON, V. C. P. Officers of the Bengal Army, 1758-1834. Parts I and II, A to K. London, 1927-28.

Inscriptions on tombs and monuments in Assam. Shillong, 1902.

List of books, etc., on Bengal to which are added a few books on Assam, etc. Pub. K. Paul Trubner & Co. London, 1887.

List of books and articles relating to Assam, compiled by the Librarian, Imperial Library, Calcutta. Calcutta, 1906

Preliminary bibliography bearing on the geography and ethnology of the counrties within and adjoining the Himalaya. North-West Provinces Gazetteer, Vol. X, 1882.

PRINSEP, H. T. and DOSS, RAMACHANDRA. Register of the E. I. C.'s Bengal Civil Servants, 1790-1842. Calcutta, 1844.

REID, J. F. M. Chronological tables containing corresponding dates of different eras used in Bengal, 1764-1835, Continued upto 1875 by G. C. Tarkalankar. Calcutta, 1875.

THORNTON, EDWARD. A Gazetteer of the territories under the government of the E. I. Company and of the native states on the continent of India. London, 1858.

YULE, HENRY, and BURNELL, A. C. Hobson-Jobson, a glossary of colloquial Anglo-Indian words and phrases. New edition, ed. by W. Crooke. London, 1903.

A. ORIGINAL MATERIALS.

(1) Unpublished

(a) *English*.

INDIA OFFICE RECORDS:

Bengal Judicial Consultations.
Bengal Board of Revenue Proceedings.
Bengal Revenue Consultations.
Bengal Political Consultations.
Bengal Secret and Political Consultations.
Bengal Public Consultations.
Bengal Letter to Court.

Court's Letter to Bengal.
Court's Book.
Committee of Correspondence Report.
Home Miscellaneous Series.
Miscellaneous Letters Received.
Bengal Civilians.
Personal Records.
Writers' Petitions.
Fowke Manuscripts.
Buchanan-Hamilton Manuscripts.

IMPERIAL RECORD DEPARTMENT, Calcutta, now in Delhi. Examined in April 1930. Copies of Assam letters in the Persian Correspondence Series, 1777 and 1780, were obtained in 1930.

BENGAL SECRETARIAT RECORD ROOM: Copy of Hugh Baillie's letter in the Board of Trade Proceedings, 1776, was obtained in 1937.

ASSAM SECRETARIAT RECORDS. Examined in May to June 1930, and a preliminary report was submitted to Assam Government.

(b) *Assamese.*

1. ASSAM BURANJI, by Maniram Datta Barbhandar Barua Dewan, entitled "Buranji-viveka-ratna", Part II, dealing with the political, administrative and religious history of the Assamese people. Compiled in 1838. Acquired by the D.H.A.S. from Srijut Trailokyasobhan Chandra Goswami, Sarujana Dihing Satradhikar of North Gauhati, through Srijut Upendra Chandra Lekharu.
2. ASSAM BURANJI, by Padmeswar Singh Naobaicha Phukan. From the earliest Ahom rulers to the advent of the British, with chapters on Ahom institutions and customs, etc. Compiled about the year 1900. Obtained by the D.H.A.S. from the author's son Srijut Chandreswar Naobaicha Phukan of Sibsagar, through Mr. A. H. S. Fletcher, I.C.S., and Mr. C. K. Bhuyan, A.C.S.
3. ASSAM BURANJI, a collection of 192 letters exchanged between the kings and officers of Assam, and the courts of Delhi, Dacca, Cooch Behar, Jayanta, Cachar, Sylhet, etc. Compiled from the original Buranjis under the supervision of the late Srijut Hemchandra Goswami. Obtained

by the D.H.A.S. from the Commissioner, Assam Valley Division, after Mr. Goswami's death in June 1928.

4. ASSAM BURANJI, containing a list of the military outposts and fortifications of Assam, compiled about the year 1681. Incomplete manuscript. Obtained by the D.H.A.S. from Srijut Upendra Chandra Lekharu of village Rudreswar in North Gauhati.
5. ASSAM BURANJI, from Swargadeo Pratap Singha to Ratnadhwaj Singha Sulikpha Lora Raja, 1603-1681. Obtained by the D.H.A.S. from Srijut Sarat Chandra Goswami, B.A., son of the late Srijut Hemchandra Goswami.
6. ASSAM BURANJI, from the invasion of Mirza Jahina to Swargadeo Siva Singha, 1630-1744. Obtained by the D.H.A.S. from Srijut Sarat Chandra Goswami.
7. ASSAM BURANJI, from the earliest times to Swargadeo Gadadhar Singha's recovery of Gauhati from the Moguls in 1682, with several historical letters. Obtained by the D.H.A.S. from Srijut Sarat Chandra Goswami.
8. ASSAM BURANJI, from the earliest times to the death of Swargadeo Rudra Singha in 1714. Obtained by the D.H. A.S. from Srijut Sarat Chandra Goswami.
9. ASSAM BURANJI, containing accounts of miscellaneous events from the earliest times to Swargadeo Rudra Singha, with a chapter on Rungaddin Padshah's conquest of Delhi. Obtained by the D.H.A.S. from the Ahom Juvak Sammilan, through the late Srijut Anandaram Gohain and Srijut Deveswar Gohain Rajkumar.
10. ASSAM BURANJI, from Swargadeo Jayadhwaj Singha to Chakradhwaj Singha's recovery of Gauhati from the Moguls, 1648-1667, being a few pages of transcript. Obtained by Dr. S. K. Bhuyan from Srijut Umanath Gohain, B.A., A.C.S., now retired.
11. ASSAM BURANJI, a digest of the events of the reigns of Ahom monarchs from Khunlung and Khunlai to Swargadeo Rudra Singha. Obtained by the D.H.A.S. from the India Office Library, London.
12. ASSAM BURANJI, containing an account of the wars with Raja Ram Singha, entitled *Ram Singhar Yuddhar Katha*. Fragmentary and incomplete, and the text archaic and mutilated. Obtained by the D.H.A.S. from Srijut Nagendra Nath Gogoi, B.Sc., of Cherekapar, near Sibsagar town.

13. ASSAM BURANJI, containing an account of Ahom clans, royal matrimonial alliances, etc., from King Sukapha to King Pramatta Singha, 1228-1751. Obtained by the D.H.A.S. from Srijut Ripunath Dilihial Buragohain of Dilihial Gohaingaon, District Sibsagar.

14. ASSAM BURANJI, containing an account of the events from the reign of Swargadeo Pratap Singha to Laluk Buraphukan's delivery of Gauhati to Sultan Azamtara's deputy Nawab Mansur Khan, 1603-1679. Obtained by Dr. S. K. Bhuyan from Srijut Ratneswar Phukan of Cinnamara, Jorhat, a descendant of Lachit Barphukan's family.

15. ASSAM BURANJI, from Suhungmung Dihingia Raja to King Pramatta Singha, 1497-1751, incomplete, and with many irrecoverable gaps. Obtained by the late Srijut Hemchandra Goswami for the Government of Assam from the Adhikar Gosain of Bengena Ati Satra in Majuli, Jorhat Sub-division.

16. ASSAM BURANJI, from Swargadeo Jayadhwaj Singha to Rudra Singha's Kachari wars 1648-1707. Obtained by Dr. S. K. Bhuyan from the American Baptist Mission, Gauhati.

17. ASSAM BURANJI, a detailed chronicle of events from the last few years of Swargadeo Rajeswar Singha's reign to the first eight years of Swargadeo Lakshmi Singha's reign. The folios are in a pell-mell condition. Obtained by Dr. S. K. Bhuyan from the American Baptist Mission, Gauhati.

The above list represents the more important of the unpublished Assamese Buranjis or chronicles consulted by me in the compilation of this book; and references to them have been occasionally cited as "MS. Assam Buranji No. 1", "MS. Assam Buranji No. 2", and so forth. Fuller information about the indigenous historical literature of Assam, can be obtained from:

1. J. F. BLUMHARDT. *Catalogue of the Bengali and Assamese Manuscripts in the Library of the India Office*, London, 1905, pp. 17-18.
2. J. F. BLUMHARDT. *Catalogue of the Marathi, Gujarati, Bengali, Assamese, Oriya, Pushtu and Sindhi Manuscripts in the Library of the British Museum*, London, 1905, p. 1.
3. H. C. GOSWAMI. *Descriptive Catalogue of Assamese Manuscripts*, 1930, Part I. MSS. Nos. 9, 39, 40, 113, 114, 149, 150, 151, 155 and 156.

4. S. K. BHUYAN. *Report and Conspectus of the Kamarupa Anusandhan Samiti or the Assam Research Society,* Gauhati. 1927, pp. 71-79.

5. S. K. BHUYAN. Assamese Historical Literature, published in *Indian Historical Quarterly,* Calcutta, for September 1929; and also in the Proceedings of the Fifth Session of the All-India Oriental Conference, held at Lahore in November 1928.

6. S. K. BHUYAN. Bulletins of the Department of Historical and Antiquarian Studies in Assam, Gauhati: No. I, 1932, pp. 27-43; No. II, 1934, pp. 50-58; and No. III, 1936, pp. 20-23.

7. S. K. BHUYAN. Bibliography under Assam Buranjis, in *Lachit Barphukan and His Times,* D.H.A.S., 1947, Appendix V, pp. 217-221.

8. S. K. BHUYAN. Assamese Historical Literature: Bibliographical Note, in *Annals of the Delhi Badshahate,* D.H. A.S., 1947, Appendix B, pp. 202-208.

(2) Published

(a) *English*

AITCHISON, Sir C. U. Treaties, Engagements and Sanads. Revised and enlarged upto 1929. Vol. XII, Parts III and IV, Assam and Burma. Calcutta, 1931.

BARUA, GOLAPCHANDRA. Ahom Buranji. A chronicle of Assam in the Ahom language, with parallel English translation. Shillong, 1930.

BARWELL, RICHARD. Letters of R. Barwell. *Bengal: Past and Present,* 1914-1917.

BHUYAN, S. K. Translation of the Assamese chronicle by Srinath Barbarua, 1671-1806, with additional matter bringing down the history to 1826. Pub. Oxford University Press. Bombay and London, 1933. References are made to this English version, entitled "Tungkhungia Buranji, or A History of Assam, 1631-1826 A.D."

——Annals of the Delhi Badshahate. Translation of *Padshah-Buranji.* Pub. in *Islamic Culture,* Hyderabad, Deccan, 1933-1934. Pub. in book-form in 1947 by the D.H.A.S.

BHUYAN, S. K. Press list of records in the Assam Secretariat, with index, Letters received from Government, Vol. II, 1823-24, in *Preliminary report on the Assam Secretariat* records, App. A, pp. 27-52. Shillong, 1931.

BUCHANAN-HAMILTON, FRANCIS. General view of the history of Kamarupa, written in 1808-9. Inserted in S. K. Bhuyan's *Kamrupar Buranji*, Appendix C.

——An account of Assam. Pub. in *Annals of Oriental Literature*, London, 1820. Mostly reproduced in Martin's *Eastern India*, Vol. III. Since published by D.H.A.S. in 1940.

Burma and Assam. An account of the Burman empire and the kingdom of Assam, compiled from the works of Wade, Cox, Buchanan-Hamilton etc. Calcutta, 1839.

Calendar of Persian Correspondence. Vol. V, letters between Company's servants and Indian rulers and notables, 1776-1780. Calcutta, 1930.

Chandernagore papers, 1778-1783. *Bengal: Past and Present*, 1909-1910.

DEWAN, MANIRAM. Native account of washing for gold in Assam. J.A.S.B., July 1838.

——Abstracts of the receipts and disbursements in the province of Assam during Purnananda Buragohain's administration. In Mills's *Report on Assam*, Sibsagar, Appendix, K-B.

FIRMINGER, W. K. Rungpore District Records, 6 vols. Calcutta, 1914-28.

——Sylhet District Records. 4 vols. Shillong, 1913-19.

FORREST, SIR GEORGE. Selections from the letters, despatches and other state papers preserved in the Foreign Department of the Government of India, 1772-85. 3 vols. Calcutta, 1890.

French East India Company in Bengal. Reports from Provincial Councils etc., 1794. *Bengal : Past and Present*, January-March, 1909.

HILL, S. C. Catalogue of the Home Miscellaneous Series of the India Office Records. London, 1927.

HUNTER, SIR WILLIAM. Bengal Manuscript records. Selected list of 14,136 letters in the Board of Revenue, Calcutta. London, 1894.

KAYE, G. R. and JOHNSTON, E. H. Catalogue of the Mss. in the European languages in the India Office Library. Vol. II, Part II, minor collections and miscellaneous manuscripts. London, 1937.

LONG J. Selections from the unpublished records of Government, 1748-67. Calcutta, 1869.

MARTIN, ROBERT MONTGOMERY. The history, antiquities, topography and statistics of Eastern India. 3 vols. London, 1838.

Narrative abstracts of General Letters to and from the Court of Directors in the Revenue, Territorial Revenue, Territorial Financial and Miscellaneous Revenue Departments of the Government of Bengal, 1771-1858. Vol. I. Calcutta, 1937.

Papers relating to the frontier tribes of North-East Frontier. Calcutta, 1855.

Parliamentary Papers. Reports of the Select Committee of the House of Commons, 1772-73.

——Reports of the Committee of Secrecy appointed by the House of Commons, 1772-73.

——Papers relating to East India affairs, *viz.* discussions with the Burmese government, 1825, Vol. XXIV.

——Report from the Indian Law Commissioners on slavery in the East Indies. Return to an order of the House of Commons, 1841, No. 28.

Press list of ancient documents preserved in the Secretariat Record Room of the Government of Bengal. Revenue Department, Series I, II and III. Calcutta, 1915-19.

Press list of copies of ancient documents obtained from the India Office. Vol. I, 1749-86; Vol. II, 1787-99. Calcutta 1914 and 1921.

Press list of ancient documents preserved in the Imperial Record Room of the Government of India. Public Department, 1748-1800. 20 vols. Calcutta, 1898-1922.

RHE-PHILIPE, G. V. de. A narrative of the First Burmese War, 1824-26. With reproductions of original despatches, Calcutta, 1905.

ROSS, CHARLES. Correspondence of Charles, first Marquis Cornwallis. 3 Vols. London, 1859.

Selection of Papers (1825-46) regarding the hill tracts between Assam and Burma and on the Upper Brahmaputra. Calcutta, 1873.

Select index to the General Letters from the Court of Directors, preserved in the Bengal Secretariat Record Room. Judicial Department, 1795-1854. Calcutta, 1924.

Select index to the General Letters to and from the Court of Directors in the Revenue, Territorial Revenue, Territorial Financial and Miscellaneous Revenue Departments of the Government of Bengal, 1771-1858. Vol. I Calcutta, 1926.

SETON-KARR, W. S. and SANDEMAN, HUGH. Selections from the Calcutta Gazette, 1784-1823. 5 vols. Calcutta, 1864-69.

SHORE, SIR JOHN. The private record of an Indian Governor-Generalship: Shore's letters to Henry Dundas, 1793-98. Ed. Holden Furber. Cambridge, Massachusetts, 1933.

VANSITTART, HENRY. Original papers relative to the disturbances in Bengal, 1759-1764. London, 1765.

——A narrative of the transactions in Bengal from 1760 to 1764. 3 vols. London, 1766.

——A description of Assam by Muhammad Cazim. Translated from the *Aalamgir-Namah*. Pub. in *Asiatick Researches*, Vol. II, No. 11, 1792.

WADE, JOHN PETER. An account of Assam, compiled during 1794-1800, Ed. Benudhar Sharma. North Lakimpur, 1927.

——Geographical sketch of Assam, compiled during 1796-1802. Ed. S. K. Bhuyan, and pub. in *The Assam Review*, Vols. I-II, 1928-29, under the title *Assam in the Eighteenth Century.*

——Memoir of the reign of Gowrinath Singha, late monarch of Assam, compiled in 1795-6. A few pages found at the end of *Geographical Sketch of Assam,* India Office ms., reproduced in S. K. Bhuyan's *Tungkhungia Buranji,* pp. 231-32.

WELSH, THOMAS. Report on Assam, 1794, with additional observations by David Scott, 1826. Reproduced in Mackenzie's *North-East Frontier of Bengal,* pp. 377-394.

WILSON, HORACE HAYMAN. Documents illustrative of the Burmese War. Calcutta, 1827.

(b) *Assamese.*

Arunoday, an Assamese magazine, pub. from Sibsagar by the American Baptist Mission. Portions of *Kamrupar Buranji, Deodhai Assam Buranji* and Lakshmi Singha's Buranji were pub. in the volumes for 1850-53 and 1860.

BHUYAN, S. K. Barphukanar Git, or the ballad of Badanchandra Barphukan. Gauhati, 1924.

——Assam Buranji by Harakanta Barua. D.H.A.S., Gauhati, 1930.

——Kamrupar Buranji, D.H.A.S., Gauhati, 1930.

——Tungkhungia Buranji, 1671-1806, by Srinath Barbarua, D.H.A.S., Gauhati, 1932.

——Deodhai Assam Buranji. D.H.A.S., Gauhati, 1932.

——Asamar Padya-Buranji, two metrical chronicles of Assam by Dutiram Hazarika and Bisweswar Baidyadhipa. D.H.A.S., Gauhati, 1933.

——Padshah-Buranji. K.A.S., Gauhati, 1934.

——Kachari Buranji. D.H.A.S., Gauhati, 1936.

——Jayantia Buranji. D.H.A.S., Gauhati, 1937.

——Tripura Buranji. D.H.A.S., Gauhati, 1938.

DAS, BHARATCHANDRA. Adi-charit, chronicle of the Bhuyans. Authorship attributed to Madhabdeva. Gauhati, 1920.

GOSWAMI, CHIDANANDA. Mayamara Satrar Vamsavali, metrical chronicle of Aniruddhadeva and other Mahantas of the Mayamara Satra. Published by Nakulchandra Chetia. Tinsukia, Assam, 1933.

GOSWAMI, HEMCHANDRA. Darrang Raj Vamsavali. Metrical chronicle of the Koch rulers. Shillong, 1917

——Purani Asam Buranji. Gauhati, 1922.

PHUKAN, HALIRAM DHEKIAL. Assam deser itihas, or history of Assam in Bengali. Calcutta, 1929. Analysis in English in I.O. Tract, vol. 166.

PHUKAN, KASINATH, and BARBARUA, RADHANATH. Assam Buranji. 1st edition, Sibsagar, 1844 ; 2nd ed., Calcutta, 1906.

(3) TRAVELS AND OTHER CONTEMPORARY PUBLICATIONS

AIME-MARTIN. Lettres edifiantes et curieuses. 4 vols. Paris, 1838.

BERNIER, FRANCOIS. Travels in the Mogul Empire, 1658-68. Translated and edited by Archibald Constable. London, 1891.

BOGLE, GEORGE. Mission of George Bogle to Tibet and the journey of Thomas Manning to Lhasa. Ed. Sir Clements Robert Markham. London, 1876.

BOLTS, WILLIAM. Considerations on Indian affairs. 3 vols. London, 1772-75.

BOWREY, THOMAS. A geographical account of countries round the Bay of Bengal, 1669-79. Edited by Sir Richard Carnac Temple. Pub. Hakluyt Society, Ser. II, Vol. XII. London, 1905.

BUTLER JOHN. Sketch of Assam, with some account of the hill tribes. London, 1847.

——Travels and adventures in the province of Assam. London, 1855.

CHIJS, J. A. VAN DER. Dagh-Register int Casteel Batavia. Covers the period 1624-93. The volume for 1663 contains references to Mir Jumla's invasion of Assam. Batavia and The Hague, 1891.

COX, HIRAM. Journal of a residence in the Burman Empire. 1797, London, 1821.

GLANIUS. A relation of an unfortunate voyage to the kingdom of Bengal. London, 1682.

GRIFFITH, W. Journals of travels in Assam, Burma, Bootan and Afghanistan. 2 vols. Calcutta, 1847.

HANNAY, S. O. Further information on the gold washings of Assam. J.A.S.B., July 1838.

——A short account of the Moa Morah sect. J.A.S.B., August, 1838.

HASTINGS, WARREN. Memoirs relative to the state of India, London, 1786.

HUGON, THOMAS. Silkworms and silks of Assam. J.A.S.B., Vol. VI, 1837.

JENKINS, FRANCIS. Report on the Revenue Administration of Assam, 1849-50. Selections of the records of the Bengal Government, No. XI. Calcutta, 1853.

——Report on the progress and prosperity of the province of Assam. In Mills's *Report on Assam,* App. B., 1854.

——Diary in Cooch Behar and notes. Calcutta, 1868.

Maasiru-l-umara, translated by H. Beveridge. Bibliotheca Indica, pub. Asiatic Society of Bengal. Vol. I, Calcutta, 1911.

MACLEOD, D.A. Sketch of the medical topography of Biswanath, Calcutta, 1837.

MANUCCI, NICCOLAO. Storia do Mogor. Translated and edited by William Irvine. 4 vols. London, 1907-8.

MILLS, A. J. MOFFATT. Report on the province of Assam. Calcutta, 1854.

NEUFVILLE, J. B. On the geography and population of Assam. Pub. in *Asiatick Researches,* Vol. XVI, 1828.

PEMBERTON, R. B. Report on the Eastern Frontier of British India. Calcutta, 1835.

——Report on Bootan. Calcutta, 1839.

PHILIPPART, SIR JOHN. East India military calendar. 2 vols. London, 1823.

PHUKAN, ANANDARAM DHEKIAL. Observation on the administration of the province of Assam. In Mills's *Report on Assam,* App. J.

RENNELL, JAMES. Journals, 1764-67. Ed. T. H. D. La Touche. Memoirs of the Asiatic Society of Bengal, Vol. III, No. 3. Calcutta, 1910.

——Memoir of a map of Hindustan or the Mogul's Empire. 2nd ed., London, 1785.

ROBERTSON, T. C. Political incidents of the first Burmese War. London, 1853.

RYLEY, J. HORTON. Ralph Fitch, England's pioneer to India and Burma. London, 1899.

TAVERNIER, JEAN BAPTISTE. Travels in India. Translated and edited by V. Ball. 2 vols. London, 1889.

TURNER, SAMUEL. An account of an embassy to the court of Teshoo Lama in Tibet. London, 1800.

VALENTYN, FRANCOIS. Oud en Nieuw Oost-Indian. 5 vols. Amsterdam, 1724-26.

WHITE, ADAM. Considerations on the state of British India. Edinburgh, 1822.

——Memoir of the late David Scott, Esq. Edited by Col. Archibald Watson. Calcutta, 1832.

WHITE, W. A political history of the extraordinary events which led to the Burmese War. London, 1827.

WILCOX, R. Memoir of the survey of Assam and the neighbouring countries, executed in 1825-6-7-8. Pub. in *Asiatick Researches,* Vol. XVII, 1832.

WILSON, C. R. The early annals of the English in Bengal. 3 vols. Calcutta, 1895-1917.

WILSON, H. H. Historical sketch of the Burmese War, prefixed to his *Documents.* Calcutta, 1827. Also published separately.

B. SECONDARY WORKS

(1) *English*

ALLEN, B. C. Assam District Gazetteers. Shillong, 1905-7.

ASCOLI, F. D. Early revenue history of Bengal, and the Fifth Report. Calcutta, 1917.

ASPINAL, A. Cornwallis in Bengal. London, 1931.

Assam Review. Founded by W. H. S. Wood. Silchar, 1928-30, Calcutta, 1930.

Assam since the expulsion of the Burmese. Pub. in the *Calcutta Review,* Vol. XIX, January to June, 1853.

Assam: Sketch of its history, soil and productions, with the discovery of the tea plant and of the countries adjoining Assam. London, 1839.

Bengal: Past and Present. Calcutta, 1907.

BHUYAN, S. K. Mir Jumla and Ram Singha in Assam. Pub. in *Journal of Indian History,* Madras, December 1926.

——An Assamese Nur Jahan or Phuleswari Devi, queen regnant of Assam, 1717-1731. Gauhati, 1926.

——Stray notes on David Scott. Pub. in *Assam Review*, Silchar, May 1928.

——Early British relations with Assam. Shillong, 1928.

——New lights on Mogul India from Assamese sources. Pub. in *Islamic Culture*, Hyderabad, Deccan, 1928-29.

——Assamese historical literature. Pub. in *Indian Historical Quarterly*, Calcutta, September, 1929.

——An early historian of the East India Company: Dr. J. P. Wade. Pub. in the Proceedings of the Indian Historical Records Commission, Gwalior session, 1929. Calcutta, 1930. Pub. also in *Bengal: Past and Present*, January-March 1930.

——Preliminary report on the Assam Secretariat records Assam Government office file. Shillong, 1931.

BLOCHMANN, H. Koch Bihar, Koch Hajo, and Assam in the 16th and 17th centuries. J.A.S.B., 1872, Part I, No. I.

BRADLEY-BIRT, F. B. 'Sylhet' Thackeray. London, 1911.

Cambridge History of India. Vol. V, British India, 1497-1858. Ed. H. H. Dodwell. Cambridge, 1929.

CARDEW, F. G. A sketch of the services of the Bengal Native Army, to the year 1895. Calcutta, 1903

DODWELL, H. H. India. Modern States Series, No. IX. London, 1936.

DUNBAR, SIR GEORGE. Frontiers. London, 1932.

ELIAS, NEY. Introductory sketch of the history of the Shans. Calcutta, 1876.

Frontier and overseas expeditions from India. Compiled by the Intelligence Branch of the Chief of the Staff Army Headquarters. Vol. V, Burma. Simla, 1907.

GAIT, SIR EDWARD. A history of Assam, 1st ed., Calcutta, 1906; 2nd ed., 1926.

——Report on the Census of Assam, 1891. Shillong, 1892.

——Koch kings of Kamarupa. J.A.S.B., 1893, Part I, No. I.

——Assam Land Revenue Manual. Shillong, 1896.

——Report on the progress of historical research in Assam, with a bibliography. Shillong, 1897.

GHOSE, J. M. Sannyasi and Fakir raiders in Bengal. Calcutta, 1930.

GHOSE, M. N. Religious beliefs of the Assamese people. Shillong, 1896.

GLAZIER, E. G. Report on the district of Rungpore. Calcutta, 1873. Also prefixed to Vol. I of W. K. Firminger's *Rungpore District Records*.

——Further notes on the Rungpore records. Vol. II. Calcutta, 1876.

GOSWAMI, S. C. The night-worshippers or Rati-khowa sect of Assam. Pub. in *The Work of the Kamarupa Anusandhan Samiti.* Gauhati, 1920.

GURDON, P. R. T. Notes on the Morans. J.A.S.B., 1904, Part I, No. I.

——The Ahoms. In Hastings's *Encyclopaedia of Religion and Ethics.*

HALL, D. G. E. Early English intercourse with Burma. London, 1928.

HALLWARD, N. L. William Bolts, a Dutch adventurer under John Company. Cambridge, 1920.

HARVEY, G. E. History of Burma. London, 1925.

HILL, S. C. Bengal in 1756-57. 3 vols. London, 1905.

——Three Frenchman in Bengal. London, 1903.

——List of Europeans and others in the English Factories in Bengal at the time of the siege of Calcutta in the year 1756. Calcutta, 1902.

HIRST, F. C. and SMART, A. B. A brief history of the surveys of Goalpara. Shillong, 1917.

HUNTER, SIR WILLIAM. A statistical account of Assam. 2 vols. London, 1879.

JOHNSTONE, Sir JAMES. Capt. Welsh's expedition to Assam, 1792-94. 1st ed., Shillong, 1877; 2nd ed., 1912.

MACKENZIE, SIR ALEXANDER. History of the relations of Government with the hill tribes of the North-East Frontier of Bengal. Calcutta, 1884.

M'COSH, J. Topography of Assam. Calcutta. 1837.

MALCOLM, SIR JOHN. Life of Lord Clive. 3 vols. London, 1836.

——The political history of India. 2 vols. London, 1826.

MONCKTON-JONES, M. E. Hastings in Bengal. London, 1918.

MUDIE, ROBERT. China and its resources etc., with a notice of Assam. London, 1840.

Notes on some industries in Assam, 1884-95. Shillong, 1896.

PHAYRE, SIR ARTHUR. History of Burma. London, 1883.

Report on the administration of the province of Assam, for 1874-75 and 1875-76; and for 1882-83. Shillong, 1877 and 1884.

ROBINSON, WILLIAM. A descriptive account of Assam. Calcutta, 1941.

ROY, C. C. A Note on J. B. Chevalier and Montigny. *Bengal: Past and Present,* Vol. XVI.

SHAKESPEAR, L. W. History of Upper Assam, Upper Burma and North-Eastern Frontier. London, 1914.

——History of the Assam Rifles. London, 1929.

STEVENS, EDWIN. Description of Assam and its inhabitants. Pub. in the *Chinese Repository*, Pekin. Vol. V, Nos. 2-3, June-July, 1836.

WARD, SIR WILLIAM ERSKINE. Note on the Assam land revenue system. Shillong, 1897. Originally pub. as introduction to Gait's *Assam Land Revenue Manual.*

WESSELS, C. Early Jesuit travellers in Central Asia, 1603-1721. The Hague, M. Nijhoff, 1924.

WILSON, C. R. Old Fort William in Bengal. 2 vols. London, 1906.

(2) *Assamese*

BARUA, GUNABHIRAM. Assam Buranji, 1st ed., Calcutta, 1876.

——Life of Anandaram Dhekial Phukan. Calcutta, 1880.

BARUA, INDIBAR. Jivanadarsa. Short life-sketches of Purnananda Buragohain, Piali Barphukan, Haliram Dhekial Phukan, Maniram Dewan etc. Sibsagar, 1889.

BEZBARUA, LAKSHMINATH. Lives of Sankardeva and Madhabdeva. Calcutta, 1916.

BHUYAN, S. K. Ahomar Din. An account of the administrative system of the Ahoms. Jorhat, 1918.

——History of the reign of Rajeswar Singha, king of Assam, 1751-1769. Pub. as a serial in *Banhi,* Vols. XV and XVI. Gauhati, 1925-26.

SHARMA, BENUDHAR. Rangili, an Assamese consort of a Burmese monarch. Pub. in *Banhi,* Vol. XV. Gauhati, 1925.

SUPPLEMENTARY BIBLIOGRAPHY

The Bibliography on the previous pages was mostly compiled in London in May 1938. The following books have come out in the meantime,—

BANERJEE, A. C. Annexation of Burma, Calcutta, 1944.

——The Eastern Frontier of British India, Calcutta, 1944.

BHUYAN, S. K. An account of Assam, compiled in 1807-1814, by Francis Hamilton, formerly Francis Buchanan, D.H.A.S., Gauhati, 1940.

——Assam Buranji, obtained from the family of Sukumar Mahanta. D.H.A.S., Gauhati, 1945. Referred to as *Assam Buranji, S. M.*

——Lachit Barphukan and His Times, D.H.A.S., Gauhati, 1947.

——Annals of the Delhi Badshahate, being a translation of the old Assamese chronicle "Padshah-Buranji". D.H.A.S., Gauhati, 1947.

CANTLIE, SIR KEITH, Assam in former times, a pamphlet for the troops. Shillong, 1944.

GOHAIN, U. N. Assam under the Ahoms. Jorhat, 1942.

KHAN CHAUDHURY, Amanatullah Ahmed. A history of Cooch Behar, in Bengali, Part I, Cooch Behar, 1936.

SEN, SURENDRA NATH, Prachin Bangala Patra Sankalan, Records in Oriental Languages, Vol. I, Bengali Letters. Calcutta University, 1942.

LIST OF AHOM KINGS OF ASSAM

1.	Sukapha	A.D. 1228–1268
2.	Suteupha	1268–1281
3.	Subinpha	1281–1293
4.	Sukhangpha	1293–1332
5.	Sukhrangpha	1332–1364
6.	Sutupha	1364–1376
	Interregnum	1376-1380
7.	Tyao Khamthi	1380–1389
	Interregnum	1389-1397
8.	Sudangpha, Bamuni-kowanr	1397–1407
9.	Sujangpha	1407-1422
10.	Suphakpha	1422–1439
11.	Susenpha	1439–1488
12.	Suhenpha	1488-1493
13.	Supimpha	1493–1497
14.	Suhungmung, Dihingia Raja I	1497–1539
15.	Suklenmung, Gargayan Raja	1539–1552
16.	Sukhampha, Khora Raja	1552–1603
17.	Susengpha, Pratap Singha, Buddhi-swarga-narayan, Burha Raja	1603–1641
18.	Surampha, Bhaga Raja, Jayaditya	1641–1644
19.	Sutyinpha, Naria Raja	1644–1648
20.	Sutamla, Jayadhwaj Singha	1648–1663
21.	Supungmung, Chakradhwaj Singha	1663–1670
22.	Sunyatpha, Udayaditya	1670–1672
23.	Suklampha, Ramadhwaj Singha	1672–1674
24.	Suhung, for 20 days only	1674-1675
25.	Gobar Raja, for 20 days only	1675
26.	Sujinpha, Arjun, Dihingha Raja II	1675–1677
27.	Sudaipha, Parvatia Raja	1677–1679
28.	Sulikpha, Ratnadhwaj Singha, Lora Raja	1679–1681
29.	Supatpha, Gadadhar Singha	1681–1696
30.	Sukhrungpha, Rudra Singha	1696-1714
31.	Sutanpha, Siva Singha	1714–1744
32.	Sunenpha, Pramatta Singha	1744–1751
33.	Surampha, Rajeswar Singha	1751–1769
34.	Sunyeopha, Lakshmi Singha	1769–1780
35.	Suhitpangpha, Gaurinath Singha	1780–1795
36.	Suklingpha, Kamaleswar Singha	1795–1811
37.	Sudingpha, Chandrakanta Singha	1811-1818
38.	Purandar Singha	1818-1819
39.	Chandrakanta Singha, 2nd time	1819-1821

1821-1824, Burmese rule, with puppet Ahom monarch Jogeswar Singha.

1824, British conquest of Lower Assam.

1825, British conquest of Upper Assam.

1826, February 24, Treaty of Yandabo, by which the king of Burma ceded Assam to the British.

1833-1838, Purandar Singha ruled in Upper Assam as a tributary prince.

GENEALOGICAL TABLE OF THE TUNGKHUNGIA DYNASTY

AHOM KINGS FROM GADADHAR SINGHA TO PURANDAR SINGHA

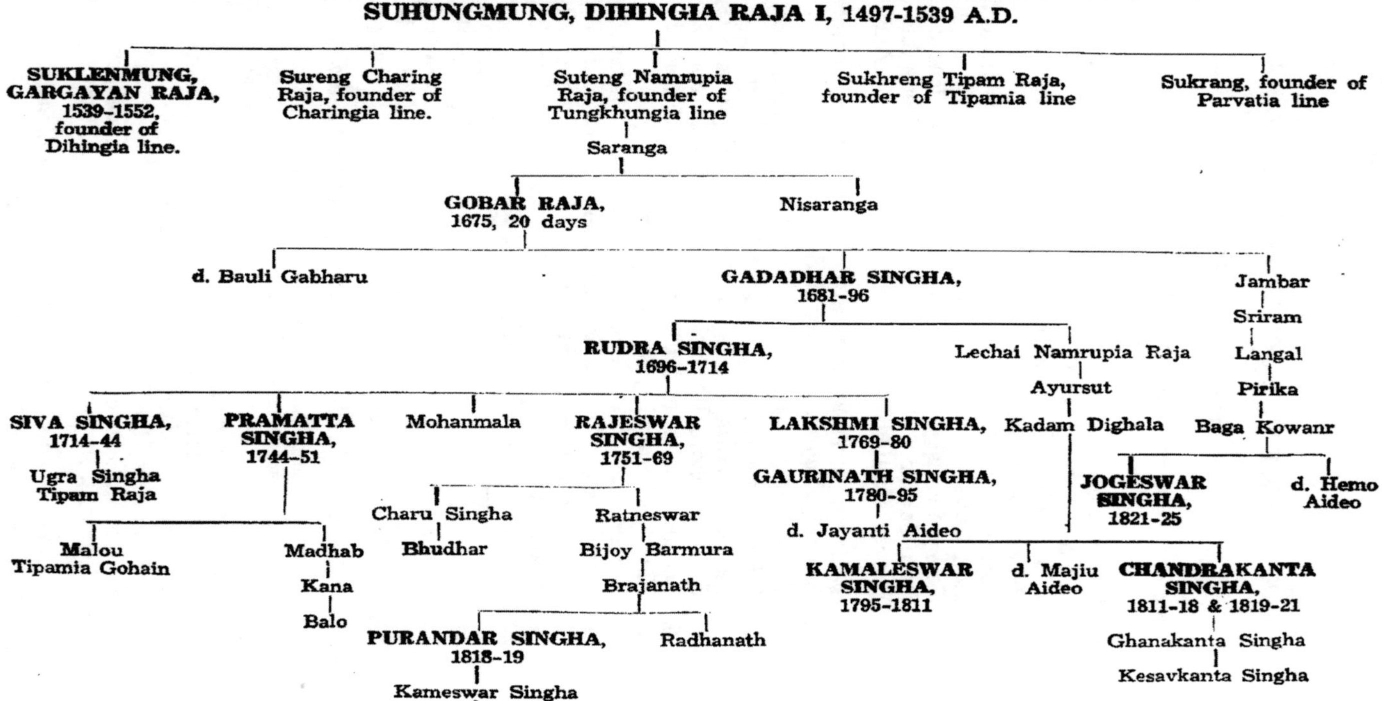

HEADS OF E.I.C.'S GOVERNMENT IN INDIA

From 1752 to 1858

Presidents and Governors of Fort William in Bengal:

		From
1.	Roger Drake	June 1752
2.	Colonel Robert Clive	June 1758
3.	John Zephaniah Holwell	January 1760
4.	Henry Vansittart	July 1760
5.	Spencer	December 1764
6.	Lord Clive	May 1765
7.	Henry Verelst	January 1767
8.	John Cartier	December 1769
9.	Warren Hastings	April 1772

Governors-General of India, appointed by the United Company of Merchants trading in the East Indies

1.	Warren Hastings	October 20, 1774
2.	John Macpherson	February 8, 1785
3.	Earl Cornwallis	September 12, 1786
4.	Sir John Shore, Baronet	October 28, 1793
5.	Lt.-Gen. Sir Alured Clarke ..	March 17, 1798
6.	Earl of Mornington, afterwards Marquess of Wellesley ..	May 18, 1798
7.	Marquess of Cornwallis, 2nd time ..	July 30, 1805
8.	Sir George Barlow, Baronet ..	October 10, 1805
9.	Baron Minto	July 31, 1807
10.	Earl of Moira, afterwards Marquess of Hastings	October, 4, 1813
11.	John Adam	January 13, 1823
12.	Baron Amherst	August 1, 1823
13.	William Butterworth Bayley ..	March 13, 1828
14.	Lord William Bentinck	July 4, 1828

Governors-General of India, appointed by the East India Company:

1.	Lord William Bentinck	June 16, 1834
2.	Sir Charles Metcalfe, Baronet ..	March 20, 1835
3.	Baron Auckland	March 4, 1836
4.	Baron Ellenborough	February 28, 1842
5.	William Wilberforce Bird ..	June 15, 1844
6.	Sir Henry Hardinge, afterwards Viscount Hardinge	July 23, 1844
7.	Earl of Dalhousie	January 12, 1848
8.	Viscount Canning	February 29, 1856

Lord Canning was Viceroy and Governor-General under the Crown from November 1858 to March 1862

INDEX

C

D

H

I

J

K

Q

R

S

T

THE END

Government of Assam

DEPARTMENT OF
HISTORICAL AND ANTIQUARIAN STUDIES, ASSAM

PUBLICATIONS FOR SALE

ASSAMESE

1. ASSAM BURANJI.—A history of Ahom rule in Assam, 1228-1826 A.D. An enlarged version of Kasinath Tamuli-Phukan's chronicle, by Harakanta Barua. Pp. xii + 152. Cloth, Rs. 2-8; Paper cover, Re. 1.
2. KAMRUPAR BURANJI.—A detailed history of the Ahom-Mughal conflicts, with chapters on ancient Kamarupa. Pp. xvii + 152. Cloth, Rs. 2-8; Paper cover, Re. 1.
3. DEODHAI ASAM BURANJI.—A collection of old chronicles dealing with earlier Ahom history, neighbouring tribes, Ahom customs, etc. Pp. lxx + 222. Cloth, Rs. 3.
4. TUNGKHUNGIA BURANJI.—A history of Assam from 1681 to 1806 A.D. in Assamese, by Srinath Barbarua of the Duara family. Pp. xlvii + 186. Cloth, Rs. 2-8.
5. ASAMAR PADYA-BURANJI.—Two metrical chronicles of Assam, 1679-1819, A.D., by Dutiram Hazarika and Bisweswar Vaidyadhipa respectively. Pp. lv + 278; Synopsis in English, pp. 279-308. Cloth, Rs. 3.
6. KACHARI BURANJI.—A history of Cachar from the earliest times to the reign of Kachari Raja Tamradhwaj Narayan and the Ahom King Swargadeo Rudra Singha. Pp. xxxiv + 124; Synopsis in English, pp. 125-143; and an Episode in the history of the Kacharis, pp. 144-49. Re. 1-8.
7. JAYANTIA BURANJI.—A history of Jayantia from the earliest times to the reign of Jayantia Raja Lakshmi Singha and the Ahom King Swargadeo Siva Singha; Jayantia matriarchal system; History of Khyrim. With an Introduction by Mr. S. K. Dutta, B.A. (Cal.), B.Sc. (Lond.), Barrister-at-Law, Honorary Deputy Director of the Department of Historical and Antiquarian Studies, Assam. Pp. xxiv + 177; Synopsis in English, pp. 179-190. Re. 1-8.
8. TRIPURA BURANJI, or TRIPURA DESAR KATHA.—A historical and descriptive account of Tripura, with special reference to the events of 1710-1715 A.D., by two Assamese ambassadors of King Rudra Singha, 1696-1714 A.D. From the original manuscript in the British Museum, London. Pp. xx + 103. Re. 1-8.

9. ASSAM BURANJI.—A history of Assam from 1648-1681 A.D. With appendices: Chronology of events in the history of Assam from 1468 to 1825 A.D.; List of Ahom Kings and their period of reign, etc. Pp. xx + 67; Synopsis in English, pp. 69-84. Re. 1.

10. ANKIA NAT.—Containing the extant dramas of Sankardeva, Madhabdeva and Gopaldeva. Edited with an Introduction and a Synopsis of the dramas in English. Pp. xxvi + 269. Rs. 3.

11. NITILATANKUR.—A treatise on Indian politics and warfare compiled by Bagis Sarma at the instance of Duara-Phukan, an Ahom military official of the reign of King Siva Singha, 1714-1744 A.D. Edited by the late Mr. S. C. Goswami, I.S.O., with an elaborate English Introduction. Pp. xii + 40. Re. 1.

12. ASSAM BURANJI, or a chronicle of Assam from Sukapha to Gadadhar Singha, from an old manuscript obtained in the family of the late Srijut Sukumar Mahanta of North Gauhati. With Preface, Analysis and Introduction in English. The Introduction elaborates sixty-three characteristic anecdotes and observations depicting the old-time political ideology of the Assamese people. Pp. lxxxv + 154. Rs. 3.

ENGLISH

13. TUNGKHUNGIA BURANJI.—A history of Assam from 1681 to 1826 A.D., with Genealogical Tables, Bibliography, Glossary and Index. Published by the Oxford University Press. Pp. xxxii + 262. Cloth Rs. 11.

14. BAHARISTAN-I-GHAYBI.—A history of the conflicts of the Mughals with Assam, Bengal, Bihar and Orissa during the first three decades of the seventh century, by Mirza Nathan, Mughal Fouzadar at Gauhati. Translated from the original Persian by the late Dr. M. I. Borah, M.A., B.L. (Dac.), Ph.D. (Lond.). In two volumes, Pp. xxix + 933. Cloth, Rs. 10 per set.

15. BULLETIN No. 1.—With an Introduction by His Excellency Sir Laurie Hammond, Governor of Assam, 1927-1932. Pp. viii + 48. Re. 1.

16. BULLETIN No. 2.—With an Introduction by His Excellency Sir Michael Keane, Governor of Assam, 1932-1937. Pp. xii + 76. Re. 1.

17. BULLETIN No. 3.—Containing (1) the Speech of His Excellency Sir Michael Keane, Governor of Assam, at the Opening Ceremony of the Narayani Handiqui Historical Institute; (2) Honorary Provincial Director's Speech; (3) Account of the Opening Ceremony; (4) Introductions to Bulletins 1 & 2; (5) Extracts from D.H.A.S. Publications. With portraits of His Excellency Sir Michael Keane, Srijut Radhakanta Handiqui, Mrs. Narayani Handiqui, Sir Edward Gait, Narayani Handiqui Historical Institute, etc. Pp. iv + 52. Re. 1-8.

18. BULLETIN No. 4.—A souvenir of the Unveiling Ceremony of the portrait of the late Mrs. Narayani Handiqui held on February 7, 1940. Containing (1) The Hon'ble Miss Mavis Dunn's Speech, (2) Honorary Provincial Director's Speech, (3) Honorary Assistant Director's Speech, etc. Pp. ii + 46. Re. 1.

19. ASSAMESE: ITS FORMATION AND DEVELOPMENT.—A scientific treatise on the history and philology of the Assamese language, being the thesis approved for the Ph.D. degree of Calcutta University, by Dr. Banikanta Kakati, M.A., Ph.D. Pp. xxxiv + 400. Cloth, Rs. 10.

20. ACCOUNT OF ASSAM.—Compiled in 1807-14 by Dr. Francis Hamilton, formerly Buchanan. Text from a copy in the India Office Library, London. Pp. x + 104. Re. 1-8.

21. LACHIT BARPHUKAN AND HIS TIMES.—Or a history of the Assam-Mughal conflicts of the period 1667-1671, with a life-sketch of Raja Ram Singha of Amber; notable utterances of Assamese kings, ministers and commanders; diplomatic epistles; and a Bibliography. Pp. xiv + 221. Cloth, Rs. 4.

22. ANNALS OF THE DELHI BADSHAHATE.—Being a translation of the Assamese chronicle *Padshah-Buranji*, with Notes. The Introduction deals with Assam's contact with the Muslim world, Padshah-Buranji manuscripts, etc. Pp. xi + 244. Cloth, Rs. 5.

23. ANGLO-ASSAMESE RELATIONS.—A history of Assam's relations with the East India Company from 1771 to 1826, and the earlier years of British administration. The Introduction deals with Assam's contact with Europeans from the earliest times, the ruling power in Assam, relations with border states and hill tribes, Assam's commercial and foreign policy, exports and imports, etc. Thesis approved for the Ph.D. degree of London University, with Map, Bibliography and Index. Pp. xxiii + 636. Cloth, Rs. 25.

N. B.—Of the above books:

Nos. 1-8; 12-13; 15-17 and 20-23 have been edited, compiled and written by Dr. S. K. Bhuyan, M.A., B.L. (Cal.), Ph.D. (Lond.), Provincial Director, D.H.A.S.;

No. 9 by Mr. S. K. Dutta, B.A. (Cal.), B.Sc. (Lond.), Barrister-at-Law, Honorary Deputy Director, D.H.A.S.;

Nos. 10 and 18 by Dr. B. K. Barua, M.A., B.L. (Cal.), Ph.D. (Lond.), Honorary Assistant Director, D.H.A.S.

In addition to the above, the following books published by the Assam Government Press, Shillong, are stocked by us for sale,—

1. DESCRIPTIVE CATALOGUE OF ASSAMESE MANUSCRIPTS.—Contains description of several representative ancient Assamese and Sanskrit manuscripts, compiled by the late Pandit Hemchandra Goswami. With Preface and "A

Note on Assamese Manuscripts" by Dr. S. K. Bhuyan, Pp. xxxvi + 256, and Index pp. 257-274. Cloth, Rs. 5.

2. AHOM BURANJI.—A history of Assam from the earliest times to the end of Ahom rule, in Ahom character with parallel English translation. Edited and translated by the late Srijut Golap Chandra Barua. Pp. xi + 388. Cloth, Rs. 6.

3. ASSAM BURANJI.—A history of Assam from 1228 to 1833 A.D., by Kasinath Tamuli-Phukan. Pp. 1 + 136. Cloth, Rs. 2-8.

4. GHORA NIDAN.—A hand-book on the diseases of horses and their remedies: Assamese text with parallel English translation. Edited by the late Srijut Tarini Charan Bhattacharjee. With an Introduction by Dr. S. K. Bhuyan, Pp. viii + 91, and Glossary, pp. 93-108. Cloth, Re. 1-6.

5. KAMARATNA TANTRA.—A book dealing with the Tantrika-shat-karma, etc. Edited with parallel English translation by the late Pandit Hemchandra Goswami. Pp. v + 110. With various mystical diagrams appended to the same. Cloth, Re. 1-8. (*Sale restricted*).